THE FLICKERING MIND

THE FLICKERING MIND

The False Promise of
Technology in the Classroom and
How Learning Can Be Saved

TODD OPPENHEIMER

RANDOM HOUSE / NEW YORK

Grateful acknowledgment is made to *Le Nouvel Observateur* for permission to
reprint an excerpt from an interview entitled "L'enfant-ordinateur," published in a special
supplement to the *Nouvel Observateur*: SPECIAL FUTUR, N.O. 993, 2 December 1983.
Copyright © 1983 by Le Nouvel Observateur. Reprinted by permission.

RANDOM HOUSE and colophon are registered trademarks of Random House, Inc.

Library of Congress Cataloging-in-Publication Data
Oppenheimer, Todd.
The flickering mind : the false promise of technology in the classroom
and how learning can be saved / Todd Oppenheimer.
p.   cm.
Includes bibliographical references.
ISBN 1-4000-6044-3
1. Educational technology—United States. 2. Educational change—United States. I. Title.

LB1028.3 .O555   2003   371.33—dc21   2002037019

Printed in the United States of America on acid-free paper
2 4 6 8 9 7 5 3
First Edition

Book design by J. K. Lambert

Contents

Author's Note

Throughout almost all of the school scenes in this book, the names of teachers, schools, and most students are real. I've taken this step for the sake of credibility, and to aid the inquiries of other researchers who may wish to follow my trail. However, in a small number of schools I have disguised identities for various reasons. In one case, a teacher asked to remain unnamed; in most other scenes, I've given students pseudonyms or used only their first names, to protect youngsters who may feel overly exposed by having their comments and behavior fully described. In all of those instances, the disguise is clearly pointed out. Whenever students' identities are revealed, it is because their names have already appeared in other media or they and their parents have given me permission to identify them.

Introduction

I n the fall of 1998, just days after the midterm elections for the United States Congress, a group of tenth graders from Blair High School, in Montgomery County, Maryland, made the pages of *The Washington Post* with an unusual school project. As part of their government-studies class, they'd accepted an assignment from the *Post* to make predictions on the year's congressional and gubernatorial races and match their choices against those of the pros. Five days before the election, the students decided to run counter to the prevailing political wisdom at the time, predicting that the Republicans would not gain seats in the House of Representatives. Not only were the students correct, but they also outguessed all thirteen of the professional pundits and political commentators to whom the *Post* had given the same assignment. "I admit it. I was beaten by a bunch of 10th-graders at something I get paid to do for a living," Laura Ingraham, a political commentator for MSNBC, wrote in a mea culpa for the *Post*'s Sunday "Outlook" section.

The students apparently won the day because, with the aid of computers, they'd done their homework with a kind of thoroughness that the pundits had neglected. They began with quick guesses on nearly four hundred races, which had been selected by their teacher as relatively easy calls. Then, with the seventy hotly contested races that remained, they embarked on weeks of serious research. They had a few standard print materials at their disposal— political almanacs and statistical abstracts, among other literature—but they spent most of their time trawling the highways and alleyways of the Internet. "They became little mini-demographers," recalls R. B. Lasco, a Blair librarian who assisted with the project. By the end of October, the class had burrowed into each district's economic history, looking for troubles such as factory closings or military-base shutdowns. They studied race, gender, and income profiles; past voting patterns; the candidates' campaign war chests; and signs of political blunders or public opinion shifts as reflected in local newspaper coverage. Then they called it, right on the button. "How could so many of us who follow politics not have heard the Democratic freight train rounding the political bend?" Ingraham wondered. "Probably because we were talking to politicians and to each other instead of listening to voters."[1]

A year later, I watched a group of eleventh graders in Worcester, Massachusetts, engage in quite a different civics project at Worcester's Accelerated Learning Laboratory. The ALL School, as it's commonly called, is the flagship institution of the Co-nect program, the only one of the big, national school-reform initiatives to organize itself around modern technology. On this particular fall day, the eleventh-grade social studies class was working on reports about the powers of Congress, constructed as "PowerPoint presentations" (named after Microsoft's ubiquitous business-presentation product). The projects were nearly finished, and the teacher was feeling pleased with the results. When I asked to see one, she steered me to a young man whose report she felt was in particularly good shape. Sure enough, as the student clicked through the presentation, I was immediately struck by the clean graphics and the digestible writing. Then, suddenly, he was done. This was the extent of his report. But its content was no deeper or more complex than what one commonly sees in civics papers done elsewhere, with pencil and paper, by seventh and eighth graders. Mystified, I asked the student how he'd used his time. He estimated that he'd spent approximately seventeen hours on the project, only seven of which had been devoted to research and writing. The rest went to refining the presentation's graphics.

Surely, I thought, this can't be a fair representation of what's going on at this school. Not only was ALL supported by the Co-nect organization, but Co-nect was in turn supported and funded by the New American Schools Development Corporation, the huge, $130 million school reform consortium formed by a collection of corporate leaders. All of which had brought the ALL School advantages that most others only dream about—not the least of which were small classes. This social studies class, for example, had no more than six or seven students. Since small classes are generally synonymous with generous teacher attention, and by extension good academic work, I took a seat in the social studies class to watch some more. The students proceeded with their computer work for a while; then, toward the end, the teacher took a moment to review their knowledge of the subject they'd spent much of the term studying. When she asked them a few elementary questions about the purpose and powers of Congress, there was an uncomfortable silence. Half the class didn't know the answers. Later, as diplomatically as I could, I asked the teacher if she ever worried that the computer's multimedia appeal is distracting the students from studying the subject matter at hand. "Not at all," she said. "I use technology as a tool. This is their first PowerPoint presentation. Next time, we'll incorporate video. So it's like a building block."

Wait a minute. If the thin academic experience in this class is now considered by a model school's teacher to be an educational building block, then we have entered a new world. We have arrived at a time when our entire sense of what it means to become an educated person has been turned on its head.

As I explored the way the ALL School and others use technology, it became clear that technology itself has sometimes caused this confusion; often, however, the prevalence of computers is simply an outgrowth of a school's general academic breakdown. In that respect, technology serves an oddly useful purpose—as a kind of red flag warning of deep, fundamental decay. Fortunately, as readers of this book will discover, remnants of education's sturdier traditions—practices that constitute real building blocks—are still available. These traditions are now scattered through a random assortment of schools across the United States and other countries, like archaeological artifacts. With occasional modification, their example offers great hope for American education. In fact, a collage of these practices could open up a whole new direction in education policy—a turn to what might be called enlightened basics.

Until this occurs, the contrasts between the nation's real schools and its more numerous unthinking trend-followers, like Worcester's ALL School, seem to grow wider every year. Indeed, the intellectual distance between the PowerPoint presentations in Worcester and the election project at Blair makes me think of the old Chinese definition of the word *crisis*. In Chinese script, *crisis* consists of two opposing characters, one symbolizing danger, the other opportunity. The tension in this duality exemplifies what has been happening lately in schools as politicians and education leaders in nearly every community in the world have been making their largest investment ever in state-of-the-art technology.

This trend became front-page news in the latter half of the 1990s, when the emergence of the Internet made the high-tech classroom seem like education's long-awaited savior. With missionary zeal, technology's promoters defined this initiative as nothing short of a revolution. It was supposed to do more than any reform in recent memory to revive our weakened schools and prepare today's students for tomorrow's increasingly high-tech jobs. In the ensuing years—partly because of growing skepticism about classroom technology, and technology in general, and partly because of the fickleness of public attention—the topic has somewhat receded into the shadows. In the meantime, though, the education world has been quietly investing in technology without pause. Many schools are spending small fortunes to upgrade systems that not long ago were state-of-the-art but are now going out of date or beginning to break down.

As the twenty-first century began, the nation's schools, vulnerable as they've always been to academic fads, have been reshaped again and again by another wave of promising "cures." Several of the latest examples are the voucher and charter-school movements and the nationwide emphasis on testing and school accountability promoted by President George W. Bush's administration. Sometimes, classroom use of computers has conflicted with other trends of this sort; quite often, it accelerates them as entrepreneurs and school administrators find ways to couple and simplify policy makers' differing edicts. In this fevered world, technology has become the ultimate innovation, the device that will let schools get closer to their academic dreams no matter what the goals may be. Or so the theory goes. The reality, which this book aims to report, is crushingly discouraging.

One of the most powerful and fascinating aspects of technology's story in schools is the way that the mere arrival of computers seems to transform education's entire culture. The situation is difficult to comprehend, because people's actual experience while using computers is so intangible and so novel. This is why technology advocates often turn to analogies or metaphors when trying to explain the computer's great power. William Gibson, the science-fiction writer who coined the term *cyberspace* in his 1984 novel *Neuromancer*, described the coming electronic universe as a computer-generated landscape of "unthinkable complexity," with "lines of light ranged in the nonspace of the mind, clusters and constellations of data. Like city lights, receding . . ."[2] A decade later, Nicholas Negroponte, the founding director of the MIT Media Lab, wrote in his book *being digital* that computerized media was becoming so prevalent that it is "being taken for granted by children in the same way adults don't think about air (until it's missing)." Eventually, Negroponte predicted, people will live in "digital neighborhoods in which physical space will be irrelevant and time will play a different role."[3]

These metaphors have their grains of truth. But the real effects of embracing computers are rather more complicated than technology's evangels would have us believe. One could also say that in the realm of education, technology is like a vine—it's gorgeous at first bloom but quickly overgrows, gradually altering and choking its surroundings.

Those surroundings, as will be shown, are remarkably wide. Computer technology is redefining the continuing inequities in our methods of teaching the rich and the poor, toying with the requisites of the human imagination, and altering public hopes about school reform. It is recasting the relationships that schools strike with the business community, warping our beliefs about the demands of tomorrow's working world, and reframing our systems for researching, testing, and evaluating achievement, not only in individual students but also across state school systems. In the process, computers are also reshaping nearly everyone's sense of how people are strengthened or weakened by the tools we use. Technology's influence has spread through this terrain so effectively over the years that educators, politicians, and many average citizens have forgotten what the academic ground looked like before computers got there.

As these transformations have taken root, one of their most potent fertilizers has been the technology industry itself. Schools, after all, are wonderful seedbeds for business development. They offer a stable, ever growing market. Their young customers are trusting, impressionable, and enthusiastic, which turns them into perfect advocates for follow-up sales in the nation's homes. Furthermore, new waves of computer technology are commonly regarded (and pitched) as efforts to help society as a whole prepare for the future—a matter of such overriding public interest that it requires big new commitments from both business and government. The result has been an urgent sense of synergy. Suddenly, a new gold mine of investment opportunity has seemed to open up, somewhat akin to the way the health-care market was stimulated some years earlier by the sudden convergence of public need, government interest, and scientific discoveries. Of course, any new business frontier has its rough spots. In the education world, as might have been expected, those troubles have been illuminated as an assortment of clever technology entrepreneurs has found opportunities to capitalize on educators' innocence. Over the years, their ever expanding vigor has left classrooms vulnerable to a host of corrupting forces, from the financial to the pedagogical. By now, across a vast swath of the nation's schools, computers have so sped and dressed up the classroom with titillating distractions that the business of learning has become another enterprise altogether—one that is often incompatible with proven traditions of learning.

This is why technology's story in schools is far more than an account of how children use computers. Like most every public institution, education poses challenges so large and amorphous that it is almost impossible to get a handle on them; equally slippery is the task of arriving at public agreement about what a big institution's central job must be. The institutions of education suffer more than most from this dilemma, partly because so many people and competing organizations have differing opinions about how its business should be conducted. In this respect, though, computer technology offers a great gift. Because it has arrived so quickly and is so powerful, it can brightly illuminate realities that surround it, like a lantern suddenly dropped into an old, dusty cave. And because its gear and its costs are so tangible, it can focus public discussion on broad, nagging questions about learning that have long been seen as impossibly abstract.

———

To many people, the classroom computing campaign may feel like a relatively new idea; in actuality, its roots are ancient. Crusades to revolutionize schools through mechanical devices of one form or another have been with us almost as long as the system of public education itself. With each new technological cycle, the campaigns for change have increased in size— carrying greater experimentation, greater hopes, and greater expense. This most recent version, involving computers, has spread with unusual speed, exciting virtually everyone it touches, from students and teachers to parents and politicians.

In the decade that ran from the early 1990s to the first years of the twenty-first century, technovangels in city after city have been creating new schools and restructuring old ones, spending approximately $70 billion on new programs that revolve around the computer.[4] While this is but a fraction of the $4.67 trillion that federal and state governments have spent on K–12 public education in the last decade, it is a fraction that matters. That $70 billion is roughly what it would have cost to hire approximately 170,000 additional public school teachers—more than twice the number employed in all of New York City. This is an interesting alternative, considering the education world's loud complaints recently about the national shortage of qualified teachers.[5] Looked at another way, slightly more than half of every dollar that schools have spent on educational supplies recently has gone to technology.[6] These high-tech supplies start with all manner of sophisticated networks—large industrial servers, high-speed telecommunications wires, and so forth. In the classroom, they include everything from standard desktop computers to laptops and New Age palm-size devices. Students are now using this gear to learn to read, often through dazzling cartoonlike multimedia games; as students are able, they are also doing much of their writing on computers, along with standard classroom exercises— and many that are not so standard—in subjects such as math, science, and social studies, often with prodigious research material delivered through the great conveniences of the Internet. Meanwhile, the non-technical supplies now competing for budget allocations with computer supplies—and often taking second place—include everything from textbooks and supplementary literature to beakers, Bunsen burners, pencils and paints, test materials, and other familiar classroom mainstays.

The result of this shift in educational spending has been a real crisis, in the Chinese sense. And as the classroom has become an increasingly technological place, the pedagogical consequences have remained largely invisible and therefore widely misunderstood. Public discussion on the subject, in both educational and political circles, has become woefully polarized. When technology's boosters look at a computer, they see almost nothing but opportunity, an educational messiah. Technology's critics, meanwhile, see merely danger, a mechanical devil that encourages the death of humanistic traditions.

The truth, of course, has its feet in both sides of the debate. This book aims to sort through the two camps, in search of their various myths and paradoxes. In the process, I hope to weed out the excesses in these discussions, and to conclude with some alternatives that will help parents and educators calmly face the increasingly technological facts of modern life.

In pursuit of this goal, I crisscrossed the country for three years, visiting dozens of schools and hundreds of teachers and education leaders. I concentrated on public schools, partly because our greatest needs lie here, but also because private schools enjoy myriad advantages (small classes, extra funding, and choice students, just to name a few) that most public schools can only dream about. Because education in America continues, strangely, to be sharply divided between poor schools and rich ones, I focused on schools that serve society's less privileged children; most of the time, I picked schools that have been considered leaders in the way they use technology. During the course of this research, I think the computer promoters and I reached agreement on several fronts; there are many others, however, where I'm sure we remain far apart. This book is my presentation of that mixture, and I offer it with the hope that it will stir a fair debate.

The essential questions in the debate are those that have worried educators for decades: How do children really learn? What does society really need from schools, from technology, and from its students? These questions concern students' roles not only as future workers but also as future citizens, especially as they inherit our increasingly dangerous responsibilities in international relations. Finally, how should we spend the vast amount of money and other resources that America devotes to this yawning terrain we call education?

—

Among America's various major institutions—government, the legal system, the military, and the health-care system, among others—education may be the most insecure and the most impressionable. The reason stems from a by-product of institutional culture that can stultify any group—that peculiar tendency to gather people of primarily like minds and sensibilities. In education's case, the institution fosters a trusting culture, as befits its clientele: a student body that is, presumably, innocent, well intentioned, and full of potential for growth. For proof of this gullibility, one need only look at the many volumes that have been written about the wild zigs and zags that American public schools have taken over the decades as they've sought to follow one fad or another.[7] This reality has made schools remarkably susceptible over the years to big, shiny promises that are eventually broken. Much of the time no one notices, however, because by then the students have graduated, administrations have changed, and parents who might have fought for the students' interests have long since moved on.

Such institutional uncertainty is much of what has helped turn schools into ripe prey for charlatans and unscrupulous profiteers. And these are not just an odd collection of petty criminals. They include some of the captains of American industry—executives of the telecommunications giants, leading software developers, even designers of education's twenty-first-century God: standardized tests. Because the education community is so large—comprising roughly 218,500 public and private schools, some 4 million teachers, and the families of more than 60 million students, to say nothing of the various businesses and government agencies attached to schools—a huckster's vision has many chances to take hold.[8] Delusions are easily born in such a culture, and easily spread throughout society as a whole, skewing everyone's view of how the world works.

One example of these delusions is the chronic campaign to close what's come to be known as the "digital divide"—the shortage of technological gear that has supposedly cheated the poor out of social and economic opportunities, but which is actually a very different problem. A related delusion involves our desperate attempts to prepare students for the professional world of the future and the prevailing beliefs about technology's role in those studies. These nostrums typically emerge when debates about the computer's effectiveness in school reach an impasse. Suddenly, most everyone dismisses knotty questions about teaching practice and argues that despite its problems, classroom computer experience is crucial for success in tomorrow's high-tech workplace. This might count as technology's dominant article of faith. Yet it is difficult to overstate how severely this line of reasoning misreads history, misunderstands the demands of the workplace, even the high-tech workplace—in short, how gravely it shortchanges students.

The skills and characteristics that students do need in order to prosper over the long term, both in the world of work and in modern society in general, involve many other things. These include a rich inner life, strong values and work habits, broad knowledge, the capacity to observe and think critically, a fertile and flexible imagination, and some feel for the art of discussion. Paradoxically, many of today's educational trends have been moving students in quite the opposite direction. And some of those trends, such as the recent obsession with standardized testing, are being rapidly accelerated by computer technology. This, unfortunately, is a logical development. America has long been a data-obsessed society. And as our cultural and economic mores are spreading to other countries around the world, blind faith in data is being exported along with them.

Our desperation for objective information also propels one of Americans' dominant habits, illustrated nowhere more gorgeously than in the field of education. I am speaking of our tendency to promote any new concept by invoking volumes of quantitative "research" that ostensibly proves its value. This is a time-honored game in public policy debates, and technology advocates have played it expertly when it comes to claims about what computers will do for student achievement. As it turns out, the vast bulk of their research is surprisingly questionable. And as will be seen, the lengths to which some companies will go to weave these webs of deception are almost worthy of Hollywood awards.

The flawed groundwork on this front, and throughout this story, illustrates a fascinating peculiarity of the educational technology world: that many of its leading players live with elaborate illusions about what computers do. Whenever I looked closely at technology practices in schools, students' academic experiences were often precisely the opposite of what technology's promoters (and sometimes its detractors) say is occurring. This made for many moments when I tripped over points of irony, making for a trail of rhetorical red flags. I would have resorted to other warning systems, but I know of no word other than *irony* for one of the central patterns in this tale—that educators fall, seemingly unaware, into the same traps over and over again. Eventually, these traps and paradoxes became so prevalent that I took to giving them their own name: *e-lusions,* in honor of the e-ification of what sometimes feels like every corner of today's Internet-obsessed world.

By taking aim at educators' illusions, I do not mean to suggest that schools should never dream or never make mistakes. Error is inevitable in public policy; trying to solve problems without taking risks would only shirk society's responsibilities. It would also be antithetical to the American spirit of innovation and democracy, which propel our search for new ways to expand opportunity. Yet with all that is known about education by now—after the hundreds of different models, high-tech and otherwise, that have been tried over the decades and the volumes of literature and academic studies on their results—there is no reason for schools today to stray too far down an ineffective path, particularly one that is costly. Corrective wisdom is everywhere. And any new twists on this wisdom, such as a new technology, should be thoroughly tested and refined before they replace their more vetted forebears—science experiments with test tubes, for instance, or art with real paints and brushes.

The computer trend in education—building as it does upon so many of education's previous false crusades—has brought us to a worrisome moment. Our schools have now become institutions that foster what could be called a culture of the flickering mind. The phenomenon is yet another layer in this story's crisis, defining a generation poised between two possible directions. In one, today's students have a chance to become confident, creative masters of the modern tools of their day and, subsequently, to move our world a step closer to meeting its growing challenges. They can also, however, become victims of the commercial novelties we are visiting upon them.

While both paths are still open, the current trend is not promising, which yields an even more discouraging possibility. America's students, as will be seen, have become a distracted lot. Their attention span—one of the most important intellectual capacities anyone can possess—shows numerous signs of diminishing. Their ability to reason, to listen, to feel empathy, among other things, is quite literally flickering.

In the end, after the digital dust has settled, a pair of simple questions will remain: How should America's public schools function so as to intelligently serve both the privileged and the underprivileged? And what role should new devices like computers play in the scholastic mix? A good way to start is to follow an old educational maxim—that the best way to teach is to set an example. That is, students might learn to approach novelties shrewdly, with restraint, if adults in the education world did that too. As will be shown, education's policy makers, from local school officials on up to state legislators, governors, and even our presidents, have by and large failed that responsibility. At nearly every stage of the computer's evolution they have fallen for its temptations, including its damaging ones, while squandering a good many opportunities to make technology, and school as a whole, truly meaningful. It doesn't have to be this way.

PART I

FALSE PROMISES

CHAPTER 1

Education's History
of Technotopia

"I believe that the motion picture is destined to revolutionize our educational system," Thomas Edison said in 1922, "and that in a few years it will supplant largely, if not entirely, the use of textbooks. I should say that on the average we get only about two percent efficiency out of textbooks as they are written today." A decade earlier, Edison had been even more pedagogically expansive, saying that film makes it "possible to touch every branch of human knowledge." Now he added: "The education of the future, as I see it, will be conducted through the medium of the motion picture, a visualized education, where it should be possible to obtain one hundred percent efficiency." Three years later, Edison's vision was undiluted: "In ten years textbooks as the principal medium of teaching will be as obsolete as the horse and carriage are now. . . . There is no limitation to the camera."[1]

Almost as curious as this snippet of grandiose soothsaying from one of America's greatest inventors is the context in which it was presented. Edison's outlook was reported in a 1939 book, by which time the author had already found reason to be skeptical of technologists' promises to schools. The book was entitled *Motion Pictures As an Aid In Teaching American History*, by Harry Arthur Wise, who used Edison's quotes to prove an axiom. "Like many new educative devices," Wise wrote, "the motion picture was received into the school with a confidence and an enthusiasm not well founded." Educators' faith in films was particularly unjustifiable, Wise asserted, because it was "more far-reaching and all-inclusive than can be justified by the findings of more recent educational research." Wise, a specialist on this subject, arrived at this conclusion after reviewing seven previous studies of teaching through films and finding mixed results; he then conducted his own study, which carefully used equivalent experimental and control groups and other measures of scientific validity current at the time. Here's what he found: The group treated to films did the best, with test gains deemed "statistically significant." The films proved particularly valuable in engaging the students' imagination and in giving them a sense of the historical atmosphere of the period. The boys benefited more than the girls did. The films encouraged low-ability students to learn factual information while helping high-ability students in "acquiring spirit and atmosphere."

Overall, however, Wise found the benefit of classroom films so dependent on the circumstances—the particular subject matter, the course objectives, the students' knowledge base, and the skill of the teacher—that they could be endorsed only for use "as a supplement." Nor, Wise counseled, should teachers feel pressured to abandon their normal routines. "The teacher who is interested in making effective use of any type of visual aid does not need to assume that existing courses of study should be thrown aside and that new units should be built up around particular devices." Not surprisingly, Wise closed by stressing the need for better teacher training. The film, he noted, "is not self-operating and its use requires much time for preparation if it is to function effectively." Instructing teachers in how to do just that, he said, "is a matter of paramount importance . . ."[2] As the years progressed, most schools did not follow Wise's advice. Classroom films—as most of us remember—eventually became a rare occurrence, treated more as a welcome moment of relaxation and entertainment than a study aid.

In 1945, six years after Wise's book came out, William Levenson, the director of the Cleveland public schools' radio station, had a whole new technological vision. He claimed that "the time may come when a portable radio receiver will be as common in the classroom as is the blackboard. Radio instruction will be integrated into school life as an accepted educational medium."[3] It wasn't long before the famous psychologist B. F. Skinner joined the chorus. "I was soon saying," Skinner observed while reflecting on the first days of one of his great inventions—the behavioral "teaching machines" of the late 1950s and early 1960s—"that, with the help of teaching machines and programmed instruction, students could learn twice as much in the same time and with the same effort as in a standard classroom."[4]

Soon after the teaching machines' moment in the sun, President Lyndon Johnson spoke, in 1968, to a school in American Samoa about the next technological hope. The "one requirement for a good and universal education," Johnson said, "is an inexpensive and readily available means of teaching children. Unhappily, the world has only a fraction of the teachers it needs. Samoa has met this problem through educational television."

Johnson's remarks were something of an understatement. Education in American Samoa was in such a shambles that students were being taught in antiquated one-room schools, and not a single teacher on the island possessed a teaching certificate from the U.S. mainland. In response, Samoa's governor, H. Rex Lee, had made the overhaul of the school system his top priority. In so doing, Lee rejected the standard solutions—pouring money into the school system, retooling the curriculum, hiring mainland teachers, and retraining Samoan instructors—all of which had been recommended by his aides and by local educators. But Lee wanted fast and total change. So he set out to invest in television. In 1964, Congress came to Lee's aid, giving American Samoa $1 million for a system of televised instruction—an amount equivalent to approximately $200 per student. Two years later, four of every five Samoan students were spending from a quarter to a third of their class time watching TV. The rest of their day was spent preparing for the telecasts and, later, following up with activities related to the shows they'd watched.

Unfortunately, the proliferation of classroom televisions in American Samoa far outpaced indications of academic achievement. By 1972, three out of four high school teachers and administrators wanted to cut back heavily on classroom telecasts, and over half the elementary school students and 70 percent of the high school students agreed with them. Samoan policy makers soon began returning more control for school management to the teachers, which did not bode well for the TV campaign. In 1979, Wilbur Schramm, a mass-communications specialist, concluded that classroom telecasts had been relegated to "a supplemental enrichment service, to be used when and if the teacher decided it was appropriate."

Back on the mainland, the attitude toward televised learning was on a similar trajectory. By 1961, $20 million had been invested in classroom television by the Ford Foundation's Fund for the Advancement of Education. A year later, President John F. Kennedy plowed another $32 million into the venture. As of 1971, public and private sources had spent a total of $100 million on classroom TV.[5]

The reader of this abbreviated history will undoubtedly notice the parallels to today's hot classroom technology. One could rewrite each of these anecdotes, substituting the word *computers* for the words *motion pictures* or *radios* or *televisions* and most people would think they were recent news reports. Not too many years ago, in fact, President Bill Clinton was in the news with his own rendition of technology's old song. In 1995, during his second presidential campaign, he pitched the nation on "a bridge to the twenty-first century . . . where computers are as much a part of the classroom as blackboards." Despite the fact that this latest technological messiah was estimated at the time to cost somewhere between $40 billion and $100 billion over the next five years, Clinton's Republican adversaries were happy to sing along. Newt Gingrich, talking about computers to the Republican National Committee as Speaker of the House in 1996, said, "We could do so much to make education available twenty-four hours a day, seven days a week, that people could literally have a whole different attitude toward learning."

If history is again repeating itself, the schools are in serious trouble. In a 1986 book, *Teachers and Machines: The Classroom Use of Technology Since 1920*, Larry Cuban, a professor of education at Stanford University and a former school superintendent, observed a pattern in how schools handled each round of technology that mirrored and elaborated Harry Wise's tale. The cycle always began with big promises, backed by the technology developers' research. In the classroom, teachers never really embraced the new tools, and no significant academic improvement occurred. This provoked consistent responses from technology promoters: The problem was money, or teacher resistance, or the paralyzing school bureaucracy. Meanwhile, few people questioned the technology advocates' claims. As results continued to lag, the blame was finally laid on the machines. Soon schools were sold on the next generation of technology, and the lucrative cycle started all over again.

Today's technology evangels commonly argue that we've learned our lesson from past mistakes. As in each previous round, they say that when today's technology (the computer) is compared with yesterday's machine, today's is better. "It can do the same things, plus," Richard Riley, the former secretary of education, told *The Atlantic Monthly* in 1997.[6] In a 2002 interview, John Bailey, the director of educational technology under President George W. Bush, bolstered Riley's view. There is a great opportunity with computers, he argued, that is not yet realized but seems entirely possible: to "personalize and individualize" instruction—pinpointing certain students' weaknesses, for example, or customizing homework assignments—in ways that their mass-media predecessors couldn't.

Considering the obvious power of today's personal computers, Riley and Bailey might appear to be right. However, since schools have been badly burned by so many of technology's unfulfilled promises, it's worth pausing a moment to ask an obvious question: What does the record on school computing so far really show? Apparently, hindsight has airbrushed its history quite heavily.

A NEW DAWN, TAKE ONE

In January 1975, a new machine appeared on the cover of *Popular Mechanics.* It was a funny-looking device—a square box with flip switches on its front plate, connected to a Teletype machine. The machine was called the Altair 8800 personal computer kit and manufactured by H. Edward Roberts, the president of a small outfit in Albuquerque, New Mexico, called Micro Instrumentation Telemetry Systems, or MITS. The Altair offered 256 bytes of memory, an immeasurable speck by today's standards, and sold for $397. MITS was promptly bombarded with thousands of orders, and the personal computer was born. One of the people captivated by the *Popular Mechanics* story was a young Harvard student named Bill Gates, who subsequently ditched Harvard and traveled to Albuquerque in search of a job. Before long, the Altair was shipping with an old mainframe programming language specially adapted for this machine by Gates and his future partner, Paul Allen. Soon, Microsoft too was born, along with a whole new industry, called software.[7] Two years later, in 1977, a handful of machines, called microcomputers, most of which looked like today's large microwave ovens, were shown off at the inaugural West Coast Computer Faire. One of these was a long, slim, sloping package called the Apple II. The world was suddenly treated to an assortment of computers being manufactured in a form that was relatively small and inexpensive (the first Apple IIs, equipped with a mere 4K of memory, sold for $1,298, a sharp drop from the $18,000 to $20,000 for which a mini-computer had been selling).[8] It was only natural now to start promoting these nimble machines in the nation's classrooms.

Perhaps it's a reflection of the personal computer's increasingly compressed intensity; perhaps it's simply fate. Whatever the case, this machine's history in schools repeats, in quickened and more dynamic form, technology's entire education story. As the years have rolled on, the aspirations attached to each version and function of the computer have washed over the schools in noisy successions of swells and crashes. Indeed, the somewhat quieter discussion we see at the turn of the new century about classroom technology (and computer technology in general) is a predictable ebb, sliding back from the high computer frenzy of the late 1990s. The pattern is not terribly different, in fact, from the nation's first big flood of computopia, which hit in the early 1980s.

———

From the personal computer's debut in 1975 through most of 1981, its manufacturers (and their enthusiasts in the schools) primarily busied themselves with getting their houses in order. Commercial breakthroughs and innovative programs steadily popped up, and schools began the slow process of buying and installing these new machines—in computer labs, in school libraries, and, occasionally, in a few classrooms. Not surprisingly, some of the first innovative classroom uses of the PC arose in its Silicon Valley seedbed. Some of those early visions were quite ambitious, aiming for the same pedagogical goals that twenty-first-century technology leaders would be striving toward two decades later.

An example was the Crittenden Middle School in Mountain View, on the northern edge of the valley. In 1981, Crittenden was already using PCs to make simple graphs, execute geometry exercises, and navigate problem-solving activities. As one teacher, Steve King, put it, the computer let students simulate science experiments "that otherwise would be too expensive or difficult to perform." King also said he was taken with the computer's apparent ability to adapt to each student's individual pace—the same gold mine that John Bailey, George W. Bush's technology chief, would still be dreaming about in 2002. Crittenden never found that pot of gold, for reasons that the John Baileys of the world might do well to remember. In fact, despite Crittenden's herculean efforts, computer technology continually failed to take hold at the school in general. Steve King, the technology enthusiast, is of course long gone by now. But Sue Nelson, a longtime language arts teacher at Crittenden, remembers those days quite clearly. "We never got any support," Nelson said. "Anyone who is any good with computers is out working in industry making big bucks." Nelson, who had been at Crittenden since the early 1980s, recalled numerous attempts to scale up the school's computer program that were continually foiled by system crashes, which have continued to this day. "The teachers then spend a day and a half rebuilding everything. The computers have been absolutely frustrating. We've got all this potential with three labs on campus, but that's all it is—a lot of potential."

While plenty of technology obviously did take hold elsewhere in Silicon Valley, it was years before California launched any organized campaign for computers in schools. It wasn't even the first state to do so; Minnesota had seen the digital writing on the wall almost a decade earlier. In 1973, it formed the Minnesota Educational Computing Consortium (MECC), an ambitious and, in time, a nationally influential cooperative of state agencies and Minnesota colleges and universities. As an early sign of the coming academic attitude, Don Rawitsch, MECC's manager of user services, told a reporter in late 1981, "We've got to get computers away from the image of being separate from everything else."[9]

In the following months, the national campaign in schools for "computer literacy" (a term that had been coined almost a decade earlier, by the computing author Arthur Luehrmann) began to gather steam. One of the best portraits of the technological fever of these years was provided by a small publication called *InfoWorld.* Founded in 1980, *InfoWorld* started its life as a biweekly newsmagazine to cover Silicon Valley's fast-growing personal computer industry. By the fall of 1981, it was clear that biweekly coverage couldn't begin to keep up with this business, and the editors decided to go weekly. That summer, they had also hired a reporter named Scott Mace, whose beat would be technology in education. For the next four years, Mace was the man on the scene—whenever Apple or IBM made big donations to schools; whenever some irreverent little start-up came out with some promising new software; whenever the field's adherents gathered for their first national "educational technology" conferences; and whenever politicians jumped on the bandwagon of the miraculous personal computer. "This was the high-water mark," Mace told me when I spoke with him many years later, in the summer of 2001. "It was the time when people thought, Let's have PCs everywhere." By his own reckoning, Mace was sympathetic to that view. And why not? Almost anytime news broke on this subject, it looked like the dawning of a new age.*

"There's a personal computer being turned out once every six seconds," said Joe Roebuck, Apple's director of sales development, in a keynote address to a Southern California conference on classroom computers in the spring of 1982. "One day's production of them would fill twenty football fields." Amid all the heady new hopes at the conference, there were a few

---

*Unless otherwise noted, the bulk of references to news events during this first heady period (1981 through 1984), and their related quotes, come from articles written by Scott Mace for *InfoWorld.* My reason for drawing so heavily on this source is that this magazine and Mace were providing the media's most consistent coverage of the suddenly burgeoning world of educational technology during this time. Through the years, the magazine published hundreds of articles on the subject, a complete listing of which would overwhelm these pages. As time went on, other publications, such as *Education Week*, the daily newspapers, and some new publications devoted specifically to this market niche, began more regular coverage. In their cases, they are individually cited.

hints of trouble to come. To those struggling to find cash for computers, for example, one school administrator suggested drawing from school building funds—a recourse that many schools pursued. Over the years, this has caused a number of imbalances in school construction, some of which were recounted at this very conference. Right there in Anaheim, a high school built a computer lab only to discover that the school building didn't have enough electricity to run it. But that wasn't stopping anyone. In a sign of the optimism of the time, Apple's Roebuck issued a strong prediction: "Education," he said, "is the reason people will buy computers."

Hyperbole aside, Roebuck hit a nerve. It's always an artificial science to pinpoint, in hindsight, the exact moment when a world-shaping trend reaches critical mass. It never does, in fact, unless a multitude of factors happen to coincide.[10] But a sure sign of any new trend, if only a temporary one, is a big story in one of the national newsweeklies. Such a moment occurred on May 3, 1982, when *Time* published a cover story entitled "Here Come the Microkids." Written in the newsweeklies' standard breathless prose, the article was full of sensationalist accounts of genius children doing computer programming and other wondrous things with personal computers. "By bits and bytes," the story's subtitle said, "the new generation spearheads an electronic revolution."[11]

The magazine noted that interest in classroom computing had now reached such a state of passion that parents were raising money for computers by staging cake and candy sales, carnivals and tree-plantings, weekend car washes, and in one case a bike-a-thon. In Utica, Michigan, a principal told the magazine, "Moms and dads are coming in and telling the counselors they have to get their kids in computer classes because it's the wave of the future." One survey noted that the number of computers in schools had tripled in eighteen months, reaching 100,000 by the spring of 1982.[12] By 1985, *Time*'s sources projected, the figure might reach 300,000 to 650,000, a number that proved to be nearly on target.[13] Apple chairman Steve Jobs was talking about giving schools, free of charge, more than 80,000 computers. This was almost as many computers as they already had, and a contribution that *Time* estimated to be worth $200 million on the retail market. But it was money well spent. In an interview many years later, Bud Colligan, an early Apple education specialist who is now a venture capitalist, told me that Apple always knew that its school initiative was an ideal way to seed its market. As children became devoted to a brand, the parents would too. And that relationship was likely to last for many, many years.

Mingled among *Time*'s facts and figures were quotes from various technology leaders that undoubtedly stirred a reader's imagination. Bill Holloway, a professor of computer education at the University of Kansas, called the spread of personal computers in the classrooms nothing short of an avalanche. Others believed they were witnessing a leap in human potential as computer programming, *Time* said, promised "to shape—and sharpen—the thought processes of the computer generation." Stephen Toulmin, identified as a University of Chicago "Philosopher of Science," predicted that computers would "re-intellectualize" the television generation. "TV relieved people of the necessity to do anything," Toulmin said. "Computers depend on what you do yourself."

Twenty years later, Toulmin had some difficulty describing how computers had fulfilled his vision of a "re-intellectualized" generation. During a 2002 interview, after he had retired and moved to Beverly Hills, Toulmin said, "To a certain extent, you can't intellectualize people. You can't resolve, for instance, to turn yourself into a mathematical genius." But even those who fell for Toulmin's earlier predictions had plenty of warning that his forecast might not turn out. Buried at the tail end of the *Time* article were a few prescient, cautionary notes. "In a typical computer class," the magazine said, "only about one in five students become seriously involved." This was followed by warnings from several high-level skeptics. One was Joseph Weizenbaum, the renowned MIT professor of computer science. Weizenbaum feared that the sudden emphasis on programming problems was leading children to ignore "a whole world of real problems, of human problems." George Miller, a Princeton psychologist, took the long view. He doubted that "a few years of thinking like a computer can change patterns of irrational thought that have persisted throughout recorded history." George Steiner, described by *Time* as a "Humanist Critic," predicted that children "will be out of touch with certain springs of human identity and creativity, which belong to the full use of language rather than mathematical and symbolic codes."

In its final word, as might have been expected, *Time* put its money on the kids. "More so than adults," the magazine said, "the young know the computer for what it is." It then quoted Shawn Whitfield, an eleven-year-old growing up on the northern edge of Silicon Valley. Every Tuesday night, Shawn and his older brother, Scott, visited the Menlo Park library for computer instruction, because, Scott said, "We'll probably never get a job if we don't learn how to use computers." For young Shawn, it was a matter of destiny. "When I grow up," he said, "it's going to be the Computer Age.

It won't affect parents. They're out of the Computer Age. They had their own age."

The digital fever quickly spread. School demand for "courseware" had grown sufficiently intense that in late May 1982, one education-research firm predicted it would outstrip supply by a ratio of two to one for the next five years. The company, Talmis, projected a $75 million demand for educational software by 1985—nearly seven times what it had been in the previous year. Another consulting firm said that by 1987, the courseware market would increase by a compound growth rate of 71 percent a year—a vision whose exponential proportions didn't quite come to pass.[14]

Before long, IBM, which was fast catching up to Apple's success with personal computers, joined Jobs's campaign in the schools. "As people are exposed to personal computers in the schools, this will become an excellent way to interest folks in home computers as a supporting educational device," Bob Wallace, IBM's manager of education-industry marketing, told *InfoWorld* that summer. Wallace said the purpose of computers in the schools was to "take up the slack teachers are leaving now." He was specifically talking about math and science, which were suffering from teacher shortages at the time. In Wallace's view, computers could fill this gap by adding an extra year of math or biology instruction, even without good teachers. Then he added a reassuring note. "Obviously, we don't want to replace teachers."

As the courseware industry blossomed, the education world grew desperate for experts. One of the first to emerge was a man named LeRoy Finkel, the much beloved instructional-computing coordinator of the San Mateo County Office of Education. Partly because of the fervor of the times, and partly because of Finkel's expertise, by the fall of 1982 Finkel's mornings were often jammed with phone calls from across the country. His tiny operation went by a delightfully unappealing acronym, SMERC (for San Mateo Educational Resource Center), but it quickly developed one of the nation's first public-domain software libraries, called Soft Swap. And educators across the globe were eager to trade. Launched in 1980, SMERC was soon singled out by then-governor Jerry Brown, who eventually scheduled a brief visit to the office and proceeded to spend three and a half hours there.

COMPUTER PROGRAMMING WARS

At the beginning of the 1982–83 academic year, the College Entrance Examination Board (CEEB) made a decision that ramped up the financial stakes in school technology. The CEEB, which oversees the notorious

Scholastic Aptitude Test (SAT) and the tests on Advanced Placement courses, concluded that it was time for AP options in computer programming. And it chose a programming language called Pascal (named after the seventeenth-century French mathematician Blaise Pascal). One problem: As is often the case in the software world, there were warring camps in computer programming. In fact, most schools had begun to use a programming language called BASIC (which stood for Beginner's All-purpose Symbolic Instruction Code). The BASIC loyalists firmly believed their program was more accessible to grade school students than Pascal and that it offered more flexible opportunities to think creatively—a logical argument, since Pascal was a tightly structured language used by university computer scientists and professionals. Perhaps more important, shifting to Pascal's more rigid demands would not be cheap. By some estimates, the schools would have to spend millions, not only upgrading their software but also buying mammoth new "microcomputers," since they were the only sort at the time that could handle Pascal.

In the years following the CEEB's decision, Pascal gradually faded into the wings—but paradoxically enough, only after causing some extra trouble for schools. But that's getting ahead of the story. Actually, in a double paradox, BASIC proved to have considerably more stamina than Pascal. It has held on to this day (most recently, in an updated version called Visual BASIC) and remains one of the programming world's most powerful tools.

When the CEEB first cast its lot with Pascal, one of the many people who disagreed with this decision was a man named Bob Albrecht. In any history of the personal computer's early, Silicon Valley beginnings, there is a small family of irreverent, 1960s-style counterculturalists whose names figure largely in its folklore. Bob Albrecht's is one of those names. It is mentioned alongside his passion for dragons and teaching people Greek folk dancing as often as it is with computers and what they can do for youngsters. The son of an affluent Iowa cattle and turkey farmer, Albrecht taught himself computer programming in 1955, on the "machine language" developed for the early IBMs. In 1966, possessed by the computer's as yet untapped potential, Albrecht headed for San Francisco (suitably, in a convertible VW bug, which, upon arrival, he paired with a red VW van). Before long, he'd moved to Menlo Park, where he, LeRoy Finkel, and several others started a great number of enterprises.

One was the Portola Institute, which served as the seedbed for Stewart Brand's legendary *Whole Earth Catalog*. Another, in 1968, was DYMAX, one of the first educational publishing houses to focus on computing in schools. Yet another was a journal for computer hobbyists called *Dr. Dobb's Journal of*

Computer Calisthenics and Orthodontia: Running Light Without Overbyte. The journal was hungrily received (and, under a shortened title, is still published to this day). Albrecht was known at the time for having a new idea every three minutes, and he was just getting warmed up. In 1972, he and Finkel started the People's Computer Center, the nation's first drop-by shop, where people could buy recreational computer time. The center actually grew out of a raggedy monthly, called *The People's Computer Company Newspaper,* which looked like something published out of a basement in Haight-Ashbury. A look inside the newspaper, which grew fat with ads during its five-year life, proved that it had much more than free computer love in mind. With unalloyed ebullience, it urged readers to support two outfits that it deemed to be educational technology's leaders: Digital Equipment Corporation (DEC) and Hewlett-Packard. From 1970 to 1973, Finkel once wrote, he and Albrecht and several colleagues "barnstormed California in Bob's VW van, loaded down with DEC and Hewlett-Packard support materials." They stopped at almost every University of California campus, from Riverside to Berkeley, offering a class entitled Computers in the Classroom-X402 and "turning on more than 500 teachers to computers."[15]

In 1979, with a man named Ramon Zamora, Albrecht launched another first: ComputerTown USA, a community computer literacy project that worked to get personal computers donated to libraries. Albrecht knew he was more of a starter than a manager, so by 1980, most of these ventures had either migrated into new directions or were safely in the hands of others. Albrecht therefore began studying how children learn and writing books about how their learning might be helped by programs like BASIC and, eventually, other pieces of modern technology.

Today, nearly five decades and more than thirty books later (some of which have sold hundreds of thousands of copies), Albrecht's fervor and vision have hardly dimmed. I noticed the fire in his imagination myself when we met several times during the summer of 2001. Albrecht, seventy-one at the time, still writes about technology and still works with elementary, high school, and college students, as both a classroom volunteer and paid tutor. "I'm just really getting started, in a way," he told me. In the years since *The People's Computer Company Newspaper* put a pencil sketch on its first cover of a tiny ship sailing into a huge, rising sun, Albrecht has seen a plethora of technological ideas travel through the schools. Some have stuck; most have not. This experience has left him with a sobering perspective on technology and education.

For years Albrecht was, by his own admission, a BASIC evangelist, partly because few other computer program options were available. In 1968, he wrote the nation's first textbook on the program and then helped teach it in dozens of schools.[16] Before long, Albrecht noticed that while some students were wildly enthusiastic about the program, most weren't. "As long as the use of computers in school would be tied to learning a programming language—whatever programming language—it wasn't going to do much. It would grow a little bit, mostly involving bright kids and innovative teachers. And then it would level off." Schools that pushed that boundary only asked for trouble. "You're beating your head against the wall to teach teachers programming," he said. And those who seemed to succeed soon discovered they had won at a losing game. "Today's hot programming language," Albrecht said, "is tomorrow's forgotten dialect."

Chastened by these experiences, Albrecht began to roll with the times. As each new software program arrived on the scene, he enthusiastically threw himself into its opportunities—without deluding himself that it was the answer, that it would last long, or that it deserved an entire course of study. "I don't teach any of these programs," Albrecht told me. "I just use them as they come up." His point is that computers, and their software programs, are merely tools, to be picked up and dropped the way a carpenter shifts from a hammer to a screwdriver to a measuring tape. In fact, if he were a school official, Albrecht would suggest avoiding any program built specifically for schools. "Students and teachers should use the same tools in schools that they're using in the real world."

COMPUTERS AND POLITICS, TAKE ONE

Politicians are like everyone else—they like to bet on winning horses. And in the fall of 1982, computers in schools looked like society's runaway winner. Earlier that year, Arizona's then-governor, Bruce Babbitt, placed the political world's first bet on this innovation, proposing a tax write-off for companies that donate computers to schools. Not to be outdone as a futurist, California governor Jerry Brown quickly proposed a similar idea. At a time when his state was projecting a billion-dollar budget deficit, Brown proposed a $48 million education initiative centered on technology. His plan was to create nineteen "Computer Demonstration Centers," which he said would inaugurate "the second American education revolution." In a speech to Computer Using Educators (an organization founded by LeRoy Finkel, widely known by its acronym, CUE, and still very much in existence), Brown spelled out his vision. "This new educational revolution," he told the crowd, "can be a qualitative leap in which we vastly increase the quality of this public education and realize the age-old dream of empowering each person to reach the limit of his or her ability." In another serving of vintage Jerry Brown earnestness, he described his initiative as being all about "the three C's—computing, calculating, and communicating with technology."

The California legislature was all ears. By September, Brown had a bill signed and ready to go that freed companies from paying taxes on 25 percent of the market price of any computers they gave to schools for the coming year and a half. Weeks later, he added a $1.2 million sales tax refund for custom-software developers. Across the country, political officials were treating audiences to similar messages. At one conference of three hundred educators in New York City, Robert Maurer, the city's executive deputy commissioner of education, said that computers, which he called "brain enhancers," were ushering in a revolution no less dramatic than the industrial revolution.

The popular perception of the technology industry is that it is inhabited by a special breed—a corps of pristine innovators that, until Microsoft's trouble with antitrust regulators, has had little if any need for the dirty business of politics. The record of the 1980s casts this story in a rather different light. In reality, technology's corporate leaders proved to be as quick and effective in learning the game of politics as they were with the microchip.

In October 1982, for example, Congress made several moves to ante up for the computer industry after intense lobbying from Apple chairman Steve Jobs. At the time, companies could take tax write-offs for computer donations, but only when the recipients were colleges and universities. That fall, a Senate committee approved a bill extending the tax break to cover donations to grade schools and high schools. And this tax break would go further than the college measure, letting companies write off roughly one and a half times the cost of each computer. In the House, those carrying Jobs's idea went further still. Representative Pete Stark, a Democrat from Jobs's Silicon Valley district, proposed making the tax break worth up to twice the cost of the computer donations.

As Congress deliberated, the chorus of cheers from California grew. In early November, a San Jose CUE conference gathered a record two thousand attendants—a third more than it had drawn to its previous conference, just six months earlier. During one of the conference's 250 sessions, IBM's Bob Wallace told the audience, "We're confident that [the computer] does teach." Since IBM had only recently begun catching up with Apple's presence in the classrooms, Wallace began by eating a little humble pie. IBM, he acknowledged, is "the new kid on the block." But Wallace also struck a shrewd note of optimism. IBM was confident, he said, that it had come into the game with an armful of strong products. "We should have," he said. "We took longer to do it." His company made it plain that it planned to back up its boasts with data. Having recently donated PCs to school districts in five states, the company expected positive results soon from various tests. Solid evidence of the equipment's benefits never did materialize. But in the midst of the CUE conference's technological fervor, that possibility seemed remote.

During the conference, teachers and students had a chance to try out some of the software being promoted. To do so, they sat down at Commodores and Ataris and other machines whose names have long since become relics of the PC's stone age. One of the most prophetic of those was the widely sold TRS 80, named after its maker, Tandy/RadioShack. Soon nicknamed the Trash 80 because of how quickly its tinny, monochrome box with green type went out of style, the machine gave schools a small taste of technology's rapid and costly cycle of obsolescence. But those troubles were a long way from anyone's mind in 1982. "There's been a lot of excitement here, and also a sense of historical importance," an aide to Governor Brown said during the conference. In a nod to the urgency of the moment, a state education official told *InfoWorld* that "we're running to catch up" with what he termed "the grass-roots use of technology in schools."

As the year turned, *Time* once again took center stage to define the meaning of the moment. For the first time in fifty-five years, the magazine chose not to put a human being on its cover for Man of the Year. Instead, it chose an artist's rendering of a personal computer. Under the headline "Machine of the Year," the magazine said, "Several human candidates might have represented 1982, but none symbolized the past year more richly, or will be viewed by history as more significant, than a machine: the computer." In recapping its reporting that year, *Time* said the computer was transformed from an image synonymous with Big Brother to a small, highly personalized device. (In an anecdote that the magazine obviously considered a cute sign of the times, it noted that throughout its 1982 coverage the editorial department had been plagued with computer crashes. In fact, in writing the main story for its "Machine of the Year" issue, Otto Friedrich, a senior writer for *Time*, ended up tapping out his copy on his favorite machine of all: a fifteen-year-old Royal typewriter.)[17]

In early 1983, struck by a sudden spread of cheap personal computers, *InfoWorld* decided it was time for a statement of its own. "The public is running out of reasons to hold off on buying a computer," Mace wrote in an editorial. After months of marketing pressure about "computer literacy" (a term used again in the 1990s, without irony, as though it were an untried concept), the industry had made the idea almost irresistible. It was now producing simplified versions of the PC for $200 or less. "At These Prices, Why Not?" *InfoWorld's* headline asked. While many of these machines were not yet sufficiently "user-friendly" (another term reinvented in the 1990s), Mace nonetheless urged readers to act now, if only to get a head start on computer programming skills, which were seen as critical for keeping up with the times. The times did indeed seem to be racing in technology's direction; even theater troupes began commenting on the change. In February 1983, the venerable South Coast Repertory started touring Southern California with *Bits & Bytes*, a play about what a young girl can and cannot get from technology. Despite all these signs of people's growing interest in technology, back in Washington the nation's political leaders remained circumspect. Nonetheless, in the months ahead, Congress would toy with numerous ways to help the computer industry reach its goals in the schools.

FALSE PROPHETS

In the midst of 1983's frenzy about computing, a product was announced that would have a very long echo. In February of that year, a company called Digital Research released a new version of a program called LOGO, built for the IBM PC market. LOGO was an ambitious children's programming language developed by BBN Technologies and spread by one particular BBN consultant: MIT computer-science whiz Seymour Papert. The program had been available previously, for Apples and some other machines, but this new release started LOGO on its rise toward wide scholastic use.

From the beginning, LOGO had a lot going for it, propelled as it was by the aura that surrounded its champion. Papert not only possessed a rare intelligence, he also loved helping children work with computers and was fascinated by how they learn. If that wasn't enough (and, as any teacher will tell you, it usually is), Papert had spent five years studying with the twentieth century's first authority on childhood development, Swiss psychologist Jean Piaget. That experience left Papert—a man already prone to grand visions and rarefied theories—with even more lofty ideas about how human intelligence could be expanded, this time by computers. A short, stocky man in spectacles, and now with longish, thinning gray hair and a long, bushy gray beard, Papert looks like—and is—the quintessential math genius. To talk with him is to engage with someone whose mind is only half with you; the other half seems to be wrestling with questions on some faraway, higher plane. All of this created a compelling package and helped transform Papert into America's leading guru on children's technology. Papert's rise was aided by the comparatively looser laws that surrounded intellectual property in those days. Before long, a number of firms like Digital Research had made their own versions of LOGO and were vigorously spreading them in the public domain.

With Digital Research's announcement of the new version of LOGO, Gary Kildall, the company president, did not miss his opportunity to seek a competitive edge. He contrasted his new programming tool to the schools' current favorite—BASIC. Schools had been heavily investing in BASIC, and in computers that could run it. However, Kildall said, BASIC "turns out to be a very poor approach to teaching someone how to use computers. In many cases, it's very limiting to a child."

Kildall's line wasn't surprising, considering his proprietary interest in trouncing a competitor. In the following years, though, a number of schools bought his argument as it was repeated over and over by IBM, Papert, believers in artificial-intelligence software, and other LOGO enthusiasts. The upgrade parade now went around the block one more time as schools spent time and money junking systems built around BASIC, which now seemed obsolete, for another program that suddenly seemed state-of-the-art.

———

The LOGO story offers, in hyper-microcosm, an allegory for the whole educational technology tale. As LOGO's leader, Papert has long managed to live in his own semifictional world, shaped by the same prophecy playing over and over again, in an endless loop, for thirty years. The central message is that computers have a perfectly good excuse for failing to have much effect in the classrooms. It's not the hardware or software that's to blame; it's the schools. But thanks to the computer, schools are about to change.

In 1975, for example, Papert delivered a speech to a technology conference in which he said, "If you asked me whether the practice of education will have undergone a *fundamental* change through the impact of computers in either five years or twenty-five years, I could answer with complete confidence 'NO' to the first question and 'YES' to the second . . ."[18] Here he is again in 1980, in his widely distributed book *Mindstorms: Children, Computers, and Powerful Ideas*: "Increasingly, the computers of the very near future . . . will gradually return to the individual the power to determine the patterns of education. Education will become more of a private act."[19] Four years later, in an article for *Popular Computing* magazine, Papert still saw revolution coming sometime soon to a school near you. "There won't be schools in the future," he stated flatly. "I think the computer will blow up the school. That is, the school defined as something where there are classes, teachers running exams, people structured in groups by age, following a curriculum—all of that. . . . But this will happen only in communities of children who have access to computers on a sufficient scale."[20] Then this, in the late 1980s: "Nothing is more ridiculous than the idea that this technology can be used to improve school. It's going to displace school and the way we have understood school. Of course, there will always be, we hope, places where children will come together with other people and will learn. But I think that the very nature, the fundamental nature, of school that we see in this process is coming to an end."[21]

On and on it went. "The pundits of the Education Establishment have failed to provide leadership in this area," Papert wrote in 1993, in an article for *Wired* magazine, one of the leading chronicles of the recent technological wave. "Perhaps the readers of *Wired*, who can see farther into the future, have a profoundly important social role in stirring up such debate."[22] Finally, by the middle of the 1990s, Papert began to adjust his vision, but only slightly. In a 1996 interview, he admitted that education had not much changed, saying schools had reacted to the invasion of computer technology the way any living organism would. "A foreign body comes along—the computer—and the organism's immune system and defense mechanism takes over. So we saw a shift in the 1980s. Before then computers were being used in exciting ways. They were in the hands of visionary teachers who were trying to use computers because they were dissatisfied with how schools did things. By the end of [the] 1980s, the larger number of computers were under the control of the school bureaucracy. . . . There were still visionary teachers, but they were being neutralized." Papert still had hope, though. Noting that more computers now resided in the homes than in schools, he predicted that households were the new opportunity zones for learning. Once children seized their chance, it was only a matter of time before schools fell. The young, he said, "are the power that will change schools. . . ."

Just recently, during a 1999 gathering of LOGO loyalists at one of his "Mindfest" conferences at the MIT Media Lab, Papert was still at it. This of course was nearly the hour that Papert had first predicted back in 1975— the moment, twenty-five years hence, when he could say with "complete confidence" that "education will have undergone a *fundamental* change through the impact of computers." Despite Papert's italicized certainty about this tectonic shift in education, come 1999 the world was still waiting. And he was still predicting. "School as we've known it has got twenty more years or it's dead," Papert said at one point, ushering in yet another twenty-year wait. By now, Papert had become completely exasperated with the education system, including its save-the-world reform movements. At the MIT conference, Papert dismissively ticked off several: vouchers, charter schools, the rise in home schooling, to name but a few. These, he said, are "not an answer but a symptom of the schools' failure." And the latest obsession—standardized testing—is, to Papert, "the last twitch of the dying dragon's tail."

All of these trends, along with the severe troubles that have recently beset school systems in various American cities and the public's continual concern about schools, are evidence to Papert that he was right—computers *did* change the system. In a 2002 interview, he told me, "If you had asked me ten years ago, I would have said I was wrong, that it will take fifty years. But now, I would say it's apparent the system is breaking down." But did computers cause all these signs of tumult? "The whole digital age has caused them, and anything that goes with that—globalization, the accelerating pace of things, and the changing media."

The incisive sting in all these remarks demonstrates some of Papert's great appeal. Indeed, his line couldn't have drawn such a following for so long if there weren't something to it. Yes of course, schools have needed to change. But what's curious about Papert is that he has long seen computers—and even more strangely, a programming language like LOGO—as the key to this change. In *Mindstorms*, for example, Papert elegantly describes how children's work with LOGO can make mathematical concepts come alive. Just exploring the program's procedures, he writes, leads to physical activities and logistical problems in which children "explore 'naturally' domains of knowledge that have previously required didactic teaching." This, he argues, puts youngsters "in contact with the 'material'—physical or abstract— [which] they can use for Piagetian learning."[23]

For a select number of students, especially those who have received careful guidance from skilled adults, Papert has been gloriously and touchingly on target. (The few dozen young geniuses at his 1999 Mindfest gathering offered an eye-opening illustration. They were nearly delirious from having such a rich, high-end playpen at their disposal and being surrounded by adoring grown-up geniuses morning to night for two days.) Most youngsters, however, have had a very different experience. If the independent studies of LOGO and other academic computer programming languages are any guide, the verdict is as follows: The vast majority of students have never understood programming, have never sustained much interest in it even if they did understand it, and have never been terribly changed by it in any case.[24]

Papert does not differ with these studies' conclusions; in his mind, they only confirm his hunches about organized education's failure. "I never thought a few hours a week of LOGO would make much difference," he told me. "Nothing will change unless it's complete"—that is, until computers are used intensively, pervasively, throughout the academic day. The "complete" change that Papert wants entails far more than classroom activities; it involves the whole culture of school, which still operates, he believes, on a nineteenth-century design. "School has probably changed less than other major institutions," he said. "The evidence that we got it right in school and got it wrong everywhere else is pretty slight." When making this argument, Papert delights in using a favorite metaphor for what happens when schools introduce computers: It's as though some "nineteenth-century imaginative engineer had invented the jet engine and attached it to a stage coach to see if it would help the horses." Computer technology, Papert acknowledged, really is "a disruptive technology. It should be so. School was designed for a different medium."

During all the years that Papert has hammered at this message, he has regularly worked with small groups of youngsters in one venue or another to prove that his programming visions were more than those of an idle dreamer. At the beginning of the twenty-first century, Papert was still at it— teaching LOGO and other programs to the residents of a juvenile detention center outside Portland, Maine. By all available accounts, Papert (with the help of Gary Stager, a fresh-thinking and similarly irreverent instructor from Pepperdine University) was producing some wonderful results. I tried several times to visit the Portland project, but Papert was always reluctant. I was therefore left to the evaluations of the various professors and other experts who have studied Papert's initiatives over the years. Virtually all of them dismissed the grand conclusions that Papert draws from his success with these tiny experiments. Their assessment, in short, was as follows: Papert and his crew succeed because they are exceptionally bright, energetic, and creative; because they haven't lost faith in children who don't achieve in traditional academic environments; and because they come in with a team that can give each youngster intense individual attention. By extension, this means that any teaching group with similar attributes could produce similar results—with paints, books, Socratic dialogues, any number of materials and techniques, a point that Stager acknowledges would also be the case in Portland. Papert, however, is not so inclined to concede defeat. During our last conversation, he argued that the "gradual, steady encroachment of electronic media" in the professions, and throughout all of society, still bodes unfulfilled promise for a similar revolution in education. "School textbooks aren't a good way to learn history," he said. "In fact, they are an extremely bad way to learn about history. The best way to handle knowledge and information is through electronic media. It's not that electronic information is anywhere near where it could be. But things are developing."

—

It's hard to argue with such shiny conjurings of future possibilities—undoubtedly another reason that Papert's pitch has held its magnetism for so long. Actually, some of today's electronic media partly prove Papert's point, having clearly contributed more social good than bad. Documentaries are an obvious example. But what about the Internet and its voracious little brother—e-mail? These media forms are undoubtedly permanent fixtures throughout society and, in some form, in all of our schools. During the course of my visits to schools, I had plenty of chances to examine Papert's beliefs about technology—even in schools that followed his dictum: They had attempted "complete" change, or something fairly close to it, through computing. As it turned out, their accomplishments were probably not quite what Papert envisioned. But that's getting ahead of the story.

At this point, Papert's argument should be assessed in one of two ways. The safest, most conservative approach is to go by the historical record. By that measure, Papert's pitch for technology fails miserably. The history of education and psychology shows that many kinds of study, including the "didactic" teachers that Papert deplores, are required for the full child development that Papert as well as Piaget have envisioned.[25] Computers can of course be part of this mix; for certain mathematically oriented youngsters, they absolutely should be.* But the record also indicates that it may be unrealistic to think that any innovation—technological or otherwise—would bring radical change to an institution as old, as large, and as established as

---

*The work of Mitch Resnick, a colleague of Papert's and an MIT associate professor of learning research, underscores this point. Resnick developed a name for himself by helping start a national network of "computer clubhouses"—after-school centers where youngsters can explore games and other computer projects, according to their curiosities. Many of those projects, of course, aren't terribly educational. But some are. "If you want to play with math much beyond first grade," Resnick once told me, "you need computational devices of some kind, so you can create and explore patterns, modify a variable, and watch the real effects of that happen."

education. Yes, change is badly needed, and it is possible. But the kind that has succeeded has been incremental, unthreatening, and compatible with education's long-standing organizational structure rather than revolutionary. For all its troubles, and all its vulnerability to silly fads, there is a hard core to America's system of education that has long been immovable. Some of the system's habits (the firm divisions between subject areas; the superficial, fact-laden nature of tests, and sometimes of the curriculum itself; the dusty, deadly quality of most teacher-training studies) would make little sense in a more ideal world. Others (the large number of students that teachers must supervise; the low common denominator of academic goals; the short class periods; the sameness of tasks within each class, despite the great individual differences among students) appear to make little sense, but they actually do—once we remember the schools' enormous job and the public and political demands for measurable scholastic progress.[26]

There is an uncomfortable truth in this history: Education is an institution dominated by the pressures of mediocrity. Schools are places where treating average needs with average amounts of resources has long been the rule—a fact that, unfortunately, has become extremely comfortable and therefore deeply entrenched. Strangely, the educational policies of the nation's most recent president, George W. Bush, merely dig this trough deeper. As will become clear throughout this book, if schools really are going to "leave no child behind," to paraphrase the title of Bush's new education law, and if they proceed to do so on the simple measures that Bush has emphasized, then most teachers will have time and energy for little more than pulling the whole class a foot or two beyond the middle. The syndrome in evidence here is somewhat like Winston Churchill's famous statement about democracy—it's the worst system in the world, except for all the others. Churchill meant his remark as a compliment, but education's policy makers don't generally treat their institutional realities with quite the same respect. Schools might find more realistic opportunities if everyone did.

The other way to evaluate Papert's call is to take society's technological shift more seriously. While Papert's timing may be off, the media evolution he champions does seem to be occurring. If that's the case, there is still a need for adjustment in the classrooms. Significant social trends generally have a way of taking care of themselves; if anything, they sweep across the landscape too quickly, too haphazardly, leaving swaths of damage in their wake. (Modern examples include the industrialization of farming, the globalization of commerce, and, in this case, the spread of electronic media.) As youngsters try to adapt to today's accelerating world, with its rapid onslaught of simulated images, perhaps it is the schools' job to slow things down. Education, after all, is supposed to help youngsters understand and cope with both the positive and negative elements of the adult world they will encounter. It is also supposed to make sure they appreciate its humanist traditions.

THE DIGITAL DIVIDE, TAKE ONE

In the spring of 1983, a report came out that many years later would give some experts a serious case of déjà vu. The document, written by International Resource Development (IRD), a market-research firm in Norwalk, Connecticut, pointed to a growing technology gap between rich and poor children.

Any reader of the news in recent years has seen lots of hand-wringing about today's supposedly sudden discovery of a "digital divide." The contrasts that have created this delineation, as we'll see in the following chapter, do not fall the way the public has been led to believe. Nonetheless, for those who think we should do whatever we can to arm the underprivileged with computer technology, it's not as though we haven't had plenty of advice on how to do this. In an observation that people today are only beginning to appreciate, IRD noted that as schools emphasize computer work, wealthier students who have computers at home would increasingly gain an unfair advantage. IRD considered the problem serious enough that it thought poorer communities and school districts might someday file legal challenges. In making this case, IRD noted that inequities between the academic opportunities for rich and poor have long been known, and traditionally have been solved by the libraries, through bountiful supplies of books. It doubted, however, that the libraries could ever offer an equivalent amount of computer access.

Several weeks later, the mainstream media came out with its first serious report questioning the way the school computer campaign was being handled. In early April 1983, *The Wall Street Journal* published a story in its business section noting that across the country, schools that had invested heavily in computers were often encountering tremendous problems.[27] In Broward County, Florida, for example, the school district bought 900 Apple IIs under a $2.1 million computer expansion plan launched six months earlier. Yet in one elementary school, only a few of the teachers and students had even tried the machines. The computer campaign apparently irritated a number of teachers, whose salaries averaged $19,300 a year and whose school board had recently imposed a labor contract that paid them even less than they'd been hoping for. In New Jersey, one state official observed a pattern of chaos in his state's school districts. "First they buy the machines, then they buy the software," the official said. "Then they start to think, 'Why did we get into this in the first place?'"

Prophecies of trouble littered the *Wall Street Journal* article. Complaints abounded, for example, about the quality of the educational software. In a typical opinion, the head of the English department at a Florida high school said that nearly all the software she reviewed recently was "horrendous." Her opinion, it seemed, was more than anecdotal. The year before, a newly formed group called EPIE (Educational Products Information Exchange), in consortium with *Consumer Reports,* had begun to offer schools the nation's first independent evaluation of education software. In its first review, of fifty products, EPIE concluded that only a fourth got a grade of 60 percent or better. A number of computer drilling programs in particular failed, said EPIE director Ken Komoski, because they let students "guess their way through." Many years later, the experts' evaluation of the courseware field was much the same, if not worse. In 1997, in a typical comment, Judah Schwartz, co-director at the time of Harvard's Educational Technology Center, told *The Atlantic Monthly* that "99 percent" of educational software programs are "terrible, really terrible." In the fall of 2001, Schwartz, by then a professor emeritus at both Harvard (in education) and MIT (in engineering science and education), considered the situation not much changed. In a note to me, Schwartz wrote, "The overwhelming majority of educational software is indeed terrible, having in large measure not been written by educators nor motivated by important educational considerations." Access to the Internet has "increased the amount of educationally valuable material," Schwartz added. "Unfortunately," he said, "it has increased the amount of mediocre material to a far greater degree."

Compatibility problems proliferated early on as well. *The Wall Street Journal* reported that at Homestead High School, in Apple's own hometown (Cupertino, California), teachers had tried to share software by networking their computers—an effort to stretch the district's $275,000 computer investment. Unfortunately, most software available at the time wouldn't work on networked systems. The article's final note was a prescient word of advice from Marc Tucker, a Washington, D.C., analyst of classroom computer policies. Tucker said schools should spend only 25 percent of their technology budgets on software, 25 percent on hardware and maintenance, and the remaining 50 percent on planning, teacher training, and other support services. Over the years, various technology specialists—including those who advise businesses—have recommended dividing technology spending into roughly the same proportions. If anything, they've suggested reserving the largest pot of money for maintenance and upgrades. But the advice hasn't mattered. Decades later, schools were consistently pouring the bulk of their cash into raw consumption, leaving no more than 10 to 15 percent for both maintenance and training.[28]

—

As the 1983 school year drew to a close, Governor Bruce Babbitt began to fear that Arizona wasn't moving toward technology's future fast enough. In an April speech to an educational computing conference at the University of Arizona in Phoenix, Babbitt proposed making computer literacy so important that incoming teachers be denied certification if they lacked this skill. Babbitt's panic, shared by many others at the time, was stoked by a national insecurity about the country's place in global competition. This was in the day, brief as it was, when Japan's economy was smugly ascendant and pundits of every stripe were blaming the schools for letting America fall behind. It was also the year that a federal commission published a report entitled "A Nation at Risk," which landed with a loud bang, drawing newspaper headlines across the country for months to come.

The report did not focus on technology but on the state of education in general. In essence, it said, through decades of efforts to make education more fun, more relevant, more sensitive to this crowd or that, schools had gradually corroded their standards of learning. What was now at hand was nothing short of a "crisis." Babbitt clearly agreed, and used the Arizona conference to pile on some additional complaints. He pointed out that Japan was graduating 50 percent more engineers than the United States, and that Soviet high school students took two years of calculus while in the States, only one of ten high school students was doing so. These failures, he argued, had infected the teacher corps as well. In a recent year, he said, his own state had not graduated a single student from its schools of education who had majored in mathematics. Arizona was not alone; other reports later revealed that teachers in training were spending excess time with "methods" courses about teaching and phys ed classes, instead of mastering math, sciences, and the liberal arts.[29] For the country as a whole, Babbitt thought the message was clear: The shortage of teachers properly trained in math and the sciences, he said, amounted to "unilateral economic disarmament."

As parents tried to sort out these various messages, they began to take matters into their own hands—with a little help from another new technology industry. Across the country, entrepreneurs had founded "computer camps," which could cost up to $250 a day. Some were lavish overseas ventures, coupled with special tours of Europe, running at more than $3,000 for a four-week excursion. First started in 1977, the camps initially tried to simply give children a general familiarity with computer technology. By 1983, camp organizers thought it was time to specialize. Some designed programs that focused almost exclusively on LOGO; others concentrated on competitors like BASIC and Pascal. There were spreadsheet camps competing with database camps. A Michigan camp director, fittingly named John Camp, had such high aims that his program read like a school curriculum description. For the media, the camp craze provided a valuable service. Through the years, and continuing to this day, news stories about almost any development in the school computer world have been accompanied by essentially the same photograph: a shot of a computer on a desk, surrounded by one or more adorable young children, a teacher often supportively joining in, all beaming with eye-glistening enthusiasm. Now the papers had a new photo op: a kid at camp, kneeling in front of a mammoth desktop computer inside her tent.[30]

DIGITAL DRILL SERGEANTS

In the heat of that summer of 1983, another innovative product, called Dial-A-Drill, was released by a company called Computer Curriculum Corporation, a firm that was and would continue to be one of the biggest players nationwide in the educational software market. Dial-A-Drill, CCC's first commercial offering in sixteen years, was a little different from most of its competitors. It was delivered as an automatic recording, over the phone, which students (or adults) could pick up at appointed times. They'd then hear a computerized voice that would put them through reading, spelling, and arithmetic drills, which they'd answer by punching buttons on the phone's keypad. As students recorded their answers, the phone-bank computer responded with occasional hints and words of praise ("Excellent work!"). It also adjusted the drill as the phone call progressed, delivering harder problems for skilled children or easier ones for those who were struggling. That made Dial-A-Drill "computer-adaptive," as testing experts call it, a feature that would become all the rage many years later (see chapter 9).

Dial-A-Drill was developed by CCC founder and president Dr. Patrick Suppes, another legend of the academic-computing movement. In the 1960s, while in his forties, Suppes became one of the earliest and most fervent advocates of computer-aided instruction (CAI), the family of computerized drill and practice routines that became widely popular in the 1980s and early 1990s. One of the things that put Suppes on the map was an influential article he wrote in 1966 for *Scientific American,* "The Uses of Computers in Education," in which he predicted that it would not be long before we had computers that could talk to children—a theory that Dial-A-Drill tried to put into practice. The article was widely reprinted, and translated into at least four languages.[31]

Suppes approached CAI as a science, which he studied intensely and promoted through an unusual double career. During his twenty-four years as CCC's president, Suppes also served as a professor of mathematics and philosophy at Stanford University and the director of its Institute for Mathematical Studies in the Social Sciences. In 1990, Suppes sold CCC to Simon & Schuster. But he stayed at Stanford, and as of 2002, he was still affiliated with the university, teaching classes as a retired professor of philosophy, emeritus. By this time, Suppes's curriculum vitae was as distinguished as his website portrait, in which a lean and tanned Dr. Suppes gazed contentedly at his readers, his fine patrician features and wavy, graying hair nicely crowning the accomplishments underneath. Those accomplishments run for approximately fifty pages. There is a C.V. with scores of academic honors and appointments; a twenty-seven-page "intellectual autobiography"; and lists of hundreds of related papers, from 1951 to present, in six different categories: "Methodology, Probability, and Measurement"; psychology; the brain; the "Foundation of Physics"; "Language and Logic"; and "Computers and Education." This last category is Suppes's most extensive, numbering 146 different journal articles and conference presentations over a forty-year period.[32]

To read through even a slice of Suppes's material is to be treated to a worldview that, while appearing archaic, has cropped up repeatedly in modern times. It is the scientist outlook in the extreme—the assumption that anything worth bothering with can be objectively identified, consciously induced, tightly controlled, and empirically measured. This outlook has often shaped the way American society works—how it evaluates children, as well as adults, and how it awards merit to each of us. Indeed, the recent enthusiasm for standardized academic testing, generously fed by George W. Bush's administration, is but the latest example of the modern appetite for such endeavors. One of the most influential early proponents of this philosophy was James B. Conant, the mid-twentieth-century Harvard chemistry professor and, later, university president who created the Scholastic Aptitude Test. (Conant, widely regarded as the father of standardized testing, also brought the nation its modern culture of large, "consolidated" high schools, as well as a system for labeling student abilities. Such a system, Conant believed, would help society "track" students, steering them into high scholarship at one extreme or vocational education at the other—a habit that educators are still trying to outgrow.) An equally famous adherent of the ultra-scientist view was a Conant contemporary, the behavioral psychologist B. F. Skinner, whose view that people were—or could be—essentially trained like animals ultimately fell into disrepute. While Suppes took pains to point out his differences with Skinner, he sometimes sided with the old man, describing himself at one point as "the White Knight of the Behaviorists."

If Suppes was right, Dial-A-Drill was going to be his white horse. When the program was released in 1983, Suppes called it part of a "broad societal response" to the need for computer-assisted instruction. The telephone drills, he said, created "a regular and organized time, in clear contradistinction to what you can do with a home computer." The product did have economy on its side. Courses cost $15 to $18 apiece (less in bulk purchases). That fee bought three to five calls a week, with each call estimated to take only six to ten minutes. It also brought monthly reports in the mail and an "overlay" card, which turned the phone's keypad into a simplified calculator. The voice system was a special innovation—"a bit-sliced machine of our own design," CCC said. If students dodged the machine's calls, their parents would hear about it in the monthly reports.

As strange as this product sounds, Suppes based it on a set of purposeful learning theories, some of which he had articulated a decade earlier, in a conversation with the editors of *Saturday Review*. Pictured then as an earnest, young fuzzy-headed professor in heavy black-rimmed glasses and a dark ascot, Suppes faced off in the magazine's pages with Bob Albrecht, whose open-ended approach to computer programming clearly irritated the Stanford professor. "One of our most important concerns," Suppes said, "is the people who say that because they have all these facilities and technology, teachers will write their own courses. I think that's no more true than it's been in publishing—that the average teacher would write a textbook. I think it's less true." What particularly irked Suppes were the idealistic celebrations of the computer as a creative tool. "The real problem with romantics," Suppes said, "is that their intellectual level is so poor. . . . Nobody says that you can produce a first-class basketball or football team just by horsing around. Or suppose we trained pilots that way: let's take an airplane and horse around—it's a nice technological device; you don't need any training—just play around with it, take it up, and see how you like it. That's crazy!"

Condescension aside, Suppes had a point. The problem was translating his theory into computer reality. When *InfoWorld* looked into Dial-A-Drill, it was less than overwhelmed. After observing a demonstration, reporter Scott Mace wrote that the program's synthesized speech "was noticeably flawed." And certain words and phrases were so patched together that they came through the phone "with abrupt and unnatural changes in inflection." Later, in an editorial, *InfoWorld* called the program "a high-tech hickory stick," likening it to the tool used in the fearsome old nursery rhyme about reading, writing, and 'rithmetic. "It is classic drill and practice," the magazine said, "the ultimate in 'back to basics,' flying in the face of all educational innovations developed in schools and on personal computers during the last 15 years."

As it turned out, most people didn't want to be bothered with automated phone calls anyway. It probably should not have taken the wisdom of hindsight to realize that taking the telephone, a system that mechanizes communication, and layering it with yet another mechanized system was not likely to produce a happy new generation of smart kids. But in Suppes's eyes, the value in the program's automated voice system was never appreciated and was mistakenly shoved aside by classroom computers. "I loved that program," he told me during an interview years later. "I was sorry to see it go." In a concession to the times, CCC then threw its energies into the more standard systems of computer-assisted instruction whereby students could sit in class in front of a real computer to practice their lessons.

The new direction paid off. After some stutters in the 1970s, CCC revenues rose—by 20 percent a year through the early 1990s.[33] In 1997, one of the peak periods of the technological go-go years, revenues for the company reached $128 million. By this time, CCC had become one of the leaders in what was soon called the courseware industry. In the following years, CCC appeared to remain strong, even after the CAI approach to computing faded. As of 2001, its software was reportedly being used by 10 million students in 16,000 schools.

Any instructional system that becomes this pervasive will, at some point, be put through some rigorous evaluation. Throughout the 1970s and 1980s, many researchers did just that with computer-assisted instruction. One such evaluation was conducted by EPIE, the courseware-watchdog group. At the end of the 1980s, a time when CAI software was at its peak, a team of EPIE evaluators set out across the country to survey the whole CAI landscape. EPIE's findings weren't pretty. "Teachers were tending to use the program as a dumping place," EPIE director Komoski recalls. The reason is that the CAI drilling routines relieved the teachers of having to teach. EPIE found that CCC actually encouraged this trend by sending in its own staff to show teachers how much easier their lives could be with CCC software. As for the students, many enjoyed the program at first, but they "tended to get bored after a while," Komoski said. As an indication, Komoski remembers a thirteen-year-old in Michigan telling him that all the work seemed to be the same thing, over and over. Others had horror stories of wrong answers, which it took the companies months to correct, if they ever did. All of this might be understandable if the programs saved schools money; but they didn't. They started at around $100,000; Komoski recalls $800,000 price tags being typical, with some programs costing well over $1 million.

In the mid-1990s, when the latest wave of computer enthusiasm rolled in, CCC's "drill-and-kill" model of learning began falling into disfavor. The company's cause was not helped much by the growing number of more empirical studies that had been accumulating on CAI, most of which indicated that any boost in academic skill brought on by these programs was superficial at best and often only temporary. Not surprisingly, these gains often showed up in standardized tests, whose rather one-dimensional material was well suited to computerized drills. As researchers looked further into these gains, they found that the students doing the best with CAI were the low achievers. This group always has lots of academic room to grow and its members can often build their skills with computerized drills. In the ensuing years, studies also found that these low achievers could be helped by drills in any number of formats: oral exercises, flash cards, or—best of all—with a tutor. High achievers, meanwhile, whose skills generally can't be much expanded (or measured) without sophisticated work, made little discernible improvement with CAI programs.[34]

———

Curiously, in Patrick Suppes's C.V., there is no mention of the company he led for nearly three decades. And despite his voluminous papers on computerized instruction, there is only the briefest discussion of this work in his lengthy "intellectual autobiography." There's an even shorter reference to his tenure with CCC; not until page 22 does he even bring it up.* (He does, however, thank Stanford for assisting his work with CAI. "Without the sophisticated computer facilities at Stanford," he writes, "it would not have been possible for me to pursue these matters in such detail and on such a

---

*When Suppes founded CCC, in 1967, he did so with several partners, one of whom was Richard Atkinson, who went on to become the president of the University of California system. Strangely, Atkinson is as reluctant to talk about the company's history as Suppes was in his autobiography. When I called Atkinson to talk about CCC, he sent word that he did not want to discuss that phase of his history.

scale.") What Suppes does emphasize are his prodigious efforts to improve student performance and its evaluation.

How does he think he did? Like Papert, Suppes accepts the academic community's grim verdict of his programs. And, also like Papert, he blames the schools' weak bureaucracy for these failures. When asked in 2001 about his 1960s prediction that computers would soon talk to children, Suppes acknowledged that he "was too optimistic" about the proximity of that development. "That's a tough problem."

In these latter years of his life, Suppes is still publishing and teaching and still trying out new ideas with CAI. His latest was a program that would let gifted students from kindergarten through high school try their hand at advanced work in math and the sciences. Like most of his CCC products, the program wasn't heavy on teacher interaction. "It was designed not to require a tutor," Suppes said. "They're just for troubleshooting"—that is, responding mostly through e-mail. Suppes does differ from Papert, however, in that he has no illusion that his products will revolutionize education. He is simply trying to find a way around weak teachers, which he seems to regard as education's Achilles' heel. "There's a lot of bullshit about teachers. Let's not think they're all beautiful flowers about to bloom. We'd all like to be tutored by Aristotle. But that's not possible."

THE DIGITAL DIVIDE, TAKE TWO

Not long after the country was introduced to Dial-A-Drill, another red flag went up about the growing gap between rich and poor as regards technology's opportunities. Following a *USA Today* survey, which found that 91 percent of the U.S. population believed students needed to learn how to use computers to be prepared for the future, EPIE, the watchdog group on educational software, launched a small pilot program to start including the poor. Today's seemingly sudden discovery of what everyone calls the digital divide had a name then, too. EPIE's Ken Komoski called it the "virtual ghetto."

That ghetto was growing fast, even in 1983. Congressional studies at the time estimated that 25 percent of the nation's children—a total of 10 million youngsters, by Komoski's count—were living in or near poverty. Other studies indicated that two times as many rich schools had computers as poor schools did.[35] So, armed with a $150,000 grant, EPIE got a handful of schools in the San Francisco area to help their students' families get discounts on computer gear. Komoski knew full well, however, that the gear alone would accomplish very little. "We're all caught up with, 'Well, I'm going to get my home computer and I'm going to have my youngsters learn as much as they can,'" Komoski said. "If we don't take a broader social vision, I think we're really buying a great deal of trouble."

To make a stab at that broader vision, Komoski planned to give these families computers only after they had come to school for training. He also tried to coax computer companies into helping out—by making donations to high-poverty schools; offering up to 35 percent discounts to those schools' families; providing the families with software evaluations; and building software and hardware libraries. Knowing companies might not be thrilled with this idea, Komoski tried to explain. "The school is becoming a very great help in marketing computers to homes," he said. "Fifty percent of the retail price of a computer is marketing costs. So if a school is helping to reduce those costs, the manufacturer or vendor can well afford a discount." Komoski's initiative did get a little funding from foundations, but it quickly petered out. Apparently, Komoski recalled years later, the whole plan required far too much support, technical and otherwise, to sustain.

COMPUTERS AND POLITICS, TAKE TWO

In the fall of 1983, Apple kicked off its first big school donation. This phase of the campaign was limited to California schools, since Jobs had failed to get a tax break from anywhere but his home state. However, with national subsidy prospects still lingering in Congress, Apple's California campaign was watched carefully by everyone—politicians, educators, and other computer manufacturers.

By all appearances, the computer's moment had arrived. When thousands of educators gathered earlier that year, for the spring 1983 CUE conference, there was a noticeable electronic charge in the atmosphere. Before the conference's big banquet dinner, Jobs worked the room like a political pro, passing out buttons for his computer donation campaign that said KIDS CAN'T WAIT—APPLE COMPUTER. Although Jobs was still waiting for traction on federal tax credits for computer donations, he'd recently scored on a few other fronts. The California giveaway (greased by Governor Brown's 25 percent state tax credit) was set for September, when Jobs hoped 10,000 Apple computers, loaded with the latest software, would land in classrooms across the state. And earlier that spring, Apple had made its first big arrangement with a college—3,000 specially designed Apples were sold to Drexel University, an unusual work/study institution in Philadelphia that had recently required each student and teacher to buy a microcomputer. (The students were paying the school $1,000 apiece for their machines; Apple wasn't talking about what its price was to Drexel.)

"We can actually change the world in a small way in the next six months," Jobs told the CUE crowd. Some players in the nation's capital apparently hoped so, too. In calling for more high-tech equipment in schools, Dr. Nolan Estes, former associate U.S. commissioner of education, told the audience, "By the time kids in your kindergarten graduate, 74 percent of them will become employed in the information industry." Estes's projections were a little off. A kindergartner in 1982 would have graduated high school in 1995. By then, according to the U.S. Census, less than 1 percent of the workforce was employed in "the information industries." (Specifically, 1.13 million people were employed in "computer and data processing services" out of a total labor pool of 124.9 million.) If Estes was talking about the year these youngsters would graduate from college, that would be 1999, by which time the figure had climbed to about 1.5 percent.[36]

Apple began its giveaway in August 1983, with 4,000 machines, expecting that number to rise to 12,800 by the end of September. When the bundles of software and discount coupons were figured in, each computer was valued at $2,300—a total donation worth $29.4 million. To get these machines, however, at least one person from each of the 9,400 schools involved had to go through a little computer training. Those training sessions ended up being something of a crash course. Offered at dealerships, typically with large pools of teachers, they ranged from a half-day's session to, more commonly, brief one- or two-hour overviews. This process made more than a few school administrators uneasy. Everyone realized it was unlikely that the dealerships would continue the training; this would of course leave schools with a new and heavy burden, which they'd been given few, if any, resources to handle. A computer coordinator in a Sacramento-area school district said he was "frightened" about superficially trained teachers coming in to class thinking they could now teach complex programming languages like LOGO.

While the schools struggled with the pros and cons of Apple's gift, the dealers seemed to be in heaven. When *InfoWorld* contacted several stores, they said the giveaway—which put, on average, no more than 1.4 computers into each eligible school—was generating additional sales, to both schools and parents. It was also spawning giveaway campaigns from other computer manufacturers, which generated additional business for dealers— and politicians.

Before the 1983 school year started, Jobs shopped his wares once more in the nation's capital. His prospects looked a little better that year, since President Reagan, after initial resistance to the tax breaks, had finally given the concept his blessing. This led Representative Pete Stark to reintroduce his plan (with some refinements) to give computer manufacturers tax breaks worth up to twice the cost of the machines they gave to schools. Despite the auspicious new signals, the bill's promoters knew it was by no means a sure thing. "There were those who thought the deduction was just too rich," an aide to Stark acknowledged. "They won't be satisfied any more this year than they were last."

In late September, as Apple was shipping its last few machines to California schools, Congress again took up the question of whether to help spread the program nationally. By this time, Jobs was no longer the only Good Samaritan on the block. Other computer manufacturers, such as Hewlett-Packard, IBM, and Kaypro (another feisty dinosaur of the PC's early days), were also getting into the act. Not surprisingly, each company had a slightly different donation plan—a better deal for the schools, in each one's view, in return for the subsidies they sought. In some ways, the timing was not terribly good for the proposals, coming as they did not long after President Reagan's massive tax cuts and simultaneous defense buildup. Those twin initiatives had given the nation a rising federal deficit, which would grow to more than $200 billion a year by the middle of the decade. Neither Congress nor Reagan was keen on granting tax breaks in such a nervous climate; nonetheless, the computer campaign seemed to hold its own appeal. "There is a lot of interest in and out of Congress in expanding the legislation to include other things," said the aide to Representative Stark, who was spearheading what had come to be known as "the Apple bill."

Indeed there was. At least eight different computer-donation bills were now making their way through various stages of congressional debate, all pushed by different corporate interests. (For example, one proposal, pushed by Tandy/RadioShack, would provide teacher training in exchange for a tax write-off on computers worth 125 percent of their value. For its part, Apple was seeking a 200 percent tax write-off on its computer donations, without throwing in any training at all.) Those pushing the "RadioShack bill," as it was soon called, and several others that called for teacher training, were doing so partly because they had learned their history lessons. In the 1960s, the federal government partly subsidized companies that gave schools audiovisual equipment; however, since little if any support services were included, much of this expensive gear sat unused in school closets.

In proposing one of the computer-donation initiatives, Representative

Tim Wirth, a Democrat from Colorado, joined the growing phalanx of observers who were worried about widening opportunity gaps between the rich and poor; Wirth even coined a few phrases that would become major themes a decade later. He spoke of "information haves" and "information have-nots," a description heavily used by former vice-president Gore and myriad lieutenants in the Clinton administration's Department of Education. Interestingly, only one bill focused on getting computers to poor schools. And it wasn't Wirth's; it was pitched by Representative Brian Donnelly, a Massachusetts Democrat and former teacher. In the fall of 1983, the House finally, and enthusiastically, passed Steve Jobs's tax break (by a 323–62 vote), but the Senate demurred. Complaints that the initiative amounted to a one-company bill led to filibuster threats, and the bill never got to the Senate floor for debate. In the end, none of these bills ever made it through Congress, which left computer giveaways to be an isolated occurrence in those states, like California, that decided to be generous.

ORWELL'S GHOSTS

As the fall of 1983 cooled into winter, the technology industry's new roses began to show their first sign of fading. Atari closed its two commercial training centers, before even trying to expand the concept nationally, because of a lack of profits. That year, computer dealers prepared for the holiday buying season with a new sense of hesitation. The easy sells—to what is commonly called the early-adopter or pioneer-buyer market—were over. And some of those customers were now coming in with complaints or complicated needs. Potential buyers hung back, fearing they were in danger of buying a system that would soon be obsolete or, worse, an orphan (that is, made by a company that disappears). "The personal computer market may be nearing a first-phase saturation," said Norbert Aubuchon, a Pennsylvania marketing consultant, based on an October 1983 study of the market.

Aubuchon's study noted that sales of any new commercial technology—cars, VCRs, computers, whatever—often take off quickly at first, because the machinery's technical challenges look like fascinating adventures to the technology pioneers. To the larger contingent of more average buyers, those challenges are ordeals, if not roadblocks. "Right now, the computer people are getting away with their shortcomings," Aubuchon said—an assessment that would crop up again when the general public rediscovered computer technology in the mid-1990s.

By now, the public was being peppered with a few more critical reconsiderations of educational computing. In a small Q & A published in *Harper's* magazine and entitled "The Computer Fallacy," Joseph Weizenbaum, the MIT computer scientist, treated the computer frenzy to a severe dressing-down. Weizenbaum was the creator of Eliza, a computer program he invented in the early 1970s that became famous for its capability to carry on a faux conversation with its user. (He named his program after Eliza Doolittle, the famous flower girl in George Bernard Shaw's *Pygmalion*, who was gradually taught upper-class manners and speech.) Weizenbaum was also the designer of the first computerized banking system and the author of *Computer Power and Human Reason: From Judgment to Calculation*, a bestselling 1976 account of his thoughts, partly sparked by his horror that people began taking Eliza seriously, as a potential new fix in the workplace and even in psychotherapy. In the *Harper's* item (a reprint of an interview with the French periodical *Le Nouvel Observateur*), Weizenbaum offered some devastating observations of the computer's effects on education, including the work of his MIT colleague Seymour Papert:

N.O.: Computers are arriving everywhere—in offices, in schools, in the home. Shouldn't this delight you?

Weizenbaum: All I can hope is that the technology I helped to develop be used well. But it isn't—far from it. . . . A new human malady has been invented. . . . Now it's computer illiteracy. The future, we are told, will belong to those familiar with the computer. What a joke this would be if only it didn't victimize so many innocent bystanders. . . . The infatuation with television, that other "educational" instrument, also comes to mind. Thanks to TV, kids didn't make as much noise as before. And from that people concluded that TV taught them good behavior.

N.O.: But you wouldn't compare television, which renders the viewer passive, with the computer, which develops creativity?

Weizenbaum: Why not? With television, a kid will watch a fighter pilot shoot down a plane piloted by another human being. With video games, the child "becomes" the fighter pilot. The difference? In both cases, the child inhabits an abstract world in which actions have no consequences, in which violence is truly mindless. Video games are, if anything, more harmful than TV, because they *actively* teach dissociation between what one does and the consequences of one's actions.

As for the computer, I think it inhibits children's creativity. In most cases, the computer programs kids and not the other way around. . . .

My colleague Seymour Papert claims he has a radically different approach: with his system, he says, the children program the computer. He made a film that was supposed to illustrate his thesis. In it one sees children working on LOGO in Senegal, Scotland, and Texas. As if by chance, they all drew exactly the same picture on their computers: a flower made out of ellipsoids strung together. Strange, isn't it?

N.O.: Even so, don't you think that the use of computers reinforces a child's problem-solving ability?

Weizenbaum: If that were true, then computer professionals would lead better lives than the rest of the population. We know very well that that isn't the case. There is, as far as I know, no more evidence that programming is good for the mind than Latin is, as is sometimes claimed.

N.O.: Would you deny that the computer revolution will affect social equality?

Weizenbaum: . . . If you want to reduce inequality, the solution is to give the poor money, not computers.

N.O.: Do you think, then, that France is making a mistake by trying to put computers in everyone's hands?

Weizenbaum: If that is what France is doing, then, yes, it's making a mistake. The temptation to send in computers wherever there is a problem is great. There's hunger in the Third World. So computerize. The schools are in trouble. So bring in computers. The introduction of the computer into any problem area, be it medicine, education, or whatever, usually creates the impression that grievous deficiencies are being corrected, that something is being done. But often its principal effect is to push problems even further into obscurity—to avoid confrontation with the need for fundamentally critical thinking.[37]

Before long, other seeds, planted only a year or two earlier, began showing signs of rot. That fall, just as the 1984 school year was beginning, Apple admitted that it had run into trouble fulfilling its computer-donation commitments. (Apparently, the company was beset with production backlogs.) This complicated the lives of more than a few teachers, who had planned both training sessions and classes around the promise of an Apple computer. The difficulties of evaluating the material on these computers were also becoming clear. Of the many organizations now attempting this job, one was the National Education Association, the nation's largest teachers' union. For some curious reason, the NEA decided not only to issue "certifications" of software value but also to sell them. (The NEA also charged companies to evaluate their software, and hit one company with a bill for $18,000.) Not surprisingly, teachers were then concerned when the organization started approving a lot of software that EPIE, the independent evaluation house, had rejected. Eventually, after being blasted in the press for conflicts of interest, the NEA tried to establish more distance between itself and its product-evaluation firm, but the link remained, as did the taint. Before long, the union gave up altogether on evaluating software.

That November, in a fitting epitaph for a technologically foul year, the nation's colleges served up some crow for the great College Entrance Examination Board. Two years earlier, the CEEB had started Advanced Placement exams in computer programming and had chosen Pascal as the appropriate programming language for a test. Now that the policy had been in place for a year, the colleges were harvesting the first fruits of their decision. For the past two summers, teachers across the country had attended training sessions in both Pascal and its AP requirements. By the fall of 1984, an estimated 300,000 high school students had enrolled in yearlong computer science courses, many of which focused on Pascal. There were indications that the AP enticement was raising the level of programming work in some high school classes. Overall, however, the program wasn't working terribly well. Large numbers of students had failed the first AP exam, given the previous spring, and educational computing experts were saying it was unreasonable to expect most teachers to learn such a complex program. To make matters worse, many schools found that their computer systems weren't sophisticated enough to run Pascal, as had been predicted. So they had to buy new gear—or give up.

As if all this weren't discouraging enough, a number of top universities were refusing to grant credit for the AP courses, even to students who passed the new test. "I can't look at a score from the Advanced Placement course and know if the student can program or not," said Michael Clancy, a lecturer in computer science and director of introductory programming courses—which included Pascal—at the University of California at Berkeley. The problem, Clancy explained, is that students who pass the AP test have proven they can handle about 50 lines of code; his beginning courses typically required 300 to 1,000 lines of code, plus the ability to make subtle modifications. Those who created the AP course said they were considering making the exam more demanding. But that didn't solve the problem. Leonard Gould, the undergraduate officer of MIT's department of electrical engineering and computer science, pointed out that MIT didn't even use a specific language in its introductory computer science courses. And other universities used such a broad range of programs (Fortran, BASIC, Lisp, to name a few) that it would be impossible to design an AP test that would satisfy the full gamut of university demands.

This was not quite what the CEEB had expected. Writing in a fall 1984 issue of *The Computing Teacher*, David Rime, chief reader of the test and a professor of computer science at Western Illinois University, said, "Students who make a high score on the Advanced Placement Computer Science exam . . . will be highly recruited by some colleges and universities." By the early 1990s, Pascal had been long since superseded by the next hot programming language (C+, then C++, and so on). This of course forced CEEB to change directions yet again—and left a generation of students with rather obsolete programming skills.

All this mayhem provided a potential moral for schools, particularly where technology is involved, which derives from the old biblical advice about false prophets: Beware of rushed decisions. It has also made for a strange coincidence. The first big school computing boom, which had arrived with the personal computer in the late 1970s, ended in 1984—the legendary Orwellian symbol of doom. The next gold rush, tied to the commercial birth of the Internet, would also last for roughly a half-dozen years, during the latter part of the 1990s. And that one ended at another prophetic moment: during the first months of the new millennium, when Y2K and other disasters were supposed to destroy us all. George Orwell would have delighted in watching us pass both of these trembling milestones.

A NEW DAWN, TAKE TWO

Amid the many stumbles with school technology in its early days, isolated but important victories did occur. With the proliferation of word-processing software, a number of teachers found that students were getting engaged in writing projects that had never much interested them before. As researchers looked more deeply into the phenomenon, they found that while computers clearly boosted enthusiasm for writing, the quality didn't necessarily follow. (Students did clearly write more. But on the whole, they didn't put the work through much revision—a situation that has not much changed to this day. Instead, they generally limited themselves to perfunctory corrections—many of which are automatically performed by spell-check software—then used the word processor's seemingly limitless space to write on and on.)[38]

The one exception to this rule was special-education students. Some researchers believe it is due to the simplicity of the machine's functions; some think it's because of the computer's infinite patience, which lets students calmly attempt the same task over and over and over; and some think that the computer's assortment of stimuli, visual and auditory, can suddenly reach a student who has long since shut down to the idea of trying. Whatever the reason—and whatever the individual nature of the problem—students with learning disabilities have, on the whole, made strides on computers much more consistently than has the general school population.*

Hanging around these accomplishments, unfortunately, were a few old ghosts. One popped up in California in June 1989, concerning the grant program started by Governor Jerry Brown that had furnished schools with more than $50 million of computers and electronic learning aids. Backers of the program now wanted to continue the grants for another three years, starting with $14 million in 1990. None of this sat too well with Brown's successor, Republican George Deukmejian. During the program's four years of operation, it had produced no evidence of having any effect on learning. And, according to a report from the state's legislative analyst, black, Hispanic, and rural students had been slighted during the grant distributions. To make matters worse, there was a widespread sense that the donations had turned into a boondoggle. "The spending has been extremely haphazard," said Ken Hargis, a spokesman for one of the legislators who was championing a bill to keep the program alive. Many in state government viewed the concept, he said, as "a pork-barrel bill to provide VCRs for vice-principals' offices."[39] The criticism stalled the technology initiatives for a while, but it didn't kill them. Within a few years, the legislature was approving new programs that would spend far more on school technology than Jerry Brown ever did.

---

*There is a small but consistent assortment of research literature on this topic. Examples include a 1989 experiment with laptop computers, which drew a 10,000-word essay out of a special-education student in Seattle who had previously had trouble composing a single sentence. "Print is an exclusionary medium," David Rose, a neuropsychologist who heads the Center for Applied Special Technology in Peabody, Massachusetts, explained some years later. "Print just can't work for some kids. They can't hold a book, or don't have vision, or they can't decode printed material." The modern computer, he found, could combine text, sound, pictures, and animation, increasing chances that these children could find some "access route" to literacy. Other specialists, from Rutgers University and the University of California at San Francisco, have used computers to draw out sounds, like an old record playing too slowly, so that children with language problems can hear the components of consonants and vowels. Laura Meyers, a research linguist at UCLA, has found that with the proper sequence of text and computer-generated speech, children with disabilities eventually could learn to work freely, without being dependent on machines of any sort. See "Expanding the Literary Toolbox," by David Rose and Anne Meyer, Scholastic Research Paper, Vol. 11, 1996; "Your Child's Brain," by Sharon Begley, *Newsweek*, February 19, 1996.

California's chaotic spending spree may have been eye-opening, but it wasn't unusual. A year earlier, in 1988, it became clear that most schools weren't giving much thought to how to tie their new technology in to the daily business of teaching. This conclusion was offered in a report compiled by an unusually heavyweight team: the Control Data Corporation and the National School Boards Association's Institute for the Transfer of Technology to Education. "We asked for technology plans. We tended to get computer documents," said James Mecklenburger, director of the NSBA Institute.[40]

Anyone who has followed the news on technology in the years since the NSBA report has seen its findings repeated throughout the 1990s. The conclusion would seem to be that school officials are incompetent spendthrifts. The real explanation is that like most of us, they're just trying to do their best. Faced with pressure from all sides to computerize, and staffs and budgets stretched thin to begin with, they don't have a lot of options. Their standard solution? Buy first and plan later—if they have the time.

When the education community entered the 1990s, it was greeted with a new, improved technological opportunity. For many teachers and administrators, videodisks were the answer they'd long been waiting for. And Texas, which loves competing with California for front-runner status, jumped on this innovation quickly.

In January 1990, Optical Data Corporation, a New Jersey–based firm, pitched the Texas Textbook Committee with a bold idea. It wanted the state to consider using its videodisk series *Windows on Science* as an alternative to textbooks for grades one through six. When Optical Data made this proposal, videodisks had already failed in the home market, partly because they couldn't take recordings and therefore got trounced by VCRs. But the industry thought the disks' huge stores of information made them ideal for schools. (Each disk could hold text, audio files, and either an hour's worth of film or 54,000 photos, along with a system for searching the material.) Equally important, the disks were on the forefront of technology's next new wave: multimedia. And virtually everyone thought multimedia would be hot. "Expansion, rapid expansion, is the best way to characterize the videodisk industry today," wrote Richard Pollack, president of Emerging Technology Consultants, in an introduction to a 1990 compendium of 600 videodisks from 94 different companies.

And schools were their new, very willing target market. In California, the Department of Education proposed making videodisks an integral part of seventh-grade science instruction and was working on some slick productions with the National Geographic Society and Lucasfilm Ltd., the production studio of *Star Wars* fame. In the South, the Florida Institute of Technology was developing a science videodisk with $169,000 in state and university grant money. In Ohio, the legislature dedicated $1 million to set up interactive videodisk learning centers in each of the state's vocational school districts.

Despite the size of these funds, they didn't cover much ground. A single computerized videodisk player—which used the old analog technology rather than a digital system—ran about $1,100. And a full package for a school curriculum cost considerably more. (A fifteen-unit physical science curriculum, for example, had recently sold to the Texas School Boards Association for roughly $17,000.) Even the individual disks were expensive—as much as $90 apiece, ten times the price of their counterparts for the home market. But educators weren't looking at costs. "We're going to see stations where kids are using disks themselves as resources, like encyclopedias. And that is when we're really going to see the power," said Geoff Fletcher, director of educational technology in the Texas Education Agency. George Peterson, the director of educational media for the National Geographic Society, agreed. Videodisks, he said, "have the potential to be the presentation tool of the '90s."[41]

Eleven months later, in November 1990, the Texas Board of Education adopted Optical Data's *Windows on Science* for its elementary-grade science curriculum, along with two science textbooks. The decision was widely cheered, even by traditional publishing houses. The videodisk industry estimated that the decision could lead to the purchase of 10,000 videodisk players in Texas alone. William Clark, Optical Data's president, was so delighted that he indulged in technology's time-honored tradition—a bit of prognostication. Basking in a surfeit of glowing national news media coverage, Clark said Texas's move was likely to have a "lasting national impact."[42]

A few years later, the videodisk industry tanked. Texas stuck with its investment as long as it could, spending some $16.2 million on videodisk technology over the course of ten years. But it wasn't long before no one was creating much new material for what was supposed to be "the presentation tool of the '90s." Of course, Texas has never let itself be hobbled by the lessons of the past, as evidenced by its lead role over the decades in boom-and-bust economic cycles. So too with the state's approach to schooling. As but one example, in 2001, the Texas Education Agency set off in a whole new direction with a handful of educational publishing firms. For an annual cost that started at approximately $1.7 million, the publishers started replacing the old videodisk machines with CD-ROMs—just in time to get in on the tail end of that round of high technology.

PUTTING APPLE'S MONEY WHERE ITS MOUTH IS

O f all the various initiatives to put computers in schools, none was as focused on changing the art of teaching as a special project initiated in 1985 by Apple Computer. Called Apple Classrooms of Tomorrow (ACOT), it was coordinated with experts at twenty different universities and research institutions. The project wrapped up ten years later, in 1995, at which time it was perhaps the most ambitious effort to date, and the most intensively studied, to teach core academic subjects using computer technology.

After picking a handful of schools that represented a national demographic cross section, Apple set out, as one of its evaluation teams put it, to "install and operate computer-saturated classrooms as living laboratories in every grade [K–12]." ACOT planned to accomplish this by weaving "state-of-the-art technologies into the instructional fabric of schooling." Each student and teacher started out with two computers—one at school and one at home. The ACOT home-computer program eventually proved unmanageable, as did previous home-computer initiatives, and was mostly dropped. But the classroom array remained: There were printers, scanners, laser-disc and videotape players, modems, CD-ROM drives, and abundant choices in software. Whenever new technologies became available, new machines appeared in the classroom. Throughout the project, Apple provided training to every teacher and put a staff member at each site for both technical and instructional help. Over the course of a decade, ACOT encompassed thirteen different schools and cost Apple $25 million.

Once all the evaluations were compiled, in 1997, the feedback was mixed but ultimately positive. Getting to that point, however, was not easy. In the beginning, ACOT managers had taken a very relaxed approach, merely supplying the teachers and students with gear and sitting back to see what would happen. The result was something of a mess. No real advances in learning or teaching occurred. In fact, the time and trouble the new technology required were causing some of the more innovative teachers to regress. (These teachers were already doing what education experts often recommend—divide classes into distinct groups according to students' individual needs, then create and supervise different activities for each group. Now, to compensate for the time they had to devote to mastering the technology—and teaching it—they had resorted to the standard method of teaching to the whole class.) In time, however, as teachers grew accustomed to the machinery—and as Apple staff members offered more active assistance—progress seemed to blossom.

The view from Apple of what had been achieved, and from most (but not all) ACOT teachers, was well summarized one day early in 1996. The *San Jose Mercury News*, published in Apple's Silicon Valley home, had just run a series pointing out that high-tech schools in the state were actually faring worse on test scores than low-tech schools.[43] Several weeks later, the *Mercury* published an opinion-page response from Terry Crane, an Apple senior vice-president. "Instead of isolating students," Crane insisted, "technology actually encouraged them to collaborate more than in traditional classrooms. Students also learned to explore and represent information dynamically and creatively, communicate effectively about complex processes, become independent learners and self-starters and become more socially aware and confident."[44]

There were two facts that Crane did not mention: After a decade of effort, Apple had found scant empirical evidence of greater student achievement. (While test scores for the ACOT schools did not decline, as those in the *Mercury*'s sample did, they did not rise, either.) Worse, one follow-up study by four well-credentialed professors from Memphis State University found that after the ACOT students returned to their normal classes, what improvements they had shown disappeared. "Overall, the ACOT students were indistinguishable from their peers on the basis of school accomplishments," the evaluators said. After returning to a "traditional environment," they were once again "educationally at-risk."[45]

To many critics, that would constitute a final verdict. But in today's education world, it's just the beginning of the inquiry. Consider the test-score issue. Educators on both sides of the computer debate acknowledge that tests of student achievement remain so crude that the picture of learning they offer is extremely limited. They're especially weak in measuring intangibles such as enthusiasm and self-motivation, the hallmarks of ACOT's accomplishments. But those victories only obscure the deeper story, which concerns two questions.

The first regards the quality of Apple's evaluations. In the years since the ACOT reports were published, independent researchers have had trouble judging the meaning of what Apple found. Not only is there an absence of quantitative measures (on standardized tests or on other admittedly limited scales), there is also a paucity of objective assessments in general. Throughout the many journal articles, company reports, and, finally, a 210-page book on the ACOT experience, almost all of the evaluations came from paid

Apple consultants, who were reporting little more than the anecdotal evidence that teachers told them.[46] These teachers volunteered for ACOT, and did so at least partly because they had faith in technology.

The second question regards the quality of the ACOT schoolwork, by whatever assessment one uses. This issue will be more fully dealt with later, during visits to one of the ACOT schools in Silicon Valley. For now, this much can be said: While it's clear that the majority of ACOT participants (teachers and students) were charged up by the project, Apple's computers bear less responsibility for that change than Terry Crane suggested. As Jane David, a consultant Apple hired to study its classroom initiative, once told me, all this "had less to do with the computer and more to do with the teaching. If you took the computers out, there would still be good teaching there." ACOT's leaders admit the same thing, although not quite so boldly. Keith Yocam, a longtime ACOT leader, noticed that as time wore on, whenever he gave presentations on educational technology, he'd end up saying very little about computers and talking almost exclusively about teaching.

A NEW DAWN, TAKE THREE

By the latter part of the 1980s, as the novelty of the computerized classroom fell to the side of the media's attention, schools reached a saturation point—at least on their first-round goal of putting at least one computer in each school. There were now approximately 1.5 million computers in the public schools and as many as 400,000 more in private institutions. This meant an average of one computer for every thirty students and at least one machine in 95 percent of the nation's schools.[47]

To one relatively obscure bureaucrat in Washington, D.C., Linda Roberts, this wasn't nearly enough. Roberts at the time was a project director in the Office of Technology Assessment (OTA), a respected but now defunct operation that long served as Congress's private scientific think tank. In 1986, when Congress commissioned OTA to examine technology's status in the schools, Roberts got the lead role. She responded two years later with a 246-page document that made no pretense of being neutral: Entitled "Power On! New Tools for Teaching and Learning," the report said students were currently getting only "spotty access" to computer technology, and it challenged the federal government to take "principal responsibility" for fixing the problem. Its job, as Roberts saw it: "make the computer a central element of instruction."

OTA called on Congress to require agencies to focus their research efforts on educational technology and suggested putting an additional 12 million computers in the nation's public schools. By the OTA's count, this would give one computer to every three students. At the very least, OTA said, schools should have one computer for every six students, which would cost a 600-school district like Chicago $130 million. To OTA, those sums were peanuts. If the schools were going to have sufficient access to computer technology, the OTA said, the government, over the next six years, would have to spend $25 billion—an amount equivalent to a third of the Department of Education's entire budget for instructional materials.

Despite the weight of this request, OTA thought the timing was perfect. Its report asserted that students in poor schools had "significantly less" access to computers than their counterparts in wealthy schools and that limited English speakers had the least access of all. But now, suddenly, the nation had the resources to solve this problem. "Research in cognitive science," the report stated, "allied with developments in computer-based technology in the schools and teachers willing to experiment, create today's 'window of opportunity' for improving education."

Anyone who hears the term *window of opportunity* should always pause for a moment of reconsideration. The image suggests an important, sudden opening—some marvelous chance that won't last long. The opportunity may well be real, or at least some part of it may be, but its imminent disappearance is often a fiction. It is the pitchman's rhetorical device, and it plays gorgeously to the American penchant for urgency and novelty. This was certainly the case here. In fact, anyone who had been watching would have realized that OTA had been crying wolf about the need for one version or another of school technology for a long time. In 1983, the agency urged teachers to show students how to program computers using BASIC. In 1984, LOGO was the answer. In 1986, the agency pinned its hopes on computerized programs of individual instruction. Now, in 1988, OTA was pushing computer proliferation, coupled with word-processing programs. (In the ensuing years, OTA would continue this routine, promoting curricular specifics like history databases in 1990, hypertext multimedia programming in 1992, and the miracles of the Internet in 1994.[48] Mercifully Congress finally put the agency to death in 1995.)

At first, Linda Roberts's 1988 report met with great enthusiasm in the education world. Then, shortly after its release, the nation was treated to a change in presidential administrations and a White House (headed by George H. W. Bush) that had little taste for futuristic approaches to academics. For the next few years, Roberts's labor of love sat on the shelf like so many other earnest Washington reports. Then, in the mid-1990s, the nation discovered the Internet. Before long, such cultural luminaries as John Perry Barlow, a former songwriter for the Grateful Dead, were calling the Internet "the most transforming event since the capture of fire."[49] For a while, it seemed as if the country had fallen into a permanent state of technological obsession. In a poll taken in early 1996, teachers ranked computer skills and media technology as more "essential" than the study of European history, biology, chemistry, and physics; than dealing with social problems such as drugs and family breakdown; than learning practical job skills; and than reading modern American writers such as Steinbeck and Hemingway or classic authors such as Plato and Shakespeare.[50]

That summer, a California task force responded in kind. It urged the state to spend $11 billion on computers in its schools, which had struggled for years under funding cuts that had driven academic achievement down to levels that were among the lowest in the nation. The task force, composed of forty-six teachers, parents, technology experts, and business executives, concluded: "More than any other single measure, computers and network technologies, properly implemented, offer the greatest potential to right what's wrong with our public schools." Other options mentioned in the group's report—reducing class size, improving teachers' salaries and facilities, increasing hours of instruction—were considered less important than putting kids in front of computers.[51]

By this time, a number of other states, as well as some private organizations, seemed to agree. In 1990, Kentucky legislators had passed an ambitious education-reform law that committed their state to spend $230 million on technology over the next five years. (Two years later, the state was still struggling with the program, the cost of which had grown to $400 million.) In 1991, the Annenberg Foundation and the Corporation for Public Broadcasting announced a $10 million grant program for math and science instruction with technology. The same year, Service Marketing Group, of Garden City, New York, reported having given $100 million worth of computers to schools across the nation. The donations were financed by an ingenious sequence of consumer purchases, which started at the local grocery store, and that ultimately proved to be quite lucrative for the marketing firm that organized the campaign.* Two years later, in 1993, Robert-

---

*The program, widely known in the early 1990s as the Apples for Schools program, worked this way: First, customers collected their cash-register receipts from participating grocery stores and brought them to school. In the meantime, the grocers bought computers to have on hand from the program's organizers, Service Marketing Group. Once the school had a sufficient pile of receipts, school officials would return to the grocer, which then gave the school a computer. In the end, however, there wasn't much of a free lunch. It took $160,000 in receipts, for

son, Stephens & Company, an investment banking firm in New York and San Francisco that dived into new technology with uncommon aggressiveness (and later went out of business), gathered five hundred people for a national first: a conference on the investment opportunities in educational computing.

In a keynote address at the conference, Senator Bob Kerrey, a Nebraska Democrat, asked for the investors' help in building "a concrete vision of a home-based learning center," something, Kerrey said, "our current educational institutions are probably incapable" of doing. The investors had been well primed for Kerrey's message. Robertson, Stephens had handed out a report defining the educational technology market as a $2.2 billion-a-year enterprise, an investment opportunity that the firm called "one of the nation's most promising." The company's analysts also noted that "several powerful forces are beginning to converge that are now driving technology into a central, mainstream role of delivering curriculum into classrooms, reinforced by products used in homes." That notion—that we'd come upon a time of sudden "convergence"—popped up frequently in the mid-1990s, animating both business and public perceptions that a "new economy" had finally arrived. (As indication of this fact, one of the new magazines launched to focus exclusively on technology in education was called *Converge.*) Drawing on the companion public perception that schools were failing to prepare students for this new world (or for the old one), Robertson, Stephens said it was time for a "new paradigm" of lifelong learning. That paradigm, the firm argued, was a ripe business opportunity, because when compared with the cost of standard textbooks, the new technologies would be seen as a bargain.[52]

All of this led the nation's top policy makers to suddenly get very serious about school technology. In December 1995, the Clinton administration issued a report entitled "The Kickstart Initiative," which gave birth to the

---

example, to get one Apple IIG; a Wisconsin school proudly announced that it had collected $500,000 in receipts to buy two computers worth roughly $3,000 apiece. In other words, for every dollar that people spent at their grocery stores, the schools got seven tenths of one cent worth of credit toward a computer. As small as this cost was for the grocers, market analysts at the time fully expected the stores to pass this cost back to the consumer. For its part, Service Marketing Group also seemed to be doing well. After buying the computers wholesale from Apple, it sold them at close to retail rates to the grocers—a markup estimated to have been approximately 40 percent. See " 'Apples for Students': Computers for Schools, Profits for Marketers," by Peter West, *Education Week*, October 23, 1991; *Giving Kids the Business: The Commercialization of America's Schools*, by Alex Molnar, Westview Press, 1996, p. 23.

federal government's first nationwide campaign to computerize the classroom. The report drew heavily on the research done years earlier by Linda Roberts, whom Clinton had now picked to be his top adviser on school computing, serving as director of the Department of Education's Office of Educational Technology.

The Kickstart Initiative was bolstered by yet another report, from a presidential technology task force composed of thirty-six leaders of industry, education, and assorted interest groups. In its report, the task force cited numerous studies ostensibly proving that computers significantly enhance student achievement. As academic experts and the media attempted to digest this material, the quality of the evidence for these claims was occasionally called into question. But why would the White House generate such problematic data? Part of the answer may have resided in the makeup of its task force. According to accounts of the task force's deliberations, all thirty-six members were unequivocal technology advocates. Two thirds of them worked in the high-tech and entertainment industries. Perhaps not surprisingly, when I asked several members what discussion the group had had about the potential downside of computerized education, they said there hadn't been any.

Soon after the launch of Kickstart, the schools were treated to another national initiative, called NetDay. Volunteer enthusiasts with drills and screwdrivers were sent to schools across the country, where they scrambled to retrofit old school buildings for Internet access. The first state to capitalize on the NetDay buzz was California, which launched a statewide campaign in March 1996 to wire 12,000 schools in one day. When the wiring day arrived, school participation was far below expectations (numbering around 4,000), even in technology-conscious San Francisco. In the city papers, school officials wondered how they were supposed to support an Internet program when they didn't even have the money to repair crumbling buildings, install electrical outlets, and hire the dozens of new teachers recently required in order to reduce class size.

Naysayers may want to lump in the Internet with televisions, radios, video players, and other powerful technologies that are huge cultural mainstays but that somehow didn't make much of a dent in schools. That fate may someday befall the Net. But at this point, its power seemed far too vast, its resources far too prodigious, and its presence far too pervasive to be so casually dismissed. In a sense, the Net almost supplanted the computer. By the turn of the new century, many people in and outside school were making little use of the high-end software that was abundantly available online and in the nation's computer stores. Aside from some word-processing programs and other simple tools, for a huge swath of the American public, the power of the computer was unidirectional: what it delivered from the Net.

———

In early 1996, an eye-opening perspective on the Internet age appeared in the pages of *Wired* magazine. It was a lengthy Q & A conversation with Steve Jobs, Apple's restless, provocative, charismatic co-founder. The interview took place toward the end of Jobs's forced hiatus from Apple, while he was head of NeXT Computer, Inc., and was trying to position NeXT to take advantage of corporate activity on the Internet. That new focus left Jobs free to look at school computing without considering his self-interest in its development—a fact that made for a bold moment of candor. "This stuff doesn't change the world," Jobs said at one point. "It really doesn't. . . . The Web is going to be very important. Is it going to be a life-changing event for millions of people? No. . . . It's certainly not going to be like the first time somebody saw a television [or] as profound as when someone in Nebraska first heard a radio broadcast. . . . We live in an information economy, but I don't believe we live in an information *society*. People are thinking less than they used to. . . . We're already in information overload. No matter how much information the Web can dish out, most people get far more information than they can assimilate anyway."

Eventually, Jobs—who accurately boasted that he had "probably spearheaded giving away more computer equipment to schools than anybody else on the planet"—was asked about technology in schools. "I used to think technology could help education," he said. "But I've come to the inevitable conclusion that . . . what's wrong with education cannot be fixed with technology. No amount of technology will make a dent. . . . You're not going to solve the problems by putting all knowledge onto CD-ROMs. We can put a Web site in every school—none of this is bad. It's bad only if it lulls us into thinking we're doing something to solve the problem with education."[53]*

---

*It's worth noting that several years later, after Jobs had returned to Apple, he somehow managed to find religion again. An example occurred in the spring of 2001, when Jobs sealed a historic $18.5 million deal with a Virginia school district. The arrangement let the schools lease 23,000 Apple laptops, one for each of its middle and high school students, as well as their teachers, with an option to buy them after four years. In announcing the project, Jobs said, "This is mammoth—the single largest sale of portable computers in education ever. Some people have wondered if our commitment to education was as strong as it once was. I can assure you, if anything, it's stronger." See "Laptops to Transform Learning for 23,000 Virginia Students," *eSchool News*, June 2001, p. 12.

COMPUTERS AND POLITICS, TAKE THREE

In the pages of the Clinton administration's Kickstart report are profiles of a dozen select schools from across the country, most of which suffered from a history of poverty or academic failure—until computers arrived on the scene. The most interesting example of this political interpretation of history involved the Christopher Columbus Middle School, just outside New York, in Union City, New Jersey, the nation's most densely populated city.

In 1989, the Union City schools were failing on almost every front. Roughly 75 percent of the district's students were poor or did not speak English. State auditors checked 40 of 52 categories measuring a school district's educational and physical health; Union City failed miserably on many of them. (Among other things, facilities were worn down; finances were a mess; many teachers weren't certified or even properly evaluated; and test scores were abysmal.) The situation was so dire that New Jersey officials gave the city's schools an ultimatum: Improve within five years, or we take over. Union City responded with a massive improvement campaign. A $27 million bond initiative in 1990 helped refurbish aging classrooms. The district also got $9 million of extra state aid, roughly $2 million of which was dedicated to the district's purchase of 775 computers—enough, the Kickstart report claimed, to provide one computer for every eleven students. Then, in September 1993, Christopher Columbus launched a two-year trial, which gave all 135 seventh graders even greater access to computer technology. Courtesy of Bell Atlantic, the school put additional computers in their classrooms and in their homes, and did the same for all of the students' teachers. Throughout the Kickstart report, the Clinton team wove electronic rhapsodies about the network's "very high-bit rate digital subscriber lines and audio/visual server technology," and how this let students, parents, and teachers communicate, and carry out "a wide range of curriculum activities."

By 1995, the Clinton team was ready to declare victory. "Recent test scores and other data demonstrate just how successful the program has been," Kickstart concluded, noting that scores in reading, math, and writing were now more than ten points above the state average. Absenteeism was down as well, and the dropout rate, according to the report, was "almost nonexistent." To dramatize the story, President Clinton paid a visit to Christopher Columbus Middle School himself. The media responded enthusiastically, splashing TV newscasts and newspaper stories with scenes of students happily making great strides on their computers.

The academic strides were true; the problem is that they had little or nothing to do with the technology. The computers didn't actually arrive until 1994, but eighth-grade test scores had doubled and tripled by 1993. So what did turn the school around? The answer is a handful of embarrassingly well known, basic changes: smaller classes and longer class periods; new books and extra time for teachers to prepare their lessons; encouragement of exploratory reading instead of sticking to drills and textbooks; an emphasis on school projects and student collaboration; strict dress codes and behavior rules; and an after-school program for help with homework. All of these changes cost considerably less than the computers, recalls Bob Fazio, the school's principal during those years, who was later moved to another school to carry out the same low-tech approach. "Bell Atlantic has not in any way, shape or form, in my opinion, changed in a basic way what goes on here," Fazio said. And Bell Atlantic executives agreed.[54]

How did this story get so tilted? Part of the answer obviously lies in the power of political spin; the other part involves the public's unflinching gullibility and the media's role in the pattern. For illustration, consider the coverage by ABC News. ABC was one of the television networks to jump on the Christopher Columbus story, broadcasting heartwarming scenes of students' recovery through technology. Several years later, after the print media had disclosed the rest of the story, ABC returned to update its coverage with a decidedly critical report on *Nightline*. During the Q & A that followed—with Linda Roberts and Jane Healy, an educational psychologist—an aggrieved Ted Koppel put the screws to Roberts.

> **Koppel:** Let me just ask you, Dr. Roberts . . . if you've got all that evidence [that computers boost learning], why in heaven's name was the president taken to a school that disproves it?
>
> **Roberts:** You know, I was there at that school and the kids are continuing to learn and their test scores are accelerating.
>
> **Koppel:** But the test scores went up. They doubled before the computers showed up.
>
> **Roberts:** But they have . . .
>
> **Koppel:** Why take the president there to make that particular point?
>
> **Roberts:** Because you have to look at how the kids are spending their time in that school and you have to look at how the tool, the computer, is an amplifier of the goals that this school has. I think . . .
>
> **Healy:** It's a very expensive one, I might add.
>
> **Roberts:** Well, it's a very important tool, and you should talk . . .

Healy: Well, teachers would be the best amplifiers.

Roberts: That's right, but teachers and parents and kids in this school really believe that computers have added, have added to the quality of education for them.[55]

THE DIGITAL DIVIDE, TAKE THREE

As the 1990s drew to a close, public discussion of the digital divide had become so incessant that it was almost a cliché. Almost every school district, and any organization involved in putting computers into these districts, had some piece of its program dedicated, in one of former president Clinton's favorite phrases, to "bridging" this fabled divide. And passionate crusaders were not far behind. "If we're going to resolve this achievement gap between students of color and white students, and high-poverty and low-poverty students, we have to give them access to the same educational opportunities," Lugene Finley, Jr., the chief technology officer for the Illinois state school board, said in 2001. "And technology does that. It can be an equalizer when you provide the tools."

Things weren't quite so simple. By this point, the great divide actually had become something of a fiction. An expansive review of technological offerings in schools across the country in 2001 by *Education Week* found that computer gear was now so common that student-to-computer ratios were much the same in poor schools as they were in wealthy schools (roughly five to one). The same was true of Internet access, which existed in almost every school in the country, whether rich or poor. Even when fancy high-speed connections became the criterion, the divide was virtually nonexistent. (About 68 percent of schools that primarily draw whites or the wealthy enjoyed high-end Internet services; among schools that mostly serve the poor or minorities, the percentage was about 63 percent.) Beyond school walls, a comfortable 95 percent of the nation's public libraries now offered Internet access. These facts led Michael Powell, the chairman of the Federal Communications Commission, to describe the digital divide as being more of a "Mercedes divide." In other words, *Education Week* said, "everyone would like to have one, but you can still get where you need to go with a less expensive machine."

The divide somewhat reopened, however, when it came to finer questions. One was the matter of teacher savvy. Principals and other administrators in wealthy, white schools classified only 25 percent of their teachers as technology "beginners," whereas more than a third got this tag in schools heavily attended by the poor and minorities. Not surprisingly, the kind of computer activities that students pursued in advantaged schools as compared with disadvantaged institutions fell along similar lines. One study done in Hawaii found that private school students were often engaged in sophisticated simulations or were off on field trips, tying technology to complicated, real-world inquiries. Students at poor schools, meanwhile, tended to get stuck trying to master the technology itself (with word processing or Web-page designs); when they did get around to doing projects or papers with computers, the work tended to lack academic rigor. No one could say, however, that these concerns weren't getting attention. One group (the Benton Foundation) listed no fewer than 20,000 different services devoted to eliminating technology's inequities; the services included free Internet access and technology training, computer gear in youth-service organizations, and hordes of other options. And the corporate world was largely to thank for these opportunities. The library buildup, for instance, was partly created by $2 billion in equipment and software donated by the Bill and Melinda Gates Foundation. Late in 2000, Gates followed up with $100 million from Microsoft to help put technology centers in every Boys & Girls Club in the United States.

All of this activity led some education activists to get sick of the whole digital divide discussion. "Clearly, the vibrant PC market is doing more than an adequate job of providing computing technologies to all Americans," wrote Adam Thierer, an economist with the Heritage Foundation, a Washington, D.C., think tank. "Free computers and inexpensive technologies are filling any digital divide that remains." Some thought the issue was getting too much attention at a time when schools were struggling with teacher shortages, inadequate salaries for those teachers they had, overcrowded classes, and buildings in need of basic repairs or wholesale refurbishment. Others meanwhile resigned themselves to the issue, seeing it as a cultural constant, a sociological offspring of technology's upgrade parade. Andy Carvin, the Benton Foundation's specialist on questions of technological equity, told *Education Week* that the problem may never be solved. "At the point where you get low-cost Internet access, there's a new technology that comes along that recreates the divide, such as broadband or wireless technology."[56] Indeed, the wireless systems were already on the march—a cruel joke on the enthusiasts who had just spent billions wiring all the schools.

⸺

Toward the end of President Clinton's second administration, he gave the digital divide one last high-profile stab. When people make repeated efforts to solve a problem, they usually learn from their previous mistakes, which helps them move forward. The Clinton team seemed to go in reverse. In exchange for a remarkably transparent giveaway to the computer industry, the Clinton team got what turned out to be a dumbed-down version of the 1983 EPIE plan, which tried, in vain, to put computers into the homes of the poor in San Francisco.[57]

In his final State of the Union address, on January 27, 2000, President Clinton offered the nation a cousin for Kickstart, his big technology initiative in underprivileged schools. Dubbed Clickstart, this venture was designed to arm whole families of the poor across the country with computers and Internet access. January 2000, of course, was mere weeks before the Internet high of the 1990s began to wear off. So there was little reason at this point for the government to pick its digital shots with great care. It was the end of the party, a hazy, intoxicated time when no one was paying much attention to loud belches of largesse.

The plan sounded great: For the next three years, the government would hand out monthly vouchers, at $10 apiece, to some selection of the nation's poor families. Each family would then chip in $5 a month of their own money, and—*voilà:* They'd have a full-service computer with Internet access. The initial sum was paltry—$50 million, a mere asterisk in the budget of the Commerce Department. Not surprisingly, this would cover only a small percentage of the nation's poor. But the plan was supposed to grow substantially, eventually reaching all 9 million households that received food stamps.

The catch was in where the money went and what it bought: During his State of the Union speech, Clinton said, "I thank the high-tech companies that are already doing so much." For whom? All of the money here, from the families and the government, went solely to the companies that were "donating" the computers. Coincidentally, after three years, those contributions would total $540 per household—precisely what these low-end computers were going to be worth on the open market. Garrett Gruener, a Silicon Valley venture capitalist and the founder of Ask Jeeves (a dot-com that soon had one of the Internet age's most dramatic moments of rise and fall), admitted that one company was planning to build a computer specifically for this market and would happily fulfill every order.

No wonder. During the three to five years envisioned for this initiative, the price of computers was expected to drop precipitously, which meant that any firm that got in on this deal would do quite nicely. Gruener hoped that as prices dropped in the ensuing years, the program sponsors would compensate—by giving away more computers or by dropping the families' contribution requirements. But there was nothing in the Clickstart business plan spelling that out. In fact, the Clickstart initiative was never supposed to be philanthropic. "I don't have any problem with these companies making money," said Gruener, who incidentally sat on the board of Be, Inc., the company slated to be a supplier of the computers. But once again, the technology leaders managed to sell their plan on a grander plane. Eric Schmidt, a software development executive at Novell and another Clickstart organizer, said, "Our feeling is that while this is good for us, it's also good for the world." His comment recalled the famous line from Charles E. Wilson, the former president of General Motors: "For years, I thought that what was good for the country was good for General Motors, and vice versa."[58]

Citizens today would, obviously, debate the proposition that Charlie Wilson gave the country a good deal whenever he helped General Motors.* As regards Clickstart, while the plan might help computer suppliers, there was precious little indication it would help many others. As a reflection of how intoxicating the prospect of just having a computer was in 2000, the Clickstart plan included no provisions for training, maintenance, or any other sort of support from government overseers or from the computer suppliers. It left this job entirely to community groups—without giving them any of the resources needed to handle the job.

Those who organized Clickstart had plenty of warning that their plan might not work. Not only were there the lessons from earlier failed efforts in this realm, but there was also advice aplenty from community group leaders, who knew what this work entailed. Daniel Ben-Horin, president of CompuMentor, one of the nation's largest providers of technology assistance to non-profit organizations and schools, pointed out that the kind of assistance a poor household needs is not the sort the computer industry is used to—what's typically referred to as technical support. "Support doesn't mean waiting for people to call with questions," Ben-Horin pointed out. "Often, they'll never call. They accept the hype about computers being plug-and-play machines, and they feel stupid for having problems." In a large

---

*While the arrival of the automobile has brought its share of rewards, it is worth noting that among the various titans of the car industry, General Motors holds what may be the industry's golden distinction in doing the most to serve its own technological interests at civic expense. In the 1920s, GM was the company that persuaded cities throughout the country to make room for cars by tearing up their old trolley tracks, which at that time were the nation's sole system of inner-city mass transit and which produced considerably less pollution than automobiles did. See "The StreetCar Conspiracy," by Bradford Snell, a former counsel to the U.S. Senate. The article originally appeared in *The New Electric Railway Journal*, Autumn 1995, and is currently available at www.lovearth.net/gmdeliberatelydestroyed.htm.

household with one phone line, he explained, a computer and a Net connection "can be a source of conflict and frustration rather than empowerment."

In the end, no one remained terribly committed to the Clickstart plan. In the spring of 2000, one company, People PC, launched a tiny debut of the initiative, giving away about fifty computers at a community center in Oakland, California. As Ben-Horin and others had anticipated, the center soon found itself with a few uncovered support expenses. But when Congress failed to fund the initiative, the computer companies found themselves with responsibility for a sustained philanthropic campaign. No one was up for that, so Clickstart quickly died.

A few years later—as the economy faltered and as yet another presidential administration took hold—school policy toward technology shifted once again. But the changes were slight. As might have been expected, the collapse of the Internet boom shook out a number of commercial technology suppliers, dropping private investment in "eLearning" from $2.7 billion at its peak in 2000 to $400 million at the end of the year.[59] This of course left more than a few schools in the lurch for technical support and equipment upgrades. As for federal policy, Rod Paige, the new education secretary, didn't take on many new technology initiatives, as befitted his boss's preference for local control of school decisions. There were, however, a few notable exceptions. One of those was to insist that a larger percentage of federal funding be spent on training teachers in technology. Coupled with that directive, the administration contributed $10 million to create a brand-new program for teacher training at Western Governors University, the college started in the 1990s by a collection of governors in the West, at which courses are taken entirely online. Although enthusiasm for the initiative was generally high, a few errant observers wondered about the worth of teaching credentials gained through a modern-day version of correspondence courses. As we will see, this medium has never had a great track record, and it might be particularly inappropriate for a profession that is about personal interaction, as teaching is.[60] When I asked John Bailey, President Bush's director of educational technology, about those questions, he acknowledged the online medium's limitations. The goal, he said, was simply to offer an alternative for aspiring teachers who cannot get to, or who cannot afford, a campus education. "It's a niche," he said.

During a lengthy conversation with Bailey, it was clear that aside from the online university, the Bush administration was trying to take a small step back from the buying frenzy that characterized school technology policy in the Clinton years. "There's been way too much hype," Bailey said. Schools "need to tell us what they're going to use [computers] for, more than

just access to the Net. What is that doing for the students? You need to proceed cautiously with all this stuff." To help schools do that, the Department
of Education launched yet another round of study (this one was expected to
consume five years and $15 million) to see what kinds of computer applica-
tions really do boost achievement.

Despite Bailey's cautionary tone, there was not much indication that the
school technology world was slowing down. Large, bureaucratic institutions like those that oversee education are similar to oceangoing tankers:
Once they set a course, they don't change directions as quickly as the commercial winds do. In the 2002 budget, the Bush administration dedicated
$850 million for school technology—about the same as what schools re-
ceived in the final year of the Clinton administration and considerably more
than the annual average for the previous decade. This turned the schools
into one of the technology industry's most stable markets in the midst of a
recessionary economy. The software industry association happily reported,
therefore, that in 2002 it expected to see school spending on technology
"continuing the general upward trend." As one software research executive
put it, "education and educational technology expenditures are not going to
go away overnight."[61]

———

At the close of *Teachers and Machines,* his 1986 history of technology in
schools, Professor Larry Cuban draws an analogy between the schools' approach to technology and the widespread release of the mentally ill from
state institutions during the 1950s and 1960s. The latter initiative occurred
because of another promising technology—tranquilizers and other new
drugs, which suddenly gave hospitals hope that they could treat the mentally ill quickly and cheaply, without having to care for them day in and day
out. Hordes of tranquilized troubled souls soon began appearing on the
street. Cuban quotes a number of health specialists who grew to regret their
decision, realizing that they should have put the "de-institutionalization"
program through tougher questions at the beginning. Others admitted they
had "oversold" the idea, partly because the political community wanted to
save money.

"The push for classroom computers is certainly not as dramatic or as
wrenching as what happened to hospital patients," Cuban acknowledged.
Yet he saw enough of a link to draw a lesson. "In dealing with lives, young
or old," he wrote, "patience and public reflection on both the anticipated
and unanticipated consequences of policies are in order, rather than the
headlong plunge into change followed by a heartfelt apology years later."

In 1941, just a few years after the publication of Arthur Wise's warning about the schools' rush toward "educative devices" such as motion pictures, the great essayist E. B. White offered some perspective. White wasn't thinking about technology, or even about education. He was in Florida, enjoying a brief respite on the beach, and this had set him to meditating on modern society's peculiar restlessness. "The sea answers all questions, and always in the same way," White wrote, "for when you read in the papers the interminable discussions and the bickering and the prognostications and the turmoil, the disagreements and the fateful decisions and agreements and the plans and the programs and the threats and the counter threats, then you close your eyes and the sea dispatches one more big roller in the unbroken line since the beginning of the world and it combs and breaks and returns foaming and saying: 'So soon?' "[62]

CHAPTER 2

Fooling the Poor with Computers:
Harlem, New York

On a leafy spring day, I am climbing fences in Harlem one morning with Carlton McKinson, a technology coordinator for New York City school district 5. Having taken the wrong subway, we are now two highways and an old, crumbling baseball stadium away from our destination: a local elementary school. This means we are late for one of McKinson's standard appointments—to connect some computers to the Internet in several stressed-out, underfunded sixth-grade classrooms. For the teachers who await McKinson, however, this would be anything but a standard day.

Since the early 1990s, national politicians and local policy makers have talked almost incessantly about the importance of halting the development of a society of technological haves and have-nots. Some of the most ambitious initiatives to result from these pitches have occurred in New York City, which is an ideal test tube for this kind of work. More than 70 percent of the city's students are Hispanic or black, and large numbers of them are commonly classified as financial have-nots. One would think that several decades of frustration in trying to rescue the poor through technology would provide these activists with sobering lessons. However, as is commonly the case with recurring public policy drives, by the time a new iteration of the concept comes along, almost everyone has forgotten what happened the last time. In the meantime, new lessons were available that could be of enormous value, if only everyone wasn't looking the other way.

The current governmental approach to the idea of computing equity was perhaps irrevocably set during the Clinton administration, helped in no small part by Vice-President Al Gore's enthusiasm for all things technological and the public's simultaneous excitement during the 1990s' high-tech boom. As Linda Roberts, director of the Office of Educational Technology under Clinton, wrote in 1997, the department was "investing in technology as a form of seed capital to attract state, local, private, and nonprofit investments, and to help close the educational-technology gap between rich and poor."[1]

While the George W. Bush administration has taken a somewhat calmer approach to this issue, it has nonetheless continued to make it a priority, by accelerating technology funding for poor schools. When the computers finally arrive in the poorer classrooms, however, reality casts this "educational-technology gap" quite differently than it has been depicted by either administration. Those differences, if seen clearly, could redefine popular images of what people mean when they speak of the digital divide. Whatever the contours of this picture are, they can be easily seen in Harlem, a place that has become legendary as the quintessence of inner-city poverty.

INTERNET DREAMS

After checking in and teaming up with two installation technicians, McKinson takes his entourage to a sixth-grade classroom and knocks on the door. Immediately, the teacher next door, a small, feisty man in his thirties whom I'll call Ben, bursts out of his room. "You're here to fix the computers?" he asks. "I can't believe it. Come in here. You gotta see this." In the far corner of his classroom is a cluster of four computers—a scene that had recently been duplicated in all of the city's sixth-, seventh-, and eighth-grade classrooms. Their arrival—roughly thirty thousand of them, at a cost of $100 million to $150 million (including installation and training)—was part of a 1996 mayoral initiative called Project Smart. Its largesse was supposed to trickle down to grades four and five and, ultimately, to every other classroom in the city. But the funding never got that far.

"These things haven't worked since day one!" Ben says. "They spend fifteen thousand dollars on each room and then they forget about it." After some exploration, it turns out that two machines do work properly but lack Internet connections; one works intermittently; and one, whose hard drive cries repeatedly like a broken mechanical doll, can't move beyond its opening screen. The school had been wired for the Internet four months earlier, but no one had ever come to make the connections. Recently, after Ben had waited a year for technical help, some technicians finally arrived. But they couldn't find the keys to the computers. "They never even asked the teachers," Ben says. "They never even came up to the room. They came and then they left. Typical board of education. It's been mismanagement, incompetence, and corruption every step of the way."

Ben then escorts us to his computer corner, whereupon his students go into a free-for-all. Two boys stand up and dance by their desks, singing, "We got Internet! We got Internet!" In between futile efforts to discipline them, Ben tries to understand what is being installed and why it has taken so long. "We have eight hundred schools to hook up," one of the technicians explains. "We're now on sixty-five." Soon, with the computers only partly in service, the technician has to move on, but before he leaves, he gives Ben a manual and a small connection wire and tries to tell him how to finish the job himself, in case McKinson gets too busy. Shaking his head, Ben returns to his class, occasionally coming over to watch McKinson, who pops in and out as he tries to satisfy several other impatient teachers.

"What are you doin'?" Ben asks as McKinson wires the modem. "You have to explain all this to me. How am I going to work this when you're not here?" McKinson, an affable young technician who is largely self-taught, picks up the modem and points out the different ports, explaining which are for uplinks, which are for downloads, and so forth. "What are all these numbers?" Ben asks as his students begin tossing things at one another. "This is a port—it's number eight," McKinson replies. "You know," Ben says, interrupting, "I don't even care. Give me the Internet. I spend six months waiting for this to work and I care about numbers?"

When an Internet connection is finally made, McKinson, relieved, offers Ben a seat in front of the screen. "What do you click on?" Ben asks. "What is this? What's the Internet? I don't even know how to use it." McKinson demonstrates a few links. "How do you keep them from going to Satan or violence?" Ben asks. "Um," McKinson says, "supervision."

——

A couple of dozen blocks south and east, in what public officials and the media dramatically call the heart of Harlem, is a large middle school where Lisa Nielsen serves as the school librarian and, according to official honors at the time, the district's best technology educator that particular year. Like the vast majority of New York public schools, this one goes by its institutional number: I.S. 275 (to signify a middle, or "intermediate," school). Despite some notable exceptions, there's a certain truth to the image these numbers connote—of a massive processing system, a kind of American stalag. In New York, education's institutional taste is particularly bitter. For it follows an unusually ambitious and often successful history of daring school reform effort.

Many of these reform drives, which follow and even define education's liberal "progressive" wing, came to life during the restive decade of the 1960s. Frustrated by the constraints on minorities that prevailed at that time and inspired by the decade's burgeoning egalitarian ideals, both educators and common citizens fought for, and often won, permission to set up new schools, which tended to be far smaller than the big institutional models that had become common by then. The new schools were also based on wildly alternative curricula and teaching methods. As might be expected, some of these reforms tried to flesh out 1960s-vintage political visions. They strove, for example, to connect schools to their neighborhoods; to let students actively guide their own learning experiences; to use the classroom as a laboratory for democracy; and to treat education as a vehicle for social change. Many of these schools created what became known as open classrooms, a pedagogy that let students in a given class break into different groups, where they could engage in different tasks, the sequence of which sometimes became a multidisciplinary project; they established free schools, even "street academies," that brought grade-school study into the outside world.

Perhaps the most famous product of these reforms is Central Park East (CPE), the Harlem public elementary school started in 1974 by Deborah Meier. Like her progressive peers, Meier believed that the key to learning was not so much in the accumulation of factual knowledge but in developing children's inner capacities of inquiry. Skeptics of progressive reform often argue that such an open-ended approach to academics is only suited to more advanced students, who have already built a knowledge base and mastered the principle of discipline. But Meier did her work with a tough crowd. "We've got kids not just with broken homes but with no homes," says Alice Litsky, a longtime CPE teacher. "They're looked after by the cousin of the brother's grandmother." Over the years, Meier made such strides—by doing little more than treat these students to the same respect and creative opportunities that wealthy, white children routinely get—that she eventually won a MacArthur prize for her work.[2]

Today, the forces of school reform in New York, and in many other cities, have exploded into a bitter feud between education's warring parties. Broadly speaking, the reformers fall into two distinct camps: the liberal progressives, like Meier, and the more conservative traditionalists. (While many schools obviously borrow from both philosophies, those on the front lines of reform have tended to be purists.) In New York's case, the progressive leaders include, in the more affluent neighborhoods, the Manhattan New School and P.S. 234; and, for the less well-off, the two CPE schools and Urban Academy High School, which is profiled later in this book. The conservative, back-to-basics wing, which represents the New York reformers' smaller camp, can also claim a few high-performing schools in poor neighborhoods. Their exemplars include Brooklyn's Clinton Hill School, whose combination of reform packages includes E. D. Hirsch's Core Knowledge program, a curriculum that stresses academic basics and the old mainstays of classroom literature; and Harlem's Frederick Douglass Academy, where results get an extra boost because the school is selective about which students it admits in the first place. Unlike their progressive peers, the traditional schools have not sought to break or even shape the system; their goal has been to teach students to accept school as it is—to understand its rules and requirements and to rise unapologetically toward its top.*

One can obviously debate these competing schools of thought, and education's intelligentsia often does, with long, impassioned streams of verbiage. The arguments can be enlightening but they don't much matter. What does matter is that in nearly all successful schools—traditional or progressive—there is a simple, common thread: a culture of high expectations. The expectation might be that these youngsters can all be creative writers, that they can all do well on the state's standardized tests, that they can all be good citizens, or whatever. Regardless of what they are, the expectations generally start with the school principal and extend outward—to teachers; to school counselors, if there are any; to students; and, perhaps most important in the eyes of many education reformers, to the students' parents.[3]

---

*One reason for the vigor of education reform in New York (and, undoubtedly, its progressive tilt) is the existence of a number of well-organized progressive reform organizations, such as the Center for Collaborative Education, the New Vision Schools, and a vibrant alternative high school movement. Bolstering these programs are nationally renowned teaching colleges in the area that have drawn from and extended the once-radical theories of the famous turn-of-the-century education reformer John Dewey, who held that children learned best by being engaged in challenging real-world projects. Foremost among these teaching schools are the Bank Street College of Education and the Teachers College at Columbia University. Another reason for the underrepresentation of education's conservatives in reform initiatives is that, in a sense, they already own the farm. When these activists set out to reform a school, they aren't seeking a new direction; they simply want more of what traditional schooling has always been about. Not surprisingly, many communities believe their schools are already set in that direction.

A number of the schools that turned these philosophies into academic results remain robustly in business today, and they stand, like the city's Statue of Liberty, as beacons for the myriad others that are lost in the shadows, offering visions of what could be. I.S. 275 is one of those places in the shadows, a school for which a statistical identity feels oppressively fitting.

I.S. 275 houses 1,100 students in a three-story building that is without drinking fountains; that, despite a regular summer school program, has lived without working air-conditioning in all but the principal's office; where getting into the locked bathrooms is so difficult that Nielsen once told me, "We've had kids have to go home because they've peed in their pants." For years there have been no art classes at this school; no shop or science lab; no dance or movement classes; and only patchy attempts at some music instruction. At the time of my visit, because of construction, I.S. 275 hadn't even held regular phys ed classes for the past two years. Which is not to imply that there aren't isolated efforts to compensate for these shortcomings. Directly across from the school's front door lies an oasis so beautiful and so out of place that it hurts. It's a small garden, with a pastoral trellis that's surrounded by a few exotic trees, a tiny pond and bridge, and carefully pebbled paths. On both sides of the garden are houses with blown-out windows. Their jagged edges stare down at the garden, as if laughing at its pretenses, or crying. Teachers occasionally hold environmental-science classes in this garden, but it's not the most comfortable place for discussion. Up and down the block, bedraggled men and women, young and old, loiter throughout the school day.

As Nielsen sat in the school library listing the trials she faced each day, half a dozen students who had cut class and were marauding the halls intermittently pounded on the library door. This continually interrupted whatever work Nielsen was doing, forcing her to answer the door, even though the answer she had to give each visitor was "No. You should be in class."

As unruly as this atmosphere is, Nielsen and her predecessors have managed to keep the library shelves filled with an array of books, a feat that is doubly impressive considering that the district had consistently reneged on its contribution to the annual book fund. (Public schools in New York are supposed to receive $4 per student for books, which would mean $4,200 for Nielsen's library, but the city has consistently come up short. The year I visited, Nielsen had gotten less than half of the book fund she was promised.) But the school has invested in computers—more than 200 of them by 2002, which have cost the school district and its benefactors roughly

$350,000. It's worth noting that precise tallies of these expenditures, even at individual schools, are nearly impossible, because new equipment is constantly arriving at schools, financed by myriad different sources. As a result, no one in New York—and most other cities around the country—can readily identify what school computing costs or who is paying for which aspect of the system.

When I first visited I.S. 275 in the spring of 1999, Nielsen was still waiting to get stable connections to the Internet for the sixteen computers in her mini-lab. "In September I was told I'd have the Internet, then November, then December, then the end of the year. Now it's supposed to be September again." Two years earlier, the city's Project Smart initiative did give her two newer machines with Internet connections. Armed with that gear, Nielsen began devising some potentially stimulating projects. In one class, for example, she had each student compose brochures on a different country, based on research done both online and in encyclopedias; when the projects were completed, students' parents came in for a "slide show." Sometimes she'd give an online news quiz, compliments of *The New York Times*'s website. But there was an unusual amount of stumbling along the way on all these endeavors, which was not helped by the technology. Most students couldn't type—a problem that pervades schools everywhere and seems to go almost entirely unnoticed by teachers. This of course made basic writing proceed at glacial speeds. Nielsen also found that the students couldn't download roughly half the material that was available on the Internet. Digital photography that students produced didn't work, nor did a number of CD-ROMs. Twice, district technicians came by promising to upgrade the equipment; both times they left without doing so. In the meantime, the computers were plagued with corrupted disk drives—and frequent theft. Digital cameras, at $200 each, regularly disappeared, as did floppy disks, CD-ROMs, and even the little gray balls in the computer mouses.

When I talked to Nielsen the following fall, she said she had just been told that Internet connections wouldn't be delivered to her at all this round— she'd have to wait for the next upgrade. And that upgrade was already delayed, because the money earmarked for it now had to go to reducing class sizes. Which raises a point: If the main problem with technology in poor schools is simply money and insufficient attention to technical issues, as many argue, then the nation's schools need gargantuan amounts of both— far more, even, than they're getting now—to solve the technology problem. Nielsen's predicament was a perfect illustration. The technical obstacles here were all the more frustrating because Nielsen had almost gotten her lab up and running on the Net, thanks to a technically astute friend, who put in nearly a hundred hours of his own time. Just before they were done, however, Nielsen and her friend discovered they needed certain codes and passwords to make the lab work. The district, however, wouldn't release them.

At times, when Nielsen was able to connect to the Internet, she had difficulties accessing certain sites—a problem that has plagued other public schools in New York and elsewhere. After some exploration, it became apparent that the city's Internet filtering system was afflicted with some serious snafus, which demonstrate one of governmental policy's most enduring patterns: the law of unintended consequences. In education's case, those consequences are sometimes made all the more glaring by technology. Educators may believe that once computers are properly installed, their technical problems will end or at least greatly diminish. In reality, that's when the serious challenges begin.

—

Nothing illustrates this pattern more colorfully than the Internet and the schools' feeble efforts to manage the way youngsters use it. Unfortunately, dynamic change is eternal with technology, which means that attempts to keep up with it through electronic safeguards may be futile.

When students first started connecting to the Internet from I.S. 275 (and every other New York public school), they quickly discovered they were blocked from legitimate sites as well as undesirable ones. These included government sites, like the White House's; any number of research sites that employed potentially offensive terms, such as *breast cancer, anorexia,* and *bulimia;* and sites devoted to drug abuse, child labor, AIDS, gay and lesbian concerns, and support for abortion—but, strangely, not the sites of groups that oppose abortion. One filtering product blocked an online brochure called "Marijuana: Facts for Teens," published by the National Institute on Drug Abuse; another blocked the official website of House majority leader Richard Armey, an ardent supporter of the federal filtering law.[4]

As recently as 2002, problems of this sort were still plaguing schools across the country—so much so that some districts resisted investing in filtering technology altogether, despite a new federal law requiring schools to install filters if they accept federal funds for Internet systems. The filtering troubles were partly caused by the shaky economics of the technology business, which was robbing the whole filtering enterprise of its basic infrastructure needs. As an example, in 2002, N2H2, a Seattle firm that claims the largest share of the K–12 filtering market, was employing only fourteen website reviewers to serve 25,000 schools and 17 million students. And despite all their imperfections, filtering systems were still costing up to $50,000 for a district of little more than a dozen schools. Schools that shelled out that kind of cash sometimes found themselves in the lurch as the companies that developed filtering software became victims of the dot-com crash.[5] Even the core systems were having problems, caused by the technology's inherent complications. A 2001 study that reviewed a range of filtering products concluded that excessive blocking "stems from the very nature of filtering." By mid-2002, according to one estimate by the National Research Council, the Internet comprised more than 2 billion publicly accessible Web pages; 400,000 of these were for-pay adult sites. With a minimum of manpower available to monitor this multitude, and with more questionable material being posted on the Web all the time, every system has to rely on automatic keywords. In other words, mistakes are inevitable. "The downsides are greater than the gains," concluded Les Moore, the technology director for a Eugene, Oregon, school district. "It's just not worth it." Earlier in 2002, another study by the University of Oregon charged that Internet filtering was tainted by bias, partly because the big companies handling this job were heavily allied with religious or conservative organizations. That summer, after a researcher tried to find out what sites the N2H2 company blocked but was rebuffed, the American Civil Liberties Union filed suit to challenge the filtering law. And, in November, the U.S. Supreme Court agreed to weigh in on the issue, at least as far as public libraries are concerned.[6]

Lisa Nielsen clearly shares the school administrators' frustrations, and added another complaint widely uttered by teachers. "I want my kids to learn self-censoring," she told me. "I don't need people to go in and monitor what they're doing." When Nielsen and other New York teachers complained, school officials tried to keep a list of wrongfully blocked sites, which they would then check out and release one by one. Before they'd made much progress, of course, resourceful students and teachers had already found their way around the filtering system. I watched a number of kids spend lunchtime, recess, and a surprising amount of surreptitious class time touring sites that offered music videos, wrestling, and, occasionally, pornographic teases.

In some schools, teachers have established enough control in their classrooms so that students steer clear of the most egregious material available on the Internet. But such discipline is a rarity. All of which leads to what may be educational technology's first e-lusion: the belief that high technology in classrooms can be controlled. In some ways, efforts in that direction are contradictory to what technology is all about. As Gary Stager, an adjunct professor of education at Pepperdine University and a passionate veteran of school computing, once told me, "It's ironic that the concern is about kids looking up inappropriate material when the dominant metaphor is 'Use the computer to look stuff up.'"

=

The next week, when I return with McKinson to Ben's school, I find Ben all smiles. "We were on it all day yesterday," he tells McKinson. "Awesome. Awesome." Apparently, Ben's class has already found its way around the district's Internet blocks; when we walk into the class, his students are happily cruising ESPN's sports site.

Two hours into our visit, one of Ben's computers crashes, and students attempting to log on to the Net are being greeted with one of those messages that raise every computer user's blood pressure: "The application Netscape Navigator 3.02 has unexpectedly quit because an error of Type 2 occurred. You should save your work in other open applications and restart your computer." Ben follows the computer's suggestion. No luck. He tries again. No luck. Apparently, he now admits, they had the same problem with another computer yesterday. After a few more attempts, Netscape fails entirely—this time because of the computer's insufficient memory. The fourth computer is still crying like a broken doll.

As McKinson sets up the classroom computer with a new version of Netscape, he tries to show Ben how to repeat the procedures should the problems recur. "Now what do I hit?" Ben asks. "Return?" "Yes," McKinson says, growing impatient. "You have to explain everything!" Ben says, "I don't know this stuff!" McKinson repeats the basics but, seriously late by now, soon has to move on to another class. For a few minutes, Ben works on his own while his students chaotically entertain themselves, but before long he gets stuck. He tries to recall the procedures McKinson explained, then tries to guess his way around those little steps that technicians always leave out. "This is a nightmare," Ben tells me. "It worked for one day."

Unable to bear Ben's despondence, I try to help. But it's a high-tech catch-22. Since Netscape doesn't work, we need a new version. But we have to be online to get it. And we can't get online, of course, because all we have is Netscape. And Netscape doesn't work. "I tell you, the problems never stop," Ben says. "We're teachers. We're all computer illiterate! We're not in the business world." I suggest using one of the two working computers for another stab at the download, but Ben, thoroughly exasperated by now, doesn't want to push his luck. "I mean, they're working," he says.

Midway through the class, while Ben struggles with his four computers, students who can't find a seat at his elbow or are too restless to wait for something to happen onscreen pass the time playing games. Five girls play patty-cake. Several others doodle on binder paper. Four boys busy themselves with a Game Boy, the palm-size progenitor of today's computer games. Others leap around, occasionally hitting or tossing things at one another. "Yo!" Ben intermittently yells. "Have a seat! In a chair!" The students promptly do so, for a moment.

This may appear to be just another undisciplined class—one that any diligent teacher should be able to avoid. Unfortunately, as we'll see, this kind of disorder is remarkably common in high-tech schools.

A TEACHABLE MOMENT

During my visit to I.S. 275, as I sit listening to tales about the lack of drinking fountains, air-conditioning, and art classes, I watch several classes file in and out of a very different computer area—the school's one well-appointed computer lab. Clean and well kept, this room was formerly used for typing classes, a program that has since been dropped. Now it's filled with thirty-five of the school's newest computers, which are lined up back to back in three long rows. These are state-of-the-art machines—mostly Apple PowerMacs—which cost the district roughly $2,000 apiece. They are capable of the most sophisticated kinds of data processing that an average consumer can manage. They can help an architect, for example, multitask his way through both design and financial proposals for a large shopping mall. They can execute mind-numbing database analyses while the user is reading his e-mail and present the results in full-color multimedia productions.

The riches in this lab create such an oasis amid the chaos in this school—and such a contrast to Nielsen's antiquated computer room—that I am curious to see how students put them to use. Computer labs are severely disparaged by the vast majority of school-computer enthusiasts. In their view, the labs turn technology into a dumping ground, where teachers and their classes file in and out without giving much thought to what they'll do there. The more promising scheme, technologists argue, is to put computers inside individual classrooms—as New York had begun doing. This makes them more accessible and thus more easily "integrated" into normal classroom work. Plenty of teachers agree with this argument, but a few old hands in educational technology still support computer labs. Their opinions are well founded, for reasons that will become clear at the end of this story.

———

Around 11 A.M., after a free period in which students used the lab mostly to play games, two dozen eighth graders arrive for a social studies class. Their assignment: create a detailed advertisement to recruit employees for a fictional business that one might start.

Despite the supervision of two instructors (the classroom teacher and the lab coordinator), the students are noisier than they were during the previous free-period class. Many aren't even working on the assignment and instead spend their time fooling around with computer games.

At one point, the teacher, Winston Duckett, stops to work with a girl I'll call Tasha, who is grappling with the assignment more diligently than most of her classmates. Tasha has laid plans for a hair-styling business and is now trying to come up with the right logo. Duckett seizes the opportunity to teach some economics. What, he asks, would the materials for such an operation cost? How about the monthly bills, for expenses such as electricity and taxes? Tasha doesn't know, but Duckett forges on.

This is the sort of interaction teachers long for, what some call a teachable moment—one of those rare times when a youngster's immediate interest (in this case, hair styling) intersects with academics. Duckett asks Tasha to think about what her own shampoo and conditioner cost; how that would multiply in a full-time business; and what the rent might be, based on what her mother pays for their apartment. Tasha grows increasingly discouraged. Eventually, she returns to her drawing. Duckett watches for a moment, then moves on to other students, who are yelling out questions or yelling at one another.

What's going on here? Obviously, teachable moments like this can fail in any class, high-tech or low-tech. Obviously, the disorder is perhaps the biggest hurdle, a problem that can and does occur in classrooms without computers. And obviously, Tasha is overwhelmed by Duckett's questions for complicated reasons, both scholastic and personal. But computers are adding something extra to this scene that greatly affects a teachable moment. Teachers know that when a student like Tasha becomes stymied, the best thing to do is to sit down and talk her through her frustrations. If other students meanwhile spin out of control, it is the teacher's job to muster whatever verbal force he can to return the students' attention to their books. Any teacher in a disorderly school knows that simply establishing an atmosphere of study is hard enough; doing so in a computer lab is even tougher. In this class, for example, Duckett is constantly yelling out pleas for quiet, each of which is heeded only briefly. With thirty-five computers in this lab—thirty-five large electronic boxes that hide the students' faces—the technology, and its myriad options, become the class's main event.

And each student is off on a different course. Some are doing word processing and are having trouble saving, or copying, or enlarging fonts, or picking fonts. Some are trying out graphic designs, which aren't laying out the way they're supposed to. Some are daring to try a little math. And some are well into Internet sites or other programs that have nothing to do with the assignment. As Duckett whips around the room trying to attend to each student and maintain group order, his technique becomes clear: answer a couple of questions, get the student started, move on.

Not surprisingly, as soon as Duckett leaves one student to help another, the first student gets stumped again. After briefly trying to solve the problem on his own, this student, like most of his neighbors, simply gives up and turns to a more inviting computer option, usually a game. Some resort to a high-tech version of an age-old classroom trick: They copy their neighbor's work. "How you do that?" one boy asks his buddy in the next seat, who then tries his best to explain. Technology promoters sometimes point to interactions like this as an example of one of the computer's primary classroom benefits—the way it encourages "collaborative learning." Indeed, the moment may be collaborative, but it doesn't seem to involve much learning. What attracts this boy is the speed at which his friend is moving through a graphics program, an activity that seems to be more fun, and a lot easier, than writing up some fake advertisement.

When I speak to Duckett about his hour in the computer lab, he has few complaints; in fact, he's rather proud of what a few of these students could do. This is part of the problem. There are lots of people just like Winston Duckett—well-meaning teachers who don't realize that academic work can get a lot better with or without computers. During my cross-country visits, I watched countless students "working" on such projects and repeatedly saw teachers and visiting adults observe this scene with admiring awe. It's strange, almost as though the computer emits some kind of technological cloak of legitimacy, which turns whatever is underneath it into something it's not.

There are many teachers who do see what's really happening. They know the sort of classroom atmosphere they need, and they know how the computer is influencing it, even when all the gear is working properly. "Kids doing all sorts of different stuff is a problem," Shareese, one of Ben's colleagues, once told me about her experiences in the computer lab. "They all look at each other's stuff and don't pay attention to their own work. You kind of want everybody in sync." Even at Deb Meier's risk-taking Central Park East Elementary School, the librarian who manages the computer lab is ambivalent about the value of what she's doing. "I would take four more of me before I'd take another piece of equipment," she told me during my visit. "What we're lacking is people." Teachers at CPE also noticed that once computers arrived in the school library, students began neglecting the library's books. Interestingly, CPE never asked for its allotment of computers from the city's Project Smart initiative, and many teachers didn't want them. But they got them anyway.

DIGITAL ARTISTRY

Shortly after Duckett's social studies class at I.S. 275, another group comes through the computer lab for a free period, which many students spend doing art projects on the computers. As the class begins work, I am immediately impressed. Most of what I see are rich, abstract sketches full of intricately woven geometric patterns. The work is so sophisticated that even when it isn't much tied to the assignment, the teachers are content to let the students experiment.

At one point, I stop to watch Jabril, an eighth grader, who is creating a drawing reminiscent of M. C. Escher—all angles of taut perspective, finely nuanced, with careful layers of shading. As he works, I am amazed at how quickly he's willing to erase large sections of exceptionally detailed work. If these programs enable a student to create such detailed work and toss it without even a thought before plunging into a second draft, then perhaps, I thought, the teaching power of these machines in art may indeed be significant.

Suddenly, Jabril deletes the entire drawing. I am stunned. Just as I bend down to ask why he would kill all that hard work, he mouses over to a menu bar and sets up another drawing. Immediately, new sections with perspective angles and detailed shading automatically pop up. I feel a wave of dismay. The aesthetics here, I now see, are almost entirely computer generated. Jabril has not had to learn a single one of the bedrock principles in this work—nothing of the geometry on which perspectives are based; none of the eye-hand coordination and control normally required to shade sections with dots or fine cross-hatching; none of the emotional or psychic attachment that one normally gains by creating something through the sweat of one's brow.

I ask Jabril if he ever does any drawing with pencil and paper. A mumble, apparently a negative. Any interest in it? "I don't have no problem with doing it," he replies. "I just don't." His answers are much like those I heard in other schools that sit students in front of computerized art programs. Even in more well-off communities, the trend was apparent: The more attention the schools paid to computers, the more attention the students did as well. When graphic functions are available, students find their splendors so convenient that, most of them told me, they no longer bother much with pencils or crayons. And they almost never tangle with anything messy, like paint or clay. Jabril tells me he also has a computer at home. I ask what he does with it. "I just play the games."

A few seats away from Jabril, several classmates are doing some original drawings on their computers. Upon inspection, I notice that most are cartoons with a violent theme—the sort that if they were being done with pencil and paper most teachers would discourage. At one point, the teacher stops to compliment a boy who is piecing together a particularly refined sketch of a half-human monster armed with a dagger and a gun. He even helps the boy color it in.

Several days after my visit to I.S. 275, I spend a Saturday morning swimming with a friend and her two children in a local pool. When we return to their apartment, the elder of the children, Mary, a kindergartner who is interested in art, asks if she can draw me. I of course agree, whereupon she sits me down at the kitchen table and begins outlining a portrait, frequently glancing back and forth from my face to the paper. Mary is just finishing her first year at P.S. 874, an alternative public school that goes by a non-institutional name, Midtown West. The school was founded partly by unsatisfied Manhattan parents and the Bank Street College of Education, a private teaching college that has long been known for cultivating some of the nation's most sophisticated progressive teaching methods. Not surprisingly, Midtown West, which sits in the heart of the city's theater district, tends to draw from families, both rich and poor, that are interested in the arts. (Chorus, art, ballet, and chess are regular parts of the Midtown West curriculum; there's also an after-school program in music, gymnastics, and environmental studies—frequently held in an adjacent mini-park that was built by parents and school staff.) Despite these advantages, and despite the fact that Mary's parents work in the arts (her mother is a publicist at Lincoln Center for the Arts, her father a musician), it soon becomes apparent that there is nothing particularly exceptional, at this young age, about Mary's rendering skills. But there is something exceptional about the quality of her efforts. As this small five-year-old works, she studies me with a kind of attention that, after a few minutes, puts a lump in my throat. It's as though she has shed the superficial way most of us observe each other and looks not only at my nose and ears but also under my skin, to how I feel, who I am. Part of the reason for my emotional reaction is that her demeanor is in such stark contrast to the quality of attention I had noticed that week at I.S. 275. Mary's gaze is open, pure, profound; at I.S. 275, I couldn't even get the eighth graders to look up from their computer screens.

To be fair, Mary has grown up in a relatively solid middle-class family—a privilege not available to many of the students I visited in Harlem. But that doesn't excuse the differences here. Plenty of education techniques exist, as will be seen later in this book, that develop the same qualities of attention in the poor that Mary demonstrated that Saturday afternoon. That's why I felt so sad. Everyone is worried about schools like I.S. 275 being left out of the technology revolution. I began to worry about what they're missing out on now that they have computers. And I'm not the only one. "Every couple of months, I hear an artist or an art historian announce . . . that 'nobody knows how to look anymore,'" writes Jed Perl, the art critic for *The New Republic.* There has arisen an "almost universal feeling," Perl argues, that "art ought to be taken in quickly, instantaneously; that a painting or sculpture should hit you with a bang. . . . What people are no longer prepared for is seeing as an experience that takes place in time." Nor do they understand, Perl says, that works of art form "a structure with a meaning that unfolds as we look," in a careful process of "relating part to part. . . . If you can unlock a moment, you can enter a realm of freedom. . . . To look long is to feel free."[7]

Obviously, Perl is describing sophisticated skills, whose acquisition or loss occurs for all kinds of complicated reasons. But there are increasing signs that today's digital culture, with its relentless speed and mechanistic style, isn't helping matters. Computerized sound recording programs have become so prevalent that pop musicians increasingly survive and thrive without understanding basic music theory and other fundamentals. The trend has led even young musicians to complain that music is losing its raw qualities and thus its "soul."[8] In San Francisco, when a group of poor inner-city youngsters was taken out for a day at the beach, they were surprised at how much fun they had. "When I'm at home, all I do is play video games," one boy said. "This is way better."[9] Discoveries of this sort should not be news; education's cognoscenti have been fretting about a shift away from the personal for decades. As but one indication, when the editorial staff of *Forbes* was debating how optimistic the magazine should be about technology in schools in 1984, one of the editors wrote a cautionary memo to his colleagues. "In the end," he said, "it is the poor who will be chained to the computer; the rich will get teachers."[10]

It's already happening. A few years ago, I.S. 275 had art classes. "When we incorporated computers, the emphasis was put on technology," Sharon Hayes, the school's assistant principal, later told me. "One thing had to sacrifice for the other." Valorie Williams, who, as the computer lab coordinator, would presumably support the new emphasis, is actually saddened that the school cut art classes. So she tries to preserve what she can. "We do have an art corner over there," she says, pointing to a small section on one of the computer lab's walls on which are posted a handful of drawings. I walk across the room to look them over. They are all printouts of computer-generated sketches.

Ironically, on the wall outside the I.S. 275 computer lab is a poster with the sort of picture that has become the standard educational technology photo opportunity: Sitting on a classroom desk is a large, gray desktop computer, surrounded by several bright-eyed, eager youngsters and a teacher leaning in supportively from behind. In bold type under the photo is a quote: "The real problem is not whether computers think but whether people do." The message carries a legitimate punch. But, like most promotional campaigns, it leaves its meaning hanging in our imaginations so that we can fill in the blanks with that most dependable of all forces—the American consumer's relentless optimism. In that respect, the poster is a perfect metaphor. On either side of its gauzy, pastel image classes rage on during every minute of I.S. 275's school day. Education policy makers like to think this chaos can be quickly calmed—with a little extra money, perhaps with more rigorous testing, or at least with some decent computer gear. But the chaos isn't calmed. It's only transformed—made to seem insignificant, part of technology's supposedly temporary growing pains.

In the end, what is I.S. 275 accomplishing with computers? It has devoted tens of thousands of dollars and countless hours of effort to letting students pursue the following activities: some random games; electronic self-portraits and other drawings that would be better done with paper and colored pencils; a few ambitious projects that generally disintegrate because there is insufficient support—both technologically and academically—to make them work; and elementary writing exercises that, while valuable, could be done perfectly easily on simple, old, used computers, which many firms will happily donate to schools in return for tax write-offs. As economical as this idea might be, school administrators don't want the hassle of fixing and maintaining used equipment. Like the rest of us, they can't resist the latest shiny new toys. As Ray Porter, a longtime computer recycling expert with San Francisco schools, once told me, "Parents, school boards, and the reporters only want to see razzle-dazzle state-of-the-art."

Three years after my initial visit, the situation at I.S. 275 had not much changed. If anything, things had become worse. The student-teacher ratio at the school got so bad that one teacher was handling ten classes two or three times a week—with a total of three hundred different students. Student performance meanwhile declined so markedly that the state put the school's seventh and eighth grades on academic probation. Not surprisingly, the computer program got neglected as well. "They never really did get my lab wired," Nielsen told me. In schools like these, technical problems don't end.

Like a number of her fellow computer instructors, Nielsen eventually gave up. In June 2000, she left the district and took a job at the Teachers College at Columbia University, helping to instruct teachers in classroom-management skills and other basics. By early 2002, the network at I.S. 275 was so unstable that her old computer room had been shut down, and Internet service in the fancy Macintosh lab next door was repeatedly crashing. During her own days at I.S. 275, she recalls, "I had students who had pen pals in China. But they couldn't do anything about it because they couldn't send e-mails."

HIGH-TECH CARROTS AND STICKS

It's 8 A.M. in the computer labs at Ralph Bunche Elementary, a central-Harlem school celebrated for its achievements with technology by the Clinton administration, *The New York Times, Fortune,* and even Bill Gates in his book *The Road Ahead.* This is the hour before academic classes begin, and Paul Reese, the school's veteran technology coordinator, has come in early of his own volition, as he does every weekday, so that students, and their parents, can work in his computer labs for an hour before school begins.

Reese moves fast—partly by nature, partly because of the amount of territory he must track. In 1986, at Reese's urging, Bunche Elementary took three large, underused classrooms on the school's top floor and turned them into computer labs. These became the heart of a special mini-school that would carry out a double mission: It would provide computer access, which would then be made effective through a disciplined academic setting.

A tall, intense man in his fifties, Reese has a take-no-prisoners air. After having been involved in school technology for more than twenty years, Reese has earned his demeanor, evidenced by the respectful way he's treated at educational technology conferences. His bearing helps as well. His large face is crowned by an unruly mop of gray-brown hair, a kind of scientist's pompadour that, as summer approaches, gets wilder as he administers his antidote to academia's constraints: He spends as many days as possible on his sailboat. Throughout Bunche's three labs, signs of Reese's school-year obsession (technology) are everywhere: in the jerry-built wiring taped across the ceiling and the walls; in the boxes of software that fill his closet; in the jumbled piles of modems and cables and dusty hard drives that spill out of the shelves in the back of the lab; in the crusty refrigerator in the corner, which holds Reese's lunch so that the lab can run nonstop from 8 A.M. to 5:30 P.M.

By 8:10, roughly a dozen students from the school's fourth, fifth, and sixth grades have arrived, most of whom rush breathlessly to their keyboards. Each student immediately pulls up a program that looks like a game: Various cartoon images fill their screens, complete with the standard, dopey sound effects; as students make their choices, the screens advance to another set of cartoons. Upon closer inspection, I realize that the games are posing some basic reading and math problems. It turns out this only looks like a game; underneath, it's what's called an integrated learning system, or ILS—a software package that combines exercises in various subjects into one comprehensive program.

ILS packages—also known as computer-assisted instruction or "drill and practice" programs—have, as we've seen, long been controversial among educators, even those supportive of computers. But they have their pluses. Their material is convenient and seemingly extensive; they contain some flexibility, with difficulty levels that can be individually adjusted upward or downward, based on how students fare in their answers; and they are the soul of patience, capable of working through exercises for hours on end until a student gets them right. This is why ILS programs often raise standardized test scores. While education's visionaries may scorn such work— whether it's with computers or flash cards—certain basic principles of language and arithmetic do need to be mastered. Many of those lessons are not fun—to study or to teach. And a good many academics, including some technology skeptics, believe that a little computerized drilling, in moderation, can be of great help to the harried teacher.[11]

But the way students actually interact with the software has five significant disadvantages. First, despite some capacities for individuation, ILS procedures are fundamentally inflexible. They generally lock students into the software designer's instructional choices, leaving the teacher little room for elaboration or creative departure. That leads to their second problem: Because of the ILS approach to drills—by repetition, without even the pretense of human interaction—knowledge gains seem to take only temporary hold in a student's mind. This is why jumps in test scores prompted by ILS work often don't last. Third, while ILS costs have come down since the 1980s, when prices ran as high as $1 million or more, the programs still aren't cheap. A basic package today costs $20,000 to $30,000; a top-of-the-line model can run well over $100,000. Fourth, the very extensiveness of ILS programs, in many educators' eyes, causes a problem of its own: It encourages teachers to abandon their role as active supervisors. Which leads to the fifth and perhaps most profound problem with ILS packages: the questionable way they motivate students. This morning at Ralph Bunche offered a perfect demonstration.

"I use it as a carrot and stick," Reese says as he whips around the computer lab fixing glitches and crashes. As the hour progresses, the peculiar mix of these carrots and sticks becomes clear. "They love to come here," says Barbara Saunders, the mother of a fourth-grade girl and one of two or three parents who routinely visit Reese's lab. "She's up early every morning, here at eight." One reason the students are so enthusiastic is that once they've completed two ILS lessons, Reese lets them play computer games or surf the Net. Over time, it also gets easier and easier to reach the carrots. Like many ILS programs, the scheme of Reese's system, as well as many of its math and reading problems, tend to repeat themselves. As a result, dedicated visitors are soon knocking these lessons out in fifteen to twenty minutes, which gives them most of the hour for computer play.

But this is before-school time, when any student should be free to play. The real measure of these ILS exercises, then, is in the ways Reese uses them during periods of academic study.

"TECHNOLOGY GIVETH, AND TECHNOLOGY TAKETH AWAY"

As Reese checks on his students, he finds one girl laboring through what should be a simple math exercise. Her screen displays a cute, old-fashioned scale, which moves as she tries to balance various blocks, each of which is assigned a different number. The problem, he suggests, is that her working materials are incomplete. "How can you figure out what the numbers are without a piece of paper?" he asks. "If you had figured out what the numbers were, you wouldn't have needed twenty-eight moves to do this." Embarrassed, the girl digs in her knapsack for her notebook and a pencil. Another girl nearby who is having trouble isn't using a pencil and paper, either. She's using her fingers. To developmental psychologists, this is a sign that she has not spent enough time with "manipulatives" (beans, colored blocks, other tactile objects), which build a sensory understanding of numbers. Developmental gaps of this sort are common in poor schools. But there's no time to fill them in now. At Reese's urging, this girl starts digging for her pencil and paper as well.

Reese's emphasis on old-fashioned basics surprises me. Computers are usually sold to schools on the assumption that they will teach children how to compute—in basic math and, ultimately, with complex digital programming—and do so more effectively than a pencil and paper can. "This is not about learning how to compute," Reese tells me. "It's clearly a practice thing. It's not the greatest of high-order thinking skills. I even encourage them to use a calculator with some of this."

Now I am really confused. Reese is known for being an early pioneer with school technology and a committed educator. He has survived many cycles of technology's repetitious hopes and failures. Wouldn't he, of all people, have found a practical way to execute technology's more sophisticated possibilities?

Not really. His decades of experience with classroom computers have turned Reese into a hardened pragmatist. Take, for example, the Geometric Supposer, one of the more ambitious programs on his shelf. It is designed, as Judah Schwartz, the program's creator and the former co-director of Harvard's Educational Technology Center, told me, to let students "make and explore conjectures." Schwartz's description conjures wonderful possibilities—of students diving into vast undiscovered realms, where they can chart new geometric patterns and hone advanced forms of analysis. And Schwartz says he has seen high school students occasionally do all those things. Reese's view of such programs? "They're funded by eggheads who don't live in the real world." He may be right. Most technology teachers I spoke to who knew of Geometric Supposer, or other programs like it, had been unable to make them work. An offspring of the Supposer, the Geometer's Sketchpad, is used at one of New York's alternative high schools, the School for the Physical City. When I asked several students there about it, they said they liked it. "It makes geometry easier," a senior said. "You can do it much faster." It turns out that the most obvious function the program performs is to carry out complicated geometric procedures automatically. This is not what Schwartz had in mind: a program that shortcuts the analytical struggle—in essence, an advanced calculator.

Or take another program, LOGO, the programming language developed by MIT professor Seymour Papert that is the granddaddy of classroom-computer products. Work with LOGO begins by directing the computer's cursor (in LOGO's case, a cute little turtle) to move in geometric patterns. To do this, the students write a sequence of commands that tells the turtle how far to move and when to turn. Those commands constitute what is essentially a tiny computer program. And writing these programs is supposed to help students understand how a computer processes information, how this action leads to that one, and so on. This, LOGO's creators believed, would teach youngsters the power of "procedural thinking." In most schools, however, the dream never took hold. Students weren't interested, teachers weren't interested, or, sometimes, the intellectual goodies were too elusive. Reese's experience is a perfect illustration. "The amount of work and scaffolding that you have to do," Reese tells me, "is really not worth the effort."

Today, most classes that bother with LOGO use an updated version called MicroWorlds, which has created a whole new set of problems. These become apparent one morning, in between my visits to Ralph Bunche, when I watch a class of sixth graders use MicroWorlds in a computer lab in another school. This one is a computer-savvy midtown Manhattan school called, appropriately, the Computer School. Founded in 1982, in the dark basement floor of a larger elementary school, the Computer School was designed with twin goals: to be the first school in New York to make technology a centerpiece of its curriculum and to do so within the framework of progressive education reform. The Computer School no longer emphasizes technology as much as it once did. But that's part of what makes its use of LOGO so intriguing—the school's routines are now the product of nearly two decades of experience with technology.

As the Computer School sixth graders navigate MicroWorlds, the work appears to be standard LOGO fare: A turtle whirls around the screen outlining whatever fancy shapes the students tell it to make. But something seems to be missing, and it's soon pinpointed when, by coincidence, the veteran education critic Herb Kohl drops by. "I don't see any kids doing programming," Kohl tells the principal. There is a reason: They don't have to. In an effort to improve the program's interface—in LOGO's case, the complex coding work that has put off many students and teachers—LOGO's creators loaded it with simpler functions. Among other things, they added text commands, which these sixth graders are now using. For example, when students want to create a series of squares or other shapes on their screen, they write in: "Forward 90, right 20," and so on, instead of having to come up with a mathematical equation, such as, for a circle, $(x-a)2+(y-b)2=R2$.

More recently, the LOGO developers added other treats. One connects LOGO to Lego, the highly successful children's set of plastic blocks and motors. (The partnership lets children make a motorized device—a little tractor or a robot, for example—and then use LOGO to tell it what to do.) The Lego-LOGO kit is high-end stuff, and thus has made it into only a small selection of the nation's classrooms. A more recent invention, more widely used than Lego-LOGO, is a souped-up version of the basic LOGO package. With this upgrade, the developers added computing power, what's called parallel processing, which lets students create two simultaneous sets of procedures. They also wrapped these capabilities inside some graphic functions. This may seem like a step forward (and with a smart teacher, it can be). But it also allows many a classroom to essentially dumb down the academic work. While the old bedrock programming language remains, its mathematical guts have been so buried by now underneath a surfeit of easier, more visually appealing functions that for most students, the mathematics are little more than procedural artifacts. Hidden alongside these archaeological digs are some of the virtues, such as they are, that might derive from mastering the fine points of "procedural thinking."

This was certainly the case that day at the Computer School, and Kohl isn't the only one to have noticed the loss. A trainer at Portal Elementary, a school in Cupertino, California, that has long been a test bed for Apple's Classrooms of Tomorrow, once told me that she too has been disappointed in LOGO's evolution. As updates of the program have become available, she has passed on buying them, because she finds the earlier versions to be more instructive. Even Marvin Minsky, a Papert colleague who helped design LOGO's turtle icon, takes a jaundiced view of his creation. Minsky is an MIT professor of electrical engineering and computer science, as well as media arts and sciences, and is renowned for his pioneering work in a number of computer-oriented frontiers: artificial intelligence, advanced technology for space exploration, cognitive psychology, knowledge representation, symbolic graphical description and symbolic learning, computational geometry, computational semantics, neural networks, "machine perception," and intelligence-based mechanical robotics, to name but a few. "LOGO is limited because it's all ninety-degree angles," Minksy once told me. "It would be nice if they could include a machine where you could make your own parts and your own fittings. Learning rule-based programs is useful, but it's low-level programming."*

—

If a supposedly advanced program like LOGO has such grave shortcomings, I began to see why, during my visits to Ralph Bunche, Paul Reese concentrates on simple carrots and sticks. Even his ILS software is far from being state-of-the-art. (Reese started using the program in the early 1990s and, as is commonly the case, technical support for the program lasted only a year or two after that. For most of the 1990s, therefore, the system at Bunche Elementary was held together mostly by Reese's will and technical creativity—or, as he puts it, "by string and chewing gum.") Sometimes, though, the system's carrots become interesting. During one early-morning session, I arrive to find Reese intensely engaged at the blackboard with a fourth-grade boy. The boy is stumped by one particular mathematical cartoon in his ILS lesson. So Reese, who majored in mathematics, turns the boy's frustration into an opportunity to advance his understanding of arithmetic. At the moment, fortunately, there are only a few other students around, so Reese is able to devote his full attention to this one student's confusion. For a while, it seems, the boy can't manage to calculate any of the addition or subtraction combinations Reese presents, no matter how much Reese simplifies them. Finally, he gets one, which Reese quickly ratchets one step higher; the boy gets that one, too. Reese showers him with enthusiasm. "You see!" Reese tells me later. "That's what this is about. If this lab wasn't

---

*The whole LOGO story is made stranger still by an odd contradiction. In Papert's speeches, and in his popular book *Mindstorms,* the professor talks passionately about his experiences as a young boy working on cars with his father. During hours of tinkering, Papert apparently developed a deep fascination with gears, and with their abundant, tactile, connective possibilities. He therefore offers today's children the art of computer programming, which he hopes will become their generation's great field of gears. There's a flaw in this evolutionary theory, however, which Papert himself once pointed out without realizing it. During a speech at his 1999 Mindfest gathering, when Papert spoke about how much he learned "from these early automobile experiences," he added a depressing coda: "Today, you open up a car and it's hopeless." The same frustration, he said, greets someone tinkering with a radio, an exercise that Papert says once inspired early inventors. "With an old radio, all these tubes and other things lit up," Papert said. "If you open a radio today, there's nothing." Obviously, today's high-powered radios and cars operate on more than "nothing." Among other things, they're packed with hundreds of microchips and other computerized materials, the standard "gears" of modern automation. The cogs on these gears aren't terribly visible, though, and are somewhat less gripping than polished steel and cathode tubes. If the digital version of this machinery is incomprehensible and boring to someone like Papert, it's probably unreasonable to hope that it will inspire large numbers of children.

here, that lesson would never have happened. *That's* what makes all this worthwhile."

Something of rare value does seem to have transpired here, but something also is going wrong. Reese's exchange with this student had all the trappings of learning. He is an able and energetic teacher, and their interaction very likely advanced the rapport and trust between them. It was, in a sense, another one of those rare teachable moments. Reese's term for it is just-in-time teaching—an instant when a youngster suddenly needs an academic lesson to get what he wants: time to play on the computer. But that premise—that learning can be leveraged with rewards—has a long and troubled history among education's intelligentsia.[12] If the research is any guide, Reese cannot depend on this boy's newfound enthusiasm for math to last long.

There is another reason Reese jumps on teachable moments with such gusto. He knows he's in a constant struggle against the floods of commercial mediocrity that pour through his computer labs. "If you look through what's on these machines," Reese admits one afternoon, "you will see a fair amount of crap." Some of that "crap" comes automatically loaded on the machines' hard drives; more is brought in by teachers who've been gulled by a fancy box or a software salesman's promises at education's ubiquitous technology conferences. Reese takes steps with this software that most teachers don't dare. "The crappy games last for a while," he says with a mischievous smile, "then they somehow disappear." But even in his labs, it is increasingly difficult to exert control, because students are becoming more and more adept at downloading demonstration games from the Internet. "I tell parents that unless you are prepared to spend a lot of time with this, you will end up with a very expensive game machine," Reese says. "We have all this hype about this stuff. There are important things that you can use, but it's not going to make you a good teacher. It's not going to revolutionize the school system."

In some ways, Reese is too self-critical. The mini-school's history is littered with a number of ambitious special projects. Three to six times a year since the mid-1980s, Reese's students have published a school newspaper, which they began posting on the Web in 1993. They designed online surveys and took on special writing projects, drawn from Internet research, the best of which are proudly posted on the fourth-floor walls. Interestingly, some of what gives this writing its quality is a simple but rare step that Reese and other mini-school teachers took: They put the students through numerous drafts until they got it right. This procedure may seem obvious—especially with computer technology, whose word processing programs make revisions, even complicated ones, remarkably easy. Yet in school after school, even good ones, I talked to students and teachers who rarely if ever bothered with multiple revisions or complex editing of any kind.

The mini-school's work on these and other special projects does seem to have had some crowning effects. Any visitor can see the thrill on students' faces when someone e-mails them from across the country after being impressed by articles they have written. That sense of accomplishment is what many teachers point to, rightly, when they argue for some amount of computer and Internet access in their schools. The catch is that even among the mini-school students, only a small portion of their computer time—at most 20 percent, by Reese's estimate—is spent on academic exercises of this sort.

While walking around one day, Reese and I come upon a scene that shakes up the neat conceptual framework I'm beginning to form around school technology. It is lunch hour and in one of the labs, Reese points out a ten-year-old boy, whom I'll call Jorge, who is working intently at a computer at the far end of the room. No one else is around. Reese tells me he's worried about Jorge. He's a child who exhibits almost no emotion and is a loner as well. "If he joins the other kids for lunch, they tease him and beat him up," Reese says softly. "This at least sparks him. But . . . I don't know."

Intrigued, I approach Jorge to see what he's up to. He is playing games, starship shoot-'em-ups, and is completely absorbed. I ask a little about the games, in both English and Spanish, but it's no use. He is as catatonic as a child mesmerized by television. Not quite, actually. As he guides his space-ships across the screen with the computer mouse, his head tilts slightly, unconsciously, to follow them. This is some of what computer promoters mean when they talk about how "interactive" computers are, and how that capacity makes them much better than television.

Like Reese, I don't know whether to be pleased that Jorge has found something to play with that won't beat him up, or to lament the fact that he has contented himself with friendship from a machine. Perhaps the fairest assessment of the situation comes from the technology critic Neil Postman in his book *Technopoly*. ". . . A bargain is struck," Postman writes, "in which technology giveth and technology taketh away."[13]

THE PACE OF REFORM

As yet another sign of the fickleness of reform initiatives, Bunche's mini-school was dismantled in the fall of 1999. The reasons pile absurdity upon confusion. The previous summer, the media urgently reported that many New York schools, Bunche among them, had fared poorly on test scores. The superintendent of district 5, which governs the Bunche school, was summarily fired, and the emphasis on technology was redirected. (The district soon got a generous new round of computer funding, which was spread rather haphazardly throughout the entire district.) Months later, the company that administered the tests (CTB/McGraw-Hill) admitted it had made a massive scoring error: It turned out that New York City students hadn't done as poorly as everyone thought and that nearly nine thousand students had gone to summer school unnecessarily.[14] But the changes that had been wrought in response to the erroneous scores remained in place. At Bunche, Reese was also let go, and the mini-school was turned into a set of more typical computer labs.

A few months after the mini-school's conversion, I traveled to New York to take another look at several schools, including Ralph Bunche. The visit was depressing. Reese was gone; so were a few of his handpicked teachers, several of whom were ancient masters of the art of classroom discipline. The labs remained, available now to the whole school. This change had its obvious pluses. But, perhaps inevitably, the computers there were being used far more loosely than they had been under Reese. (During my visits, for instance, students spent their time with relatively plodding attempts at typing and fussed with a jazzy graphics product called Kid Pix. Like its better-known competitor, HyperStudio, Kid Pix is essentially a children's version of PowerPoint.) Both Kid Pix and HyperStudio consume oodles of time and expense. Yet both are no more instructive than a pencil and paper, a box of crayons, a pile of magazines or old photos, and some scissors and glue. In fact, some teachers say their students find these simple materials to be more useful and, often, more fun. In addition to enjoying entertainment like Kid Pix, the students spent time randomly searching the Internet—that is, when Net service was working. By 2002, the Internet system at Bunche— once the high-tech king of Harlem's schools—was suffering from network instabilities just like I.S. 275.

One crisp November afternoon, I met up with Reese at an Upper West Side coffee shop for a little postmortem. Despite the circumstances of his dismissal, he was only mildly bitter. His attitude was no doubt buoyed by the new position he had found before he even left Bunche, as a sort of roving technological fix-it man for the district. The experience had him juiced up all over again, this time over the shockingly varied state of technical skill he found from one school to the next and from classroom to classroom. Even now—several years after the Project Smart initiative that spread computers throughout most of the city's middle school classrooms—Reese was still finding computers sitting in the corners, unused. In one school, Reese said, "I told the principal, 'I don't care what they do, but you've got to tell the teachers to take the dustcovers off.' " Other teachers he's worked with have been technologically willing but pedagogically resistant. "I can't touch a computer—I've got to teach to the Regents," a math teacher told Reese, referring to the state's notorious standardized tests, which determine every student's chance of advancing to the next grade.

The pervasiveness of encounters like these had led Reese to reconsider the city's approach to classroom technology. "I would not buy a bunch more computers," he told me. "I would re-evaluate what we have. And I'd rethink the movement away from computer labs." When I followed up later with Lisa Nielsen, the computer coordinator at I.S. 275, she had the same opinion. Their point is a simple one: At this early stage of the personal computer's history, the technology is far too complex and error prone to be smoothly integrated into most classrooms. And this is particularly the case in schools like theirs, where teachers must pour every ounce of energy they have into classroom management. The labs, on the other hand, offer a worthwhile escape—a separate environment designed with only technology in mind. When the labs are properly staffed, teachers can set the whole class on a specific, technological assignment instead of handing this treat to a select few students, which is what happens when there's only a handful of computers at the back of a classroom. (Proper lab staffing is of course a question unto itself, but Reese was full of ideas on how to make it happen. Teacher's aides, for example, are inexpensive and perfectly capable of handling technical problems and helping establish order; so, too, are many college students.) As we've seen, computer labs create plenty of challenges and distractions of their own. But in a school's early years with high technology, a lab's hurdles may be more surmountable than those confronting stressed teachers trying to "integrate" computers into their classrooms.

―――

The day after our coffee klatch, I spend a morning shadowing Reese at a couple of these schools. He's right. The average Harlem school, if these samples were any guide, is in a very different position than everyone thinks when it comes to absorbing expensive new initiatives. In some cases, they seem to have a lot more already going for them than their would-be reformers appreciate.

We begin at Isaac Newton, an East Harlem school that shares an old, hulking brick building with two other schools. While I wait for Reese to assemble his materials in the school's storage room, I fall into conversation with Steven Levy, a seventh- and eighth-grade social studies teacher, who is sitting here taking a break. I ask him if he's putting computers to much use in his class. Levy shakes his head. "You have two masters," he tells me. "You have the requirements that come down from the state. And you have the computer saying, 'Feed me, feed me.'" Since these two masters share some common ground (the classroom), one would think they would talk to each other. But they usually don't. "I have never had a software company come in," Levy adds, "and say, 'What would you like us to write?'" What they say instead, in his experience, is: "We've made this. Would you like to buy it?" Levy, a small, graying man, offers these comments calmly, somewhat dejectedly. I somehow find myself inclined to dismiss them; he seems like a worn-out white man in a black school, someone who has little hope of finding any connection with these students, with or without technology.

Twenty minutes later, I find out how wrong I am. When Reese and I stop by Levy's class, he's in the middle of a lesson on American history. "Why was there no slavery here? Why were the Southerners in these states being so gracious?" he asks, rapping the blackboard with his knuckles so hard that I'm surprised he's not recoiling in pain. Virtually every student is paying attention. "When you say *agrarian,* you mean . . ." A pause, then a couple of students yell out, "Cotton!" "And wherever there is cotton, there will be . . ." The students answer again: "Slaves!" "It's that simple," Levy says, walking toward his desk, this time to pound an overhead projector for emphasis. "No cotton! (*pound*) No slaves! (*pound*)." Occasionally, Levy ambushes a student, nailing him with a surprise question. In one case, when one of his targets can't answer, Levy hits him again right where he lives. "You're gonna get ripped off," he tells the boy, "because you don't understand this." The boy quickly gets the point, and noticeably pays more attention through the rest of class. I am stunned—not just at the difference between this personality and the one I saw in the storage room but at Levy's capacity to sustain this quality of energy and suspense while teaching basic history.

As the academic fireworks proceed, Reese fiddles around as quietly as he can with a computer in the corner. The students hardly notice—a sharp contrast to the scene I witnessed several days earlier, at Ben's school, where the mere arrival of the computer technician sent the class into disarray. After we leave, I ask Reese why he'd want to complicate this man's finely honed routine with computers. Reese explains that he has nothing of the sort in mind. All Levy wants at this point is a simple database so that he can keep a record of the headlines on news stories that his students regularly bring in. Reese is less than thrilled with this skimpy idea, but he likes its simplicity; at least, it will let Levy get used to computers slowly, by giving him something that will take only a few minutes each day.

Moving slowly has another advantage—it keeps teachers from wasting their time while the high-technology sector works out its kinks. One of the great secrets of the industry is that manufacturers of computer hardware and software often know their products are hampered by significant limitations. Yet they rarely hold back from going to market with this gear, because they also know that most if not all of those problems will be fixed with the next upgrade, the release of which will simply net more sales. Not only is this syndrome bothersome and costly for consumers, but the flow of these upgrades is too fast for schools, and especially teachers, to keep up with. "I wish I could put a moratorium on new versions of everything," Reese tells me at one point, during a moment of mechanical exasperation. As an illustration of his complaint, Reese's district had recently required schools to buy a new version of Microsoft Word. But, Reese notes, "It won't run on half the machines we have."

Later, Reese finds himself struggling with even lower level complications. He's been called to the school next door, where the teachers have no desks suitable for a computer terminal and a keyboard. After an hour or so watching him try to jury-rig a computer nook (and painfully teach one delighted little girl how to find the *t*, *h*, and *e* keys on the keyboard), I decide I've had enough. As I head for the door, I turn around for a moment to see what Reese will be up to next. He's just spied the school principal and, after drawing a very deep breath, stops him in the hallway. "We need to find your shop," Reese says. The principal looks blank. "Our shop? What are you talking about?" Reese explains that he needs to make keyboard racks for the four computers in one of his classrooms. "We don't have a shop," the principal says. Reese draws another breath and starts looking around for other options.

Shop classes used to be routine in decently equipped schools but are now essentially relics of the past. As will be discovered throughout this book, eliminating them has been a grievous mistake. I consider joining the conversation to raise these points, but I realize that it would be cruel. I decide instead that it is time to go, knowing full well how easy it is for someone like me to walk away from all these troubles.

DREAMS OF CASH

It's odd that such a culture of poverty would continue to afflict New York schools. The city not only has its valiant education-reform history, it also has years of evidence that the state's system of funding schools has been inadequate and unfair. Since the early 1990s, New York's governors and other officials have repeatedly fretted that schools weren't preparing students for proper jobs and that school buildings were falling into disrepair.[15] Finally, in 1991, the education writer Jonathan Kozol startled the academic world by publishing *Savage Inequalities*, a harsh account of the economic discrimination visited upon schools in poor communities across the country. One of Kozol's main case studies was New York City, where schools had been receiving less than half the money their suburban counterparts got ($5,585 per student in the city, for example, versus $11,265 in Great Neck, Long Island, or $11,372 in Manhasset). In some respects, the numbers were worse than they appeared, because the cost of doing academic business in New York (materials, salaries, and so on) is far higher than it is in the suburbs. Kozol also included an assortment of statements from those who justified these imbalances. *The Wall Street Journal*, for example, argued in a 1989 editorial that "money doesn't buy better education." To prove its point, the *Journal* noted that over the years, measures of educational achievement had remained static across the country while per-pupil spending had risen. Clearly, the paper concluded, "increasing teacher salaries" or "hiring teachers with advanced degrees doesn't improve schooling. . . . It's parental influence that counts." So what are we supposed to do when parental influence fails? The best recourse probably is not an Internet connection but a good teacher. Moreover, as Kozol pointed out, if money doesn't matter, there would be no reason to give so much more of it to schools in richer communities.[16]

A decade after Kozol's book became a bestseller, New York officials had an opportunity to revisit their school funding inequities. In 2001, in response to a six-year lawsuit, which was brought by a group of frustrated educators and activists and which produced a nine-month trial, the state supreme court issued a decision that appeared to settle matters. "New York State has over the course of many years consistently violated the State Constitution," said Justice Leland DeGrasse, "by failing to provide the opportunity for a sound, basic education to New York City public schools." To be crystal clear, DeGrasse held that the state's constitution makes it plain that this "sound, basic education" should be defined as follows: "the foundational skills that students need to become productive citizens capable of civic engagement and sustaining competitive employment." And that, DeGrasse argued, required a range of improvements that New York students had long been denied: a "sufficient" number of qualified teachers and staff; "appropriate" class sizes; "adequate" school buildings; "up-to-date books, supplies, libraries, educational technology and laboratories"; "suitable curricula, including an expanded platform of programs to help at-risk students"; and, finally, "a safe, orderly environment." It was soon estimated that making those improvements would bring city schools as much as an extra $1 billion each year.[17]

The city's education leaders were, naturally, overjoyed. Then, a year later, their hopes were dashed. In June 2002, in a 4–1 ruling, the state supreme court's appellate division reversed DeGrasse. In the appellate court's eyes, New York's constitution does not require the state to prepare students for "competitive employment," as DeGrasse had reasoned. All they needed, the court concluded, was enough skill for the most basic kind of employment. "Society needs workers in all levels of jobs," the appellate court wrote, "the majority of which may very well be low level." This could be achieved, the court declared, with nothing more than an eighth- or ninth-grade education in reading and a sixth-grade education in math. Furthermore, the court said, the real causes of the city's academic problems are "demographic factors such as poverty, dysfunctional homes, and homes where English is not spoken." For this, "more spending on education is not the answer . . . the cure lies in eliminating the socioeconomic conditions facing certain students." In other words, helping students who struggle with school is not the schools' problem. It's someone else's.*

The circumstances that led to the appellate court's reversal merely added to the dissonance of the moment. To begin with, the appeal of DeGrasse's

---

*Bizarre side stories abound in this case, which was brought by a coalition of academics, activists, and New York City school districts, called the Campaign for Fiscal Equity. One involves the state's lead expert witness—David Armor, a part-time professor at George Mason University, who had been hired in approximately forty cases (and was paid $250,000 for this one) to offer analyses like the following: "I don't think there is very much that can be done to overcome the gaps you see between the poor and the non-poor." Another oddity involves the appellate court's response to the plaintiffs' claim that books are "antiquated" in New York City schools. "Surely, a library that consists predominantly of classics should not be viewed as one that deprives students of the opportunity of a sound, basic education," the court said. Well, perhaps. But the problem is that there aren't any classics to speak of in New York City school libraries. "Antiquated" here means tattered social studies books that identify Ronald Reagan as the current president and chemistry books with outdated reference tables. When teachers want to assign reading, they often have to line up at the photocopy machine to make duplicates of book

decision was filed by New York governor George Pataki, who, like many other governors in the 1990s, had been consistently lacing speeches with promises to offer his state a "world-class education." In one State of the State address, for instance, Pataki said, "In every aspect of our educational system, we must set the highest standards for student success, and settle for nothing less." But when the appellate court said the state didn't need to meet such high standards (or, as the lone dissenting justice put it, "logically, it has no obligation to provide any high school education at all"), Pataki, a Republican, was among the first to applaud the ruling.

Pataki's rationale was that he was already giving more money to poor schools. This was only partly right. Pataki had indeed been increasing education funding during the wealthy late 1990s, but only after being prodded to do so by the state legislature. And most governors increased school funding, albeit a little more generously than Pataki did. By 2002, the funding gap in New York between school districts heavily populated by the poor (as New York City is) and wealthier districts was still the widest of any state in the country—standing, on average, at $8,598 in more well-off districts versus $6,445 for their poorer cousins. While these inequities had begun to narrow across the country as a whole, a real divide remained. In two thirds of the nation's states, schools in wealthy districts still got a larger share of state and local funding than poor districts did, by an average of nearly $1,000 per student. Schools that were predominantly white (typically wealthier than heavy minority schools) also tended to offer students the longest school days and the most time for extras such as art and music, sports, and general play. If this imbalance wasn't worrisome on its own, evidence was accumulating in the South that schools had begun to re-segregate along racial lines.[18] To make matters stranger in New York, there was Pataki's personal history. The son of a Hungarian immigrant who worked as a mailman and spoke no English, Pataki rose in life partly by getting the sort of help he now thought New York City children didn't need. Pataki and his brother both attended Yale, through work-loan scholarships that were won through their father's fervent pleading. In his 1998 auto-

---

chapters; many of these copies end up being too faint or blurred to read. As Robert Berne, vice-president of academic affairs at New York University, put it, "No judge on that panel would send their kids to a school that provided for the kind of education that they say is adequate for New Yorkers." See "Pataki's Poster Boy," by Nate Schweber and Wayne Barrett, *The Village Voice*, Aug. 7–13, 2002; "Classics Go from Xerxes to Xerox," by Joyce Purnick, *The New York Times*, July 1, 2002; "The Bare Minimum," by Bob Herbert, *The New York Times*, June 27, 2002.

biography, in fact, Pataki said his father made him go to Yale because the university had been "so responsive to our particular needs."[19]

After its defeat, the group that had sued the state vowed to renew its fight, this time before the state court of appeals (which in New York's case is the state's highest court). No one expected a ruling on the appeal to come before mid-2003. This gave Pataki a nice reprieve from the supreme court's onerous mandate to increase spending in New York City schools. And there was a special bonus, which the appellate court, most of whose members were Pataki appointments, undoubtedly noticed. If the governor ultimately lost this fight, he wouldn't have to pay its price until well after the fall 2002 election. In the meantime, he could keep talking about setting high academic standards while New York's impoverished schools kept limping along.

Breaking Down Rural Isolation:
Hundred, West Virginia

As you drive from the big East Coast cities into Hundred, West Virginia, population 344, you drive by Tenants' Funeral Home and Storage, whose proprietor is also the local financial planner. "It's one-stop shopping," Shelly Harter, the local high school math teacher, likes to say. A few curves past the funeral home is the town center, marked by Hundred's only stoplight, whose permanent yellow blink defines the town's cultural rules. It's easy does it around here. A right turn at the light takes you through Hundred's commercial complex: a couple of tanning salons, several used-furniture stores, and some dusty gift shops. The shops sit peacefully, like sleepy grandmothers, under the sagging wooden balconies that shade the town's two raised sidewalks. Within several hundred yards, you've passed the church, the fire department, Cindy's Liquor Store (which doubles as the town's American Red Cross office), the sole motel and café, and then you are heading out of town.

The economic boom of the 1990s was pretty much foreign news in this valley. Hundred, named after a Civil War veteran who was called Old Hundred for living to 109, sits about dead center near the state's northern edge. This is the top of West Virginia hill country, a region caught between two eras. As in much of the state, the economy here was once fueled primarily by coal mines. The coal is still plentiful, but the deposits in this area are high in sulfur, which the utilities now try to avoid because of its contribution to acid rain. Over the last decade, therefore, all but a couple of the dozen mines that used to put food on people's tables have closed. The sources of most remaining local income are the local gas company, the school system, a state prison fifty miles away, a sprinkling of small businesses, and welfare checks.

Into this hungry maw the state has dropped an unusual combination of classroom computer systems. These begin with some basic but intensive drill programs for students in the elementary grades and move up to a futuristic Internet system, which was first test-run at the local high school.

The building that holds Hundred High School suggests a counterpoint to the community's poverty simply in its appearance. The façade is redbrick modern, the floors tiled with shiny linoleum, the halls lined with rows of graffiti-free new lockers. It would be an easy movie set for high school scenes in any small town, complete with a peppy sign out front announcing that this is the "Home of the Hornets." If visitors look up after walking through the front doors, however, they take a leap into the future—or one hopeful version of it—in the four bloodred, space-age plastic orbs affixed to the ceiling's acoustic tiles in every room. These are infrared sensors, put here in 1997 to provide wireless connections to the Internet. Students beam information from them, and to them, through equally high-tech wireless laptops.

School-issue laptops may conjure worries of theft and breakage, which could waste up to $288,000, the total of what a mere 180 of these machines cost. (The laptops, called StudyPros, from a California firm called NetSchools, went for $1,600 apiece.) But at Hundred—and, by all indications, most other schools that have invested in laptops—there's been remarkably little theft. As for the possibility of damage, these computers are built with an almost indestructible magnesium case. Heavy as they are (they weigh more than seven pounds), students generally toss them into backpacks along with their schoolbooks, because the laptops have to be hauled home each night to recharge their batteries.

Watching youngsters use this network stretches one's image of what high school is all about. Which is probably called for in some fashion. High school is arguably the stage of education most suited to computer use. Students are generally mature enough at this age to negotiate the computer's complications and to resist being manipulated by at least some portions of Internet trash, such as pornographic videos and incessant commercial messages. (The temptations of other Internet abundances, such as bomb-making instructions, may, unfortunately, be quite another matter for hormone-addled teenagers.) Most important, high schoolers are only a step away from the world of work, where basic computer skills, at the least, are an increasingly common requirement. Understandably, this fact tends to excite politicians, most of whom see vast opportunities in school computing. Listen, for example, to Cecil Underwood, West Virginia's recent governor. In 1998, Underwood visited Hundred High and was so pleased with what he saw that he later wrote a column about it in the local paper. "The classroom demonstrations I witnessed at the school showed the tremendous potential of using computers in West Virginia classrooms," Underwood said. Claiming that West Virginia was the first state in the nation to wire every school for the Internet, and one of the first to make use of this fancy infrared network system, he said the scene confirmed the wisdom of one of his main goals: to make technology opportunities available to every student, the rural poor as well as the affluent. This, Underwood proclaimed, is "preparing them for better opportunities in higher education and future employment."[1]

Inspired by visions like Underwood's, a smattering of school districts across the country began making aggressive investments in unusually futuristic technology in the early years of the new millennium. Many abandoned relatively new, or at least workable, desktop computers in both classrooms and computer labs to buy the next new game: "portable" devices like laptops—roughly 200,000 of them nationwide, by one estimate.[2] Which raises a few questions: What is the effect of such a rash of mechanical novelties? And how do students in America's rural shadows fare when life suddenly includes a portable computing device? Technology promoters fervently and consistently argue that their world becomes markedly better; that the round-the-clock connectivity possible with portable computers opens fascinating new challenges, new communication options with the outside world, and, along the way, a satisfying new sense of achievement. I went to West Virginia to see whether this was true.

The initial evidence here suggested that it might be. When the Department of Education assembled a 1999 website of several dozen school systems around the country that were doing exemplary jobs with educational technology, West Virginia districts were featured more frequently than any other state's. Hundred High School was a particular favorite of Department staffers, because state officials had dared, in the middle of backwoods mountain "hollers," to go for the gold—and to spend it, too.

IT'S JUST A TOOL

The day I visited Shelly Harter's senior algebra class, the assignment was to practice turning basic formulas—$Y = 3x - 4$ was the first example—

into visual graphs. Before getting started, the students arranged their desks into clusters under each of the room's four red orbs (to work, the laptops must be positioned within a few yards of a sensor). Within minutes, the students had beamed into the school's server, which responded by opening each laptop to a sophisticated graphing program. The students proceeded to manipulate these graphs with options that yesteryear's students never dreamed of. With a simple tap on their touch pads, they could adjust the size and layout of each graph and even its format—bar, line, or circle graph. "It takes away the probability of an error," Harter told me. And, she said, "you can go from one to the other almost instantly. You don't have to draw the circle over and over. It takes the time thing to another level."

As the class proceeded, Harter spent roughly twenty minutes just getting each student on the same page, so to speak—with the same graph on each student's screen. As the students caught on, she introduced more math problems. I glanced at the textbook, which advises using any of various tools: "pencil and paper, mental math, or a calculator." Harter reminded them that in this case, a calculator means the computer. "All this is, is a tool to use," she told them. "You don't have to force them into each situation." The students barely looked up from their screens.

After watching the class work for a while, I asked one student, Henry, whether he felt that he was learning more with these tools, or did they just make math more fun? "A little bit more fun and a little bit learning more, because it makes it easier," he answered as he tested out the slope for his formula in four or five different positions on the screen. To give me another example, Henry told me about the way they're using the laptops to do research on the Internet in social studies classes. "You don't have to read it or anything like if you look it up in a book. All you have to do is use your fingers and just look." What did he do when he found sections he wanted to include in his written report? That's one of the best parts: He simply hit select and copy commands, pasted it into his own file, then reworked a little of the language to put it in his own words.

At issue here, on a superficial level, is one of a student's oldest games— copying someone else's work. Indeed, surveys indicate that as Internet connections have become more common in both schools and students' homes, so have incidents of scholastic plagiarism.[3] One might argue, as most technology defenders do, that cheating is cheating and that a teacher's responsibility on this front remains the same as ever: Check students' work. But the power of the computer has made that worldview obsolete. When students wrote reports in pre-Internet days, it wasn't terribly difficult for teachers to evaluate the papers' sources. Today, the number of Internet sources at a student's disposal is so high, and changing so constantly, that a teacher would never dream of keeping up with them all.

On a deeper level, however, Henry's routine provokes one of technology's oldest arguments—concerning the evolution of society's relationship with tools. When technology's critics get exercised about youngsters' worrisome activities on computers, technology defenders frequently try to defuse the argument with a version of Harter's warning: "It's just a tool," they say. And like any tool, it has to be used wisely. As it turns out, however, the computer is not just a tool.

In one sense, Henry was doing what human beings have always done: He was using a new tool to collapse a series of difficult, time-consuming procedures into a few simple, quick ones. His forefathers did the same thing to change the process of cutting grain, which was managed for centuries with backbreaking and tricky sweeps of the scythe. With one wide upgrade, daily labors on the farm were reduced to driving a machine across a field. So, too, with the device computer technologists typically point to as their primary forebear: the printing press, which obviously did much to relieve yesteryear's scriveners from the painstaking task of lettering books by hand.

When work gets simplified, however, something is always lost. The question, of course, is the value of what's been lost compared with what's been gained. Clearly, in his social studies class, Henry might benefit by putting more effort into his own research and analysis. In fact, that endeavor would stand a somewhat better chance if he were cribbing from written reports. Even if a student borrows liberally from those documents, the act of physically transcribing the material requires that he read and think about it, at least temporarily, word for word. And even if he doesn't adjust much of the language, that physical task forces a student to run the material through his head, which gives its meaning a chance to stick. Not so today. The computer's copy-and-paste function has tossed that process onto history's scrap heap, next to manual typewriters and buggy whips. Technology's supporters of course hold a different view, countering that with the Internet, especially in library-poor schools, Henry has access to many more sources of information than just an encyclopedia or a few magazine articles. That may be right or wrong, but the essential choice is no different than it has always been—breadth versus depth. When time is limited, a researcher has to choose one or the other.

Arguments like these seem interminable, as old as machinery itself. On one side, writers like Wendell Berry have written profound texts about how modern agricultural technology has steadily broken our sense of connection to the land and the spiritual satisfactions that can be derived from it. Meanwhile, techno-visionaries like Nicholas Negroponte and Howard Rheingold wax just as poetical about the way the Internet builds meaningful new connections with imaginative possibilities and between distant and needy people. Answering Rheingold's camp have been a wide range of computer critics—from traditionalists such as MIT computer scientist Joseph Weizenbaum to more radical commentators such as Theodore Roszak and Neil Postman—all of whom utter warnings about what computer technology steals from the art of thinking, if not from our very soul.[4]

Weizenbaum, in particular, does a masterful job of explaining the circular relationship that humans have with their machines in his classic work *Computer Power and Human Reason*. It is through our imagination that we first develop our tools. But over time, Weizenbaum explains, those tools (from the ax to the machine gun, from the cotton gin to the computer) shape our picture of the world and thus our capacity to imagine the next stage of invention. Before long, tools like computers come to be regarded as an indispensable part of progress. But in truth, we consistently choose routes of invention that depend on our machines; we then ignore, and soon forget about, non-technical answers to the same challenges that might be just as effective, if not more so. As an example: "The very erection of an enormously large and complex computer based welfare administration apparatus," Weizenbaum wrote, "created an interest in its maintenance and therefore in the perpetuation of the welfare system itself." So, too, he argued, with the pillars of our economic system—banks, commodity markets, various manufacturing firms, and so on—all of which have developed in ways that bring increasing automation rather than greater humanization.*

---

*One of the most provocative arguments about tools is offered in the opening pages of Postman's 1992 book *Technopoly*, where he retells an old story about the old Egyptian King Thamus, from Plato's book *Phaedrus*. According to Plato's story (originally relayed by Socrates), the god Theuth, an inventor, visited King Thamus to pitch the wonders of his latest ideas: numbers, calculation, geometry, astronomy, and writing. Regarding writing, Theuth said he'd discovered something that would vastly improve the Egyptians' skills, "a sure receipt for memory and wisdom." King Thamus begged to differ, saying those who use this tool will not build their memories but will come to rely on writing instead of "their own internal resources." As for wisdom, the king said, "your pupils will have the reputation for it without the reality: they will receive a quantity of information without proper instruction, and in consequence be thought very knowledgeable when they are for the most part quite ignorant. And because they are filled with the conceit of wisdom instead of real wisdom they will be a burden to society." For an extra twist of the knife, Thamus told Theuth that the "discoverer of an art is not the best judge of the good or harm which will accrue to those who practice it. You, who are the father of writing, have out of fondness for your off-spring attributed to it quite the opposite of its real function."

Undoubtedly, there will always be fervent voices on both sides of the debate about what technological tools do for us, and to us. But that doesn't excuse what happens in the classrooms, where students cannot choose their camp of loyalty. At most schools, a student's role is pretty simple: Work with the tools and assignments you're given.

THE VIRTUAL TEACHER

To show off another aspect of Hundred High's laptop system, David Cotrell, the social studies teacher, staged a special class for me called thematic science—the same demonstration he'd arranged for the governor. To Cotrell, science studies offer a particularly good illustration of the new intellectual worlds that the Internet can bring to small, isolated schools. The previous year, for instance, his class studied high-altitude climatology at a time when an Everest expedition was under way. Through the Net, students tracked the expedition's daily bulletins, complete with photos broadcast by expedition team members. As the expedition progressed, Cotrell said, the students watched the climbers navigate phenomena such as changing weather conditions and Everest's ungodly temperatures—"a lot of the things kids in this school will never see," Cotrell said.

Cotrell's pitch made great sense to me, so I was eager to see it in action. That afternoon, Cotrell had one of his classes explore wildlife on the Internet. Shortly after class began, however, technological reality descended like a wet blanket. Students couldn't get connected, and most of those who did went to the wrong sites. (One student, searching for foxes, ended up at a site for Michael J. Fox, then a second one for fox terriers; another, studying coyotes, got the Phoenix Coyotes, an Arizona ice hockey team; a third, who was looking for bears, arrived at an Internet banner that said "Welcome to the Black Bear Bar & Grill Web Site.") Finally, fifteen minutes before class was over, a few students found sites that really were about animals, which of course left almost no time for discussion, to say nothing of time to think about animal science.

As it turned out, the problems here stemmed from two unusual circumstances that limit the generalizations that can made of the scene, at least to some degree. First, this class's Internet searches occurred in the pre-Google days of search engines, when the sites you didn't care about came up much more often than those you wanted. One could also argue, however, that this problem simply underscores the myopia of technology fervor. Most schools across the country, desperate to join the "information superhighway," wired themselves to the Net in the mid-1990s; in fact, many got there long before Hundred High did. In the ensuing years, they all had the privilege of watching the Internet's various systems for finding and sorting information rattle through their awkward infancy. In the meantime, millions of students wasted hours of precious classroom time much as Cotrell's students did.

Second, Cotrell staged this demonstration with a special-education class, for whom the scholastic bar is typically kept relatively low. For instance, when I asked Cotrell if he might not get further with conventional materials—books, encyclopedias, even some paper handouts—he said, "Not with special-ed kids. 'Cause there's only so much they'll pick up on anyway. And this gives them a break and takes their attention to something."

Once again, the theory in Cotrell's remark was persuasive. However, the chaos of the academic atmosphere in his class, even allowing for its special-education status, was too close to what I had seen in other classes, here and in other states, to ignore. Why, I kept wondering, is the Internet's great abundance of information poorly used so repeatedly? Watching students use the Net, I began to feel that I was witnessing education's institutional embrace of raw media consumption rather than a passing on of the great habits of intellectual exploration, synthesis, and analysis. Indeed, even with Cotrell's class that followed the Everest expedition the previous year, the thrill appeared to be in what the students *saw*, not in what they made of it.

It is certainly laudable to try whatever method is available to break down the barriers that isolate people; indeed, one could argue that in today's "global economy," education must increasingly strive toward this goal. But couldn't a good book on Everest or on foxes—even a single copy that, in a poor school, must be passed around—do that, too? It might even leave a larger opening for discussion, simply because a book imposes such a humble presence. In contrast, whenever a fabulous Internet site is found, teachers and students both tend to say little more than "Wow!"

—

By many accounts, one way the computer can reach beyond the glitz of websites and really break through geographical barriers is in its capacity to facilitate something called distance learning. This is a system that lets students in one place communicate with teachers or experts in another place— either in type over the Internet or visually through fancy two-way television sets, in what is normally called videoconferencing. Either way, these networks are essentially the digital age's version of old-fashioned correspondence courses, but they've become quite popular at remote schools—and, with even greater enthusiasm, on college campuses. They also have a long history, dating back as far as 1928, which has led to prodigious appraisals of distance learning's value.

Today, with computers and the Internet being all the rage, distance learning has enjoyed quite a renaissance as college administrators have seen potential profits in being able to offer courses to more paying students—without having to house those students on campus or even hire many more professors. And high schools, even grade schools, have been fast following suit. In the fall of 2000, for example, Illinois set aside $370,000 to create a "virtual high school" available to all 630,000 students in the state. Nine months later, Michigan joined in, spending $18 million on the Michigan Virtual High School, which would offer twelve Advanced Placement courses and an online library of seven hundred "information technology courses." Other states, such as Pennsylvania, Colorado, and Texas, have set up "virtual charter schools" in the elementary grades, providing online curricula to children as young as kindergartners.[5] By mid-2002, seventeen states had established or were developing online high school programs and twenty-five states were allowing online charter schools, popularly known as cyber schools. (One venture, the Virtual High School, was developed by the Massachusetts-based Concord Consortium, which is devoted to the concept of "ubiquitous computing." As of May 2002, the consortium had signed up two hundred high schools in twenty-eight states and eight countries.) This is big business in the education realm. According to one calculation, $482 million in venture capital was invested in 2000 in companies building online tools for higher education; by 2002, universities had chipped in another $100 million of their own. The International Data Corporation went so far as to predict that e-learning, as it is sometimes called, would increase 33 percent a year from 1999 to 2004, making online instruction a $12 billion industry.[6]

The scale of these ventures has started to redefine the concept of academic credentials. From Dartmouth to Berkeley to the community colleges, administrators at approximately five thousand schools of higher education have added distance-learning courses with such fervor that many people are now sporting degrees from some of these hallowed halls that were earned mostly or entirely online. At some, online degrees cost more than standard, on-campus versions (at Duke's Fuqua School of Business, for example, a "blended" online MBA program costs up to $90,000, as compared with $60,000 for a traditional MBA). According to the International Data Corporation, the number of students enrolled in online college-level courses totaled two million in December 2001 and should reach five million by 2006. The most dramatic example of the growth of online higher education is the

University of Phoenix. By early 2003, the university was operating 180 campuses and "learning centers" in 37 states and had become the largest private university in the United States, with more than 141,000 students—57,000 of whom attend school via the Internet. The privately held university, which charges $400 to $500 a credit (or $23,000 for an MBA), reported an 82 percent rise in income in 2001, to $32 million. It is now publicly traded on the stock exchange, with a market value in early 2003 of $2.9 billion. Success like this has attracted plenty of off-campus organizations. The U.S. Army, for one, gave PWC Consulting a $453 million contract to create "eArmyU," which lets recruits pursue their studies at 24 different colleges no matter where they are stationed. Corporate spending on "e-learning" is expected to skyrocket, rising from $4 billion in 2001 to $18 billion in 2005. As auspicious as these trends seem, distance-learning entrepreneurs see even greater opportunity beyond U.S. borders. They are particularly eyeing developing nations, many of which have growing desires to educate their citizens but a lack of facilities and professors to handle the job.[7]

All of this activity has spawned a small but passionate rebellion among the professorial class. As might have been expected, many instructors are not thrilled about having to deal with online dialogues and hundreds of e-mails each day in addition to their traditional duties. Beyond insider controversies, however, the question on the minds of the average student and parent is fairly straightforward: Are distance-learning courses, whatever their cost, a helpful addition to the school day?

The answer, judging from decades of studies, is not particularly promising. One professor, Thomas L. Russell, of North Carolina State University, has become so intrigued by the constant desire to examine this question that he has collected the studies in a book, which he continually updates as new research accumulates. (By Russell's last count, in 1999, the number of studies came to 355.) As might be surmised from his book's title—*The No Significant Difference Phenomenon*—Russell believes the record shows that students in distance-learning courses, however they are structured, perform just as well (no better, no worse) as do students in traditional courses.[8] One problem, though: Many other specialists on this phenomenon believe that the core research Russell has been collecting is shoddy, superficial stuff, thereby weakening any conclusions he drew from it. For instance, most of Russell's base research simply evaluated the grades and testing performance in each class of students. This fails to account for the dropout rate along the way, which by all accounts is significantly higher in online courses.[9]

The critical aspect of distance learning's high dropout rate is its causes, which suggests the concept may create a meaner bargain than many school administrators realize. Andrew Hunt's experiences are a perfect example.

When I visited Hundred High, Andrew was a senior and one of the school's stars. A short biographical essay he wrote for a college application listed no fewer than seventeen extracurricular activities, half a dozen of which included honors. He was active in student government, wrote for the school paper, was a lead musician in the school band, and played lead roles in two school plays. He was also a finalist for a National Merit Scholarship and won first place in extemporaneous speaking at a state contest. Andrew's dynamism is important, because self-motivation is supposed to be the key to a successful experience with distance-learning courses. (Even its advocates acknowledge that those who lack motivation are likely to fail at distance learning.) But Andrew's experience with a distance-learning class in English composition seems to have been a failure on its own terms. If anything, his frustrations were compounded by the ways in which the course could not match his passions.

"I would *really* rather have a real teacher," Andrew told me as he sat in class one morning pecking away at his laptop for an online assignment. Andrew was one of ten seniors being taught by Dr. Terry Craig, an English professor at West Virginia Northern Community College, which lies about thirty bumpy miles west of Hundred, in New Martinsville. Craig has shared Andrew's frustrations. "We all miss the contact," she says. "The chief problem with distance education is the distance."

Craig's class struggled from the beginning. This was the first year with this class, and technical problems had plagued them all. At one point, Andrew's system was so bollixed that Craig couldn't read several weeks' worth of his work. (She did finally read his essays in person, during one of her few visits to his school; by then, Andrew felt it was impossible for her to give his pile of work any serious critique.) Nonetheless, Andrew has tried to look at the experience from the high ground. "It's a new concept," he told me, "so I guess they'll always have some teething problems. The further we dive into it, the smoother things seem to run." Yet even when the technical bumps were smoothed out, fundamental problems remained. Dr. Craig clearly tries to be responsive to questions from her students, logging on to her e-mail several times a day. And occasionally, when students have important assignments, she logs on during their class time so that she can respond within minutes. Most of the time, though, she fits in her online work as she can. That is supposed to be distance learning's great beauty. Across the country, in fact, when teachers and students are polled on their feelings about distance learning, they consistently applaud the way online work lets people do their work on their own time—a great boon to anyone juggling many demands.[10] But as that freedom intersects with education's organizational requirements, trouble can arise. In West Virginia, for example, hours usually elapse between the students' queries and Dr. Craig's replies. By then, the class period has long since passed and with it the students' time and ability to make use of any answers to their questions. "If anything is due that day," Andrew said, "that may be all the time you have to work on it."

There are other pluses to online studies. Foreign-language classes, for one, can be greatly enlivened by online dialogues with fellow students from distant cultures. There can also be a certain efficiency to the experience. During one class, Andrew and four of his classmates sat clustered together working on an online essay assignment, which asked whether the students believed in love at first sight. Within twenty minutes, Andrew had ripped out an e-mail about why he was late with an assignment, had quickly scanned some other students' essays on the subject, and had fired back an articulate essay of his own (yes, he does believe in love at first sight). But there was little joy on his face during the exercise. Occasionally, the students conferred with one another, but their conversation wasn't terribly focused. "I'm a really interactive person," Andrew told me at one point. "When you have everyone sitting around in the same room, you can talk to each other."

Andrew's remark was dripping with unintentional irony. *Interactivity*, as everyone knows, is the ubiquitous buzzword that has fueled the computer age.* Yet that is precisely what Andrew felt was missing—by the term's pre-technological definition. Adding to the irony was the fact that the lower-achieving students in Andrew's class—the ones who did not qualify for his high-tech opportunity—got to engage in more "interactivity" than he did. On the few days a week when Andrew and his distance-learning teammates were online, these students sat on the other side of the classroom reading and discussing British literature, face-to-face, with Cindy Kocher, the

---

*Typifying this perspective is the following remark from Leslie Conery, interim chief executive officer for the International Society for Technology in Education: "We know that if you want interactive, engaged learning, an online course has the greatest potential for that." When Conery made this statement, in the spring of 2002, evidence was abundant that, with some exceptions, online learning was falling well short of its promoters' promises. One study, a long-term examination by SRI International that began in 1996, found consistently less interaction between teachers and students in online courses than in traditional classes. In Florida, which pioneered one of the nation's most extensive systems of "virtual high schools," students indicated in a poll that they've been satisfied with their interactions with teachers. But they were clearly displeased with their lack of contact with other students. See "Technology Counts 2002: E-Defining Education," a special issue of *Education Week*, May 9, 2002, pp. 8, 13–24, 27–29, 37–38.

school's regular English teacher. Kocher told me she had seen some advantages in the distance-learning experiment but had been less than thrilled with it. Having once taken a distance-learning course herself, she said she could understand the students' frustration with the absence of personal interaction. Asked for her judgment of the overall quality of the students' experience, she said, "I don't know how to answer that. They get college credit. And they learned how to write a research paper and how to get information off the Internet. But I taught them that last year." After a pause, she said, "I guess they're getting more from her online than they've gotten from other college professors who have come in here in the past." Apparently, most of those professors never followed up at all.

By all indications, the sharp contrasts between different students' opportunities in Kocher's class and their varying degrees of satisfaction are typical. In a survey conducted at Cornell University, only 30 percent of the respondents expected to get the same or better interaction with instructors in online classes as compared with a traditional course. At Ohio University, when the Ford Motor Company gave fifteen thousand employees opportunities for some free distance-learning education, only nine employees took advantage of the offer.[11]

The reasons for such wariness may be partly explained by one unusually nuanced study. As part of her doctoral work at Berkeley, Cathleen Kennedy tried to refine the über-analysis of Tom Russell of North Carolina State. Part of her findings mirrored the scene at Hundred High. "There is a zone where online learning is good—but it is a very narrow zone," Kennedy told me. She drew this conclusion from a relatively well controlled examination— she evaluated three different community college classes (traditional lecture, student-directed study, and student-directed study online), all taught by the same instructor: herself. The nuances in her findings, which are consistent with other research on the subject, are telling. Highly self-directed students, particularly those who like working alone, did very well with online distance learning. But these students are not the mainstream, even among achievers. Most good students like personal interaction, either with other students or with the teacher, and these students did poorly—and were often angry about getting a class that emphasized online work. So did new students, whose study habits were not yet well formed.[12] In short, Kennedy said, online distance learning "does nothing for the typical good student. If you require online interaction, those students just drop out like flies. The more capable the student, the more they drop out."

Several years after Andrew had graduated from Hundred High, Dr. Terry Craig was still teaching online English classes there and at several other local high schools. By this point, she had become even more ambivalent about the concept. Having mastered the technical kinks—a problem that "goes with the territory," she said—she was finally having fun designing her Web postings. But the task was still proving to be surprisingly onerous. As a general rule, she spent two to four hours organizing class material on the Web—preparations that would take her only an hour for a traditional face-to-face course. And she missed Andrew Hunt. Most students, she said, weren't nearly as assertive as Andrew; in the current year's class, for instance, students were so shy that Dr. Craig had little sense of how they were doing. "I have real mixed feelings," she said. For further illustration, she pointed to the situation at her community college. "We haven't had a traditional class in so long in some departments, it's scary," she said. "And we *need* them." Prime examples, she said, were philosophy classes, where face-to-face discussion is critical. "For the last few years, those classes have just been online. And some students really want a traditional class."

Andrew Hunt also looks back on his experience with bitterness. After graduating from Hundred, Andrew found that in college English courses he had to repeat things that he'd studied in his high school distance-learning class, because he'd learned so little online. "I feel like I'm learning it all now for the first time," he told me in 2003. In the intervening years, Andrew had traveled to Ukraine, done an internship with West Virginia's House Education Committee, and majored in political science (with a minor in philosophy) in preparation for law school. By this point—six years after the laptop system was introduced at Hundred—Andrew thought he'd be hearing tales from friends and his younger brothers, who were still there, about the school finally making advances with the system. Instead, he heard the reverse: The laptops had become gradually less important; students didn't take them home very often anymore; and teachers slowly reverted to pre-digital teaching methods—all of which left Andrew with a sense that he'd been somewhat used by his old high school to justify its investment in distance learning. "I really feel like I bought those course credits," Andrew says.

——

It's a shame that school administrators didn't listen to the world's Andrew Hunts and Terry Craigs. On the college level, soon after they set up distance-learning programs at a number of the nation's campuses, administrators discovered that the troubles and costs of doing so were much greater than they had anticipated; meanwhile, student participation in these programs—even from unenrolled working adults, who might have been captivated by an interesting correspondence course—was much lower than expected. As a result, by the middle of 2002 many colleges and universities were scaling back or entirely shutting down their distance-learning ventures. "University presidents got dollars in their eyes and figured the way the university was going to ride the dot-com wave was through distance learning," said Lev S. Gonick, vice-president for information services and chief information officer at Case Western Reserve University in Cleveland, and a man who had once been gung-ho about distance learning. "The truth is that e-learning technology itself, and those of us who represent the e-learning environment, have thus far failed."[13]

It wasn't long before distance-learning enterprises for the younger grades—the growing number of cyber schools—were afflicted with similar problems. And their difficulties were more serious. By the middle of 2002, about fifty of these virtual institutions had been set up, serving some fifty thousand students in a manner that confused and angered school districts across the country. Riding the public's appetite for "school choice," the cyber schools organized themselves to take advantage of many of the same financial freedoms recently granted to charter schools. This meant that when a cyber school enrolled a fifth grader from a different school district, that district was obligated to make payments to whatever district the cyber school calls home. As can be imagined, this hasn't sat well with many school officials. "We think too much money is going out of the district for what they are delivering," says Charles Stefanski, superintendent of Pennsylvania's Cheltenham Township school district, which joined 120 Pennsylvania school districts in multiple lawsuits against the Einstein Academy, the state's biggest cyber school.

Pennsylvania has been something of a hotbed for cyber school start-ups—largely because of its 1997 charter-school law. The law, which was passed under then-governor Tom Ridge, sought to encourage charter schools by granting their operations broad latitude, and feeding them with the milk of public funding. The opportunity in Pennsylvania, and other states with similar charter-school laws, was quickly seized on by commercial entrepreneurs, who have founded the majority of the nation's cyber schools. As the ventures took shape, the new schools' managers soon realized why school bureaucracy is so complicated. At the Einstein Academy, for example, while student enrollment skyrocketed, administrators had difficulty finding teachers. State funding didn't come through, either—a setback that was aggravated by school districts' refusal to cover departing students' tuition. Soon, the cyber schools weren't functioning quite as instructively as advertised. Equipment didn't arrive, teachers were forced to improvise, and e-mail—a cyber school's lifeblood—went unanswered for days. "I was constantly e-mailing and calling, trying to figure out what was going on," says Shannon Hoffman, a mother of a thirteen-year-old student at Einstein. Hoffman said the school's teachers didn't seem to know that her son had several learning disabilities. "These teachers were acting as though he was brilliant."[14]

In the summer of 2002, Pennsylvania took steps to stanch the chaos by passing a law that put cyber schools under state supervision and partial state funding. This, everyone hoped, would start to clean up the funding disputes between school districts. But concerns lingered that cyber schools were still taking on more students than they could handle, without hiring an equivalent complement of teachers or establishing much quality control over the curricula. These worries were not helped by the news that Pennsylvania officials were planning to approve two new cyber schools in the fall of 2002. Farther west, in Ohio, the state's largest cyber school (eCOT, the Electronic Classroom of Tomorrow) ended the 2001–2002 school year almost $4 million in debt. Apparently, the school told the state that a few more students had enrolled at the school than were actually there, which prompted the state to ask for some of its money back. eCOT also had to write off almost four hundred computers that it failed to get back from students who left the program before the school year was over. The problems prompted controversial proposals for legislative fixes in Ohio, where the state's five cyber schools were expected to receive $28 million in state aid in 2003. As problems proliferated with distance education for the young, state officials throughout the country struggled to devise new ways to control these operations, and to require that teachers meet students for some minimum amount of "face time." This wasn't always easy. Cyber schools have become a favorite of the home-schooling crowd, and of many others who support an uncompromised definition of the American ideals of freedom and self-determination. To these parents, e-learning has become the long-awaited safe harbor, a refuge for education's own small but growing family of survivalists.[15]

ELECTRONIC MATH FRONTIERS

Bernard Shackleford is the quintessential high school math teacher. Short, bespectacled, with a gray goatee and a dry, gravelly voice, he visibly delights in trigonometric complications. After teaching at Hundred High for thirty-one years, he became similarly fascinated by the school's New Age computer system and quickly transformed himself into its main technical-support expert. That savvy is increasingly needed, sometimes for less than ovbious reasons. As in any school that dares to put an Internet connection in each student's hands—through desktop, laptop, or, the new trend, Palm devices—some students at Hundred had become quite skilled at hacking through the system's firewalls. They had also found new, high-tech versions of age-old excuses. During study hall one day, one of Shackleford's math students claimed that she didn't bring in a printout of her math homework because her dog had chewed through her computer cords. "Just the printer cord?" Shackleford asked skeptically. "No," the girl said. "All of them." Between hysterical giggles, a classmate asked whether the dog had gotten shocked. "I think he got shocked a few times," the girl said, "because now he runs away from them." Shackleford just smiled.

Later that day, Shackleford sat in the school's technical-support office, amid several small piles of laptops in need of repair, conversing with the rep from StudyPro. At one point, as they were discussing the troubles that students had been having with the machines, Shackleford reached for one particularly sick laptop, drew a deep breath, and said, "I need more hours in the day for this." As does anyone in his position. New technical snafus pop up all the time for schools that have gone the laptop route. Batteries die. Power cords are in short supply. Files get lost. Screens get cracked if students absentmindedly leave pencils or other things on their keyboards when they close the lid.[16] And integrating these futuristic systems into academic life is a challenge in itself. At one high school in Cupertino, ground zero of California's hip Silicon Valley, calculus students decided to drop laptops after a year because none of their other classes would support the machines.[17]

There are also a few stratospheric problems just with the networks. Infrared systems enjoy advantages that standard, radio-wave wireless-communication systems don't. (Interference is minimized, security is enhanced, and, potentially, so is performance.) But infrared technology also lacks important powers. It can't pass through walls or travel long distances without a series of big surfaces (particularly ceilings) to bounce off. This forces schools to put beams and sensors and gear all over the place—a costly necessity. Perhaps most important of all, development on infrared may well stall, and potentially for good. In 2001, technology companies had already begun shifting their development money into radio-based networking. "It just hasn't taken off commercially, and I see no signs that that's going to change, unfortunately," says Joseph M. Kahn, a professor of electrical engineering and computer science at the University of California, Berkeley, who researched infrared technology for most of a decade.[18]

This of course raises some uncomfortable upgrade questions for the many districts that invested large amounts of their budgets in laptops—

infrared and otherwise. By the fall of 2001, NetSchools, Hundred High School's supplier, was doing business with 68 public and private schools, up from the 10 it started doing business with in 1997. One customer was a district in Bloomfield, Connecticut, where the school board cut teacher's aides (and held back on standard PCs) to fund a $2.1 million, five-year program. The investment bought an infrared system and a mere 850 laptops. In Maine, Governor Angus King at one point persuaded state legislators to dedicate $50 million to buying portable computers for every seventh and eighth grader in the state, starting in 2002 with a $37 million contract with Apple. (A good portion of that money—as much as $20 million—was going to come from the state's $32.6 million surplus, a cushion that soon disappeared. This was at a time when some legislators were grumbling about basic renovation needs in Maine schools, estimated to cost roughly $100 million.) By the end of 2002, similarly expansive laptop ventures, at similar costs, had been launched in New York City, Michigan, Virginia, and California, and more were coming in other states. The prices schools were paying, however, varied wildly. For example, while a district near Richmond, Virginia, spent $19 million on a networking package and 23,000 Apple laptops, the San Lorenzo, California, school district spent essentially the same amount on a third as many machines. But no one was looking at costs. "The computer lab is a thing of the past," proclaimed Arnie Glassberg, assistant superintendent of San Lorenzo schools. Glassberg's district went to some effort to buy these laptops, pulling together a federal grant, a school bond, and interest on the district's savings account. San Lorenzo's teachers were expected to respond in kind, incorporating laptop projects into every subject they teach.[19]

All of this activity gave new meaning to an old adage: You reap what you sow—in this case, upgrade frenzy. As all of these schools were investing in costly laptops and complex networking systems, dozens of others were already on to the next new thing: Palm organizers and "pocket PC" devices.[20] This meant that before any lessons had been learned from the old system, a new round of technological chaos began to descend. As an example, some students were getting left out of these handouts, prompting new complaints of inequities. Computing's fundamental pedagogical holes opened up as well. One stems from the very opportunities that make technology so dynamic: As the computer industry continues to innovate, more and more services are offered on one device, for both productivity and entertainment. As this trend has reached down to the gizmos in students' backpacks—not just pocket PCs but also cell phones—teachers and administrators are having increasing trouble figuring out which devices they should welcome at school and which should be banned. "They don't know what to do with them or how to set them up," said Elliot Soloway, a cognitive scientist and education professor at the University of Michigan in Ann Arbor, and an avid technology watcher. "There's no curriculum. We're going to make the same mistakes again."[21]

This endless circle of obstacles has left Bernard Shackleford with a keen sense of computer technology's constraints and some wariness about how machines are used in his own courses at Hundred High. In one of his calculus classes, for example, while a few students from another class sat in the back visiting Internet chat rooms during their study hall, Shackleford's students toiled away in front with pencil and paper, their fancy laptops sitting quietly at their feet. "When it comes time to take the AP exam," Shackleford explained, "a lot of this equipment isn't legal. So they've got to get used to working it out on their own." His answer seemed curious, and led me to ask him two questions: Are the testing services lagging behind the times? Or have they rightly concluded that there's real virtue in old-fashioned figuring? To Shackleford, the truth seems to fall somewhere in the middle. While the testing companies have begun to let students do some figuring on graphing calculators, the establishment may be right to defend some old-fashioned traditions. As an indication, Shackleford pointed to one software package, a high-end math program called Derive, which he wouldn't allow his students to use. "It's too powerful," he said. "It does all their thinking for them. I have one copy, and I keep it locked in my cabinet."

So what, for Shackleford, is the point of all this equipment? "In some ways, it has enabled me to teach in more depth. I've been able to get into topics I've never gotten to before." As an example, he said that just covering the basics in Algebra II used to consume so much time that he never got to logarithms (exponential functions) or matrices (advanced methods of solving equations). Now he does. Did he worry that the computer's automated functions let students move through the fundamentals too quickly? No. "Why should you take two weeks to learn to graph the sine curve when kids can take their computers and do it in three minutes? That's tedious stuff."

RURAL RESULTS

It's not entirely clear, as we'll discover in many of the following chapters, that avoiding this tedium pays off. Just in the simple matter of test scores, the results are somewhat mixed. Hundred High's experience offers a small illustration. Being one of the poorest high schools in the county, Hundred has never been a particularly strong performer when it comes to test scores. And the arrival of the laptop system has not much changed its standing. (Shackleford considers that record a victory, since he thought the new toys would initially provoke a drop in achievement.) The one exception has been the school's math scores, which rose shortly after the laptop program was adopted and stayed up through 2002. While some of that gain could be attributed to the school's computer system—with its new frontiers for graphing, spreadsheets, and formula-crunching—Shackleford acknowledged that there might be other explanations for the growth. One powerful possibility, he said, was a more sophisticated set of math textbooks, which arrived at roughly the same time the computers did.

The same fuzzy situations have dogged other laptop programs around the country. In Bloomfield, Connecticut, reports suggest that the laptops' arrival certainly brought a new sense of vitality to the academic atmosphere. Students were writing a lot more, and by some teachers' accounts writing better, because they were doing more revision. Test scores in Bloomfield were up slightly, but the district had initiated a set of new reading and math programs just as it bought the laptops, and the only score that had risen much was eighth-grade reading achievement. Reading skills, however, are not obviously linked to laptop work and are easily boosted by traditional study methods. Caveats like these led Bloomfield school officials to give their laptop program a hard look. When they began weighing the facts against their hefty annual expenditures at one tiny middle school, Jerry Crystal, the district's technology coordinator, was moved to ask an uncomfortable question: "Are we getting $500,000 of improvement out of these kids?"

The same questions were being asked in Virginia, where school officials had to recall their laptops for fixes after discovering that students were using them mostly for instant-messaging their friends and swapping game and movie files. So too in Seattle, where the private high school that is Bill Gates's alma mater started requiring students to own laptops. The decision provoked such a backlash (apparently because the school could furnish no pedagogical justification for the laptops) that one parent, a computer specialist at Evergreen State College, launched a website called Laptop Moratorium Now![22]

The laptop trend has of course done wonders for the cause of Internet accessibility—but not always with desirable results. By early 2003, laptops with wireless Internet connections had become so prevalent in college lecture halls that professors had to fight for students' attention: One boring professorial moment meant everyone suddenly heard the tapping of computer keys. Some professors actually enjoy the competition. "It's an audible vote," as Jay Mallek, a professor at American University's business school, put it. But Mallek's view is far from universal. Other professors have relegated laptop users to the back of the lecture hall, where they won't disturb the other students. "When you see twenty-five percent of the screens playing solitaire, besides being distracted, you feel like a sucker for paying attention," says Ian Ayres, a professor at Yale Law School. At a law school in Texas, a professor banned laptops from his classes, even for note taking. "It has made an enormously positive difference to shut those computers off," he says. Interestingly, the Texas professor's first move was to disconnect his classroom's wireless transmitter. Students quickly protested, and the college administrators told him to plug it back in.[23]

—

Doubts of this nature about the classroom computer have led technology proponents over the years to regularly look for harder evidence of its value. A brief sample of these statistical adventures occurred in West Virginia in 1999, when a group of outside evaluators examined the computer program used to practice basic skills in the state's elementary grades. After compiling students' gains on state tests, they concluded that 11 percent of the yearly improvement, and perhaps a good deal more, was caused by the computers. This study was heavily publicized for a while, partly because of the high profile of some of its authors. The researchers were three university professors and a doctoral student from Hofstra and Columbia universities, whose work was sponsored by the Milken Exchange on Education Technology, a formerly vigorous but now defunct non-profit think tank started by junk bond veteran Michael Milken. The main reason for the study's prominence, however, was its bold and definitive conclusions. In a world where solid, tangible evidence of academic gain is hard to come by, this was big news.

The program the evaluators examined worked this way: For ninety minutes every day, students in grades K–6 sat down in front of computer terminals for math and reading exercises akin to the work that Paul Reese's students did at Ralph Bunche. The program started in 1990 with a $7 million investment from state authorities, which bought an automated system from either of two companies—IBM or Josten's Learning Corporation, one of the nation's leading school-software suppliers. The programs' designers tried hard to steer clear of the "drill-and-kill" routines that had given this technology such a bad name. (This, school officials hoped, was achieved by asking students questions about a book they had read or a math assignment they'd worked on—questions that required reflection and rumination rather than rote reactions.) When the Milken group studied the program's results, it came to a few conclusions that are somewhat at odds with most such evaluations. It found no difference between black and white students' achievements, and greater gains among students who did *not* have computers at home. The data convinced the researchers that computerized drilling had generally boosted test scores; they were so certain about this, in fact, that they concluded that the computer program was more cost-effective than hiring more teachers or reducing class size.[24]

When I started poking around in elementary schools, in both Hundred and other West Virginia small towns, I heard a rather different view; if anything, there seemed to be a lot of grumbling among both teachers and principals. "To be honest with you, I'm not real enthused about the program," Paul Huston, principal of Hundred's Long Drain Elementary, told me. "I think the state of West Virginia threw a big chunk of money down the drain," he added without so much as a smile at his mournful pun. In a nutshell, the word from the teachers I spoke with was this: Despite its designers' efforts, the automated reading-and-math system was extremely simplistic, offering only the most rudimentary kinds of drill, often with little if any correction or explanation. It broke down a lot ("on a daily basis," Huston said); it was more costly than other, more attractive curriculum measures; and it locked schools into constant upgrades with its suppliers. At Long Drain, for example, Huston cast his lot with the Josten's system. Before long, he discovered that it was incompatible with other software, so all upgrades had to be bought from Josten's. "We're sort of locked into what Josten's put in there ten years ago," a teacher from another school that used Josten's told me. "They gotcha," Huston said. At Keyser Elementary, in Mineral County, a more urban community several valleys east of Hundred, the story was much the same.

What, then, is to be made of all the gains reported in the Milken study? The answer says a lot about the potential and the limits of drilling work in basic skills on computers, or in any other medium.

At both Keyser and Long Drain, there wasn't much sign that the computer drills had done anything (scores hadn't fallen since the program started, but they hadn't risen, either). In the opinion of Brenda Williams, who managed the program for the state's department of education, this may well be because the teachers in these schools didn't use the program in the most enterprising manner. Across the state as a whole, scores did indeed rise, just as the Milken researchers claimed. The reason, says Williams, is that many teachers found ways to combine the computer drills with non-technological activities—exercises with toys or blocks to build arithmetic skill, for example, or reading stories aloud to expand students' sense of language. This, education experts have long pointed out, is how any good instructor should teach—with or without technology. Yet the researchers felt certain that the added element of the computer had made the difference in this case; as proof, Williams says that before the computer program was introduced, many teachers had been using many of the same low-tech activities to teach basic skills without seeing nearly as much improvement. When the computers arrived, she said, it was like having "seven intelligent little helpers who have patience to the nth degree." Those helpers freed up teachers' time so effectively, she said, that by the end of the year, some told her that almost all their students were at grade level, for the first time, in both reading and math. Those who were not at grade level by then were set up for summer school work—on the computer program.

Educators who are familiar with academic studies are a little more circumspect about these claims. Some point out that the computer program extended the time students spent practicing basic skills, a change that should produce results even if computers were not involved. Some criticize the quality of the computer routines themselves, noting that schools have been gradually turning away from computerized drills, choosing to use technology for creative projects instead. "Therefore," wrote Jeff Fouts, a professor of education from Seattle Pacific University, who evaluated the Milken study, "those who point to this research as supporting the increased availability and use of technology in the classrooms in general . . . are using the findings inappropriately."[25] And some argue that the computer program's expense—which grew to $42 million by 1998—could have gone to hiring living, breathing "little helpers," who might well have produced even greater gains. This point is at least partly debatable, since those funds, amounting to $7 million per year, would pay for a mere 330 teacher's aides, not nearly enough to spread throughout the state's 6,000 or so elementary school classrooms.[26] Score one for Milken's cost-benefit analysis.

But the most critical of all these concerns is not the quality of the software but the quality of the academic gains. A fair case can be made in West Virginia and other states that have launched similar programs that simple academic exercises on computers—whether by drill and kill or by some more reflective routine—can raise test scores. But what is that accomplishing? Not much, in the eyes of Debbie Wallizer, a twenty-five-year veteran of Keyser Elementary. "When [the computer system] first came, they loved it," she told me as her students quietly went about their business during a reading hour. "Now, it's boring to them. If you gave them a choice, they'd rather read books." Wallizer has noticed that when her students are exposed to books, their reaction is the exact opposite of what it had been with the computer program. "Initially, they hate reading books. Eventually, they see that it opens up. When you realize it can create a visual picture, as *you* choose it to be, they start to get interested."

Money, Bureaucratic Perfection, and the Parenting Gap: Montgomery County, Maryland

A fter visiting a number of schools, it became obvious to me, as it would to anyone, that the same computer programs can be used in a fashion that is exemplary or dismal; in fact, such contradictory practices often can be seen in the same school building, and sometimes in the same classroom. Some of these contradictions appear to be bumps on a learning curve that would afflict any large institution attempting massive change. But that begs some natural questions: What will computers deliver once all the equipment is in place, the teachers are trained, and all the kinks are worked out? What, in other words, is the most we can expect when schools are a little farther down the technology road?

These questions matter—not only intrinsically but also because of education's latest trend: standardized testing. Whenever computer initiatives fail to produce a rise in test scores, as they often do, their promoters argue that the value of computing can't be measured by test scores. Their case is a fair one; indeed, practitioners of many enterprising low-tech classroom exercises say that test scores don't fairly reflect their practices and visions, either. To give all these pioneers their due, it's best to take what might be called a holistic look at what's going on in education. After all, over the long haul the personal and sociological aspects of the scholastic experience generally count for more than what can be tallied by numerical measures.

One way to consider long-range cultural issues such as these is to look at a school that has already spent years wrestling with innovations like technology. Ideally, one would pick a big school, where academic activities run the gamut. And, to give computer promoters their complete due, one should choose a school that enjoys both adequate funds and a wealth of administrative support. A school that fits these criteria quite neatly is Blair High School, in Montgomery County, Maryland.

Blair is a classic example of the modern educational institution—a hulking redbrick building that squats on the crest of a gentle knoll just outside the District of Columbia. On a first visit, the most notable parts of the Blair facility are its maze of clean, pastel halls; its gaping football stadium just outside the door; and its wildly heterogeneous student body of nearly three thousand teenagers. Over the years, Blair has been widely celebrated for its special "magnet" program in computer science, general science, and mathematics. Launched in 1985, the program has gained a national reputation, drawn some of the country's brightest teenagers, and developed some of education's most sophisticated uses of technology. Indeed, this is the birthplace of the great 1998 school politics project that was featured in *The Washington Post* and noted in this book's Introduction. Former president Clinton once paid the school a happy visit and claimed it as a relative: a descendant of the Blair line of his family.

Blair High School has also drawn money—or, more precisely, the whole district has. Between 1995, when the Montgomery County school district launched its formal classroom computer program (called Global Access Technology), and 2002, it has spent $267 million—just over $33 million a year—on various items related to technology (this includes the computer hardware, the wiring, the teacher training, the whole works). In the totality of the district's annual budget, $33 million is a mere asterisk, less than 5 percent of what, in 2002, was a $1.3 billion fund. Nonetheless, with a mere 136,000 students, Montgomery County has been able to spend nearly $10,000 a year on each one of its students.[1] This includes roughly $250 a year on technology for each pupil—more than twice the national average.[2] If computers aren't fulfilling public expectations at Blair, one has to wonder if such expectations can be met in any school.

Underneath the pile of money lies an equally rich set of questions. In fact, anyone who wants a fair look at the entirety of the computer experience in school—its glories, its shortcomings, and its confounding complications—should visit Blair. The story revolves around two questions in particular: How does this school handle the gap between its technology stars and its other students—the poor, the middle-of-the-road achievers, and the assorted others who make up more than 75 percent of the student body? More important, what causes this gap, and what effect, if any, does technology have on it?

Blair's students are so varied that they're divided into several additional subgroups, leading some teachers to joke that Blair is really six schools in one. There's the magnet program (with 400 students); a program for a set of brains who are media enthusiasts, called the Communication Arts Program (285 students); a program of classes in which English is used as a second language, for the 330 students who, in a recent year, traced their lineage to 42 different countries; the special-education program, for those with specific learning disabilities (150 students); another remedial program, for students who are two years behind in reading ability (150 students); and finally, the school's "regular" students, that mass of 1,500 or more whites, Hispanics, Asians, and African Americans who are emblematic of suburban public high schools everywhere.

In an effort to reduce the contrasts between these groups, Blair's teachers try, among other things, to give their underachievers computer experiences that are as meaningful for them as NASA explorations are for the school's annual stream of National Merit scholars. This is, of course, the suburban front on the great national campaign to close the digital divide. Here, too, however, the process has proven to be something of a struggle. To understand why, it is best to begin with a sample of what made Blair famous.

MISSION POSSIBLE

E very weekday morning since 1985, Mark Curran has been teaching one of Blair's most unusual and most popular classes in what amounts to a modern-day machine shop. The shop resides on the second floor, amid a network of hallways so long and circuitous that students have given them street names: Maryland, Montgomery, and Silver Spring avenues; Blair Boulevard; and the longest, Sligo Creek, at the end of which sits Curran's Engineering Technology Laboratory. As with about 10 percent of the classes at Blair (85 out of 950), this course is reserved for Montgomery County's magnet students (who must pass highly competitive entry exams) and anyone else at Blair who has conquered the prerequisites for these classes and dares to take them (most, of course, don't). Five times a day, twenty-five or more students file in and out of this shop. Numbers like that would seem to be an invitation to exhaustion, until one watches this class at work.

The course, which Curran teaches in a three-year sequence (with his partner, Ed Johnson), is called Research and Experimentation/Problem

Solving. In many respects, the class, and the shop where it's held, is the heart of Blair's magnet program. It's where students learn the practical skills they'll need for the crowning jewel of their tenure at Blair: an in-depth research project that becomes the focus of their junior and senior years. A crucial step in that process occurs in the tenth grade, with what Curran calls Mission Possible. That mission? Come up with a plan to investigate some problem or question related to earth science. (These have involved something as local as monitoring pollution runoff into the Chesapeake Bay or as exotic as looking at the deterioration of the ozone layer, earthquake developments in California, or the three geologic plates that are splitting apart in East Africa's Rift Valley.) All this work is preparation for today's eleventh-grade class in engineering, which has a mission of its own: invent a new safety device for some personal, industrial, or commercial purpose, design a prototype with a computer-drafting program, then produce a real, working model.

This is no fake academic exercise. Students have to confirm the uniqueness of their ideas through patent research. In past years some students have come up with ideas so intriguing that they've managed to sell their patents, often for a tidy sum. One student put himself through college on a patent for a special wheelchair brake that made it easier for the handicapped to travel uphill; another won $40,000 for his design for a digital metronome. In today's class, a student is building an automatic massager that fits under a mattress and is operated by a series of wooden rollers, pulled by a belt drive. Another is making a simple Plexiglas wheel guard for Razor scooters. (At the time, this popular device, designed largely for tricks and competition, had nothing to keep its front wheel from pivoting 360 degrees, which is one reason that so many of its riders ended up in emergency rooms.) Another student, named Jossi, is designing a heated snow shovel. I asked him why. "Because now, my dad always hurts his back and then I have to shovel the snow off the driveway myself." His only problem at the moment was that he couldn't figure out how to turn the shovel on.

"Why won't it work?" Curran asks. Jossi shrugs. "Okay, how do we *find out* why it doesn't work?" "Take it apart?" Jossi asks. "Right." Curran also suggests that Jossi poke around in his "odds-and-ends bin," where he might find a similar switch, whose dissection would yield "a magical answer." About fifteen minutes later, Jossi brings Curran a partly chewed up thermal switch and a puzzled expression. "Get in there!" Curran says. "Destroy it some more! How else are you going to find out what's wrong?" Jossi smiles in sheepish delight, returns to his workbench, and starts jabbing away with a screwdriver and pliers. Before long, he thinks he's fixed the problem. "Let's turn it on and see if it blows up," Curran says as he checks the connections. "Okay, ready?" Jossi grins but can't help taking a few steps back before plugging it in.

While it's not hard to see why a class like this is fun—and that Curran's talents as a teacher have a lot to do with it—there's considerably more here than meets the eye. Students cannot take this class without also studying a daunting array of related subjects. The magnet students (typically, the only ones in the class) couple their work here with studying the fundamentals of computer-chip technology, structured computer languages, pre-calculus mathematics, and some assortment of electives in fields such as matrix algebra, linear programming, statistics, thermodynamics, and quantum physics. As Curran puts it, explaining his class, "This doesn't substitute for the basics. This is where they apply it."

Not surprisingly, Blair's annual list of magnet research projects reads like a compendium of reports from the National Academy of Sciences. Some samples: "Effects of LPS on VP expression and receptors during chronic osmotic stimulation," a project in neuroendocrinology mentored by a doctor from the National Institutes of Health; and "Detection of human telomeric repeats by fluorescent in situ hybridization," a biotechnology project mentored by a scientist from the National Institute of Standards and Technology, an office where national standards are set for the study and manufacture of almost every conceivable material, from metal alloys and football helmets to disease tissues and DNA. Other student projects have drawn from fields such as astronomy, engineering, psychology, "fluid dynamics," even artificial intelligence. And there are dozens more every year.

But a lot of what makes this class work is the inherent talent of the students themselves. As Kathleen O'Connor, a local college placement consultant, told me, "We do a fabulous job of taking silk purses and turning them into silk purses." And that raises questions about how easily the technological achievements of a class like this can be exported to other schools—or even to other classes at Blair. Among these silk purses, the math brains seem to constitute a particularly special product line. You can see it in their eyes; they are a presence in nearly every school, and have been through the generations. During my visits to Blair, I began to wonder whether this crowd's success with high-level computing goes beyond their hyperintelligence to some alternative system of psychic wiring. Consider the way they respond to a question: gaze often focused somewhere off to the side, answers typically delivered in a rapid-fire monotone through a faint but constant smile. It's as though the logical connections in their thoughts are so complex, the algorithms so intense, that all they can do is watch in bliss as their brains deliver their voluminous readouts. Why would they, or anyone else, want to dilute this elegant process with superfluous data, especially the unpredictable sort generated by another human face? No wonder these students are often most comfortable working at a computer.

OH, JULIO!

Then there's the scene downstairs. In a classroom off "Blair Boulevard," John Kaluta teaches a class called Technology Innovations and Applications for all grades of Blair's regular students. Kaluta is a midsize, affable man in his early forties who is enthusiastic about his subject, the sort of energetic, regular guy whom everyone hopes they'll get as their science teacher. He has specifically designed this class to give average students some version of what their magnet counterparts get from Curran's Mission Possible, so that they too get a chance to elevate their problem-solving skills. The class, in other words, is a perfect test of what happens when a smart use of the computer is presented to a group of difficult students.

This semester, Kaluta's class had been making a blimp out of eight Mylar balloons. The project was meant to teach students about subjects such as structural design; density, flotation, and load limits; and how to handle the kinds of computer-assisted design programs that are used by engineers and architects in the real world. To build a sense of a professional atmosphere, Kaluta tried to mimic an engineering lab: About two dozen desks with computers are grouped here and there in five different pods. The computers are set up in a circle, so that each group of students faces in toward the other members of the group. Around the edges, the class's remaining desks are pulled together so that other students can go over their work in teams. School administrators have lent Kaluta's efforts a little extra support by giving this class a leisurely ninety-minute period—Blair's version of an increasingly popular innovation, called block scheduling.

The day I visit, Kaluta spends most of his time strolling the room checking on his students, each of whom is engaged in a different stage of the blimp project. As he passes one computer terminal after another, it gradually becomes clear to him that most of his students have accomplished very little. He stops by one student, Julio, who is working on an "FAQ," a list of frequently asked questions about the blimp, which is to be posted eventually on the class's website. Julio has one question typed on his screen. "Oh, Julio!

Julio!" Kaluta moans. "You're killin' me! Other students have twenty-five to thirty questions all typed out. What have you been doing?" Julio shrugs endearingly.

At one point, after I'd gotten the lay of the land, I played a little game—a routine I performed in most classrooms I visited. First I would follow the teacher as he or she perused the class. Then I would walk the room by myself. In virtually every heavily computerized classroom, the differences between what the teacher saw and what I saw on my own were so dramatic that it was sometimes hard to keep from laughing. In this class, for example, Kaluta and I pass a group of students who are entering data into a spreadsheet; when I return for my own look, they're well along on a news exchange about their families' favorite sodas. In a second computer pod, a student who earlier was diligently working solo is now, during my pass, deep into the intricacies of the Dallas Cowboys' website. A third group has been working fairly diligently, recalculating the blimp's load limits. They're finished, however, by 8:20, which means they have the rest of the class period—a full forty minutes—to themselves. As I might have expected, they turn to Netscape's latest offerings.

At one point, Kaluta stops to help a student who is trying to calculate cubic meters of helium for the balloon. He takes a good five minutes with this student, who seems to be one of the few taking the project seriously. "Now, if you *really* want to get thorough, go to howstuffworks.com. It's a great website." He then stands by while the student types it in, gets it wrong, tries again, gets it right, then watches the system crash. Kaluta reels in frustration, angrily shaking his head. Apparently, the computer system at Blair has been crashing regularly. With a deflating sigh, Kaluta looks around and notices the many students who, having been neglected for the last five minutes, are now fabulously off task. "Oh well, keep trying," Kaluta tells his helium analyst, then heads for a particularly noisy group on the other side of the room.

The noisy group has what some might think is the best job of all: They are actually building the blimp. The group (four students) is seated around a box of uninflated balloons, bags of ultrathin sticks of balsa wood, a canister of helium, some glue, some measuring devices, some string. But they're not doing anything; they're talking lazily. As soon as Kaluta questions them, their eyes light up. "I couldn't put that section in," one student says, turning to a teammate, "because he got the measurement wrong!" "Nuh-uh," his teammate answers. "I didn't get it wrong!" Eventually, Kaluta settles the group down, clarifies what they're responsible for, and moves on. They return to their tasks for a bit, then go back to their conversations.

All these difficulties are somewhat surprising, particularly the network troubles. Blair's budget for technology is so lavish that it has earned the school fame for being one of the most wired in the nation. It was such an early participant in the Internet (starting in 1989—it was the first school in the state to be hooked up) that it was able to get one of the nation's shortest public school Internet addresses: mbhs.edu. Furthermore, Blair's Internet service is provided by what should be an unusually reliable host—the National Institutes of Health. But all that takes a distant second place to the reality of school bureaucracy and its overarching rule of scarcity: scarcity of time; scarcity of teachers; and scarcity of money. Even in this well-funded school, there are constant cries for new equipment, more maintenance staff, and more training and support for everyone.

<hr />

But what about the tenth grade's famous achievement—outperforming thirteen professional pundits in predicting the 1998 congressional elections? One of my visits to Blair occurred exactly two years after the school's big victory and just weeks before the 2000 congressional elections—and a potential repeat performance. Once again, two long banks of computers in Blair's massive library were filled with government-studies students working on another rendition of this assignment. Now, I figured, I would see how smart academic computing is conducted.

When I watched these students, I was surprised to find very few of them doing much work. Confused, I later sought some explanation from R. B. Lasco, one of the school's two librarians (or, in the lingo of the digitally equipped school, the media-resources teacher). It turned out that the pundits in 1998 came from the Communication Arts Program, the school's liberal arts magnet group. In other words, these were not your average tenth graders. The couple of dozen students I was watching in the library now *were* average tenth graders. "They'll ask you how wide the margins have to be," Lasco said, "and that will be the end of it."

As a school librarian, Lasco gets a chance to see every one of Blair's three thousand students, along with their teachers. This has left him with a view of the school's academic efforts that is not particularly forgiving. In Lasco's opinion, today's high school students are influenced by forces far more powerful than anything schools can devise. And that in turn leaves teachers, even good ones, relatively impotent. Not coincidentally, Lasco likes to cite the book *Beyond the Classroom*, by Laurence Steinberg, an intensely researched treatise, which argues that students' will to learn has been increasingly trampled by an excess of extracurricular activities and after-school jobs, and by diminished attention to parenting, among other things.[3] "It's part of the whole media-consumer society," Lasco tells me. "They're constantly bombarded with the message 'You can get whatever you want. Now. The customer is always right.' I've finally realized that I have to take extra care to be absolutely, perfectly clear in any instructions and any material that I give out. Because when I don't, if they have trouble with something, it's immediately my fault: 'You didn't *tell* us we had to do that. You didn't put that on the handout.'"

What does all this have to do with computers? At the end of the blimp-building class, John Kaluta offered a few connections as we sat together reviewing what had occurred. It had seemed to me that it would be difficult to stage a better creative technology experience for this population of students than the blimp project. It was challenging, varied, group-oriented, and tied to a real object; it offered freedom within relatively firm expectations and was supervised by a committed, no-nonsense teacher, who clearly had rapport with his students. Yet the class still wasn't finished with this relatively simple construction task, despite having spent three to four and a half hours a week on it for the last six weeks. What went wrong? The exercise seemed somewhat inefficient, I suggested to Kaluta.

"Yes, it's horrible," he quickly replied. "This group idea looks good, but one student can sit there and not do the work, and you'll never know. Plus, the project has taken so long. So by now they've lost interest." The delay was not entirely the students' fault. "We were going to do [the initial design] with AutoCAD [a computerized drafting program]," Kaluta said. "But guess what. We don't have AutoCAD yet. So we did it by hand. We'll draw the finished product with AutoCAD when we're done." I joked that the students probably learned more by doing the drawings by hand. Kaluta smiled, then nodded vigorously.

Humor aside, Kaluta's experience is remarkably representative of an academic scene that most schools would be happy to achieve. Kaluta is blessed, by most schools' standards, with an unusually large number of computers in his room. He has twenty-one relatively state-of-the-art machines. Yet by his lights, that's still not enough. With thirty-one students, it means "ten kids are sitting next to another kid who's doing the work for some period of the class. And some will be perfectly happy to sit and let the other kid do all the noodling around." Kaluta knows, however, that getting thirty-one computers is not only unrealistic (many classes at Blair are without any computer at all); it also isn't the answer. "With computers," he said, "if you tell them exactly what to do, they won't learn much. But if you let them flop around but lead them, *then* they really learn something." With a large class, however, Kaluta said he's found it impossible to gently lead each student. The net result? "They generally go waste time until they're caught." The pattern has left Kaluta with some dark conclusions. "Idle time on the computer," he said, "is worse than idle time with your head down."

One change that Kaluta thinks might ease his troubles is smaller classes. Having fewer students to watch over would give him time, he believes, to see to technical troubles as well as individual students. He's right. When I've visited high-tech schools with ten or fifteen students per class (mostly private institutions), I've noticed that they've often done a wonderful job of managing their myriad challenges. But the same benefits are gained in small classes that *don't* use computers. That's why nationwide support for smaller classes is one of the constants on the political agenda of the teachers' unions. It costs a lot more, however, to hire new teachers, whose salary requirements keep rising, than it does to buy computers, whose cost continually drops.

Even if schools did invest in more teachers, students in smaller classes will only go so far. "Some students just aren't ready to do what I'm asking them to do," Kaluta said. This is a sentiment echoed by many a teacher today, which made me wonder if, in many cases, it might be best to concentrate on the fundamentals and leave the fancy, technological approaches to later. In other words, I asked Kaluta, would it have been a problem to teach this class without the technology? "No, not at all," he replied. "That's what they do upstairs." Kaluta was referring to a technical-concepts class given to students for whom English is a second language. I once visited that class, too. Coincidentally, it was a small class, of maybe a dozen students. There was very little goofing off. And the teacher showed me, with evident pride, what a firm grounding in the basics he felt his students were getting with nothing more than balsa wood and glue, a smattering of math formulas on the blackboard, and plenty of discussion to connect the whole puzzle.

SCIENCE VS. CALCULATORS

When I move upstairs, this time for a magnet course in earth sciences, I immediately feel like I've joined a college seminar. Moments after the bell rings, the teacher, an earthy young man named Leslie Rogers, is already into a brief lecture, complete with overhead slides on the ten principles of solar energy, the dynamics of energy flux, the albedo effect, and other arcane concepts. "We are trying to discover the reasons for the seasons," Rogers says, "and to quantify those reasons." He then turns the class loose to work in two-person teams on the eleven computers that line the classroom's walls, where they will download live NASA data through a fancy piece of computer code called a Java applet. Rogers occasionally yells out directions, but he has to ask for the students' attention only once. Anyone not listening (invariably because students are arguing about their research procedures or because someone can't pull his nose away from the computer screen) is quickly disciplined—most of the time not by Rogers but by a fellow student.

Which is not to say these students are always on track. At one point, I notice a student, the spitting image of Harry Potter (gangly, long face, electrified hair, thick spectacles), who gets so involved in what he's exploring that he can't sit in his chair. Instead, he perches on it like a bird, crouching, with his feet on the seat. To anchor himself to his perch, he keeps one hand on the back of the chair while he pecks at the mouse and keyboard with his other hand. Apparently, this is a boy who likes to work solo. Before long, Rogers comes by, pulls him off the chair, and assigns him to a team. "*You*," Rogers says, "need a partner. You've been working alone *too* much." The student blinks, glances at his new partner, looks at what's on this computer screen, and finds a new perch. Soon Rogers has to take stronger action. "Everyone stop for a minute! I want you to know that who is jumping ahead, who is not following directions . . . is *plain . . . as . . . day.*" Dead silence. Rogers surveys the class. "You need to bridle your enthusiasm a little." They promptly do so. Obedience and diligence are the norm in this class. No wonder these magnet kids are famous.

Partway through this class, about when Rogers has finished his opening lecture and slide show, George Herman, who teaches an equivalent course to Blair High's regular students, has hardly gotten started with his class next door. He spends the first ten or fifteen minutes of class at his desk, listening to students who come up, one by one, with questions on homework they couldn't figure out, excuses for work they didn't do, and so forth. While these dialogues continue, it's social hour for the rest of the class, which for most means an opportunity to either zone out or cut up. Herman regularly steps in to restore order, which of course makes the conversations at his desk take that much longer. Eventually, he hands out the day's assignment, their first heavy math exercise with graphing calculators.

For anyone born before 1970, these are exotic implements. Slightly larger than the standard palm-size store-bought calculator and costing up to a hundred dollars apiece, graphing calculators are built to do everything yesteryear's students did with pencil and paper and slide rules, and then some. They compute trigonometric functions such as tangents and cosines, perform statistical analyses, convert fractions into decimals, and draw small tables and graphs. The more inventive students will plug a couple of them together and play video games with each other.

The handheld calculator, graphic or otherwise, provides a small but clear window onto several general discussions about technology. In fact, the issues surrounding its use in school are much the same as those that surround computers, but in simpler form. And the calculator has an even longer history to go by, because the use of the calculator has been a subject of debate and controversy for decades. Opponents see this device as an evil crutch; in their eyes, when students become dependent on a machine like this for more and more of their work, they're left without a solid, internal understanding of mathematical procedures. Calculator supporters counter that today, the intricacies of those procedures have become relatively unimportant; in their opinion, if a device can free students to spend their time with more advanced concepts, in the end they're ahead of the game. Regardless of which side sounds more persuasive, it's important to note that the studies on calculator use have not been terribly auspicious.* All of which left me curious, when I was in Herman's class, to hear what the students thought. Did they find themselves doing more or less math with calculators as compared with more basic tools?

"Oh, less math—definitely," one student says. "It makes it so much easier." The other three students at her table heartily agree. I turn to another group of six students and ask how many can do the graphing calculator functions on their own. "No one!" says one student with a laugh. "It's *hard!*" "Unless you're a frickin' genius!" her friend says. More laughs.

When I later relay these answers to Herman, he tried to explain. "You can cube something on paper," he said. "But the possibility for large errors is quite high. As long as they understand what they're doing and understand

---

*One of the most recent studies of calculator use, and one of the most widely circulated, was a Brookings Institution report entitled "How Well Are American Students Learning? Focus on Math Achievement," published in September 2000. The study found that the more students used calculators, the worse their math skills were; it also found that minority students were using calculators much more frequently than whites. In reporting this story (on December 15, 2000), *The Wall Street Journal* found additional evidence of similar patterns. Maine, for example, offered a portrait that was free of racial factors (98 percent of the population there is white). Nonetheless, of fourth graders who reported using calculators almost every day, 47 percent didn't meet state math standards—even on tests that allowed calculator use. In contrast, of the students who said they used calculators only two or three times a month, only 23 percent fell below state standards. Interestingly, in the years leading up to this study, the National Council of Teachers of Mathematics, the National Research Council, and the National Science Foundation have all vigorously (and financially) supported calculator-friendly curricula.

the formula, it's okay to let the calculator do it for them." After a pause, he added, "Of course many don't, and they just write down the answer or copy it from a friend." As we talked further, it became clear that the graphing calculator was aggravating inequities in many classrooms but that it could also ameliorate them. There are two stages to this situation. The first has to do with free-market economics; as such, it's a micro-illustration of the digital divide's stubborn persistence. Many students can't afford a one-hundred-dollar calculator, so they pick up a five- or ten-dollar version. Since the cheaper machines can't do nearly as many functions as the pricier models, the less wealthy students tend to lag even farther behind their peers. That said, the top-of-the-line calculators have so much power that students don't need much understanding of math principles to perform their calculations. "If you have one of the fancy ones," Herman told me, "it makes it real easy." Enter stage two: the opportunity to close some inequities. Thinking back on my moment of jest with Kaluta, I asked Herman if, in another paradox, the students who are stuck with cheaper calculators might not, in the end, learn more math. "You certainly appreciate distances once you get through entering everything in," he replied. By then, of course, the better-equipped students are on to the next set of problems, whether or not they fully understand what they're doing.

This conversation reminded me of several points that came up during my discussion with Kaluta, stemming from his remark that his students weren't ready to do what he was asking of them. That, of course, is the teacher's eternal challenge. But it comes up with unusual frequency when technology is involved. Which made me wonder: Is the average student ready for the sophisticated techniques that some of the most interesting computer assignments involve? Computer promoters typically argue that it's self-defeating to think this way and that it's unfair to withhold technology from people, particularly young people. In essence, they say, you get skilled at something by doing it. "You work out the kinks in something by trying it out," Gary Stager, a veteran of educational technology and an adjunct professor of education at Pepperdine University, once told me. "You can't say, 'Well, because the technology isn't perfect yet, let's keep the computers out of the schools.'"

The logic is persuasive, but it's missing something. At Blair High, computer use works with the magnet students not only because they're smart but also because they've built up their base. They've learned the math, the computer logic, the entire understructure that anchors the work and permits students to eventually launch into creative explorations of their own. Interestingly, when I ask Rogers, the magnet science teacher, about his students' use of graphing calculators, he too says the presumption is that they understand the principles underlying the calculator's functions. Then he says, "Actually, I've found that a lot of these kids don't know the pencil version, because they've been using graphing calculators since middle school. So I've had to start again from scratch." Even the math stars, it seems, have to regularly repair their foundations.

THE PARENTING GAP

When I've relayed stories like these to the computer campaign's leading advocates, their tendency is to blame the teachers—or the less than ideal amount of attention schools typically pay to housekeeping necessities such as teacher training and computer maintenance and upgrades.* On both charges, however, things are not quite as they seem.

Let's start with housekeeping issues. One reason it's interesting to study Blair—or any other school in Montgomery County, Maryland—is that the school district has long been far more dedicated than most to all sorts of administrative support for technology, even in comparison with other states that have spent generously on computers. (On teacher training alone, the district spent $28.7 million between 1996 and 2002.) As for the computer network, very few of the school's peers can boast of having Internet service through a backbone as robust as what Blair gets from the National Institutes of Health. So it lacks logic to blame Blair's computer woes on the poverty of its computer support systems; that's like blaming malnutrition in America's children on insufficient choices in our supermarkets.

Now, let's look at the teachers' shortcomings. During my visits to Blair, I had several occasions to talk at length with Herman and another teacher, Joe Bellino. Herman, who teaches science to both regular students and

---

*For a glimpse at the heavy pressure continually placed on schools to devote as many of their resources as possible to teacher training and computer-system maintenance, one need only survey *Education Week*'s special issues on technology, called "Technology Counts." Each issue is full of charts and graphs and anecdotes from across the nation—all suggesting that schools are not yet doing enough to integrate computer technology. As but one example, in the issue published May 10, 2001, a student survey asked this question: "When you don't understand something, do any of your teachers use a computer to help you understand the problem in a different way?" The pie chart reflecting the answers included a heavy black section indicating that a dismal 71 percent of teachers failed this test. Any teachers who have favored nontechnical material for adding to students' understanding clearly got the message: Technology is indeed what counts.

those for whom English is a second language, has been at Blair since 1997; Bellino, who juggles a range of responsibilities (he directs the English-as-a-second-language program, including its publication of a quarterly newspaper, and does extra duty as the school's data-systems administrator), has taught there since 1975. Because Blair High School has been experimenting with technology since the early 1980s, Herman and Bellino, along with many of their colleagues, have already made the mistakes with innovations that less experienced schools still see as answers to their problems. So when outsiders stop by to inquire about popular hopes for technology, Herman and Bellino reply with a certain weary wisdom.

At one point, for example, Herman was telling me how teachers try to coordinate technology and science classes at Blair so that the two will "reinforce each other." To make his point, he took several bricks out of a cabinet so I could see how something as simple as these objects could teach the principles of force, matter, and energy. I asked how that exercise compares to what he can do with computer technology. "I think if you understand how this works, you have the basics. This is Bruner and discovery learning," he said. Herman was referring to Jerome Bruner, a leading pioneer of the "constructivist" theory of education, which holds that students learn best if they discover, or construct, their own knowledge through having to work out real problems, preferably with raw, three-dimensional materials.[4] "You've got to see how *this* goes," he said as he helped a brick slide down a fulcrum on his lab table. Plus, he added, "It costs six dollars for these bricks."

At Blair, Bellino explained, "a lot of our kids aren't sure that what they're seeing on the computer is real. It's very abstract. It's a game." When teachers send students to do research on the Internet, Bellino said, the students often have no sense of the differences between various sources of information. "We try to start them with encyclopedias, then move them to magazines and books," he said. The point of that sequence is to help students understand the layers of information that constitute authoritative evidence and knowledge. "*We* know what that is, but they don't," Bellino said. "If they find comic books on the Web, a lot of these kids don't know the difference." Herman agreed. "I think things like the Net should be used gradually," he said. "It's so overwhelming. A lot of these students lose track of what they're being assigned to do. They end up lost, or just look at pictures."

This conversation stunned me and then inspired me to ask an entirely different question, tied to the field of psychology. Most educators are familiar with the principles of child development that have evolved from the theories of Jean Piaget and his revisionist contemporary Lev Vygotsky. While small twists and turns have been added to child development theory since the mid-twentieth century, when these men dominated the field, the crux of their beliefs has long stood tall. In essence, it is that children generally are ready for certain challenges only at certain stages. That readiness can open up considerably if a child is treated to sensitive coaching or is given unusually rich experiences, particularly those that stimulate the senses. But by age eight or nine, according to traditional theory, a child's sensory foundation has been pretty well constructed and his or her most formative years of development are supposedly over. While there is plenty that can still be learned, certain fundamental windows of opportunity for learning have closed—if not fully, then most of the way.

This is why we all learn sports and languages more easily when we're young and why master musicians usually started practicing on their instruments when they were very small children. And it's why most critics of classroom computing—from technology skeptics to mainstream medical and child-development experts—have focused their worry on a child's younger years. In the late 1990s, however, scientific breakthroughs in the study of the adult brain suggested that the windows of learning opportunity might not be so rigid after all. So I asked Herman and Bellino if they saw new possibilities in these older students. In other words, were they making a conscious effort with these teenagers to make up any lost ground in Piaget's famous stages of development? "Yes," Bellino said. "These students have missed so many steps growing up. The tactile stuff is still really important."

I left this discussion entirely befuddled by the computer advocates' chain of logic. How can they see computers, with their constant flood of flattened images and simulated experiences, as the answer to an unmotivated student's problems? And when technology fails to be the answer, how can they blame that on insufficient technical support or on the shortcomings of teachers like Kaluta and Herman and Bellino? That line of reasoning highlights a general education e-lusion, which technology seems to encourage: the tendency among education critics to cast blame in the wrong places. When people go looking for reasons for poor student performance, usually the last place they point their fingers is at the students themselves or at the pressures, or lack thereof, in those students' homes and personal lives. Yet if the preponderance of research on this topic is to be believed, that is precisely where the heart of the trouble lies.

This does not exempt schools from attending to these troubles. But it does shift our notion of what action schools need to take. If students' academic lives are suffering from problems in their extracurricular lives, we should all do whatever we can to right whatever is askew. In the meantime, schools' responsibilities only rise. For poor-performing, unmotivated students, what needs attention is the parenting gap, not the technology gap. Obstacles on the technology front are just that—essentially technical problems. Those kinds of challenges will take care of themselves once students gain the confidence, discipline, and imagination necessary to work at life's difficulties, whatever those may be.

Strangely, despite decades of experience with this reality, schools are still trying to find their proper role in this story. And today's hyperventilation over technology is another sign of how lost the education world continues to be. And it's why, at a school as technologically sophisticated as Blair, teachers like R. B. Lasco find themselves muttering about schools, computers, and the consumer culture in the same breath. Yes, Blair's magnet students are indeed benefiting from technology. However, as O'Connor, the college placement consultant, indicated when referring to them as permanent "silk purses," those students would clearly learn a tremendous amount from almost any project that presents a challenge. For the rest of the student body—mostly average souls, with average levels of motivation and high levels of distraction—computers are simply another consumer toy. They fit right in with these students' need for tasks that are easy and fun, and that can be abandoned with impunity when problems occur.

This is not to glorify the good old days of three R's and no nonsense— a time that, judging by any straight look back, probably never even existed. For most of the twentieth century, the public schools were stuck in different ruts, many of which were unnecessarily repressive and more off-track than the initiatives of today's reformers.[5] Comparatively speaking, though, yesteryear's schools did understand the principles of discipline and concentration—concepts that have a hard time surviving around computers. Here in affluent suburbia, we have one of the nation's most technically sophisticated schools, yet for the vast majority of its students, more access to technology seems to mean more ways to misuse it.

During another after-class conversation with John Kaluta, I asked him if he saw any merit to taking a different tack, to being stingy instead of generous with technology. In other words, if it were politically possible (a doubtful proposition), would it make any sense to insist that students be asked to earn their time on computers? Those who had done their work, who'd mastered their prerequisites, would get computer time; those who didn't—well, back to the blackboards and the balsa wood. Kaluta found the concept tempting, to a point. "A carrot-and-stick approach?" he asked. "I don't know. If you hold [the computers] back, some students would end up never getting them. A lot of these students don't get time on computers anywhere else. And even those who don't excel do get used to the computer. By the time they finish this class, they've written a Web page, and there are tons of kids out there who don't even do that." What if it could somehow be done without unfairly favoring the privileged students? After pausing for a moment, he said, "It's an intriguing idea. It might work if it was sort of a *Father Knows Best* kind of thing, where the students did eventually get the computer." Then, as he reflected on his own class, he said, "I know what my father would have done. He would have taken the computer away."

THE LAW OF HALFWAY MEASURES

School computer initiatives generally follow some cruel rules—tied, not surprisingly, to money. No one disputes the fact that educational technology, if "done right," requires a substantial amount of financial support. Indeed, much of what motivates the nation's technology policy makers is their fervent belief that schools aren't getting anything close to the amount of money they need to put working, up-to-date computers at everyone's fingertips, to properly train their staffs, and so on.[6]

Their panic is not without reason. Look at the schools profiled thus far in this book. Several are considered stars of the educational technology movement. Yet it's abundantly clear that if each one doesn't devote an inordinate amount of money, time, and support to this innovation, many of the technologists' most ambitious academic efforts will remain a great disappointment. And all the computer campaign will have to show for itself is a scattering of halfway measures. This is not unusual. All sorts of reform efforts suffer from such treatment. It could be called the law of halfway measures, and it's one of the things that government does best. From food safety to environmental protection and financial auditing standards (of the kind that gave birth to the 2002 Enron fiasco), government oversight is riddled with insufficient safeguards. So too with public education, an undertaking that seems particularly ill suited to carrying out complex, highly sophisticated, and fast-changing visions. During discussions about school reform, educators here and abroad commonly say that teachers need four to six years to incorporate major new initiatives. Yet when computers arrive in the classroom, carrying their own imperatives, teachers are suddenly asked to keep up with technologies that become outdated every two or three years. It should come as no surprise years from now if many graduates and parents realize that their classrooms were used as dumping grounds for technology's throwaways.

And here in Montgomery County, despite its riches, computer technicians are still crying "Poorhouse." "Some schools with computers bought six years ago can't keep up with the county's requirements for Internet work," Peter Hammond, Blair's computer maintenance technician, told me. Hammond is all too familiar with student and teacher complaints about the system in his school constantly crashing. "We've got 800 computers and three maintenance staff. That's a ratio of one person for every 250 machines. In industry, you hear the ratio should be about one to 20." Interestingly, despite industry's greater investment in technical support, frustrations run rampant in its hallways as well. As an indication, when the nation's corporations were surveyed about their satisfaction with technology suppliers in the fall of 2002, more than half weren't terribly pleased with their service. A third indicated they would be happy to switch to another provider but probably wouldn't do so. Apparently, the attendant trouble and expense was too high, which left them feeling trapped into remaining with their original suppliers.[7]

There is a way to manage the technology dilemma, and it begins by realistically confronting its eternal troubles and costs. Strangely, this is a solution that most schools overlook.

Judging from spending patterns so far, the average school district isn't nearly as serious about technology as Montgomery County, or in any financial position to do anything about it even if it were. And at some point, the public may well want to cut back on the money it is devoting to school technology anyway. Signs of this shift occurred as early as the fall of 1999, when National Public Radio reported an extensive national survey that attempted to rank the public's multiple concerns about education. Responses indicated that the public's fervor for student access to technology had already faded dramatically; it ranked behind such issues as desires for smaller classes, increased parental involvement in school, improved school security, and control of student violence. In fact, computers and technology was at or near the bottom of a lengthy list. Only "discrimination against children because of race or gender" was considered less of a national problem. (Interestingly, when the school technology newspaper *eSchool News* asked several computing enthusiasts about these findings, some said the poll simply proved that the nation needed to spend still more money on school technology—to show everyone how significant computers can be.)

Technovangelistic fervor aside, it is pretty clear that the vast majority of the nation's schools will continue to function, for some time, without the financial support necessary for state-of-the-art systems to work properly. They will, in other words, have to find some way to work with the law of halfway measures rather than against it. There's no shame in halfway measures—as long as everyone admits that's just what they are. What's wrong is to attempt ambitious visions—and to enlist innocent parents and school administrators as supporters of those visions—and then fail to give the schools sufficient resources to carry out their grand plans.

Poverty can also be a blessing where technology is concerned. Curran's Mission Possible class is a prime example. Here's one of the school's most sophisticated classes, a course where students explore the confines of computer modeling in preparation for their final graduation projects. The machines a visitor finds in Curran's lab, however, are always six or seven years old. Curran doesn't mind. "I could teach robotics," he told me, "on an Apple IIe and BASIC"—a computer and a programming language that are 1970s technologies. "I could do the same things I do now." In fact, Curran and Johnson, his co-teacher, take great delight in their ability to make use of machines that others consider obsolete. "Just before they go to the dumpster, they come to me," Curran says with a laugh. Since these are computers that no one cares about any longer, the students feel free to tinker with them. They take them apart, try experimental programs, crash them, rewire them and, in the process, learn quite a bit about technology.

A handful of other schools around the country have been learning the same lesson. Mississippi, for instance, signed up high school students in 2002 to build six thousand computers for the state's schools. Not only did the students learn something about the inside of a computer (and, thus, some useful job skills); they also made some money (eight dollars an hour), and were expected to save the state nearly $2 million. As this program got off the ground, it suffered some instructive stumbles. Many computer parts never arrived at schools that signed up to build computers, and staff turnover crippled what little computer construction could be done. By mid-2003, one of the program's customers, South Delta Elementary, had gotten only four new student-built computers; it therefore returned to the open market, where it had better luck. "We're still behind, because technology, it changes so quick," said Lucille Lovette, South Delta's principal. "The money is just not available to keep up with it."[8]

Some classes at Blair make the case for an even tighter focus on computer basics. On a couple of occasions, I dropped in on a course humbly named Business Technology. This is where students learn their way around the standard computer functions of the modern workplace—spreadsheet programs, word processing programs, even typing. One instructor, a large, matronly woman, delivered her lesson in a didactic, matter-of-fact tone, without any of the charm and gusto the classic good teacher manages to muster day after day. As uninspiring as this class may sound, that's not how it struck the students. These were some of the most attentive, well-behaved students I saw during my visits. And the classes weren't even small. One had nearly thirty students, who were scattered throughout computerized cubicles in a long, L-shaped room. The instructor taught the class from a console at the center, where she sat slowly guiding the students step by step through Excel, Microsoft's ubiquitous spreadsheet program, occasionally burnishing a few of their math skills in the process. The Business Technology classes draw from Blair's non-magnet crowd, more than half of whom typically do not go on to a four-year college. These students know very well what technical skills they'll need under their belts when they leave Blair. And they're here to learn them.

———

While we're on the subject of debunking technology promoters' arguments, let's consider one more: In debates about the importance of classroom basics, the technologists often argue that they aren't trying to displace solid fundamentals. Technology isn't meant to be a replacement, they say, it's a supplement. This line has been uttered so frequently that it's become an educational computing mantra. But it's hollow, another e-lusion.

As we have seen all too well in Montgomery County, trying to fully support technology initiatives is extremely costly. Beyond the financial expense, there are the demands that computers make on a school's time and energy—to say nothing of a valuable commodity called public faith in school reforms. These are not flexible resources; every community can offer only a fixed amount of each one, and any amount devoted to technology leaves less available for other practices. So when technovangels argue that technology is only meant as a supplement, they're either fools or liars. It would be like stocking a school lunch cafeteria with cake and cookies and candy and saying that the sweets aren't meant to discourage students from eating the salad and potatoes at the end of the buffet; they're only a "supplement."

This axiom was demonstrated repeatedly at Blair, even with the school's magnet students. One morning, when the teacher of an Advanced Placement history class started students on a research exercise, noting that both computers and a nearby cart full of books were available as resources, the students spent the first part of class surfing the Internet. Eventually, when half of them had found little of interest and the other half had been frustrated by system crashes, most of the students turned to the books. By then, class was almost over.

This is how it goes. This is how schools, from the elite of Montgomery County to the small-town toilers in rural West Virginia, believe they're filling in modern society's parenting gap. This is how education is being defined in the twenty-first century. At least that's how our older, more entrenched school cultures have been treating the challenge.

CHAPTER 5

Starting from Scratch
with a Computer on Every Desk:
Napa, California

Walking the halls of New Technology High School, a bold new public school in Napa, California, visitors hear almost none of the noise commonly found in American public schools. This is partly because the school is small (only 220 students, all juniors and seniors), but it's mostly because of physical design. There are no bells, and each room and hallway is covered with wall-to-wall carpeting, which drapes the school in a kind of corporate quiet. Classrooms are separated not by the standard concrete walls of institutional yellow or green but by large glass panels. Peering through them, one sees classes of up to fifty or sixty students seated behind large computers, which are on every desk, and teachers holding forth like corporate trainers—marking up white boards, sitting behind elaborate workstations of their own, or quietly facilitating discussions from the side of the room. Workplace white and gray are the dominant colors—on the desks, on the computers, on the walls. The only notable exceptions are thick purple bundles of cable, which circle the ceilings like grapevines in some sci-fi Napa Valley of the future. Students seem happy, collegial, motivated. There's not a streak of graffiti anywhere.

New Tech's professional atmosphere grew out of its unique origins—the desire by its founders to create a state-of-the-art model training center for the workplace demands of tomorrow. The venture also produced an intriguing by-product. It gave the Napa community a chance to start over, educationally speaking, with a small, experimental academy that could be a school reformer's dream. This led to an enterprise that goes a long way toward answering one of education's most persistent questions: Is whole-scale school reform possible, or even desirable?

To accomplish their goal, New Tech High's founders set up a collaboration between the school district and a consortium of more than forty-five businesses, many of them high-tech firms. "We want to be the school that business built," Robert Nolan, the founding principal, told me in 1996, just before the school opened. "We wanted to create an environment that mimicked what exists in the high-tech business world." One of Nolan's partners, Ted Fujimoto, a local business consultant, told me that instead of just asking the business community for financial support, the school would now undertake a trade: in return for donating funds, businesses could specify what kinds of employees they want—"a two-way street."

Almost as soon as this vision was put into place, the school became a darling of the nation's educational technology community. Within a year of opening, it was turned into a "U.S. Department of Education Demonstration Site," and in 2000 the Department honored the school again, designating it as one of fifty-nine high schools across the country that were listed as a "New American High School." Many schools display multiple honors, but New Tech has been able to regularly pull in hard cash, too. During the Clinton administration, the Department of Education's vocational education division donated $300,000 to the school, and it was often singled out enthusiastically by Linda Roberts, the Department's former director of educational technology. In addition, the California Department of Education set up an ambitious contract with New Tech, making it the lead player in a statewide "Digital High School" initiative. In return for $250,000, New Tech has been conducting seminars roughly every month or two on how other schools can follow in its footsteps. High-profile corporate money has also joined the party. Several years after New Tech opened, the Bill and Melinda Gates Foundation gave the school $300,000 to refine its program. The Gateses are actually spending $5 million, over the course of five years, to start ten high-tech high schools throughout Northern California—part of their $350 million drive to build small high schools across the country. In California, they designated New Tech High as model number one.

The high-tech press, smelling an easy news sensation, has responded in kind. In late 1998, *Converge*, the glossiest of the many new publications that celebrate educational technology, ran a lengthy feature on the school, penned by JoAnne Miller, New Tech's director of External Relations, under the headline IF WE CAN DO IT, ANYONE CAN! Several months later, *Technology*

& Learning magazine joined in with a glowing account by the magazine's editor, entitled "New Technology High School: Preparing Students for the Digital Age." Miller, who is no longer with the school, used to beam over these accomplishments. "New Tech High," she once told me, "is the only school in the country that fully integrates technology well."

Before long, the school was drawing so many visitors—more than five thousand from its opening up to the spring of 2000—that anyone wishing to come for a look was scheduled for one of the school's bimonthly formal tours. Guests have included assorted luminaries, including Tipper Gore during her days as Second Lady. Over time, the tours have become quite an operation, led by a specially trained corps of student guides. "These are our product, our consumers, and our bosses," Miller said one spring morning, pointing to the three students who were leading a tour I was about to join.

One of the first stops was a large, relatively empty room that looked like an oversize control booth. It had glass walls on three sides and, sitting against the back wall, two gargantuan servers for the school's computer system (by 2001, the number had grown to four).

"This is the equivalent of our library," Daniel, our lead guide, says with a faint smile. But I notice there isn't a book or journal in sight. "There are thirty thousand feet of wiring in the school," Daniel tells us with another smile, this time because of the stunned look on his listeners' faces. Up front, a few standard desktop computers are connected to what the school calls its electric library, named after a commercial database of periodicals and texts.

As our guides lead us through the building, it is clear they have been well trained to lay out the school's story. Before New Tech even opened, they point out, school officials spent four years in planning with its various business partners, most of whom are local and wanted to create employees for new, "non-polluting jobs" in the Napa Valley. Not surprisingly, the facility, a refurbished former elementary school, is now the district's magnet school for technology. And its academic structure seems as futuristic as its building. There are no quizzes, no final exams. Admissions are deliberately non-exclusive (the only requirement is a C average), to attract students who may be perfectly capable but who, as JoAnne Miller wrote in *Converge*, "drift aimlessly through high school only to find themselves without direction when they graduate." Most of New Tech's students started at larger, traditional high schools, where they were unhappy, and came here in search of an environment that was more relaxed and intimate; many come from the area's poorer families, and almost a third are minorities. Yet Miller was confident that the environment at New Tech offered special stimulation; as proof, she would frequently point out that after students have been at New Tech only a semester or two, their grades usually rise, sometimes significantly.

After surveying the grounds, we poke our heads into a few classrooms. In a social studies class, a sprawling group of nearly fifty students has just been given a new assignment. As is the custom at New Tech, the first step entailed dividing the class into numerous groups of three and giving the students several relatively detailed pages outlining the requirements for a report due at the end of the week. As we look on, the students for the most part ignore us. Some flip through the new handout; some grumble or goof around, as teenagers do; a good number continue working on their computers. I glance at what they are doing at their keyboards. It's the same old story: e-mail, chat rooms, Internet sites that offer music, motorcycle products, and various other non-educational artifacts of the new information economy. "Ladies and gentlemen! Please!" one of this class's two teachers suddenly yells. "I want you off e-mail! I want you in your workstations. Now!"

Welcome to the all-new, all-digital high school classroom. So much novelty, so much possibility for both the ingenious and the shallow. All in all, it's quite a mixture. Alan Lesgold, a professor of psychology and the associate director of the Learning Research and Development Center at the University of Pittsburgh, once told me that the computer functions like an "amplifier," because it exaggerates both good study practices and bad ones. If Lesgold's metaphor is apt, if this machine really is turning up the volume on every routine it touches, it is in intensively computerized schools where the echoes play loudest. But what is the quality of those sounds? To get some indication, over the course of several years I kept returning to New Technology High School.

If computers are only partly fulfilling expectations at a large, well-funded, and technologically sophisticated school like Blair High School in Montgomery County, Maryland, that certainly gives well-deserved pause. But it also opens up another possibility: When educational technology's intelligentsia talk about their most annoying obstacles, most point to the institutional habits of the nation's older schools—their calcified bureaucracies, their dusty academic requirements, their tired, lifeless methods of teaching. To fully unleash the computer's power, they argue, schools have to entirely reconceive their methods of teaching and learning in general. For this crowd, technology is the essential ingredient in that pedagogical revolution, its academic sine qua non.

"Sure, changes in how schools teach have to happen, no matter what you do," Cheryl Lemke, a leading educational technology advocate, formerly with the Milken Family Foundation, once told me. "But they're not going to happen without technology." If Lemke's view is correct, then technology's best chance is at a school that can start afresh, building its entire program around technology—a place, in short, like New Tech High. And if schools are to take the message here seriously—"If we can do it, anyone can!"— they'll need to dissect what "it" really is.

THE COMPUTER'S REAL EDGE

Despite the computer's array of technical challenges, there are places where it can work wonders—primarily in school management. Boring as that may sound, these changes can have profound effects on a school and on how students feel about their daily experiences there. In this realm, schools like New Tech High have come up with a few innovations that really should be exported to other schools.

Perhaps surprisingly, most schools have been remarkably slow to take advantage of this opportunity, even those in hip urban centers. During one of my Napa visits, a group joining our tour was from Leland High, a large and somewhat elite public school of seventeen hundred students in San Jose, California. San Jose, of course, is the hub city in Silicon Valley, the buzzing epicenter of today's much-vaunted information age. Despite such futuristic surroundings, at the time of these students' visit there was no high school in their area that was anywhere close to being as wired as New Tech. So Leland's assistant principal and an assortment of student leaders had come north looking for ideas.

After the tour, when I interviewed Lily Sarafin, a student leader of the Leland brigade, the first item on her list of what she liked about New Tech was its method of delivering school-wide bulletins. Dubbed digital announcements, these messages are sent to each student's computer through e-mail, thereby obviating the noisy P.A. announcements commonly delivered by loudspeaker. People who don't work inside schools may not realize it, but P.A. announcements blare constantly in the vast majority of the nation's public schools; in fact, many teachers turn livid on this subject. They disrupt students' work and the flow of the class hour with mostly inconsequential bureaucratic notices. And their standard delivery, loud and crackling with static, conjures sensations of being in a prison rather than a school. Turning these annoyances into quiet e-mail is a blessing—and a small but solid hit for technology.

Another smart idea is to equip teachers with computers (once they've received sufficient training). One of the most unappreciated facts of life in education is the public's unrealistic yet ever growing demands on its teachers. These people—who survive on a secretary's salary—are expected, among other things, to push their students harder; provide individual attention; nurse youngsters through myriad social problems; and prepare them for a growing number of standardized tests. Now come politicians, from President Bush on down, who expect even more "accountability" from schools, which means more time devoted to bureaucratic reports on school amenities and ethnic breakdown, to say nothing of the annual assessments of students' academic performance. For a teacher to track all this information by hand is a nightmare, and nothing is lost by turning over a good bit of this chore to the computer.

As an illustration, as students were filing out of Paul Curtis's political studies class at New Tech one day, he showed off the speed at which he could generate evaluations of their work. Within thirty seconds, he'd tabulated a set of ratings into a one-page report. "Go pick up your evaluation—it's printing out right now," Curtis told one girl. "At the north printer?" she asked on her way out. Curtis nodded and started on another. Speed is not always helpful in learning, as we'll discover throughout this book. But it can have its advantages, especially for stressed-out teachers. "Do you know how long it would take me to do that on paper?" Curtis asked me. "Four hours. This allows me to spend more time on the creative part of my job."

The technology can also give outsiders prompt, detailed pictures of how students are faring. The mere existence of e-mail, for instance, has revolutionized the way teachers can talk to their students' parents. As proof, Kristine Fife Johnson, a teacher at Christa McAuliffe Academy, a private high school in Yakima, Washington, that operates entirely online, once offered the following experience. When she worked in a traditional school, she said, "The only time I could call parents was at five-thirty, in the middle of their dinner. It was not very realistic for us to have a meaningful conversation." With e-mail, Johnson and the parents could communicate at their convenience, by phone or online.[1]

As can be imagined, e-mail is just the beginning of computer technology's power to help schools communicate with the outside world. In 2001, a number of schools around the country began posting student-performance data on the Internet (partly in response to a looming federal directive). The result was a useful and burgeoning national database of "report cards" on schools of all kinds, which parents and others can review as time permits. Some school districts have also set up Internet forums, which have allowed school board members to poll parents on proposed ideas or to get detailed comments from them on controversial questions. One hopeful venture in this direction was something called Xchange: Strengthening Schools Through Board Discussions, launched in 2000 by the National School Boards Association with support from America Online. "Every shred of evidence tells us that the number one predictor of improved student learning is increased parental involvement," said then-chairman and CEO of AOL Steve Case in announcing the Xchange venture.[2] Hyperbole aside, Case was on to something. And while parents haven't used Xchange quite as consistently as Case and the school boards association expected, school superintendents have generally found that the system helped board members get better acquainted with their constituents and with technology's obstacles and true potential.*

As school-information networks have developed, they have revolutionized the concept of record keeping—with good and bad results. Some districts have created financial disasters for themselves by trying to update or add onto massive but problematic old computerized administration systems. (These networks are disparagingly referred to in the trade as legacy systems. The reason is that if a district goes too far down the road with a bad system—one that's old, flawed, or simply incompatible with newer technology—it can find itself chained to that system's troubled legacy for years.) Other districts—those unburdened by old systems or wealthy enough to make the digital leap to a new one—have found themselves in a field of bureaucratic riches. As early as the mid-1990s, schools in Henrico County, Virginia, were already putting individual education plans for their special-education students online, where administrators, teachers, and parents could review them anytime. It wasn't until the first years of the twenty-first century, though, that high school students could register for classes online, thus sparing themselves the hassles and long lines that characterize registration day. Still, by 2002, this was an option in only a handful of the nation's schools.[3] While back-office advances are a boon, schools such as New

---

*The potential of administrative computing systems has attracted considerable industry attention as well. In 1997, the Annenberg Foundation gave Florida $33.4 million to help principals and school administrators get up to speed with computing. In 2001, Microsoft's Bill Gates and his wife, Melinda, through their foundation, gave funds for similar purposes to several states, with a goal of donating $100 million to all fifty states by 2003. Such heavy commitments from the technology and philanthropic communities could offer government budgets some welcome relief. There certainly seems to be little harm in leaving more of the expense of the schools' administrative computing systems to the technology industry, which seems to have found some steady customers. See "Students to Teach School Administrators About Technology," *eSchool News*, August 2001, p. 16.

Tech High believe the computer's academic rubber doesn't meet the road until they dare to put these machines in front of each one of their students.

EXPLORING THE WORLD FROM YOUR DESK

"You see the computers here," Daniel says during our tour. "But that's not the focus. It's project-based learning—the new style of learning." Daniel laughs slightly as he adds this last comment, knowing it has become New Tech High's mantra. Project-based learning has become so central to the school's self-image that New Tech regularly offers special one- and two-day "institutes" on the concept. In the school's view, project-based learning is the academic counterpart to the way people will increasingly work in the "new economy."

While this approach to teaching has a lot going for it, it's also old news. It was originated in Europe in the mid-1800s by Friedrich Froebel, the inventor of kindergarten. Here in the United States, it was promoted by the famous turn-of-the-century education reformer John Dewey, and schools have been incorporating the practice to varying degrees ever since.* The idea sounds like common sense: let students spend several days or several weeks conducting true inquiries—independent, in-depth explorations, ideally with a multidisciplinary orientation—and they will more fully engage their curiosity. It also seems more like the way people work in real life. When an architect, for example, tackles a design problem, she uses mathematics, the fine arts, history, and even anthropology and psychology. But a multidisciplinary approach to schoolwork has never been widely accepted. Indeed, when debates arise among big-name education reformers, much of the

---

*Although Dewey is widely considered to be the father of learning by doing, he didn't always practice what he preached. Dewey did demonstrate his theories, by launching an exceptional, small private "laboratory" school at the turn of the century at the University of Chicago, which continues to this day in altered form. But the bulk of his own teachings took a different turn. At the college level, Dewey promoted his philosophies while standing at the front of the room lecturing in high traditional style, usually in rather abstract terms. It was William Heard Kilpatrick, a professor of history and education at Teachers College at Columbia, who developed, popularized, and somewhat diluted Dewey's ideas, beginning with a 1918 essay for *Teacher's College Record* entitled "The Project Method." Though not well known today, Kilpatrick attracted a vigorous and loyal following during the first half of the 1900s—and the continuing enmity of education's traditionalists. See *Dewey's Laboratory School: Lessons for Today*, by Laurel N. Tanner, Teachers College Press, 1997; *And There Were Giants in the Land: The Life of William Heard Kilpatrick*, by John A. Beineke, Peter Lang Publishing, 1998; *Left Back: A Century of Failed School Reform*, by Diane Ravitch, Simon & Schuster, 2000, pp. 178–83.

argument concerns the virtues—or the emptiness—of teaching through projects. For example, E. D. Hirsch, founder of the Core Knowledge school-reform movement and the leading traditional theorist, believes that while projects may feel good, they weaken the rigor of old-fashioned, fact-based lessons and leave too much material uncovered. Nonsense, today's progressives counter—students don't remember half the facts they learn anyway. If students are truly engaged in exploration, the progressives argue, they'll see meaning in what they're doing, which will lead them to retain the factual material that matters. And so this debate has gone for decades, through wave upon wave of reform.[4]

Now comes the computer, education's eight-hundred-pound gorilla, landing in this debate with a thud. Not surprisingly, it made its nest a little differently on each side of the discussion.

While traditional schools have begun using computers, they've generally done so, as might be expected, in traditional ways (that is, by sticking to the three R's—reading drills, computerized math exercises, and some standard writing and Internet research). One of the most curious traditionalists to promote school computing is William J. Bennett, who was education secretary under President Ronald Reagan. In his exhaustive 1999 book *The Educated Child,* Bennett was quite skeptical about whether computers could do much for student achievement. A year later, in December 2000, he started a for-profit education enterprise called K12, which sought to deliver classroom materials, surprisingly enough, via computers, beginning with the very youngest students—kindergarten through second grade. In forming his company, Bennett pulled in some big names. One was David Gelernter, a Yale professor of computer science and a frequent critic of school technology, who signed on as K12's technical adviser; another was Lowell Milken, who runs his own education company, Knowledge Adventure, with his brother, Michael Milken, the formerly imprisoned junk bond financier. (The Milkens reportedly invested an initial $10 million in Bennett's venture.) While computer skeptics have called Bennett hypocritical for commercially embracing what he once called nonsense, Bennett has justified his venture by structuring it around his conservative values. K12 distributes curriculum materials that are relatively traditional—back-to-basics lesson plans in science and math, for instance, or phonetic reading drills, all of which are dressed up slightly with multimedia effects for today's image-needy youngsters. Primary markets for K12's products have been the cyberschools, which are growing in number, and the homeschooling crowd, whose cause Bennett vigorously applauds. "We say 'traditional learning, powerful technology,'" Bennett said.[5]

Bennett's enthusiasm aside, the teachers who have embraced technology most wholeheartedly have tended to come from education's progressive wing. To this group, which includes the staff of New Tech High, the computer is the perfect device: It freshens what has long been a somewhat radical philosophy with an air of legitimacy and cutting-edge modernity. In fact, the progressives argue, today's computer's powers are so significant that they fundamentally change the potential of class work. And that potential is perhaps most fully realized in student projects.

To many if not most visitors, a lot of New Tech's way of putting that argument into practice is impressive. The visiting students from San Jose, for instance, got very excited about the way a project approach to learning seems to open up a class, giving it a broad, interdisciplinary scope. The day they arrived, students were studying the Great Depression in a class called American Studies, which blends history and English. On the surface, assignments are the typical high school routines: biographies of famous figures, reports on World War I, or other projects, large or small. Students also venture out occasionally into the community for interviews with local residents or professors at the nearby community college. After touring a few New Tech classes, Patrick, a Leland senior and the student body president, said, "It seems like the motivation isn't trying to get the grade but how to get the skills. There's no cheating, because there's no tests. It's more like a workplace."

The normal approach, taken at the vast majority of American schools, both public and private, can be deadening in comparison. It's all too familiar to Lily Sarafin, the student leader and documentarian of the New Tech field trip. "At our school," Lily told me, "when you study the Depression, you sign up for a history class. Then you go to a lecture, you take notes, you take a test, and you forget it." Literature on the Depression is then handled in an English class, if at all; and the economic lessons of the period, which can have fascinating sociological overtones, get delegated to economics classes, where they're homogenized into abstract textbook theory. "Nothing is connected," Lily said.

Those connections are what New Tech High hopes to make vibrant, largely through computer projects. By the end of our visits, however, both Leland's seniors and I had noticed numerous signs that New Tech wasn't exactly closing the loop. At first, the gaps looked like typical computer-room chaos. Upon closer inspection, however, it became clear that in New Tech's computer-intensive culture something different was going on. The school was indeed modeling new standards for how students and teachers each do their jobs.

HIGH-TECH TEAMWORK

One spring morning, Paul Curtis was trying to teach his seniors an extra lesson about adult responsibilities: For several weeks, he let them teach his government-studies class. The students were grouped into teams (of two, in this case), each of which took turns assuming the helm for three days. Their job was to devise assignments that would cover a single chapter in the class's history textbook; they could also choose how the students' work would be evaluated—through multiple-choice tests, writing assignments, or public presentations. At the end of their three-day stints, Curtis would grade each team on how much the class as a whole learned.

The exercise was the quintessence of New Tech pedagogy. "It's more being treated as equals," Kyle Lewis, a senior, said in the article for *Converge*. "There's a lot of respect going both ways." To Lily Sarafin, of Leland, it seemed like "students weren't really being taught; they were learning by themselves." New Tech's administrators and teachers credit computers for this apparent shift, as do most outsiders who have visited the school.

On this particular day, a pair of Curtis's student teachers is asking the class to examine, and then orally argue, an assortment of significant United States Supreme Court cases. I join a trio of students who have been given the 1964 libel case *New York Times Co. v. Sullivan,* a dispute tied to the civil rights protests of Martin Luther King, Jr., which provoked a ruling that has guided lawsuits against nosy reporters ever since. After failing to find material on the case in the school's "electric library," my trio of students tries the Web. "Oh come on," complains one student, whom I'll call Stefan. "There's no information on the Internet. You should know that." Stefan's peers ignore him and continue searching. Or, more precisely, one does. The class is given roughly a half-hour to look into its cases; during that time, the actual hands-on research (that is, managing the computer mouse) is commonly done by just one member of the team, which leaves the others to fend for themselves. In a few groups, the second or third members of the team take the initiative to look for material in their textbooks. But most just wait for the computer to finish its searches, during which time they behave like any student given a break: They mess around, talk to their friends, or stare into space.

Eventually, the team I'm watching finds a useful article on the case in the school's electric library (after getting help from their teacher). They then proceed to engage in one of New Tech High's special pedagogical tricks— a role-playing exercise: One student plays the prosecuting attorney, one represents the defense, and the third will advise. "I don't have any facts," Stefan says as he sits down at his computer to write his argument. "I'm just going on the morals." One of Stefan's partners, whom I'll call Peter, turns to his terminal and pounds out three impassioned sentences. The central problem in this case, Peter writes, is that Sullivan's rights were violated [in a newspaper ad] and he is justified in being "flaming mad" that people are spreading lies about him. All around, other students compose similar stabs at analysis on other cases. The real teachers meanwhile sit quietly at the side of the room, content with how their students are fully in charge of their own learning.

After roughly an hour, each group presents its findings, taking turns at the front of the room to speak as a panel. While a number of students are quite articulate, their presentations seem remarkably short on substance. During the question period following my group's presentation, for example, one student wisely asks what the original ad in *The New York Times* actually said. "I don't know," Peter says. "We weren't given the ad."

VIRTUAL RESEARCH

There are clearly many things wrong with this picture, some of which could be controlled with a little common sense. But the root causes of the intellectual disarray, in the students as well as the teacher, are more subtle. And those roots are growing, to varying degrees, in other schools that attempt to be on technology's leading edge. Let's start with the students and their method of doing research. When I asked JoAnne Miller, the New Tech external relations director, whether classes like Curtis's could engage in the same projects but with more traditional research materials, she responded with an often heard answer: "Yes, you could do these same things without technology," she said. "It's just easier with it."

One might argue the reverse, at least during the stage of technological progress in which the schools found themselves at the beginning of the twenty-first century. Take what happened in Curtis's class as my group foraged for useful information. At one point, I asked Stefan why he'd become disenchanted with the Internet. The reason, he said, is that he finds the material gathered by electronic search tools insufficient. "If you want to find real knowledge, go to a library or ask someone who knows. Don't look on the Internet."

Stefan is partly right, for reasons we'll get to in a moment. The problem is that, like most of his peers, Stefan doesn't spend much time in a library. There are several available nearby—a city library is downtown; others, at the two neighboring high schools and at the local community college, are not far off. And the teachers ask students to visit them. But their requests don't pack much punch, partly because, on research papers and other projects, books are not routinely required to be among students' sources. With online options so easy and seemingly so sufficient, most students visit outside libraries infrequently, if at all. As Stefan told me, "I usually just go and get what the teacher tells me to do."

But why does it matter that students go to a library? The material available online would seem to be more than enough for a high school research project. Not only is there the ever-expanding Internet, but New Tech students also have their "electric library," with its hundreds of books and periodicals. As prodigious as both resources sound, they're cursed with some significant limitations. Some are obvious; some, including the most serious, are not.

Take the school's electric library, which is named after the commercial service that supplies the school with its material. One of the students' most frequent complaints was that the system wasn't kept up-to-date, which should be its primary virtue. In perusing the system myself, I also noticed that the commercial Electric Library website boasted "2,000 complete works of literature," a "complete encyclopedia," a dictionary, a thesaurus, books of facts, and "premium content" from hundreds of periodicals. Digging a layer deeper into each of these, I was surprised by what was really included and what was missing. The encyclopedia was *The Encyclopedia of Australia,* and the books were largely an odd assortment of obscure specialty books, hardly what most would call "works of literature." In the newspaper section, journalism's mainstays—such as *The Wall Street Journal, The New York Times,* and the *Los Angeles Times*—were strangely absent. So too with the magazine section, which included *Time, Newsweek,* and some business and commercial special-interest magazines but did not list most of the media's in-depth publications—magazines like *The New Yorker, The Atlantic Monthly,* or *Harper's.* The absence of some of these publications, such as *Harper's* and *The New Yorker,* couldn't be directly blamed on the Electric Library, because they weren't yet available in electronic form. But when schools pay $2,500 to $3,000 a year, which is what a subscription to the Electric Library costs, one would think that they would be shrewd enough to demand a service that contains some of our most sophisticated sources of news. Failing that, they might at least subscribe to these magazines in traditional form—an expense that would be less than 5 percent of the Electric Library's cost. But to the New Tech Highs of the world, the frontiers of the online world are so intoxicating that no one thinks about tired old magazines and books. So they get material that, in the Electric Library's case, is often somewhat less than neutral. Curiously, the state has given New Tech High special funds each year to buy books; until recently, however, the school had seen no need to do so. By the spring of 2001, its book budget had an unspent fund of $16,000.

———

But what about the wide wonders of the Internet? The research picture here, it turns out, has been mixed at best. Consider the following facts: By the middle of 2000, by one estimate, roughly half the world's research materials were already online, and more than a million Web pages were being added to the Internet each day, many of which have contained some interesting educational material.[6] Nonetheless, a survey in the spring of that year reported that three out of four search attempts were still leading to the wrong information. Two years later, about 20 percent of the public websites that had existed nine months earlier had disappeared because their authors had gone out of business; others, suffering from neglect, no longer worked properly or were long out of date.

It was also clear at the time that more trouble was on the way. By early 2002, use of the Web, by both developers and consumers, was already starting to decline. One poll, by the Pew Internet and American Life Project, found a dramatic drop in the number of people who said the Internet helped "a lot" in enabling them to learn new things. (In 2000, about half the respondents agreed with this assessment; by March 2002, that figure had fallen to 39 percent.) More and more, it seemed, people turned to the Internet simply to get something done quickly—not to expand their horizons of knowledge.[7] Soon informational disappointments in the digital world only worsened. As investment capital continued to dry up for Internet ventures that were more educational than profitable, business prospects for the Internet began imitating other cycles of media development in the past: By the middle of 2002, what increasingly filled the Internet's void were hundreds of lucrative sites serving up pornography, swindles, and various other samples of sleaze.[8] By the end of the year, websites oriented to the education market were proving to be so evanescent that researchers monitoring the phenomenon created a term for it: "link rot."[9] Meanwhile, whenever the computing public was hit with another wave of virus attacks, technology experts noted that legitimate coding development—in software design, in security systems, and for search engines—wasn't moving nearly as fast as the arcane tricks that hackers devise.[10] Those tricks aren't just viruses; they also involve ingenious ways to manipulate data such as website rankings, which tends to make research findings unreliable.

Smart teachers and determined students should be able to pick their way through these obstacles, just as everyone else has to. But for an average high school student—to say nothing of a child in the younger grades—those Internet obstacles can be overwhelming. They go far beyond the material that is continually sensationalized in the press—the wacko information, the myriad consumer temptations, and the other detritus of today's hyper–market oriented culture. If anything, these distractions have begun to serve an almost accidental function: They give people a false sense of shrewdness. Once anyone penetrates the Net's first few layers of junk, it's easy to think that the hard work has been done and that whatever information remains should be relatively solid. When it comes to learning the principles of academic research, however, nothing could be further from the truth.

The problem was well explained to me at one point by Garrett Epps, a professor of constitutional law at the University of Oregon. Epps, a former journalist and the author of several books, is an avid Internet user and quite expert in technology. The Internet's problem, he believes, is that it's "essentially ahistorical." When researchers go to work, Epps notes, one of their primary jobs is to place any information they're looking at in context. This means finding out what thinking or beliefs are dominant in that field, or were dominant at the time of someone's writing, and how that thinking has evolved through the years. It also means learning what in particular authors may be reacting to in their writing, what elements of the research are their own original findings (called primary research) and which parts are secondary (from other sources, which writers glean, as Epps put it, "from the received wisdom of their time"). These issues constitute the "layers" of information that several teachers at Maryland's Blair High School found so difficult to impart to their media-saturated students. Leafing methodically through a solid book is one good way to clarify these levels of knowledge.

This work is not done simply by perusing the listings in a book's index—literature's equivalent to keywords on an Internet search engine. A well-researched non-fiction book offers a multifaceted portrait of its author's worldview. At its reader's disposal are an organizing table of contents, various appendices, detailed bibliographies, endnotes and footnotes, and the thought-provoking serendipity that comes from imaginatively browsing the entire pile. This, Epps explains, provides "a sense of a writer's theory of knowledge and how he selects his information. You don't pick that up on the

Net. If you're doing your research online, there's no context to it. There's this sort of eternal present."

The Net also makes little distinction between good information and bad, a more commonly heard concern. It might seem simple to alert students to those distinctions, but it isn't. Even traditional literature sometimes goes to pains to blur marks of quality—all the more reason to school youngsters in the notion of textual refinement before they jump into Internet research. "There's good secondary [source material] versus weak secondary," as Epps put it, "and weak secondary versus nuts." Epps is just one of several university professors I've spoken with who have noticed a gradual deterioration in the quality of research in students' papers. There's a reason for this decline. According to a survey released in late 2002, roughly 60 percent of the nation's high school teachers no longer assign basic research papers (of three to five thousand words), and 80 percent no longer assign more extensive papers, even in Advanced Placement (AP) courses. Apparently, with the growing pressures of standardized tests and increasingly fact-stuffed curricula linked to those tests, teachers don't have the time to evaluate research papers. They also don't feel much need to, since the state tests and graduation requirements rarely demand research skills. Even when teachers do assign research papers, fewer and fewer students know how to do the work. "It's very challenging material," says Lynda Motiram, a social studies teacher in Millersville, Maryland. "We have to first spend time on basic things. . . . I am constantly surprised by the poverty of the writing skills of these extremely smart and insightful students." Not surprisingly, when college professors and employers were surveyed recently, three fourths of them rated the writing skills of high school graduates as fair or poor.[11] In many cases, students have become so habituated to the Internet that if they don't find what they're looking for online, they assume it doesn't exist—or that it isn't significant. And when they do find something online, their treatment of the material often raises more questions than it answers. Teachers everywhere talk about students, even in AP classes, who copy large portions of their papers off the Internet. Epps said he's amazed by how often he sees even law students "ginning up these quotations that are unattributed to anyone. They've become the urban-legend version of research."

Undoubtedly, the Internet will steadily improve. More and more material of all kinds will be published there; search engines will likely increase their power and specificity; and both teachers and students have every opportunity to get smarter about how they use these tools. But that doesn't justify the romanticized ways that schools used the Internet in the 1990s. And it didn't much help matters for the immediate future. For an entire decade of many students' academic lives—if not longer—shelf after shelf of research materials available in the physical world haven't been available on the Internet. And those materials will be months if not years late when they finally do appear, if they appear at all. (In 2001, the Supreme Court slowed things down even further, with a ruling that requires online databases to secure writers' permission before publishing their work.)[12]* Also included on physical library shelves are reams of useful documents: decades of old (and new) scholarly journals; numerous out-of-print books; storehouses of historic government documents; and hundreds if not thousands of Ph.D. dissertations, to name but a few of the primary-source materials that, to the uninformed Internet researcher, might appear nonexistent.

Whenever the day comes that this material is online, the databases required to hold and organize it will have to include searching systems that are far more sophisticated than anything available, or even envisioned, today. Navigating those systems may be easy technically, but it won't be any easier intellectually. Researchers will still need the ability to identify subtle but telling distinctions in their sources of information—distinctions that the Internet tends to pave over.

Ironically, those who will be at an advantage in this work will not be the ones who spent their academic years leaning on their computers. It will be those who forced themselves to confront the complexities and contradictions that lurk inside the stacks of our nation's libraries. Technology's job, in other words, is not to make research "easier." Its role is to add electronic resources, particularly the most current materials, to the treasures that exist on paper and in one's own observations in the real world. The computer should help research become more varied, more complex, more nuanced, more multifaceted, more up-to-date—and more complete. It should not make it easier. But at schools like New Tech, we get the reverse idea. When a school celebrates electronic resources as limited as the "electric library," the value of traditional resources gets crowded out in the most insidious way: People simply forget about them.

*For some indication of what effects copyright law has on the material available on the Internet, one only has to look at Project Gutenberg—an ambitious, non-commercial venture started in 1971 to make entire books available on the Internet (*promo.net/pg/*). By early 2003, the service had posted approximately seven thousand books. Because of copyright obstacles, however, virtually all of these had been published before 1923. None of this discouraged Lightning Source, an e-book wholesaler, which forged a deal with Palm, Inc. to offer five hundred of the very same public domain books to schools for a fee: $750 a year. See *Publishers Weekly Newsline*, February 5, 2003.

A KINDER, GENTLER TEACHER

Obviously, there are multiple ways that smart teachers can avoid the Internet's black holes. The common perception is that teachers everywhere are taking advantage of computers—and of the Net in particular—to make great academic breakthroughs. During several years of work on this subject, people constantly told me about teachers who were doing just that, and I did see some illustrations of their argument. In Moorhead, Minnesota, for example, the Robert Asp Elementary School linked all the computers in its main lab and connected the teacher's terminal to an overhead projection screen. When it was time to explore the Internet, the teacher could demonstrate his recommended research paths and get all the students quite literally on the same page. In other classes—usually in a high school, where a little extra maturity could be counted on—teachers occasionally managed to keep research standards high, forcing students to go beyond the easy Internet sites when composing their papers.

As the Internet develops, sophisticated teaching methods are occasionally growing along with it. The one-year anniversary of the September 2001 terrorist attacks demonstrated the Net's scholastic potential quite profoundly. As the tragedy's anniversary approached, all kinds of intriguing materials sprouted on the Internet—impassioned discussion sites praising America (and blaming her); collections of relevant poetry; emotional photo-essays; curriculum plans on Islamic history and on how to properly fold the study of religion into social studies, to name but a few. Any of these could produce thoughtful classroom discussions, writing assignments, and a variety of research projects. What stunned me, however, is how smart activities like these consistently proved to be the exception. Almost every time I visited classrooms where the teacher, or someone else, had boasted that great technological learning was going on, the actual exercises staged were nearly empty of intellectual content. How could the contradiction between perception and reality be so severe? Why would teachers get so close to something useful and then miss its opportunity so profoundly?

Perhaps there's something in the very burn of electronic technology that distorts the vision. Look again at the methods of New Tech's teachers, which begin with the idea of grouping students into teams. This practice is celebrated at many high-tech schools, for two reasons. First, it's generally believed that teamwork, like projects, is becoming the professional norm, especially in the high-tech industry. "It's much more realistic," Paul Curtis says. "There are far fewer jobs where it's just you." Second, the computer, with its great dynamism, seems like the perfect tool to keep a team busy with multiple tasks. Nearly all the academic projects at New Tech are therefore done by student teams.

The practice sets in motion some curious dynamics. To begin with, groups have a tendency to defer to their most dominant member—and teenagers are particularly susceptible to this tendency. At New Tech, whenever I watched a class divide up into teams, it was clear within minutes who the dominant student was and who was the most passive one. (Team members are allowed to "fire" non-performing members, but understandably, students at this age almost never do this to one another. Their other option is to complain privately to the teacher later—a seemingly less appealing solution but one that is frequently used.) Teachers are well aware of these obstacles and often try to bypass them by mixing up the teams. But the pecking order usually recurs, with different players.

The math on New Tech's vision of teamwork isn't particularly pretty. With trios as the norm for student teams, this means that on any given assignment, a lesson can be weakened—sometimes severely—for up to two thirds of the class. Then there's the effect on social relationships. Since new projects are constantly being assigned, students are forced to act out popularity contests weekly, if not daily. In one class I watched, in which the students were allowed to sort themselves into groups, a young man had to ask the teacher after class to find him a team, since no one had chosen him. After school, I happened to see this student leaning against the school building, in tears, while a female classmate tried in vain to console him.

Once the teams have been set up, the main piece of New Tech's pedagogy begins—seen in Curtis's method of sitting back a bit, inserting himself only occasionally as a facilitator for the students' individual explorations. The style is widely celebrated by education's technology enthusiasts, who consider the computer's powers and offerings so substantial that students can often be left to their own devices. There's a larger context to this methodology, however, which takes some of the shine off the computer advocates' boasts. Two points are at issue.

First, as with student projects, this approach to teaching was invented long before computers hit the classrooms. It has been around since at least 1921, when A. S. Neill founded the famous Summerhill School in England, shoving progressive education theories into the limelight once again. Educators even have a catchy phrase for teachers who practice this philosophy: "the guide on the side instead of the sage on the stage." It isn't easy to make the concept work, but I've seen plenty of teachers do it. They're usually among a school's most talented: bright, exceptionally knowledgeable, intensely curious, and blessed with genuine regard for young people's capabilities. Perhaps most of all, they're comfortable with a certain amount of chaos—the second point of concern.

No matter how comfortable a teacher feels about being "the guide on the side," the laws of physics still apply: The greater the number of directions that the class as a whole pursues with students' individual projects, the less time there is for the teacher to attend to each one. And computers don't much help the proportions here. They take the normal student inquiry and quickly multiply it into an array of complications, involving not only technical difficulties but also myriad research choices. Before long, the questions become too numerous and complex for most teachers to properly attend to. As we've seen, this happens so regularly that I began to think an atmosphere of disorganization in the high-tech classroom has become commonplace. While this may be the norm, it often leaves students feeling frustrated. At New Tech, many students never found particularly good material for their class projects, simply because they never got one-on-one time with the teacher.

An interesting by-product of this dynamic is an overall atmosphere of laziness. In school after school, we have also seen that as teachers struggled to give individual students the attention they needed, others had little to do but socialize. It's tempting to say this is a teacher's fault, that he should have given the students other tasks to do while they were waiting. But it gradually became clear that turning to serious work at such moments doesn't make much sense for the waiting students, because they must also keep an eye out for the teacher—and for the computer's intermittent bursts of success or failure. Both students and teachers realize this. That's why Net-searching classes tend to collapse into a social hour. This yields a whole new form of classroom disarray. It's school as a party, sanctified and institutionalized by education's authorities. After a while, as I watched a number of such classes around the country, I began to feel as if I were observing some modern version of the Heisenberg effect: The mere existence of computers in the classroom seems to alter the atmosphere. And more often than not, it encourages everybody in the room to go off task.

In Curtis's class, it was particularly obvious what everyone missed. As it turns out, there actually are online resources on the famous libel case Curtis asked my group of students to research; in fact, by using another one of the standard Internet search sites, I later found the entire opinion—a twenty-six-page document that one would not likely find in full in school textbooks. Finding trenchant analysis of the opinion, however, especially of a sort that's synthesized enough to be comprehensible to high school students, was another matter. That, of course, is why schools have long depended on standard resources: namely, good books (including some textbooks) and good teachers. By all appearances, Curtis is a good teacher—whenever he engages with students, it's clear from the exchange that he knows his material, can discuss it in an interesting manner, and enjoys the students' respect. But Curtis was so enthralled with how computers let students take charge of their own learning that he didn't feel the need to use his teaching skills—stepping in, say, to refine his students' inquiries, or simply to introduce other research sources.*

This is the what high-tech academic culture does to itself. In school after school, when teachers, even good teachers, embrace technology, their next step is to believe that the computer's power relieves them of many of their didactic responsibilities. As proof, in my follow-up conversations with Curtis, it was clear that he too noticed the shallowness in his students' work that day. Yet he was untroubled by the situation. If anything, he was quite proud of the dynamic he had staged and of how the students had taught the class by themselves. The scene epitomized New Tech's ideal and the philosophy that it is vigorously exporting to other schools.

WHAT MATTERS IS "WHAT YOU SHOW"

One March morning, I joined several dozen visiting teachers and administrators in the New Tech High cafeteria for one of the school's workshops (or "institutes") on project-based learning. The cafeteria is a standard school lunchroom (big, windowless, with long brown tables everywhere), with one striking difference: The walls are adorned with a dozen large banners from technology's big boys—Microsoft, Lotus, Hewlett-Packard, Pacific Bell, among others—and a few local business leaders. "This is not advertising," JoAnne Miller told us as she welcomed the group to the school. In fact, she said, the school had asked for these banners. "This is a thank-you from us to our partners." At each seat lay a two-inch-thick gray binder filled with printed material that aimed to document each stage of the school's academic process.

---

*One might ask what Curtis could have offered his students if he had stepped in, and had stooped to include materials that aren't so cutting-edge. In the *New York Times* case, a pretty complex lesson could be created simply by giving students a copy of the original ad, an account of the decisions from the lower courts, and a passage from any one of the many good books on these incidents, such as *Pillar of Fire*, by Judith Tarr, or *Make No Law*, by Anthony Lewis.

After some general remarks, Miller turned the floor over to Mark Morrison, the school's clean-cut, folksy principal—or, as he's listed on the school website, its CEO/Director. Morrison began by expanding on why the school considers project-based learning (PBL in New Tech High–speak) so critical. In the coming years, Morrison said, companies around the world will need more and more people with high-tech, quasi-scientific skills, as exemplified by the growth in the biotech industry. The demand will become so intense, Morrison fears, that students will need to come to college with a head start on these skills; otherwise, employers will increasingly fill their higher-paying jobs with recruits from overseas. "We might as well join the club rather than fight them," Morrison told the crowd. To do its part, Morrison said, New Tech set out to "build a technology-rich, project-based, subject-integrated curriculum. Where do you buy that? There's nowhere. And we looked around." Thus was New Tech's pedagogy born. "It's about educators really lettin' go," as Morrison put it, "lettin' the students almost take over."

To illustrate what he meant, Deborah Aufdenspring, the social studies teacher, showed several students' projects. Each one was a high-end multimedia slide show, known in the technology trade as a PowerPoint presentation. (Named after Microsoft's popular PowerPoint program, the term has become embedded in today's lexicon, just as "Xeroxing" has for photocopying.) A few of these projects showed depth and creativity. One, for example, was about a boy's father's experiences in Vietnam; the presentation offered an array of interesting photos, snippets of interviews the student had conducted with his father's fellow veterans, and a sprinkling of background history. In most projects, however, the academic content was pretty thin. Once again, while the graphics were almost always impressive, the analytical material—the variety of sources used, the depth of material from each one, and the quality of the writing—was surprisingly simplistic. After a paragraph or two, most students considered their job done.

Later, when I returned for New Tech's day of gathering outsiders to evaluate students' year-end portfolios, the problem was even more evident. One project, by a young woman I'd been introduced to earlier as one of the school's best students, consisted of reviews of two simulation games. Simulation programs are quite controversial in technology circles because of their artificiality and, many experts contend, the hidden bias that often guides their structure. As a result, there are many opinions on these games, each one backed up by stacks of literature. Strangely, the girl's reviews explored none of these critiques. Her website, like those of her peers, did carry numerous statements promoting what she felt she had learned, such as: "I think I demonstrate a lot of critical thinking."

One of my fellow evaluators—Cynthia Bulger, who administers a local group serving at-risk youth—was shocked by what she saw. "How are you going to get into a university with those kinds of writing skills?" she asked me. "I have an eighth grader who's already doing more than this." Bulger is no opponent of technology; her organization, the CyberMill Clubhouse, is one of a growing number of "Digital Clubhouses" started by the MIT computer whiz and LOGO enthusiast Mitch Reznick. Nonetheless, after looking at one portfolio, in which a student with aspirations in music had written about little more than her hopes and dreams, Bulger couldn't believe the teachers hadn't required more work. "You want to be a musician? You want to play the guitar? Go research it. This isn't really showing me anything. All in all, I think they kind of missed the boat on what portfolios are all about. I mean, if we're going to stick all this money into technology . . ." Several visiting teachers I spoke with at New Tech's workshops were similarly underwhelmed, and said they had seen more robust examples of project learning at schools that were much less high-tech.

It may seem odd that students would do so little hard analysis and then fill their reports with statements professing their analytical skill. But in a sense, this is what they're taught to do. As New Tech political studies teacher Paul Curtis told us during the evaluations, one of the school's slogans is "It doesn't matter what you know. It matters what you show."

TRUST

In fairness, New Tech's emphasis on public presentations has some value. I spoke with several graduates who felt that doing this sort of work had strengthened their confidence and their ability to express themselves. "It probably led to more development of my social life than my academic life," Daniel told me about a year after he'd graduated. Yet, like many of New Tech's achievements, this has nothing to do with technology. I visited plenty of schools where students learned to work together and articulate their ideas, orally and in writing, without computers having much of a role in the process.

The same pattern of self-delusion afflicts a feature of New Tech's culture of which teachers and students are particularly proud—what the school calls its "community of trust." Everyone here loves to point out that students are on a first-name basis with the administrators; that they easily hang out in the principal's office if they've got a problem or just want to chat; that students are free to walk in and out of class without having to get hall passes; that they're allowed to come in after hours and on weekends to work with the computers, or anything else, as long as a teacher is around; and that there's virtually no school crime. Safety is so widely felt that students commonly leave backpacks and wallets on their desks without fearing they'll be stolen. This atmosphere—and the students' devotion to it—is among the qualities that most impress outside visitors, particularly those who come from public schools where vandalism and punishment have become an accepted part of daily life. "If you treat someone responsibly, so they will act," Patrick, of Leland High School, said after his tour. Alicia, a New Tech senior, told me, "It's like a family here compared to other high schools."

Statements like this come up all the time—from teachers, from students, and in virtually every press account on the school. From all indications, they're essentially true. But when this point of pride is mixed in with the school's commitment to technology, visitors are led to believe that if their schools would only invest in the same kind of computerized curriculum, they will get trustworthy students who behave like professionals, too. But the trusting atmosphere has nothing to do with technology. It derives from the school's small size. With 18 staff members for 220 students—in a building the size of most high school gyms—it becomes only natural to build closer, trusting relationships than are possible to achieve in big schools. Smallness almost forces their creation.

It should be remembered that technology also creates new opportunities for students to abuse a school's trust. While New Tech administrators constantly boast about how much time students put in on their computers—coming in on their own at night and on weekends, for instance—the truth on this score is another matter. Judging from numerous accounts from students, a good bit of this after-hours work occurred because the students weren't attending to their work during class. And that happened because of what they *were* doing: playing the same games I'd seen in virtually every other heavily computerized classroom. "You know what they were all doing in class?" Lily Sarafin, the Leland student leader, asked me after she and her schoolmates spent a day shadowing New Tech students. "They were e-mailing each other. And trying to hide it when the teacher came around."

By one measure, the prevalence of these tricks is nothing new—schoolchildren have been passing notes behind teachers' backs and hiding magazines inside their textbooks since the beginning of educational time. By another measure, though, the computerized version of these games is quite different indeed. In yesteryear's classroom, an attentive teacher could see a passed note or a hidden magazine; on computers, the "toggling" function can render an e-mail or an unauthorized Internet site invisible in seconds.

When I've questioned New Tech's teachers about problems like these, they've seemed partly aware of the situation—and also untroubled by it. The school's literature emphasizes that students here are treated like adults so that they'll learn how to manage their time. "Most students realize," the school notes on its website, "that no one is going to 'get them through' or force them to succeed—it's up to them. Those whose grades go quickly down in NTHS's relaxed environment either fix the problem or go back to a more traditional atmosphere." The site includes quotes from students who apparently have so appreciated being treated this way that they've found themselves liking school for the first time.

But there's a second—important—reason that students are having such fun here. New Tech's teachers have been so taken in by the power of their technology that they've seen little need to ask their students to do what many schools would call hard work. All that's typically required on research projects are three sources: one website, one book, and one other source of a student's own choice. Teachers often allow up to several weeks for these projects, yet many students procrastinate until the last few days—without suffering any consequences for it. Homework assignments are minimal as well—generally an hour a night, at most. A write-up on the school's website boasts about this, noting that classwork is so efficient that students rarely have homework. (The website also explains the reasons for this: When students work at home—with a household computer or a borrowed school laptop—they can't be hooked up to the school network. Any digitally intensive assignment therefore becomes difficult to manage. In New Tech's view, this glitch is perfectly acceptable—"practical reasons," as the school puts it, for why there isn't much homework.) Whatever the reason, it's been a relief to the students. "Compared with the high school I came from," Stefan told me, "it seemed like an extremely, extremely light workload."

The grading is lenient too. "They don't grade us hard, but they criticize us hard," said one of the school's tour guides. By all indications, the first part of his assertion is an understatement. During the portfolio evaluations, when New Tech teachers joined in the voting, I noticed that they consistently gave students much more positive ratings than community members did. And to the extent that standardized tests are any measure, the performance at New Tech is nothing exceptional. (While the students solidly outperform Napa's two other high schools on state tests, their scores on the

SATs fall short—below the district's other high schools, and often below state and national averages.) All of this raises obvious questions about the pride that everyone at New Tech—students, teachers, and administrators—takes in how dramatically students' grades rise after they come to New Tech High. Technology's blinding effects clearly spread wide.

THE DIGITAL CURRICULUM

D uring the school's project-based learning workshop, Mark Morrison, the principal, explained that at New Tech "we organize our curriculum around what it would be like to work at Silicon Graphics or Microsoft." In press accounts, school administrators frequently point out that one of their main goals is to produce graduates who are "industry-ready." The futuristic vibrations in statements like these are strong, and undoubtedly they have drawn many of the school administrators who come to Napa looking for answers. What, then, does such a curriculum look like? And what does it say about other schools' prospects for aggressive scholastic reform?

The New Tech curriculum is a curious assortment. There are some catchy twenty-first-century offerings: Computer Applications/Communication Technologies I & II; Multimedia Design and Criticism I & II; highly technical classes in computer networking, through one of Cisco Systems' ubiquitous "Networking Academies"; and, new in 2002, an "Oracle Academy," sponsored by the Oracle Corporation. There are some basics: "Integrated" Math II & III and Physics; and, in social studies, two more hybrids—Political Studies and American Studies.

While this may sound like an industry-ready program, Napa's two other public high schools—both of which are big, stodgy exemplars of education at its most traditional—offer a course lineup that many might regard as much more suited to twenty-first-century professional success. In the technology arena, for example, the course offerings at New Tech's competitors include laboratory studies in applied physics, beginning and advanced electronics, engineering and technical drafting, computer maintenance and repair, and several courses in telecommunications. They also offer myriad courses in areas in which technology is commonly applied—subjects such as biology, environmental science, aviation, automotive mechanics, and video and television production. This is in addition, of course, to a rich variety of courses that New Tech doesn't even offer, including such basics as fine arts and the performing arts, sports, and forty different classes in various foreign languages. A good number of these are Advanced Placement courses, which New Tech does not offer and which many educators, including the Department of Education, promote as vital preparation for college.[13]

Perhaps the most telling comparison between a program like New Tech's and the version found at clunky old institutional high schools is in their math classes. Until recently, the most advanced math course at New Tech covered only algebra and pre-calculus (in 2000, the school finally added a course in calculus). At San Jose's Leland High School, algebra and pre-calculus classes are often taken in students' sophomore and junior years. By senior year, many are studying differential equations and college-level calculus. "They can finish all the math required for an engineering major," Setterlund says. Leland, of course, is a somewhat elite school, but the same contrast exists in the math programs at Napa's two traditional public high schools, where the student demographics are much the same as New Tech's. One of those schools even offers AP statistics.

The paucity of New Tech's math program points to yet another irony in the school's high-tech value system, and this one is rather cruel. Anyone involved in the guts of today's technology age knows that having a rich background in mathematics and a vivid grounding in physical science and engineering principles is essential in this field; this kind of background is critical for work in high-level computer programming—an option that New Tech High students are supposed to be prepared for most of all. But when a school concentrates instead on teaching students how to handle today's computer programs, it is not simply missing the boat. It is pointing students to the wrong port. "By the time they get into the workforce, [the computer programs they learned in school] are totally obsolete," Marjorie Bynum, vice-president of work-force development for the Information Technology Association of America, told me.

Despite the novelty of New Tech's computing emphasis, the school is repeating a very old pattern. "This is computerized vocational education," says Judah Schwartz, the former co-director of the Harvard Center for Educational Technology and professor emeritus at Harvard and MIT. Ever since vocational schools were founded, Schwartz recalls, administrators repeatedly found that they couldn't keep up with the rapid technical innovations in the business world. Of course, mastery of those innovations constituted these schools' entire reason for being, which is why they have long been regarded as education's slums. Now come New Tech and dozens of similar schools polishing up this routine and selling it as a promising new game. But in some ways, it's actually worse than its predecessor. When New Tech graduates finally get their first jobs, many of the new computer programs then in use—or taking shape in the labs where today's students might work—will undoubtedly be pretty sophisticated. The most powerful of them will require an understanding of complex math principles, particularly differential equations, which these students did not have the opportunity to learn.

—

School reform doesn't have to go down a path of such intellectual starvation—even in a small school. Elsewhere in the country, schools that are even smaller than New Tech have devised curricula that are more varied, more ambitious, and considerably more effective. Generally, the most successful haven't aimed for whole school reform. Instead, they pick their shots and leave education's bureaucratic beast alone to continue dozing. One could even argue that the entire concept of "whole school reform" has become a term of art—framed by who looks at it and from what perspective. Practically speaking, it is nearly impossible to remake a public school's "whole" program anyway; far too many rules and organizations are attached to the system. In such a world, *reform* becomes a subjective term— painted as marginal by its critics or as big and systemic by its supporters.

One attempt at reform—the New American Schools (NAS), of which New Tech is now a part—illustrates this point quite colorfully. Launched in 1991 to create a national family of "break-the-mold schools," NAS is regarded as the most ambitious school reform initiative in modern times. Over the years, NAS also has enjoyed great political support and extremely generous financial backing. Some has been private (in 1993, Walter Annenberg, the media-mogul-turned-philanthropist, stunned the country by giving NAS $50 million, one of the largest donations to K–12 public education in history). Some money has come from government. (In 1997, the project also became the primary beneficiary of a new, $150 million federal program aimed directly at comprehensive school reform. By 2001, some 3,000 NAS schools existed across the country and were generously supported by states and local school districts.) But whenever hard-nosed evaluations have been attempted of academic achievement at NAS sites, or to see whether they have in fact broken the mold, the program has come up woefully short. One 2002 history of NAS goes so far as to argue that in order to survive the pressures of the education and political system, NAS gradually abandoned its revolutionary mission, becoming merely another educational handservant dedicated to feeding the system it once sought to change.[14] This does not mean that bold academic visions are impossible. But it does mean, as we'll eventually see, that school reform should be defined rather differently than has been education's habit.

APPLE'S REFORMS

It would obviously be unfair to judge the entire concept of high-tech school reform through one institution; that's why I strove to visit as many of the fully wired schools around the country as I could. One of the more illustrative examples lay not far from New Tech—in the middle of Silicon Valley. This area may not have had a high school that could fully demonstrate high-tech visions for education when the Leland students went prospecting, but it has long had a very wired grade school: Cupertino's Portal Elementary. In the late 1980s, Portal was singled out by Apple Computer to be one of the test beds for the ambitious, ten-year $25 million experiment called Apple Classrooms of Tomorrow (ACOT). Since the literature on the ACOT reform effort is so prodigious—and so lacking in tangible measures of progress—I decided to see what could be learned through several personal visits to Portal, in 1999 and again in 2001.

Portal sits in a quiet, pastoral corner of Cupertino, just a few miles from Apple Computer headquarters. The school doesn't suffer from typical public school pressures; it's small and draws its students from a professional, well-heeled community, where children start their school day with a full stomach and a diligent attitude. This means that the positive aspects of the school may draw more from the students' personal advantages than from technology's power. By the same measure, though, any technological weaknesses at the school carry more weight. One could argue, in other words, that in a school like this, there is little excuse for failure.

During my first visit, I immediately saw why ACOT trainers and evaluators end up focusing more on teaching style than on technology. The scene in class after class, especially for the younger grades, was the epitome of progressive teaching methods at this level—what one New York technology veteran calls "teaching on the rug." Small groups of children were everywhere—on the floor, at computers, at desks that were clustered in circles—all attentively working at different tasks. Even the normal age and class divisions were porous. Portal had set up its classrooms in a kind of modular arc, with retractable walls to encourage team-teaching. Classes were also grouped together, so kindergartners joined first and second graders; third graders joined fourth graders, and so on. In one class, students at computers were making their own crossword puzzles, turning vocabulary lessons into a game. In the fifth–sixth grade room, another collection of students was absorbed in Internet searches. (Although they often got stymied by computer crashes, most of the students just rebooted their machines and calmly carried on.) Right behind each of the computer users, their peers were toiling away at plain old tables with the same level of enthusiasm—just reading, or writing stories with pencil and paper in looseleaf booklets. From all appearances, academics were an adventure here, no matter what medium was being used.

Late one morning, when I camped out for a while in a fourth-grade class, the more complicated reality underneath this picture began to emerge. This was the day for student project presentations, a main portion of which was done with HyperStudio, the ubiquitous classroom multimedia tool. Because of how time-consuming it is for young children to master HyperStudio (and how rudimentary their multimedia creations typically are), I asked the teacher, Linda Lamay, if the projects could have been managed without HyperStudio. "Oh yes," she said, "but the presentation is so much more interesting to the other students with HyperStudio."

This kind of account fills ACOT literature. However, if one takes a passage from this literature and simply removes the word *HyperStudio,* or any other term describing a computer-related activity, substituting something like *independent projects,* the sentences read just fine—as an accurate but not terribly newsy description of good classroom practice. Take this example from one of the dozen research reports done on ACOT by Apple employees or outside evaluators: "Students used [independent projects] to complement both the development and presentation of ideas. [Projects] served to stimulate the processes of thinking and writing." In this case, the deleted words were *computer graphics*—a nice tool in the right hands but hardly essential.[15]

A few minutes later in Lamay's class, her own students demonstrated this axiom. Once their computer presentations were done, the students pulled out the physical models they had built. In every case, the other students in the class rushed forward, crowding around the project, examining it in detail, and peppering the designer with questions. ("How did you make that?" "What did you use for the roof?" "How did you get the smoke over the volcano to stay on?") Lamay eventually had to call for order.

It certainly seemed that student interest in non-computerized projects was plenty high. When I checked my impression with Lamay, it turned out that she wasn't comparing the HyperStudio work to the physical projects but to mundane traditional reports—the kind done on sheets of paper. This is why important caveats don't show up in research like the ACOT reports. Computer activities are consistently compared with old, boring activities, the sort of routines that can be easily trounced by almost any new idea.

Leaving aside student projects, where measures of performance can be woefully subjective, what about these students' abilities with old-fashioned academics? For example, how were their reading skills? I asked. "Extremely high," Lamay said. And their comprehension, their imagination? She squinted with uncertainty. "When I ask them why do you think a character felt such and such, they say, 'It's not in here!' (pointing to their books)." ACOT's organizers partly understood this danger. When setting up their classrooms, they didn't try to replace materials that teachers have long used to stimulate creativity with computers. Textbooks, workbooks, tactile math manipulatives, and tools for the arts such as crayons and pianos—all this remained at hand. In Lamay's class, for example, she had placed buckets of crayons and colored markers, yet the students rarely used them. At other schools where Lamay had worked, she said, "when I gave out worksheets, nine out of ten would color them. Here only one out of ten will." If she asked for some artwork, she said, students would say, " 'Do we *have* to color?' They're just not interested in creating that beauty on the paper."

When I returned to Portal in 2001, I got another tour. The atmosphere was much the same, and the art program had been expanded (courtesy of a parent fund-raising drive, after the district cut back its arts budget). This year, the teachers were particularly excited about some "i-movies" that the sixth graders had produced with the video functions on the new iMacs. So I asked to see one. My tour guide happily corralled a sixth-grade girl who, she said, had made one of the better films—of the famous Icarus story, as part of a social studies course on Greek myths. The film was indeed entertaining— the students had memorized all their lines (with a few amusing exceptions) and they delivered their performances with delightfully clumsy enthusiasm.

When the film was over, I asked the girl what meaning she had gleaned from this particular myth. She seemed startled by the question, paused to think for quite a while, and finally said, "Don't fly close to the sun." That was it? She nodded. Suspecting the girl was merely feeling shy in front of a reporter, I asked if they had engaged in much discussion about such topics in class. She said they had not. Now I was startled. In schools throughout the country, I observed and spoke with students at low-tech schools who were much younger than this girl and much poorer (a number of whom are featured in the latter chapters of this book). During those visits, I heard students discuss many subjects, including Greek myths, and most could talk me to death about what the stories meant—to them, to society, to history, and on and on. What was going on here? Clearly, this young lady had all the advantages anyone would need to engage in such discussions. If anything, perhaps she had too many advantages. Her school day was so full of captivating electronic distractions that she rarely felt much need to get beneath their surface. Nor, apparently, did her ACOT-inspired teacher.

THE FUTURE'S REALITIES

W hat, then, retards the reform efforts of futuristic schools like Portal Elementary and New Tech High? Part of the answer is the extent to which these schools have equated novelty with progress. On a more immediate level, where high-tech education is concerned, the answer lies once again in one instructive word: *money.*

Consider the budgetary realities at New Tech High. By law, the school must spend the same amount on its program as every other high school in the district. That figure, in 2001, was $5,935 per student. But New Tech's real costs, by Morrison's estimate, are nearly twice that amount. That's where the school's grants and donations from Bill and Melinda Gates come in—to make up the difference. But Morrison notes that even the Gateses' $5 million "won't begin to build these kinds of schools." At New Tech High, for instance, most of the extra cash goes to sustaining the school's technology system and to financing constant system upgrades. Those costs explain why New Tech students don't get art or a science lab—to say nothing of AP classes in Spanish or calculus. This, apparently, is what a curriculum looks like when it is organized, as Morrison put it, around "what it would be like to work at Microsoft or Silicon Graphics."

New Tech's administrators are not entirely oblivious to the school's curricular handicaps, and they've tried to compensate for them. They've made arrangements at the local community college for students to fulfill a few extra requirements in subjects like science and math; they've also won privileges at neighboring high schools for students to take classes that New Tech doesn't offer and to play sports on their teams. The plans have been only moderately effective. Aside from some basic language classes and a few others required by the state for graduation, most New Tech students haven't bothered to take advantage of these offerings. In the spring semester of 2000, for example, only eighteen students were taking any classes at the other local high schools. Most everyone does take classes at the community college, either on campus or through special classes given at New Tech. But most of these are either business classes or entertaining electives. In the spring of 2001, for example, only twenty-three of the school's 200-plus students were taking the college's calculus courses. One could argue that this is not New Tech's fault, that as long as it makes these options available, it has done its job. But that's not terribly realistic. It should have been obvious to someone that teenagers were not readily going to abandon their friends for a class with people they didn't know, at a school that is a hassle to get to, especially a large high school that they intentionally avoided in the first place.

One of the school's other innovations, with community service, has produced some unusual relationships with New Tech's industrial sponsors. An increasing number of high schools include programs of this nature, sometimes called service learning. In most schools, administrators see these endeavors as serving a triple role—they teach students the meaning of altruism, provide valuable work experience, and help the community in the process. At New Tech, the culture is so wrapped up in the commerce of technology that almost nothing of the kind has taken place. Here, community service is defined as an internship in "technology, business or education." Morrison frequently tells his students that the internships are very much about giving back to the community; since New Tech was started and equipped largely by businesses, including local firms, in Morrison's view, these companies are the community. Not surprisingly, the vast majority of student internships are offered at private companies, often some of the school's own business partners, and often at conveniently low wages. Over time, students themselves found the program's focus so limited that they asked school administrators to accept internships oriented to true public service—and to make allowances for run-of-the-mill jobs. Before long, students were getting credit for flipping burgers at McDonald's, as long as they also operated the restaurant's computer. As for the internships in "education," aside from a small initiative to teach computer skills to city residents, the bulk of this work constituted hours that students donated to New Tech High—fixing computer systems or guiding the school's monthly promotional tours.

It looks like New Tech co-founder Ted Fujimoto was not blowing smoke when he talked, back in 1996, about the "two-way street" he hoped New Tech High would develop with business. Over the years, the school has kept traffic flowing nicely in both directions.

That might be fine—if it gets students where they want to go over the long term. Right now, most of New Tech's graduates tend to go on to junior colleges. About 25 percent enter four-year colleges; the rest move right into the workforce. Not surprisingly, the largest block of these students (fully half, according to a 1998 class poll) want to pursue careers in technology and business. They may have the basic technical skills to do so—for the moment. But what will happen down the line, when the "new" economy's constant upheavals revolutionize the work world yet again?

CHAPTER 6

Computer Literacy: Limping Toward Tomorrow's Jobs

O ver the years, there has been no shortage of excitement about the vast changes that computers are supposed to bring to the working world and about what students must do to prepare for that transformation. As recently as the summer of 2001, well after the collapse of the Internet boom, Bill Rodrigues, vice-president of Dell Computer's education and health-care sector and co-chair of the CEO Forum on Education and Technology, outlined a widely shared view. "Information technology is transforming the global economy and drastically changing the way business and society operates," Rodrigues declared. Because of this, he considered it imperative that students learn how to use technology in a multitude of endeavors: "to locate and evaluate information; to learn, reason, make decisions, and solve problems; and to collaborate and work in teams. . . . Without a serious and significant investment in these skills, curricula, and accountability, our schools face the almost impossible challenge of trying to produce graduates for a 21st-century work force."[1] Sentiments of this flavor have, in one form or another, laced years of press accounts and public discussions on school computing. They have operated almost as technology's first commandment. And why not? From all appearances, it looks like the most logical of rationales. Supporting evidence pops up all the time.

The campaign that launched the Clinton administration's big push for computers in schools offers a graphic illustration. When that initiative first began, in 1995, a White House report compiled a few persuasive numbers. In the decade since 1984, it noted, the number of jobs requiring computer skills had increased from 25 percent of all jobs to 47 percent. By 2000, the report estimated, 60 percent of the nation's jobs would demand these skills—and would pay an average of 10 to 15 percent more than jobs involving no computer work.[2] Throughout those years, other readings of the economic temperature touted the gains in productivity that computers, and the entire technology industry, have brought to the United States. By the time the year 2000 actually arrived, however, the numbers on each count were a little more complicated than exuberant policy makers had anticipated.

In the economy as a whole, the long-term numbers showed remarkably little change. From 1870 to the early 1970s, productivity increased at an average rate of approximately 2.3 percent a year. It then slowed to about 1 percent a year, and even in the gusto of the 1990s it merely resumed its previous pace.[3] The reality on the technology job front, as everyone now knows, has been even grimmer. In the first six months of 2001, companies laid off more workers than they had hired in the course of the entire previous year. (Specifically, this amounted to 268,437 layoffs, according to one industry count, as measured against 234,800 new hires in all of 2000, the final year of the decade's Internet frenzy.) Of course, by 2001, recession had begun to shake a number of industries across the country. But the technology sector contributed more than its share to the process. By the middle of that year, tech layoffs accounted for 41 percent of the 652,510 job cuts that had been announced throughout the economy.[4]

Although big projections made by policy makers are typically unreliable, it is a safe bet that computer skills of some kind *will* be needed for a growing proportion of tomorrow's work force. But if the nation's schools are going to embark on a nationwide campaign, some specific questions must be addressed: Can any solid projections can be made? What kinds of technical skills are we talking about? How should those capabilities be developed? What do employers themselves say about what they need? And, ultimately, how does such a focus fit into the schools' overall responsibilities? In other words, what priority should computer work be given among other studies—not just old mainstays like the arts and sciences but also studies that prepare youngsters for becoming citizens in today's unpredictable world?

Asking questions is always easy; the hard part is answering them. Fortunately, this is one domain where most of the answers are readily available. And they are very different from what most people imagine.

REAL JOB TRAINING

L isten to Tom Henning, a physics teacher at Thurgood Marshall, one of San Francisco's more high-tech high schools. Henning has a graduate degree in engineering, and he helped found a Silicon Valley company that manufactures electronic navigation equipment. "My bias is the physical reality," Henning told me one day as we sat outside a shop where he was helping students rebuild an old motorcycle. "I'm no technophobe. I can program computers." What worries Henning is that computers at best engage only two senses, hearing and sight—and only two-dimensional sight at that. "Even if they're doing three-dimensional computer modeling, that's still a two-D replica of a three-D world. If you took a kid who grew up on Nintendo, he's not going to have the necessary skills. He needs to have done it first with Tinkertoys or clay, or carved it out of balsa wood." David Elkind, a professor of child development at Tufts University, holds a very similar view. "A dean of the University of Iowa's school of engineering used to say the best engineers were the farm boys," Elkind recalled, because they knew how machinery really worked.[5]

Apparently, urban business executives share this view as well. One of the plainest illustrations of this fact was produced in April 2000, by a group of business leaders quite sympathetic to computer skills. The Information Technology Association of America (ITAA) produced a report that month entitled "Bridging the Gap: Information Technology Skills for a New Millennium." The report from ITAA, which represents a cross section of the economy, was compiled at perhaps the peak of new-economy frenzy, just weeks before it started to crash. Not surprisingly, the association projected big demand for "IT [information technology] workers" and a grave shortage of applicants who possessed the appropriate skills. Specifically, it foresaw the creation of 1.6 million new IT jobs in the year 2000, more than half of which would go unfilled.

When the employers who were fretting about this gap were asked what skills mattered to them, this is what they said: Most important of all was a deep and broad base of knowledge. "Want to get a job using information technology to solve problems?" the report asked. "Know something about the problems that need to be solved." This statement reflected the sentiments of nearly two thirds of the association's members. Following far behind this priority was "hands-on experience" with technical work, which less than half the nation's IT managers considered critical. (Most apparently felt perfectly capable of teaching those skills on the job.) Even for high-tech jobs, a large portion of these employers' priorities (more than a third) were non-technical. They included "good communication, problem-solving, and analytical skills, along with flexibility, and the ability to learn quickly."[6]*

A year later, ITAA came out with its 2001 report. Surprise: Opportunities for IT workers in the year 2000 hadn't been nearly as robust as the association had predicted. Over the year, the industry had created only 400,000 new IT jobs, a somewhat different figure from the 1.6 million it had advertised and the nearly 800,000 of those it had expected to fill. Obviously somewhat sobered, the association adjusted its projections for 2001. But it was still plenty upbeat. This year, it said, there would be a demand for 900,000 workers.[7] Since the ITAA report was put together in early 2001, it's quite likely that it didn't have a chance to factor in the year's many fatal pileups on the "information superhighway." That answers the question about what kinds of solid projections are possible (very few).

As confident as employers are about being able to teach the hard skills they need for their particular professions, they are just as uncertain that they can do the same with the "soft skills"—the background knowledge, the taste for problem solving, the people skills, the concepts of discipline and reliability—that technology business leaders indicated are their priority. "Employers don't think that can be taught on the job," Marjorie Bynum, vice-president of work-force development for ITAA, told me. "If they're not learning those at school, where will they learn them?"

---

*Anyone who wants additional ammunition against the all-tech visions of groups like the CEO forum might find reassurance in the views of Peter Drucker, the legendary business guru. Drucker has a good deal of faith in the powers of high technology, both in the business world and in school—in the latter camp, largely to relieve teachers of mindless drill work, so they can give students more individual attention. As for students, Drucker believes there is much they too could get out of technology. However, Drucker has deeper experiences in mind than schools typically offer—a whole range of endeavors that help people understand "the dynamics of technology." Interestingly, though, Drucker most heavily stresses a revived concept of basic skills. Tomorrow's "global" workers, he says, must be able to "appreciate other cultures . . . *understand* the various knowledges . . . present ideas orally and in writing . . . work with people." Managers of the future, he writes, will need "self-knowledge, wisdom and leadership . . . all the knowledges and insights of the humanities and the social sciences—psychology and philosophy, economics and history, the physical sciences and ethics." See *The New Realities*, by Peter Drucker, HarperCollins, 1989, pp. 245–47; *Post-Capitalist Society*, by Peter Drucker, Harper-Collins, 1993, pp. 24–29, 196–207, 213–17.

"KNOWLEDGE OF THE HANDS"

For some insight into the precise kinds of skills needed, at whatever stage of industry's cycle of rises and falls, it may help to examine the way seasoned professionals look at workplace competence. Consider this from Kris Meisling, a senior geological-research adviser for ExxonMobil. "People who use computers a lot slowly grow rusty in their ability to think," he once told me.

Meisling's group creates charts and maps—some computerized, some not—to plot where to drill for oil. In large one-dimensional analyses, such as sorting volumes of seismic data, the computer saves vast amounts of time, sometimes making previously impossible tasks easy. This, Meisling believes, lures people in his field into using computers as much as possible. But when geologists turn to computers for interpretive projects, he finds, they often miss information, and their oversights are magnified by the computer's captivating automatic graphing and design functions. This is why Meisling still works regularly with a pencil and paper—tools that, ironically, he considers more interactive than the computer, because they force him to think implications through. "You can't simultaneously get an overview and detail with a computer," he said. "It's linear. It gives you tunnel vision. What computers can do well is what can be calculated over and over. What they can't do is innovation. If you think of some new way to do or look at things and the software can't do it, you're stuck. So a lot of people think, 'Well, I guess it's a dumb idea, or it's unnecessary.' "

I have heard similar warnings from people in other businesses, including high-tech enterprises. A spokeswoman for Hewlett-Packard, the giant California computer-products company, told me the company rarely hires people who are predominantly computer experts, favoring instead those who have a talent for teamwork and are flexible and innovative. Hewlett-Packard has been such a believer in hands-on experience that in five years in the mid-1990s, it spent $2.6 million to help forty-five school districts build math and science skills the old-fashioned way—with real materials, such as dirt, seeds, water, glass vials, and magnets. Much the same perspective came from several recruiters from film- and computer-game-animation companies. In work by artists who have spent a lot of time on computers "you'll see a stiffness or a flatness, a lack of richness and depth," Karen Chelini, the director of human resources for LucasArts Entertainment, George Lucas's interactive-games maker, told me. "With traditional art training, you train the eye to pay attention to body movement. You learn attitude, feeling, expression. The ones who are good are those who as kids couldn't be without their sketch book."

Many jobs, obviously, will still demand basic computer skills if not sophisticated knowledge. But that doesn't mean that the parents or the teachers of young students need to panic. Joseph Weizenbaum, professor emeritus of computer science at MIT, once said that even at his technology-heavy institution, new students can learn all the computer skills they need "in a summer."[8] This seems to hold in the business world, too. Patrick MacLeamy, an executive vice-president of Hellmuth Obata & Kassabaum, the country's largest architecture firm, recently gave me numerous examples to illustrate that computers pose no threat to his company's creative work. Although architecture professors are divided on the value of computerized design tools, in MacLeamy's opinion they generally enhance the process. But he still considers "knowledge of the hands" to be valuable—today's architects just have to develop it in other ways. (His firm's answer is through building models.) Nonetheless, as positive as MacLeamy is about computers, he has found the company's two-week computer training to be sufficient. In fact, when he's hiring, computer skills don't even enter into his list of priorities. He looks for strong character; an ability to speak, write, and comprehend; and a rich education in the history of architecture.

Indeed, it is often the intangible knowledge and abilities that make for exceptional work. Another architect, an Italian named Matteo Pericoli, recently taught New Yorkers a thing or two about knowledge of the hands. As *The New Yorker* magazine put it in an article on his work, Pericoli "draws obsessively. He draws buildings, he draws maps, he draws birds. And last year . . . he drew the entire West Side of Manhattan." Pericoli did a line drawing, in black ink, of the way the city looked to him during boat rides on the Hudson River and put it on a thirty-seven-foot roll of paper. It took him a year, during which time he kept the drawing rolled up in his apartment, where he'd work exposing just a few feet at a time, never erasing or changing anything once it had been drawn. Before setting ink to paper, Pericoli shot photographs, more than four hundred of them. "In Pericoli's fine lines every building is benign," the magazine wrote, "and together the buildings seem almost to be swaying softly in a chorus line along the Hudson." When Pericoli reflected on his work, he said, "Every building has character; to draw it is like drawing a face, the things that give it soul. If you draw something, it is fixed in your mind forever, it is a miracle." Not coincidentally, this article on Pericoli's landscape, which was exhibited at New York University, began by mentioning that when the noted architect Charles Gwathmey spoke that year at Princeton, he complained that young architects no longer knew how to draw.[9]

Eventually, those weaknesses can show up on a company's bottom line. A senior partner at a prominent contracting firm in the Northwest told me of his pleasure in seeing how computerized design programs have sped up his firm's productivity. At the same time, he said the blueprints they receive are riddled with so many more errors these days—and are often so at odds with construction reality—that he's had to more than double the number of engineers on his payroll, just to fix design problems. These troubles trickle down to work sites, too. In Minnesota, builders have complained that young hires are so incapable of solving basic construction problems that supply companies are increasingly labeling materials with letters, to make it obvious how the parts fit together.

Part of the explanation for these deficiencies may lie in some of the software students use. In a lengthy 1996 *Business Week* article on computer games, for example, academics and professionals expressed amazement at the speed, savvy, and facility that young computer jocks sometimes demonstrate. Several pointed in particular to computer simulations, which some business leaders believe are becoming increasingly important in fields ranging from engineering, manufacturing, and troubleshooting to the tracking of economic activity and geopolitical risk.[10] The best of these simulations can of course be a valuable supplement to any discipline. But they can also teach some bad habits.

A good illustration of this point lies in research done by Sherry Turkle, professor of sociology at MIT, who has studied youngsters using computers for more than twenty years. In her 1995 book *Life on the Screen: Identity in the Age of the Internet*, Turkle described a disturbing experience with a simulation game called SimLife. After she sat down with a thirteen-year-old named Tim, she was stunned at the way "Tim can keep playing even when he has no idea what is driving events. For example, when his sea urchins become extinct, I ask him why."

> **Tim:** I don't know, it's just something that happens.
> **ST:** Do you know how to find out why it happened?
> **Tim:** No.
> **ST:** Do you mind that you can't tell why?
> **Tim:** No. I don't let things like that bother me. It's not what's important.[11]

One reason Turkle was pestering Tim is that simulations are by nature built on hidden assumptions, many of which are oversimplified if not highly questionable. All too often, Turkle once wrote, "experiences with simulations do not open up questions but close them down."[12] Turkle worries that such software fosters passivity, ultimately dulling people's sense of what they can create and change in the world. There's a tendency, Turkle once told me, "to take things at 'interface value.'" Indeed, after mastering SimCity, a popular game about urban planning, a tenth-grade girl boasted to Turkle that she'd learned the following rule: "Raising taxes always leads to riots."

SOFT SKILLS, HARD TEACHING

The essential message inside all these accounts is not news. In fact, if the economic prognosticators had chosen to look back just a few pages in technology's history, they could have found plenty of warnings that the path to career success isn't nearly as straight as they'd have us believe.

As early as 1982, high-technology firms were telling educators not to neglect non-technical skills in their rush toward computer proficiency. During one educational technology conference in San Jose, representatives from such firms as IBM, Pacific Telephone, Pacific Gas & Electric, National Semiconductor, and Lockheed all urged educators to remember the three R's. Robert Preston, manager of technical education for National Semiconductor, particularly stressed the importance of communication skills and the ability to "guesstimate" fractions, ratios, and other numbers without the aid of calculators.[13]

Actually, the tendency of the business and political communities to point fingers at the schools as the cause of, and solution to, their own problems enjoys an extremely long history. Business has been lobbying for changes in the classroom since the turn of the twentieth century. The path of education reform is littered with the titles of their campaigns, often waged in partnership with government. In 1905, for example, the National Association of Manufacturers urged the schools to help solve what was seen at the time as a productivity crisis, saying, "We must act at once because of the stress of foreign competition." This was soon followed by the Smith-Hughes Act of 1917, which initiated vocational education. In the 1930s, school-business partnerships became somewhat discredited by the Great Depression; with the New Deal, however, the government put a work-force focus back in the lead with the creation of the Civilian Conservation Corps and the National Youth

Administration. Later, President Lyndon Johnson's "War on Poverty" in the 1960s gave birth to the Job Corps, Mobilization for Youth, and a host of industrious-sounding acronyms: MDTA, HARYOU, CETA, among others.[14]

While some of these initiatives brought welcome energy to the nation's classrooms, none of them gave large populations of students skills that held long-term value. Rather, the emphasis was generally guided by labor-market needs that turned out to be transitory; when the economy shifted, workers were left unprepared for new jobs.

As but one example of how business has habitually blamed schools for its own problems, the Stanford historian Larry Cuban took note of an awkward irony in a 1983 account of corporate involvement in schools. The year before, the California Business Roundtable had issued a report declaring that "data on student performance show that California secondary school students are not being adequately prepared for college or work." In a comment for a subsequent news story, one Roundtable leader added, "In investigating urban unemployment, we came to the conclusion that the real problem was education itself." The oddity was that the Roundtable made this call in 1982, one of the worst periods of recent national recession. It was a time when unemployment was in the double digits, when young adults with master's and doctorate degrees were driving taxis or working in secretarial pools. How, Cuban wondered, could business suggest that its complex troubles would ease if the schools simply turned out more of these people?[15]

Whenever they have, it certainly hasn't had much effect. Other accounts indicated that in the economy as a whole, performance trends in our schools have shown virtually no link to the rises and falls in the nation's measures of productivity and growth. "The link between education and the national economy is pretty tenuous," observes Peter Capelli, co-director of the National Center on the Educational Quality of the Workforce at the University of Pennsylvania.[16]* This is one reason that school traditionalists push for broad liberal-arts curricula, which they feel develop students' intellect

---

*As self-evident as it would seem that more education brings greater economic progress, the hard data on this question is chronically ambivalent. As but one example, in 2002, when the school-reform journal *Education Next* enlisted a pair of experts from conflicting camps to fight out this argument, both leaned on the exact same information—international gross domestic product measures—to prove opposing points. Eric Hanushek of Stanford's Hoover Institution argued that across the globe, increased test performance is linked to a slight, eventual increase in GDP; William Easterly of the Center for Global Development and Institute for International Economics in Washington, D.C., lists evidence, particularly in Third World countries, that as education has increased, productivity has often declined. How can this be? For one thing, *education* and *economics* are big terms and cover a multitude of sins. Hanushek, taking

and values, instead of focusing on today's idea about what tomorrow's jobs will be.

Through the years, there have been indications that labor policy makers have gotten somewhat more farsighted. In 1991, as fears were rising about another phase of weakness in the nation's economic future, the Department of Labor issued a report entitled "What Work Requires of Schools." Dubbed the SCANS report (after its authors, the Secretary's Commission on Achieving Necessary Skills), it boiled down a year of conversations with employers, managers, union leaders, and workers of many kinds. In some respects, its message was familiar. (As Larry Cuban once described earlier clarion calls: "The lyrics might be different but the melody was the same.")[17] In essence, SCANS said, the days of high pay for low-skill work were over; higher levels of ability were now needed just to get into the game. However, the report warned, "More than half of our young people leave school without the knowledge or foundation required to find and hold a good job. . . . These people . . . face the bleak prospects of dead-end work interrupted only by periods of unemployment."

To halt this possibility, the report compiled a list of skills deemed to be today's keys to success. While the list was much like what ITAA and many of its predecessors had outlined, there was a new sense of scope. SCANS started by outlining some familiar foundations (the three R's; speaking and writing abilities; a facility for creative and analytical thinking, problem solving, decision making, and "knowing how to learn"; along with such personal strengths as responsibility, self-esteem, self-management, sociability, and integrity). The report also listed five special "competencies," which it said could and should be learned in tandem with the basics. These were the ability to: handle resources (money, time, materials, people); teach or work as a team with others (particularly those from diverse backgrounds); manage and interpret complicated information, often by using computers; un-

---

the more macro view, looks at one overlayer of these sins, while Easterly looks closer to the ground, country by country, and counts very different troubles. (He also out-facts Hanushek by almost three to one.) It should be noted, though, that economics has never been quite the hard, authoritative science that many assume. Just as a measure of growth, the GDP itself is quite limited. It does not count the progress made when families become healthier, handle their own child-care duties, or entertain themselves with simple activities at home. In fact, by the GDP's measure, people contribute most to our economic growth when, in addition to their work, they churn the economy with frequent costly troubles—at hospitals, or at attorneys' offices when filing for divorces or paying penalties for various legal violations, including acts of environmental pollution. "The Seeds of Growth" and "Barren Land," *Education Next*, Fall 2002, pp. 10–23; "If the GDP Is Up, Why Is America Down?" by Clifford Cobb, Ted Halstead, and Jonathan Rowe, *The Atlantic Monthly*, October 1995, pp. 59–73.

derstand and design "social, organizational, and technological systems"; and select the right equipment and tools for the job, troubleshooting technical problems as they occur.

To inspire educators, many of whom had become immune to cascades of fervent recommendations, SCANS painted a picture of "the School of Tomorrow." It described a school where students are constantly working on real-world projects, which spontaneously fold in studies of biology and math, writing and presenting, teamwork and analysis, the whole shooting match. For extra verve, SCANS noted that its vision was compatible with a proposal sent to Congress just weeks earlier, by then-President George H. W. Bush, which outlined a plan to be accomplished by the year 2000. Called the AMERICA 2000 Excellence in Education Act, Bush's bill included the ambitious New American Schools project, which sought the creation of 535 "break-the-mold" schools across the country.[18]

Few people had much quibble with SCANS's proposals; the problem was carrying them out. In fact, schools had been trying to teach through problem-solving exercises for years. "Ever since the early 1980s, you couldn't sell a textbook in California if it didn't have problem solving in it," recalls Henry Levin, a professor of education at Columbia University's Teachers College and a veteran school reformer himself (he was the founding director of the Accelerated Schools Project). To meet that need, Levin said, textbook publishers "added a whole bunch of trivial stuff." And schools fell for it. The result, in Levin's view, has been a rash of "contrived" student projects, where students are working on endeavors with predefined solutions when they should be given real-world problems that are full of ambiguity and trouble. There is a perfectly logical reason for this: Both students and teachers need lessons to finish on schedule, and real-world problems don't always cooperate. Teaching through this methodology therefore takes inordinate amounts of patience—and time.

When the much-anticipated year 2000 finally arrived, education's landscape once again was quite different from what the federal visionaries had expected. By now, more than two thousand New American Schools had been created, but the reforms that shaped them soon proved to be somewhat less than effective. (In an exhaustive, 250-page evaluation in 2001, the RAND Corporation found that of 163 schools it had data on, only half did better than their district counterparts in math and less than half performed better in reading.)[19] Many other schools also weren't delivering the sorts of measurable results that education critics wanted. Despite its merits, SCANS would soon be forgotten in favor of the next new answer: testing and accountability.

THE "NEW" ECONOMY

I t often seems as though computer hype, and public belief in it, is a quintessentially American affair. In truth, these themes have been playing quite well overseas as well. Consider the tenor of some presentations made during a conference I was part of on education technology in September 2000, in Glasgow, Scotland.

This event, grandly billed as Fusion: Global Learning Summit 2000, was organized by four Scottish academic and government organizations. This was not your average conference by American standards. In the United States, gatherings of this ilk generally are organized and financed entirely by the technology industry, whose employees are then heavily represented as speakers. At this conference, American big guns such as Apple and Microsoft were brought in only as supporting sponsors and featured sparingly in the conference presentations. Nonetheless, the computer industry had little trouble getting its message into each day's sessions.

Throughout the conference, panelists talked about how important it was for students, and everyone else, to stay in step with the new, information-age economy. "E-learning will be absolutely fundamental to our economic success," said Charlie Watt, senior director of e-business at Scottish Enterprise, a governmental economic development agency. "Everyone in this room knows that the fundamental shift of our age is the very rapid transition from an industrial to a knowledge economy." This "knowledge-driven economy," he said, "will impact on every area of our lives." Watt's sense of urgency was caused, in part, by some odd demographic shifts on the horizon. According to his figures, emigration and birth trends in Scotland were such that in the coming years the country would steadily lose young employees, while the ranks of elderly workers would swell. Calling this trend a "population time-bomb," Watt, and most other British speakers at the Fusion conference, spoke repeatedly of the need to develop systems for "lifelong learning."

In a PowerPoint presentation, Watt outlined the changes he thought this new knowledge economy was bringing on:

- Jobs are less standardized
- Routine manual tasks [are] replaced by technology
- Core attributes [are] increasingly important: creativity, flexibility, computer literacy, problem solving, interpersonal skills[20]

As Watt and others hammered on these themes, which were already becoming clichés to anyone who had been watching technology over the years, the potential holes in their message began to dawn on me. To justify all this urgent change, its advocates point incessantly at the tumultuous approach of a whole new economic world, defined both in the United States and abroad by the same handful of ubiquitous descriptors: the *information economy*, the *knowledge economy*, or, most frequently, the *new economy*. Commonplace as these terms have become, they have always confused me. And despite the river of ink that the press eventually spilled chronicling the new economy's downfall, its basic assumptions live on vigorously. As but one indication, as late as September 2002, well after the high-tech market's collapse, Angus King, the Independent governor of Maine, waved the information-economy banner to justify his $37 million initiative to give laptops to every one of Maine's seventh- and eighth-grade students. "The vision is simple," King wrote in a *USA Today* opinion column: "to make Maine's people the best educated—and the most digitally literate—in the world, a goal rendered urgent as our nation makes the difficult transition to an economy relying primarily on the acquisition and use of information."[21]

But what exactly *is* an "information economy"? Why is work today—including the digital products and services that the technology industry delivers, and the rules it lives by—so different from yesterday's horses and carriages, railroads and bridges, that it constitutes a *new* economy?

Clearly, the Internet and technology in general have ushered in some valuable new industries. And just as clearly, the computer's powers with data analysis and visual displays have opened up plenty of opportunities in old industries, from medicine to oil exploration. The Internet in particular has created new customer-communication avenues, quickened business transactions, and cut labor costs. (It should also be noted that labor savings for a company always mean job losses for some of its workers—particularly clerical workers such as phone order operators, bank tellers, and other paper handlers.) But the coming of new jobs and the going of old ones is an ancient economic story running throughout American and even world history.[22] What's so special about these changes that they constitute a "knowledge economy"? Don't new jobs always require new knowledge? Furthermore, is there really all that much change going on? Even allowing for some of the most obvious differences to the consumer (with one, things can be purchased while you're sitting at your desk; the other requires getting out of your chair), aren't there lots of products from the "old" economy that we still need? Maybe I've missed something, but people still seem to be buying food, clothes, and houses, cars and trucks, heating oil and beds, and a good many other clunky things.*

Since the panelists in Charlie Watt's closing session were distinguished leaders in education, business, and politics from Scotland, Australia, and the United States, I decided to pick their brains. Could they offer some explanation, I asked, as to what, specifically, a "new" or "knowledge" economy is? Of the four speakers on this panel, two chose to respond. One was Watt; the other was Peter Peacock, a minister of the Scottish Parliament and deputy minister for Children and Education. Watt, who spoke first, shrugged for a minute, then ticked off some of the various businesses that make up the new economy: the hardware manufacturers, the software developers, the telecommunications industry, and a few others. And that was it. Then Minister Peacock spoke. "You can be as skeptical as you like about the knowledge economy—I personally am not," he said. "But nonetheless, the bigger question for me is having got the technology available to us, how do we exploit that to improve and change our education system."

The contrast between the two men's answers seemed revealing. Watt's list struck me as a satisfactory description of the high-tech industry—hardly the vast new frontier that needed a shimmering "new economy" label, but a perfectly accurate rundown of the welcome vigors that these businesses have brought to the modern world's industrial portfolio. For Peacock, this wasn't nearly enough juice for a "Global Learning Summit." So he foamed and fumed about the great possibilities of the "new economy," and about his abiding faith in it. But he never managed to add anything to Watt's definition of what it is. No doubt the gaps in these answers go a long way toward explaining why Internet industries enjoyed such a brief moment of

---

*Perhaps the fairest way to characterize the evidence on the new economy is to say that it seems to be a subjective term—one based on the perspective of those who invoke it. Good illustrations of the two sides here (no, there's nothing new about this economy; yes there is, it's a whole new world) were offered in two lengthy, contrasting magazine articles. The first, published on December 6, 1999, by The New Yorker ("Clicks & Mortar," by Malcolm Gladwell), argued that the "E-commerce" revolution really happened off-line, primarily in the laborious shipping of all the stuff that everyone was ordering online. The second article, published in January 2001 by The Atlantic Monthly ("The New Old Economy: Oil, Computers, and the Reinvention of the Earth," by Jonathan Rauch), argued something of the opposite. Rauch said, "Knowledge, not petroleum, is becoming the critical resource in the oil business." After spending considerable time in the field, Rauch discovered that getting the last drops of petroleum out of American oil fields required sophisticated tools and sophisticated technical skills. But so does each new wave of industrial progress. In the end, of course, the oil business is still about oil—and about the same old analytical skills that Kris Meisling of ExxonMobil described—which is precisely why Rauch had to call today's moment "the new old economy."

economic glory. Undoubtedly, their strength will return someday, in humbler form, to be appropriately fit in among the rest of the world's business enterprises. In the meantime, it would be nice if the new-economy visionaries who visit their prognostications upon the young showed some of the same humility. The expectations of today's students might then be more realistic, and their choices of college studies and careers more durable. This would free us all from what may be the computer loyalists' biggest e-lusion: that a rush toward technology is the best guarantee of security in the years ahead.

"OUR FUTURE DEMANDS MORE"

In his 1998 book *The Productive Edge*, Richard Lester, director of MIT's Industrial Performance Center, argued that the modern business environment—increasingly crowded as it is with new products and marketing techniques, mobile capital and far-flung competition abroad—contains more uncertainty than it has at any time in the last one hundred years. Business's main task now, Lester argued, is to figure out how to deal with ambiguity, volatility, and profound change.[23] The computer seems to be ideally suited to this challenge; that's partly why technology enthusiasts push it in schools so aggressively. But this misses high technology's real economic story. In a review of Lester's book, *The New York Times* observed the following: "Among the greater ironies of the computer age is the fact that information is cheap and accessible, and so no longer very valuable. What is valuable is what one does with it. And human imagination cannot be mechanized."[24]

This is precisely the reason that one of Lester's MIT colleagues, Joseph Weizenbaum, published his modern-day warning way back in 1975. "Man, in order to become whole, must be forever an explorer of both his inner and outer realities," Weizenbaum wrote in his groundbreaking book, *Computer Power and Human Reason: From Judgment to Calculation*. "What could it mean to speak of risk, courage, trust, endurance and overcoming when one speaks of machines?"[25] Weizenbaum, the inventor not only of the first talking computer program but also of the first computerized banking system, was not someone to push mysticism. He had his mind on something real—our internal architecture of values and morals, our aesthetic sensibilities and imaginative capabilities. Federal policy makers have sometimes talked this way as well. The second paragraph of the SCANS report's opening statement—which it addressed to parents, employers, and educators—said:

"We understand that schools do more than simply prepare people to make a living. They prepare people to live full lives—to participate in their communities, to raise families, and to enjoy the leisure that is the fruit of their labor. A solid education is its own reward." The next paragraph closed by saying, "We are not calling for a narrow work-focused education. Our future demands more."

As the 1990s have faded into the past, and with them any memories of the SCANS report's fine points, the power of computer technology has redefined education's message, sending commerce's call down into younger and younger grades. "Should you be choosing a career in kindergarten?" Helen Sloss Luey, a social worker and a former president of San Francisco's Parent Teacher Association, once asked me. "People need to be trained to learn and change, while education seems to be getting more specific."

———

In some states, schools have dared to approach the entire notion of education more broadly, setting up a range of projects outside school that engage youngsters in the social challenges of the day. In North Carolina, for example, an alliance of community, business, and political leaders has established the North Carolina Civics Education Consortium, which brings nonacademic adults into the schools and draws the students out to mix it up a little in community problems. Interestingly, many state constitutions contain language suggesting that one of the public schools' main jobs is to develop students' civic sensibilities. Yet most states have forgotten this promise.

"Schools in many ways have lost their civic souls," Terry Pickeral, of the Education Commission of the States, once told a Washington, D.C., conference. Some states actively discourage attention to these themes, seeing the stuff of politics and civic affairs as controversial and therefore dangerous.[26] Fortunately, prospects for the future on this front are much brighter. Community-service programs at schools (commonly called service learning) seem to be expanding dramatically. From 1984 to 2000, the percentage of the nation's high schools offering these programs more than tripled, growing from 27 to 83 percent.[27] Following the September 2001 terrorist attacks in the United States, there were indications that interest in civics might expand even further. Books, articles, and Internet material proliferated on the topic, many of which spawned healthy classroom discussions.[28]*

---

*As might have been expected, some schools interpreted the September 11 anniversary as a time for political persuasion—in some cases telling students how great America is, in others stressing how miserably it has failed the world. The smarter teachers avoided propaganda and instead used the anniversary as a chance for students to ponder the new complexities in inter-

An interesting example of such discussions was launched by Eric Liu, a writer and former deputy domestic policy adviser in the Clinton White House. After returning home to Seattle following his stint in federal politics, Liu was struck by all that he had needed to know in order to function in Washington—and how little school had prepared him for the task. Soon, Liu started volunteering in Seattle community groups, trying to teach youngsters what he considered the basics of citizenship: "How to form an argument, how to run a meeting, how to speak up at a meeting. How to protest," Liu says. His list goes on: "How the media works. How to choose someone to vote for. How to get involved in effective community service, not just make-work service. When students graduate, they'll be doing these things a whole lot more than using quadratic equations in chemistry. Plus, these are things where all kids begin equal—and the learning of which helps them *remain* equal."

Interestingly, at least one relatively solid study backs up Liu's hunch. In a data analysis that took pains to control for outside influences (like family background and school quality), Norman Nie, director of Stanford University's Institute for the Quantitative Study of Society, found that the playing field for civic affairs was remarkably level—at least in school. Specifically, in a long-term study of 10,800 college graduates, Nie found that civic involvement was just as robust among students with high grades and test scores as it was among lower-performing students. There was, Nie concluded, "no evidence for a general intelligence factor on our measures of political engagement and public orientation."[29] At last, schools may have found an area of true equal opportunity in their desire to prepare youngsters for the complications of adult life. And it's an avenue that is far grittier and more real than what is available on a computer screen.

—

It would be nice if the challenges that parents and policy makers face when confronted with fads like school technology consisted of nothing more than the basic pedagogical questions: What is the purpose of school? What is the true nature of academic work? If that were the case, education's problems could be solved by reviving a few long-forgotten guidelines about how people learn. Unfortunately, however, our love affair with technology in

---

national relations (sometimes through role-playing) and to pursue the questions that arise from such exercises. For one articulate outline of such an approach, see "Sept. 11 Goes to School: Patriotism and Psychobabble in the Civics Classroom," by Eric Liu, *Slate*, September 3, 2002; slate.msn.com.

school has gone on far too long, and has run far too deep, to be cooled by an appeal to common sense. We have come upon a time when the institution of education has finally lost its center. At this point, the American public has become thoroughly habituated to hearing stern warnings about the schools—a steady stream of them, lurching back and forth, from one point of view to another, each one resulting in dramatically different (and painfully expensive) new policies, issued by everyone from local school board members to state governors to the nation's presidents. The pattern has become so constant that almost no one believes in the concept of truth anymore. Education's bitter debate has become the new norm.

In the midst of this confusion, the assumptions that must guide a large public institution like education have become so thoroughly cooked, so basted in subjectivity, that they now belong to the marketplace's highest bidders, who can then present them in any fashion that the public will swallow. These assumptions are central elements of our social foundation: the building blocks necessary to develop a youngster's imagination; the need for solid facts to guide big policy changes, and the odd turns that academic research has taken to generate those facts; the limits of free-market capitalism, especially when it comes to forging partnerships between business and schools; and, finally, the boundaries we draw around the art of teaching. The troubles in these domains are not nearly as obvious as are the ones found in the daily garden-variety chaos of the high-tech classroom. But their effects in the long term are far more dangerous.

PART II

HIDDEN TROUBLES

CHAPTER 7

Bulldozing the Imagination

One morning in the spring of 2001, as Mark Abbott, a fifteen-year-old at Pittsburgh's Oliver High School, sat typing out an assignment in the computer lab, he turned to a reporter and offered his assessment of the lab's machines. "These things are garbage," Abbott said. His opinion was understandable. The labs at Oliver High, one of the city's poorest and lowest-performing high schools, were equipped with Tandy 1000s—computers that were older than most of the students and that still transferred data on obsolete floppy disks. Broken printers sat nearby gathering dust, their replacement parts long since out of production. But things had recently started looking up. In 1998, the city had begun investing heavily in new computer hardware and software for Oliver High and the many other schools in the city that were filled with antiquated computer gear. By late 2001, the total of the city's new technology purchases came to $24 million.

Presumably, this is how it's supposed to be. A district plagued with old gear eventually faces the music and puts down real money for some good machines. The interesting aspects of this particular investment were the pressures that surrounded it. As school officials were readying their computer orders, the district faced a rather severe deficit—totaling $37 million by 2000.[1] By law in Pennsylvania, as in most states, schools cannot operate in the red, so district officials took some drastic action. They cut back spending on teachers and supplies, shut down twelve elementary schools and sent their students to other schools, and raised taxes by 20 percent. Meanwhile, they let a $35 million wish list accumulate, on items such as career-education classes, social workers, student counselors, and year-round schooling. But they didn't forgo their computer upgrade. This made for some odd juxtapositions on individual campuses. At Oliver High, for instance, while students were now without a machine-shop class and a vocational-education instructor, students down the hall from the old Tandy lab were happily typing away at $1,300 workstations, which included state-of-the-art Dell computers, scanners, and digital cameras. The full price tag on these items at this school: $192,409.

These trade-offs, as we will soon see, extend far beyond the curricular, cutting deep into the experiences that build students' inner foundations, and their imaginations. And Pittsburgh is far from the only community making shifts of this sort. New Jersey cut state aid to a number of school districts in 1996 and then spent $10 million on classroom computers. Across the country, in Union City, California, one single school district spent $37 million shortly thereafter to buy new gear for a mere eleven schools; to sustain this investment, the district has consistently cut back expenditures on science equipment, field trips, and other academic mainstays. The Kittridge Street Elementary School, in Los Angeles, killed its music program in 1996 to hire a technology coordinator. In Mansfield, Massachusetts, administrators dropped proposed teaching positions in art, music, and physical education and then spent $333,000 on computers. Throughout the country, phys ed classes have been on a steady decline. Art programs also have been a casualty, their spacious accommodations often seen by administrators as ripe for transformation into computer laboratories.[2]

As national spending on school technology has increased, some states have shifted portions of their book funds into computer funds. Ironically, one of the states that has been the most aggressive in this regard is Texas. As noted in the first chapter, Texas education officials decided in the early 1990s to let schools spend book budgets on soon to be obsolete videodisk technology. In 1998, just a few years before Texas gave up on videodisks, Jack Christie, then chair of the state board of education, proposed (unsuccessfully) that schools stop buying books altogether and replace them with laptops.

In many states, some of the curricular domains that have been replaced by computer programs appeared at first to deserve it, since they seemed to be relics of an earlier time. Take shop classes, for example, which have been almost entirely replaced by "technology education programs." In San Francisco, a community whose modern identity is linked to high technology, by the late 1990s only one public school—the lone vocational high school—still offered a full shop program. But appearances are deceptive with programs like shop. As numerous employers have explained, experience with tactile materials is critical to expertise in a vast range of professional pursuits. Sometimes, it's needed just to land a job. "We get kids who don't know the difference between a screwdriver and a ball peen hammer," James Dahlman, chair of the vocational program in San Francisco, told me. "How are they going to make a career choice? Administrators are stuck in this mind-set that all kids will go to a four-year college and become a doctor or a lawyer, and that's not true. I know some who went to college, graduated, and then had to go back to technical school to get a job."

The further irony, of course, is that in today's world, computer access is becoming ubiquitous, while access to tools and other materials needed to build physical things has become almost extinct in the schools. And policy makers continue to accelerate this trend. In the fall of 2000, Tom Ridge, then-governor of Pennsylvania, made news with a dramatic initiative to spend $3.2 million over the next two years to put toddlers on the fast lane by giving computers with Internet access to more than four thousand day-care centers. The director of the program (this one was called CyberStart) went so far as to argue that tots would develop their fine-motor skills as they learned how to use a computer mouse. "It's as simple as this," Ridge said. "Children who understand computers and the Internet are more likely to succeed in the new technology-based economy of the 21st century."[3]

Beyond this tired and wobbly argument about high-tech job skills, Ridge is making a deeper case: that if children don't get started on technology when they're very young, they will fall seriously behind. Parents certainly have been sympathetic to this view. As evidence, the hottest-selling toys in 2002 were high-tech gizmos designed to give young children a leg up—talking books and robots, beeping alphabet boards, and the many other computerized products that the industry calls "electronic learning aids."[4]* But here, too, a fuller account of the evidence suggests that parents' faith in technology's power may be quite a misconception—yet another educational e-lusion. In some communities, parents and teachers seem to have been aware of this fact. As far back as 1996, when the school superintendent in Great Neck, Long Island, proposed replacing elementary-school

---

*The runaway leader in this market has been Leapfrog Enterprises, which in 2002 was making eight of the top ten bestselling electronic toys. Leapfrog is a division of Knowledge Universe, an innovative educational products company co-founded by Michael Milken, the former junk-bond king.

shop classes with computer classes and training the shop teachers as computer coaches, the move provoked such a parental backlash that the superintendent rescinded the plan.

THE BODY'S BRAIN

I n raising their concerns, the Great Neck parents have had plenty of company. Over the years, specialists in childhood development have grown
increasingly dubious about the wisdom of giving young children intense exposure to computer technology. Their greatest concern involves the very
young—pre-schoolers through third graders. Those are the years when a
child is most impressionable. Child-development experts therefore consider
it crucial to give children at this age a broad base—emotionally, intellectually, and in the five senses—before introducing something as technical and
one-dimensional as a computer. In their eyes, the primary materials for that
base—those critical building blocks pointed to throughout this book—are
experiences in the human and physical world.

The importance of this foundation as a prerequisite for learning may
be most apparent when it's missing. During one of my school visits—to
Sanchez Elementary, which sits on the edge of San Francisco's Latino
community—I watched a teacher struggle in a computer lab with a frenzied
bilingual special-education class, full of second, third, and fourth graders.
"It's highly motivating for them," the teacher said as she rushed from machine to machine, attending not to math questions but to computer glitches.
Then she noticed a girl counting on her fingers and her mood changed.
"You see," she said, "these kids still need the hands-on"—meaning the opportunity to manipulate real objects, such as beans or colored blocks. The
value of these materials, child-development experts believe, is that they
deeply imprint knowledge into a young child's brain, by transmitting the
lessons of experience through a variety of sensory pathways. "Curiously
enough," the educational psychologist Jane Healy wrote in a 1990 book,
Endangered Minds: Why Children Don't Think and What We Can Do About It,
"visual stimulation is probably not the main access route to nonverbal reasoning. Body movements, the ability to touch, feel, manipulate, and build
sensory awareness of relationships in the physical world, are its main foundations." The problem, Healy wrote, is that "in schools, traditionally, the
senses have had little status after kindergarten."[5] In a 1998 follow-up, *Failure to Connect: How Computers Affect Our Children's Minds—for Better and
Worse,* Healy expanded on this theme. She wrote that abstract reasoning,

according to psychological research, grows out of "physical experience of action." And that lasting motivation comes from activities that grow with a child's curiosity—a process too individual for most computer programs to sustain for long.[6]

Plenty of educators share Healy's views. I even found teachers in extraordinarily high-tech schools making similar points. One such school is Cary Academy, a brand-new, lavishly funded K–12 private school in North Carolina's Research Triangle Park. Cary Academy was started by the president of the SAS Institute, one of the giants of the software industry, partly to serve as a test bed for SAS's high-end visions for computing in schools. The academy has virtually everything a school could wish for—an immaculate, country-club-type campus done in Georgian architecture; computers for every student; small classes (its student-teacher ratio is a minuscule eight to one); varied tactile exercises for the elementary grades; and labs stocked with every piece of science equipment imaginable. Despite all this, Gray Rushin, the school's science teacher, is no cheerleader about computerized approaches to science. "I'd give up [the computers] *way* before I'd give up the lab," Rushin told me. "All these virtual labs—that is garbage, real garbage. The computer is a tool to explain real things students have seen." Rushin favors what teachers in his field call wet science: the test tubes and fluids and solid objects that students can handle and push and transform with their own hands. A physicist in Ohio agreed. "My concern is that we are tending to expose students to too many contrived, controlled versions of reality, rather than nature as its raw untidy self. If our schools' curricula included an hour of bird watching or rock collecting, or fossil hunting or astronomical observing for every hour spent in virtual reality, I could be content. But increasingly, that seems not to be the case."[7]

The subject at issue here is what educators call kinesthetic experience—what youngsters learn through the experience of their own bodies. One of the most focused examinations of this notion is *The Hand*, a 1998 book by Frank R. Wilson, a neurologist and the director of a program for performing artists at the University of California School of Medicine in San Francisco. In this exhaustive treatise, Wilson accumulates prodigious amounts of material—part scientific and part anecdotal, in the form of personal profiles of people whose success stems from early experiences with intense, tactile work. Other studies seem to confirm Wilson's case.[8] The overall picture suggests that the sensory capacities of the human hand send powerful signals to the brain, helping it learn and develop.

While science only partly understands these dynamics, some researchers believe they've seen enough to put the brakes on computing. "When people are using computers the way they do now, it's all visual, with a little bit of auditory activity," says Susan Lederman, a professor of psychology and computing and information science, and the author of one scientific study on the hand. "If you use them a lot, you are cutting off the natural kind of interaction with the world that you get with the hand. The hand and eye complement each other." But with the simulated dynamics of computing, "there's no forced feedback. You are depriving the system." The simplest version of these theories was once put to me by a former teacher. It had been some years since this teacher had been in the classroom, but she still remembered the maxim her school had lived by: "The more muscle, the more memory."

Despite kinesthetic insights of this sort, when the Clinton administration first launched its nationwide scholastic computer campaign, shop classes were one of the curricular areas it suggested schools consider cutting—to provide money and empty rooms for computers. All of which may suggest a new role for classroom computers: as canaries in the academic mine. When enthusiasm for technology reaches unusually high levels, it may be a sign not of success but of trouble—a signal that the scholastic program is ailing and that money and attention should be directed elsewhere. As David Elkind, of Tufts University, once told me, "You need computers to motivate kids if you have the kind of system that isn't stimulating to begin with."

THE MYSTERIES OF THE IMAGINATION

With such a swirl of worries surrounding computer technology, questions eventually arise about what may be humanity's most intriguing attribute—the imagination. Jane Healy has certainly raised alarm bells on this front, arguing in *Failure to Connect* that computer games distract children from engaging in physical play. The latter, she believes, teaches children how to pretend, which in turn develops the imagination. Across the country, teachers also report a marked decline in children's ability to play and create imaginary worlds. This is not a minor problem. A healthy imagination allows youngsters to develop into accomplished artists, writers, and scientists. It helps all of us see and appreciate the concepts in books, movies, or any other kind of exceptional work. And it certainly fuels the fun everyone has when people know how to be playful with one another, and by themselves.

So what solid information really exists about how computer activities affect the imagination? Perhaps the most that can be said is that there is limited, speculative, but intriguing material on both sides of the argument: Computerized media may well build the imagination in a few spheres, and tear it down in many others.

The best way to begin this inquiry is to look at some related but better-traveled ground—the effects of television on children. Computer proponents understandably get annoyed when technology critics say that computers repeat television's sins, dulling children's curiosity and turning them into passive sponges that soak up anything that spews from the screen. In their view, the computer's dynamic, "interactive" requirements make those links off-base. "It's not like the TV," Don Taylor, headmaster of the high-tech Cary Academy, told me. "Those comparisons go about two inches deep." However, more than a few psychologists dare to make just those comparisons. "I think it's quite legitimate to raise the same questions with computers as we did with television," says Dan Anderson, a professor of psychology at the University of Massachusetts at Amherst. "The history is the same. There's been this naïve optimism about helping kids learn in fabulous new ways. Then there has been great alarm about violent content, then more alarm that kids are not getting smarter, and might be getting dumber."

To be fair, no responsible voice in psychology and child development (Anderson included) goes so far as to say that the links between television and computers are definitive or even precise. For all its recent advances, research on the brain remains sketchy. And computers are so new that their effect on the brain is still a mystery. "No one has done any serious study yet," Jerome Singer, a leading researcher in child psychology at Yale, told me in the fall of 2001. Singer and his wife, Dorothy, a professor of psychology at Yale's Child Studies Center, are among a handful of experts who have tried to establish some firm grounding on these questions. Over the decades, the husband-and-wife team has written a number of books on the effects of television and other elements of the media on children's imagination and creative play. In their recent volume, *The Handbook of Children and the Media,* they found only one area that clearly diminished "imaginative play"—violent material, both in television and in video games.[9] "There is a clearly shown association with overt violent behavior, and less cooperation," Jerome Singer told me. "The data is very clear about this, in a number of studies."

But when it comes to television's general effect on the imagination, the data is somewhat mixed. In one of the Singers' earlier works (*The House of Make Believe: Children's Play and the Developing Imagination*) researchers compared two groups of children exposed to the same story—one on television and one on radio. The TV group had better recall of the story's details.

But the radio group did a better job of remembering the dialogue, the expressive language, and the sound effects. This group also produced "more imaginative drawings" about the show (with "more details . . . portrayed from unusual perspectives").[10] Not surprisingly, the Singers also found that when children who were heavy TV watchers were compared with light viewers, the heavy watchers had weaker language skills, which are an obvious building block for the imagination.

But what about computers? While technology promoters may have hyped the medium's interactive powers, this machinery clearly offers a range of activities that television can't. Some academics have even argued that computer games expand children's imaginations. High-tech children "think differently from the rest of us," William D. Winn, the director of the Learning Center at the University of Washington's Human Interface Technology Laboratory, once said. "They develop hypertext minds. They leap around. It's as though their cognitive strategies were parallel, not sequential."[11] But once again, child psychologists have generally argued the opposite. They see most computer programs narrowing information rather than opening it up. The reason is that the computer, whose heart is inevitably digital, is fated to be a linear mechanism. Psychologists therefore suspect that computers tend to exercise mostly one half of the brain—the left hemisphere, where primarily sequential thinking occurs. The right brain can meanwhile get short shrift, yet this is the hemisphere that works on different kinds of information simultaneously. It's the domain that shapes our multifaceted impressions, the engine of creative analysis.

Computer promoters of course dismiss these worries, noting that in most schools, computer hours are far too limited to do much damage. To a number of developmental psychologists, that isn't the point. They argue that the schools' enthusiasm for computer technology sends the wrong message: that the mediated world is more significant than the real one. "It's like TV commercials," Barbara Scales, the head teacher at the Child Study Center at the University of California at Berkeley, told me. "Kids get so hyped up, it can change their expectations about stimulation versus what they generate themselves." Coming to much the same conclusion, Jane Healy has been inclined to urge great caution. "A prudent society controls its own infatuation with 'progress' when planning for its young," she argued in Endangered Minds. "Unproven technologies . . . may offer lively visions, but they can also be detrimental to the development of the young plastic brain. The cerebral cortex is a wondrously well-buffered mechanism that can withstand a good bit of well-intentioned bungling. Yet there is a point at which fundamental neural substrates for reasoning may be jeopardized for children who lack proper physical, intellectual, or emotional nurturance. Childhood—and the brain—have their own imperatives. In development, missed opportunities may be difficult to recapture."

To underscore this point, Healy mentioned an English teacher who could readily tell which of her students' essays were conceived on a computer. "They don't link ideas," the teacher says. "They just write one thing, and then they write another one, and they don't seem to see or develop the relationships between them." Healy concluded that the pizzazz of computer-generated schoolwork hides these analytical gaps, which "won't become apparent until [the student] can't organize herself around a homework assignment or a job that requires initiative. More commonplace activities, such as figuring out how to nail two boards together, organizing a game . . . may actually form a better basis for real-world intelligence."[12]

This may be one reason that computer programs that attempt to replace old-fashioned book reading don't get the best of reviews. One small but carefully controlled study went so far as to claim that Reader Rabbit, a reading program used in more than 100,000 schools, caused students to suffer a 50 percent drop in creativity. Apparently, after forty-nine students used an early version of the program for seven months, they were no longer able to answer open-ended questions, and showed a markedly diminished ability to brainstorm with fluency and originality.[13] Teachers have occasionally noticed the same signs. At Expo Elementary, a progressive-methods school in St. Paul, Minnesota, one teacher told me that after trying Reader Rabbit with her kindergartners, "That zombie look kicked in. I found it really scary."

While some of these concerns are not based on hard science, nature, as we know, abhors a vacuum. And computer skeptics have rushed to fill this one with alarm. "Nobody knows how kids' internal wiring works," Clifford Stoll wrote in *Silicon Snake Oil*, "but anyone who's directed away from social interactions has a head start on turning out weird. . . . No computer can teach what a walk through a pine forest feels like. Sensation has no substitute."[14] In the fall of 2000, approximately eighty leading academics, doctors, psychologists, and other experts joined forces to make an even stronger statement. The group was gathered by an organization called the Alliance for Childhood, which was publishing a report entitled "Fool's Gold: A Critical Look at Computers in Childhood." In compiling its document, the Alliance assembled mounds of literature, each piece of which added to the sense that the hurried embrace of computers might really be damaging children—not only their social and cognitive development but also their physical health.

While the Alliance report had its share of arguments from confirmed technology doubters, it was also laced with concerns about computers from established conservative sources. One example was Marilyn Benoit, the president-elect of the American Academy of Child and Adolescent Psychiatry, who spoke at a 1999 State of the World Forum about what she called "dot.com kids." Benoit was afraid that "children's constant exposure to rapid-fire stimuli to the brain" from the onslaught of digital media had contributed to the rise in hyperactivity disorders, their inability to handle frustration, and a general condition that she termed childhood narcissism. The trend has given birth to a whole new psychological label: "explosive children." Other experts endorsing the Alliance's report included such august figures as the child psychologist Robert Coles; education author Jonathan Kozol; Daniel Goleman, the author of *Emotional Intelligence;* the famed primate researcher Jane Goodall; Diane Ravitch, the education author and former assistant secretary of education under George H. W. Bush; and Joseph Weizenbaum, MIT professor emeritus of computer science. Once all their material was assembled, it made enough of a case that the experts joined the Alliance in calling for a moratorium on computers in the elementary grades, at least until a decent study of these questions could be done by the surgeon general.[15] The moratorium call landed like a bomb, producing headlines across the country. But within months, the public's fervor for the shiny promise of computers resumed, and all the experts' warnings were largely forgotten.

THE POTENCY OF THE ARTS

A nyone who surveys the research landscape looking for scientific reasons to turn one way or the other in education—to go with computing, say, or with wood-carving—will, as we have seen, trip over debatable studies seemingly everywhere. The problem is certainly understandable. *Learning* and *achievement* are subjective terms. The mere suggestion that their foundations have been discovered raises inevitable questions: By what standard? By whose measure? According to what proof?

It's somewhat helpful, therefore, when research comes along that offers proof so tangible that it is physical. Such was the case with a German study, completed in 1995 by Dr. Gottfried Schlaug, who subsequently went on to Beth Israel Deaconess Medical Center in Boston. Schlaug decided to examine the brains of a group of musicians and to do so with magnetic resonance imaging—popularly known as an MRI scan. One group was a set of nine string players, and the MRI revealed that all of them had a larger brain mass than non-musicians did—specifically, in the section of the somatosensory cortex dedicated to the thumb and fifth finger of the left hand. Musicians who had perfect pitch turned out to possess an unusually large hunk of cortex in the left hemisphere's planum temporale, an area that may help process both sound and language. Interestingly, Schlaug found in all these musicians that any expansion of the brain's cortex was most influenced not by how many hours the musicians played but how young they had started. In fact, when comparing non-musicians with those who had started playing music as young children, Schlaug found that the musicians had a larger mass of nerve fibers connecting the brain's two hemispheres.[16]

The implications of this last finding are significant. A person's creativity and analytical skills depend greatly on the ability to think with both hemispheres of the brain; yet many of us lack this agility, as indicated by how often we joke about being either a left-brain person or very right-brain. It's not surprising, then, that the education world has been pelted with additional research (there were nearly a dozen more studies by 2001) that confirmed or expanded on the core point here: that certain kinds of music education in the early years, including the elementary grades, holds value that has long been unrecognized. A few of these findings included traditional measures of academic achievement, such as gains in standardized test scores.

As word has spread about music's potential, some policy makers have fallen for claims that turned out to be rushed and thin—just as they have with computer technology. Such was the case, for instance, with the much-vaunted "Mozart effect," a theory advanced by a 1993 study, which showed that college students who listened to as little as ten minutes of Mozart before taking IQ tests increased their scores in spatial reasoning by nine points. The Mozart buzz had such reverberation that the governor of Georgia, for example, raised $100,000 in private funds to give classical music CDs to families with newborns.[17] Eventually, it became known that the college students' IQ gains were only temporary, lasting not much longer than the sonata—a mere ten or fifteen minutes.[18] In other words, just listening to music probably won't do much more than help someone relax; learning to play it might. The results of follow-up studies have mostly been tentative, but they suggest some powerful associations. In one, for example, Swiss and Austrian researchers tried an experiment with a group of students that had been studying the standard range of courses, one of which was a music class in which they actually learned to play an instrument. The researchers increased the frequency of students' music lessons, from once or twice to five times a week while actually cutting back on math and language studies. After three years, the experimental students were as good at math as students who had stuck with the standard curriculum, and even better at languages. Researchers found the intensive music students to be more cooperative with one another as well.[19]

Several American studies conducted around the same time produced additional surprises. One, a survey of SAT test takers from 1990 to 1996, indicated that students who had been taking courses in the arts scored higher on both the math and the verbal parts of the exams. Specifically, students who had been taking classes in theater, art history, music performance or appreciation, dance, or studio arts consistently got at least 30 points more than students who hadn't been taking these courses, and often scored up to 50 or 60 points more.[20] In the younger grades, another study looked at four classes of children, ages five to seven, who were enrolled in a special program that emphasized music and art; two other classes, acting as control groups, stuck with standard lessons. When it was time to test the children seven months later, the researchers discovered a mistake: The kids in the arts program weren't the random sample they hoped for but were a group of underachievers. Yet they still caught up with the standard classes in reading, and surpassed them in mathematics.[21]

—

While these studies sound persuasive, they beg some chicken-and-egg analysis. First, regarding the SAT study, it is likely that arts classes draw students who are top performers before they even step foot in an arts class. These youngsters may have unusually broad interests, the capacity to keep up with a number of electives, well-off families who encourage cultural and intellectual pursuits, or some combination of all three. Music classes are particularly susceptible to this kind of self-selection, because mastering an instrument requires such exceptional self-discipline. As for the young underachievers who did so well after some arts studies, this comparison posed another problem: the arts and non-arts groups each got different teachers, which left open the possibility that the arts students were treated to more inspired classes.

Some of these eventualities may be explained by what's popularly called the Hawthorne effect—the notion that any new environment, and any new level of attention from overseers, will boost productivity whether or not the change is worthwhile. (It's also worth noting that the Hawthorne effect may suffer from its own illusions; several examinations of the original studies, conducted with factory workers in a Chicago electric plant in the late 1920s, suggest the effect was either nonexistent or too small to matter.[22]) When it comes to children, however, Hawthorne's ghost seems plenty real. Any practical activity—with a computer or with a cello—is likely to get a youngster's blood flowing, especially if it's new or the teacher is enthusiastic. A more recent study underscored this fact. After sixty-three fourth-, fifth-, and sixth-graders took individual piano lessons, they marginally bested a control group in spatial reasoning after the first and second year, but did no better after the third year.[23] This is disturbingly reminiscent of the Apple Classrooms of Tomorrow (as described in chapter 1). In that program, outside researchers found a few of the same gains that the arts classes produce (students are enthused and proud of their work; teachers are stimulated; and so forth). Once the Apple students went back to their regular classes, however, their improvement mysteriously evaporated too. So, yes, exciting new activities do often lead to nice treats, including rising test scores. But the juice is not in any particular tool as much as it is in the task-activities that continually marry interesting challenges with creative freedom.

As we can see, many claims about the value of music, and the arts in general, sound a lot like the claims made about computer technology. Both camps encourage schools to fund and plunge ahead with their programs despite the paucity of "hard" proof of their scholastic merit. In both camps, the teachers generally see a change in their students' behavior, and that's proof enough for them. "Art turns a light on with these kids," says Bob Sotelo, who has taught art for twenty-one years at Maple Lane School, which sits inside a maximum-security facility for juvenile offenders in the state of Washington. Sotelo devises class projects that mix art with math and language studies, often culminating in public exhibits. This scheme, he's found, has minimized behavior problems and strengthened the students' confidence. "They're surprised they have ability." And the opportunity to show their work, he says, "gives them an outlet, a voice—some kind of positive interaction with society."[24]

But technology promoters talk about the exact same benefits from publishing on the Internet. There are several important differences, however, that are generally overlooked. When schools take their chances on the Internet, they commit to a heavy up-front financial investment in work that, for a child, is simulated and virtual rather than tactile and real. And that work is presented to an audience that is extremely iffy, composed largely of strangers. Meanwhile, a small show in a local community center or even a parents' night in a school hallway will, for most youngsters, carry just as much punch, if not more.

Ultimately, the arts might well help raise test scores and any other measures of achievement. Or they might not. To most of the researchers who specialize in the arts, that isn't the point anyway. In their view, the arts should be taught for their own sake, not for their peripheral effect on "hard" subjects like math and science. Two Harvard researchers who hold this view are Ellen Winner and Lois Hetland, who examined 188 different studies of the arts since 1950. In all that literature, the researchers found precious little well-controlled proof that the arts are dependable boosters of academic performance in other subjects. (The only exceptions to this rule have been Schlaug's scientific studies of instrument playing's influence on the brain, cited earlier; and drama classes, which consistently improve students' reading, writing, and speaking skills.) Yet the researchers still remain loyal to this field. "The arts are the only disciplines," Winner and Hetland concluded, "in which recognizing and expressing deep personal feelings and thoughts, often in nonverbal form, is the essence of the enterprise."[25]

A more aesthetic explanation of this argument was made in a *New York Times Book Review* article on books that aim to teach art to children. After surveying five different fancy and densely referenced texts, the reviewer settled on her favorite, a simple book called *Harold and the Purple Crayon*. What appealed to the reviewer was the book's uncluttered path to the imagination. "There's just little Harold in his pajamas, heading out on an ordinary night to draw a line that runs on forever, a line that forms a moon to light his steps and a path to walk on and nine kinds of pies to eat—as if one well-worn, stubby crayon could allow you to dream up a whole universe. Which of course it can."[26]

As seductive as this case for the arts may be, it's also vulnerable in its very softness. That's precisely why Howard Gardner, the Harvard education professor who also helps direct the university's Project Zero, wants to protect arts classes. "If arts live by instrumental arguments, they may also die should those arguments prove faulty—or should someone find a less expensive way to raise IQ or spawn imaginative businesspeople."[27]

Of course, the same arguments could be made, once again, about technology. That's why—with some limited exceptions, such as repetitive practice of basic drills—computing will be most effective if it is left for the upper grades, where students can explore technology for its own sake. At that age, they are ready to understand and appreciate the intricacies and limitations of programming languages, digital circuitry, and other fine points of high technology. Of course, not every student will want to tinker with the inside of a computer or devote Saturday afternoons to designing Web pages. Nor will every student want to play an instrument or be in a school play. This is why schools have always tried to follow one of the oldest clichés in the book: Variety is the spice of life.

EDUCATION'S ECOSYSTEM

In a small town in the center of Long Island—southeast of the Great Neck school district, where the superintendent once tried to cut elementary school shop classes to make room for computers—sits a small, working-class, public elementary school that pursues an unusual vision. The school is called Otsego Elementary, and its principal, Joan Delle Valle, is an advocate of paying attention to students' individual "learning styles." The concept has a long but spotty history. First popularized in the 1970s by a number of educators and psychologists (primarily Rita and Kenneth Dunn), it essentially suggested that teachers try to cater as best they could to each child's cognitive idiosyncrasies. While some children, for instance, may perform best in traditional classroom settings, others will shine if allowed to listen to music while reading, sprawl on the floor, or even procrastinate for a few hours, turning to their homework just before bedtime.

While experts like the Dunns have marshaled research proving that the concept works, it has never been heartily embraced. As can be imagined, most teachers—and their bosses—have not felt confident that such a melange of environments and expectations could be accommodated in the public school regimen. In recent years, though, the notion of attending to children's different learning styles has gotten a new lease on life, thanks largely to some of the recent scientific study of the human brain. Some of those studies led to a popular set of theories about people's "multiple intelligences," as developed by Harvard's Howard Gardner. In a nutshell, Gardner believes each of us has some combination of eight distinctly different kinds of ability: spatial, musical, *inter*personal (the knack for dealing with others), *intra*personal (the knack for dealing with oneself, sometimes called self-awareness), bodily-kinesthetic, naturalistic (a feel for nature), logical, and linguistic. By Gardner's definitions, schools have routinely done a very good job of addressing the last two—logical and linguistic. But they've failed miserably, he argues, at attending to the rest.[28] Once Gardner's theories were coupled with other things that were being learned about the genetic development of the brain, it yielded a renaissance of interest in human potential.

Today, Delle Valle happily supports her students' desires to, say, kick back with a textbook on big beanbag chairs, dim the lights, or eat at their desks. While one would think every student would want such treats, Delle Valle has found that over time, students whose true learning styles don't fit this routine eventually gravitate back to hard desks and brightly lit rooms. "It's taken the negativity away from being different," Delle Valle told me. In addition to the many environmental options, Otsego offers quite a curricular cornucopia as well. Hands-on science activities are a big priority; so are the arts and a range of other tactile endeavors. One of Delle Valle's requirements is that teachers deliver their lessons three or four different ways—to improve the odds of catching each student in the room.

Otsego doesn't have much computer technology in its school. More important, Delle Valle made sure that no area of the curriculum was cut to find money for what equipment it does have. "Everything fits together," she said. "When you cut something out, you may lose something academic along the way that you may not realize." Her comment reminded me of the lessons that ecological scientists learned in the 1980s, following the Reagan administration's vigorous policy of allowing clear-cutting in the national forests. At the time, timber companies argued that they could reseed these forests and manage their ecosystems for renewal in the process. Within a few years, scientists realized that the variety of flora and fauna in virgin forests was so dense, so full of hidden webs of life, that if they were heavily logged, it was impossible to fully revive them. This led to a more restrictive approach to logging during the Clinton administration, and ongoing environmental battles ever since.

Now the same lessons are being visited upon schools. Many of the districts that cut certain subjects in order to fund technology have already started having visible troubles. In Union City, California, for example, the district that spent $37 million in 1996 had to spend another $5 million in 2001 to upgrade its system—this at a time when district enrollment was falling, a turn that in itself cost the district $6 million in state funding. "It is killing us and we are not alone," says Pat Gibbons, Union City's deputy superintendent. "After four years all the basic computers were antiquated immediately. We started having teachers saying, 'This is too slow, we won't use it.'"

As the economy faltered in the early years of the twenty-first century, school funding naturally shrank as well. By 2002, school districts across the country were looking for new places to pull back on spending. In the following months, some spread their cuts across their entire curriculum, but a good many did not. In Northern California, for example, district officials started closing elementary schools, laying off teachers or freezing salaries for those who remained, adding students to already crowded classrooms, and, of course, cutting music classes and other programs in the arts. But they did not touch their technology budgets. Other states, especially Arizona, Illinois, Indiana, South Dakota, and Utah, actually increased their spending on school technology in 2002.[29]

In New York City, the budget for technology in the nation's largest school district grew dramatically through the late 1990s. (One category in district budget documents offers some illustration. From 1997 to 2000, spending on "computer support services" grew more than fivefold, from $19.7 million to $118.6 million.)[30] Meanwhile, funding for textbooks and other books in New York schools has declined. In late 2001, New York City's budget woes were further aggravated by that fall's terrorist attacks, and the city's schools found themselves facing a $406 million deficit. To cover those losses, school officials laid off administrators and cut back many areas they deemed nonessential. These included after-school and arts programs, the latter having enjoyed a brief growth spurt during the prosperity of the 1990s. But the city stuck by its classroom computers. When it came time to set the 2001 budget, school officials included an estimated $250 million for technology—a sum that could have bought nine hours of one-on-one tutoring for every student in the city; or 5 million new textbooks; or 7,800 new teachers, which would amount to a 10 percent increase in teaching staff.[31]

The same trade-offs could be found, in varying degrees, in many smaller districts across the country. The question, of course, is what will happen to graduates from these communities. Those students now have to navigate college studies, along with the increasingly complex challenges that the adult world presents, after having built their intellectual foundations in schools that were robbed of books, teachers, the arts, "wet sciences," and other basic building blocks. The situation could be called the educational equivalent of Maslow's hierarchy of needs.

In the 1960s, the psychologist Abraham Maslow etched what is likely to be a permanent place for himself in the annals of history by defining personal evolution as a pyramid. People can make little use of the upper levels of human needs and desires, he argued, until their base requirements have been fulfilled. For Maslow, the base of life's pyramid consisted of physical requirements, such as food, shelter, and clothing. On the next level is personal safety, followed by a network of nurturing relationships (family, social). On top of that are our more amorphous needs: the sense that we're being treated with respect; the satisfaction of our curiosities (education fits here); our aesthetic desires; and finally, self-actualization—that is, fully realizing one's potential on one's own terms.[32]

Education, being the construction site for a variety of individual skills, forms a pyramid of its own. Judging from the literature on psychological development, the first layers of this pyramid should consist of a variety of exercises that build up and enrich students' internal capacities—their ability to observe, listen, reflect, and imagine, among other things. On top of this foundation is the ability to think critically as one strives to solve life's complex problems. Following this layer, and somewhat mixed within it, is hard, factual knowledge about how the world works. Somewhere higher, near the top, come opportunities to use fancy tools. That is probably where technology should come in—as but one of a number of extra options.

This, of course, assumes that schools can afford extra options. Since financial constraints seem to be a constant in public education, one would think that schools would make a priority of handling their money shrewdly. One would also think that when businesses get involved in schools, they would do their best to compensate for classroom shortages. What's surprising is how often they don't, and instead bring in initiatives that multiply a school's troubles.

CHAPTER 8

The Spoils of Industry
Partnerships

On a drizzly September day in Marietta, Ohio, in 1991, then-Governor George Voinovich broke virtual ground on what was supposed to be Ohio's educational wave of the future. With assistance from Ohio Bell, the governor linked up by live video transmission to an audience at Ohio University in Athens; he then dropped in via a second feed to observe a class in progress in the Appalachian Mountains, at Whitwell Elementary, in Ironton. "In order to fulfill my administration's commitment to excellence in education," Governor Voinovich said, "we must explore projects like this, which work to eliminate the problems our rural schools are experiencing. This distance-learning project is a fine example of a public/private partnership at work to give our children access to educational resources otherwise not available to them."[1] Hours after the demonstration, the network wasn't transmitting a thing. As it turned out, the system was still more of a concept than a reality. And the reality was so difficult to make work that Ohio Bell had to bring in a temporary version that morning to get everyone through the demonstration. Its transmissions, which were powered by high-end microwave technology, emanated from a pair of costly corporate trucks that were temporarily sitting outside purring quietly in the school parking lot.

The system promoted by Voinovich that day was a new video network promised by Ameritech, Ohio Bell's parent company. Despite everyone's high hopes for the project, it was a full year before Ameritech got the system in place at Whitwell and a half-dozen other schools. In the following years, problems crashed the system so persistently that in 1999 the schools abandoned it altogether. "In the last year, it was down more than it was up," Teresa Franklin, an Ohio University professor of education who served as technical expert for the project, told me. "Anytime the governor wanted to hook up with Ironton, Ameritech made sure it all worked wonderfully. Wonderfully. An hour later, we couldn't get the two schools to even connect."

The network problems in these Appalachian schools, and their mounting costs, were shared in one form or another by scores of schools in the 1990s across Ohio and other states in the Midwest. Unbeknownst to the general public, these troubles were caused in no small part by the schools' presumed benefactors—the nation's telecommunications giants and the political leaders who carried their water. By the latter part of the decade, federal authorities, through the telecom industry, encouraged schools to go even further in building high-end networks through a multi-billion-dollar federal subsidy called the e-rate. On the surface, the e-rate's purpose was to discount a poor school's costs when it came time to get wired, and many schools have used its support wisely. But a good many have not. Quite aside from educational questions, which are legion with any of these fancy networks, the e-rate program has created some serious problems, which have remained largely hidden from public view. These include an assortment of unusual financial opportunities for the companies that provide schools with network services—and some outsize costs to schools and the general public.

The abuses that certain schools have suffered over their telecommunication networks, along with a few more isolated games that unscrupulous entrepreneurs have played, illustrate an extra layer to education's vulnerabilities with technology. Gary Stager, the educational technology veteran from Pepperdine University, once put it to me this way: "I don't want to be anywhere near the schools when the bill for all this stuff comes due." Most of the time those bills are perfectly legal, but they are questionable on ethical grounds, constituting a kind of soft corruption. Sometimes they're also questionable on legal grounds, complete with indictable crimes.

THE DEREGULATION SHUFFLE

The story of the telecom industry's high-tech ride through the schools begins during a brief but powerful moment of political and legal history: the drive for industry deregulation. From the latter part of the 1980s through the 1990s, deregulation was regarded as the answer of the day in a range of fields—everything from phone service to airline travel to gas and electricity supplies. But by 2001, as California sank into an energy crisis and the Enron corporation's house of cards started collapsing, deregulation's rose began to wither.[2] Around the same time, the telecom industry fell into severe debt and other financial trouble, suggesting that the merits of deregulation in that industry might someday be reinterpreted as well.[3] Should that day come, an intriguing element to the story will lie in the way telecom firms used the schools to make lucrative deals with state officials.

Some of the clearest demonstrations of this phenomenon were the arrangements made by Ameritech. Now a subsidiary of the Texas telecom giant SBC Communications, Ameritech was the primary supplier of phone service in five Midwestern states throughout most of the 1990s. In 1994, two years before telecom deregulation made its federal debut, Ameritech sought state deregulation in Wisconsin. And it did so through an ingenious, multi-million-dollar shell game. In the end, the game turned on those who played it. First it stung the schools; eventually it ensnared the states' taxpayers. To understand why, it helps to briefly revisit the history of telecom deregulation, both nationally and as practiced in the Midwest by one company.

When federal regulators under the Reagan administration broke up the AT&T monopoly in the 1980s, the progeny, as most everyone knows, was a feisty, nationwide family of Baby Bells. By the mid-1990s, about a decade after these companies were born, the telecom world was suddenly populated with enterprising upstarts—cell phone outfits, independent phone companies, and similar operations. To fight the vigor of these new businesses, Ameritech, like most of its Baby Bell cousins, sought even greater freedom from state regulators. As these new companies refined their pitch, it became remarkably consistent in state after state. In Wisconsin, the pitchmen were Ameritech and a coalition of its telecom cousins, large and small. In essence, the industry wanted to trade the old system of regulation, whereby the state controlled its profit margins, for a new system that only set prices on services. Then, if companies held prices relatively steady but cut costs, profits would rise and the new income would be theirs.

The timing of the coalition's move was certainly fortuitous. Just as serious discussions began, regulators in a number of states, Wisconsin included, began noticing that phone rates were becoming exorbitant. In response, Indiana regulators cut rates by $57 million a year; Missouri ordered a cut of $84.6 million. To follow suit, Wisconsin state officials were drafting a telecom bill that would significantly lower their phone rates. But before the idea could gain traction, the industry coalition made a counter-proposal. At this particular moment, the world was just becoming aware of the much vaunted wonders of the "information superhighway." And this was a concept that the telecom firms were perfectly positioned to define, market, and build. Ameritech therefore offered to make the state a leader in the development of this superhighway. In exchange, Ameritech hoped, the state would not cut phone rates but would freeze them for three years.[4]

Unfortunately, the telecom bargain wasn't terribly fair, on two counts. First were some unmentioned changes in the industry's financial picture. "The cost of providing local phone service has been going down," David Merritt, then executive director of the state's Citizen Utility Board, said at the time. As a result, Merritt estimated, a rate freeze would give Ameritech an extra $50 million a year "to do whatever they want." As concern spread about the shortcomings of this deal, Ameritech sweetened its offer. It still wanted a rate freeze, but would first cut phone rates by 10 percent—approximately $14 million. It also put hard numbers to its commitment to help build the information superhighway. Over the next six years, Ameritech said, it would invest $700 million in Wisconsin's telecom infrastructure through its Wisconsin subsidiary, Wisconsin Bell, Inc.[5] As part of that investment, Wisconsin Bell would lay wire capable of videoconferencing and other high-end transmissions "to the doorstep" of every hospital, library, and school across the state.

As generous as the offer sounded, it was quite deceptive. Ameritech's pronouncements suggested it would now spend extra money on Wisconsin, but as it turned out, little if any special investment was planned. This twist, which yielded the second unfair element of the Ameritech deal, came to light late that spring when the state's utility regulators, the Wisconsin Public Service Commission (known as the PSC), produced a report dissecting Wisconsin Bell's financial record. The report was a stunning accusation, but one of its authors was in an unusual position to make it. His name was Glenn Unger and before becoming a chief engineer for the PSC, he'd spent twenty-five years working for Ameritech in a range of departments, including capital and expense budgeting.

To figure out Ameritech's promises, Unger charted Wisconsin Bell's investments in wiring and related infrastructure since 1968. The chronology suggested that the assistance Ameritech was offering was simply business as usual. If anything, it was a substantial cutback. During the previous five years, for example, the company had invested a total of $915 million in new infrastructure. Now it was pledging only $700 million for the coming six years.[6] "They were going to do those jobs anyway, and they made it sound like it was extra," Unger told me years later. "That kind of rubbed me the wrong way."

The PSC report sparked a brief period of public questioning, which Wisconsin Bell responded to by arguing that the financial trends were not quite what they seemed. Infrastructure costs in the telecom industry had dropped so dramatically, the company said, that a $700 million investment actually reflected a spending increase. But this wasn't quite true, either. System costs had been declining for decades, and during many of those years Wisconsin Bell had raised spending quite generously. Even now, during the sudden efficiencies of the digital age, telecom firms in other states were dramatically increasing their investments in infrastructure. Furthermore, the PSC discovered that Wisconsin Bell forecasts of rising investments presumed that without this commitment, the company would have spent nothing. But that was absurd. Since 1978, the company had consistently put at least $130 million a year into new business opportunities in Wisconsin.

Negotiations with utilities are often a mathematical maze, which can consign regulators to months of searching for openings in financial statements. Knowing this, the PSC had tried to begin its discussions with Wisconsin Bell with some common figures. It asked the company, for instance, to furnish a baseline of expenses reflecting "business as usual." Wisconsin Bell (referred to as WBI) declined, saying it didn't have those numbers and couldn't produce them. This struck the PSC as a little odd, since other states' telecom providers (such as New Jersey Bell) had recently done just that when submitting their deregulation proposals. "Staff finds it difficult to believe that a company with WBI's talent and resources no longer produces planning scenarios," the PSC report stated. Noting that such reports had been performed in the past, the PSC found it doubly strange that this time, "WBI preferred to define 'business as usual' at a zero level." As for the company's promises to schools and other public institutions, Unger saw holes here too. Some of those initiatives were leftovers from previous years' plans; others had already been accomplished. (An example was a commitment to provide high-speed ISDN services to "more than 80 percent of customer lines"—a quotient the company had already fulfilled.) "All of a sudden they roll out the targets and make that their new plan, and everyone applauds," Unger recalled.

But this was the mid-1990s, when desire for an information superhighway was at a fever pitch, and no one was in a mood for technical quibbles. That summer, then-governor Tommy Thompson called a special legislative session for what was soon dubbed "the information superhighway bill."

After some brief wrangling, the bill quickly passed by a wide margin. (Not surprisingly, the telecom industry was generous with its lobbying efforts, spending roughly $1.4 million in the process—nearly half of which came from Ameritech. Governor Thompson's vote may have come more cheaply. By one tally, in 1993 and 1994, Ameritech donated only $14,000 to the governor's re-election campaign fund; once the bill passed, donations shrank markedly, to $1,000 in 1995, $1,450 in 1996, and just $800 in 1997.)[7] The telecom coalition also doled out a few political favors—protections for consumers, labor, and other groups that had a stake in the coming changes. "It was a very professional, very broad-based fix, as telecommunications deregulation efforts always are," Barry Orton, professor of telecommunications at the University of Wisconsin at Madison, told me. "When they play this game, they bet on every race and every horse. And they bet to win, place, and show."

One of those bets was on the schools—specifically, a commitment to establish ongoing funds to help schools get wired. Ameritech made this offer in each one of its service areas, for a total donation of $97 million in five different states.[8] The interesting aspect of this donation is its context. Take Wisconsin, for example, where Ameritech agreed to contribute $13.5 million over five years, or 57 percent of the entire state fund for educational technology. As generous as this donation seems, from Ameritech's point of view it was a very good deal. If the deregulation bill under negotiation at the time had become law a decade earlier, according to another University of Wisconsin telecommunications expert, it would have netted Ameritech an extra $487 million in income; it also would have increased costs to consumers by 27 percent.[9] Overall, this made for pretty good odds: Ameritech would get a new income scenario worth nearly half a billion dollars in exchange for a donation to the schools that would cost the firm less than a third of 1 percent of that revenue.

In the years since those heady days, when the Internet was just becoming a global force, the image of an information superhighway became an unusually well worn cliché—so much so, in fact, that critics had great fun extending its metaphors, pointing out potholes and wrong turns, unfinished on-ramps and kitschy roadside clutter. Crude as these literary devices may be, their analogies have some merit. Both asphalt and digital highways are often built in haste, and to serve a narrow set of purposes. Both usually take longer to build than anyone expected and run way over budget. Both quickly prove incapable of handling their growing traffic. And both tend to pass their problems and real costs on to others.

Virtual reality on the digital highway first hit the schools when it came time to set up their new systems—those state-of-the-art high-bandwidth networks that Ameritech said it would wire to every institution's "doorstep." As it turned out, the job of running high-bandwidth service from those doorsteps to some closet inside the school building, and then to classroom systems, was no small task. Since this wasn't Ameritech's responsibility, a number of educators suddenly had to become instant telecommunications specialists as they sought bids, negotiated wiring contracts, and paid the bills on huge obligations that were not in their budgets. Ameritech played this game brilliantly, sometimes telling anxious school officials that they couldn't predict what these jobs would cost. As the contracts progressed, schools in more rural parts of the state discovered they were paying heavy service fees, some coming in at close to $4,000 a month. Those prices were more than twice what wealthier schools were paying in the urban centers of Madison and Milwaukee, where telecom lines had long been concentrated. No one anticipated such a contrast, since Ameritech had promised to shoulder the cost of laying wire to each school in its service area, no matter how far away it was. But things had changed since then. In the years following its 1994 promise, Ameritech sold off most of its far-flung territories to smaller, independent telecom outfits. These firms weren't part of the deregulation bargain, and they were free to charge whatever their services cost.

Sensing trouble on the horizon, Governor Tommy Thompson soon stepped in to erase these inequities. Beginning in 1998, the telecom firms started paying into a state fund that would cover the bulk of the schools' network expenses. The fund was set up to be a $500 million aid program, deftly entitled Technology for Educational Achievement, or TEACH Wisconsin. It allowed every K–12 school in the state to pay a flat rate for the services— $250 a month; TEACH paid the rest. One problem, though: The telecoms didn't really have to pay for their TEACH contributions—Wisconsin taxpayers did.

The taxpayers' new responsibility broke into two parts. First, about 80 percent of the $200 million that TEACH would end up spending over the next five years came from the state's General Fund (in other words, from tax receipts). The other 20 percent (roughly $40 million) came from the telecom sector. But the companies were allowed to pass on the costs of that contribution to the taxpayers as well, in extra surcharges that were added, and sometimes hidden, in their customers' phone bills.

The handoff was a little odd, considering the telecom industry's big promises to help the schools several years earlier in exchange for the new profit-making capabilities they'd won with deregulation. But no one in the state legislature could resist another emotional call to help the schools. The governor's plan passed quickly, with little discussion about forcing the telecom industry to live up to its old bargain.

Years later, in 2002, a few Wisconsin legislators became concerned that they weren't quite getting the services out of TEACH that they had paid for, so they ordered a state audit of the program. When the audit came in, it was not entirely flattering. It found no information on how the money had been used over the years, how it had changed teaching practices, or what else had been achieved. "The limited information available shows," the audit said, "that a relatively small number of students participate" in the networks the state had spent so much money to install. For example, during the 2000–2001 academic year, TEACH spent $61.3 million to wire just one third of the state's 55,000 classrooms. One part of that expenditure was $3.2 million for 161 school video links—a cost of nearly $20,000 per school. The auditors also found that these systems, which the state had worked so hard to make state-of-the-art, were being used by only 13,019 students—less than 2 percent of the state's school population.[10]

As Ameritech developed its school networks in other states, problems sprouted. Annette Massie, the principal of Ohio's Whitwell Elementary School in the Appalachian Mountains, remembers being promised a high-bandwidth network so her students could engage in videoconference sessions with the Columbus Zoo or the Center of Science and Industry. "We got the computer," Massie recalls, "but we couldn't hook it up. The technology was never put in place." Some aspects of Whitwell's network did work for the first few years, but once it was time for an upgrade, things began to fall apart. Incompatibilities occurred, high-tech consultants and gung-ho supervisors grew restless and moved on to greener pastures, and Ameritech's attention to teacher training and other matters started to flag.

Practical troubles only aggravated the core dilemma with distance learning: its pedagogical weakness. Under the right circumstances, these systems can be a gift—in fact, their offerings are much like the standard text-only distance-learning programs discussed earlier, only at a much higher level. As an example, Mike Weller, president of the networking firm Access Wisconsin, fondly recalls a biology teacher describing how his overhead video camera had let him, in one instance, project close-ups of a dissection of the human eye. The images of that operation reportedly sparked interest—and higher test scores—in both his distance-learning class and in his own students, who suddenly became more interested in the details they saw on the projection screen than in the live dissection occurring at the front of the class.

But high-end gizmos also spawn high-end problems—a fact that Weller and most other video-network enthusiasts readily admit. Certain problems, however, tend to go unacknowledged. Proponents of this technology may demonstrate its educational possibilities by showing students talking history or science with real university experts hundreds of miles away. But one of the first things distance learners learn is that those vaunted experts aren't always available when you need them. This points up an important difference between video distance-learning systems and the standard discussions conducted through written text. One of the great conveniences of online dialogues, as we've seen, is that people don't have to contribute at the same time—a great help to the busy professional. Video dialogues, however, have to occur in what technologists call "real time"—live, that is, at a moment when everyone can join in together. If a key participant has a conflict, the exercise is shot.

Even when everyone is available, the technology spawns other problems that seem inescapable. What happens, for instance, after some big-shot lecturer has just conducted a distance-learning class with hundreds if not thousands of different students all around the country—or even around the world? Do the promoters of this technology really expect that he'll follow up with all these students or with their teachers? And there's the question of the quality of these conversations, which don't always seem to be worth their expense. "It's really stressful," a German teacher in Ohio's Appleton East High School observed after using its video network to work with students at a nearby school. "The most negative thing about it is not being able to hear the students on the other side of town as well as the students here. It kind of depersonalizes the teaching. I don't feel like I really know those kids over there." Transmission capabilities can improve, of course, and they undoubtedly will. But no matter how good the technology eventually gets, wires will never bring people together face-to-face, the domain where communication, especially of the nonverbal variety, thrives. A teacher in Minnesota put the matter plainly. "I could care less about my students connecting with people in Japan," he said. "What about connecting to the person next to them?"

As might have been expected, students who worked with the Appleton system were generally underwhelmed.[11] So was Todd Alan Price, an assistant professor in research and foundations at National-Louis University in Madison, Wisconsin. While Price was a graduate student at the University of Wisconsin at Madison, he focused his doctoral studies on video distance learning, specifically Ameritech's Appalachian projects. "In lieu of giving the schools funds for real learning programs," Price told me, "Ameritech gives them wire. They hook them to a university and some other schools, and it's nothing, really. And now they don't even have that."

—

Ameritech, understandably enough, has its own interpretation of the network's history. Randall Pickering, an executive with SBC Wisconsin, was a leading spokesman for the company during its pre-SBC days in the early 1990s, when it was promising to wire the schools in exchange for looser regulation. Pickering told me that he doesn't recall the PSC report, well publicized as it was, which questioned the math in the company's infrastructure promises. But he does remember what the company did, and insists that it more than fulfilled its promises in Wisconsin, finishing its work ahead of schedule. Furthermore, he points out, the state now holds telecommunication firms responsible for making sure that a new network in any school (and any hospital or library) is error-free for thirty days before the state signs off on the job. From all accounts, the Internet networks in Wisconsin schools have indeed begun to improve, at least on a mechanical level. However, other problems have remained—in Wisconsin and elsewhere. In Ohio, for instance, Micheal Kehoe, vice-president of external affairs at SBC's unit in that state, remembers the struggles everyone had in the handful of Appalachian schools that served as early test sites. One reason for the troubles, he said, is that once the network's advocates at Ohio University moved on, commitment to the system "began to wane." And, of course, the company's subsidies lasted only so long—ending after eight years. In Kehoe's view, Ameritech fulfilled its end of the bargain just by laying wire to the school basement and offering some basic help; any system problems beyond that— that is, within the building—were justifiably the school's responsibility.

Legally, Kehoe is right. Ethically, it's a matter of perception, and of high technology's continually moving targets. Whitwell Elementary's principal, Annette Massie, like most educators who became technical administrators, remembers numerous difficult meetings with telecom representatives, with confusion coming from both sides. "The phone companies were arguing about technical issues back and forth, because they were new to it, too." To believe that a company's job is done once the system is put in place "is not really fair," Massie argues. "It's always new. There are always technical hassles. Once you're in it, you've got to stay in it."

Staying in it unfortunately carries a responsibility that is bigger than most educators realize—and than most technologists will admit. Bonnie Beach, an Ohio University professor who served as a consultant and co-director for the Ohio network throughout most of the 1990s, recalls countless breakdowns, answered by fixes that didn't last. "Sometimes it would be hour to hour," she told me. "I'd have a big plan one day and test it at two P.M. and it would be fine. By the time class started at three, [the system] would be down."

Sometimes the repair would involve technology's classic solution: an upgrade to an entirely new system. Beach remembers one idea, an expensive one, that blew through her schools in the mid-1990s—mini-video cameras that would sit on top of classroom computers, an early version of the webcam system for continuous broadcasting. "Every school in Athens City now has one of these on their computers," she said. "We paid for special ISDN phone lines for these for a year, and we never got one of those things to work." Beach generally tried to solicit Ameritech's help, but that usually led to protracted negotiations, where, as Beach recalls, "I didn't know when Ameritech was selling me a bill of goods."

The lesson, Beach concluded, is that schools should actually avoid being on technology's cutting edge. "We got in while the technology was evolving," Beach said. "We should have waited until it settled down." When I asked whether she thought such a moment really existed, Beach paused, then said, "Probably not." As proof, she noted that schools were already moving away from ISDN lines and into the new, faster version—DSL service. And telecom companies across the Midwest and many other regions of the country, particularly in rural areas, were having great difficulty delivering on their promises with DSL, even to technically savvy business customers.[12]

"EVENTUALLY, IT BITES YOU IN THE ASS"

As schools struggled to work out their high-tech kinks, Ameritech had reason for not always attending to their troubles. In the years immediately following deregulation, its business spun out of control. At first everything looked rosy. Wisconsin subsidiary WBI, for example, enjoyed dramatic increases in profits, from $70 million in 1994 to $260 million in 1998. Ameritech managed this feat partly by cutting costs in various realms—primarily maintenance, system upgrades, and labor. The labor cutbacks were particularly robust. Throughout its five-state region, the company cut 21,500 people from its 62,000-member work force.[13] (There was bitter irony in this fact, since one of Ameritech's promises in 1994 was that deregulation would bring thousands of new jobs by helping the company build the great information superhighway. Ameritech also reassured old-line workers that they would be retrained for high-tech, a promise that went largely unfulfilled.) By 1999, the cost-cutting began to exact its pound of flesh. The telecom boom was nearing its peak, and Wisconsin Bell profits fell that year to $83 million.[14] But when the company looked around to see what could be done, it found an operation that was a shell of its former self. In the view of Gary Kitchens, president of the company's network services division, Ameritech's former managers "sucked the marrow" out of the company." Marc Jones, president of the local Communications Workers of America and a former Ameritech technician, was equally graphic. "The former management just raped and pillaged the company before they left," he said, "and now we're all paying."[15]

By the fall of 2000, 8,300 Wisconsin customers were without phone service, and repair and outage complaints were up 270 percent from the previous year. Some customers were put on hold for up to an hour when they called to report their problems; others were told they'd have to wait up to three weeks to get a working phone line. As troubles mounted, Ameritech was so slow in responding to them that the Wisconsin legislature ordered an investigation, which ultimately resulted in customer credits for service outages and a $2.5 million fine.[16] By this time, however, service in the other four states Ameritech served was disintegrating as well. Illinois, for example, was considering fining the company $34 million for its troubles, and Ohio regulators were considering a penalty of $122 million.[17] As Wisconsin officials tried to fix their Ameritech mess, they encountered a surprise: In forging their deregulation agreement with the telecom industry, legislators had given away much of their oversight leverage. "When the states found out that service had gone to hell, they also found out they couldn't do much about it," Barry Orton, the University of Wisconsin telecommunications professor, told me.

Glenn Unger, the former PSC engineer who had spent decades working for Ameritech, believes he saw the seeds of these problems long ago, in the terms of the company's first bid for deregulation. At the time, when Ameritech promised to spend $700 million over the next five years as compared with $915 million spent the previous five years, Unger knew what was missing. "That other $215 million they cut was for basics, and those are the parts right now they're having trouble with," he told me in late 2000. In prior years, those basics included a forty-person division devoted solely to solving customer complaints and rooting out their internal causes. After the AT&T breakup brought an era of free-market pressures to the telecom world, the division was dismantled, and its staff was spread into other divisions. "In the old days," Unger recalls, "their objective was zero complaints. If they got forty in a year, they thought they were doing poorly." This compared, in the time between 1998 and 2000, to an average of 3,400 complaints each year. "Initially, you can live without staff functionality and service," Unger said, "but eventually it bites you in the ass."

Even without the inside knowledge of a Glenn Unger, the hollowness of Ameritech's promises—to the public and to schools—could have been apparent long ago. Barry Orton remembers that when Ameritech first promised to make Wisconsin a leader on the information superhighway, it was "making the same argument in Indiana and Ohio. And each state bought it." (This matches the recollection of Craig Glazer, former chairman of the Public Utility Commission of Ohio. Glazer, an early proponent of the video network, remembers that when Ameritech brought its superhighway promises to Ohio, his staff also found that the company's new spending plan was "identical to what [it] would otherwise invest.") In the end, Orton said, "I don't think they brought wire to within a mile of any school with anything more than they would normally do. It was a very good effort by a feed company to give away horses."

By the end of 2001, complaints about Ameritech's service were still heavy and state officials still lacked the regulatory teeth to do much about it. (Interestingly, many regulatory experts, including Craig Glazer, had also concluded that customers were paying more for their services than they would have if there had been no deregulation.) As for the schools, the situation had become a financial mixed bag. On the positive side, Ameritech and other Midwestern vendors were steadily paying into various state funds, administered by new government agencies that increasingly shouldered the practical problems involved with keeping school networks running. Some of these funds drew much of their capital from the fines that states assessed the telecom industry for poor service. This was a turn that many school tech administrators considered very much their due, after having spent years waiting for Ameritech to pay attention to their digital troubles. But the payoff was only partly helpful. As time wore on, many school officials found that the job of paying for high-bandwidth services was increasingly their responsibility, as first-round discounts and onetime grants ended.

Evidence on this score arose as school contracts for line costs and related services came up for renewal, and telecom outfits held firm on prices; some even raised their fees. This was despite the fact that costs for fiber-optic cable and other digital equipment had been cut in half just in the last few years of the 1990s. At some schools, it was also despite written promises that fees would drop with any contract extensions.* Come the turn of the millennium, as the decade's economic high wore off, schools found themselves, once again, with minimal resources for fancy extras like high-bandwidth computer networks. Some tried to content themselves with technological basics, but even that was hard. In Ohio, for example, Whitwell Elementary was so short of cash that Annette Massie, the principal, resorted to pirating software. "I'd tell people, 'Either buy me some software or come visit me in jail,'" she said.

The technology industry, meanwhile, was well buffered from the schools' financial troubles, at least for a time. In the latter part of the 1990s it got a sumptuous new treat to chew on, elegantly served by Congress. As part of the massive Telecommunications Act of 1996, which deregulated the industry on a federal level, Congress called on the telecom sector to help low-income schools with their wiring projects through the e-rate (education rate) program. As it played out, the e-rate program actually widened the technology industry's income-generating options further into the realm of the unorthodox. It also drove those opportunities far beneath the bureaucratic surface, where only a small group of insiders and contractors could tally its spoils.

NETWORK EXCESS

The e-rate was essentially a federal version of Wisconsin's TEACH program. Telecom firms contributed to a government fund; when schools had a computer network project sketched out, they applied for funding, which typically covered the bulk of their costs. The more poor students a school served, the greater its funding could be. (Some schools got up to 90 percent of their costs covered by e-rate disbursements.) And, as with the TEACH fund, the telecoms were free to pass the costs of their e-rate contributions on to consumers, through a small line item on phone bills, labeled

---

*While reneging on contractual promises would seem to be illegal, and therefore preventable, the fluid nature of computer technology makes written commitments rather flimsy. An example is the contract that Access Wisconsin signed with Bob Hannu, director of WONDER, a network serving thirteen schools around Wausau, Wisconsin. (Being college campuses, Hannu's schools weren't covered by TEACH subsidies.) Hannu's contract promised a reduction in fees with any extension, but at renewal time his service, Verizon, raised its fees. When Hannu objected, Verizon pointed out that the network in the whole region had been upgraded over the years. That changed his level of service, which made the old promise obsolete.

"Federal Universal Service Fee." When the e-rate first started, the surcharge was a mere 3 percent of a customer's long-distance charges. Over the years, however, as long-distance revenues have declined, the telecom firms gradually increased the surcharge. By early 2003, it averaged nearly 10 percent.

Congressional Republicans, a crowd that has never been sympathetic to anything that looks like a new tax, were wary of the e-rate from the start. And the actions of telecom firms didn't much help. In 1998, just two years after they agreed to fund the e-rate out of their own pockets as part of their deregulation package, industry leaders were back in Washington fighting to reduce their commitment. And they succeeded, albeit temporarily. After AT&T, Sprint, and MCI spent $10 million on lobbying, Congress cut the industry's contribution to e-rate funding that summer by 40 percent. As the program went into effect, however, full funding—at $2.25 billion a year—was restored by the Federal Communications Commission (FCC), which oversaw the e-rate system.[18] None of this sat terribly well with a group of Republican leaders, including Senator John McCain of Arizona and then–Speaker of the House Newt Gingrich.

The congressional critics thought the FCC's method of handling the e-rate fund had exceeded the commission's authority, and the intent of the 1996 Telecommunications Act. Concern focused on the entity that the FCC had set up to administer the fund, the quasi-independent Schools and Libraries Corporation (SLC). And questions were already arising about weaknesses in SLC oversight. Shortly after Congress voted to cut e-rate funding, a federal audit by the General Accounting Office (requested by Senator McCain) found that the SLC was sending out letters of commitment to school districts before evaluating the schools' proposed computer systems. Noting that the corporation had yet to set up procedures for auditing funding applications, the GAO suggested that the SLC get confirmation from its auditor that it had developed safeguards against waste, fraud, and abuse. The audit also indicated that the fund created duplicative procedures for funding technology in schools, an initiative for which some $12 billion in federal money was already available. Ira Fishman, the SLC's chief executive officer at the time, agreed with the GAO's findings and promised to act on its recommendations; but he also insisted that the SLC had a system of controls that was working. The following year, in February 1999, congressional opposition to the program resurfaced. Calling the program a "backdoor tax," a group of House Republicans mobilized to abolish the e-rate, with a bill pointedly called the eRate Termination Act.[19]

Yet congressional support was high for what was fast becoming a kind of educational industrial complex, and the fund survived. The FCC responded by immediately putting poor schools on a "fast track" for funding, whereupon things started to get interesting. That May, one of the nation's largest e-rate projects to date—a $28.7 million subsidy to a consortium of fourteen school districts around Atlanta, Georgia—started to unravel. At the time, the federal gift to this consortium was more than the e-rate fund had given to thirty-four entire states. Despite this generous freebie, six of the fourteen districts concluded that the project wasn't worth their time and trouble.

The project was supposed to install a vast state-of-the-art system to deliver video programming "on demand," along with "interactive" teleconferencing between classrooms, to 315 Georgia schools. However, as it came time to bill each district for its share of the project, school officials glimpsed the parameters of their upcoming commitment. While federal authorities were taking on 80 percent of the project's total cost (approximately $34 million), that still left an expense of roughly $5 million to a group of very poor schools. "Our schools probably have greater needs than interactive video in the classrooms, where we need to be teaching reading," said John Peterson, technology director at the Rockdale County school district. Others thought the project would merely duplicate existing wiring and video delivery systems. "Our principals told me for this amount of money, they didn't believe it would be an improvement over what we have already," said Penny Angel, the technology director in Marietta.[20]

As understandable as the administrators' concerns were, they raised a troublesome question. Why did federal administrators of the e-rate fund approve the massive project in the first place? Clearly, if these schools had chosen to, they could have taken the full $28.7 million that e-rate administrators had offered and built lavish systems they didn't need or wouldn't use. The question is particularly curious considering the questions the General Accounting Office had raised a year earlier about poor oversight of the fund and SLC director Fishman's assurances at the time that auditing safeguards were firmly in place.*

———

During the following year, it became clear that federal administrators still weren't examining e-rate proposals with much care, as evidenced by a deba-

---

*Fishman's assurances about spending controls in the e-rate program are doubly curious considering his own history. A former White House lobbyist and fund-raiser for Al Gore, Fishman resigned from the SLC after just nine months, amid controversy over his $200,000-a-year salary and $50,000 annual bonus. After leaving the SLC, Fishman founded HiFusion Inc., a Baltimore company that, not coincidentally, sold Internet services to schools.

cle in San Francisco that was far larger and far less understandable. At the time, San Francisco was a city covered with red flags when it came to financial dealings in the public schools. Throughout the 1980s and 1990s, corruption so riddled the school district that one tally showed school officials having lost or misspent up to $100 million.

The mismanaged funds were proceeds from a series of school bonds, which had raised $337 million over the years for school renovation and construction projects. In early 2001, after state auditors had raised questions about the district's financial management systems, local reporters began tracking school funds. They discovered that nearly a third of the bond proceeds ended up in odd places: with contractors who never finished their projects, and in many cases never started them; in the budgets of a newly bloated school bureaucracy; and in the salaries of non-teaching employees, several of whom became the subject of corruption investigations. To make matters worse, when parents and school board members raised concerns about the lack of progress on school repairs, district officials, including the superintendents, went to extraordinary lengths to conceal misspending. Unabashed, superintendents then turned to the voters to seek, and win, even more money through additional bond measures.[21]

Signs of these troubles were accumulating throughout 2000, when the Universal Service Administrative Company (USAC)—a new oversight agency that replaced the SLC—was evaluating a bid from San Francisco for even more school funding. That October, the USAC (which is run by a board of directors, the majority of whom are telecommunications company executives) approved an e-rate grant to the district of $50.2 million. The grant would finance the lion's share of a $68 million project—an extremely sophisticated network of high-speed broadband Internet connections in forty-six of the city's neediest schools. Eight months later, to everyone's great surprise, San Francisco turned the grant down.

The reason the superintendent gave publicly sounded much like the reluctance voiced in Georgia: "We'd have to come up with between $7 million and $9 million and, given our financial situation, we have to weigh it against other considerations," said Arlene Ackerman, San Francisco's relatively new superintendent, who came into office determined to root out corruption. "When we consider all of the other things we need, like doing minimal repairs and cleaning our schools, is this technology the most important thing at this time? Do parents want high-speed Internet connections or good clean bathrooms for their kids?"[22] Later, in a letter to the *San Francisco Chronicle*, district officials updated their estimate of their share of the costs to $18 million.

The district's private reasoning, meanwhile, was considerably more revealing. In reality, the district had been very much interested in a new high-speed Internet system. The problem was that the bid that won the San Francisco contract, and which was scheduled for e-rate funding, would have taken everyone for a very big ride. The contract was so overblown, in fact, that senior district technicians discovered they were better off not only rejecting the whole package, including the $50 million federal subsidy, but financing the entire project themselves. Apparently, the schools' normal retail costs for the system's components were so much less than the bid prices that the technicians realized it would be cheaper to do the whole job themselves. This meant the cost of paying for the entire system with city funds would come to less than paying for 20 percent of it as structured under the federal e-rate package—that is, less than $18 million.

This is a stunning finding. It is, in essence, the educational equivalent of the $640 toilet seat and the $74,000 ladder—those famous artifacts of an earlier federal spending spree, when the Reagan administration launched its historic military buildup in the early 1980s.[23] During this early phase of the e-rate's heyday, there was no way to tally the full extent of overcharges in the nation's schools. But there were plenty of indications that the abuses were widespread. In early 2002, for instance, the FCC examined eighteen districts around the country that had received e-rate funding. Presumably, the review was at least phrased with some care. The accounting firm that conducted the examination was Arthur Andersen, which was on the hot seat at the time, facing a criminal indictment for its own abuses in the unfolding Enron scandals. The examination found possibilities of fraud in one (unnamed) school district and signs of various other kinds of infractions in most of the other seventeen districts. In New York City, for example, Andersen's auditors said school officials and Verizon, its e-rate service provider, could not specifically account for the $2.6 million of e-rate money that was given to each city school. In Los Angeles, they said, "it could not be demonstrated with certainty that program funds were used for eligible services."[24]

Throughout the following year, signs of scandal spread. In fall 2002, an audit by the FCC's inspector general found questionable financial dealings of one sort or another "at nearly all locations" it examined. That December, federal prosecutors charged a New York firm, Connect2 Internet Networks, Inc., with eight counts of federal crimes, including wire fraud and obstruction of justice. (Apparently, the firm bought more expensive gear than its customer schools could afford, created fake invoices to suggest the schools had paid their share, then coached school officials to lie about the arrangements. In the few years since e-rate funding had begun, Connect2 had done more than $9 million of business with 36 schools.) That same December, USAC killed an $18 million e-rate job in Ysleta, Texas. Auditors concluded that the district's vendor—industry stalwart IBM—had set up the job in such a way that it precluded bids from competing Internet contractors. IBM denied the charges, but government regulators said, "The record reflects that the overriding goal of the IBM-Ysleta relationship is to maximize the . . . funding, not necessarily to promote educational goals." IBM, which offered the same "sole source" option to many districts around the country, was not a small player in this game. Over the years, it had received $351 million of e-rate money. The total value of the projects for which it sought funding in 2002 came to $1 billion—nearly half the program's annual budget. As the various scandals unfolded, government authorities complained about their inability to keep up with them. The FCC's Office of Inspector General, for instance, employed only three full-time auditors, at a time when the e-rate program was generating more than 40,000 networking proposals every year.[25]

Not surprisingly, by spring 2003, some of the e-rate's old congressional critics started taking yet another look at the program. At that point, except for rare cases like Connect2, none of these scandals had progressed far enough in the legal system to offer easy portraits of how unscrupulous technicians were going about their business. If anyone had bothered to look beneath the bureaucratic surface, however, a number of dark trails would have been discovered long ago.

Consider a few details in the winning bid in San Francisco.

The company that got the e-rate job here was NEC, the international network and computer hardware firm (2001 net sales: $43 billion) based in Tokyo and Los Angeles. And what a prize it was. The district had called for huge Internet servers in every classroom, a total of two thousand in just the first year. Each school would also get six high-speed T-1 lines, capable of handling video. There were autosensing Ethernet switches and fiber-optic wiring; LANs and WANs (Local Area Networks and Wide Area Networks), which were the latest in top-of-the-line communications systems. All this would be laid on an ATM backbone, a sophisticated data transmission system defined as Asynchronous Transfer Mode.[26] "I don't even have that in my company," a technical marketing manager of Bay Networks, a California company that installs similar systems, once told me. San Francisco's extensive specifications also left NEC with opportunities to get creative.

Those opportunities were seized in January 2000, when NEC submitted a

$75 million bid on the San Francisco job. When the USAC finally approved NEC's bid, the project had been scaled back to its final $68 million level. But this merely reduced the number of schools being covered—not the price of the work itself. And that's where all the fun was.

An example: For one stage of the job, NEC proposed installing 130 Internet switches of a particular type, called a 3512. The company bid them at $5,924 apiece. Once additional costs were factored in—for the warranty ($2,266), freight ($191), and installation ($1,900), the price of each switch grew to $10,281. On the retail market at the time, these switches were selling for a base price of approximately $2,000 from Cisco Systems, a top-of-the-line manufacturer (or about $4,000 with warranty). Once NEC's markup was multiplied out for 130 switches, that yielded a profit margin of roughly $780,000, on this one item.

"This is outrageous to me," Jim Levine, a systems manager in the San Francisco district's Information Technology office, told me. "A 3512 for $10,000? You know what that is?" he asked, gesturing to indicate a small, thin box measuring roughly 24 square inches. Installing this switch, he said, requires "a few bolts. It's a unit that needs to go into nineteen-inch rails. You plug it in, and maybe you label it, with some configuration and address information. It takes less than an hour—if someone knows what they're doing." Levine's reaction was much the same to the item preceding this one—another switch, called a 3508, that NEC bid at $12,829, or $24,431 with freight, warranty, and $4,000 for installation.[27] Cisco sold those items at the time, without the warranty and other extras, for approximately $5,000. What if the district added its own labor? Levine shrugged. "You unbox it, put cables in, and connect it. My God—for $24,000?"

As if this weren't painful enough, schools sometimes add still more to contractor profits through bureaucratic overkill. Once a contract is signed, district procedures are often so slow and convoluted that it can be a year or more before the equipment is actually delivered. During that time, as any observer of the technology market well knows, prices for computer components usually drop dramatically. Yet the schools are often on the hook for the previous year's prices, and the contractor gets to pocket the difference.

Presumably, a school district could avoid contracting abuses. In fact, competitive bidding was long ago made standard in government contracting specifically for that purpose. If a variety of firms got a well-publicized chance to submit the lowest bid on a job, the theory went, then government contracting would cease to be an avenue for doling out political favors. Not so, it seems, in San Francisco schools. The contracting process here has turned into its own kind of animal—one so ugly, in fact, that at the time of the NEC contract, the city attorney's office and the FBI were both looking into indications that a few district employees had engaged in bid-rigging, illegal kickbacks, and numerous other abuses.[28]

==

One would hope that tricks like these would be restricted to fat, fuzzy programs like the e-rate. But they are used more often than many realize. In New York City, home of the nation's largest school district, for example, officials found a way to cut some of the administration's budget deficit by robbing their own schools. (This was managed through an ingenious shell game, involving contracts with the city's various computer suppliers. In early 2002, the city's central school administration purchased 11,000 computers, along with service and installation, at wholesale prices ranging between $1,200 and $1,300 apiece. When it came time to distribute these machines to individual schools, administrators marked up the price nearly 30 percent, in some cases beyond retail, thereby netting an estimated $6 million for the cause of school bureaucracy.[29]

Technology's contracting opportunities are of course far too lucrative to be restricted to the back offices. When New York technicians got out into the field to work on basic rewiring of the city's schools, a few teachers and principals watched in amazement as the technicians returned again and again, for hours at a time, without getting much done. Once they did get the schools wired, it wasn't long before they were back again for another upgrade. "We just got wired again last month," said a New York City high school principal who did not want to be named. "Every time they do this, that's supposed to be it—the next generation of technology. But it lasts about six months, and then they're back again." In Philadelphia, a competitive bidding scandal in the school district led to a $36 million bill for a flawed computerized accounting system that was initially supposed to cost only $15.6 million. In Arizona, four executives from Qwest Communications created $33 million of false revenue—by fudging the accounting on a statewide contract to wire 1,383 public schools—then covered it up. And in Huntsville, Arkansas, a district superintendent who set up his own computer supply company filled machines with low-level components, then sold them as high-end machines. According to a state prosecutor, the maneuver cheated the schools out of as much as $100,000. Interestingly, the superintendent's trick might never have come to light if he hadn't sold the computers to his own district, thereby violating a state law that prohibits self-dealing.[30]

One response to abuses of this sort would be to pull the plug on lavish partnerships with corporate interests, especially those that are built so elaborately around technology. In some cases, that may be warranted. A wiser approach would be to simply scale back the number and scope of these projects and double up on the oversight. Obviously, there are some schools, principally those serving older students, that can make good use of high-end computer networks—although by all indications, their number is considerably smaller than federal administrators imagine. And these schools are now getting shortchanged by other districts' contracting excesses. "It's going to the wrong people," says San Francisco's Jim Levine. "Those funds were destined for education. If that was happening, then a lot more schools would have a lot more money."

EDISON'S NEW LIGHTBULBS

Discouraging though all this news may be, it does not mean that industry is incapable of partnering with schools in a helpful fashion. An example of one such arrangement has been the relatively recent and growing national movement to forge apprenticing arrangements at local businesses for high school and college students. Initiated in the early 1990s and known by the uninspiring moniker School-to-Work, these alliances are, in some cases, making the stultifying old image of vocational education obsolete. There are, of course, many disappointments with these apprenticeships—employers who neglect to give youngsters much attention, who stick them with menial jobs or train them to fill that firm's immediate need, which disappears or changes by the time the students graduate. But there are plenty of counterexamples—the Siemens Corporation, for one, has dared to teach youngsters broad, durable skills, sometimes in fields that have little to do with its own business, or that might even favor a competitor. Encouraging results seem to have followed. From hospitals in Boston to high-tech firms in Austin, Texas, and law offices in Portland, Oregon, hundreds of students have begun to understand why numbers matter, how to work with professional teams, how to handle the public, and, perhaps most important, what it means to be conscientious and reliable. In some internships, at mechanics' garages or local newspapers, for example, they are also able to make sense of how computer technology works in the modern industrial world. Not surprisingly, some of these students have said that they got more out of these experiences than in all their years of school.[31]

While the School-to-Work movement has obvious value, it is a mere ripple on an ominous, rising tide in education that is known as the privatization movement. This movement has grown so dramatically, in fact, and has so often left the schools tied up in the strings of various firms' commercial self-interest, that one university professor in Arizona has dedicated his career to tracking these developments.

In 1996, Alex Molnar, a professor of education policy (then at the University of Wisconsin, Milwaukee, and subsequently at Arizona State University), wrote a book called *Giving Kids the Business: The Commercialization of America's Schools*. Molnar's story detailed one shocking anecdote after another as he illustrated the extraordinary lengths that businesses were willing to go to in order to sell their wares in the schools or to promote their point of view.* Molnar's account pointed out that the privatization movement, like so many education trends, has been one of the schools' most constant dance partners, albeit not always a gracious one. In the 1960s, for instance, industry and federal officials colluded to sell the schools on the idea of having private firms manage their affairs, under a concept called performance contracting. The rationale then, as now, was that the private sector could handle education's job more effectively—and more cheaply—than the bloated government bureaucracy. Within a few short years, evidence accumulated that this promise had not been fulfilled and that private companies had actually abused the schools' trust, in some cases looting their accounts. By 1972, after facing widespread criticism, performance contracting withered away—for a time.

Several decades later, privatization of government functions was back in style. By then, Molnar was at Arizona State, directing the university's Educational Policy Studies Laboratory, a division of which became a collection pail for news on privatization in the schools. As of 2002, the lab reported, 36 for-profit companies were managing 368 schools in 24 states—a 70 percent rise over the previous year. (The vast majority of these were charter schools.) Throughout Molnar's studies, one entity in particular has been the target of his fire: the Edison Project, a venture that quickly became the nation's largest private-sector operation in school management.

Founded in 1991 by Chris Whittle, a marketing whiz from Tennessee,

---

*One of the bolder examples was an advertisement from Lifeline Learning Systems, a company that distributes free supplies to schools sponsored by three hundred different businesses and whose corporate cousin is the *Weekly Reader.* "IMAGINE millions of students discussing your product in class," the ad states. "IMAGINE their teachers presenting your organization's point of view. IMAGINE your corporate message reaching their parents through literature the students take home . . . let Lifetime Learning Systems take your message into the classroom, where the young people you want to reach are forming attitudes that will last a lifetime." See *Giving Kids the Business: The Commercialization of America's Schools*, by Alex Molnar, Westview Press, 1996, p. 35.

Edison Schools, Inc., as it was formally called, was designed to run schools at a profit for Whittle's investors, and to improve academic performance in the process. Whittle's name was plenty familiar by this time; a year earlier, in 1990, he had launched Channel One, an enterprise that aimed to bring television advertising into the nation's classrooms through a twelve-minute current-events show, with ten minutes of news and two minutes of ads. (In exchange for the free TV program, schools had to promise to show it to roughly 90 percent of the student body nearly every school day.) Reactions to Channel One—from educators, politicians, and editorialists—were not exactly glowing. Critics called it "educational junk food" and "academic acid rain." As might have been expected, studies of the TV show (which, it turned out, contained only six minutes of hard news) indicated that students weren't learning much about current events from Whittle. But they did remember a great number of commercial products, and made increasingly positive associations about them.

For a while, Whittle seemed to be making a nice profit on the venture. One of the few public accountings on Channel One, made possible when a Texas tax assessor found that Whittle had failed to pay property taxes on his equipment, concluded that Whittle's costs for an average-size school totaled a mere $18,373—not the $50,000 he had continually claimed in press accounts. Meanwhile, Alex Molnar wrote in *Giving Kids the Business*, "advertisers were paying Whittle close to $200,000 every time a thirty-second commercial was broadcast on his program." Eventually, the Channel One venture began stumbling, and in the mid-1990s it had to be sold off in pieces. But in 1991, Channel One was looking pretty good, and Whittle was feeling inspired at the possibilities for expansion.

The centerpiece of Whittle's new plan was a generous dose of still more technology. According to one account of the Edison Project, Whittle envisioned a family of futuristic schools in which each student would get a "computerized learning station, without textbooks or classrooms, and each teacher will have an office, 'just like real people—with phones.' " In promoting his venture, Whittle made yet another promise to bring private-sector efficiency into education: "The new system will not cost more than the current system," Whittle said. "We don't need more cash. We need more creativity." Whittle estimated that "it would take $1 billion and four years to develop a prototype suitable for replication in the 50 states." The first 200 schools would open in the fall of 1996, serving 150,000 students. By 2010, enrollment would reach 2 million.

It wasn't long before things started to turn very sour. Investors shied away from Whittle's project, seeing no way to make any money. And educators failed to sign up. Then news leaked out that Whittle wasn't going to use all the funds he raised for schools after all. (Apparently, most of the $750 million he sought during the first round of financing would have to go to Time Warner, an early investor, which meanwhile had gotten cold feet and wanted to be bought out.) Soon news reports started surfacing that Whittle's various operations were losing money—badly. In late 1993, Whittle shifted course, announcing that rather than start new schools, the project would now rescue old ones—specifically, "a select number of failing public schools."[32] While not as futuristic as the schools in his original plan, these too would be graced by the twenty-first-century energy of computer technology.

Whittle's new vision was more realistic, at least in part. Over the next decade, the Edison Project managed to sign up nearly 150 schools in 22 states, giving the company an estimated enrollment of 75,000 students. But here too the news has not been exactly upbeat. Edison has claimed that test scores rose in 84 percent of its schools after the company took over. Studies by the districts themselves, or by outside evaluators, tell a different story, leading critics to believe that Edison has slanted its data.* While the company has had some successes (three schools in Baltimore and one in San Francisco are examples), Whittle's customers by and large have not been amused. "We looked at Edison schools' performance compared to the rest of the district, and it was not what we had been promised nor what we expected," said Ken Zornes, school board president in Dallas, Texas, in announcing the board's unanimous vote to revoke Edison's contract in August 2002. This followed similar contract cancellations earlier that summer in

---

*One of the angriest surveys of Edison's performance was conducted by Chaka Fattah, a Democratic congressman from Philadelphia, where Edison had been embroiled in a controversial $60 million five-year contract to run twenty of the city's lowest-performing schools. In opposing the arrangement, Fattah said his office had conducted its own survey of performance in twenty states and Washington, D.C. "The data reveals," Fattah wrote in December 2001, "that in nearly 90 percent of Edison schools—61 out of 69 schools—for which results were available, students perform substantially below standard levels set by the state compared to other students." In October 2002, the General Accounting Office, Congress's fiscal watchdog agency, attempted to finally settle the dispute. After conducting an eleven-month study of performance at schools run by Whittle and two other for-profit school management firms, the GAO concluded that these operations were having no effect either way. In other words, academic performance at their schools was neither rising nor falling. See "Edison Schools Perform Poorly Nationwide," by Chaka Fattah, *EducationNews.org*, December 18, 2001; "U.S. Report Makes No Call on For-Profit Schools," by Diana Jean Schemo, *The New York Times*, October 30, 2002.

Macon County, Georgia, and at Boston's Renaissance Charter School, which became one of Edison's flagship customers when the school was founded in 1995.

The Edison Project's fortunes have not been helped by its own behavior. In some cases, it has refused to furnish information on its schools—both test-score results and financial data. "Every time I ask a question, I never get the same answer twice," said Robert Mitten, business manager for the York City schools in Pennsylvania. As if this weren't trouble enough, in the spring of 2002, the Security and Exchange Commission found that Edison had exaggerated its revenues, requiring a settlement; later that year, the Department of Education's inspector general embarked on an investigation into whether Pennsylvania school officials had inappropriately swung the state's $60 million contract to Edison. In the meantime, losses for the company were accumulating; by December 2001 they had reached $240 million. This was somewhat strange, since Whittle had consistently claimed that he could operate his schools at a lower cost than a district does, and since Edison received more money than districts get to educate the same students. (This was partly because of Edison's vigorous private-sector fundraising efforts, and partly because Edison typically billed districts according to a calculation of student costs that was more generous than the districts used themselves.) Despite these advantages, by the end of 2002 Edison had never made a profit. To offset its losses, Edison typically paid its bills and covered its debt by issuing new shares of stock. But that option was closing fast too. In October 2002, for example, the company's stock was trading at only 52 cents a share. This was a sharp drop from the prices listed during Edison's three previous issues of new stock, when the company was trading at anywhere from $18 to $35 a share. (Edison also had to deal with three class-action lawsuits filed by investors who charged that the company had misled them.) As Edison sought additional ways to cut its losses, officials at some of its customer schools noticed that Edison wasn't delivering many of the materials it promised, or sufficiently training its teachers. In Philadelphia, Edison staff members carted textbooks and supplies away from several schools, saying they were unneeded, and set up executive offices in others. Unimpressed, Philadelphia's school superintendent ordered the Edison executives to move out.[33]

In many of its customer districts, school officials have been particularly disappointed in how Edison had managed one of its top priorities: computer technology. In York, for instance, after Edison took over one elementary school, which became the Lincoln-Edison Charter School, the school lost its connection to the district's computer network. "The technology in that building has taken a step back as far as I'm concerned," Mitten said. Stranger still were the conclusions that one outside evaluator drew of Whittle's other big promise—to whip public schools into shape with some tough private-sector-style management. Gary Miron, a researcher with Western Michigan University's Evaluation Center, found that Edison's troubles were caused by three main factors: The company was having more trouble than most schools in retaining teachers; its curriculum often veered away from state standards; and, most ironically, the operation functioned under a costly business model. "In reality," Miron said, "too much money goes to the control of the central office and not enough to the schools."[34]

While these kinds of private-sector arrangements with schools may look promising to entrepreneurs and politicians, they seem to hold no special appeal for the general public. In one 2002 poll, when eight hundred registered voters across the country were asked to rank their priorities for education, the concept of letting commercial firms manage schools came in dead last, with a mere 1 percent of respondents showing any interest in the idea. (The voters' top priority was raising teacher quality, followed by equalizing funding between rich and poor schools; the year before, the top choices were exactly the same.)[35]

Parents, it seems, want to stick with measures that have proven to give children a solid education. But what counts as proof?

Education's myriad reformers, particularly those attached to computer technology, obviously believe they have good, statistical proof—just as Whittle claimed he did—that their programs stimulate learning. And their cause has been helped greatly by shifts in the political winds. With uniform standards and school accountability rising to the top of the nation's educational agenda under President George W. Bush, school administrators across the country have been desperate for anything that will help them raise test scores—and raise them fast. To the shrewd entrepreneur, this has opened up a new horizon for software products that can be marketed to the very heart of a school administrator's latest anxieties. It has also brought education's propensity to e-lusion to one of its finest hours. But no matter. When there seems to be such solid scientific evidence of scholastic achievement, and when those gains seem to be inextricably tied to technology, who are we to question them?

CHAPTER 9

The Research Game:
Faith and Testing in Las Vegas

During the woeful debates that have come to characterize Americans' relationship with their schools, one of the most consistent subjects of hand-wringing is our failure to properly teach children how to read. Impassioned promises to break the nation out of this pattern are much of what helped President George W. Bush win the White House, and his initiatives on reading soon led his domestic agenda. Chastened by the schools' history of failure with loose education fads, Bush coupled his efforts with some academic tough love: Before schools adopted new programs in reading instruction, or any other curricular domain, the programs had to be scientifically proven to be worthwhile. The president was so adamant on this point that his signature education package, the No Child Left Behind Act, repeated the words *scientific* or *scientifically* 115 times, and the word *research* 245 times.[1]

As auspicious as the president's priorities seem, they have created a new dilemma: How are schools, and the public at large, supposed to evaluate the complicated claims of scientific research? Hundreds upon hundreds of studies of one kind or another have been conducted over the years to see what effect, if any, technology has on student achievement in reading, and many other subjects.[2] Experts in the private sector and the academic world have built entire careers around this question; some have even sought hyperobjective relationships with the research by devoting their energy to studies of the studies—a rarefied family of science called meta-analysis. Taken together, the body of research is wildly varied and seemingly inconclusive. As an example, one of the largest and most frequently mentioned reports—a 1991 meta-analysis of 254 studies by James Kulik—was cited by the Clinton administration when it launched the first large-scale federal campaign to get computers into schools in December 1994. Kulik reported that this survey—one of many he had done before and has conducted since—showed that computers helped students learn 30 percent faster than they do when receiving traditional instruction. But Kulik's studies haven't held up to scrutiny particularly well. One such examination was conducted in 2000 by Jeffrey T. Fouts, a professor of education at Seattle Pacific University and the lead evaluator for the Bill and Melinda Gates Foundation. Fouts found that Kulik's surveys suffer from a bothersome meta-analytic habit: They continually recycle the same old pool of research, and add new material as it comes in. In Kulik's case, the drift in his conclusions has been muddied further by the fact that most of the studies in his original pool lacked standard scientific controls.[3] In the face of complications like these, promoters of the dominant competing points of view—those who think technology works in school and those who think it's a failure—have had every opportunity to shop for facts that bolster their side.

To most people involved in education today, disputes of this sort have a perfect solution: standardized test scores. These simple statistics are wonderfully understandable, ostensibly objective, and easily tallied. They would seem to be the ideal tool to cut through polarized debates about "why Johnny can't read," ending decades of costly educational missteps. Bush, too, has heartily embraced standardized tests, thereby accelerating their popularity. As it turns out, this three-pronged drive—in reading, in research, and in standardized tests—has introduced the schools to a whole new set of vagaries, some of which are far more consequential than those of the past. From all indications, the education world is not terribly well prepared for the challenge.

One of the best ways to look at the trouble caused by these three developments is to begin at the ground level, with the teachers and their attitudes toward the task of teaching youngsters to read. One unusually intense illustration of the teacher's worldview played out for three spring days in 2001, in Nevada, at Las Vegas's MGM Grand Casino and Conference Center. The occasion was the second annual national conference of Renaissance Learning, Inc., a Wisconsin-based firm that, in the early years of the twenty-first century, was one of the largest and most profitable publicly traded companies among those devoted solely to educational software. It was also far and away the number-one manufacturer and seller of software aimed at improving reading skills. At the time of the Las Vegas conference, Renaissance's customers numbered 55,000 schools, from nursery school through high school. Roughly 50,000 of those were public schools (more than half the nation's total). By the company's estimate, this meant that since its founding in 1986, Renaissance Learning had shaped 300,000 teachers and 20 million students with its products. To achieve that level of success, Renaissance Learning has built a large, aggressive, multifaceted organization based in large part on prodigious amounts of research that, according to the company, definitively prove that its products powerfully stimulate learning.

Renaissance Learning's product line comprises a handful of remarkably simple software packages designed to help a teacher test and track students' progress in math and, most of all, in reading—a scholastic domain that has stubbornly refused to show much progress over the years. Not surprisingly, with the level of market penetration that Renaissance Learning has achieved, the publishing world has begun to take notice. Virtually all the big firms that supply classrooms with textbooks—Harcourt Brace, Houghton Mifflin, and Macmillan/McGraw-Hill, among others—now send out promotional brochures and catalogs that are tied to the Renaissance program. Some even bundle the program free of charge with textbooks and other materials that schools buy.

Somewhat coincidentally, Renaissance Learning's work is now center stage in the country's political discussions—at least when the public's attention has been on education. This is because the company's emphasis on reading, and on a systemized assessment of reading progress, dovetails nicely with the latest trends in Washington. It has not hurt that education itself had, until the 2001 terrorist attacks, become the nation's hottest sociological obsession. Chief among the people thusly obsessed is President George W. Bush, who sees standardized measures of achievement in reading, and other subjects, as the key to his education plan's ultimate goal: school accountability. None of this has been lost on the computer industry. By 2002, software makers were happily producing new programs and supplementing old ones that could keep teachers fed with evaluation data all day long.

—

By 8:15 A.M. on the Renaissance conference's opening day, the MGM Grand Arena, which has been a venue for everything from Rolling Stones concerts to heavyweight title boxing matches and professional bull-riding contests, was packed with close to 6,000 teachers and school administrators. Vegas, of course, is the town built on synthetic themes, and the MGM Grand is abundantly in step. Once the largest hotel in the world, the MGM Grand bills itself as "the city of entertainment." Under one air-conditioned roof, it offers a 172,000-square-foot casino, 15 theme restaurants, and more than 5,000 hotel rooms. Running throughout the complex's 115 acres is a special, supplementary theme of grandness. Among other sites, there's the Grand Pool Complex, a Japanese restaurant called the Grand Wok, and the Forever Grand Wedding Chapel. Phone conversations with hotel staffers typically close with MGM's customized good wishes: "Have a grand day."

Renaissance Learning designed its conference to fit the atmosphere here perfectly. As the audience assembled, a pop choir from a local performing arts high school warmed them up with a classic Vegas song-and-dance show performed to Carly Simon's "Let the River Run." Renaissance directors had chosen this number because of one line, which became the conference slogan—"Dreamers, Wake the Nation"—and which was projected, along with the performance, onto four oversize screens at the front of the arena. Before a word had been spoken about teaching or software, swarms of educators were on their feet shouting and clapping and ready to go.

A few minutes later, as the performers waved their good-byes, Loy Ball, a senior Renaissance Learning consultant from Tennessee, who served as conference emcee, took to the podium. Smiling and shaking his head at the auspicious beginning, he reminded the audience of the previous year's successful first annual conference, called Take the Next Step, which had been held in the capital of his home state. "Many of you left Nashville ready to take that next step," Ball said. Now, he continued, "we hope you are ready to wake the nation to a Renaissance education." This too was met with whoops and widespread applause. "We believe," Ball told the crowd, "that with technology, we have found the future of education." With these products, he claimed, "I saw kids succeed who had never had success before." (More whoops.) In the coming days, Ball said, "You will see why Reading Renaissance is the most effective comprehensive school improvement model in the country." Ball closed by promising them "the best three days of professional development I think you're ever going to experience in 2001. And I say 2001 because we're going to do it again next year, and we're going to get even better."

Ball then introduced the opening keynote speaker, Christopher Paul Curtis, a former auto plant worker and now successful children's-book author, who delighted the crowd with tales of his hard-luck past and hilarious readings from one of his homespun stories. Most of the teachers in attendance were familiar with Curtis's work. His books are among the nearly 50,000 in

Renaissance Learning's database, which is the raw ore for Accelerated Reader, the company's flagship product.

Accelerated Reader is the company's oldest and most successful piece of software. Ball calls it "the most successful and widely used educational program of all time." It's also the company's simplest. The program is built around computer disks filled with short quizzes about books, with one quiz keyed to each volume. The books used on these disks are those the company deems educational and within the normal range of abilities for a particular grade, kindergarten through high school. When students pass a given book's quiz, they receive a certain number of points. Passing these tests is purposely made relatively easy (it can often be done by getting a mere 60 percent of the answers right), to put a sense of achievement within reach of those who've long been treated as average, or even poor, performers. Once students have accumulated sufficient points, they can be awarded prizes, which vary at each school. Some schools have offered candy and toys, fancy treats like color TVs and, in one case, even a car. (This happened in Dallardsville, Texas, where the principal of Big Sandy High School bought a used truck to give away in a drawing. The more Accelerated Reader points the students earned, the more ballots they could fill out for the drawing.) Other schools stick with academic prizes, preferring to give out pencils, books, or psychic honors such as recognition at school assemblies or lunch with the principal.

One of the beauties of the program is that it doesn't require much technology. In a pinch, a single classroom computer can handle the job. The computer doesn't even have to be terribly up-to-date. (In schools that are low-tech, teachers from different rooms have even shared a computer.) As students finish reading their books, they simply pull up a chair for a five- to ten-minute, multiple choice test. By focusing on work done away from the computer, Accelerated Reader actually stands apart from the typical educational software product. In fact, Terry Paul, chairman and co-founder of Renaissance Learning, counts himself as something of an iconoclast about educational technology. "The research has proven, with a few exceptions, that computers are not a great teacher," he told me during a conference luncheon. Their real value, Paul believes, is in helping teachers manage their growing piles of student-performance data. The challenge of handling that task is fast becoming educational technology's new frontier; one firm predicted that spending on school technology would rise dramatically to a record $15 billion in 2002 as administrators rushed to meet President Bush's expectations on school accountability.[4] Terry Paul is well positioned for this shift. Assessment, classroom management, and record keeping are what the Renaissance system is about.

—

In other respects, Renaissance Learning is very much like the educational software of yore. It piggybacks on tried-and-true approaches to learning (in this case, basic book reading). It offers itself as a conveniently automated, comprehensive system—an attractive prospect for any school. And, like its competitors, it requires a commitment—not only of faith and time but also of money. A bare-bones approach to the company's reading program could be had at the time of the conference for as little as $499 (this buys four disks, each one holding quizzes on up to fifty books). Bigger packages, of twenty disks, are to be had for $1,499. For $2,999, a school could buy a Super Kit, comprising twenty disks and some reading-evaluation software. But the company doesn't consider this product-only approach terribly effective. Its trainers usually suggest that schools invest in the company's comprehensive program. This includes the full Renaissance product line, along with training and consulting. For a small school, one of, say, six hundred students, the price is approximately $135,000 over two to three years. For an entire district of roughly 15,000 students, it's $3 million.

The question, of course, is what a school gets in return. As with most educational software, the power of Renaissance Learning's products derives from the many other things the computer manages to leverage. For poor and generally failing schools, those other things quickly add up, in the company's view, to a new culture of success. The most dramatic portrait of this kind of turnaround was delivered, as the conference climax, by Don Peek, at the time the executive vice-president of the School Renaissance Institute, the company's private think tank. Days later, he was named the Institute's president, a promotion that would come as no surprise to the teachers and principals who laughed and cried over and over as they listened to his tale.

"NOTHING SHORT OF A MIRACLE"

The crowd's heartstrings were vibrating before Peek even began. He was introduced by Judi Paul, Terry Paul's wife and Renaissance Learning's co-founder. She spoke in the MGM Grand Arena via video, in yet another oversize broadcast on the arena's gigantic projection screens. Judi couldn't be there in person, she explained, because her daughter had just had triplets (shown on screen) and she was needed at home. Nonetheless, Judi told the assembled educators, "I want to personally thank each of you, because *you* [she then pointed firmly at the camera] are the heroes." Judi proceeded to relay the story, well known to any Renaissance regular, of the Pauls' son, Alex. "I want to take a few moments to talk about dreams," she said. As the story goes, Alex had shown so little interest in reading as a child that Judi was moved to come up with a game to motivate him. Sitting at their kitchen table, and later in their basement, she devised a paper-and-pencil version of what was to become Accelerated Reader, and Alex soon became a real reader. Today, he's a graduate of law school; at the time of the conference, he was clerking for a state supreme court judge.

After Judi's warm-up, Peek walked onstage and took his position front and center. No podium. No video projections. It was just Peek and a microphone. A compact middle-aged man with a wide smile, Peek stood there with his arms hung away from his sides, like a wrestler ready for a match—which in some ways he was. He had come, he said, to tell what he called the Pittsburg story. That's Pittsburg as in Pittsburg, Texas. Peek is Texan through and through, as are, curiously, a good number of Renaissance presenters. After a few days at a Renaissance conference, one begins to see why. A knack for wrapping a pitch in a good story seems to run in Texan blood; its disarming charm is much of what once put Ross Perot within striking distance of the White House. Don Peek is so good at it that he can hit the same folksy marks every time he tells this story, which he has done hundreds of times. In fact, some of the quotes in this retelling are exact replicas of things he said in his first big speech, which he delivered during the company's inaugural national conference the year before. A videotape of it is even sold by the company.

The Pittsburg story began, Peek said, twenty-eight years earlier, when he was a young teacher at Pittsburg Middle School—a "dirt-poor" place deep in northeast Texas where the sole local industry is poultry: "We have millions and millions of chickens." Economic and academic difficulties are so severe in Pittsburg that during Peek's time there, the federal government gave 50 percent of the students lunch free of charge or at a reduced cost, and 60 percent of them received additional financial help under the federal Title One program. Having grown up in Pittsburg, Peek had attended this middle school and was filled with anticipation at the opportunity to return as its teacher. "Ahm 'on tell you something," he said. "That first day of school, they wheeled in those textbooks—ratty ole pink-lookin' textbook that looked vaguely familiar to me. You guessed it. Our school board in their infinite wisdom had turned down the last two [textbook] adoptions. I was going to teach world geography from the same textbook from which I had been taught. One child had a special treat. He had my book."

About six weeks later, Peek made a discovery. "All those wonderful discussions I wanted to have, I couldn't have. Because those kids couldn't read." Many, he said, were reading two to three grade levels below their age; some were four to five years behind. "By mid-term, this young, naïve teacher was down at the principal's office knockin' on that door," asking the principal to make him the Title One reading teacher the following year. "Folks, you may find this hard to believe, but there was not a long line behind me for that job."

After working for seven years to build reading skills at the middle school, Peek was named assistant principal, then high school counselor, whereupon he started noticing that the kids coming down to his office for being in trouble—or because they wanted to drop out—were the same ones he'd seen with reading problems in middle school. Eventually appointed middle school principal, Peek decided to find out why teachers were having such difficulty teaching kids to read. To reassure the crowd that he wasn't pointing fingers at elementary school teachers' failures, he reminded them that his wife taught first grade at the time. "You start pointing fingers about first-grade reading problems in my house, that's a quick way to go to bed without your supper." What it's really about, he said, is "taking kids *where* they are and movin' 'em forward—as fast as they can go."

Despite Peek's efforts, the middle school chronically struggled with state tests. In 1991, less than half the school passed the reading exam on the state's notorious standardized test, the Texas Assessment of Academic Skills (TAAS); even fewer (43 percent) passed in math. Shaken, Peek called a faculty meeting. The core problem, everyone agreed, was weakness in reading; it affected even math scores. In the arithmetic sections of the test, the math teacher pointed out, "Every problem was a stated problem"—that is, the problems were framed verbally. If you can't read, you can't do the math. This dilemma feeds into one of Renaissance Learning's operating maxims— that reading controls everything. Terry Paul has gone so far as to calculate, as he once told me, that "70 to 80 percent of academic performance is predicted by reading ability." In less statistical terms, President George W. Bush makes a similar point when he makes such a priority of reading instruction.

"That day," Peek told the audience, "we decided that reading was the largest problem we had. And our focus, our money, our time and attention was going to go on reading." Peek essentially declared war. He ordered his faculty to go to any workshop on reading they could find, to bring him any book or magazine article on the subject, to visit any school that might offer lessons. His own explorations brought him to a 1983 study, by John Good-lad of the University of Washington, that surveyed schools to measure what portion of the school day a typical public school student devotes to reading. By Peek's recollection, the statistics were as follows: 6 percent in elementary school, 3 percent in junior high, and 2 percent in high school. For middle school, Peek noted, "that translates to eight minutes a day." Like almost everyone in the audience, Peek couldn't believe these figures. So he embarked on an observation of his own school and found the count remarkably accurate.

There's a simple point to these findings, Peek explained: "You cannot talk the skill of reading into a student. You cannot talk the skill of anything into anyone." Any decent educator realizes, he said, that "we must teach them short bursts of skills and then we must do what? Practice. Practice. And more practice." To underline the point, Peek asked the audience to compare those eight minutes of reading to the two hours students typically spend at athletic practice, or more during football season. "I don't know what it's like where you come from," he said, "but in Texas, if you lose last Friday night's game, that two hours can stretch to five in a heartbeat."

Eventually, Peek said, he came across a magazine ad for a program called Accelerated Reader, which promised to raise school reading scores dramatically. All the program asked was that schools set aside a chunk of time each day for students to read freely in one of the books on the company's list. Skeptical as he was about an ad, Peek noticed that the program was relatively inexpensive, so he ordered it. Right away, he realized it offered new methods of "accountability," and therein lay "a true gold mine." Peek immediately telephoned the company and asked to talk to the president. ("I am not a slow mover," Peek said. "I'm a whole-hog-or-none man, myself.") After crying poorhouse for a while and bemoaning the sorry state of his school's test scores, Peek asked Terry Paul to make Pittsburg Middle School one of the company's first test sites. If Paul would throw in some extra software, Peek would provide him with detailed information on student performance. Terry Paul lives on data, so they had a deal.

There was a catch, however. Peek's teachers had to faithfully follow the Renaissance routine. And apparently they did. Beginning in the fall of 1992, they carved out sixty minutes each day for students to silently practice independent reading (this is the company's mantra). They fit students to books that suited their abilities, had skilled students tutor those who were struggling, and persuaded local businesses to donate a small collection of prizes. Library circulation quickly doubled. Four months later, Peek said, his students posted a full year's growth in reading skills, as measured by a Stanford University diagnostic test. By year's end, the passing rate on the TAAS reading exam had risen from 49 percent to 65 percent. This brought in $49,000—the state's bonus to the school for a job well done. The faculty elected to invest the money in staff training, but there was a decent chunk left over for some real prizes, which Peek had five students round up in a marathon shopping spree at a Wal-Mart superstore. When they returned to campus, it became clear to all that a new day had arrived. "Folks, I don't know what Wal-Mart shopping bags do to kids in your part of the country," Peek said, "but it can whup northeast Texas kids into a frenzy in a heartbeat." To make his new priority crystal-clear, Peek cleaned out the school trophy showcase ("There were only third- and fourth-place trophies in there, anyway") and filled it with Wal-Mart booty. One morning, he saw a little boy talking to the librarian about a basketball in the cabinet. "Please don't sell that basketball," the student apparently pleaded, "cuz I'm readin' as *fast* as I can."

The next year, Peek said, students' scores on the Stanford test jumped even more dramatically, rising 2.23 grade levels. Peek asked the audience members how they would feel if their students' skills rose more than four grade levels in two years. "Would that make a difference in your job? Would that make a difference in those kids' lives? You better know it would." Peek knew, however, that Texans don't care about tests from Stanford. So when the district superintendent called in spring 1994 to tell him his school's TAAS scores were in, Peek told him to stop right there; he hopped into his truck, rushed across town, and opened the box "with trembling hands." The results: 90 percent of his students had passed their reading exams. "I guarantee you, we were pumped." And things only got better. In 2001, sophomores at Pittsburg High School, who were also using the Renaissance program by then, posted 98 percent passing rates in reading and 100 percent in math.

News of the school's success spread, bringing visitors, Peek said, from 150 different Texas schools. "Folks," he noted, "you don't come to Pittsburg, Texas, by accident." What pleased him most, however, was what the new program seemed to do for the school's most poverty-stricken students. After starting with what he calculated to be a 35 percent performance gap between the advantaged and the disadvantaged, by 1999, he said, that figure had shrunk to less than 8 percent. To Peek, the message is quite plain, and it's one that has echoed in the speeches of President George W. Bush. "It doesn't matter what your skin color is in Pittsburg, Texas," Peek said. "You're going to read, and you're going to learn. And we expect it from every one of our children."

Peek closed by telling the story of his own son, Nick, a seventh grader at the time, who Peek said was a perfectly capable reader but just didn't like books. Intrigued with the prizes, the boy started reading some easy books, enjoyed them, and continued checking out more—at least during the school year. After Nick's graduation, Peek noticed that over the summer his son went to Wal-Mart to buy six or seven books. "There were no points. There were no prizes. There was no Accelerated Reader. He was reading out of pure enjoyment." Peek calls the whole experience—with his son, with his school, and with the rest of the Pittsburg district, which soon adopted the Renaissance program—"nothing short of a miracle." The audience seemed to agree, judging by the long and heavy applause.

THE NUMBERS

While most school stories involving Renaissance products aren't as dramatic as Peek's, similar tales, with much the same tone of sin and salvation, abounded in Las Vegas. Numerous teachers reported that the program had doubled their schools' library circulation. One, from the Peggy Heller Elementary School, in Merced, California, told me that when reading hour is over in her class, students now beg for more time and get frustrated when the computers fail and they can't take their reading tests. Another teacher, from Mesa, Arizona, said the software lets her track progress individually, something "that's almost impossible with this many kids" but that "most teachers have tried to do on their own for years."

Dozens of additional testimonials are sprinkled throughout the Renaissance marketing material. A rural Kentucky school reportedly rose from the bottom of the state's barrel in 1994, when only 5 percent of its students met state reading standards, to near the top, with 70 percent now passing. In a fifth-grade class in Georgia, reading abilities apparently rose 2.2 grade levels in seven months, and test scores jumped 30 percent. At a school in Oxnard, California, the library collection was said to grow from 2,000 to 10,000 books in two years, and students reportedly have been asking to give up recess to do their Renaissance work. The school (Our Lady of Guadalupe) now has a waiting list, the leaflet says, "for the first time in many years." To round out the picture, quotes from satisfied customers are highlighted in company catalogs. "When I introduced Accelerated Reader, it was like magic!" says an elementary school teacher from Niagara Falls, New York. "Students had their noses in books everywhere I turned." In another catalog, the superintendent in McKinney, Texas, says, "No other school-improvement program or process provides me with the ability to ensure district-wide accountability and improvement." A principal in Memphis, Tennessee, adds, "In 33 years as an educator, I have never encountered a program that could transform a school the way Renaissance has transformed ours."

One would think accounts like these would provide more than enough proof that a company's programs improve student achievement. But they don't for Terry Paul. He is constantly searching for more proof, more data, more information. Paul is so obsessed with these issues that at the time of the conference, he was writing a book on the application of information theory in the schools (specifically, how technology can generate "information feedback loops" to the teacher). "You've got to be able to prove this stuff works!" Paul told me at one point. In some ways, Paul believes he already has, in spades. "I've got more data on reading behavior and math behavior than anybody in the world," he said. That's a big statement, but anyone perusing Renaissance Learning's literature might be inclined to believe him. One of Paul's proudest documents is a sixty-page booklet entitled "Research Summary." Put out by the company's School Renaissance Institute, it consists of a series of brief write-ups on approximately seventy-five different studies—"field reports" from different schools around the country, "white papers" from the institute itself, and evaluations done by outside experts.

The studies reflect a curious phenomenon found throughout the field of education research, and many areas of scientific research as well. It's an intellectual disconnect that has become an integral part of the research game. Researchers will frequently tell you, with accepting calm, that most education research is horribly flawed: full of limitations, biases, or odd influential factors that researchers did not see or did not acknowledge. In the next breath, most of these same researchers will tell you why their research is solid. Terry Paul is no exception.

"The Accelerated Reader is a reading researcher's dream," says one of his key, early studies. "For the first time, all the major elements required to measure reading practice (quantity, level, and score) have been reduced to the simple statistic of reading points." Billed by Renaissance in 1994 as "the largest study ever of literature-based reading," the study (called the 1992 National Reading Study and Theory of Reading Practice) looked at 4,498 students from 64 schools across the United States. It claimed "statistically significant correlations" proving that this program "can more than double the growth in students' reading ability."[5] An update and expansion of the study a year later offered additional evidence of what Paul called the "Reading Fallout Theory," his notion that new reading skills lead to new skills in other subjects—in this case, mathematics. The study produced a number that Paul often invokes: 68 percent of math gains, the study found, can be traced to increased reading skills.[6] The company says that by 1996, it had distributed more than 400,000 copies of these studies to educators across the United States.

Later studies piled on additional approaches to educational research, and arrived at equally noteworthy conclusions. One of Paul's favorites is a massive project—one he now refers to as "the largest study ever done on whether technology makes a difference in schools." Delivered at a 1996 National Reading Research Center conference in Atlanta, Georgia, this study looked at 6,149 schools in Don Peek's home state of Texas. It was chosen partly because Accelerated Reader (AR) is so widely used there (at the time, the study said, more than 40 percent of Texas schools had bought the program). To draw a comparison, the study chose two kinds of schools—those that had bought AR (2,500 fell into that camp), and those that hadn't (about 3,500 fit this category). The study found "statistically significant evidence that schools which owned AR performed better than non-AR schools on virtually all subject tests, including reading, math, science, and social studies."[7]

The company was so pleased with the results of its Texas study that in its marketing materials, it went on to say that "schools that purchased Accelerated Reader show students improved" in a number of important new ways. Not only did students do well in traditional, rote standardized tests, but they also improved in what's become the latest trend in state-sponsored tests: evaluations of such things as "critical thinking" and creative skills. This is done by giving students "performance-based" tests, which generally are a series of essay questions or multifaceted tasks. Challenges like these, the theory goes, are ones that students can execute only by invoking both factual knowledge and analytical savvy.

Interestingly, although Paul has co-authored or helped design many of the large-scale studies of his company's products, he has no special training in statistical research. His degrees are in economics, business, and law. "I'm just a numbers guy," he told me one afternoon as we walked toward a conference session he was hosting in Las Vegas, called, not surprisingly, Research Symposium. "I'm just a quantitative person," he said. "Either you're a 'quant' or you're not." Paul's session did indeed feel like a researcher's dream. Half a dozen specialists, most with university affiliations, delivered presentations that were stuffed with scientific analysis. Most were accompanied by a barrage of slides full of statistics, charts, and carefully worded but noticeably bold claims about the power of Renaissance's products.

Those claims have helped the company seek a position of some respect within the education reform movement. During one conversation in Las Vegas, Stuart Udell, then president of the School Renaissance Institute, told me that the company considers its record to be superior to the dozen or so big school-reform models that have become national names. Schools across the country have happily contributed to this image by dramatically reorganizing some or all of their academic routine around Renaissance concepts.

To encourage this, the company has set up two prizes for its adult customers. One is essentially a free consulting service, which helps interested schools apply for grants that will fund the Renaissance program—an onerous process that many schools can't manage on their own. The other is a system to reward teachers, schools, and entire districts with special certifications for having achieved "model" status. That accomplishment (which brings schools numerous freebies, a Renaissance press release, and showers of recognition at the national conference) is so coveted that teachers in Las Vegas were on the edge of their chairs when it was time to announce new model inductees. Some became teary-eyed when they weren't chosen. Education organizations, children's software reviews, and business publications have added to all of this buzz, treating the company to more than a half-dozen different product awards and commendations over the years.

THE EMPEROR'S CLOTHES

There is another way to look at these accomplishments. When one begins rummaging around in Renaissance Learning's closet, it becomes clear that the company's materials are not as carefully woven as they look out in the bright lights. Some start to unravel rather badly, in fact, once they get tangled up in the ongoing national debate about literacy. At a certain point, tears open around the gains that Renaissance schools seem to make on test scores; others lead to questions about the company itself and how it functions in the marketplace. The trouble begins, however, with the basics—the nature and quality of Renaissance Learning's scientific research.

In the late 1990s, in yet another wave of public panic about student competence, building up the reading abilities of America's youngsters became the ultimate political priority. Then, in April 2000, a report was released by a group called the National Reading Panel, a collection of experts whose study of literacy had been formally ordered by Congress.[8] Unfortunately, at the same time, the nation (or, more precisely, the nation's army of news editors) was a little distracted. The study came out at the peak of media frenzy about Cuban refugee Elián González, which tended to bury news reports on a tired issue like reading. But the literacy report had some afterlife. Congress was sufficiently pleased with the report that in 2001, it gave $15 million to the National Institute for Literacy, just to publicize its findings, and $5 billion to the Department of Education to carry out its recommendations.

The study did its part to earn these rewards. The mission of its fourteen-member panel (composed mostly of educators, along with one physicist and one parent) was to find the best, solidly proven way to stimulate reading ability. To do this, the panelists spent two years combing through the scientific literature on reading—specifically, 100,000 studies published since 1966 and 15,000 others published previously. By early 2000, the panel had boiled these studies down to approximately 400 that met the gold standard of scientific research—that is, they were conducted as controlled experiments, or nearly so (i.e., quasi-experimental), with results published in a refereed journal.

With this exemplary pool, the panelists started looking for solid instructional possibilities. In the process, they were required to take one more step: hold their meetings in public. This was partly to avoid the troubles that had beset other high-level, fix-it commissions that tried to go about their work quietly. The public vetting also lent the panel's final recommendations some extra credibility, since by then it had heard from parents, other researchers, and an array of educators whose job it is to carry out academic ideals in the less-than-ideal real world.

When the panel finally issued its conclusions, it offered both old news and, for outfits like Renaissance Learning, whose emphasis is on independent reading, it presented some revelations. In essence, the report said that while certain practices were more effective than others, it was clear that there was no one method of teaching reading that could carry the day. The most effective approach of all, the panelists concluded, was a mixture of practices: exercises that help beginning readers distinguish sounds and then associate letters and words with those sounds; reading aloud to children and having them read aloud as well; adult coaching and discussion; and, most important, a variety of activities that build comprehension and the capacity for literary analysis.

Buried in the middle of the panel's report was a section innocently titled

"Encouraging Students to Read More." The idea sounds elementary—a predictable garnish on a report that was aiming to be comprehensive. However, the findings in this section were not so easily digested. The panel had found ninety-two different studies conducted over the years that had looked at the effects of simply getting students to read more literature of their own choosing, what educators call free reading. As with every other issue under the commission's purview, the panelists first winnowed the pile to those studies that met some basic scientific standards. The tally came to fourteen, two of which concerned Accelerated Reader.

The panel's evaluation of the AR studies, presumably the company's best, was not pretty. Basically, its report said, the studies were so handicapped by design flaws that it was impossible to tell what was going on. Students may well improve their reading scores while using AR, but it's equally likely that something other than AR may be causing the rise in scores. The possibilities include everything from new books to extra hours of study, an atmosphere of higher standards and expectations, increased involvement by parents, or nothing more than a re-energized staff of teachers. In fact, judging from other teachers' stories in Pittsburg, Texas, some of these other factors were the main causes of rising test scores in Don Peek's school. "Even if you buy a bad program, if the staff is committed to it, it will work," says Joel Hodes, the principal of Schurz Elementary, on a Nevada Indian reservation, who was a participant at Renaissance's Las Vegas gathering. The National Reading Panel members had similar impressions. "For the most part," their report said, "these studies found no gains in reading due to encouraging students to read more. It is unclear whether this was the result of deficiencies in the instructional procedures themselves or to the weakness and limitations evident in the study designs."

In one example, the panelists looked at a 1994 Accelerated Reader study that examined two North Carolina schools, comparing 50 ninth graders in a school that used AR with 50 in a school that didn't. The researchers tracked these students for five years; this gave their results some longitudinal flavor, a welcome icing on any researcher's cake. They measured these students from third through eighth grade, according to their performances on the standardized California Achievement Test.[9] But the national panelists discovered, strangely, that the Renaissance researchers calculated their numbers by subtracting scores on a third-grade test from scores on the ninth-grade test, an exam so much more advanced that it's almost an entirely different test. A separate evaluation of this AR study—which was conducted by a researcher at California State University, Fullerton, and which the panel did not see—found further errors. According to this review, the two groups of students, at least in the ninth grade, had drastically different levels of exposure to books—five to six hours a week in the AR school, versus two to three hours in the "control" school.[10] Even without this insight, the Renaissance study was so much a case of comparing apples to oranges that the national reviewers had no recourse but to declare its statistics invalid.

The panel's findings in the second AR study were even odder. This study was conducted in 1999 by three researchers, one of whom was a Scotsman named Keith J. Topping, a paid Renaissance consultant and one of its most heavily promoted academics. Of all the AR studies, this was the only one (at least in the peer-reviewed literature) that attempted to follow a basic rule of experimental research: You take one group that's engaged in the activity you're trying to study (in this case, AR) and compare it with another group that is similar, and is in similar circumstances, but that isn't involved in the activity under review. In other words, while the first group is feverishly practicing with its exciting new toy, the students in the second (control) group should not be catatonically sitting at their desks as a teacher drones on about the waning of the Middle Ages. To be fair, the control group should get a promising new toy too, just a different one.

This is what Topping did—sort of. According to his summary of his own research, Topping looked at one Scottish class that was using AR, one class that wasn't, and a third class that was using "an alternative intensive method."[11] The problem is that the class using AR was also practicing some other reading instruction—coincidentally, some of the very same alternatives that the American reading panelists reported to be effective. "If you have AR combined with something that works, showing that it still works doesn't tell me much," Tim Shanahan, professor and director of the Center for Literacy at the University of Illinois, in Chicago, and a member of the National Reading Panel, told me. "That's like saying, 'If you're sick, I'll give you some penicillin and pray for you. And in five to ten days you'll be better.' That doesn't prove much about prayer." In sum, Shanahan said, "The two AR studies were just dismal. They couldn't have possibly answered the questions being asked."

Not surprisingly, Terry Paul has not taken too kindly to the NRP report. "Every study that's ever been done has significant flaws," he told me. "I could go through the accepted NRP studies and find flaws." Paul's deeper complaint is that the NRP misunderstood AR, seeing it as a "free reading" program, when in his view it is more of a management tool, which teachers use to supervise reading. To Shanahan, that distinction is flimsy, especially since Renaissance so aggressively markets AR as a full reading program. Either way, the NRP's dour assessment of AR, and other programs like it, has not been fun for Paul to live with. "The NRP sits there like a big ugly frog," Paul said in an e-mail to me as recently as mid-2003.

—

But what about the basic premise here—the old adage that practice makes perfect? The idea seems so obvious that at the Las Vegas conference, Renaissance presenters constantly drew laughs and applause by citing instances where schools, and high-minded experts like those on the reading panel, seem to blindly ignore it. Can this maxim actually be wrong? Are we really supposed to believe that students' reading ability won't improve when they do more reading?

Shanahan, who sits on the board of the International Reading Association, chairs the reading committee for the Department of Education's high-profile National Assessment of Educational Progress, and has helped design a number of state testing programs in reading, gets questions like these from audiences all the time. To answer, he sometimes plays a game. He first asks for a show of hands from people who play the piano. He then asks whether they think they'd play better if they devoted more time to practicing; virtually all nod vigorously. He then asks those who don't play piano if they'd improve with more practice; virtually everyone laughs. The point is obvious: Unless you have at least some basic skills—and, ideally, a complement of more advanced skills, too—practice is meaningless. "The assumption that just reading a book and taking tests about it will improve reading ability is a poor assumption," Shanahan argues. In Accelerated Reader's case, "It's probably too much practice, too much unguided practice." But the primary concern, Shanahan said, is that "it's stealing instruction time."

Misconceptions of this sort are much of what has hurt the nation's academic performance over the years, but not quite in the fashion that's popularly believed. While President Bush and other politicians publicly fret about little children who can't read, international scores show that young readers in America outperform everyone except Finnish children.[12] The falloff hits later, in fourth through eighth grades, and it hits hard. By eighth grade, American students lag behind a dozen countries in reading. In presentations, Shanahan has made this clear to the Bush administration. Nonetheless, in 2001, Bush proceeded to devote $5 billion to boosting reading skills among the relatively unneedy: children in kindergarten through third grade. Campaigns about suffering eleven-year-old skateboarders apparently don't tug the political heartstrings the way doe-eyed six-year-olds do.

Whatever age level is in question, the panelists' report concluded that top-of-the-line reading instruction is not complicated; it's not even terribly new. It does take some time. And most important, Shanahan pointed out, none of the panel's suggestions require schools to buy fancy or expensive products, whether low-tech or high-tech. "If I were teaching the class," Shanahan said, "and was asked if I could do more interesting things to teach a book than just have them read it, I'd like to think I could."

Those things, according to the panel's recommendations, fall into a simple sequence. For unskilled readers—many of whom can be found in junior high school—the panel strongly recommended a complex of exercises that build facility with sounds and word recognition.* The panel's other big emphasis was on the nettlesome challenge of teaching comprehension, an issue that becomes increasingly important, and increasingly elusive, as poorly educated readers advance in age.

Smart ways to teach comprehension can get complex; they can also be a lot of fun. Some entail intensive discussions about a work's characters and themes or about how the writer manages to set a particular tone. If the text is nonfiction, the discussion style should help students learn how to evaluate facts and to reconcile conflicting accounts of historical events. Nontraditional exercises in comprehension—having students compose loose diagrams that lay out a story's dramatic structure or having young children act out a story—have been shown to have great results. At the same time, one of the most effective ways to deepen a reader's sense of a literature's meaning is as old-fashioned as it gets: basic writing exercises. These include not only standard book reports, which summarize what's been read, but also creative essays, which invite students to focus on one point of fascination or to use what they've read as a launching point for their own stories. Curiously, Renaissance Learning says—as a selling point for AR—that its program makes book reports unnecessary.

---

*Some educators who were displeased with the National Reading Panel's conclusions complained that the panel was biased. The most commonly heard complaint is that its report merely perpetrated the long-standing "reading wars" between "phonics" loyalists and defenders of "whole language." (For those new to this odd and unnecessary feud, whole language shuns nitty-gritty work on phonics, or individual sounds, in favor of a more "natural" approach—regular exposure to whole words and whole stories.) Some of the panel's critics, including at least one of its own members, later argued that the panel took the phonics crowd's side. But the report itself indicates otherwise. It goes to great lengths to say that exercises with natural text have their place, when combined with phonics and a number of other linguistic exercises. If anything, reading comprehension, not phonics, was the panel's main obsession, since more than half the studies in its final pool were about comprehension.

This illustrates Tim Shanahan's central worry—that Accelerated Reader leads students, as well as teachers, to ignore these basic elements of literary nutrition. "I'd like to believe a teacher could ask a harder question, or a more interesting question, about a book than what's on [AR's] tests," Shanahan observes. The possibilities, he points out, are numerous: "Unpack the plot. See how conflict works in the story. Gauge the mood and how the writer sets it." AR not only overlooks these issues, it sanctions the neglect of more basic skills as well. "What if a child is having trouble with word recognition?" Shanahan asks. "They're on their own for that. Vocabulary? They're on their own. Comprehension? They're still on their own. It's over-sell. It's hype."

Shanahan is in a unique position to know. Shortly before Terry Paul headed off for Las Vegas, he hired Shanahan to conduct a private review of Renaissance Learning's primary pieces of reading research. When Paul returned to Wisconsin, he was greeted with some sobering news: "They seem to take the same old handful of studies and keep repeating them with larger and larger samples," Shanahan told me, summarizing what he'd reported to Paul. As a result, "the mistakes they make initially continue to be the same ones you see on down the line."

———

Some of those mistakes are pretty serious. Consider Renaissance Learning's bedrock studies, particularly the 1992 national study on the "Theory of Reading Practice." This study, which was designed and written up by Terry Paul himself, goes to considerable lengths to make very definitive claims. In the study's introduction, for example, Paul writes, "Does reading practice cause reading growth? Surprisingly, reading researchers have never conclusively answered this fundamental question." Pointing to his own study, Paul says, "Now, though, the results of the National Reading Study are in. We know the answer. Literature-based reading does cause reading growth, and dramatically so."

To find these dramatic answers, Paul fudges his figures a little, which takes a moment's patience with statistics to understand. In one case, for instance, Paul cites reading growth of "2.13 grade" levels in a single year through the use of AR. To anchor this claim, he points to the "correlation for the least-squares regression." This, he notes, is "significant," and therefore "associated with dramatic growth in reading ability." The problem is that he based this huge growth on the notion that students had earned 100 AR points. But almost none of the students did. The vast majority got well below 50, and the low achievers got as few as 14. How could Paul come up with such a calculation? He used a hypothetical multiplier, then based his conclusions on the expanded result.

When Cathleen Kennedy, a computer science professor at the College of San Mateo, California, and a researcher at UC Berkeley's Evaluation and Assessment Research Center, reviewed Paul's claims on this count, then did her own calculations of the data, she was stunned. "This is not an honest picture of what this program is doing," she told me. "It's a typical dog-and-pony show used on administrators who don't know about statistics." One of the things that most galls researchers like Kennedy is Paul's tendency to play fast and loose with statistical terms, particularly his frequent claim to have found "highly significant correlations" when there are none.*

The issues here obviously descend quickly into the technicalities of statistics-speak, but those technicalities matter. As federal authorities seek proof that education reforms are based in solid ground, more and more enterprises are invoking the terms of science to lend credibility to their products. To their customers in the schools—or to anyone whose work involves taking academic research a step further—these esoteric terms are valuable guideposts. They help people distinguish the solid from the flimsy, the promising from the useless. Wherever such distinctions are blurred, there is fertile ground for hype and deception.

One question that is persistently blurred in Paul's claims is whether other factors that have little or nothing to do with AR might be driving the action in the company's studies. It's a common question in research on any education program. And it came up repeatedly in my conversations about AR with Kennedy, Shanahan, and other research experts familiar with Renaissance Learning's work.

When a school buys a program like AR, quite often that purchase simply becomes a way of organizing the staff's recommitment to teaching. (This seems to be what happened in Don Peek's school, judging by accounts from several of his teachers.) And sometimes the product is but one of many new literacy initiatives being undertaken. This may be one explanation for the superior performance by AR schools in the study that Terry Paul singled out

---

*In this study, for example, the regression statistics actually turned out to be flat, with associations that Kennedy called "extremely weak"—that is, indicating very little evidence of any cause and effect. "It's not measuring what they say they're measuring," Kennedy said, about not only the 1992 study but also the 1993 follow-up, which further attempted to link reading improvement to gains in math ability. At best, Kennedy said, the studies show what statisticians would call "statistically significant, weak correlations." The point here is that statements of "statistical significance" aren't always what they seem. They're not, as many would assume, signs of a large change or effect; they're usually only an indication of a gargantuan sample base within which a tiny change has been observed.

as a favorite—the company's massive 1996 survey of more than 6,000 schools in Texas. The study makes much of the fact that it "cross-referenced" AR information with additional data, some that came from the state education agency and some from a leading private data firm. But virtually the only thing the researchers knew about these schools was this: One group had bought the AR software; the comparison group hadn't. Whether any of these schools also expanded teaching hours, bought new books, or instituted any number of other effective changes was never examined. Nor was the very likely possibility that the AR schools were simply wealthier, and thus more likely to have the funds for fancy programs and a population of more confident students. Despite all these complications, the company's own data indicate that the final difference between the two groups is actually quite slight. Only 4 percent of the AR schools performed better than the non-AR schools.

These and other Renaissance studies are further compromised by a lack of controls for all sorts of tricks that students commonly rely on to master AR tests. Those include resorting to shortcuts, such as skimming or reading CliffsNotes, or old-fashioned cheating. (By many teachers' accounts, cheating is surprisingly prevalent on AR tests. Renaissance claims it prevents this problem by scrambling the order of its test answers. But the questions, and their answers, don't change. And since the computer disks contain only five or ten questions on each book, numerous schools report that students find it easy to crib the answers and pass them around. At many schools, students sit down for their tests with the book at their side, or with a friend who has read it, and quickly rack up a passing score.) Because of these complications, Kennedy argues, "This is not a measurement of reading practice. It's a measurement of reading performance."

When I asked Terry Paul about these criticisms, he dismissed them all. "I am skeptical of small-scale control studies in social science," he says. "The selection bias, the Hawthorne effect, the difference between teachers kind of overwhelms small studies. Big databases are the only way to filter out some of this noise."* Some researchers may agree with Paul, but from all indica-

---

*As an example, Terry Paul's original study—the 1992 report that Cathleen Kennedy criticized for misusing statistical measures of validity, and then compounding the problem with a multiplier—Paul regards as an innocent, informal piece of work. While the multiplier technique might have been buried, Paul says, "It's not something I didn't disclose." As for the experts' other concerns about the company's approach to research, Paul questions the experts' criteria. "For an academic journal," he said, "you have to qualify everything up the ying yang, talk about the fact that of course this doesn't prove causation, list the questions raised which deserved to be researched, etc., etc., etc."

tions most don't. Relying on big, uncontrolled databases, Tim Shanahan says, "is like trying to read the entrails of a goat." Federal authorities apparently agree, judging from their recent insistence that school initiatives be founded on well-controlled studies.

The tempting conclusion to draw from this story is that Renaissance Learning, Inc., is an anomaly—a company that generates unusually irresponsible research. In actuality, the kind of material the firm generates—and the claims it makes about that material—is more common than one would think. In 1998, for example, *Educational Technology Review* reviewed 834 articles published from 1991 to 1996 in leading research journals in educational technology. The journal found that "only 12 percent . . . of the work is of an empirical and objective nature." Upon further inspection, the journal concluded that "approximately five percent . . . is conducted using formal methods such as control groups with *comparative* learning outcomes"—that is, a second group whose characteristics and options are truly equivalent to the group that's armed with computers.[13] As Edward Miller, the former editor of the *Harvard Education Letter,* once told me, "The research is set up in a way to find benefits that aren't really there. It's so flawed, it shouldn't even be called research. Essentially, it's just worthless."

Considering the sorry state of the art in this field, Shanahan didn't consider the limitations in Renaissance Learning's research to be terribly serious. Many companies, he pointed out, do no research of any kind on the effectiveness of their products. "Renaissance Learning deserves some credit," he said, "just for putting themselves on the line." In fact, the gaps and odd twists in Renaissance research are so common that, Shanahan surmised, the company could probably get some of its studies published in middle- or low-level research journals—if it were willing to pull back slightly on its claims.

As its compendium of research has accumulated over the years, Renaissance Learning has done just that—to an extent. Part of the reason is that Terry Paul has arranged to have the later studies conducted by independent academics. But important weaknesses have persisted. The prevalence of such weaknesses throughout educational research is much of the reason that many private companies that work with schools have applauded Bush's higher scientific standards. In their response, however, a good number of these firms simply pasted the government's terminology on their own past research materials, to prove to customers that they are solid academic citizens. Renaissance Learning has been no exception. "Renaissance is supported by the highest-quality research, as defined by the federal government—it meets the five criteria of scientifically based research and involves control groups,"

Terry's wife, Judi, wrote in a March 2003 letter to educators. Similar comments prominently appear on the company's website. To support her statement, Judi listed thirty-nine of the studies done over the years on various Renaissance products. While the tone of some of the more recent studies' claims is more cautious, numerous reports still suggest or flatly state that Renaissance programs have led to dramatic gains in achievement measures. And, while the growth numbers may be real, there is no firm proof that Renaissance programs were the cause of higher reading test scores. In fact, the studies continue to leave open the possibility that other factors could have driven the AR schools' accomplishments—or that simple changes in instruction methods could produce even greater results. In some cases, the gains appear to be the result of nothing more than normal student growth.*

THE CREATIVE RESEARCH LAB

The story behind Terry Paul's approach to academic research is as curious as the research itself. In the early 1990s, before he formally joined Renaissance (which was actually founded by his wife), Paul was serving as president of Best Power Technology, a company that manufactured backup power systems. Best Power was a family-owned firm and had long been run by Terry's mother and his brother, Steven. Paul's tenure there yielded some creative lessons, as well as the model for the company's research division, where nearly a fifth of its one thousand employees work.

Best Power was founded in 1977, in Necedah, Wisconsin, a tiny town of less than a thousand people in the state's desolate heartland. Marguerite Paul, Terry's mother, was drawn to the community for a specific reason. Since the 1950s, Necedah had been the gathering place for a subset of devout Catholics who were followers of a woman named Mary Ann Van Hoof,

---

*An interesting example of the more recent studies on Renaissance's reading products is the work of Jay Samuels. A professor of both educational psychology and curriculum and instruction at the University of Minnesota, in Minneapolis, Samuels served with Shanahan as a member of the National Reading Panel. But he emerged with a more positive view than Shanahan did of instruction through what reading experts call "sustained silent reading"— essentially, Accelerated Reader's routine minus the company's short quizzes. In March 2002, Samuels wrote a forceful letter for Renaissance pointing to a very mixed study that, he argued, firmly proved AR's value. To make his case in the letter, which Renaissance publicly distributed, Samuels listed his credentials in some detail. Missing, however, was any mention of the fact that Samuels was paid by Renaissance to conduct his own AR studies (these turned out to have their own weaknesses) or that he serves on the company's board of directors.

who claimed to have had visions of the Virgin Mary (among other saints and angels), private knowledge of coming waves of global devastation, and the stigmata to prove it.* Marguerite Paul saw a business opportunity in Necedah, which regularly drew tens of thousands of visitors during Van Hoof's vigils. Anyone struggling to survive when the rest of the world was crumbling would need independent power supplies, and Marguerite decided to manufacture them. (The family was also drawn to this area, according to former employees, because Necedah, which sat in the state's poorest county, would be a fertile seedbed of cheap labor.) Before long, the company was selling thousands of power inverters and transformers to survivalists, private companies, and other customers across the nation.

Best Power grew slowly in its early years, aided at the time by alternative-energy tax breaks created by President Jimmy Carter. Finally, in 1980, the company had become large enough that Marguerite and Steven decided they needed some extra management muscle, so they brought in Terry. (Terry's father, Willard, while technically a founding officer of the company, was relatively absent. And Steven was busy with other interests, one of which was the development of a perpetual-motion machine.) Terry immediately saw two new business possibilities. One was to capitalize on the nation's newly developing high-technology industry by supplying backup power sources for computer users. The other was to build an impressive base of research about energy usage and backup energy needs, which could be promoted and legitimized by a separate think tank. That operation was called the National Power Laboratory and its success (its data was soon being quoted by both competitors and *The New York Times*) fed Terry's later visions in education.

By 1992, Best Power was pulling in close to $100 million in sales, an achievement that inspired the family to take the company public. But Terry was wary of the family's weaknesses as a management team. His solution

---

*Adding to Van Hoof's appeal were her regular sufferings, endured on the Fridays of Advent and Lent. During these times, Van Hoof would take to her bed and, by some followers' eyewitness accounts, endure the physical blows that Christ suffered (sometimes with outstretched, rigid arms, as if in crucifixion), and intermittently receive heavenly messages, which are now recorded in six written volumes. Today, the most visible remains of Van Hoof's teachings are a shrine that her followers started in her honor, in the belief that when devastation did come, anyone who followed her Christian teachings would be spared. The shrine—a pastoral garden and still-unfinished concrete basilica—houses roughly a dozen life-size statues, which include various apostles, George Washington and Abraham Lincoln, and Jesus Christ in a state of bruised and bloody anguish. The shrine, which was built by Van Hoof's followers, is called Queen of the Holy Rosary, Mediatrix of Peace, Mediatrix Between God and Man. It is being sustained and completed by a local organization called For My God and My Country, Inc.

was to convince his mother (and the company's board) that it was time for her to retire. Marguerite was not in a retiring mood, however. Convinced that Terry was trying to steal the company from his brother, Steven, she persuaded the board to fire Terry instead. Terry responded by suing his mother and several company board members for dismissing him without cause. This spawned a long and strange court fight, which was finally resolved in a settlement worth almost $12 million to Terry and company stockholders. While the suit dragged on, Terry joined his wife as co-chairman of Renaissance Learning, which was, and still is, based an hour's drive from Necedah, in the town of Wisconsin Rapids, and was then doing business under the name Advantage Learning Systems, Inc.

Pleased with his success with the National Power Laboratory, Terry quickly looked for similar opportunities in the education market after his arrival at Advantage Learning. He began by setting up a new, separate operation in Madison, not far from the University of Wisconsin, which did business under the name Institute for Academic Excellence. The Institute immediately adopted an academic patina, which was polished by its scholarly-sounding address: 455 Science Drive, University Research Park. In reality, there was never any tie to the university. In fact, the manner in which the Institute went about its research would have left many university researchers astounded.

But it wouldn't astonish them all. In recent years, news reports have occasionally popped up, indicating that scientific research, even at respected universities has become increasingly biased toward the private enterprises that fund it.[14] Sometimes the service being delivered to commercial interests is made plain; sometimes it's carefully hidden. In either case, statistical concoctions that look true enough to fly through the public radar tend to share common rules. Because the School Renaissance Institute turns out so many of these studies, and because those studies aim so high, the methods behind this research are unusually revealing.

One of the first things the Institute did, after Terry Paul's debut studies in 1992 and 1993, was create what looked like an objective framework for gauging the ideal level of reading challenge that any student should face. To do this, Paul went prospecting for ideas in the annals of mainstream academic literature, an approach that would become a common practice of his over the years. Eventually, Paul came across the writings of the Russian psychologist Lev Vygotsky. To many experts in the worlds of education, psychology, and child development, Vygotsky is one of the great luminaries; he's the man who, more than any other, devised a set of theories that trumped those of the even more famous psychologist Jean Piaget, who outlined the stages of child development. Vygotsky's idea, in part, was that children were entirely capable of pushing the envelope on Piaget's somewhat rigid demarcations of academic ability—if they were properly guided. As Vygotsky's work progressed, he became so fascinated with the outer limits of children's capabilities that he gave them a formal name: the zone of proximal development. For Terry Paul, that zone looked like a gold mine.

Paul realized that he could become, in essence, the zone's modern king. If he could find a meaningful way to define reading challenges and then show teachers how to push students to the pleasurable edge of their comfort zone, but not over it, he'd have a killer product. Vygotsky helped him do that. As one of Paul's reports stated, "The point between unchallenging and frustratingly difficult text, the point at which maximum growth occurs, is the zone of proximal development or ZPD."[15] Over the years, this concept has become the engine in the Renaissance reading program. "ZPD! ZPD!" Don Peek screamed out to one conference session in Las Vegas in a typical exhortation. "If you're having trouble motivating your students, you're not using the zone." After some experimentation, Paul defined this zone as any score on Accelerated Reader quizzes that falls between 85 and 92 percent of correct answers. Scores above 92 percent mean a student is reading books that are too easy; anything below 85 percent means the books are too hard. All a teacher needs to do, therefore, is watch the numbers. Simple enough, right?

Not to Terry Paul. As with most of the Institute's material, he wanted a reassuring blanket of data behind this theory. So in 1998, he put together a study of approximately 80,000 students in Tennessee who used Accelerated Reader. The study was supposed to find the exact ZPD that would produce the biggest boost in reading ability. To conduct his inquiry, Paul contracted with William Sanders, a professor at the time at the University of Tennessee, at Knoxville, and a highly regarded innovator in the nettlesome problem of linking students' and teachers' performance, and tracking the interaction, over a period of years. Paul of course hoped that such a mother lode of data—Renaissance scores from thousands of AR users, cross-referenced with Sanders's detailed achievement records—would generate some powerful statistical arguments. Once the study was done, however, Sanders found that most students using the program, even with the proper ZPD, were not showing gains of any great significance. More important, the older the students were, the less the program tended to help them. In retrospect, Sanders saw plenty of indications that the AR program could be useful—as one tool among many to teach reading. But it seemed problematic when viewed as a necessity or when used as a stand-alone solution. "There were plenty of highly effective teachers who weren't using the tool," Sanders told me. "And there were some highly effective teachers who were." While the AR teachers showed a slight edge over the non-AR teachers, the problem, Sanders said, is that "you don't know if those teachers were more effective to start with."

There might have been a reason the numbers didn't cooperate with Paul's expectations. Lev Vygotsky, it turns out, had something quite different in mind regarding an ideal "zone" for reading. At the crux of Vygotsky's work was an intriguing discovery and the theory for which he is most known: Pushing the limits of a youngster's learning zone made sense, Vygotsky realized, only when his or her efforts are robustly supported with social interaction—with teachers or skillful friends. Challenges pursued independently were another matter entirely; if anything, they framed the bottom of Vygotsky's zone. As Vygotsky himself put it: ". . . the zone of proximal development . . . is the distance between the actual development level as determined by independent problem solving and the level of potential development as determined through problem solving under adult guidance or in collaboration with more capable peers."[16] In other words, let's say we have an eight-year-old girl who is given lots of books to read at increasingly advanced levels. If she then gets to read or talk about the books with a teacher or parent, and is also paired with smart playmates to paint or build a make-believe world around the concepts she's reading about, before long she should be reading like a ten-year-old. That, at least, is Vygotsky's notion. It is not about silently poring through advanced books all by herself and then having her accomplishments evaluated by some computer software.

Terry Paul saw no reason to worry about these details. In his view, books ought to be tutor enough in themselves. If students are encouraged to pick challenging enough material, they'll be "pulled into their ZPD," as several Renaissance presenters frequently put it. The limitations in that statement are why many experts in reading and academic research, including some who have worked for Renaissance Learning, Inc., have trouble with Paul's connections. "You see how quickly this gets fuzzy," Cathy Upham, one former Renaissance employee, told me. "What Terry Paul does is he takes the most faddish theorist and creates a frame where it looks like this simple little test of his fits this complex learning theory." In doing so, Upham said, Paul "gains sexiness—by yoking what he's doing to a known learning theorist." The problem, Upham argues, is that Paul employs "none of the controls" necessary for these assertions. "To do that," she said, "you need all sorts of validity tests. And he does zero of that."

Upham, who has advanced degrees in rhetoric and writing and a Ph.D., ironically enough, in Renaissance studies, was hired by Renaissance Learning in 1997. Her job was to help boost the company's sales to high schools, a market that has not embraced Renaissance products as enthusiastically as the early grades have. To give the high school foray some muscle, Upham was supposed to design something called Accelerated Literature, poised to be one of the company's most sophisticated software packages. The product was supposed to test "higher-order thinking skills," an elusive but seductive target that educators aptly refer to by its acronym: HOTS. In Upham's view, HOTS has become "the big buzzword, although nobody knows what it is. And nobody defines it, least of all a commercial company."

Accelerated Literature's commercial life didn't go terribly well—for reasons that say something about the prospects for any sophisticated educational software. In 1998, before the product was launched, the company dropped the original concept, Upham and others recall, for two reasons. First, a true HOTS product would require sophisticated content, which could be created only by people erudite in high school subjects such as history, mythology, science—the list could go on and on. But Upham got the sense that Paul didn't want to spend what it took to hire people with those skills. Second, once the product was distributed, it did not have great prospects for spawning the ongoing profit stream that AR disks generate. "Once schools buy it," Upham said, "they wouldn't need much more." (Terry Paul differs with Upham's version of events, saying it was simply more efficient to fold HOTS efforts into their existing products.)

Before long, Upham left the company, thoroughly disillusioned. At the time of my interview, she was employed by Wisconsin's Department of Public Instruction, to help the state improve its reading and writing tests. Her comments here are not official viewpoints but her own personal opinions. They are quoted at length partly because they are widely shared by a number of former employees who were in senior positions at either the Renaissance Institute or the mother Renaissance company. Most of those former employees are reluctant to be identified, however, because they are fearful of the aggressive stance the Pauls have always taken with their critics.

Despite former employees' fears, an open discussion of the company's operations can still be had, through the views of independent contractors who have occasionally helped the Pauls do their work over the years. Many of these contractors are credentialed professionals, armed with Ph.D.s in rarefied sciences such as psychometrics, which is the statistical art of designing valid psychological measurements. These people are not so reluctant to discuss their experiences.

One such expert is Michael Beck, a well-regarded psychometrician and the founding president of Beck Evaluation and Testing Associates, catchily known, for high-tech enthusiasts, as BETA. Terry Paul hired Beck to develop a program the company called its Standardized Test for the Assessment of Reading, commonly referred to by its own evocative acronym, STAR. This program (which sells, in a basic package for 200 students, for $1,499) was to become the company's bedrock diagnostic test. In quizzing students on a specific piece of text, it is supposed to let teachers set students' reading levels and identify those students who need additional help. In that respect, it is the one Renaissance product that, ideally, would prompt teachers to provide what reading expert Tim Shanahan was crying for: individual assistance in specific areas of weakness, such as sound recognition, vocabulary, or comprehension.

Beck began the work as any researcher would—gathering lots of data, and establishing "norms" (these are basically midpoints on a national bell curve, drawn from average classroom situations, which become guideposts of where the average student should score). When it came time to convert all this information into a final product, Beck ran into unusual obstacles. Paul, he said, "became a little more inventive than was called for." A typical conversation, Beck remembers, would run as follows: "He'd say, 'How do you like this?' And I'd say, 'Well, it doesn't have anything to do with what we did.' Then Terry would say, 'We're going to put it in there anyway.' " Part of the reason for Terry Paul's frustration may be that he thought statisticians didn't crunch information properly. Beck recalls Paul frequently telling him that he had found "a better fit for the data." Part of the reason also may have been bias. "Terry would go looking for data to support his ideas," Beck remembers. Plenty of people do that, he acknowledges. But, he noted, "we don't then call it research. We call it a belief system."

Paul's evaluation of Beck's criticisms is much the same as his assessment of Shanahan—that neither of these people understands his company's products. He credits Beck for having the courage to create a test that had little precedent. But Beck's methods, he said, weren't "based in scientific item response theory. He didn't understand item response theory." Beck, who has spent thirty years working with procedures that use item response theory, is baffled by Paul's conclusions. "I don't recall ever having a discussion with Terry or any of his staff concerning the advisability of using these procedures," Beck told me.

Thinking back on her own tenure, Cathy Upham said she came to see the School Renaissance Institute as something other than what it appears. "It's a pseudo-independent research firm that really functions as a marketing tool," Upham said. "And people are being snowed to think it is a real research institute.* The stuff he does with statistics is just nonsense. He plays with it. And that's appalling. There's this thin veil of research over what's purely a marketing product." What worries Upham most is that "the educational community is not savvy enough to scrutinize this stuff." It's a concern shared by many former employees. "The education community expects people to be just like they are, that they're there because they want to help kids," one former Institute senior employee told me. "If someone comes in with a motive to make money, you've got the most gullible population in the world just eating out of your hands."

"IS THIS BOOK WORTH MUCH?"

One evening, long after Tim Shanahan had wrapped up his work on the National Reading Panel, he visited with the parents of children who attend a Chicago-area elementary school that's in a district for which he's done some consulting. When it was time to take questions, the first ones were about Accelerated Reader, although Shanahan hadn't even mentioned the program. It turned out that the school (Kimball Hill) had begun using Accelerated Reader and parents were concerned that their children would only read books that were part of the AR program. The reasoning behind the students' choice was obvious: If they read other books, they wouldn't get any AR points, and that meant no kudos and no prizes.

These troubles extend far beyond Chicago. All across the country, librarians have complained in Internet discussion forums that while AR has increased their circulation numbers, the quality of students' reading hasn't always followed. Important, well-reviewed books, both classics and new releases that librarians have gone to considerable trouble and expense to acquire, tend to be ignored once library shelves are full of books leading to points and prizes. The narrowness of the students' focus is exacerbated by the fact that teachers often use AR points for class grades. Several librarians noticed that students had trouble managing anything other than the most basic comments about books they'd read through AR. One librarian in an Iowa elementary school told me that if she asks any complicated questions about the books, the students draw a blank and will often admit that they

---

*By late 2002, Terry Paul also started rethinking the Renaissance Institute, at least in part. "People were getting confused about it," he told me. So Paul stopped maintaining the operation as a separate subsidiary and folded it into the umbrella firm, where it became simply another company division. But it retained its emphasis on educational research.

skimmed the material just enough to take the quiz. In at least one school, teachers have prohibited classroom discussion of AR books. AR test questions tend to be so simple that teachers have been afraid that, after hearing a little conversation, many students would pass an AR test on the book without having read it. Even librarians who are generally supportive of the program are concerned. "With dwindling funds, I'm finding it more difficult to provide a balanced collection," wrote Mary Givins, a teacher and librarian at Roberts Elementary School, in Tucson, Arizona. "Easy fiction and [regular] fiction shelves are crammed, and I'm having to replace and repair constantly. I could book-talk until I'm blue in the face and a lot of kids won't touch a book unless they can 'take a test' on it."[17]

Complaints of this sort, along with persistent questions about cheating, even came up at Renaissance's gathering of the faithful in Las Vegas. Amid the applause and celebrations, more than a few teachers dared to voice concerns. The most fervent protestations came from high school teachers, who were frustrated by the program's simplistic design. Some found themselves with a rare opportunity to do their own informal, controlled studies. When students arrived as freshmen, some had come from lower grades that used AR and some from grades that didn't. The differences between the two were often telling. In one session, someone asked how much "carryover" there was—in other words, did the gusto for reading last once points and prizes were no longer in the picture? "I see a big drop, to be honest," said one high school teacher, prompting a round of nods. A cursory independent study published several years later confirmed the teachers' hunches. (The researchers came to this conclusion by surveying 1,771 seventh graders from ten schools, where some had used AR in fifth grade and some had not. When they were asked to identify books they'd read, the students from non-AR schools actually identified more books than the AR students did.)[18]

In Las Vegas, the grumbling sometimes became prevalent enough that a few teachers started challenging the very basis of the Renaissance program. "Is the Renaissance Learning company aware of how weak the STAR test is and how elementary the training seems to be for high schools?" asked Sam Hack, a high school teacher from Missouri. "And are they doing anything about that?" The reply from the Renaissance presenter—a teacher herself— was rather curious. She said she wasn't using STAR much for skill diagnosis and instead relied on the basic AR program for that information. Some talked about how unrealistic the complete Renaissance program seemed to be for any school that does not want to alter its entire routine. Later, in a private conversation, several teachers said they were uncomfortable committing to something promoted solely by a commercial interest. "I'd be a lot happier if it was endorsed by the state, or some education organization I trusted," said Annette Halpern, a high school teacher from Santa Paula, California. "Everything here feels like it's about selling."

To reading professionals, complaints like these are serious enough that a few have begun to take some action. In Texas, one of the company's biggest markets, Jo Worthy, an associate professor of education at the University of Texas at Austin, became so concerned about Accelerated Reader that she embarked on an intensive study of the program. Along with three of her doctoral students, she spent several years looking at how seven different fourth-grade classes were using AR at two elementary schools. They worked from the ground up, starting with the students, and what they found wasn't encouraging.

Some students said their teachers wouldn't allow them to pick books outside their AR "reading levels." Some had become turned off to reading because they didn't like Renaissance's book selection, which is thin on nonfiction. Some were motivated for a while but stopped reading once they'd gone through the AR books that were available for their level. Ultimately, the researchers found, these constraints discouraged students from exploring challenging subjects that can often be appealing.[19] For many students, particularly boys, these tend to be works of nonfiction—books about satellites or snakes, for example, or elementary histories of Africa or of America's early days. Nonfiction titles of this sort aren't organized for the consumer market the way children's fiction is. While librarians may have the time and knowledge to overcome such obstacles, it's quite another matter for a commercial firm to pull that off.

Over the years, Renaissance Learning has tried, with some success, to broaden its selections. Yet snafus have remained. For example, when challenging nonfiction books have been included on AR lists, they've sometimes offered fewer points than easier works of fiction do. This fact is not lost on students. "It breaks my heart," wrote Julie Criser, a media specialist at Blair Elementary School in Wilmington, North Carolina, "when I hear a child ask 'Is this book worth much?' "[20]

As it turns out, there's a second element that determines the worth of AR books and simultaneously limits students' reading choices. This involves the odd scheme used by Renaissance Learning—and other mass-market reading programs—to determine a book's difficulty level.

For purposes of uniformity, almost everyone involved with reading in schools—publishers, state text-adoption committees, librarians, and teachers—chooses books according to standardized measures called "readability formulas." While these formulas come in roughly half a dozen varieties (depending on the company setting the formulas), all rate the difficulty of a text by looking for the same basic factors: sentence and word length, vocabulary choice, and a few other signs of complexity. Even in the best of circumstances, these automated ratings offer a skewed picture. A simple fiction story that's full of long sentences or a few long or obscure words, for example, is likely to be rated as more difficult than it is; conversely, a science or history book that's full of complex ideas but written very simply may get an undeservedly low rating.

Knowing this, Renaissance Learning, like many companies, has occasionally tried to add nuance to these formulas. But once again, Renaissance has introduced extra artistry to the process. An indication occurred in the late 1990s, when Terry Paul went searching for a new, improved formula, which would be linked to Renaissance's STAR test. Over the following years, Paul bounced from one testing and evaluation house to another, apparently convinced that he knew a better way to do their business. He finally ended up contracting with Touchstone Applied Science Associates (TASA), a Brewster, New York, testing outfit. The contract called for an ambitious new hybrid—a formula that would be both sophisticated and easy to use. To accomplish this, the TASA staff hoped there would be some equally ambitious new research.

Within a week of starting work on Paul's new formula, Stephen Ivens, then a TASA vice-president, walked off the project. "I knew no one was serious about doing the work," Ivens recalled. As a former director of research and development at the College Board, with a specialty in reading assessment, Ivens had some detailed opinions about how that work should be conducted. "When someone says, 'We'll have the results in three months to announce at IRA' [an International Reading Association conference], you know no serious research can be done." Sure enough, there wasn't much new research. Renaissance did embark on a massive cataloging effort, Paul says, going through 30,000 books to establish a database of some 30 million words. The company then matched this information against Renaissance performance data. In Ivens's view, this was simply recycling the company's old numbers. "They didn't collect any new data. No one was interested, for example, in the difference between how expository and fictional texts were written." In the end, Ivens said, TASA and Renaissance Learning came up with something that's "more of a vocabulary test than a reading test. And it's awfully short. It's just marketing jive. It sounded good, but it didn't do anything."

THE TECHNOLOGIES OF TESTING

As the new federal emphasis on school accountability has taken root, an increasing number of educational software companies have begun to make claims very similar to Terry Paul's. The numbers behind those claims, based as they are on standardized test scores, would seem to be real facts. So what's not to love?

As it turns out, truth is just as elusive in the test-score world as it is in readability evaluations. And it is far more consequential. With the Bush administration's new policies, it appears as though we're finally getting down to academic business. In some ways, we are. After reams of literature over the decades demonstrating that elementary and high school academics have to some extent become a loose and fad-ridden enterprise, a little rigor and some tangible measure of progress is certainly in order.[21] To its credit, the testing industry has tried to deliver just that, making every effort to improve the sophistication and nuance in these crude rituals of scholastic life. Overall, however, their success has been remarkably spotty. And it does not seem to be getting helped much by technology.

In the opening years of the twenty-first century, standardized tests began to define academic life so thoroughly that, before long, they became the dominant reality in almost every classroom, its implacable boss.[22] Test scores draw their power, first, from the realm of politics, which worships numbers and harvests them any way it can. This in turn hands power to a highly mechanized, private test-manufacturing industry, where errors and scholastic limitations are not only rampant, but have also been kept largely hidden from public view.

One of the more detailed accounts of this phenomenon was provided in the spring of 2001, when *The New York Times* published a lengthy two-part series on the companies that create and evaluate standardized tests. Horror stories abounded from employees, paid nine dollars an hour, who were asked to score tests, often in a rush, on subjects they knew nothing about. "We are actually told to stop getting too involved or thinking too long about the score—to just score it on our first impressions," said Arthur Golczewski, a former scorer at NCS Pearson, the nation's leading scoring company, which handled 300 million standardized tests in 2000. As might be expected, employees occasionally discover that they have scored a particular item wrong, creating hundreds of errors. "There was never the suggestion that we go back and change the ones already scored," said Renee Brochu, another scorer. Apparently, evaluators are also sometimes told to manipulate the scores. "One day you see an essay that is a three," Golczewski said, "and the next day those are to be twos because they say we need more twos."

Company executives have disputed these stories. Yet when the executives found errors, in numbers substantial enough to alter a school district's performance, their correction measures were rather curious. In Tennessee, CTB/McGraw-Hill randomly changed the test scores to fit a state official's estimate of where the numbers should land. In New York City, CTB sat on scoring errors for months, by which time nearly 9,000 students had spent the summer in remedial classes when they should have been on vacation.[23] These errors should not have surprised anyone, especially in New York. Years earlier, in 1980, a shrewd New York student discovered that the preferred answer on a PSAT question was in fact incorrect, which produced front-page headlines: YOUTH OUTWITS MERIT EXAM, RAISING 240,000 SCORES. As people began to re-examine the exams, errors were soon found on the PSAT, the SAT, the LSAT, and some Graduate Record Examinations.[24] Now, two decades later, the testing world's potential for profound error is being heated up further by a rash of computerized evaluation products.

———

In the spring of 1994, the *Harvard Educational Review* published a series of articles about academic testing, one of which was on its long and problematic history. The article was written by George Madaus, a professor of education and public policy at Boston College and the former director of its Center for the Study of Testing, Evaluation, and Educational Policy. Madaus looked specifically at testing as a technology, and its effects on equity in education.[25] Much of his article reads as though it had been written today, because the issues in testing have changed so little over the intervening years.

To Madaus, the system of testing has long functioned as a technology, even before the age of the computer. This is not just because of the gear that schools need to administer tests—the paper and pencils, the various sorts of scoring and rating systems. It's also because, in his view, technology and testing affect people in similar ways. In both areas, Madaus finds, people tend to be seduced to follow novelties and to forget old, worthwhile values. Furthermore, both technology and testing insidiously mask complications, and make them feel irrelevant. "Technology leads a double life," Madaus wrote. "One life conforms to the intentions of policymakers; the second contradicts them, proceeding behind their backs to produce unanticipated uses and consequences. . . . Although the benefits of technology are enormous, technology simultaneously creates problems, opens new ways to make big mistakes, alters institutions in unanticipated negative ways, and impacts negatively on certain populations." The same patterns occur, Madaus believes, in the world of testing.

The system of intellectual testing on a large scale began with Alfred Binet's invention, in 1905, of what evolved into the IQ test. Interestingly, Binet had a very different purpose in mind than the mass evaluation system that the test became. His fellow Parisians were simply looking for a quick way to identify students unlikely to succeed in "normal" classes and who therefore needed special instruction. Yet the appeal of a dominant, objective measure was too strong to resist. In the years since then, Madaus wrote, Binet's technology has been used to "misclassify and label people through most of this century." Those classification biases, Madaus argued, have particularly hurt minorities and the poor.

Modern testing technology, in Madaus's view, has only hidden the problem. "Inequity associated with a technology may be difficult to detect," Madaus wrote, "since most technologies are based on highly technical, arcane underpinnings." As a result, "most Americans usually do not inquire whether the design of a test or any other technology might produce a set of consequences or inequities along with its professed advantages." The reason, he said, is that "all those who benefited from testing, such as test makers, policymakers, and a host of different test users," have become testing's "maintenance constituency." And that constituency has "covered up, evaded or ignored their dependence on this technology, as well as the fallibility, vulnerabilities, and failures of testing."

In the early days of the twenty-first century, the vulnerabilities and failures that Madaus described seven years earlier were more alive than ever.

At almost every public school today, teachers routinely schedule regular prep sessions for students' standardized tests. Actually, it's more common to hear about these practice sessions but not see them. When testing time approaches, public schools generally go into emergency mode: no field trips, no art, music, or drama, no special programs, and no visitors. Even the usual curriculum is tabled—for weeks at a time—while students do virtually nothing but prepare for their tests. They are drilled in multiple-choice problems in reading, math, and social studies. They go over banks of historical facts. And no wonder. These exams are what educators call *high-stakes tests*—the term for a test that is the overriding criterion for a student's advancement, and for a school's ability to stay in business. Nothing else counts.

It wasn't always this way. In the past, if a girl tested poorly but racked up good grades, had been a consistent participant in class discussion, or was considered by her teacher to be capable and motivated, she could still advance from one grade to the next, and even graduate. Today, those other factors are often of little consequence. They're seen as signs of softness, and are bundled up with the new public distaste for "social promotion," the old practice of sending children on to the next grade regardless of their performance. (Interestingly, despite the odor of low expectations in social promotion, the custom may not be as irresponsible as it seems. A good many credible studies, including recent surveys of high school dropouts, have found that holding students back a grade or two can be more damaging than sending them on before they've learned their lessons. It all depends, of course, on how the low-performing students are treated; the promotion, or lack thereof, is secondary.)[26]

At a certain point, as many readers of the news have noticed, a number of schools imitated former first lady Nancy Reagan. They just said no. By the spring of 2001, from the working-class town of Harwich, Massachusetts, to the upper-class, test-savvy communities of Marin County, California, and Scarsdale, New York, both students and teachers had begun boycotting high-stakes standardized tests. In Fairport, a middle-class suburb of Rochester, New York, after parents boycotted the high-stakes state Regents exam, the school superintendent made plans to issue an alternative local diploma. In doing so, the superintendent enlisted the help of both university leaders and local businesses, in the belief that they could come up with better standards than the state's. (The head of the local employers' group was especially concerned that with so much time spent on testing drills, students were doing fewer projects and apprenticeships which, he said, "inspire the better thinking, reading and math abilities that businesses need.")[27]

But the winds of the moment are always strong. For the most part, the testing protests have been framed as permissive quibbling from softheaded liberals, whose children can't hack cold competition. (As an indication of the power of this view, in mid-2003, two years after launching Fairport's effort to create an alternative high school diploma, the district's superintendent was still trying to get it accepted.) Among the handful of different state exams that have consistently won this struggle to define achievement, one of the most prominent is the Texas Assessment of Academic Skills (TAAS)—the central plot device in Don Peek's story about his old middle school in Pittsburg, Texas.

The real story behind Peek's tale—and the truth about Texas tests—is instructive on a number of fronts, which roll out in an intriguing sequence. Obviously, Bush has drawn much of his national vision for schools from his experience in his home state; coincidentally, Texas has long been Renaissance Learning's primary market. Most of the reports about the power of

Renaissance products therefore come from that state, and from Texas achievement data. This also makes Texas one of the early leaders in taking a vigorous approach to both challenges—standardized testing and computerized methods of preparing for tests. The nexus of those pursuits is therefore likely to influence public assumptions about computerized educational products everywhere. If the data here has problems, so does Terry Paul. And so do schools across the country, as Bush's vision becomes an American reality.

——

In the middle of Don Peek's story, there is a revealing moment when he explains the history behind TAAS. He slides by it pretty fast, but he drops just enough detail to start a skeptic wondering. Before the days of TAAS, Peek noted, Texas students had to take other standardized exams—more basic ones, which were designed to evaluate minimum competency in the three R's. Each test reigned for about five years, before being replaced by a new, improved version. In each case, Peek recalled, the students and teachers had trouble in the beginning, but within a few years they'd figured out how to get their scores up. Then, in 1990, along came TAAS—a real challenge, Peek told his crowd, "an upper-level thinking test." The next thing the audience knew, Peek was telling gripping anecdotes, showing how seriously his teachers took the school's failure on TAAS the first year and what they did to improve matters the next year. Unnoticed, of course, was the repeat of their old pattern: The school was simply figuring out how to get its scores to rise on the new test. Indeed, during those years, a number of Texas school districts that had never heard of Accelerated Reader posted similar gains.

That statewide climb was soon contributing to the glow around the presidential campaign of then-governor George W. Bush. Like others who had sought the White House from a governor's seat, Bush managed to plant a fertile seed during his campaign regarding his role in a state "miracle." The concept had a nice circularity to it. In 1988, Michael Dukakis, then the governor of Massachusetts, threatened Bush's father's run for the White House with a "Massachusetts miracle." Dukakis's miracle was a state economic revival in the midst of national hard times; the Texas governor's would be a state education revival in the midst of national dismay about school quality.[28] As evidence, Bush invoked TAAS scores as proof that achievement was rising, and state dropout records to prove that more students were staying in school.

The media quickly took the bait. "Accountability Narrows Racial Gap in Texas," crooned *USA Today,* in an editorial in March 2000, which then went on to describe "Texas-size school success."[29] Even *The Boston Globe,* presumably chastened by Dukakis's doubtful miracle, picked up on Bush's theme. EMBARRASSED INTO SUCCESS announced a front-page headline in June 1999: "Texas school experience may hold lessons for Massachusetts."[30] The academic world was somewhat more skeptical, though. Before long, a chorus of critics rose to debunk Bush's miracle.

In assembling their attacks, the critics were aided by a multitude of research supposedly proving the Texas story to be more myth than miracle. A good portion of this information was generated in the course of a lawsuit against the state, brought in 1999 by a veterans' group, which claimed that TAAS discriminated against Hispanic and African American students. "An education system in which 30 percent of students overall (and 40 percent of minorities) do not even graduate from high school is one to be deplored rather than applauded," wrote Walt Haney, a professor of education at Boston College. Haney, one of the expert witnesses hired to fight Texas's claims, put together two lengthy studies that by his measure showed that academic achievement in Texas had declined grievously through the 1990s.[31] His studies were full of dramatic numbers—comparing ostensibly bogus TAAS scores with negative results from other state assessments, the SAT, the highly regarded National Assessment of Educational Progress (NAEP), dropout figures that were some of the country's worst, and survey data that quoted dozens of disgruntled teachers.

Haney's studies read like a slam dunk for the plaintiffs; yet the judge ruled in favor of the state. As it turned out, some of the bad news Haney found in Texas was no different elsewhere in the country—and not especially attributable to TAAS; other negative trends were true but offered a partial picture, were slightly exaggerated, or were caused by changing procedures that were fixed at the time of the trial. Some remain subject to differing opinions about which tests really count, since Texas high school students get up to eight tries at passing TAAS for graduation. Nonetheless, while ruling in favor of Texas, the judge acknowledged that its testing system was not nearly as effective as state officials would have everyone believe.[32]

———

One benefit of this filtering process is a relatively clean pool of information on what can and cannot be claimed about the power of standardized tests like TAAS. It also clarifies claims about any exercises connected to standardized tests, including computerized products like Accelerated Reader. So what can be known about the rise in Texas test scores? And what can be said about the value of those gains?

In winning its lawsuit, Texas emerged with several pieces of impregnable evidence that Texas students—particularly its minorities—have been more than holding their own against students in other states.[33] And TAAS seems to deserve some credit for these gains. In combination with the state's school-accountability system, the test specifically targeted low-income and minority groups, set the passing bar within their grasp, and then moved it up slowly, "like a magnet," said a report by the Education Trust, pulling them into steadily higher levels of performance. This was the system's "genius," said Uri Treisman, director of the Dana Center at the University of Texas at Austin.[34] Somewhat similar trends occurred in other regions of the country as one state after another fixated on measurable academic standards and struggled to raise them.

But when it comes to news on other fronts, standardized tests have had quite another story to tell. TAAS is a particularly graphic example. Pressures to excel on this exam have been so intense that they've given new meaning to the phrase "teaching to the test." That pressure has now created a whole new industry. In Texas, there are "TAAS camps," instructional videos for teachers, cram booklets, and tutorial software such as "Heart-Beeps for TAAS," which, by mid-2000, an estimated 1,000 schools had purchased for $4,200 a copy.[35] In many schools, classwork was largely given over to test preparation from New Year's through April.

Texas officials happily defend how seriously their schools take preparation for TAAS. That, after all, is the point of the test, and of the whole accountability system. William Mehrens, an education professor at Michigan State University and one of the testing industry's most regarded experts, puts it this way: As long as a state's curriculum and its test are closely matched, and both are sound, as he believes the Texas system is, then even if schools "teach to the test," students should come away with some real knowledge. Mehrens would be expected to defend TAAS, since he is generally a proponent of modern testing systems and served as an expert witness for Texas in the TAAS case. In fairness, a few diligent school districts have stayed true to Mehrens's vision. An example is Mount Vernon, a heavily black suburb of New York City.

In 1999, the state of New York started using a new, "English language arts" exam, which asked fourth graders to, among other things, chart the chronology of a story, understand the imagery of a poem, and write an essay using both the poem and the story. Another section of the test asked students to take notes while they listened to a story and to then write a second essay that would prove they had understood the narrative. When roughly two thirds of Mount Vernon's fourth graders failed this test (and a similar portion of eighth graders failed their version as well), Ronald Ross, the district's forceful new superintendent, got tough. After winning a 10 percent increase in the school budget, he hired a reading specialist and forced principals to get directly involved in the classroom. Teachers, meanwhile, were told to teach explicitly to the new test. So what did their students do? They started reading for thirty minutes each night, getting writing assignments in every subject, being drilled in the difference between an essay that would indicate "mastery" on the new test as opposed to one that would be considered merely "proficient." They learned a graphic method of taking notes and they took lots of sample tests. In other words, Ross did a little more than just teach to the test. As he put it, "We said, 'What are the broad areas that this test looks at?'" Just judging from the numbers, Ross's approach worked: The next year, half of Mount Vernon's fourth graders passed the English exam, and the following year three fourths did—a performance that trumped many wealthier districts in the state. One school's pass rate jumped from 13 up to 82. Perhaps equally important, Mount Vernon's students (and teachers) seemed to be enjoying the work. [36]

The problem, however, is that Mount Vernon's experience is an exception, for reasons that aren't likely to go away anytime soon. The problem begins with the fact that the United States has never had national academic standards, and despite appearances, Bush's No Child Left Behind law did nothing to change that. (While each state does have to show "adequate yearly progress" toward improved academic achievement, especially among the disadvantaged, each state was given the right to set its own standards for improvement, and to meet them in its own way.) This, naturally, allowed quite a variety of academic environments across the fifty states. When each state then goes shopping for tests that hew to its individual standards, the nation's handful of testing companies suddenly have to deliver up to fifty different products, which requires spending more time and money than the system can afford. "The states are making matters worse," says Robert L. Linn, a professor of education at the University of Colorado, Boulder, and a nationally known testing expert. "They want to test later and later. They want the results sooner. And they all want the tests customized to their particular needs." As proof of how unrealistic these expectations are, Linn points out that results on NAEP, the respected national exam, are delivered more than a year later than any state test; NAEP also costs more than ten times as much to administer. "The testing industry is stretched way too thin," Linn says. And Bush's policies, he believes, "will stretch it even thinner."

The net result, unfortunately, is quite a mess. As recently as 2002, while the curricula in various states were increasingly asking students to master broad areas of knowledge and sophisticated analytical skills, state tests were largely stuck quizzing students on their capacity for rote memorization.[37] What everyone continually fails to realize, says Theodore Sizer, a leader in high school reform and the founder of the Coalition of Essential Schools, is that "tests tend to test how one individual performs on that kind of test. It's like taking a temperature in a hospital. It's one important index, but it's only one. We're judging kids on the basis of their temperatures."

By all indications, there are plenty of ways to jigger the thermometer readings. One is an old classroom trick: cheat. In Texas, three Houston teachers and an administrator were forced to resign after they secretly corrected test answers; in 1999, Austin's school district was actually indicted for tampering with test documents.[38] Statewide, school officials added another dodge. Like many states, Texas has habitually slotted low-scoring students into special education and other programs, where they're either exempt from the tests or are excused from having their scores included in accountability measures. That, of course, boosts indications of achievement by everyone else. While Texas has begun cracking down on this sleight of hand, in 2000, the state was still excluding many minorities from TAAS exams. Fourteen percent of low-income minority students were being kept out of TAAS results as compared to 6.6 percent of whites.[39]

Inside Texas classrooms, teachers came up with other innovations. In a study for the Harvard Civil Rights project, two university professors from Texas found that while minorities were being treated to test-preparation drills, white, middle-class students were getting involved in activities such as creative writing projects, science labs, and problem-solving approaches to mathematics.[40] One particularly gross example was a largely Hispanic high school in Houston. Despite having virtually no library budget, the school spent $18,000—almost its entire instructional budget—for commercial test-preparation materials that replaced teachers' lessons. Across the state, the researchers discovered, students were learning how to look for words linked to the right answer instead of laboriously reading and thinking about a text. "In many classrooms," Margaret Immel, a Rice University reading expert, told The Washington Post, "the joy and magic of reading is being replaced by drudgery."[41] Scores may well rise, the Texas professors noted, but "high school teachers report that many of their students are unable to use those same skills for actual reading. They are not able to make meaning of literature, nor to connect reading assignments to other parts of the course such as discussion or writing." By some indications, student preparation for college isn't showing much improvement, either. A group of Houston high school seniors who passed TAAS were soon shocked when they did poorly on their college boards.[42] At the University of Texas at Austin, admissions officers say that despite rises in TAAS scores, they've seen no improvement in the skills of their applicants.[43]

It may not be surprising, then, that despite Texas's obsession with measurable achievement, some out-of-state measures of its progress aren't quite so glowing. On NAEP scores, for example, the state has never moved beyond average showings in reading. This raises questions not just about the quality of TAAS but also, by extension, about programs the state uses to teach reading, such as Accelerated Reader. Don Peek may base much of his Pittsburg story on the notion that TAAS is an "upper-level thinking test." Yet the Education Trust, which compiled its report for the Business Roundtable (a leading business lobby that was presumably looking for good news in Bush's home state), came to the opposite conclusion. "No one, including Texas education officials," the Trust reported, "would argue that the current TAAS tests do a very good job of assessing sophisticated kinds of knowledge and skills." The exams, it said, "are weighted toward less-challenging subject matter and have fairly low-level achievement benchmarks."

As proof, the Trust cited a survey by *Education Week* which found that Texas relies unusually heavily on multiple-choice questions, making it one of twelve states that include no essay or even short-answer questions on subjects other than reading and writing. In 1999, the Trust found that the tenth-grade exam (the passing of which is a prerequisite for graduation) included "far fewer items from higher-level math topics than did tests in Kentucky, Massachusetts and New York." Testing standards are so low that in early 2001, when Texas announced that the test would be revised in 2003, it issued a warning: If schools don't act soon to improve instruction, the state said, three out of five students will fail it.[44] And the testing game was reset once again.

TESTING THE NUMBERS

At this point the questions become obvious. Here we have a standardized test in one state with several unique strengths and some significant weaknesses, particularly in reading. We also have students in some schools beginning to perform well on that test after extensively using reading products made by Renaissance Learning, Inc. What are the connections? And what broader story do they tell about testing and classroom technology, and about our resulting concepts of learning?

Part of the story is told by the history of STAR, Renaissance's computerized "diagnostic" program. The background on this little program matters because STAR is structured to be "computer adaptive"—one of the bold new forefronts in testing technology. In this form of examination (which has been used for years in Graduate Record Examinations but has yet to filter down to the younger grades), as students answer each question, the computer automatically adjusts the difficulty of the next question that comes up. (Questions get harder when students answer correctly and easier when they answer wrong.) This innovation's great appeal is that it generates assessments in a fraction of the time of a traditional exam. STAR, for instance, consists of no more than several dozen brief questions and can be finished in under ten minutes.

On the positive scale, this turns a computer-adaptive test into a kind of scholastic smart bomb: By continually pushing at students' limits, it gradually zeroes in on the edge of their abilities, exposing strengths and weaknesses in greater detail than the typical test. Students at the low end, for instance, suddenly "have a chance to show you what they do know instead of just what they don't know," says Robert Linn, the testing expert from the University of Colorado. The reverse then happens for top students, who are used to acing tests aimed at the whole class and now have to face rounds of questions they can't answer. Unfortunately, this also means that students in the great, gray middle are protected from these intellectual bombardments. Since their tests will bounce up and down around the middle of the scale, assessment of average students with computer-adaptive tests has been much less exact. For all their failings, standardized exams avoid these peculiarities—first, by offering everyone more questions and, second, by making the questions the same for everyone. All of which leaves testing experts feeling simultaneously intrigued by computer-adaptive testing's untapped potential and nervous about its hidden side effects.

Some of those side effects can be glimpsed in the rest of the STAR story. Before contracting with Michael Beck to make STAR, Terry Paul approached TASA, the testing and evaluation firm that has contracted for the New York State Board of Regents exams. Stephen Ivens, the former TASA vice-president, remembers the negotiations breaking down "because we wouldn't make it short enough for [Paul]." STAR's brevity soon turned the program into a kind of McTest. To satisfy the program's promise that it will assess individual skills, Renaissance gave STAR the capacity to generate nine specific "diagnostic" reports. These comment on everything from whether a beginning reader has mastered sound and word recognition to whether an advanced reader can use indexes and glossaries, preview chapters before reading, or take notes while studying. But the assessment is something of a fiction. All it knows is whether the students did well or poorly on the STAR test. Based on that, it guesses at where the problems may lie, and guides teachers with canned bits of evaluation from the computer's database. For example, one such report says, "These scores indicate that Kim likely reads many different types of literature for pleasure. . . . He or she is able to read critically and uses reading skills to solve problems in different subjects." There is no evidence, though, that Kim can do anything of the kind. The assessment is then followed by equally general, canned bits of advice. ("Practice evaluating and making judgments about texts"; "acquire a working vocabulary of literary terms"; and so on.)

At its heart, judging from the views of outsiders who have worked on the program, STAR was meant to be only a general indication of how a whole group is doing—and, ideally, a younger group, whose variety of skills is relatively narrow. But as is often the case with testing technologies, many teachers—with Renaissance's encouragement—have begun using STAR as a more definitive measure, and at all grade levels. Some have even used it to place students in special classes—targeting them, sometimes wrongly, for either remedial work or "gifted-and-talented" programs. The test, says Michael Beck, was never designed for such consequential decisions.

That argument—that no single test should determine a student's fate, let alone an entire school's—has long been the testing experts' mantra, even for fervent testing advocates like William Mehrens. Yet year after year, schools across the country, and now national and state policy makers, ignore the experts' advice. Which only multiplies testing's inherent obstacles. The result is that, once testing administrators get a handle on one problem, such as the complications of computer adaptivity, other problems always pop up somewhere else. Suddenly, academic smart-bombing becomes a giant whack-a-mole game. Consider the situation in another corner of the Renaissance program.

When Tim Shanahan, the University of Illinois reading expert, was reviewing the studies on AR, he got a glimpse at some of why Peek's old middle school students, and many others around Texas, had been able to raise their TAAS scores. After noticing how closely Renaissance quizzes mirror standardized tests, it occurred to him, he said, "that students are just getting a lot of testing practice." The deeper problem here is that standardized tests are never as standardized as they seem; they always contain variances—caused by the way questions are asked, by the way teachers taught the material, or by confusion in test directions. When students relentlessly practice testing's routines, they gradually learn how to keep all these variables at bay. As Shanahan put it, "they get all those variance options lined up on one side of the equation. It's sort of a fake way of raising your scores."

If Shanahan's critique is on target, these troubles play out with radiance in Renaissance's other main initiative—a relatively new product called Accelerated Math. While the math program's aim is, like AR's, to stimulate work done away from the computer, it depends far more than AR does on computer technology, and is more complex. Its format is also akin to the way an increasing number of other companies, and school districts, are using computers to prepare students for standardized tests.

In essence, Accelerated Math is a system that automatically generates math quizzes and then tracks students' work on those quizzes. The product is loaded with handy functions, one of which is a scrambling procedure made possible by the program's algorithms. On any given test, each student therefore gets slightly different problems. This lets teachers turn students loose to help and learn from one another—"collaborative learning," in education-speak—without risk that they'll steal their neighbors' answers. As students pick away at their work, they go through very much the same motions that are required on standardized tests. Not only are most problems framed as multiple-choice questions (with the familiar four options), but their answers are also recorded on a narrow, computer-ready card. For each question, students fill in a tiny bubble, just as they do on the SAT and other exams. (Renaissance programmers even buy old standardized tests, which they use as a guide when creating questions.) For schools that prefer to test students with essay questions—the latest trend in testing design—the program offers what are called "extended response" quizzes, where students must show and explain their figuring. The program's complexity does require more gear—a computerized scanner and a top-of-the-line printer, since teachers typically generate hundreds of pages of quizzes each day. When everything's working properly, though, teaching can become very easy.

That ease is the math program's huge selling point, which Ann Lubas, one of Renaissance Learning's lead presenters, made crystal-clear in Las Vegas. In a packed afternoon session on Accelerated Math, Lubas told the crowd that when she first discovered the product as a teacher, she suddenly realized, "I didn't have tests to grade. I didn't have tests to take home and write. I'm *in love* with this program!" Many of her customers are also in love with the way Accelerated Math imitates standardized tests, since most test-preparation programs don't bother to go that far. "Our math scores have really come up," an elementary school teacher from Merced, California, told me. A main reason, she said, is that "the terminology for the [test] is getting reinforced."

The reinforcements don't stop there. Accelerated Math also includes a database of computerized charts that pinpoint, say, which fourth graders are struggling with long division or which high school trigonometry students still don't understand sines and cosines. The charts even include little red prompts to tell the teacher which students have been getting wrong answers for long enough that it's time to intervene.

It's hard to fault a support system that seems so dynamic, so multifaceted, and so individualized. But, here too, the classroom reality does not quite align with the picture painted by test scores.

The first reality check involves the functionality and cost of high-end testing tools like these. In Las Vegas, when I stopped by a Renaissance booth for a demonstration of Accelerated Math, over the course of an hour or so, teachers continually came up to complain about one seemingly intractable problem after another. One teacher couldn't move student records from grade to grade. Another said her school had bought the program when it was first released and that it was always crashing. The program demonstrator explained that she had bought the pilot program—a "quick and dirty" version that was full of bugs, which the company had since abandoned. The teacher didn't find this terribly reassuring. "We paid a lot for it, I think, about $1,500," she said. "I was very frustrated." Other schools have paid more. According to the company's fall 2000 catalog, a basic Starter Kit (a scanner, a year's technical support, and material for one grade) cost $1,899. A Super Kit, which merely adds the program's diagnostic test, sold for $3,299.

What teachers probably don't see is that Accelerated Math's diagnostic program employs the same kind of guesswork that the reading program does—a weakness that plagues a good bit of educational software. For example, when Sarah, a fifth grader, scores in the mid-range, the diagnostic program (STAR Math) reports the following: "These scores indicate that Sarah has a firm grasp of whole number concepts and operations. She has a basic understanding of fractions and decimals, but she needs to keep working on fraction and decimal concepts and operations." Once again, Sarah may not have learned or even practiced any of those functions. It's another canned evaluation—based on a national sample of fifth graders and its assessment of *their* skills.

When asked about this, Terry Paul pointed out that teachers are entirely free to work students through detailed understandings of what each math procedure means. If anything, Paul argues, the product encourages that kind of individual attention. "I don't think kids can get through the objectives if the teacher is not personalizing and having those conversations. A lot of teachers have difficulty transitioning from traditional lecture to individual attention. You've got to have a system that allows that without chaos." As logical as Paul's argument sounds, it leads to the second reality check with Accelerated Math—the quality of schoolwork it inspires. Some former Renaissance staffers recall being astonished at the classroom scenes they witnessed when they visited schools to help teachers work with the program. "I just shuddered," one former employee told me. "Teachers had totally abandoned the text, totally abandoned lectures. It turned a math class into a bunch of monkeys working problems." One teacher apparently concluded that the program did such a terrific job that she gave up lecturing and boxed up her textbooks.

But what's wrong with encouraging students to work problems? If a program's skill assessments have their limitations, wouldn't the specificity and relentless repetition of the assignments make up for it? The distinctions here are perhaps best explained by Judah Schwartz, the former co-director of the Center for Educational Technology at Harvard University and a longtime specialist in the teaching of mathematics.

In Schwartz's view, all classroom instruction methods fall into two main camps: those that strive to teach skills and those that aim for understanding. While the two faculties are obviously related, they are not the same, and they breed very different teaching methods. (As proof, the decades-long war over traditional and progressive education is little more than an endless restaging of this battle, with the traditionalists fighting for skills to take priority and the progressives fighting for comprehension.) This feud has become heatedly delineated in the "math wars" and "reading wars" that have been causing curriculum turmoil in California, Massachusetts, Texas, and several other states. Like many educators who have stayed out of these skirmishes, Schwartz believes that both skills and comprehension are critical and that neither should take precedence over the other. Numerous educational reform initiatives—progressive, traditional, and many in between—have faltered because they ignore this obvious fact and become far too comfortable leaning on only one leg.

This, Schwartz believes, is Renaissance Learning's handicap. "Accelerated Math *may* be a good way to develop skills," he told me. "But I don't think it develops understanding." More to the point, Schwartz says, "you wouldn't know with this program whether understanding was weak or strong." Terry Paul, of course, disagrees, arguing that students' success on

Advanced Placement tests—and later, in college math classes—proves that the program is powerful. "The AP exam is designed by professors of mathematics," Paul told me. "Most people think students who can do that have a pretty good understanding of math. On any practical method of defining understanding, it seems to work."

Things may not be quite that simple. Consider the perspective held by Mike Russell, a senior research associate at Boston College's Center for the Study of Testing, Evaluation, and Educational Policy, who has been surveying the way technology and testing interact in schools across the country. Russell found a number of teachers who are delighted with Accelerated Math and other programs like it. These teachers tend to be pleased that they have more time to work individually with students and that the computer drills can be directly aligned to the states' growing phalanx of academic standards—and thus to state tests. "When a teacher reaches that part of the curriculum standards, they can just go to the software," Russell says. But the students' intellectual experience in these classes has been another matter. Accelerated Math, Russell concluded, "seems to be good for kids that need a lot of math work. If they're good at math, it's not of much use." Accomplished students, he said, are ready to experiment widely, in a fashion that mechanized drills—no matter how much teacher attention goes with them—can't accommodate.

This is why test-prep programs have trouble shedding their curse of narrow-minded monotony. One of the most dramatic illustrations of testing's narrowness occurred in the final days of 2002. This, of course, was a hot moment for high-stakes tests, a time when more than half the states in the country were vigorously using them. Several days after Christmas, a massive study of academic testing, the largest ever thus far, reported the following: Student performance in test-intensive states may well rise on state tests. But when their performance was considered on the big national exams—the Scholastic Aptitude Test, ACT (an SAT competitor), NAEP, and AP exams—most of these states slipped in comparison with the national average. To make matters worse, the study also found rising dropout rates in test-intensive states, coupled with a jump in enrollment in programs offering equivalency diplomas. Apparently, this was not only because students are intimidated by test pressure. The researchers also found signs that administrators, in a panic about raising test scores, occasionally encourage failing students to drop out.[45]

If anything, the canned responses in programs like Accelerated Math aggravate troubles of this sort. This monotony of course can happen with any simplistic teaching methods, both high-tech and low-tech. As an illustration, a former math teacher told me about a game he used to play with high school students. "I would ask them what the sine of an angle is. They could all give me numerical answers, but no one could tell me what it means." He's found the same patterns of ignorance in advanced-math classes. "If you asked college calculus students to explain, in English, what the derivative of an equation is, most couldn't do it. But if you put an equation on the board and asked them the derivative, they'd do fine."

Considering the persistence of such weaknesses, can they be blamed on a computer program? Isn't it up to teachers to use a program any way they want—poorly or intelligently? With computer technology, those choices can be a mirage, another e-lusion. When tools are powerful, as Accelerated Math and many of its computerized cousins are, busy teachers tend to defer to their definitions of what work needs to be done and what work doesn't. The teacher who put away her textbooks is a perfect example. "The tool is exceedingly seductive," Judah Schwartz says. "People begin to forget about the rest of the teaching job, because the tool makes it possible. The machine screams for so much attention that nobody pays attention to anything else."

—

Standardized testing may have its failures, but it remains the boss. Considering the faith that millions of people continue to put into this mechanism's data, it is important to look at what, in the aggregate, computer products of this type have done for test scores. Here again, Renaissance's track record provides a fitting set piece.

With more than half the nation's public schools as customers, Renaissance Learning now has a hefty presence in American education, albeit mostly with reading instruction. Yet national reading skills during the company's period of robust growth seem to have remained stubbornly flat. Judging from NAEP scores, between 1992 and 2000 the scores of top students rose slightly, while those of low-performing students fell more significantly. Interestingly, the gap between top and bottom students widened among all racial and ethnic groups. Specifically, two thirds of the students tested fell below the level that the federal government considers proficient, and 37 percent couldn't meet even the standard of basic knowledge. (This involves the ability to get beyond simple words and phrases and to draw conclusions from what one has read.)[46] Tennessee offers a particularly dramatic snapshot of this contradiction. Renaissance's penetration with Accelerated Reader grew here during the 1990s from 20 percent of the state's schools to nearly 70 percent. During that time, reading scores in the state generally declined.[47]

In the context of such trends, why do teachers keep thinking that products like Accelerated Reader and Accelerated Math will save them? Among other things, technology's evaluation tools seem to continually get better. Once President George W. Bush's education program took hold, that trend began picking up real speed, which could be observed by any administrator who sat in a school district's buyer's chair. One person who found himself in that position is Tim Shanahan.

In late 2001, Shanahan took a leave of absence from the University of Illinois to direct the reading program for the Chicago public schools. In the following months, he was barraged by vendors selling new software products, complete with "diagnostic" programs supposedly capable of compiling profiles of each student's strengths and weaknesses. Like the Renaissance STAR products, this software breaks down test data to show performance in specific areas—reading comprehension, word recognition, fluency, and so forth. Shanahan turned down almost every one of them. "It's just a repackaging of test scores," he says. "They aren't as personalized as they seem." The reason, he found, is that in all of these programs the categorization of skills is so arbitrary, and the number of questions in each category so limited, that the data aren't reliable. The core information here is only designed to tell whether someone got an answer right or wrong, not why. Packaging that information into a "diagnostic" assessment, Shanahan concluded, "can be very inaccurate. You're telling schools to prescribe instruction based on a flip of the coin, essentially." Nonetheless, sales of this genre of software have been plenty robust. "The stuff looks so good," Shanahan says. "It looks like you're getting a lot more information, and with four-color charts. Schools believe if they teach to these patterns, they'll raise achievement on standardized tests. The evidence of that is not really there."

To be fair, the testing industry is fully aware of complications like these. It also knows that no matter what it does to make tests an accurate and sophisticated measure of learning, someone will always find a shortcut. So the industry toils on, tirelessly trying to stay one step ahead of the Terry Pauls of the world. The challenge here is plenty familiar. The promises of strict accountability and testing are old lovers in the education world. They have been featured partners during numerous back-to-basics reforms over the years—first in the 1890s, then in the 1950s, the 1980s, and now again in the early years of the twenty-first century. Interestingly, each of those movements occurred during a particularly conservative phase of America's political history.[48] This is not to slight those periods or their initiatives; the radical 1960s gave birth to their own excesses in experimental education. It should merely be remembered that any severe swing in the nation's political

mood produces fervent education visions. And those visions tend to be passing phases rather than enduring absolutes.

———

More than almost any other social enterprise—more than science, more
than art, more than literature, more even than industry itself—technology
runs on the glow of novelty. The most successful technology developers
know this; when building a new product that they hope will have legs, they
usually couple its novelty with two additional attractions: greater ease and
greater speed. This combination (it's new, it's easy, it's fast) is a powerful
triumvirate; to the modern mind, it equals progress. And that, to George
Madaus, the Boston College testing expert, is precisely the problem, especially when technology mixes with testing.

Like many old-line educators, Madaus gets nervous when something
comes along that proposes to lighten the schools' burdens. Those temptations, he argues, sideline alternative ways of doing things that might have
been more time-consuming but were also more valuable. "A danger of high-
stakes testing programs, as with many technologies," he writes, "is that
they depreciate certain ends by making other ends more attainable and,
hence, more attractive." Everyone, particularly adventurous Westerners,
wants to believe that a better technological solution always lies just over the
next horizon. And this, Madaus fears, "will blind policymakers and the public to the reality that we cannot test, examine or assess our way out of our
educational problems."[49] William F. Goodling, a former Pennsylvania congressman and chair of the House committee on education and the work
force, once put it this way: "If testing is the answer to our educational problems, it would have solved them a long time ago."[50]

The ultimate point here is painfully obvious: Learning can be only partly
measured quantitatively. It's an enterprise, rather, that is deeply psychological, frequently emotional, and thus inescapably subjective. To ignore this
fact, to force millions of teachers and students to turn all we have learned
about the mysteries of the mind and the human soul into a narrow numbers
game, is an insult to science and an abrogation of social progress. This is not
to suggest that there shouldn't be state or even national academic standards. But there must be better ways to hold a school, or a state, to this standard of "accountability." But given monumental obstacles on this front, and
the government's long history of seeking the cheap and easy way out in
America's classrooms, that seems unlikely.

One idea is to follow the testing experts' long ignored advice—that is, to
use a variety of measures, rather than a single, year-end test, to rule on the

future of a student, a school, or an entire district. One of those measures might allow more room for human judgment. This might seem impossibly subjective; it may also cost more money, since it probably requires hiring more smart adults in the schools. But if we are going to evaluate a young person's progress, it only stands to reason that the wisdom and experience of an older person, who knows a youngster outside the test room, should carry some weight.

If we avoid this challenge and continue seeking refuge in quick and easy numbers, the political world's much hoped for higher standards are likely to remain elusive. Bush's No Child Left Behind Act almost guaranteed this fact, as was signaled by its very name. Leaving no one behind means making sure everyone passes the finish line. And everyone can't accomplish that, at least in a timely fashion, unless the finish line is dropped back. In 2002, that is precisely what an assortment of states started doing with their numerical standards as they realized they couldn't meet Bush's requirements.[51] In the education world, this is known as the Lake Wobegon game—named after the mythical town in Garrison Keillor's radio show, where "all the children are above average."

GOING FOR THE GOLD

Within the educational software world, a good deal of excitement about any company's products, from both students and teachers, is always sparked by their seductive extras—"bells and whistles," as educators call them. Some companies, like the makers of HyperStudio or Reader Rabbit, use entertaining treats, such as musical ditties, multimedia cartoons, and other beguiling visuals. (HyperStudio enthusiasts take great delight in their particular multimedia excesses; at company conferences, a favorite line often shouted in unison by loyalists is "Let's Overdo It!") Renaissance Learning avoids this sort of visual chaos, choosing instead to focus on a single but powerful whistle: its system of awarding points and prizes. Whatever the scheme, all these temptations put the educational software industry squarely in the middle of yet another hot academic debate: Does it help or hurt to lure students into doing academic work with rewards?

The use of rewards in school is nothing new. For decades, teachers have been routinely handing out candy and gold stars, commendations and special privileges to students who do exemplary work. A handful of other modern reading programs, both high-tech and low-tech, draw on this tradition as well. Because Renaissance's system of rewards is so overt, it has become something of a lightning rod in this debate, which serves to illuminate the age-old question of how to properly motivate students.

Company trainers are all too familiar with the complaints about Renaissance's points and glittering prizes, and they usually try to deflate them before they even arise. During Don Peek's Pittsburg story, for example, he paused at one point to explain his school's rationale for the rewards. "Our kids were *poor!*" he told his audience. "Those points were the only money they had in their pockets. But ahm 'on tell you, after several years, we didn't really need all of that stuff. It was just a jump start, cuz we had to get 'em excited about it. Then they're going to find those favorite authors, and those favorite genres. And they're going to grow on their own intrinsically."

Peek hit the issue on the nose; he even framed it the way the experts do. The central question here is whether it's possible to boost learning purely through "intrinsic motivation" (that is, by getting students to do something for its own sake, for its own intrinsic pleasures). Or do students need to start with "extrinsic" motivators (pizza parties, hall passes, multimedia cartoons, shoot-'em-up characters—the list can go on and on)? In today's high-stimulus world—crowded as it is with commercial temptations on every corner, every channel, every website—Renaissance Learning knows what has to be done to hold a youngster's attention.

Once again, though, the data don't quite play along. Among the many critics of rewards, the most noted is Alfie Kohn, author of the book *Punished by Rewards: The Trouble with Gold Stars, Incentive Plans, A's, Praise, and Other Bribes*. Kohn expects a lot from us; one could even say that his vision is idealistic. Grades, prizes, praise—to Kohn, they're all modern implements of behaviorism, as defined and popularized in the 1960s by the preeminent lab-rat scientist B. F. Skinner. Kohn's main argument is that rewards of any type train children to behave like pets: They learn to do tricks for treats. (This is true, he argues, in the adult world as well, where incentive plans are the prime culprits.) "Do this and you'll get that," Kohn writes.[52] When a teacher, parent, or boss sets up this dynamic, Kohn believes, an underling's engagement with the activity is immediately bifurcated. Are students reading because they like the story or because they like the pats on the back and the free basketballs? It's hard to tell.

Although Kohn's criticisms may sound extreme, they're based on an impressive amount of examination. Some involves little more than rhetorical logic, but a fair portion derives from scientific studies. This is not the private, selectively presented kind of research that has characterized Renaissance literature; for the most part, Kohn's sources are carefully controlled studies, vetted over the years by a succession of neutral experts. In fact, in a different literature survey, where studies of Accelerated Reader and other reading "incentive" programs were reviewed, the conclusions were the same. As its author, Jeff McQuillan, reported: ". . . there is no clear causal relationship in any of the studies conducted so far between the use of rewards and an improvement in reading attitudes, achievement, or habits." In fact, in some of these studies, students given rewards for their work did worse than an equivalent group of students doing the same activity without rewards.

The most important question is how students do once rewards are out of the picture. "If the jump-start is to work," McQuillan wrote, "we should know if the engine is still running a few miles down the road." Apparently, it wasn't. In general, students lost interest in reading, forgot what they'd read, or drifted to books that were easy. "The internal motivation that is supposed to 'kick in' doesn't," McQuillan concluded. "Instead, the external rewards in effect short-circuit the motor. Rewarding children to read may therefore lead to less reading in the long run, not more."[53]

As might be expected, the issue is not quite this simple. In fairness to Terry Paul, there are a few important distinctions that McQuillan, Kohn, and many others in the anti-reward crowd tend to gloss over. Mike Milone, a private researcher who has consulted for Renaissance Learning (and who trained as a "behaviorist"), asserts that what matters are the specific kinds of rewards people get. To many of us, all of life is driven by rewards, in an endless array of ethical shapes and sizes. They include everything from a mother's love and smiles to short-term treats and privileges to enduring pleasures such as success and the respect of our peers. Renaissance's points and prizes, Milone acknowledges, are "the lowest kind of rewards there is." The teacher's challenge, therefore, is to show students how to climb life's ladder to the morally meaningful.

Unfortunately, the software industry's ladders may be missing a few rungs. In Renaissance's case, the main reason that academic studies show performance falling off once rewards disappear, Milone argues, is that teachers "have failed to help students make the transition to higher level rewards." The research backs Milone up. It also indicates that while this could change, the feat has generally remained beyond the skill of the average teacher.[54] It also seems to remain beyond the skill, or the interest, of the average software producer.

Consider the young life of another company's math software program, one that has stood quite tall in the family of "educational games." The program is a small, $20 adventure package called the Logical Journey of the Zoombinis. Like all good games, this one has proven substantive enough to often hold the interest of young and old alike. (Children have been so captivated by it that they've created their own Zoombini stories; some have even invented a Zoombini language.) Created in the mid-1990s by a Cambridge, Massachusetts, non-profit called TERC, the game bills itself as dedicated to "the art of mathematical play." The central plot revolves around a band of tiny people who have lost their homeland and must overcome a series of death-defying obstacles to find a new home. Since each Zoombini has slightly different physical characteristics, the fun—and the intellectual challenge—is in figuring out what it takes to navigate each adventure (specifically, which combinations of Zoombinis and which sets of choices at each challenge will get everyone through). Infantile as this may sound, the game allows for 625 possible combinations, a tiny sample of which will quickly stump most adults. These combinations, it should be noted, are structured by the rules that govern such high-minded mathematical procedures as database analysis, algebra, base-5 numbers, algorithms, and mathematical objects such as vectors. The solutions also change each time the game is played. The whole experience acquaints youngsters with important principles of logic—how to look for patterns, how to reason and organize evidence, and how to systematically test one's hunches. While the Zoombinis' journey has its share of cartoonlike effects, it quickly becomes clear that the main rewards in this adventure are relatively intrinsic—that is, they lie in the feeling of accomplishment at solving the game's logical puzzles.

As an indication of how education fads can ruin a good thing, when the Zoombini game was updated, the software producers put a little assessment system on the back end. The idea was to help teachers track student performance, in keeping with Bush's emphasis on accountability. This meant that youngsters were told, for instance, that their skills at "mudball wall" were unsatisfactory. "It's ridiculous," says Gary Stager, the adjunct professor of education at Pepperdine University and a partner in techno-rebellion with Seymour Papert, the LOGO guru at MIT. "That's like being graded in chess." Many educators hardly blinked at the Zoombini update, though, because so many educational software products have been adding equivalent functions, to the education world's general delight.

All is not bleak, however. While computers have their limitations, they are supremely capable of tracking aspects of what their users are doing, potentially in some detail. It was only a matter of time, therefore, before an enterprising scientist would discover ways to blend this power with academic work, yielding a truly potent diagnostic program. Apparently, that is exactly what several researchers in cognitive science at Carnegie-Mellon University did. After twelve years of experimental research, much of which included studying patterns of the brain, they developed a program called, aptly enough, Cognitive Tutor. It too focuses on math skills (specifically, algebra and geometry). While students work at the program, the computer creates a "cognitive model" of what they're doing—based on indications such as how long they take to solve certain problems, which questions they get right or wrong, how often they ask for help and on what topics. Like a good live tutor, the product does not simply correct students when it intervenes but asks them questions about their work, and does so with increasing specificity. This enables the program to assign additional problems, targeted with some accuracy to topics that truly need attention.

Despite Cognitive Tutor's power, its creators knew that the work it fostered was still low-level when compared with what a teacher can do—an unusual realization in the courseware world. So they turned the program into an entire math curriculum, restricting the computer work to 40 percent of class time. During the other 60 percent, students interact with the teacher, who guides discussion about the math problems. Those problems are not narrow multiple-choice questions of the sort that speckle Accelerated Math and other, similar programs; instead, students are given just a few relatively complex mathematical dilemmas, posed in text form, which they then work out in pairs or in teams. "The students are doing the mathematics, not the teacher," says Bill Hadley, who spent twenty-eight years as a teacher in Pittsburgh schools before becoming president of Carnegie Learning, the company that makes Cognitive Tutor. Like many courseware makers, Hadley believes he has definitive statistical proof that his program improves achievement. "We are the poster child for data," Hadley told me, sounding very much like Terry Paul. All boasts aside, Carnegie Learning has been more careful with its research than its competitors. Most examinations of Cognitive Tutor's effects are robust controlled studies of truly equivalent groups. And virtually all show gains that are not only dramatic but have held on for years.[55] By all indications, this program, by forcing teachers to use and then build upon pinpoint technology, develops understanding as well as basic skills.

Unfortunately, it is also relatively alone. Like all maturing industries, the courseware business has been going through a shakeout, which has of course been sped by the recent downturn in the economy and in the technology sector specifically. Research-and-development budgets have thus been slashed, which is why superficial add-ons like the Zoombini assessment have been more the norm than the intense diagnostic work of a Cognitive Tutor. Interestingly, in the early years of the new century, the brightest business opportunities in courseware lay in the higher-education market. The reason is that any economic downturn brings a rise in the number of out-of-work people returning to school. Furthermore, demand for back-office administrative services and student record-keeping systems are most intense at the collegiate level. As terrorism worries accumulated, the pressures on the whole college system only grew, following new reporting requirements on international students.*

But the K–12 market was quickly finding its second wind, helped in no small part by President Bush's emphasis on testing. The Princeton Review, Score, the Sylvan Learning Systems, Kaplan—all these old test-prep outfits were creating new computer services, both online and offline, to help students find quick ways to meet the new standards. One general development in the courseware market seems to have been a shift from products that might replace teachers, or some of their functions, to those that simply make their lives easier. "The smart companies realized the teachers would then support them instead of opposing them," says Jeffrey Silber, an education market analyst with the investment firm Gerard Klauer Mattison. Renaissance Learning clearly learned this lesson a long time ago. That insight, however, has also contributed to the company's main business problem. Renaissance has traditionally sold its wares mostly by getting teachers excited, then depending on them to sell their administrative bosses back home. By 2002, with school budgets getting tight, district officials were pulling in on the spending reins. This meant Renaissance now had to build a sales campaign that could reach district administrators. This was no small chal-

---

*A fall 2002 report by Gerard Klauer Mattison (GKM), one of a handful of investment firms that closely track the education market, offered an enlightening snapshot of the way industry looks at computerized learning. The company noted that while education spending, per student, has grown more than 130 percent since 1971, the nation's primary achievement measures during that time—the NAEP scores—"have shown virtually no improvement." Yet GKM was still "bullish." After a financially flat period in 2002 across the field, from kindergarten through adult training courses, companies that do business with schools should, it said, start enjoying an annual growth rate of 6.8 percent. This would raise industry revenues from $102 billion in 2001 to $142 billion in 2006. The firm also expected the economy to rebound as early as 2003, and total education spending to pick up soon thereafter, reaching $1.08 trillion in 2006—double what it was in 1993. Along the way, GKM said, the "greatest industry risk is government regulation." This particularly applied to for-profit education companies, such as the Edison Project, which "may be subject to decision-making that is based more on politics than on business fundamentals." Offsetting that danger, GKM said, are several "regulatory improvements." Chief among those are President Bush's No Child Left Behind law, which created incentives for new assessment mechanisms; and a June 2002 U.S. Supreme Court decision upholding the use of vouchers in Cleveland, Ohio. "As private managers demonstrate superior results," GKM said, "we believe more local and state governments will choose to outsource their schools." See "Back to School 2002," a report by Gerard Klauer Mattison, an investment firm based in New York and Los Angeles, issued September 10, 2002, pp. 2, 4, 21.

lenge, because Renaissance's competitors had already been doing business with these officials for years.

From all accounts, the founders of Renaissance Learning, Inc., have known about the limitations of their materials—or at least their conflicts with prevailing wisdom—for a long time. Over the years, various senior employees say they have repeatedly urged the Pauls to pull back on the claims they make about what their products can do for schools. Some have begged the Pauls to acknowledge what the research really shows: that once other influential factors are properly accounted for, the program (if properly used) does provide some boost—but only a marginal one. The Pauls consistently resisted these pleas. Sometimes they seemed to disagree with them; sometimes they seemed to fear them. In at least one case, they acknowledged that few schools would shell out the sort of cash and time commitment their product requires in return for only a marginal boost.

While internal questions floated around company headquarters, criticism of the program occasionally surfaced on the outside, through the media. Whenever this occurred, the company immediately went on the offensive, launching an aggressive public relations campaign to quell doubts about the program before they had a chance to catch on. Perhaps the most dramatic demonstration of the company's armored strategy occurred, not surprisingly, in its prime stomping grounds—the state of Texas.

In the fall of 1996, the *School Library Journal* published an article entitled "Hold the Applause! Do Accelerated Reader and Electronic Bookshelf Send the Right Message?"[56] The article was written by Betty Carter, an associate professor in the School of Library and Information Studies at Texas Women's University in Denton. Carter, now a full professor, drew her arguments largely from her own study of librarians and several AR-using grade schools. In addition, one of her graduate students had surveyed fifth-grade AR nonfiction books and found that 89 percent had never been reviewed by a reputable publication. And the 11 percent that had were not always reviewed positively. Carter's article did not mince words. It criticized both software programs, which function similarly, for their limited choice of material; for their emphasis on testing (which sends the message, she said, that "there is only one way to read a book"); for their drain on school budgets; and for their systems of points and prizes.

Within weeks of the publication of Carter's article, Renaissance Learning was in full siege. Judi and Terry Paul sent a four-page footnoted response to *School Library Journal* (a shortened version of which the *Journal* published as a letter to the editor), and copied it, with an urgent cover letter, to the company's entire staff. "We need to make our case directly," said company president Mike Baum, "to people who have read Carter and need to know the facts."

Things soon got worse. In April 1997, the Fort Worth *Star-Telegram* published a front-page article on AR, headlined "Reading Rewards: Program's Popularity Overrides Criticism."[57] The story was a relatively balanced account, which quoted Carter leveling a few of her earlier criticisms and further complaining about the prevalence of cheating. Judi Paul got in a few zingers, too. She called Carter "a racist white woman with middle- and upper-class views." Paul's point, an essential Renaissance theory, is that underprivileged children, particularly minorities, don't generally grow up in households where reading and learning is practiced and valued, so they need extra treats to get started. But Carter got the last word. Paul's comment, Carter said, "implies a paternalism that learning to read for poor minority children is something different."*

Scorched-earth assaults naturally leave burning embers. Carter, who was active in the civil rights movement in the 1960s, still smolders about being called a racist. In the end, what seems to anger Carter most is that automated programs like Accelerated Reader dumb down the entire library experience. In her view, they take librarians' hard-earned skills—their knowledge of literature, their knack for matching books to youngsters' developing interests and individual reading abilities—and shove them to the side. She also believes they compromise a library's central principle of freedom.

Carter makes a solid point. Computerized programs of this genre claim to expand a youngster's options, but in reality they do the opposite. In Renaissance Learning's case, when schools invest in the company's reading software, what they're really buying is a succession of contorted constrictions.

---

*After the story's publication, the Pauls went on the offensive yet again. First, Judi Paul wrote a letter to the editor of the *Star-Telegram* and sent a six-page response directly to librarians and other educators throughout Texas. "When I used the word 'racist,' " she told the newspaper, "I did not mean that the critic herself was a racist." Her point, she said, was that these criticisms "have a racist effect." And, she added, "Accelerated Reader does not dispense rewards. Educators do." Later, when Scholastic released a competing product called Reading Counts, Terry Paul distributed an internal memorandum that accused Scholastic of using "marketing spin" and "pseudo-scientific gloss" to sell a product that was "rotten at the core." See Fort Worth *Star-Telegram* letter to the editor, May 9, 1997, by Judith Paul, Chairwoman, Advantage Learning Systems, Inc.; internal communication, from Terry Paul, addressed to "ALS and Institute Employees," dated March 23, 1999.

First come shelves full of books that have been stratified by an inaccurate set of "readability levels." Next come the automated quizzes and the point system, which simplify the subtleties and variety in this material even further. Finally come the students, whose choices and sense of their own capacities have been narrowed yet again by quasi-fictionalized "zones of proximal development." Not only are all these delineations confining; not only are they costly; they're also, to Carter, unnecessary. When students pick a book, she said, "if they can't read it, they just don't."

DREAMS

B uried in the middle of the academic questions about Accelerated Reader and Accelerated Math is a very basic one, given the concerns at issue in this book. Why is a computer needed at all with these programs? At least with reading, it's certainly the consensus among the experts that the heart and soul of literacy happens in the books themselves, in the mental exercises young readers do with a story, and in their interpretative interactions with teachers, parents, and peers. So what does a machine contribute to the endeavor?

"Let's find something to do with technology that really adds something," says Tim Shanahan. "What programs like Accelerated Reader are doing is on the edge of using technology. Teachers have to do a bunch of new things to make Accelerated Reader work. They should be doing stuff to teach reading." It is also worth noting what the National Reading Panel concluded about computerized programs in general, including those that try to put technology to more active use. As a whole, the panel said, the genre seems somewhat promising. Panelists found indications that some high-end software products (such as those featured earlier in the Apple Classrooms of Tomorrow) might help students gain facility with word and sound recognition and overall vocabulary. Computers may also stimulate comprehension, the panel surmised, by offering extra avenues for understanding, such as multimedia displays and hypertext links to the Internet, and by creating a powerful tool to practice writing, which is still considered one of the best ways for a reader to build his or her own lasting sense of meaning. The panel also acknowledged the computer's capacity to boost motivation. Nonetheless, the panelists warned that the studies on computer use in reading weren't extensive or solid enough for any definitive recommendation. Regarding the machine's power as a motivator, the panel's report cautioned that "this effect may diminish as computers become ever more common."

The equivocation in these conclusions, as we have seen, enjoys a long and persistent history.[58] It may be useful, therefore, to conclude with one particularly graphic illustration of the confusing picture that high-tech schools can present.

Of the dozen or so big school-reform models that have come into vogue in recent years, only one has been dedicated to improvement through technology: the Co-nect Schools, whose flagship, the ALL School, was featured in this book's Introduction. Founded in 1992 by the Educational Technologies Group at BBN Corporation, by 2001, Co-nect had enlisted fifty-eight schools in eight states. And, as with most reform models, its literature listed a handful of schools and school districts showing gains made in standardized test scores after signing on to its program. But the Co-nect promoters wanted something a little firmer than test scores, which can of course be increased by many things, both technological and non-technological. So in 1993, it commissioned Michael Russell, of Boston College's Center for the Study of Testing, Evaluation, and Educational Policy. Russell spent five years studying more than twenty-five different Co-nect schools in Florida, Texas, Tennessee, Ohio, and Maryland. He controlled for how many years of technology experience each school had, and even compared Co-nect schools with other schools of similar demographics. "I couldn't find anything," Russell told me. "There was absolutely nothing to say." But what about Co-nect's reports of rising test scores? "Some schools did show some rises, and some were big ones," Russell said. "Others showed nothing, and others were down. When we averaged everything together, it came out to zero." Later, in 2001, a three-year study by the RAND Corporation came to similar conclusions. Almost half of the Co-nect schools it studied had made no gains at all in math when compared with neighboring schools, and more than half had made no progress in reading.[59]

=

During Renaissance Learning's Las Vegas gathering, I spent a little time, as one normally does at conferences, wandering the exhibit hall. It was filled with demonstration stands for various Renaissance products and rows of other booths, where companies that have attached themselves to Renaissance Learning could sell their wares. Housed in a cavernous room, the exhibit sat just across from a temporary "Renaissance store," where the company sold its own products, at a now-only discount rate. As I strolled past tables of T-shirts, buttons, children's books, and various prizes, I stopped occasionally to talk to some teachers. One was Gloria Rankin, an elegantly dressed fifth-grade teacher from Memphis, Tennessee, who had just finished visiting a booth that sold dozens of goodies—basketballs and soccer balls, CD players, skateboarding knickknacks, walkie-talkies, even a Lava lamp—all conveniently marked with their assorted point values. When asked what she thought of the whole Renaissance program, Rankin paused. "I'm disappointed," she said, "that we can't teach students to read without a lot of gimmicks."

Rankin came to education from the private sector, where she had helped manage an entertainment promotion company and then worked as an administrator at a private college. She started teaching in 1995, whereupon she was promptly initiated into the realities of education theory. Like many large, urban school districts, Memphis's was burdened with a student population that was largely ethnic and poor. In the 1990s, it also had a superintendent, Naomi House, who was an avid believer in school reform. In her eight years with the district, House thrashed her way through an endless series of school reform initiatives, which were drawn from the famous New American Schools project and were eventually imposed on all 160 schools in the district. Apparently, House's game plan failed. After $12 million in expense, achievement in Memphis hadn't budged; in many schools, it actually declined.[60] The last of those reform efforts was the famously dogmatic reading drill program Success for All. (Despite this low-tech program's test-score accomplishments in other districts, Memphis teachers soon renamed it "Stress for All, Success for None.") In 2000, when a new superintendent arrived, he was decidedly underwhelmed by Success for All and dumped the program, along with the rest of the district's campaigns for whole-school reform. But the appetite for novelty is hard to kill. A few schools began considering yet another reading package, called Soar to Success, sold by Houghton Mifflin; others were testing out Accelerated Reader. To facilitate these explorations, the district had sent a small brigade of administrators to Vegas. For some classroom perspective, it also sent one librarian and Rankin.

"Why do people in education keep reinventing the wheel?" Rankin asked me. "It is the biggest time waster—and money waster. When are we going to stop doing that?" And now, she said, comes George W. Bush, whose No Child Left Behind program, in her mind, is one more new wheel. Rankin had no quibble with Bush's desire to hold schools, and specifically teachers, rigorously accountable for students' progress. "But do people realize that a lot of kids aren't prepared to come to school?" Curiously absent from Bush's supposedly comprehensive campaign, Rankin noticed, is "any mention, or responsibility, given to the parents."

I told Rankin that I thought she'd hit on something, that it's odd the way everyone always points at schools and teachers but is afraid to point any fingers at parents. "It's not about finger-pointing," Rankin said. "It's about training." Her argument was that today more than ever, families, both rich and poor, are in disarray. And they need support and guidance on how to help children build a range of basic skills, reading being but one of them. "What part should they play to prepare their child for school?" she asked. But that is a big question, one far removed from the automated topics at issue that week in Las Vegas.

At the end of the Renaissance gathering, as conference-goers bade their good-byes, they were reminded of, and warmly invited to, the company's next annual conference, to be held in San Antonio, Texas, in early 2002. Renaissance staff members were clearly excited about the conference. They were already heavily broadcasting its theme: "Let the Dream Continue."

Education's Holy Grail:
Teacher Training

One morning in central Harlem, Carlton McKinson, the lone technician for this area's school district, labored for nearly an hour with a teacher's laptop. Finally, he made a connection with the Internet, which promptly delivered seventy-three new messages. Startled, McKinson asked the teacher (whom we met in chapter 2 under the pseudonym Ben) when he had last checked his e-mail. "Six months ago," Ben said, "when it stopped working." Ben had once tried to get another district computing specialist to fix his laptop, during one of the district's occasional teacher training seminars, but she couldn't manage it. Shaking his head, McKinson said he didn't have time to fool with it now and started packing up. Sensing the impending disappearance of a once-in-a-year opportunity, Ben peppered him with questions. McKinson finally gave him a steely look. "Didn't the trainer explain this?" he asked. Ben turned to me with an impish smile. "You getting all this?"

The communication gap between these two men illustrates another of education's dominant e-lusions—that teacher training will solve technology's problems. There is a reason for this. Whenever each new wave of machinery hits the schools, educators and equipment vendors are always concerned first and foremost with their most immediate technical problems—acquiring the equipment, getting it installed and working, and, they hope, linking the system to a few new pedagogical aspirations. Once the chaos surrounding this groundwork settles down, schools start noticing the missing pieces, the most important of which, everyone suddenly discovers, is training the teachers to properly use the gear. As Gregg Martin, a school district official in Vermont's Champlain Valley, once said, "I could put the same software into two classrooms, and in one classroom it's used horribly, and in the other it's fantastic. It's all got to do with the teacher."[1]

But educators have long understood the importance of teacher training; it is commonly seen as the answer to curricular innovations of all kinds, both technological and non-technological. Whenever any of these initiatives have faltered, the blame is often placed on the teachers' lack of preparation.[2] This pattern has become so consistent over the years that the notion of satisfactory teacher training could be seen as education's permanent fantasy, a kind of educational Holy Grail.

It is certainly conceivable that states and school districts could begin making headway in this direction—in technology, in the sciences, or in any of education's other constantly evolving subjects. But that takes a commitment that hasn't generally interested education's policy makers. One reason may be that proper teacher training takes serious doses of time, money, and effort. Education's institutional resistance to those investments—despite its leaders' professions of support—can be seen with dark clarity in technology, a domain that enjoys a level of interest and largesse that other academic realms only dream of.

⸺

During the subway ride back from Ben's classroom, as McKinson reflected on the day, he was still struggling to make sense of his experience. "Teachers think they can make a phone call and the computers will be fixed the next day," he said, then ruefully shook his head once again. Technical problems have become so incessant in Harlem schools that all McKinson has hoped for after setting up a system are two to three months of stable operation before the first crash. Despite this workload, the city has employed fewer than 150 trainers and support technicians for its 40 different school districts, which serve 1,200 schools and 80,000 teachers. Joe Eione, a veteran information technology officer in the city's board of education, points out that these proportions amount to roughly 17 times the workload suggested for the business world, where the recommendation is one support staffer for every 30 people.

McKinson is fully aware of these shortages, and he once thought he'd found a solution: Corral at least one teacher in each building into becoming something of an on-site techie. Teachers would be attracted to this idea, he thought, both for pedagogical reasons and for selfish ones: The first 60 teachers in his district who attended computer-training sessions would be loaned a laptop. Ben had managed to be one of those early volunteers, which made McKinson even more frustrated that he was still confounded by the Internet.

The reasons for the teachers' confusion are quite clear, at least to Ben. As is the case in many school districts, Ben's training session entailed sitting in an auditorium watching an instructor project a set of pre-programmed visuals, from a CD-ROM, onto a screen at the front of the room. "They put fifty people in a room for two hours," Ben told me. "They don't even give you the CD," Ben says. "They call it hands-on. My hands weren't on it. It's ridiculous." For Ben's training, the instructors did eventually mail out the CD, along with some support materials. By then, however, most of the lesson's fine points had long since been forgotten. This highlights a principle that any savvy instructor understands all too well: If students, young or old, don't have an opportunity to immediately practice what they are taught, they will forget the new concepts as quickly as they learned them. This is particularly the case with technology because, as any computer user knows, the tiniest missed step—an overlooked "return" or an unexercised menu option—will turn a document into a frozen mass of errors. That is precisely what happened to Ben, over and over again.

Because of such difficulties, schools in New York, like many of their counterparts in other communities, have offered extra workshops at the end of the day and on weekends. While this may seem like a practical idea and a generous gesture, for many teachers it was not much of a solution. "I can't do that," Ben said. "I have a mortgage. I have a family." Like many teachers, Ben moonlights to make extra money—in his case, with a night job at a camera store. Other teachers work as tutors. Knowing that many teachers face financial pressures of this sort, New York school administrators tried to give their technology training classes extra appeal by paying teachers $13 an hour to attend. But even that wasn't much of a lure. Tutoring opportunities, by contrast, paid more than twice as much.

Many teachers came to the classes anyway, seeing mastery of technology as important in its own right. Ben's neighboring teacher, a serious young woman I'll call Shareese, is an example. Shareese maintains a disciplined class, and at the time of my visit, she had been spending her off hours studying for a master's degree in education. This left Shareese, like Ben, too busy to make the off-hours workshops, but she had attended every school-day training the district had held. Among other things, these trainings had shown her how to get her students to make use of the CD-ROMs in the school's computer lab as research sources for school reports. In doing so, however, Shareese found most of the CDs to be inadequate or out-of-date. "If we're going to have computers, we might as well have the full program," Shareese told me one afternoon as she sat waiting for McKinson to connect her classroom's computers to the Net. "Otherwise it doesn't really work."

These facts of life have tended to put teachers who bother with technology training into two difficult categories. Paul Reese, the veteran Harlem technology coordinator from Ralph Bunche Elementary, has found that those who attend training classes are either the system's "movers and shakers" or those who don't have tutoring gigs or other side jobs and are there for the extra cash. The problem is that the first group, the go-getters, usually constitute a minority of a school's teachers; the latter group is generally unmotivated and, often, not terribly gifted at teaching. The inertia that surrounds this latter crowd has been an age-old challenge. Ken Komoski, director of EPIE, the educational software clearinghouse, well remembers his own tribulations when trying to develop teachers' technical skills in the 1980s. "We wanted to turn the teachers into crap detectors," he told me. "They didn't want that. They wanted to be told what to buy."

No wonder. For decades, the dominant trend in education has been to push teachers into technology regardless of their level of interest in these tools. A recent illustration of this philosophy occurred in the fall of 2001, when a school district in Dallas, Texas, decided to freeze teachers' salaries if they didn't master a lengthy list of computer skills in the next five years.[3] The question, of course, is whether the education system is equipped to disseminate good teaching skills on a broad scale—through technology or otherwise.

TEACHING REALITIES

In the summer of 2001, I spoke with an expert in teacher education who sadly told me about teachers she was working with in New York City who were still trying to master computer basics. "You can't believe how rudimentary the skills are out there and how little time these teachers have to improve them." Embarrassing as it may seem to outsiders, unfamiliarity with computers remains surprisingly common within education circles. In 1999, a well-circulated survey indicated that no more than 20 percent of teachers felt confident of their ability to use computers in their classrooms. The percentage has improved since then, but teachers are still unsure of how to best use these machines and how to fit technological activities in with everything else that's expected of them.[4]

What's the problem? While the teaching profession may not be drawn from among the best of every college's graduating class, it does get bright people. Teachers as a group are unusually energetic, devoted to their work and to their students, and obviously respectful of their profession's core value: learning. So why are they having so much trouble learning to use computers, and passing a sensible set of those skills on to media-loving youngsters? The answer has something to do with inherent conflicts between the culture of school—which is chronically impoverished, fundamentally nontechnical, frozen by bureaucracy, and pressured from all sides—and the culture of technology, which depends on a steady stream of money, a love of machines, constant change, and loads of free time.

But the core problem is the education world's basic approach to training its teachers in general. The contours of this issue can be understood, first, through a few facts on teaching's cycle of poverty.

In the mid-1990s, when the National Commission on Teaching and America's Future surveyed the nation's 1,300 schools of education, it found that more than half did not meet common professional standards. Among the many things missing from the training offered to teachers are studies of child development, or even minor degrees in the subjects that graduates would go on to teach. The result is that by 1996, more than a quarter of the high school students in math classes and more than half of those in science classes were being taught by teachers with no background in either of these fields. Several years later, the numbers looked even worse: One report found that nearly 40 percent of high school teachers didn't hold degrees in the subjects they taught; another found that 75 percent of seventh- and eighth-grade science and math teachers lacked certification in these fields.[5]

By the end of 2002, the trend seemed to have improved, but only slightly. Then, in early 2003, another report found that while states were building up their programs to train and keep good teachers, very few were aiming those incentives at schools that predominantly serve the poor, minorities, or low achievers.[6] In Chicago, things got so bad that many teachers were flunking their certification tests five, ten, or even twenty-four times—sometimes they never manage to pass them at all—yet they were still teaching. To make matters worse, students in Chicago schools that had the lowest scores—and the highest proportion of minorities—were roughly five times as likely as their peers to be taught by failing teachers.[7] "The quality of the staff is uneven and on the whole deteriorating," Harold O. Levy, the former chancellor of New York City schools, told me during a conversation in early 2003.*

As investment in teaching has declined, the education bureaucracy has responded mostly by feathering its own nest. Over the decades, the proportion of school staff classified as teachers fell from 70 percent in 1950 to 52 percent in 1993, while the non-teaching staff increased by more than 40 percent. By 1996, for every four classroom teachers there were six other school employees. The situation is quite different in other countries, where teachers make up 60 to 80 percent of school staff. Not surprisingly, teachers in America now have almost no free time—they get an average of 8.3 minutes to prepare for every classroom hour of elementary school and just 13 minutes for every high school hour. Meanwhile, U.S. school districts invest a mere 1 to 3 percent of their resources in teacher training and development—a sliver of what most other countries devote to this task.[8] This may partly explain why approximately two thirds of the nation's K–12 teachers—nearly 2 million tired or frustrated souls—are expected to leave the profession in the next ten years.

One might expect the nation's schools of education to make some effort to offset these trends. Instead, they've imitated them, turning education programs into financial funnels to their more commercial disciplines. As of 1998, colleges were spending about $100 less per student credit-hour on education programs than for, say, engineering (and paying education professors $11,000 less each year than their peers in other departments). Overall, it has been estimated that only about half the tuition paid by education majors is used for their own education—even though they pay the same tuition as everyone else.[9] This is a neat trick, a kind of curricular shell game. "These places are cash cows," says Linda Darling-Hammond, professor of teacher education at Stanford, co-director of the National Center for Restructuring Education, Schools and Teaching at Columbia, and the former

---

*As intuitive as it is to believe that students will learn more from a teacher who has been trained, licensed, and certified by state authorities than they would from someone who comes to teaching through other channels, this is far from certain. One of the more exhaustive reviews of the research on this issue, which includes some two hundred studies over the years, came to the harsh conclusion that teacher certification has had no significant effect on learning. This does not mean that teacher ability doesn't matter; the same review, in fact (by the Abell Foundation), found that other teacher attributes, such as verbal skill, matter greatly. The problem is that teacher certification programs have long been seen as a patchwork of inconsequential courses that in some cases have nothing to do with the teacher's field; in others, they are hopelessly mushy or tailored to political fads.

executive director of the National Commission on Teaching and America's Future.

As the teaching profession has languished, and as the school accountability movement has accelerated, education policy makers have tried to give teacher training some muscle. Some colleges have raised requirements on education majors' studies and on the grade averages they must maintain. Many states have sought legislative remedies—they've introduced new, rigorous teacher certification procedures (which many prospective teachers have flunked), raised salaries, and granted bonuses to teachers and schools that produce high student test scores. Idaho, for one, required districts to give new teachers three years of mentoring by experienced colleagues, along with ongoing supplementary training. Curiously, to win this assistance, which cost Idaho $2 million, teachers had to give up some employment protections for their first two years.[10]

As valuable as these various moves may seem, they are not unanimously viewed as a solution. Raising the bar on teacher certification may guarantee better skills, but it also blocks aspiring teachers from the classroom. At the very time that the classrooms are losing teachers (partly because hordes of veterans are just now retiring), student enrollment is rising. This could be called America's teacher time bomb. Add in the many specialties that new teachers will need in math, science (where national scores have been declining), bilingual education, and other fields that have long subsisted on teachers armed with little more than general skills, and the bomb begins to tick rather loudly.

To President George W. Bush's credit, he has tried to help matters on the teaching front. He has injected some extra cash into teacher training and opened up accreditation pathways to qualified professionals who haven't been through the standard teacher certification programs. This may sound dangerous, given the difficulty of getting teachers properly certified. (As but one indication, when California revised its standards for teachers to meet Bush's requirement that all teachers be "highly qualified," it defined the term so loosely that Bush's education department rejected the plan.)[11] But nearly everyone agrees that the nation's teacher colleges are in need of an overhaul.

The point here, as far as technology is concerned, is that the panoply of demands on America's teaching force is substantial, and rising. In the midst of all these pressures, to also ask teachers to handle technology's myriad complications—both technical and pedagogical—is, to put it mildly, expecting a lot. And now, just as teachers are starting to get comfortable with computer technology, along comes a new round of constrictions—the multitude of requirements imposed by the Bush administration's accountability initiatives. To a teacher, these can feel like very mixed messages. "We're saying one thing, but our method of motivating people is something else," says Barbara Stein, a coordinator of technology training for the National Education Association, one of the nation's two big teacher unions.

—

It should then be no wonder that many people—both in and outside education—see computers as a low priority. (Recall National Public Radio's 2000 poll demonstrating that when people were asked to rate their many hopes for education—better teachers, smaller classes, improved school safety, and so on—technology ended up ranking quite far down the list.) It's conceivable, actually, that state governments have acted with some innate knowledge of the public's sentiments. As of 2001, only half the nation's states had bothered to require teachers to have any technology training, and only three states (Idaho, Michigan, and North Carolina) required teachers to be tested on technology skills.

But what happens when teachers themselves put technology training first? It turns out that considerable obstacles still come up. Consider the experiences of Ericka McGhee, a sixth grade teacher at New York's I.S. 275. McGhee did not work a second job, so she was able to attend off-hours teacher training. Even so, she found the experience frustrating. "They don't follow up," she told me. "They immediately move on to something else totally different. So we're lost." McGhee is a little more determined than many teachers, so she kept at it. In so doing, she said, she had to let other areas of interest slide. At the time of my visit, she said these included new techniques for teaching science and math and for reaching students with learning disabilities, the latter being one of the teaching profession's most nettlesome obligations.

This is what educators mean when they talk about "opportunity costs"— the organizational euphemism for needs that get neglected when the system requires people to focus their energies elsewhere. It's a sad fact of life, and it is as true for teachers as it is for students. Technology promoters may argue otherwise; they may say—and they often do—that as teachers learn to "integrate" technology into core subjects, two masters are served simultaneously. In a computer simulation program on earth science, for instance, students supposedly get a chance to learn about both science and the art of simulations. In reality, as we've seen, students and teachers rarely have time to do justice to both challenges, or even to one. Yet another e-lusion.

The same immutable laws of nature afflict technology's great gift to communication: e-mail. While teachers, students, and parents can, with e-mail, now correspond at each party's convenience, it still takes time to type out questions and answers. In school after school that has embraced computer technology, teachers have been increasingly coming home to dozens of e-mails from students and parents, many of whom want immediate and thorough answers. This doesn't help the length of a teacher's workday. The problem has gotten so severe that in Washington, D.C., the principal of a Georgetown prep school declared a moratorium on e-mailing faculty. In Washington state, teachers went so far as to make rules and limitations on e-mail part of their collective-bargaining agreement. "A lot of us feel resentful that technology is being imposed on us," a sociology professor at Moorhead State University, in Minnesota, once told me. This may account for Stanford professor Larry Cuban's recent finding, when he studied how schools have been using technology since the 1980s, that there was no great accompanying improvement in teaching practices.* Jeffrey Fouts, the Seattle Pacific University professor and lead evaluator for the Bill and Melinda Gates Foundation, is more blunt. "In our experience," he told me, "technology in the hands of a weak teacher is a disaster."

If the schools' tribulations with computer training haven't provided proof enough that the business of mastering computer technology is complicated stuff, perhaps industry's struggles will. In the summer of 2001, a survey of corporate Internet training found that while many employees breezed through the program, most of them didn't retain much. As a result, many companies had already become disenchanted with computer usage. While corporate "e-learning" had been projected to grow massively in the coming years (by one estimate, to some $14.5 billion in 2004 revenue, up

---

*In *Oversold and Underused: Computers in the Classroom,* Cuban and a group of graduate students intensely studied computer use in a collection of schools in California's Silicon Valley (specifically, pre-schools, high schools, and one college: Stanford University). This study, which was something of an update of Cuban's 1986 book *Teachers and Machines: The Classroom Use of Technology Since 1920,* found teachers to be much more comfortable with technology, and more enthused about it, than they had been in the 1980s. But, with a few exceptions, Cuban didn't find much pedagogical change. "If anything, what we observed and were told by students suggested strongly that occasional to serious use of computers in their classes had marginal to no impact on routine teaching practices," Cuban writes. "In other words, most teachers had adapted an innovation to fit their customary teaching practices, not to revolutionize them." See *Oversold and Underused: Computers in the Classroom,* by Larry Cuban, Harvard University Press, 2001, pp. 96–97.

from $2.2 billion in 2000), overall computer usage had flattened in 2001 as some companies reported bad experiences. Industry "has tended to ignore what we know about learning," said Larry Israelite, senior vice-president of the Forum Corporation, in Boston.[12]

Educators have made a similar mistake. In 2000, schools were devoting only 17 percent of their technology budgets to teacher training—about half the standard industry recommendation. During the following year, education leaders began pushing schools, with unusual unanimity, to focus on what they saw as their last great barrier. Once again, it was technology training for the teachers. Yet by 2002, reports indicated that spending in this realm had not risen but had actually declined, to 14 percent of the schools' technology dollar.[13] This is one reason that veterans of the field often laugh when new ventures in classroom technology are sold through fervent promises of additional teacher training. A sample of this syndrome occurred in the fall of 2002, when Angus King, the governor of Maine, was trying to sell the public on his $37 million investment in laptops for Maine's seventh and eighth graders. Those trying to show they were being shrewd in their support of the program earnestly noted that if it was going to work, more resources had to be devoted to "professional development." Which prompted Gary Stager, adjunct professor of education at Pepperdine University and one of the backers of the laptop program, to say, "Let's see, does that mean we're now going to have the three-hour class instead of the two-hour class?"

THE ONLINE RESCUE

As depressing as this picture may seem, computers are offering a few promising ways out of the teacher-training morass. Over the years, a good many enthusiastic souls have been turning to the Internet, where they can continue their studies online—in technology and many other subjects—at any hour they happen to have free. Granted, distance learning for teachers is handicapped by the same limitations that constrain students (technical hassles, solitude, and the absence of face-to-face interaction). But for those who are dedicated and willing to accept the online medium's limitations, the Internet offers great solace. Many teachers also report that online discussion forums have created unique opportunities to find and brainstorm with like-minded peers. The Net also lets teachers easily follow up on questions, which traditional training often discourages. "Teachers come into a classroom after a long day and listen to someone speak at them for a couple of hours," says Timothy Stroud, of the American Federation of Teachers. And that's where it often stops.

It is important to remember, however, that the advances made by an enthusiast won't necessarily be duplicated by the masses—the great horde of average teachers, or perfectly good teachers who don't enjoy high technology. For this crowd, the smallest complication can be hit hard, sometimes with surprising speed. In the summer of 2002, for instance, when financial scandals plagued a variety of technology firms, one of the victims was WorldCom, Inc., the primary benefactor of an online teacher education program called MarcoPolo. In building this program, which combined a variety of potentially informative websites, WorldCom elicited partnerships from organizations such as the National Endowment for the Humanities, the National Geographic Society, and the National Council of Teachers of Mathematics, among many others. By fall, MarcoPolo had been adopted in all 50 states and was being used by 180,000 teachers; 2.4 million more teachers were expected to be trained and on board by 2005. Then, when WorldCom fell under investigation for accounting fraud, MarcoPolo suddenly found itself struggling for survival.[14]

The free market may be built for these upheavals, but schools generally aren't. This is why seasoned experts in e-learning often urge restraint. "Look at what you can accomplish with the least amount of technology first," says Paula O'Callaghan, director of the online program at Syracuse University's school of management, one of the oldest and largest accredited distance-learning programs in the country. In short, Callaghan says, "You should learn to crawl before you walk."[15]

The bottom line in this mess suggests a curious contradiction: If teachers are going to use technology properly, they would seem to need a substantial amount of additional training of some kind. That will obviously take more money and more of everyone's time. But education's record with money and time is not particularly auspicious, which casts doubt on technology's investment no matter how robust it becomes. The frustration that many teachers feel in such a bureaucratic maelstrom is well expressed by John Taylor Gatto, an acerbic former teacher who spent twenty-eight years in New York City schools and was twice named New York State's teacher of the year. "For 140 years," Gatto once said, "this nation has tried to impose objectives downward from a lofty command center made up of 'experts.' It doesn't work because its fundamental premises are mechanical, anti-human, and hostile to family life. Lives can be controlled by machine education but they will always fight back with weapons of social pathology: drugs, violence, self-destruction, indifference, and the symptoms I see in the children I teach."[16]

To now devote even more resources to this mechanistic domain would commit us to playing a zero-sum game. What to do? One answer might be to leave the technology expertise in each school to some small group of experts—the librarians, the increasingly ubiquitous "computer resource specialists," and, informally, some collection of teachers who love technology, who have free time, and who exhibit common sense in when to use these machines—and when not to. The other teachers, meanwhile, can concentrate their training in the sciences, social studies, and the host of other starving scholastic domains. Those who want to augment those basics with online studies should be given the opportunity to do so, as long as it doesn't steal from their primary duties. At the same time, those who aren't inclined toward technology shouldn't be forced into it.

———

One afternoon in New York I got a chance to see firsthand how teachers look at some of the conflicting demands placed on them. The moment occurred in one of the after-school technology workshops occasionally held for Harlem schools that took place in a computer lab at Ralph Bunche Elementary. As is commonly the case, the background of that afternoon's trainer was not in teaching but in computing. Yet the teachers followed her every suggestion about how to use technology in their classrooms. During this particular hour, they were learning to set up database records so that they could teach their students to file impressions of books they read into different categories ("genre," "summaries," and "opinions," the trainer explained). When I wandered around to check on their progress, I was surprised by the range of results. A couple of teachers were moving along swimmingly; most, however, seemed stumped. Only a few had the courage to ask repeated questions.

Midway through the session, the trainer realized she had not brought floppy disks. This meant the teachers couldn't take copies of their work home with them, which made it hard for them to use these lessons, such as they were, later in class. Partly for my benefit, the training then devolved into a philosophical discussion about the pros and cons of educational technology.

A special-education teacher (education-speak for those who teach children with learning disabilities) was upbeat. When her students discovered the visual appeal that computer graphics lent to their documents, the effect, she said, was "accelerated self-esteem." A math teacher was ambivalent. He saw possibilities for computer technology with today's emphasis on "constructivist math" (the teaching method that minimizes the importance of correct answers, aiming instead to have students discover mathematical principles through trial and error). But he feared that the computer's power would shortcut the analytical steps that constructivist math was all about. A third teacher voiced the argument typically heard in schools that serve minorities: "Our students are already disadvantaged. If they don't get computers, they'll be even more disadvantaged." A colleague disagreed. "Everything is computers now," she said. "They also don't know how to play games with each other. They don't even know how to talk to each other. We need to teach them that, too."

Helping teachers minister to such a range of needs may require more money and time, but it is not rocket science. Within the annals of academic literature—and, more graphically, in the halls of a handful of enterprising public schools across the country—the principles of inspiring teaching and learning are alive and colorfully on display. As we'll see, only a fool, or a huckster bent on selling rotten goods, could miss them.

PART III

SMARTER PATHS

CHAPTER 11

Getting Real at New York's Urban Academy High School

I n an aging brick building on New York City's Upper East Side, a dozen teenagers of varying ages, half of whom look like street kids, pull their desks into a circle as Avram Barlowe, their teacher, distributes several thick handouts. "You're killing trees," one particularly muscular student complains. "Yes," Barlowe says, "I'm killing a lot of trees."

Barlowe has asked these students to spend an entire four-month term intensively studying one slice of American history: the Civil War and the Reconstruction period that followed. Some will spend the whole course just studying slavery—specifically, the true causes of the slaves' emancipation and what their freedom meant to them. The course is one of four similarly focused classes on other subjects, Barlowe's alternative to the general surveys most schools define as American History. (His other three are titled Columbus and the Age of Exploration; the American Revolution and the Constitution; and the Great Depression and World War II.) In each case, students are expected to sustain a reading regimen comparable to what college students confront. In this class on the Civil War, for example, they'll be responsible for studying a variety of books and journal articles, including such rarefied selections as the writings of John Brown, the famously militant white abolitionist, and interviews with some surviving slaves written in the 1930s under the auspices of the Depression-era Works Progress Administration.

Today, Barlowe is handing out some of his favorites: three seminal articles on the origins of slave emancipation by contemporary writers, who take passionately different points of view. (One, James McPherson, argues the standard line that President Lincoln was the slaves' central savior; another, the black historian Vincent Harding, says the slaves emancipated themselves, and that a white Republican president could never have led such a radical change; and the third, Ira Berlin, takes the middle line, maintaining that the slaves were the prime movers in their emancipation but did not act alone.) It will be the students' job in the next few days to figure out these contradictions.

After the students have spent fifteen to twenty minutes reading over their handouts, discussion begins. The debate is constant and heated; in fact, students regularly have to fight their way into the conversation. Whenever the dialogue bogs down or goes off course, Barlowe quickly interrupts. "I want to hear some pieces of evidence here!" he insists. "You're going to have to evaluate the evidence of all these people's actions and decide what it has to do with the end of slavery."

At one point, Brian, a senior, calls all three writers' arguments "nonsense." Citing some congressional legislation from the period, he argues that it was the coalition of abolitionists (citizens and a few legislators) who brought an end to slavery. Several students intently nod in agreement; others passionately disagree. "For the weekend," Barlowe tells them at the end of class, "I want you to go home and look at all of Harding's evidence. He says it was just the slaves. But let's look at his evidence." This is esoteric stuff, a level of surgical thinking that many students don't get unless they attend law school. To give them a jump start, Barlowe has included several detailed sheets among his handouts, on which he's consolidated the main facts that make up each writer's evidence. He'll expect first drafts of his students' papers, he tells them, in two weeks.

The sense of urgency in this discussion is not common in public high school classrooms. It's as though the students saw Barlowe's class as their last chance to prove themselves—which in some ways it was. As part of a relatively recent alternative public school movement in New York, Urban Academy was created, in 1985, as a place for students who are failing at other schools (usually big, traditional institutions); some perform perfectly well at those schools but are simply miserable there. This is the city, after all, "where the warehouse high school was invented," writes Linda Darling-Hammond, the renowned Stanford education professor, formerly of Columbia University.[1] Not surprisingly, the need for alternatives to these factories has become pretty strong. "We call it 'the second chance school,'" Ann

Cook, Urban's co-director, later told me. "Some kids call it their 'last chance school.' "

Whatever it's called, it's different. Consider the views of a handful of college professors who were among a corps of experts that visit Urban each spring to evaluate the work of graduating seniors. One is David Thayer, a Ph.D. in microbiology from Rockefeller University. After looking at the students' work in the sciences, Thayer sat back, raised his eyebrows, and said, "This is more sophisticated than most college genetics labs, some of which I have taught. It's definitely more than most college freshmen do."

Eric Foner, of Columbia University and president-elect at the time of the American Historical Association, had this to say: "The papers are quite impressive overall. They vary, of course, as papers do. But the very good papers are at the same level of what we'd expect from students here at Columbia. We have students who are coming in from AP courses at suburban schools or who have various kinds of history backgrounds. But not a lot of them have done the kind of careful weighing of historical interpretations against each other that you find in some of these papers. Most students have to be taught to think this way. The general impression students have when they read a work of history is: 'This is true because it's in a book.' When they read something that takes a different point of view, they get rather disoriented, and they're not quite sure how to gauge [it]. Obviously, these students have been trained in this essential component of the study of history."

And this, from Judith Walzer, an English professor at New School University: "I've had the experience of teaching students or examining students where you ask a question and there's a one-sentence answer. And it's not a question of shyness or dumbness or anything like that, but the person hasn't learned how to develop an idea. How to make a statement and then qualify and describe and give examples and illustrations. Each and every one of these people could do that."[2]

Urban Academy's accomplishments certainly back up the professors' impressions. While average New York City high schools, including the "good" ones, see nearly 20 percent of their students drop out, Urban's dropout rate is half that.[3] Like many of the city's alternative high schools, Urban struggles with (and protests) the New York State Regents exams, the state's high-stakes, semi-annual standardized test. Beyond that, the school's record seems solid. SAT scores typically come in above the national average. And 95 percent of the graduates go on to four-year colleges, some of which carry some highly regarded names—Oberlin, Mount Holyoke, University of Massachusetts, Hampshire, Bennington, Brown, Swarthmore, among others. Recently, Urban has begun to accumulate a bit of public gilding as well. In

1998, the Department of Education made Urban a "Blue Ribbon" school, and later listed it as a special "Showcase" institution. In the ensuing years, Urban continued getting attention, including a visit from Rudy Crew, the city's high-profile former superintendent of schools, who took an opportunity one day to show off a few of his prized possessions to John F. Kennedy, Jr.

As I roamed around the school during several visits of my own, I began to see what makes Urban's scheme work and why students who come here, including those who had been strong students elsewhere, are often shocked by what's expected of them.

Urban Academy is not a high-tech school. Nor is it against computers. In fact, most of the staff believes that technology has an important role in education—especially in high school, which, for many students, is only a step away from the wage-earning life. Urban's view differs from the standard technovangels', however, in how the computer's role is defined, to what extent it is used, and, most important, what other activities surround computer use. Minimal as it is, Urban's approach to technology is well worth looking at. But that will be best understood later, when we can see how computers take their place inside the web of values that drive the school.

AN URBAN FAMILY

When Avram Barlowe sat down to gather the materials he distributed in his American history class, he did not pull a single one from the Internet. Even if they were available on the Net (most weren't), finding information is not what the class is about. His focus is on the dialogue. Managing that, Barlowe finds, is challenge enough. So when it comes to class readings, he generally resorts to the simple, tried-and-true world of print—specifically, the assortment of historical materials he has accumulated through twenty years of his own study and research.

"Our concern," Barlowe told me on his way out of class, "is what are their crap-detector skills. That's a big focus here." The echo between Barlowe's comment and the very same words from Ken Komoski of EPIE, the educational software clearinghouse, is telling. Both men's remarks were undoubtedly inspired by Neil Postman and Charles Weingartner, whose popular 1960s-vintage book—*Teaching as a Subversive Activity*—opens with a chapter, well-known to virtually all progressive educators at the time, exhorting them to become better crap detectors.[4] (Interestingly, these authors also borrowed the phrase, from Ernest Hemingway.) For his part, Komoski was referring to his failed efforts to give teachers discriminating values regarding software purchases; here at Urban, the teachers practice this kind of critical thinking every day—with their students. In fact, signs of Urban Academy's focus—its war against B.S. of all kinds; its web of close relationships between faculty and students; and its dead seriousness about tough-minded learning—fill virtually every corner of the school.

You see it first in the common areas. Urban is a shockingly tiny school, comprising a mere 120 students and a main campus of eight classrooms, all of which reside on a portion of the second floor of a five-story building. The building used to be one of those legendary New York "warehouse" high schools, but it was broken up in the mid-1980s into six different academies, in concert with yet another wave in the city's implacable alternative-school movement. The redesign gave all six of these schools access to facilities that would be beyond the reach of most small schools, including a three-story library equipped with Internet connections, a small theater, two gyms, and even a swimming pool.

The redesign also left a cavernous central hallway as Urban Academy's most spacious domain. Students have, however, put the area to good use—it's filled with half a dozen couches, several coffee tables, and, during almost any break period, several knots of teenagers gathered around a game of cards, a gossip session, or some horsing around, with a teacher as often as with one another. The atmosphere is particularly noticeable at lunchtime. At just about every American public school, lunch is an opportunity for any teacher not on duty to get a break. (As an indication, while touring schools I quickly learned that if I wanted to visit with teachers, one of the best tactics was to bring along a bag lunch. That usually gave me my pick of teachers to eat with, since most of them do the same thing. No one eats with the students unless they have to.) Not so at Urban. Come lunchtime, teachers and students alike pull out their lunch bags or stroll to the cafeteria or to the delis around the corner, then return to eat together in a classroom or in the school's formal common room.

You also see the school's ethic in its office, which functions as almost a second common area. The office feels like the city room at an old-fashioned newspaper. It's one long room, with no individual offices or cubicles, just a score of desks spread around for the teachers. Most of these are stacked high with chaotic piles of books and papers; there are also a few additional bookshelves or cabinets, for those with sufficient seniority or moxie to claim some extra turf. It is sufficiently crowded that anyone heading for the sink or the coffee machine in the corner has to twist sideways frequently to get there. Nonetheless, the room is a sea of moving conversation, between teachers, students, and the school's two founding directors, Ann Cook and her husband, Herb Mack. This is command central—for everybody. Whenever the office empties out a bit at the end of a break, you'll often see a teacher and student head to a third common room next door for some private conversation.

Those conversations are the center of Urban Academy's ethic. A scene in Barlowe's history class was typical. Despite the vigor of the day's debate, I noticed that before long, several students stopped participating. In fact, a couple of students felt free to put their heads on their desks and fall asleep. Oddly, Barlowe, like several of his peers, roused these students only occasionally. When I asked Barlowe about this later, he was not the least bit uncomfortable about it. "I don't think everyone has to speak to participate," he said. (To make sure students are keeping up, he said, he watches their written work.) As for those who fall asleep, that's a different problem, which he said he'd deal with separately. That morning, for example, Barlowe knew that the young woman who'd fallen asleep was a new mother. "She was up with a baby last night," he said, "so I didn't want to bother her."

The average school administrator would be stunned, if not outraged, by Barlowe's response. But the incident speaks volumes about the school's credo: This is, in almost every sense of the word, a family. Many schools talk of such goals; some sincerely try to achieve them. This school pulls them off.

Urban has achieved this by making a particular set of organizational decisions and sacrifices. Consider the numbers. Urban employs eleven teachers for its 120 students. On the face of it, this means each teacher has, as the educators call it, a per-pupil load of eleven or twelve students—a sliver of what most public schools expect of their staffs. Comparing numbers on these duties is a dizzying process, since every school tallies student loads a little differently. Some look at it by counting how many students teachers see in a day in their various classes. By that measure, the noted education writer Theodore Sizer once calculated that in the average New York City public high school, each teacher has to instruct 175 students a day; in Los Angeles, the number reaches almost 200.[5] The point, though, is this: If all schools could keep their student loads this low, wouldn't they behave like a family, too?

Maybe so. The kicker, however, is that Urban accomplishes this without spending any more money on staff than traditional schools do. Its trick? "Everybody teaches here," Ann Cook told me. "We don't suck up administrative units." What she means is that Urban doesn't employ any pure administrators. The responsibilities those staff members would have—the dozens of time-consuming tasks typically done by principals, assistant principals, student counselors, college guidance counselors, attendance monitors, student activities coordinators, secretaries—are shouldered at Urban by the teachers. Visitors to Urban are treated to a firsthand experience of what this has done to school management the moment they contact the school. Any telephone call is answered by a teacher or, even more often, by Cook herself, who like many of the teachers is often still at school past 6 P.M. While Urban's system may have increased teachers' burdens, it also keeps every adult in the building inside the visible orbit of students' lives. That's why Barlowe can leave his sleeping young mother in peace—and avoid humiliating her in front of her peers. He knows there will be a natural moment, later, to pull her aside for a private conversation about her work, her baby, or any other difficulties in her life.

And he'll do it. "Individual needs, not institutional needs, drive the school," says Herb Mack, Urban's co-director. This sounds nice, but what does it mean? Some examples: If a student arrives at school distraught, someone will cover the class of that student's adviser so that the adviser can step in to help. "Urban Academy," writes Darling-Hammond, "is a school where there are no cracks for students to fall into."[6] Students will tell you the same thing. "There is always a teacher to help you with your problems," says one. "They eliminate the problems that lead to the cracks," says another. "They do what they have to do to keep kids in school. If I need to get up early, they'll call me."

There's a rationale beyond mere empathy for handling students this way. A study of the school by Columbia University's National Center for Restructuring Education, Schools and Teaching (NCREST) noted that many adolescents, "especially those who have experienced alienation and failure in school . . . are still unsure of their capacity to commit themselves, to rescue themselves if they start to slide, to believe that the capacity to be successful students resides within themselves. This is demonstrated by the number of students who credit Urban Academy rather than themselves for their continuance in school."[7] It's also demonstrated by the bonds that are built between students and the school. One fall afternoon after one of my visits to Urban, I fell into conversation with a Hispanic student, a senior, who would be graduating the following spring. Everyone is familiar with the sense of anticipation that impending graduation stirs in high school seniors, that emotional virus commonly known as senioritis. This student seemed germ-free. He said that during the summer he was thinking, "It's only July, and I'm going to have to wait how long before school starts again?"

Earlier, I referred somewhat metaphorically to psychologist Abraham

Maslow's famous pyramid, in which he outlined an individual's hierarchy of needs. My point was that education could be regarded similarly. And, if anywhere, technology fits on one of the final upper layers but that it's too often treated as part of the pyramid's foundation, where it crowds out more basic needs or at least distracts everyone from them. At Urban, teachers seem to approach the education pyramid with a bit more architectural integrity. "The school understands," says NCREST's study, "that students' survival needs must be met before they can be responsive to the school's educational agenda." The echoes between this statement and Maslow's hierarchy of needs, established some two decades before Urban's founding, are surprisingly direct. To Maslow, survival was the first priority, the base of his pyramid; nothing else would matter until an individual's basic needs, such as food, shelter, and self-protection, had been attended to. At Urban Academy, the staff has attended to students' survival by daring to function, quite literally, as surrogate parents. In some cases, the school has found homes for students who had none or medical care for those who were sick. "Urban Academy took over where my parents left off when they died," one student said. "They made sure I got my Social Security check and I knew my tenants' rights. They even found me a job."[8]

Any public school that deals with large numbers of low-performing students knows all too well that their academic potential is compromised every day by personal obstacles of this sort. But in almost every school, when the question of how to deal with these problems comes up, teachers and administrators throw up their hands in frustration, saying there's no way that schools can teach and also serve as parents and baby-sitters at the same time. Urban Academy's operation, slender as it is, demolishes that claim. Its teachers not only take on the family's job, they go further. These values seem to take root even in small ways. Like any school, Urban has a few weak teachers—awkward sorts who lack the charisma and authority needed to command a class, especially one composed of fierce nonconformists. Yet as I visited these teachers' classes, I was surprised at how orderly they usually were. It made me wonder why, with so little outside motivation to do so, Urban's students paid so much attention to these teachers. The answer seemed to be twofold: First, they'd become partners ("stakeholders," in education-speak) in a culture based on the principle of decency—an academic version of an extended family; second, I gradually realized that students know the odds are good at Urban that something interesting and different will usually come along soon, even in a class that seems numbingly boring.

BIGGER BATTLES

The clearest demonstration of Urban's scrappy academic ethic is its course catalog. The fall 1999 lineup, for example, included nearly fifty different offerings, everything from About Men and Women to Chemical Puzzles, where students must function as scientific detectives, to So Sue Me!, where students analyze and argue facts like lawyers. There's a film class focusing solely on the work of Alfred Hitchcock; a range of classes in art and photography; a homework laboratory; an opera club; a playwriting class, in which students work with a professional playwright and stage readings of their work with New York actors; and a weekly three-hour block devoted to community service. There are also advanced classes in psychology, history, pre-calculus, and college algebra.

For such a tiny operation, this is a stunning buffet. It's also an ironic counterpart to the computer-heavy schools like those featured in the first part of this book. Those schools boast about the great service they're doing their students by giving them high-tech modern-world skills. Yet they often manage this by cutting back on offerings that—far more than computer work—are once-in-a-lifetime opportunities. Napa, California's New Technology High School—another small school that claims to serve academic misfits—is a classic example. One student there complained that she was interested in psychology and was frustrated that New Tech had no psych classes. Urban Academy does. In fairness, most students don't come to New Tech to pursue subjects in the humanities like psychology; they aspire to careers in technology—an industry for which the primary academic prerequisite is the mastery of advanced math skills. Strangely, New Tech didn't offer advanced math. Low-tech Urban Academy does.

The reason for its offering such variety is that at Urban, preparation for life after school is taken seriously. An example is the Scientific Methods class, in which students pursue independent research projects for an entire year, occasionally meeting one on one with their teacher, Barry Fox. During those meetings, Fox reviews their research methods—Socratically, that is: He rarely offers suggestions, and only after taking them through a series of questions about how they plan to solve certain complications, how they'll know if a procedure worked or failed, and so forth. He also sends them to the Internet, so they can compare their research methods with what big-league scientists have done. Those inquiries don't stop on the screen, though. Once students have found some references, their next stop is a good library. (In

Urban's case, the neighborhood library happens to be the one at Rockefeller University, home to the 1999 Nobel Prize winner in cell research.) After they've collected some good journal articles, Fox suggests that the students contact the authors, ask some questions, and try, if they can, to add something to the professional research.

There are specific styles of thinking being taught with this approach—habits of mind, as they're called in the education world, or at least by its progressive wing where they're most valued. In essence, these are the habits of inquiry, the capacity to dig into any subject as if one were a professional investigator. The method as practiced at Urban was devised by Cook and Mack, who brought it here after refining it for years in England, Chicago, and at other schools in New York City. Interestingly, one of their primary early incubators was the Bronx High School of Science, notorious as one of New York's most demanding high schools.

As I began exploring this "inquiry" style of pedagogy myself, it sparked my curiosity on several levels. First, it simply made sense. While the notes of caution seem obvious (factual and historical context, for one, can't be forgotten in the midst of a student's exploratory zeal), to address academic subjects as a professional researcher would seem to be the most exciting and, for a youngster, the most empowering way to attend school. Second, as we've seen, when technology advocates talk about which pedagogy offers the greatest promise for computers, they point most often to this method of "teaching and learning." (Those two words are generally used together for a reason; at its best, progressive education—and classroom computer use—is supposed to be equally enterprising for both the student and the teacher.) So, if computers are truly worth their weight in school, it seemed to me that high-tech practitioners of this philosophy ought to at least match the performance of schools that operate with simpler materials. But the more I looked into what goes on at Urban, the more it seemed that the computer is no match for a pedagogy like this one.

This is not to suggest that everything is perfect at Urban. In fact, there's a curious paradox in Urban's culture that might strike some people as an embarrassing inconsistency. In almost any class—even the smaller ones that focus on rigorous discussion—there's always a collection of students who aren't demonstrating what might be called model behavior. One or two typically sprawl across their desks in various poses of relaxation (some are asleep, like the new mother in Barlowe's history class; some just check out). A few slouch under baseball caps that at other schools would have to be left at the door. Some munch on snacks, drink sodas, or chew gum. When I asked Ann Cook about this, she said, "I don't want to make that stuff the issue. I want to make the hard stuff the issue." Most teachers, of course, function on the belief that it's impossible to get to the hard stuff unless there's an atmosphere of order. (And to be honest, Urban somewhat aims for the same goal but fails to achieve it. In the school's literature, prominently noted among the requirements for graduation is regular class participation.) The point, however, is that there is a bargain that Urban implicitly strikes with its students: We won't hassle you about how you sit or when you eat; in return, you will do your work. And we will hassle you about that.

It's another example of good academic tough love. If anything, this is the core of Urban's philosophy, a working relationship played out in a complete loop of support. It is particularly visible in the class called Homework Laboratory.

Many schools set aside specified periods of the day when students can concentrate on homework. At best, these are supervised study halls; at their worst, which is often, they aren't even supervised. At Urban, however, the teacher on tap works every minute. One by one, the given teacher takes students aside and works them over. "What's your plan for that assignment?" one teacher asked. "When are you planning to finish?" asked another. "Okay, what's your next step? Tomorrow, when you wake up, what are you going to do? And what if that doesn't work out?" "Realistically, what do you really think you can get done this week?" asked a third. "Realistically. How are you going to work that in?" As you can imagine, at some point during these interrogations, students often slump into a funk of defeated confusion. That's when the questions get more persistent, for this is what support at Urban is about—forcing youngsters to overcome their obstacles.

It's also about teaching the youngsters to think for themselves. As part of their art studies, Urban's students must give equal weight to a class in art criticism, where they find work they don't like, research how and why it was done this way, and explain their judgments. Urban so delights in provoking students that it has a class called Looking for an Argument.

A DIFFERENT TEST OF LEARNING

The capstone to Urban Academy's program, its version of final exams, is what the school calls proficiencies. These begin as long-term projects—research papers, science experiments, art exhibits, and so on—and culminate in a series of solo oral exams. Conducted by a panel of Urban teachers and outside experts (this is where the college professors' evaluations come in), the exams are akin to the hours that graduate students spend nervously trying to defend their theses to leading professors in their field. The exams have to be undergone six times, in front of a different evaluation team on each occasion. That's how Urban covers its six areas of emphasis (math, science, literature, social studies, the creative arts, and art criticism); coupled with these are ongoing demands in supplementary areas, such as library research, class participation, and community service.

And no one pulls any punches, as Caitlin Schlapp-Gilgoff learned when she arrived at Urban from Stuyvesant, which is the only New York public high school, aside from Bronx Science, to earn national academic honors. "In my previous school," Caitlin says, "if I hadn't really done enough work throughout the semester, I could cram at the end and I'd be okay. Or not. But it was entirely decided on the last week of classes. It didn't really reflect continual work or real ability and development. Proficiencies entirely avoid that. You really have to know what you're talking about, and work toward a goal. And it really develops your writing, and discipline, in terms of time management and all of that."[9] Watching students go through this "proficiency process" made me glad I was spared this ordeal during my own high school education. Upon reflection, though, I wish I hadn't been.

For their science proficiency, for instance, Urban Academy students are asked to design an experiment, collect their own data, control their variables, and produce an analytic paper, often including some statistical analysis, just as a professional scientist would. When they're done, they'll have to justify each decision to the science panel's evaluators. Similarly exacting study and writing are expected in literature and social studies. In math, the test is not only fluency in algebra and geometry but also the completion of a math project. (Students might build a bridge, for example, perform some statistical analysis, or create a complex computer program.) A big piece of the math proficiency requires students to solve a logic proof—an exercise of brain-twisting complexity and taught in a fashion that may well be unique to Urban Academy.

When Urban's graduates get to college, they're often stunned by how they compare with their peers. "I think I have an advantage, having written as many papers as I've written and having read as much as I read," says Kevin Kirby. "A lot of people at Stonybrook can't write papers. They struggle. I mean really, *literally* struggle." Diandre Verwayne, an Urban student who went on to the College of New Rochelle, just outside New York City, found she had a competitive edge in class discussions. "I'm not just talking off the top of my head," she says. "I challenge people. I even challenge *my* thoughts. So I know, if there's going to be people who will counteract me, with this idea, then I have to get myself prepared, in order to respond to that."[10]

TRUE TECHNOLOGICAL SUPPORT

Amid all this intellectual work sits a single computer laboratory. The lab, along with a couple of computers in each classroom, is used regularly, albeit more selectively than in most schools I visited. Why? "I think computers are great," Ann Cook told me at one point. "I think they're a low priority, though." At this school, computer work is focused on two areas: computer design and programming.

In the programming class, students spend a good bit of their time on computer games—not playing them but creating them. To refine the work, classmates play and critique one another's games, then send them back to their creators for revisions. This idea of having youngsters use computers to actually make interesting things from scratch, instead of playing simplistic, mass-marketed programs created by someone else, has a lot going for it. And it's bandied about in conversation at almost any gathering of educational technology's intelligentsia. Those conversations usually conclude with a weary sigh as everyone realizes what an impossible dream truly creative computer work is, given the gray realities of school bureaucracy and the chronic inadequacies of school funding. But here again, with the shrewdness of a poor corner grocer, Urban Academy finds a way to make academic ends meet.

All of Urban's computer classes are not quite so shrewd. I visited one, Internet Programming, where students spent hours toying with website designs; another, in computer graphics, had students practicing refinements of Photoshop, a software package primarily geared toward manipulating photographs. In each case, there was some interesting work, but it seemed surprisingly easy; no one was struggling or particularly stumped. When I asked about the looseness of the work, the teachers argued that a lot of that is unavoidable—this is how people learn to find their way around computer software. They're right, but I couldn't help wondering whether the work justified the time it took. In the fifteen-week Internet programming course, for instance, the teacher had only three goals for the class: the creation, by each student, of a small Java applet (a code that animates computer graphics), a function in JavaScript, and the design of an interactive website. "That's all I really hope to get accomplished," she said with a sheepish smile. During that time—a full forty-five classroom hours—students in other rooms will be studying the settlement of the American Southwest, learning physics through a Basic Repair and Maintenance class, solving Chemical Puzzles, mastering quadratic equations, and tracing the history of political philosophy, just to name a few competing options. Before they graduate, of course, students in the Internet class will get a chance to take many of those courses. Some, however, they will have to miss.

Whenever I asked about trade-offs like this at Urban, I was stunned to find that most of the teachers weren't terribly concerned about them. Computer classes here are just another curriculum option. Even when students get around to them late in their tenure at Urban, teachers say, most do just fine—including those who've not had much previous computer experience. "In math classes here, there's a focus on logic," said Becky Walzer, daughter of New School University's Judith Walzer, who, among other subjects, teaches computer programming, literature, and math. "Programming is similar to that kind of thinking. So I don't see kids having much difficulty with it." What about some of the more advanced software? Wouldn't students need considerable experience on the elementary versions of those programs, almost as prerequisites? Not according to Roy Reid, who teaches photography and computer graphics. "I tend to skip all those boundaries," Reid said. His reason is that the bulk of education software, even for students of high school age, isn't that complicated.

An awkward question surrounds these teachers' observations, which hearkens back to an earlier e-lusion (that children must learn computer skills as early as possible or they'll be left behind): If the risks of being a latecomer to computing are so great and the consequences so dire, what happens to the technological laggards now? Almost every class in middle school and high school contains some students who have had little if any previous experience with computers and others who've been playing with these machines for years. Are the less experienced students having great trouble keeping up and suffering greatly as a result? Upon reflection, most of these teachers say no—a view echoed by their peers in almost every school I visited, including those that are avidly high-tech. What really matters, most of them say, is motivation: They should have the basic desire to learn computer skills, a quality as readily available at age sixteen as at age six. This is why Joseph Weizenbaum, the MIT professor emeritus of computer science, once said that even at his technology-heavy institution, new students can learn all the computer skills they need "in a summer." It's also why in core academic subjects—social studies, science, or any number of others that high-tech schools love to fill with computer exercises—Urban's teachers either steer clear of technology or keep it in its place on the periphery. As illustration, in Barry Fox's science lab there are computers—two relatively old machines, that is, which were stuffed into the corner at the time of my visit. All around them were piles of old terrariums, some holding live lizards or snakes or lab rats; at other times, when Fox is teaching the Science of Household Chemistry, the lab is full of toothpaste, beakers, and other implements of what teachers call wet science—materials that many schools cut back on in order to find money and space for computers.

If there's a rush to learn any technologically oriented skills here, it's those that surround computer work, not the computer work itself. "I think it's bad to start learning how to do research on the Net," Harry Feder, a professional lawyer who teaches Urban's legal studies, told me after a class that had students poring over a famous case that is standard fare for first-year law students. Feder, who graduated from Georgetown Law School in 1991, was among the first generation of law students using online networks for legal research, and he remembers doing Boolean logic searches before they were commonplace. Feder has found that young attorneys increasingly "don't know how to use the books." This weakness is exacerbated by the fact that LexisNexis, the granddaddy of online research services, is made available to law students free of charge. Interestingly, while law schools increasingly suffer cutbacks on book budgets, LexisNexis hires students to remain in law school libraries to help others use its services, which include laser printers and free paper. Urban Academy tries to build slightly different habits. "I would rather send them to the library's open stacks," Ann Cook told me, "where they can get the right call numbers, sit on the floor, browse around, and find related stuff."

———

At one point, I asked Cook if she and Mack got many questions from parents and students who are concerned that there's not enough technology in Urban's curriculum. Apparently they don't. "If a school is working, you may get a few questions about technology," she said. "But if a school isn't working, parents will seize on that as necessary, because it's the one thing they can hold on to. I always tell parents, 'Ask where the classroom book collection is, then see what it is.' *That* tells you something."

Good point. But it still seemed to me that there are certain subjects—

mathematics possibly being the best example—where computers offer undeniable power. When I asked Cook if she would agree, a sly smile spread across her face. "You should visit a class in Wally Math," she said.

REAL-WORLD MATH

Soon after Walter Warshawsky started teaching math at Urban Academy in 1990, he became one of its legends. He walks the school's hallways like a Caucasian version of Toshiro Mifune, the late Japanese film star known for his portrayals of larger-than-life samurai warriors. Mifune was not a large man and neither is Warshawsky; in both cases, their size comes from their demeanor. They're like moving walls that seem able, if provoked, to suddenly transform and lash out like a tiger. A man in his early sixties, Wally, as everyone calls him, has a short gray ponytail, a curly salt-and-pepper beard, spectacles, and a soft, low voice. When I first met up with him, he was walking out of a class grumbling about the fact that he'd made a scheduling oversight. It was a small mistake, but it forced him to give five points to the student who was shrewd enough to catch an error—in keeping with the agreement he makes with each of his classes.

Wally, who also teaches philosophy and ancient history, approaches math differently than any teacher I'd ever seen or heard about. This is undoubtedly why everyone at Urban refers to his classes, whether they are in beginning algebra or advanced calculus, as simply Wally Math.

A typical example was a trigonometry class, which Wally began by dividing the students into groups of three-person teams. Without a word, he then turned to write out a series of puzzles on the blackboard. As he scrawled away, the students chattered, ate snacks, laughed, and generally paid little attention. Wally didn't even flinch. After a few minutes, he started explaining the puzzles. He spoke so softly that I could barely hear him above the students' conversations. That didn't last long. As soon as it was clear the day's exercise had begun, the students quickly quieted down on their own.

Trigonometry, being an advanced stage of mathematics, is offered in most high schools to their more-senior students. But Wally manages to teach trigonometry to a mix of students from ninth to twelfth grades by turning the course into a game. In the context of a story about computers in schools, there's double meaning in Wally's method. Computer advocates, as we've seen, continually boast of how much fun learning can be on a computer, especially with the software industry's wide array of math games. In Wally's class, the games are, to say the least, a little different.

In the trigonometry class, for example, the game began with a few minutes of silence as the students scribbled out their tentative formulas. (Most had calculators on their desks, but the puzzle was sufficiently complex that the calculators were of use on only a few steps in their figuring.) Eventually, I noticed some urgent whispering as each team's members began to argue with one another over their procedures. Before long, a few frustrated students started asking Wally questions—"Don't we have to know the value of x first?" "How come the sine can't be bigger than one?" When the questions became incessant or pained, he offered a few short comments, using them to redirect attention to other parts of the puzzle. But he never directly answered them. One by one, the groups announced that they'd solved the first puzzle and called for Wally to come collect their worksheets. It turned out that a couple of them had just missed, which meant that only two groups got the exercise's precious three points, their tiny step toward the three hundred points every student must accumulate each term to pass Wally's classes.

Wally has some intriguing reasoning behind each stage of these games, which, incidentally, are the subject of his master's thesis. First, he permits only one answer per team. "That makes them argue," he said. "If I allow three answers per team, they won't talk to each other." Each team has three members because, he said, "If I have four, one won't do anything. And it allows a two-to-one vote." To prevent teamwork breakdown, Wally assembles the teams himself. (At New Technology High School in Napa, California, we also saw students work almost constantly in teams; they too are composed of three students, chosen in their case by the students themselves. Most New Tech High teams therefore become mini-social clubs, with at least one weak member who does minimal amounts of work.) At Urban, Wally often groups his students a little differently each day, by emerging abilities. This ensures that smart kids will compete with one another and that the same fair contest will confront less able students. He also likes to throw curves. When I asked him what sort of problems he gave his morning algebra class, Wally said, "Mostly problems where the answer is that there is no answer. Or that there's not enough information. They hate those. I love 'em."

One of the reasons Wally uses puzzles is to make mathematics real. A common assignment from him is to read a questionable news article and look for signs of bias, missing information, or quantitative assertions that don't make sense. He also creates puzzles tied to work being done in other classes, such as science or social studies. Sometimes Wally just sends his students on a mission outside school walls.

To learn the principles behind trigonometry, for example, his students had to figure out Staten Island's proximity to particular points on Manhattan's shore. "Trigonometry is long-distance geometry," Wally says. "So what's the point of doing it in the classroom when you have a city to do it in?" In this exercise, each student began with four things: a semicircular angle ruler, a plastic drinking straw, the height of the Statue of Liberty, and an all-day field trip. Grouped once again in teams, the students spent their subway ride to the Staten Island Ferry negotiating their plans of attack, and the ride back arguing about what they had found when they peered through their straws from the deck of the ferry. With these exercises, Wally explains, "the students will get errors. Then they have to focus on why."

It's not unusual for a teacher to dream up a field trip that makes flat classroom material suddenly come to life. High-tech schools do this, too, sometimes letting students use laptops on field trips to record observations. Wally's approach moves in an entirely different direction—toward simplicity and, simultaneously, toward perhaps greater sophistication. Strangely, very few people in education think this way. During the course of my research, the one subject in which I encountered the most consistent respect for computers' ability to handle complexity was mathematics. This included university professors and high school math teachers—almost anyone who has seen this machine put through its arithmetic paces. Wally knows how these experts feel and happily sticks with his puzzles and his plastic straws.

"I don't like using the electrical stuff," Wally says, "because I want them to see how the tool is made. And that they can make one, too, out of fifty cents' worth of stuff. And they could use it to do trig instead of getting some sophisticated instrument that's going to cost them thousands of dollars to do a problem. This way they don't have to worry about the tools. They just focus on the procedure."

It's worth noting that when the students' straws were used with their angle rulers, they created sextants. An essential part of a sailor's gear for centuries, the sextant has now been rendered virtually obsolete by electronic positioning devices—obsolete, that is, until a storm knocks out a boat's electrical systems. I've spoken with sailors who tell such tales. One still packed a sextant. When a mid-Atlantic gale nearly destroyed their boat, she was very glad her captain had made everyone learn to use this simple tool.

―――

The uniqueness of Wally's perspective inspired me to sit down with him one afternoon to talk about some of the fancy exercises with computers and math that I'd seen or heard about students doing at other schools. I was pretty well convinced by then that, for high school students in particular, many of those exercises, if approached shrewdly, were well worth their expense and effort—until I ran through them with Wally.

We started with the simplest and most prevalent piece of educational technology: the classroom calculator. All over the country—even at schools admired for their sensitivity to children's nascent capabilities, including one in St. Paul, Minnesota, that modeled itself after Harvard professor Howard Gardner's famous theories of multiple intelligences—I watched both elementary and high school students happily do their math assignments on little pocket calculators. And I heard teachers everywhere defend these devices. Wally differs with all of them.

"There's nothing more sophisticated than our brains," Wally said. "Those kids don't have any number sense. If they use [calculators] in the lower grades, they don't know how to not use them. If you don't know the basic number math, you can't do the abstractions of it." To illustrate, he scrawled an elementary algebra problem in my notebook: $x/a + a/b = c$. Thus, $x=?$ "How are they going to figure that out?" The goal with mathematics, Wally believes, is to learn to compose visual pictures of whatever mathematical principle is at issue. To accomplish this, Wally's students solve their trigonometry problems with both handwritten tables and calculators, so that they can understand a calculator's automatic steps. This is what turns math skills into life skills. "When you get out in the real world, you can't have a calculator every time you have a problem with math in it," Wally said. "If you can't make the numbers dance in your head, you can't figure it out. You can't look at something and say, 'That doesn't make sense.' If they read something in the newspaper with statistics that say this or that, they won't know if it's true or hype."

The important issue here in Wally's mind is the ability to estimate. "If you're using a calculator, you never estimate," he said. "When you're watching TV, you can't say, 'Oh, that economic thing they're talking about, that's about $1 million.' Teachers can't figure out how to teach this to their students. So they rationalize, and pretend it's not necessary." Curiously, the responsibility teachers might once have taken for this choice has been conveniently diminished over the years. Since the early 1990s, students have been allowed to use calculators on their standardized tests, including testing's Goliath, the SAT. Yet to Wally, it's clear that "the ones who don't need calculators in the exam rooms get the highest scores."

One of the other scenes I discussed with Wally occurred at Blair High School, the mammoth suburban institution on the outskirts of Washington, D.C., that has been widely celebrated for its technological savvy. During one of my visits to Blair, I spent an hour watching ninth graders feed some textbook data from the 1970s into a computer modeling program to make predictions about the causes of global warming. The class was part of Maryland's Virtual High School, a traveling workshop in which the state takes great pride, having devoted eight years and nearly $3.5 million to it. When I asked the Virtual High School teacher, Susan Ragan, whether the students wouldn't learn more by doing these calculations by hand, she said, "Not with dynamic graphs and predictions like this."

The computer program that Ragan is talking about would seem to be technology's classroom ideal. Built to handle a sequence of graphs, which change shape as each successive set of data is fed into them, dynamic graphs make esoteric concepts blossom into resplendent visuals. In this particular exercise, Ragan wanted students to see what happens to plant photosynthesis when fossil fuels are added to the environment, and then when carbon levels are increased. She said they did plot one year's graphs by hand, on the blackboard, to make sure everyone understood the math concepts. "If you can do it once," Ragan told me, "you've got it. But that doesn't show you the whole thing. What happens in fifty years?" If they tried to do it fifty times by hand, she said, "by the time they got done, they'd be so tired and bored, they'd hate it." When I surveyed a few students, they were having a blast playing scientist with these mobile graphs and seemed to be relatively comfortable with the underlying math principles.

In my mind, this scene chalked up a solid point for computers. But it mystified Wally. "It's just showing the kids a movie," he said. "They're not doing it—the computer's doing it. Even after you learn the principle, you gotta keep doing it. So there's a picture in your head of what it *is*. So you can say, 'Oh, I see where that number's going.'"

At Urban, Wally explained, instead of going through Blair's computer modeling exercise, they might learn what it takes to set up a computer to carry those exercises out. He was even more blunt about the content of the Virtual High School lesson. "It's B.S.," he said. "Environmental problems aren't the only causes of global warming. There's obviously an agenda there. I try to stay away from agendas, or show why their assumptions are wrong." When I relayed Wally's critique to Ragan, she acknowledged that he had a point. "Yes, there are all sorts of things left out of that exercise. You can't say anything definite about global warming from this carbon model." It's the teacher's job, she explained, to bring in the material that sets the lesson in context, to do "a whole global warming lesson." Do they do that? Well, Ragan said, her instructors try to encourage that, but it's an open question. "With teaching, you can't be sure of anything," she said. "You get in the class, close the door, and teach what you know."

The holes in this dialogue point to the overriding purpose of Wally's work—sticking to the basics and doing it right. This, in Wally's mind, will prepare students for a self-sufficient life after school far better than can a graphic modeling program, which may or may not be available when the world's scientific dilemmas crop up. "I know it's likely that most of my students won't go on to math in college," he told me. "These are the last math classes they'll have. I want them to be able to function in society. You can't even serve on a jury today without math. If they throw DNA at you, you're sunk."

CHAPTER 12

A Word from the Army: KISS

Say what one will about the military, but when it comes to organizational management—a challenge that bedevils any large enterprise—it has learned a thing or two. The reason is obvious: The consequences of failure in a military organization can be fatal for hundreds if not thousands of people. This concentrates the mind of any manager. And it undoubtedly accounts for why, among all of society's large, modern institutions—medicine, government, the media, education, and industry—the military has been quickest to take a long, hard look in the mirror after a stumble. The most recent moment that provoked such self-correction was the Vietnam War. In the following years, each branch put itself through a period of intense, ethical self-examination that led to wide-scale reforms.[1] Clarifying many of these efforts was a catchphrase from the Army, the military's largest branch: Keep It Simple, Stupid, which was quickly popularized through its delicious acronym, KISS.

The power of simplicity obviously has appealed to more than the nation's lieutenants and drill sergeants. Some educators, even those involved in technology, have been drawn to the concept too. One such person is Tom Snyder, a former educational software maker, who consistently delivered an unusual message to audiences at some of the myriad conferences held each year on educational technology. During one such presentation in San Francisco not long ago, Snyder said, "If you guys had all been really committed to technology in schools back in 1984, *really* committed and well funded and everything, your schools would all be permanently wired for Commodore 64s. Thank you for not doing it!" Snyder's gambit prompted a huge laugh. Everyone in the room knew that Commodore 64s are ancient machines whose manufacturer has long since gone out of business, leaving thousands of orphans that could no longer be upgraded.

Snyder was something of a lone crusader for a radical idea: one computer in each classroom. The computer's job, in his view, is not to break up the traditional classroom group endeavor but to stimulate it. "Schools may be the last place," Snyder once said during a speech, "where the government is funding us to gather together into public forums to have conversations. We have got to protect that." Snyder doesn't pull any punches on this topic. In ten or fifteen years, he fears, employers will increasingly ask whether applicants were computer trained or teacher trained. Those who were computer trained, he believes, will be left out—because "they won't be able to make sense of the world."

In support of this view, Snyder designed software packages that help teachers conduct discussions. During his tenure, he says, when the members of his firm sat down to create a new product, they began and ended with one question: "Does the computer actually contribute to having conversation?" An example of how Snyder's materials tried to accomplish this is a social studies package that stages a hypothetical international crisis, complete with multiple options for the president and his advisers. Coupled with each option is screen after screen of historical information, analysis, context, further questions, and other material that forces students and teachers alike to grapple with complexities. But the overriding point is that the exercise is conducted as a group, with the teacher leading at every stage. The same format applies to the company's other products, in subjects such as history and science.

Snyder arrived at his epiphany partly out of frustration, after he and his partners once tried to design a course on the Internet, structured as most are these days, through a number of website hyperlinks. "At the end of this orgy of webbing," Snyder recalled, "my partner said, 'We still haven't figured out what the course is.' We often forget about that, because the Internet is so seductive, you can just link all day." To illustrate, Snyder pointed out what would happen if a boy wanted to study the history of the civil rights movement and began his work with a website devoted to Martin Luther King Jr.'s famous "I have a dream" speech. One popular site, he said, would send the boy on the following path: "I have a dream . . ." (hyperlink, click); this sends him to a site featuring fires during protests in Atlanta, Georgia . . . (hyperlink, click); now comes a compendium of famous, early fires . . . "You see how far away he now is from the topic?" Snyder asked. The great irony, Snyder noted, is that parents and teachers watching this boy would be thrilled by what he was doing. But, Snyder asked, "what will he be able to contribute about Martin Luther King at a party when he's twenty?"

Snyder's message clearly flies in the face of high-tech orthodoxy. Over the years, computer enthusiasts have continually celebrated the computer's ability to break up the old, constricting, linear forms of information. At the peak of "new media" hopes, in the early and mid-1990s, many in the publishing world thought that an entire new industry would be born with CD-ROMs full of multimedia material that was so interactive it would make traditional linear storytelling obsolete. Swayed by this vision, authors rallied around new companies that tried to design stories that could be structured and finished by the reader. Most of these ventures tanked along with the CD-ROM market. And they never made a dent in schools. There is a reason, according to Snyder, and his view is widely shared by education experts. Apparently, learning remains a relatively linear process.

This is not to minimize side connections, which are critical to creativity and innovation. But even the most innovative among us learn the principle of what Snyder calls "slogging through." In other words, understanding and mastery come to those who can stay on topic, face the challenges, and resolve the contradictions. (To illustrate this point, Snyder likes to repeat a story from a comedienne who, after watching television with her boyfriend, finally realized why he kept changing channels. "He clicks whenever something complex comes on.") "Let's not come back in ten years," Snyder pleaded at the San Francisco conference, "having spent the last decade congratulating kids for *leaving* ideas."

To underscore his argument, Snyder cited an old Harvard study that tried to ferret out predictors of success. Among other things, the evaluators looked at which students did well at reading comprehension from third grade on. One factor proved to be consistent: "They come from families that talked at dinner," Snyder said. "The end."[2] Obviously, it's not quite that simple; families that enjoy lengthy dinner conversation typically can indulge in lots of the other finer things in life. And almost every educator knows that family privilege and academic success are joined at the hip. However, schools can compensate for many of these gaps, as we're beginning to see.

TEN-DOLLAR TECHNOLOGY

Another great believer in a simple approach to the complex art of learning was Alfred North Whitehead, the famous English philosopher and mathematician of the early twentieth century. One afternoon, I had occasion to test out some of Whitehead's views during a visit with Bob Albrecht, the impish godfather of scholastic approaches to BASIC, the first programming language built for personal computers. Albrecht, seventy-one at the time, had been treating me to a cornucopia of academic possibilities with today's computer technologies—spreadsheet activities, the latest website-building software, and documents overflowing with hypertext links, which let students, as he put it, "just click and go, click and go." After listening for a while to Albrecht's worldview, I pulled out one of Whitehead's quotes. "The best education is to be found in gaining the utmost information from the simplest apparatus," Whitehead wrote in 1929. "The provision of elaborate instruments is greatly to be deprecated."[3] Albrecht heartily agreed, with one caveat: An extra phrase should be added to the first sentence, he suggested, so that it read: ". . . the simplest apparatus that is capable of doing the job."

Albrecht's revision wouldn't add much complication, at least not in his mind. Whenever he volunteers in schools, which he still does regularly, Albrecht arrives with an unusual assemblage of materials, the primary piece of which is a knapsack full of gizmos and gadgets. He also packs sets of documents on computer disks, which he calls his backpacks. (There's an Algebra Backpack, a Physics Backpack, a Measurement Backpack, and several others. The disks carry all those files and articles that he litters with hypertext links.) Yet when it comes to teaching, say, the laws of probability, Albrecht pulls out a Tupperware container full of dice. Some are standard, six-sided dice; some are dodecahedral (with twelve faces, each of which is shaped like a pentagon), and some are icosahedral (with twenty tiny, triangular faces). "Here," he says, waving his dice box in the air. "This is educational technology." Cost? About $10. Another Albrecht favorite is "base-10 blocks," used to teach math to very young children. "I do a lot more of that than I do with computers," he says. "Because they are powerful and they are cheap. And teachers can learn to use them."

Albrecht's point about blocks is more profound than it appears. A good many schools, including those considered models of intelligent computer use, have enthusiastically bought computer programs that simulate blocks and beans and other physical materials that have long been staples of math instruction in the early grades. "That," Albrecht argued, "is not appropriate technology." Even now, with computers in almost every school, the product exhibits at math-education conferences feature table after table of blocks in different colors and patterns, counting chips, fraction tiles, puzzles, building kits, and assorted other manipulatives—"manippies," in teacher lingo. "I could harp about tool selection all day," Albrecht told me. "If we could teach teachers appropriate tool selection, we wouldn't have these problems."

Albrecht has thought a lot about tool selection. When we first sat down together, he tossed a pile of catalogs at me—from Texas Instruments, Vernier, and other suppliers of what he calls data grabbers: small devices, with electronic sensors, built for fieldwork. A student with one of these in her hand can record, say, how far away a bird is and how fast it flies, or the temperature in the water of a polluted stream, and then plug this data into a computer for analysis. But he usually just packs the simple stuff—even when teaching advanced college mathematics.

After digging a little deeper in his knapsack, Albrecht pulled out dozens of measuring devices of various shapes and sizes. There were protractors with holes for drawing circles of different sizes; one had a little wheel on the end. There were also calipers, mostly plastic, but one was a beauty—made of solid brass. He also carries a few books, including a 276-page volume, roughly two inches square, entitled *The Pocket Professor: Over 1000 Physics Formulae: Mechanics, Thermodynamics, Electromagnetics, Optics.* Then he brought out his favorites: a set of tape measures and folding measuring sticks, all calibrated in meters. "That one will just about take you out to Mars," he said, pointing to his 1.5-meter tape. Discussing the reason with him quickly gets you to a math-and-astronomy lesson, involving the translation of solar distances to meters and millimeters. As I listened to Albrecht explain the devices piling up on my coffee table, I found myself confused, as I always was about math in school, and at the same time fascinated in an unfamiliar way.

———

Obviously, computers are brought into classrooms for more than math and science. But these two subjects, which have been discussed regularly throughout this book, merit an extra moment of attention for three reasons. First, they are the subjects that technology advocates usually point to most vociferously as the ideal domains for exploration and invention with computer technology. Second, the sciences are arguably the fields that are visiting the most change upon modern society at the moment and, perhaps, the most opportunity in the near future. Biotechnology, genetic engineering, pollution control, exploration of the climate and the atmosphere—all these fields are screaming for qualified graduates, a shortage that federal policy makers aren't doing much to alleviate.* If only by mental association, computer technology is seen as intimately connected with advancement on each of these fronts. Third, a sense of the sciences, and a firm grip on mathematics, matter a great deal, as we have seen, to any student who is looking into computing as a career option.

Albrecht is in stride with each of these points, although he steps more lightly than most academics do. In his classes, students generally have a ball with his bags of "technology," the total cost of which (absent the data grabbers) comes to less than $50. Not long before our meeting, for instance, he taught a class with one of his metric measuring sticks. "Every single kid wanted to use it," he said, "because it *folds out.*" What's striking about this story is how similar it is to the accounts from schools that invest heavily in computer technology. Almost every news account on these schools is filled with gleaming anecdotes from teachers and parents about how enthusiastically the youngsters have taken to the technology, and about the vast scholastic possibilities it opens up. What they're not seeing is the enduring truth underneath every new toy. It's not the computer that has excited the students; it's the physical machinery, the presence of a real tool, and a real-world activity. As Albrecht's experiences indicate, this excitement can be achieved with a $50 collection of hand tools as easily as it can with a computer, a single one of which can cost twenty to thirty times as much.†

---

*An illustration of this blindness occurred in 2002, when President Bush submitted his education budget. Bush initially sought $450 million for a partnership program between K–12 schools and universities that has tried to improve the quality of math and science teaching in the lower grades. That fall, the Senate Appropriations subcommittee that handles education approved a mere $25 million for the partnership.

†An interesting illustration of technology's sometimes false allure in the sciences came up in a *New York Times* review of a software package called Studyworks Science. The software aimed to equip students with all manner of sophisticated tools—a chemistry library, complete with both principles and formulas, and a worksheet full of advanced math functions—all of which moved *The New York Times* to headline the review GIVING STUDENTS SERIOUS HELP WITH SCIENCE. Yet the company claimed it would take students only twenty minutes to master the program. "That may be true, but probably only for the best students," the reviewer concluded. "And that raises a basic question about the program's usefulness. The students who are most able to make use of it probably need it the least—they know the formulas and laws, or if they don't, they at least know how to find them. Those students who have difficulty coping with science will probably find it hard coping with Studyworks Science as well." See "Giving Students Serious Help with Science," by Henry Fountain, *The New York Times*, September 23, 1999.

The message in these simple tools could alter the debate about how to close the great "digital divide." As we've seen throughout this book, the computerized activities that schools generally offer to poor or struggling students in an effort to expose them to technology are thin at best, which only puts these students at further disadvantage. That syndrome greatly troubles Judah Schwartz, the professor emeritus of MIT and Harvard, and the former co-director of the latter's Educational Technology Center. The problem, Schwartz says, is that when schools serving the underprivileged rush from one new technology application to another, at some point "the newness wears off. And then the whole system reverts to its previous inequities." In his decades of teaching, Schwartz has long tried to counter this trend with his own version of simplified technologies. He was an early practitioner, for instance, of devising math lessons for students in the primary grades around a broken calculator. (Schwartz realized that if he broke or taped over all the buttons except for zero, one, and the plus key, then told second graders to see who could be first in tallying up, say, 2,312, a very interesting lesson would ensue. As students realized they didn't have to add one 2,312 times and could in fact create combinations of 10, 100, or 1,000, they would discover, quite on their own, the meaning of place values.)

The prevalence of options like these, and their wide neglect, have left Schwartz with no great fondness for education's standard approach to calculators and most other current forms of classroom technology. "The calculator as a surrogate for how numbers work is a fraud," he says. As dismissive as his criticism sounds, Schwartz is actually aiming at a finer point. Some of the calculator's weakness, he explains, derives from the way its tiny screen condenses, and thus distorts, the arithmetic process. Those limitations, Schwartz points out, afflict every tool, even multi-gigabyte computers. And therein lies their opportunity. "All tools have their prices," Schwartz says. "A useful strategy is to turn their price into a teaching occasion." The pedagogical goal, he says, is to figure out "what *are* the limits of this particular device?"

There's something rare, delightfully realistic, and empowering in Schwartz's attitude. He persistently points out, for example, that technology is not going to go away. So we might as well learn to confront its powers—and its weaknesses. At the same time, Schwartz heartily agrees with those who want to limit very young children's exposure to computers—partly because they are not yet up to seeing through the computer's limitations.

This suggests an interesting new way of defining school policy when it comes to technology purchases. Perhaps student access should be limited to those computer programs they can fully understand. Such a policy would rule out a lot of children's software, such as the fancy multimedia programs with high-end production values that overwhelm children's imaginations. It could keep powerful geometry programs away from high schoolers who know only enough to use their shortcuts. And it could encourage simple, sensible activities. By the same token, a policy of this sort might encourage certain sophisticated simulations—but only for older students and teachers, who are capable of critiquing their omissions. Some schools have already taken this route. In Denver, Colorado, the school district set up an ingenious program that taught high school students to take apart and reassemble computers, upgrade the hardware, and diagnose problems—all on used computers donated by Dell Computer. (Pleased with the schools' success with the program, Dell subsequently expanded its initiative, giving four thousand used computers to fifteen districts across the country.) In Beverly, Ohio, the Fort Frye school district tried a similar idea, teaching its high school students to build new computers from scratch. The program soon saved the district $30,000 in computer costs.[4]

One of my discussions with Bob Albrecht makes the case for KISS-ing in another technological sphere. At the time, Albrecht was in the middle of explaining his graphing calculator, a high-end but increasingly common classroom tool that can negotiate arcane concepts such as sines and cosines, graphical analysis, statistical regressions, algebraic equations, financial functions, and matrices. Once again, I was having a little trouble following the explanation from a man who calls himself a "metric evangelist" and who does advanced algebraic equations every morning because, he says, "it relaxes me." So I asked him what he did if a young student had trouble following these concepts and if he further determined that this youngster's math foundation was weak. Does that student have to go back to working basic math problems, either by hand or with drilling software? Or is the answer to use more advanced pieces of technology, with all their possibilities for graphic explanation?

Neither one, in Albrecht's experience. "If you give him more math problems, it will destroy him. That's what got him where he is now," he said. As for the fancier technological approach, while computers offer a few new options, he's found them to be generally too abstract. The best answer, Albrecht believes, is some activity that appeals directly to the student's interests. "Hands-on experiences are great," Albrecht said. "A lot of those kids are great with their hands." These experiences include, on the higher end of the scale, Albrecht's data grabbers (if schools can afford them and have the skill to manage them). But many of the same lessons, he says, can be learned quite happily with Albrecht's knapsack and a set of real-world problems. As evidence, one of Albrecht's co-teachers told him that when he walks down his school's hallway, students who haven't exactly been the class stars often approach and say, "When are you going to do another one of those investigations?" Sometimes they even bring in their friends from other classes.

Albrecht delights in contrasting this picture—steeped as it is in the traditions of John Dewey, the legendary school reformer—with education's current fixation: standardized testing. "Whenever I go out into the real world," he likes to say, "I never see people making a lot of money sitting at their desks answering multiple-choice questions." Albrecht's folksy tale fleshes out an old truth about standardized tests: They don't, in and of themselves, predict later success—on the job or in life. Granted, good scores may build confidence (just as poor scores reinforce a struggling student's sense of inferiority). It is also true, with some notable exceptions, that general success in school usually contributes to success later; any adult can see that just by looking at the varying amounts of progress that former classmates have made. But scholastic success could be measured through any number of endeavors. The fundamental question concerns what happens to the human psyche when it repeatedly succeeds (or fails) at challenges. The result, of course, is a change in one's level of confidence. And confidence can be built many ways; yet for some reason, in today's sophisticated world, education policy makers have chosen to confine it to selecting among multiple choices on a piece of paper.

One thing that struck me about both Albrecht's and Schwartz's approaches was how similar they are to the one practiced by Wally Warshawsky, the Zen master of math at New York's Urban Academy. With all three instructors, the priority is each student's need for physical, sensual, and often idiosyncratic engagement with academic concepts. Beyond that, of course, Warshawsky couldn't have been more different from his two peers, particularly Albrecht: Warshawsky is only a step away from being a Luddite; Albrecht is a technology lover. Yet when it comes to engaging students, they're on the same simple page.

While arguing his various points, Albrecht regularly reaches into one more bag—a small, well-worn, Velcro-fastened fanny pack that seems to reside permanently on his left hip. In one motion, he whips out his graphing calculator, snaps it open, and holds it in front of your face. The speed with which he does this reminds me of a movie gunslinger; it even has a touch of the cowboy's bravado as Albrecht talks for a moment about the different things he can do with this device, then snaps it shut before you can answer and slides it back in its holster. Albrecht's delight in all these tools is plenty obvious, and plenty infectious. When I was a boy, I would have loved being equipped with backpacks like these. I would also have wanted a teacher like Albrecht, who could show me when to use the tools inside them and when not to.

Toward the end of one conversation with him, I got nervous about drawing too much meaning from his arguments. Albrecht is obviously not your average instructor. He's rarely seen without a shirt emblazoned with a large dragon, his lifelong icon; one of his hobbies is fatiguing much younger friends on hikes in the California woods. This childlike energy travels with Albrecht whenever he visits schools. (Even his face gives it away. One of his ears is curiously misshapen—by birth, one presumes. But it curls at the top into a slight point, much like a dragon's.) All of this moved me to ask him if he thought it realistic to expect average teachers to duplicate his experiences. "If you really want to solve this problem," he said, "double the teachers' salaries." To most people, that sounds about as realistic as cloning an army of Bob Albrechts. But he's onto something.

PRESERVING REFORM

One of the great privileges of being a journalist is the legitimacy it confers on one's secret desire to be a Peeping Tom. While reporting this story, I was welcomed into dozens of schools of all kinds, many of whose administrators let me wander from class to class, freely choosing either a brief glance or an extended visit. A number of these schools were among those, mentioned only passingly so far, that have become famous in education circles as exemplars of today's most effective approaches to public school reform: Some are designed around Howard Gardner's well-known theories about multiple intelligences. Some are the cream of New York City's intense traditions of progressive education. Some are called Expeditionary Learning schools, whose emphasis on real-world investigations is patterned after the Outward Bound program, which believes that the rigors of the outdoors put steel in teenagers' spines. And some are Core Knowledge schools, which follow proudly old-fashioned traditions.

Throughout all these visits, I was continually struck by a bizarre constant. No matter how varied and ingenious the pedagogy was (and in many classrooms the creativity was phenomenal), it rarely carried over into the technology program. Not surprisingly, most of these "exemplary" schools put very little emphasis on technology. But in one model school after another, once students did sit down in front of computers, the scene became strangely reminiscent of the superficial chaos at most of the high-tech schools I visited. Even more surprisingly, these observations almost always followed lengthy conversations with no-nonsense teachers and principals, who seemed to understand technology for what it is—a perfectly nice supplement but one that requires an exceptionally firm hand.

An example was New York City's P.S. 234, the innovative elementary school in the city's Tribeca neighborhood. P.S. 234 uses no textbooks, workbooks, or grades, preferring students to do their own original research, starting in kindergarten. It also hires virtually all its teachers from New York's Bank Street College of Education, which has long served as the seedbed for some of the nation's most sophisticated progressive teaching methods. (Bank Street teachers are so prized that upon graduation, they generally have their pick of jobs anywhere in the country, at both public and private schools.) During my visit to P.S. 234, I quickly saw why. In class after class, clusters of students had their noses in complex projects, even in the youngest grades. Kindergartners and first graders were designing a city block; third and fourth graders were learning geometry fundamentals in art class (sometimes their shapes are constructed with yucca, corn, and iris fibers grown by the students in the school garden). When teachers spoke to the students, they tended to do so as respectful coaches, in keeping with the "guide on the side" philosophy that propels "constructivist" pedagogy. As noted earlier, these methods are valiantly but unsuccessfully attempted at many progressive schools these days, including those that are proudly high-tech, such as Napa's New Technology High School. But here, constructivism seems to truly work, for a number of reasons, one of which is the fact that P.S. 234 projects aren't plagued with technical complications. As teachers visited each group, they quickly understood what the students were doing and what materials and challenges were involved, and they offered just enough questions and thoughts to get students to struggle toward their own discoveries.

P.S. 234's approach to reading and writing provided an eye-opening contrast to the narrow approaches taken by educational software companies, particularly Renaissance Learning and its widely used product Accelerated Reader. Throughout P.S. 234, classroom walls were covered with challenging reminders of what it takes to be a perceptive reader and thoughtful writer. In a fourth-grade class, for example, one poster noted that literature has both an explicit "over-story" and a quieter "under-story," where a writer's subtle, sometimes most enduring, messages reside. Another told students "how to linger with a book." (The tips included talking about it with somebody, just sitting back and pondering the story, rereading the first and last chapters, writing an epilogue or a new ending, or expanding on a meaningful passage—a process that teachers here call "writing off" the book.) Other advisories noted methods of finding connections between different texts to experiences in one's life, and so on. To facilitate this process, teachers do make use of a little technology: Post-it notes. This technique, advocated by Columbia University reading expert Lucy Calkins, creates an open-ended but simple way for students to capture moments of inspiration. It's also delightfully ironic. Computer advocates love to talk about the computer's capacity to facilitate creative, nonlinear work. Here was a method of doing the same kind of open-ended brainstorming, so simple that a first grader could do it—without the system crashing on her.

The intellectual vitality at P.S. 234 is so strong that it continually spills outside the classrooms. As but one indication, an atrium on the school's first floor is filled with several huge 3-D models, the results of students' semester-long endeavors. One of the more impressive was entitled "The Hudson River Study," produced by a class of second and third graders. When I told the class teacher, Lynn Handelman, that I was looking into computer use in schools, she said, "I felt bad that we didn't use the computers for this. But we used our hands and our minds. They were touching everything, looking at things under a microscope, looking at photos, reading stories." The class's curiosity was intense enough, Handelman said, that she ended up bringing in factual texts that were so advanced that she had to read them to the class aloud. "It allowed them to use their imaginations," she said. "It's a very active kind of learning." The cost? About $500.

When I spoke with Anna Switzer, P.S. 234's principal, the conceptual framework for this abundance of activity became even clearer. Switzer, who has two degrees from Bank Street, does not count herself a strict adherent to constructivism; its pure form is too relaxed, in her experience, for keeping up with today's hard-nosed state standards. So P.S. 234's version includes a touch more teacher guidance. The mix seems to have paid off. When city test scores come in each year, P.S. 234 is routinely near the top, and sometimes in first place. The power of this school's pedagogy, and its fragile subtlety, makes Switzer circumspect about computers. "I think less and less of computers as time goes on," she told me. "What discourages me is the *reality* of their possibilities. Their potential is enormous. But the reality of what teachers and students can do is another thing entirely. With the Internet, for example, I have huge concerns about the student as the consumer. In almost every class, someone gives me fifty pages from the Internet that no one wants to read. And they haven't done anything with it. Kids should be *producers* of knowledge, not just consumers. The computer is an enormous tool for that, or it has the potential to be. But not enough of it can happen without enormous adult input."

In keeping with these views, Switzer had managed to keep computers to a minimum in P.S. 234 classrooms (there are roughly two per room, and they often sit relatively neglected in the corner). But she couldn't keep an ambitious technology plan out of school entirely. Thanks to a parent drive, P.S. 234 now has a state-of-the-art computer lab.

It should be noted that most students at P.S. 234 come from educated, relatively well-to-do families. That puts some limit on how much other schools can duplicate their low-tech intellectual achievements. So once again I went searching for answers in schools that dare to test their models of reform with the disadvantaged. One of those is Harbor Middle School, in the notoriously poor Dorchester section of Boston, where one of the strangest moments of contrast popped up.

————

Harbor, a brand-new school, belongs to the Expeditionary Learning family. The practice of "inquiry" learning, somewhat akin to the approach taken at New York's Urban Academy, is at the heart of Expeditionary Learning methods. And Harbor is considered one of the family's up-and-coming stars.* Harbor, being so new, was living out of temporary digs when I visited. Overlooking the noisy Massachusetts Turnpike, these comprised several floors of a local electricians' union office, which Harbor's teachers had to completely empty at the end of each day so that the union could hold its own classes. Harbor's phys ed classes consisted of students skipping rope in the parking lot, where the teacher, a former gymnast, showed them how to do flips on a strip of lawn next to the cars.

Despite the mayhem and the school's infancy, Harbor's principal, Scott Hartel, had no trouble showing me thick piles of the students' in-depth reports on a variety of topics. One recent project was an intense study that sixth and seventh graders did of the Boston Harbor Islands. Students camped out on the islands four or five times over the course of two months, studying their history and ecological health. Their final step was to draw a set of pictures of island scenes, which were turned into postcards. The state

---

*In light of the pummeling that many schools have suffered in these pages for doing poorly on standardized tests, it is only fair to note that Expeditionary Learning schools, which have been part of the ill-fated New American Schools project, have never distinguished themselves on this front either. While this is a sign of some real weaknesses, at some of these schools students have learned to handle scientific inquiries and other "investigations" like professionals— a practice that many schools might do well to follow.

park service was so impressed with the students' work, which compiled information that the service itself had never had, that students were invited to speak at fancy dinners and display their postcards for sale at park sites.

In setting up this project, Harbor made sure that computers would be used only in the simplest of ways. (During the writing, for example, teachers stripped the computers of all but one font choice, so students wouldn't waste time toying with typeface designs.) And Hartel, an engaging, fresh-faced young man, was adamant that all the artwork be done by hand. "Clip art will not be used in our school," he said. Hartel expects computers to play a growing role in Harbor academics, but he's leery of these machines. "If we're going to encourage beautiful work, clip art will only cheapen that," he told me. "Electronic portfolios are not for us, either. We will use computers, but I fear that eight out of ten times, they cheapen rather than deepen the work."

Hartel's determination to hold the barricades made me curious to see what students *were* doing on computers at Harbor. I was particularly interested in how they might approach writing—a big priority here.

Much like at P.S. 234, Harbor puts students through a carefully layered approach to writing, which includes an initial period of random brainstorming and multiple stages of revision. In the process, students must focus not only on basic grammar but also on advanced concerns such as content, structure, and style. Many schools talk this game; very few really practice it. But Harbor does, and its piles of student reports were proof. Every one included at least three drafts, in pencil, many of which were heavily adorned with a teacher's red marks. In report after report, it was clear that no matter what level of skill or motivation students brought to the table, they were indeed pushed to "deepen" as writers. "Our writing is mostly tied to projects, because these kids have got to have something to write about. They're experience-poor," Christina Patterson, an eighth-grade teacher, told me. Since the computer's copy-and-paste functions can so easily facilitate both writing and editing, I assumed that a visit to Harbor's computer lab would be a special treat. But I was surprised to find that students weren't making the slightest use of these functions. "They basically just come in here to type up their final drafts," the lab instructor told me.

When I later shared this encounter with Hartel, he was equally surprised. At this point, I was getting pretty discouraged. If good progressive schools can't get this machine right, what's going on? I began to think that computers had become education's cultural imperialists. They were now the McDonald's of the schools, bringing a vanilla shake and a greasy burger to every culture they touch. Hartel woefully agreed.

An even stranger illustration of this syndrome occurred across town, at Cambridge's Morse Elementary School. Morse follows the back-to-basics Core Knowledge program, which was founded by E. D. Hirsch, the conservative professor of education and humanities from the University of Virginia. As an experiment, I spent most of my time at Morse just hanging out in the computer lab to see how different classes functioned here. Morse runs from kindergarten through eighth grade, and most of those classes tromped in and out of the lab when I was there for their regular computer hours. Morse, like most Core Knowledge schools, is generously funded, and this was abundantly reflected in its lab, which was filled with twenty-four brand-new Apple iMacs, all of which were networked and connected to the Internet. Yet, oddly, whenever a whole class tried to log on to the same program or website, this state-of-the-art system promptly stalled, sometimes for up to twenty minutes.

As powerful as these machines were, despite the system jams, almost every class used them for little more than typing practice. They would stumble in full of excitement, log on to whatever program the teacher chose, pull out their penciled rough drafts, wait for the computer to make a connection, wait some more, and eventually start typing. Most of these students had never had any typing instruction, a reality in virtually every school I visited. So their writing on computers, even in the upper grades, was painfully slow. After an hour or so, their screens would be full of a couple clean-looking but syntactically awkward paragraphs. Then it was time to call it a day.

While observing students in this lab and in a few Morse classrooms that use computers, I was particularly surprised at the lack of traditional academic rigor—the attribute for which Core Knowledge schools are most famous. So at one point I asked the principal, David Coady, to explain the school's approach to computer technology. "I think we're a pragmatic school," Coady said. "My priority is an orderly climate." This was not surprising. Coady, a former elementary school teacher and football coach, is a clean-cut, exceptionally fit man in his sixties; he has a military bearing, highlighted by a white shirt tailored with tucks at the waist. His explanation of the school's technology program left me a little unsatisfied, so I asked him again, this time trying to be clearer. What kinds of things was Morse specifically trying to do with technology, I asked, to carry out the Core Knowledge philosophy? Coady looked at me blankly for a moment, then said, "I more or less leave it up to the teachers to work that out."

One of the Morse teachers who had put the most effort into working that out was Karen Spalding, a science teacher. Spalding was actually something of a mole at Morse, favoring student projects that smacked more of progressive teaching methods than those espoused by Morse's back-to-basics godfather. During my visit, for example, she had eighth graders out gathering weather data for a project on hurricanes; for the sixth grade, she had set up projects drawn from a National Science Foundation program called Genscope. The program let students play around with simulated DNA combinations to create fictional dragons, to amplify a biology lesson in genetics. Interestingly, the day I watched her genetics lesson, the computer network was down. This meant that students couldn't play with the DNA combinations on their own, at the bank of terminals that lined the classroom walls. As an alternative, Spalding loaded the program onto her own computer and projected it on a screen at the front of the room. The DNA choices then became a group game, which provoked considerable anticipation, laughter, and lots of discussion. Tom Snyder would have been pleased.

The bottom-line message of this landscape is disturbingly simple: The challenge of school culture is complicated enough; invasions that further complicate the picture, such as computer technology, should be kept to a bare minimum—perhaps at even more of a minimum than the way these relatively low-tech schools use them. Much the same conclusion has been drawn by a few education experts that have studied school reform. An illustration occurred in early 2002, when the Brookings Institution convened a panel of school-reform analysts in Washington, D.C. In the new federal budget, Congress and President Bush had once again codified the need for "comprehensive school reform," increasing spending on broad reform plans to $310 million. But as the panelists exchanged thoughts, many noticed the evidence that most "comprehensive" reform plans were failing because they were trying to do too much. "Less dramatic reforms"—such as summer school, teacher training, and basic curriculum changes—"may not get the attention they deserve," said one panelist, Jeffrey Mirel, a professor of educational studies and history at the University of Michigan. These ideas, Mirel said, "could be as or more effective than whole-school reform."[5]

NAVIGATING THE SEAS OF COMMERCE

One of the great conundrums of technology is that a machine's opportunities are inextricably connected to its problems. You can't, for example, introduce students to the latest in multimedia graphics tools without also getting embroiled in befuddling technical glitches. And you can't let students freely search university scientific research on the World Wide Web without also giving them access to bogus scientific claims, to say nothing of the rest of the Internet's trash.

Then again, a few well-compiled Internet sites or a challenging software program can be worth more than a bad book. In other words, navigating technology's good and bad options may be difficult, but in the end the challenge is pretty straightforward: Technology simply presents more choices. And there ought to be a dependable "KISS" way to filter them. Indeed there is. In most cases, all that's missing is the will to do it.

An interesting illustration of this fact grew out of a meeting of the American Psychological Association in October 2000. The group had convened at the National Press Club, in Washington, D.C., to call attention to the paucity of knowledge about how media technology affects children, both positively and negatively, and to the need for substantive research. At the end of the day's presentations, the participants divided into eight groups, each of which was supposed to come up with a plan of action. Most groups made relatively obvious calls for more research on this issue or that, but a few went further. Two groups suggested creating some sort of review board for the various media products that are marketed to children, both in homes and in schools. One idea was to give this review board some real muscle, signified by its proposed acronym: PCMA, for President's Council of Media Advisors.

Before we balk at the scent of government interference, it's worth pausing a moment to consider its possibilities and its precedents. First, there is no need to saddle this process with any regulatory authority; it can instead function much like the Green Seal certification that is given to various products deemed to be environmentally safe. No company is forced to submit to Green Seal review—they do so voluntarily, when they believe their products warrant it, knowing that this seal of approval will add immeasurably to their marketing appeal. Second, as noted earlier, an organization called EPIE (Educational Products Information Exchange) once conducted a promising campaign of this sort in the 1980s but had to abandon the project because the time and costs required far surpassed what a tiny non-profit could manage. Considering the exponential growth in computer media today, reviving this process with some government funding and coordination seems perfectly sensible.*

---

*Interestingly, there already has been one version of this idea, published on the Internet by the Entertainment Software Rating Board (*www.media-awareness.ca/eng/indus/games/esrb. htm#works*). The ratings are organized much the way movie ratings are—with six general categories, according to what age level the material is suited for, from early childhood to adults

Following the APA meeting, its organizers considered proposing the PCMA idea to the National Science Foundation (NSF), along with its requests for research funding. As it turned out, the NSF wasn't interested in the organization's questions about school computing, so the APA dropped its momentary sense of urgency. Subsequent APA conferences focused on reviews of past research and discussions of its members' favorite school software. Curiously absent was any burning desire to look further into this material's effects on a youngster's mind—presumably the question that a psychological association would be most suited to address. This left the prospects of any broad action to anti-technology activists, who have always been on the issue's fringes and will likely remain there. It also leaves schools to battle the forces of commerce on their own. From all indications, it's not been a terribly even match thus far. So perhaps a few simple guidelines can be of help.

Each school, obviously, has its own curricular emphasis, and thus a slightly different priority for how computers are used. But each school might also help itself tremendously by setting up the simplest system it can. This could be a one-computer classroom, à la Tom Snyder; a few drawers full of open-ended, low-tech devices, like those Bob Albrecht uses; a handful of Internet connections in the school library for online research; and, for high schools, a true, modern-day shop class—that is, one full of computers that students can take apart. In fact, if schools wanted an extremely simple technology that could teach high-order reasoning skills, they could invest in a bunch of $15 chess games. Since the late 1800s, chess has been proven in study after study to expand players' capacity for concentration, visual memory, quick calculation, logical thinking, problem-solving, and even creativity.[6]

---

only. But as everyone knows from experience with the R and PG ratings of movies, this doesn't offer the most informative system of guidance.

Improving this process should not be difficult. The first step is to assemble a range of experts on media and child development including media enthusiasts as well as skeptics. The council would solicit submissions from those who produce electronic media for youngsters that they consider educational (movies, TV shows, computer software, websites, etc.). The submissions could include studies or other material that the producers believe proves the products' value. Then, much as the Green Seal determinants do, the PCMA would review the material and issue an Educational Seal of Approval to those deemed worthy. The council might also issue periodic reports of these evaluations, with rankings, so consumers could learn more, particularly about products that caused the council concern.

JAPAN'S EXAMPLE

O ver the decades, America has expended a lot of energy worrying about Asia, and especially Japan, during periods when its economy has been ascendant and ours has been moving in the other direction. In the early 1990s, James Fallows of *The Atlantic Monthly* found that much of America's insecurity in this regard was gravely misplaced, an argument that seemed to pan out as Japan faltered and the United States strengthened during the latter half of that decade. Fallows argued that chasing Asia's model was a cultural impossibility anyway; as with any society, Asia's peoples are shaped by conscious and unconscious values that we can never understand, let alone imitate. In a 1989 book, *More Like Us*, Fallows urged American policy makers to renew their attention to our own values—the spirit of adventure, experimentation, and egalitarianism that are among the basic attributes of our democracy.[7]

Today, Fallows's advice could apply to American schools. Over time, in fact, Japan's educational system has stolen and refined so many of America's most powerful education traditions that we'd have to become more like them to be more like us. There might be some percentage in going this route. According to the Third International Mathematics and Science Study (TIMSS), Japanese and American students are roughly on a par in science in the fourth grade; by the seventh grade, though, Japanese students are far ahead. They rank near the top of all countries that participate in this study, while American students score roughly in the middle. This puts American seventh graders 23 points lower than their Japanese counterparts—nearly the equivalent of one American grade level.[8]

In the late 1990s, a team of American researchers traveled to Japan to figure out why this was happening. They studied Japan's educational system, then spent many weeks observing science classes in the elementary grades. What they found was an approach steeped in the values of America's great education philosophers—principally, John Dewey and the Harvard psychologist Jerome Bruner. In essence, the class exercises they witnessed revolved around active exploration, argument, analysis, and reflection. Rather than rushing from topic to topic as most American schools do, in an effort to keep pace with mounting government standards and assessments, Japanese classes lingered on discrete problems, examining them from every angle, sometimes for weeks on end. Curiously, this environment is firmly at odds with the common American image of Japanese schools, which presumes that students do nothing but memorize late into the night.

As it turns out, a relentless ingestion of facts does occur in Japan, but it's part of high school culture, as a vetting process for Japan's competitive universities. In the country's elementary schools, life has been very different indeed.*

Take classroom scenes as examples, where students embark on a study of matter. As the class begins, the teachers don't start with a lecture or a reading to supply students with the facts. Instead, they started with questions. For instance, one teacher asks, "Do you think all matter has weight?" Another, launching an aquatic biology lesson, wonders aloud what killifish eat in the water, then pauses to hear what students think. The goal is to provoke students' curiosity, bring out their existing knowledge or misconceptions, and spark their imagination. From there, the teacher sends students off on a preliminary project to test their hunches. This leads to rounds of group discussion, which helps students plan formal investigations. Throughout the process, the teacher offers comments that help students see distinctions and distortions so that they can lay out their work systematically. On and on it goes, mirroring the labors of professional scientists as closely as youngsters can.

Not surprisingly, the intellectual groundwork that goes into this experimentation is equally multifaceted. Tom Rohlen, a Stanford professor of education who has studied and written extensively about Japan, has found that Japanese teachers tend to emphasize textbook work much more than American teachers do—largely because Japanese texts are so much more thorough than ours. "There aren't all the illustrations and the desperate efforts to make learning fun," Rohlen says. "They're really wonderful, elegant texts, especially in math and science." In each of these subjects, Rohlen found that where American instructors teach a topic in a few steps, the Jap-

---

*In yet another twist in the endless competition between the United States and Japan, it appeared that the tranquil atmosphere of reflection in Japanese classrooms that American researchers found had begun to fade in the early years of the twenty-first century. Students were increasingly disorderly, even violent, and dropout rates were suddenly high. Japanese started referring to the phenomenon as "classroom collapse." As educators searched for reasons, some blamed Japan's failing economy, which was sapping students' faith in the future; some blamed insufficient funding of the schools, which was leaving classrooms understaffed; and others blamed Japan's parents, who were starting to spoil children with diversions like cell phones instead of spending time with them. The result, according to one teacher, was a generation of students who were lonely and materialistic. In other words, Japan was becoming more like the United States. This of course opens up an opportunity for America to learn another international lesson and finally get ahead of Japan, at least academically, and stay there. See "Educators Try to Tame Japan's Blackboard Jungles," by Howard W. French, *The New York Times*, September 23, 2002, p. A6.

anese break the process down into numerous stages. As Catherine Lewis, a senior research scientist in the Department of Education at Mills College and the leader of the Japanese school research team, put it, "In the U.S., we do things quickly. Then we have to do them over and over again."

As Japanese science classes progress, the teachers continually invite criticism—from students and from fellow teachers, who frequently observe the instruction. Sometimes the criticism is harsh. In one class, the teacher had set up an uncontrolled experiment, in which students constructed pendulums to sort out the effects of weight, speed, and distance. In a video of the seventh of nine classes on this project, children as young as ten or eleven stood up and offered withering critiques of their classmates' procedures—and their teachers'. As they spoke, the teacher beamed with pleasure.[9]

It is complicated stuff to dissect the process of science in such detail. To allow room for the complexity, the Japanese—a people whom many Americans regard as technological fanatics, if not geniuses—stuck to simple physical materials. In each classroom, there wasn't a calculator or a computer in sight.

CHAPTER 13

The Human Touch

Driving down out of the foothills of Yuba County, California, one dawn, past wide, frosty fruit orchards and abandoned stony gold mines, I asked my escort, Ruth Mikkelsen, the principal of the local school for juvenile offenders, what the area's main industry was. "Methamphetamine," she said with a chuckle. No wonder. Yuba County lives with some of California's most dismal demographic statistics. Its unemployment rate has hovered around 12.8 percent, twice the state average. Teen pregnancy rates and the proportion of children on welfare are among the state's highest. The county consistently sends a larger percentage of its adults to prison than any other county in California. It's also had the state's lowest percentage of youngsters who go to college, its highest proportion of children classified as low income (68 percent), and the state's stingiest dads when it comes to child-support payments.[1]

Down in the flats, the fields are bordered by mile upon mile of gargantuan river levees, built by the Chinese in the late 1800s, when they were brought to this part of the world to construct the railroads. Entering Marysville, the county seat, we pass a scattering of burnt-out storefronts bandaged with dry, broken boards—reminders that until the 1950s, this town was still famous for its healthy economy of bars, brothels, opium dens, and gambling houses. Descendants of those unruly days now fill Ruth Mikkelsen's classrooms at Thomas E. Mathews Community School. "If you take all the kids who are being thrown out of school and put them in one room, those are the kids we have," Mikkelsen said. "One of those kids in a normal class will pretty much destroy that class."

It wasn't hard to see what she meant. When we pulled up to the school, a group of boys playing basketball on a crumbling court out front were guarding each other with real hostility. Inside, a dozen boys and girls, dressed in the school's official uniform of blue jeans and white T-shirts, jostled and sassed one another in the tiny common room. One hulking skin-head leaned against the wall, alone, slump-shouldered, quiet, angry-looking.

Underneath this toughness, one could also see signs of softness and hope. Before I'd even started exploring, Gary, a skinny fourteen-year-old, spontaneously grabbed me for a quick tour of what I had come to watch: how the Waldorf School movement, an old Austria-bred system of private education, is working in a new venue—a hard-boiled public institution for real troublemakers. After introducing me to each of his teachers, Gary walked me past the primary tools of the Waldorf day: the recorders every student learns to play, the numerous paintings and art projects, and a pile of "main lesson books"—lengthy creative reports in each academic subject that the students must generate every few weeks.

Later, during an English class, I noticed a fifteen-year-old I'll call Robert waving his hand desperately. A small boy with an angelic walnut-brown face, Robert had been expelled from his previous school for smoking mari-juana; soon after his arrival at Mathews, he jumped out the probation offi-cer's window and ran away. On the day I visited, about a year after his return, Robert sat attentively through a two-hour class. When the teacher finally called on him, he flawlessly recited six lines he had memorized from *The Merchant of Venice*. Evelyn Arcuri, the teacher, told me that in the early days when she would ask the students to return their materials, "they would just toss stuff at me. Now there's better control. They're more engaged." I soon noticed something similar. One twelve-year-old boy sat with me after school, regaling me, in enthusiastic detail, with a creative mixture of Greek and Roman history. The boy could barely read, but he'd been inspired by the oral storytelling that Waldorf teachers emphasize. These roughnecks even like Waldorf's focus on art. Thomas, an outgoing and restless seventeen-year-old, had found that when he was forced to draw pictures of stories he had read or heard, "you get more visual ideas of what you're doing." Arcuri believes she can see that occur. "This year kids are saying, 'Can I take this home?' We never had that happen before."

Mikkelsen and her teachers attribute these changes to the battery of skills they have learned at Rudolf Steiner College, a small private school near Sacramento that serves as the West Coast teacher-training center for Waldorf schools. Much of what teachers learn there is how to reach children through their senses. Child-development experts have long advocated multisensory approaches to learning—as a way both to deeply imprint lessons in a youngster and to accommodate the different learning styles that are bound to exist among diverse students, particularly those with learning difficulties. Yet few education systems in this country have the history with these methods that Waldorf schools do. "I now have a way to give it to them many times, in different ways," Arcuri told me. "We had tried everything with these kids," Mikkelsen recalls. "Nothing worked. You can't lecture to them. Independent study doesn't work. They need constant support and a lot of socializing." During Mikkelsen's discussions with teachers at the Steiner College, "I said to them, 'If this is so good, if Rudolf Steiner is as hot as you say, then this will work for our kids. Otherwise, it's another bunch of elitist B.S.' "

Several years later an outside evaluator dropped by the Mathews School. After his visit he told Mikkelsen that the effectiveness of her program for juvenile offenders couldn't be fairly judged because it was clear that she did not have truly problem kids. "I suddenly realized it was working," Mikkelsen recalls. John Cobb, the local probation manager, has had the same feeling. "Kids who can't make it anywhere else can make it here," he told me. In 1999, a Stanford University researcher found empirical support for Mikkelsen and Cobb's impressions. Sixty-two percent of the youngsters who had attended Mathews for as little as three quarters of the year had advanced two or more grade levels in reading and math.[2] Interestingly, these accomplishments match or trump the fixes that technology reformers promote, despite their greater costs, as being education's most effective path to improvement.

The cause of the changes at Mathews, and the unusual mixture of teaching techniques behind them, are well illustrated by the Waldorf "main lesson books," the system's academic core. The books are filled with students' careful records of field trips and classroom experiments; impressions of the teachers' regular oral presentations; and, in more advanced classes, syntheses of what the students have read in primary sources. (Waldorf teachers avoid textbooks, considering their digested information a poor substitute for original material.) Thumbing through the students' main lesson books, the first thing one notices is that they're all neatly handwritten—in fountain pen.* The books are generally accompanied by detailed drawings and poetry, some of which the students have written themselves. Playfulness is encouraged, because Waldorf teachers believe that imaginative speculation can be just as educational as objective facts and conclusions, if not more so.

This notion, that imagination is the heart of learning, animates the entire arc of Waldorf teaching. When that concept is coupled with the schools' other fundamental goal, to give youngsters a sense of ethics, the result is a pedagogy that stands even further apart from today's educational system, with its growing emphasis on national performance standards, its demand for hurried achievement in subjects such as reading and mathematics, and its increasing rigor in standardized testing—to say nothing of the campaign to fill classrooms with computers. This is not to suggest that Waldorf schools have a monopoly on contrarian ideas; Quaker and other religious schools teach ethics, too. And various alternative academies, like the renowned Montessori schools, have long taken adventurous approaches to learning. Some Waldorf practices resemble those in some of these other alternative schools. But that makes a study of the Waldorf method all the more intriguing.

It is odd, actually, that the public knows so little about Waldorf schools, because they've been operating in this country since 1928; in the process, they have collected quite a few famous followers (Waldorf parents have included Paul Newman, Joe Namath, John DeLorean, and Mikhail Baryshnikov; graduates include Victor Navasky, the publisher of *The Nation*, and Ken Chenault, president of American Express). During the past twenty-five years in particular, Waldorf schools have proliferated vigorously. By the turn of the twenty-first century, roughly 130 were operating in the United States and 700 worldwide. Waldorf schools may well be the world's fastest-growing independent school system. In the view of David Alsop, chairman of the Association of Waldorf Schools of North America, they are the world's "best-kept education secret."

The secret is slowly getting out. In the past decade, several dozen public schools have adopted Waldorf methods in an effort to enliven classrooms that many educators see as having become sterile academic factories. Unfortunately, some Waldorf methods have caused trouble of their own, both in public schools and in private Waldorf classrooms. There has been contro-

---

*As nostalgic as this may seem, there's hidden practical value to these exercises. Many schools have cut back on the time they devote to teaching cursive handwriting, a facility that students will sorely miss when, beginning in 2005, they have to compose handwritten essays for the SAT.

versy and a lawsuit, stemming largely from the attention that Waldorf teachers pay to their somewhat unorthodox form of spirituality. (To some critics, this threatens the prevailing taboo against teaching religion in a public school.) Running through these bumps, however, is a substantial record of achievement—one that has earned the respect of a number of leading figures, from Howard Gardner, the prominent Harvard professor of education and psychology, to the well-known education reformer Theodore Sizer to Saul Bellow, whose hero in the novel *Humboldt's Gift* is fascinated by the philosophy of Waldorf's creator.[3]

PROLETARIAN BEGINNINGS

Waldorf education was born one spring day in 1919, when Rudolf Steiner, a maverick Austrian philosopher and scientist, visited the Waldorf-Astoria cigarette factory in Stuttgart, Germany, to give a speech to its workers. Given the international devastation that followed the terrorist attacks on the United States in the fall of 2001, the circumstances of Waldorf's beginnings hold particular meaning. The First World War had ended just five months earlier, and Steiner, like many Europeans, was shaken by its unprecedented bloodshed. He talked about the need for a new social order, a new sense of ethics, and a less damaging way of resolving conflict.

After the lecture, Emil Molt, the cigarette-factory owner, asked Steiner if he would consider starting a school for the workers' children. Steiner agreed, insisting on some conditions, including that his school be run by the teachers. (That rule, which remains, has spawned occasionally chaotic but cooperative styles of Waldorf school management. It also prefigured the modern-day theory, popularized by the Yale psychiatrist and school reformer James Comer, that for education to work, teachers and parents must be involved in school decisions.) Steiner further insisted on a highly ambitious curriculum. "The need for imagination, a sense of truth and a feeling of responsibility—these are the three forces which are the very nerve of education," he once said.[4] Twenty years after the Stuttgart school opened, the Nazis shut it down, along with six other Waldorf schools that had sprung up by then. The reason, according to the state press at the time, was that Germany had no room for two kinds of education—one that educated citizens for the state and another that taught children to think for themselves.[5]

By then seven other Waldorf schools had been started around the world—three in Switzerland and one each in London, Budapest, Oslo, and New York City. (The Waldorf schools in Germany reopened after the Nazi regime was decimated, and the German contingent now numbers approximately 140.) Today, although the schools' Old World academic philosophy runs counter to some academic trends, it may dovetail with others. "All the things you read about public schools," Mikkelsen told me, "that you need to do this, you need to do that—hell, they've been doing it for eighty years."

Mikkelsen was referring to the myriad reforms that policy makers incessantly propose in order to reverse a range of problems besetting American youngsters: gradually weakening morality and family structure; students' shrinking attention span and declining capacity for creativity and self-discipline; their diminishing appreciation for the nuances of language in reading, writing, and conversation; their increasing turns to violence; and graduates' spotty preparation for the professional world. "The most serious problem in schools is kids not getting along," Steve Grineski, the interim dean of the College of Education and Human Services at Moorhead State University, in Minnesota, says. "The reason people get fired isn't their lack of job skills, it's their lack of social skills." That is precisely why Mikkelsen was attracted to Waldorf. "It's like learning to be a really good parent, plus tapping into every creative thing you ever thought of," she says. Ben Klocek, a high school senior at the Sacramento Waldorf School, whose family has been intimately involved in Waldorf for years, puts it this way: "Have you ever heard of that thing about emotional intelligence?" His question refers to Daniel Goleman's provocative 1995 book *Emotional Intelligence*, which suggested that IQ isn't nearly as important as personal traits such as self-awareness, confidence, and flexibility. "Waldorf," Klocek says, "gives you very high emotional intelligence."

This may be true for Klocek, a multitalented young man, who grew up with the twin luxuries of a private school education and the careful guidance of unusually well educated parents, both of whom were also master Waldorf teachers. But what happens in the gritty, underfunded, overbureaucratized world of public education, where it sometimes seems as though teachers need things like multimedia games to hold students' attention? At T. E. Mathews, I did notice a few state-of-the-art computers in one room. Yet judging from teachers' accounts and my own observations, the students were generally more interested in Waldorf exercises. This despite the fact that the school practices only some of the Waldorf program, the full complement of which is too involved for a thinly educated student body that comes and goes as this one does. This seemed curious, and it sent me to poking around other Waldorf schools in the United States for many weeks. I visited both Waldorf public schools serving the underprivileged and a good number of the system's old, private institutions—a detour from my public school regimen but one taken for specific reasons.

Deborah Meier, the founder of Harlem's Central Park East Elementary School and the legendary queen of modern-day progressive school reform, likes to offer an in-your-face answer to the question of how to help poor students: Give them the same kinds of schools the rich kids get. Traditionalists may be inclined to dismiss her suggestion, believing that public schools could never afford the kinds of experiences students get in private schools. But some intriguing private school programs aren't nearly so lavish, Waldorf being one example. (A typical fifth-grade education at a private Waldorf school, for instance, costs $8,275. This is roughly 45 percent more than what taxpayers pay for a student's fifth-grade year in public school, but it's about average by private school standards.)[6] And by all indications, the Waldorf ethic travels well—something that can't be said about a lot of school initiatives, including most that use computer technology. It also has produced some fertile cross-pollination, as Waldorf leaders learn a few things from the hard-nosed public school system. All of this made me curious to explore both the public and the private half of the Waldorf world. I wanted to see how everyone was faring in realizing Steiner's dreams of enriching youngsters' imaginations and ethical, even nonviolent, sensibilities, and then examine how those dreams were being translated in scrappy, standards-driven public school life.

A TALE OF TWO SCHOOLS

In a corner of Milwaukee's run-down northern edge, where crack-cocaine deals and prostitution have been neighborhood fixtures, lies a long, flat, modern brick building that until recently was an education researcher's dream. It was nirvana, in fact, for anyone specifically interested in the education of poor black children and how they may be helped or hindered by technology—as compared with decidedly low-tech practices. In a sense, the building functioned like a pair of urban test tubes. As part of a district initiative to test some experimental ideas, two alternative elementary schools moved into this building and operated side by side for a number of years. Each was a public school serving the same grades, K–5, with roughly the same number of students. Each drew from the same demographics: mostly neighborhood kids, mostly black, and mostly poor (roughly three quarters of each school's student body is deemed poor enough to be given a federal free lunch—public education's great dividing line for poverty). Each school got the same district funding per student, and by the turn of the twenty-first century, each one had been in operation for a decade.

That's where the similarities stop. One of these institutions, the Frances Starms Discovery Learning Center School, has energetically devoted itself to a panoply of current education-reform ideas, one of the most noticeable being computer technology. The other facility is the Urban Waldorf School, and its teaching methods are based partly on the *avoidance* of technology, especially in these early-grade-school years. Urban Waldorf has since moved to its own building nearby, to accommodate its expansion to grade eight, which has left the whole building to Starms. In late 1999, however, when the two schools operated here side by side, the contrast between their very different paths was eye-opening. One could see it in the atmosphere in their classrooms; in teachers' accounts of their experiences; in the financial costs of school operations; and, perhaps most important, in their differing results in student achievement.

The Starms Learning Center, in many ways, has had nearly every advantage that a hard-luck urban school could wish for. It has received a series of generous grants over the years, totaling $390,000. The school has not exactly poured this money into its teaching staff. (In 2002, the school had 328 students and sixteen teachers, creating a student-teacher ratio of roughly twenty to one. To somewhat soften this load, Starms has hired ten teacher's aides, a slighter larger complement than is typical for a school this size.) The various grants have, however, brought an abundance of high-technology equipment (a large, well-appointed computer laboratory, a dozen digital cameras, four computerized scanning machines, and a fancy teleconferencing system). Sugaring all this has been an assortment of initiatives that have let the school taste almost every new school-reform dish that's come along. "Every research-based innovation that was considered good for kids—every one was sort of built into the system here," Betty Hilton, the school's technology consultant, told me. Nonetheless, Hilton acknowledges, "our standardized test scores are pitiful." As an illustration, more than half the school's fourth graders have tested at "minimal" levels in reading; 42 percent earn the same low ranking in science, 33 percent in social studies, and 29 percent in math. Roughly similar proportions of students have fallen into the next higher category (suggesting that they possess nothing more than "basic" skills). Overall, between 1997 and 2000, less than 10 percent were ranked as "advanced" in any subject; on most subjects, the numbers were below 5 percent.[7] The result is that Starms students have been among the district's lowest performers. Reading skills are so weak, Hilton said, that "we can't go forward with social studies."

It doesn't take long to see why. In the computer lab, second and third graders spend hours assembling inane collections of computer graphics with Kid Pix, the ubiquitous grade-school multimedia program. For some, the simplest functions are such a struggle that the mere assembly of a few images is all the teacher expects; others easily assemble their composites within minutes, then dump them without a thought. In another class, fourth and fifth graders are preparing science reports on animals, which consumed nine weeks of research in books and on the Internet. One boy's report on lions, which reads much like his classmates', tells me the following: "A lion can grow up to 10 feet long. A lion can eat 75 pounds of meat." Along with several other similar sentences, there are photos taken with the school's new digital camera, the piece of the project of which the teacher seems particularly proud. In another fifth-grade class, history reports on "Who Really Discovered America?" contain about the same level of detail. If this is the Discovery Learning Center, where, I kept wondering, is the discovery?

A good number of Starms students are "special-needs" children— youngsters with learning disabilities of one kind or another, precisely the sort of child that computers often reach. During a tutorial hour, I watch one of these high-tech outreach efforts unfold as a teacher with a saint's patience sits with a catatonic third grader, slowly working him through a Kid Pix program that is supposed to connect to his senses. (There is a section on his screen where he can place images of things in his neighborhood that he can hear, another for things he can smell, a third for things he can touch, and so on.) Despite the teacher's labors, the program doesn't appear to stimulate any of his senses, let alone his basic understanding. Eventually, Hilton leans toward me and whispers that the boy is heavily medicated, so much so that by mid-afternoon he's toast. Okay. What about the unmedicated? Hilton shows me some projects that first and second graders have done, for which they used computers to scan in pencil sketches of their neighborhoods, then turned on the computer's microphone to tell a local story. "Younger kids can't write very well," she says with a smile, "but they can *talk* about their pictures. When you work with both art and sound, you're working with different learning styles." That sounds good. Then I realize that the Waldorf school next door gets a number of special-education cases too. How do they manage this responsibility without technology's help?

———

When I walk into a third-grade class across the hall, I find myself in one of Waldorf's famous "knitting hours"—part of its age-old custom of teaching students what it calls hand work. Knitting is so central to Waldorf's early grades that students spend almost a year knitting flute cases, which they use to store recorders that they start playing in first grade. It is autumn, and this particular class is knitting wool hats for the coming winter. Since the Waldorf school has put more of its money into certified teachers (the school has twenty-five teachers compared with Starms's sixteen), this class, like many at Waldorf, is without a teacher's aide. Nor is there quite the same plethora of progressive extras that Starms offers—the rugs and special reading corners, the brightly colored commercial posters and computers and overflowing boxes of supplies. In this class, there are just a few handmade items in the corner, a wall of books, some artwork and handwritten stories on the wall, a rolling cart with knitting supplies, and rows and rows of students at Masonite desks, all facing the blackboard.* (Waldorf classes are not small. Typically numbering twenty to twenty-five students, they're considerably larger than what's seen in many leading progressive schools but are not terribly different from the public school norm.) To set an atmosphere of calm and concentration in this crowd, the teacher has dimmed the lights. It seems to help. Quiet reigns. When students have something to say, they raise their hand or whisper.

As I tour the room, most of the students ask if I want to look at their work. When I do so, they explain their knitting with such care and innocent pride, I can't help feeling touched. Their investment in these fuzzy little hats

---

*Blackboards are a centerpiece of Waldorf pedagogy, and consciously honored (with detailed drawings and inscriptions by the teachers, among other things) far more than is customary in most schools. Interestingly, there may be more to this practice than a Luddite love of old-fashioned tools. In the late 1990s, when a research team affiliated with UCLA examined the results from the new Third International Math and Sciences Study (TIMSS-R), they came up with some surprising insights into why some students do well and others don't. After they gathered detailed video recordings of eighth-grade classes from seven different countries involved in the math and science study, one difference consistently stood out: Schools in many countries still use blackboards, but American teachers increasingly use overhead projection screens. While these screens are often praised for their flexibility, they encourage teachers to present material in bits and pieces, which come and go quickly. By contrast, in Japan, for example, teachers believe in maintaining a complete record of the entire lesson (on the blackboard), which offers both slow and fast students opportunities to revisit ideas as needed and thus deepen their understanding. This is one reason, the researchers surmised, that Japanese math and science students typically best their American counterparts. See *The Teaching Gap: Best Ideas from the World's Teachers for Improving Education in the Classroom*, by James W. Stigler and James Hiebert, Free Press, 1999, pp. 73–75.

and their appreciation for what they are accomplishing is a quantum leap beyond what I just saw across the hall in Starms's $80,000 computer lab. There, and in almost every other computerized classroom I have visited, no one but the teacher cared whether or not I looked at the students' work. While the students knit, I glance through the main lesson books at the back of the room (and, later, those of a fourth-grade class next door). The contrast between these dense booklets, illustrated with nothing more than colored pencils, and the much thinner reports of the Starms students, who were one and two grades farther along, was remarkable.

What about Waldorf's special-education students? With a minimal amount of computer technology (only fourth and fifth graders use computers, and only for writing) and nothing close to the extra grants and teaching aides that Starms has had (the only grant that Urban Waldorf has received was one $150,000 grant in 1998 for three years of staff development), the school seems to take on the special-education challenge with two strikes against itself. It's as though the Waldorfians have stuck their heads in the sand, leaving these poor students to subsist on antiquated answers. Or that's how it appears. In actuality, the school has employed two specialists to work with their learning-disabled students in small groups, where the students could relax and try out Waldorf's unique methods of learning through the senses. Although this approach may sound as fuzzy as the third graders' precious wool hats, it has plenty of pedagogical research behind it. And it has delivered solid, old-fashioned results. After stumbling a little the first few years, the school has consistently beaten both district and national averages on test scores. A table of its scores is almost the polar opposite of the Starms scores. Except for the 2000–2001 year, when the Waldorf scores dropped, most of its fourth graders have tested in the top categories ("proficient" or "advanced") in all subject areas; only a small percentage have remained at "minimal" levels.[8] One of the areas in which they're most accomplished has been reading, a domain in which Waldorf is notorious for seeming to be almost lackadaisical.

These achievements have been only mildly surprising to Dorothy St. Charles, Urban Waldorf's principal through the 1990s. St. Charles was a veteran public school principal before she ever heard of Waldorf, but she became intrigued with the program when introduced to it a decade ago by an innovative district superintendent. Since then, the practices have increasingly made sense to her. "Technology is the last thing these kids need," St. Charles told me. "They need association with people, that human touch. They can't get along with each other. They don't know how to talk to each other. They need to be able to work out problems. They need to disagree." To

St. Charles, the Waldorf system provides an exceptionally secure arena for those trials. "I think it's the best thing for urban kids," she said. The reason is a unique combination of elements that, she said, makes these children "feel safe."

THE PRIMACY OF THE IMAGINATION

R udolf Steiner believed that people actually have twelve senses—the accepted five plus thought, language, warmth, balance, movement, life, and a sense of another person's individuality. Vague as some of these additional "senses" sound, most of them have been roughly confirmed under other names by modern research.[9] Waldorf's goal, as John Bloom, administrator of the San Francisco Waldorf School at the time of my visit, explained, is "to avoid the dissonance between the messages of the inner and outer worlds. We try to connect the thinking and feeling realms. When you separate those, therapists get [students] as adult patients." On my visits to Waldorf schools, I felt as if I were watching sensory foundations being built in each class, almost in layers.

Walking into the kindergarten class at the private San Francisco Waldorf School one morning, I felt myself relax. The lights here were dim, the colors soft pastel. Intriguing materials for play were everywhere. The children had organized them into a half-dozen distinctly different fantasy worlds—there was a make-believe woodshop in one corner; in another, reminiscent of a farmhouse bedroom, two girls were putting a curiously bland doll to bed in a cradle. This doll, I learned, is standard issue in Waldorf kindergartens. It's the old-fashioned sort—simple stuffed cotton, but with one significant difference: It had almost no facial features. "The only thing an intelligent child can do with a complete toy is take it apart," a kindergarten teacher told me. "An incomplete toy lets children use their imaginations." There were also wild hats and capes, pinecones and driftwood, bowls of nuts and other items from the natural world. John Bloom explained that despite appearances, the raw materials are not meant to celebrate nature; their purpose is to challenge children's spatial creativity. Automated toys—whether plastic Lego pieces or computerized images—are built to be used or fitted together according to the manufacturer's plan; not so with pinecones or driftwood or clay.

Most adults think it's cute when children imitate whatever they see. Waldorf teachers take it seriously. Susan Kotansky, a former kindergarten teacher at the Westside Community School (a high-performing Waldorf public school in Manhattan that was forced to close when the school district needed its space for offices), recalls that at first her students imitated super-heroes they'd seen on television. In time, after they had worked with their teachers on a variety of physical projects, including cooking, and had listened to fables and fairy tales (a staple in Waldorf primary grades, partly because of their moral lessons), "their play changed and got more purposeful." As idealistic as this sounds, a juvenile prison in Texas, a state famous for being tough on crime, has found that its inmates also can be turned around through the power of fairy tales.[10] Learning through stories as well as practical experience is a concept long advocated by progressive-education leaders, particularly the great reformer John Dewey.[11] In recent years, the idea has been gaining popularity, though it is still rarely put into practice.

To my surprise, young Waldorf children appeared to understand the principles embedded in their exercises—so well, in fact, that they could comfortably explain Steiner's methodology themselves. At the original Waldorf school in the United States, the Rudolf Steiner School, a private institution housed in two limestone townhouses on Manhattan's Upper East Side, I fell into a provocative discussion one morning with a dozen fourth graders. The class was finishing a yearlong project: making mallets, which they'd later use for wood carving. The mallets had to be hewn out of stubborn pieces of hardwood, which the students were patiently filing and sanding by hand. One boy who had finished his mallet was now making a knife out of teak and regularly paused to feel its smoothness on his cheek. When he was ready to oil the finished product, the teacher gathered his classmates in a circle. This struck me as a little precious, until I heard the whole class gasp as the oil, soaking into the wood, brought out a flush of rich yellows and reds. I couldn't help smiling at the students' reaction, since by this point I had watched dozens of high-tech schools spend hundreds of thousands of dollars to provoke similar gasps with computer gear. Here, the whole class had been equally thrilled, if not more so, by very old technology worth about $10. The incident also led several of these children to explain why Waldorf students work on some kind of art project virtually every day. Recalling her early years, Eliana Raviv, a ten-year-old, told me, "We never had green or purple. We make it out of vermilion, red, yellow, and blue, *two* kinds of blue. It's important to get forms out of your own painting. That way you learn how to develop forms."

Private Waldorf students aren't graded on their work until around the seventh grade, a practice that's been sharpened for Waldorf public schools to include specific grade-by-grade standards. At one point, Eliana's classmate Maisie Weir told me about a friend in a traditional public school in Atlanta. "All they think about is tests," she said. "They don't even have recess anymore." Young students also do quite a bit of drawing with crayons—not the standard paraffin Crayolas but thick chunks of beeswax imported from Germany. Softer beeswax, which can be molded after warming in the hand, is also used to teach sculpting. In the early grades, there is an almost bland conformity to most student artwork, particularly the drawing and painting—an oddity that repels more than a few parents. But there's an explicit purpose to this routine: to build a foundation of technique. Sure enough, when I visited a year-end student art show in New York, spanning work from kindergartners through twelfth graders, I could see a steady increase in refinement and individuality. A good portion of the older students' work was so powerful it might easily have been displayed in professional galleries.

But why learn an archaic art like wood carving as we enter the twenty-first century? "You almost need it as a balance for the high-tech world," Tove Elfstrom, the woodshop teacher at the Washington Waldorf School, in Bethesda, Maryland, explained to me during my visit there. "So they can make something. To give them an innate sense of material." Intentionally or not, Elfstrom's comments borrow from scientific research into what children can learn from engagement with physical tasks.[12] As he put it, "Your finger sense develops your overall brain capacity." Waldorf teachers go even further—they believe that one of their primary jobs is to help youngsters develop a strong will. To do that, they argue, students must learn that the rewards they reap from an experience require a commensurate amount of effort—mental, physical, even emotional. Many Waldorf loyalists lay the blame for some of the troubles of today's youth on cultural forces that tilt the balance—technology being chief among them. As Douglas Gerwin, a Waldorf high school teacher, puts it, technology "promises an experience by which we don't have to do anything to make it happen." Gerwin's comment reminded me of my time in Milwaukee, where the Waldorf children were so much more engaged with their knitting than their peers at Starms were with their computer-lab projects. This is why Waldorf teachers discourage younger students from watching television and don't generally expose them to computers until the eighth grade or later. The delay doesn't seem to do much harm. Peter Nitze, a graduate of the Rudolf Steiner School, went on to graduate from Harvard and Stanford and to become global-operations director at AlliedSignal, a company that manufactures aerospace and automotive products. At an open house one night at the Steiner School, Nitze told the audience, "If you've had the experience of binding a book, knitting a sock, playing a recorder, then you feel that you can build a rocket ship—or learn a software program you've never touched. It's not a bravado, just a quiet confidence. There is nothing you can't do. Why couldn't you? Why couldn't anybody?"

Nitze is pointing to what the San Francisco Waldorf School's John Bloom considers one of Waldorf's main priorities. "We are building a capacity for concentration," he told me. And Waldorf's attention to the arts, and to the feelings that the arts can generate, feeds that capacity. Betty Staley, a senior teacher at the Rudolph Steiner College, explained the process this way: As students "live into" stories and other material by painting or drawing their impressions, their emotions inevitably become engaged. And memory, she argued, is linked to emotions. As soon as Staley said this, I recalled one of the few academic exercises I remember from my own early school years. In second grade, a teacher once had us draw abstractly, with colored chalk on black paper, as we listened to classical music. I remember the euphoria of watching my chalk marks spontaneously adjust to the rhythms of the music. I even remember some of the shapes I made.

Music is as central as art in the Waldorf curriculum. Practice begins in first grade, with the recorders the students store in their hand-knitted cases; in fourth grade they each choose an orchestral instrument. A typical Waldorf private school offers several different music classes—at least one choir, an orchestra, and a jazz ensemble in which students learn to improvise and sometimes make their own instruments. All of this helps build students' capacity for concentration. As anyone who has ever played a musical instrument realizes, mastering one takes relentless patience and perseverance—qualities, not coincidentally, that a few studies have suggested are the key ingredients to academic success.[13] Perhaps Rudolf Steiner and his followers intuitively knew what modern science has now confirmed: Music does indeed expand the mind—figuratively and physically.

I sometimes felt as if I were experiencing the genesis of these theories myself during Waldorf's musical exercises. On one occasion, when I joined a Waldorf teacher-training class, I started the day by learning a complex singing round. As I struggled to keep up, I could literally feel my brain being pushed. The process exhausted and stretched me in unfamiliar ways, and made me envious of Waldorf students. My envy peaked one evening in New York City, at a parents' night for the Steiner School. As part of a fund-raiser, several faculty members had arranged to sing cabaret songs. When they finished, some of the eighth graders, who were helping to serve food, decided that they would sing something too. Moments later, the adults sat transfixed as half a dozen teenagers put on an a capella performance of James Taylor's "That Lonesome Road," in slow, layered parts, with the polished harmony of a professional chorus. "All I could think," Chris Huson, a banker and the parent of a Waldorf second grader, told me later, "is that when my kids grow up, I want them to be just like those guys."

═

Emphasis on the creative also guides the aspect of a Waldorf education that probably frightens parents more than any other: the relaxed way that children learn to read. The issue packs an extra punch with President George W. Bush advocating early childhood reading as the centerpiece of his education initiatives.

Whereas students at the most competitive public and private schools are mastering texts in first grade, and sometimes even in kindergarten, most traditional Waldorf students aren't reading fully until the third grade. And if they're still struggling at that point, many Waldorf teachers don't worry. In combination with another oddity of private Waldorf schooling—sending children to first grade a year later than usual—this means that students may not be reading until age nine or ten, several years after many of their peers. In some circles the idea that children might come to reading later, at their own pace, is perfectly normal. David Elkind, a noted child psychologist at Tufts University, cites prodigious evidence, particularly from other countries, that late readers ultimately fare better at reading and other subjects than early readers.[14] A number of prominent figures, including Winston Churchill and Albert Einstein, were very late readers. But with today's competitive frenzy, the drive in this country is to get children to master as much as they can, in reading or any other skill, as early as possible.

It's no surprise, then, that Waldorf parents occasionally panic. Others distrust Waldorf education because they have heard tales of parents who pulled their children out of a Waldorf school in the third grade when their kids still couldn't read. "That's like a standing joke," Toba Winer, the mother of two graduates of the Rudolf Steiner School, told me. "People say, 'Oh, can your kids read?' There was no concerted effort to drum certain words into the kids. And that was the point." Before teaching sound and word recognition, Waldorf teachers concentrate on exercises to build up a child's love of language. The technique seems to work, even in public schools. Barbara Warren, a teacher at John Morse, a public school near Sacramento, says that two years after Waldorf methods were introduced in her fourth-grade class of mostly minority children, the number of students who read at grade level doubled, rising from 45 to 85 percent. "I didn't start by making them read more," Warren says. "I started telling stories and getting them to recite poetry that they learned by listening, not by reading. They became incredible listeners." Dorothy St. Charles has observed the same phenomenon in Milwaukee. "The stories make them curious," she said. "They start making connections. You don't have to *talk* about integrity and discipline and all those things. They see it."

Lending further support in Waldorf private schools is the requirement that every child learn two contrasting foreign languages (Spanish, for instance, is typically paired with German; French, with Russian). The purpose is only partly academic; it's mostly to develop students' ear for sounds and their facility with different parts of the mouth and vocal cords. From such a base, literacy generally follows quite naturally. Many Waldorf parents recall that their children were behind their friends in non-Waldorf schools but somehow caught up in the third or fourth grade and suddenly read with unusual fervor.

Still, the system isn't fail-safe. Although Waldorf teachers learn techniques, phonic and otherwise, that can pinpoint reading troubles, some have such faith in the Waldorf way that they overlook children with real disabilities—a problem that school leaders consider the teachers' failing, not the system's. Nonetheless, I spoke to several disgruntled parents whose children were later found through outside testing to have dyslexia or other reading difficulties. Such accounts obviously inflame the worries of some reading experts; others are less concerned. Lucy Calkins, a well-known reading specialist at Teachers College of Columbia University, says that in most public schools, children who start reading later tend to do worse, and Waldorf students might benefit slightly from starting earlier. (Interestingly, Waldorf public school students do just that, which may give them a leg up on their more privileged private school peers.) Overall, Calkins says, "I would not necessarily be worried in a Waldorf school. The foundation of literacy is talk and play."

THIS IS MATH?

A central objective of Waldorf teaching is to create a sense of wonder about each subject, including math. Sixth graders study geometric progression by doing graphic-art projects. In San Francisco, I observed second graders studying arithmetic by creating concentric circles of times tables and musing about their similarity to planetary patterns; later they sang out complex multiplication drills while clapping and hopping across an exercise room in syncopated rhythm—a display of mental and physical dexterity that I have seen stump a class of teachers in training. "Their numbers are in their bodies," John Bloom, the school administrator, explained.

A standard exercise in Waldorf classes is a riveting game called mental math. One day at the T. E. Mathews School, when a bunch of teenagers was being particularly disruptive, Evelyn Arcuri, the teacher, clapped her hands and said, "Okay, I'm thinking of a number." The students quickly quieted down. "If you add twelve," she said, "subtract twenty, multiply by nine, and subtract six, the answer is thirty. What's the number?" Within moments— before I could recall the arithmetic steps of the exercise or even the numbers—several students were pumping their hands in the air, promising answers, often the correct one. (The answer, by the way, is twelve.) As students get older, the formulas get more complex and are recited far more quickly.

Intriguing as all these alternatives are, they provoke a question that applies to any educational practice: Do their strengths hold? Apparently so. Beau Leonhart, who has taught math for twenty-two years at the Marin Academy, a non-Waldorf high school in California, and her husband, James Shipman, also a longtime teacher at Marin, have found that the Waldorf graduates they get tend to exhibit an unusually long attention span. "Waldorf kids aren't the ones out the door when the bell rings," Shipman says. "They're the ones who tend to linger, who want to carry on a conversation. If anything, they're a little slower, because they're thinking about it." Leonhart adds, "If they can't do it one way, they'll go at it from another angle." Shipman, who teaches aikido, among other subjects, told me, "In thirteen years I've had two black belts, both Waldorf kids. They know the meaning of focus and discipline. They have a depth—there's no way around it. They're very present." It may be no coincidence that Waldorf schools concentrate on building athletic foundations as well as academic ones in children's early years—balance, coordination, agility—before introducing competitive sports in the upper grades. It seems to pay off. School news clips are full of accounts of victories over teams from schools two or three times their size.

Waldorf students' capacity for concentration may be stimulated by an old-fashioned but increasingly rare practice: allowing time for reflection. Science classes are an example. In the average school, teachers introduce a concept first and then do a demonstration or an experiment to illustrate it. "It takes the kid out of it," Mikko Bojarsky, the science teacher at the Sacramento Waldorf School, told me. Waldorf teachers turn this process around, doing an experiment before giving the concept much discussion. "Then you let it go to bed for the night," Bojarsky said. "They literally sleep on it. A lot happens in their sleep life." The next day, he said, students generally come in with many more questions than they had the day of the experiment, often including some the teacher never considered. "Nowadays we always push people to think so fast instead of letting them reflect," Bojarsky continued. The Waldorf process institutionalizes an important principle—to let students struggle toward their answers and individual understanding. Indeed, this notion is the foundation of one of the more popular modern-day progressive reforms, the practice called constructivism. In many schools, however, constructivism's principles are so elusive that they've been far too difficult for students, or teachers, to master. "One of the things I had to learn," Bojarsky said, "was to not answer their questions, especially in the twelfth grade. If you give them answers, they'll just shut down. It's amazing what they'll come up with if you wait long enough."

A SENSE OF ETHICS

E ach morning when both public and private Waldorf students in the elementary grades get to class, they find their teacher standing in the doorway, waiting to look them in the eye and shake their hands. "You can tell so much by how they shake hands, who's a little off," Lynda Smith, at the time a San Francisco teacher, told me. Moments later, after the students have taken their seats, they rise for another Waldorf tradition: recitation of the morning verse.

This is a short poem, written by Steiner, that aims to inspire students about nature and good work. (The verse for the first through fourth grades in the private schools, for example, says in part, "I revere, O God, the strength of humankind, which Thou so graciously has [sic] planted in my soul, that I with all my might, may love to work and learn." Morning verses are a routine in public Waldorf schools too, but without references to God, angels, or other explicitly religious concepts.) When possible, classes may go for a walk to recite these verses on a riverbank in Sacramento, say, or in the school garden. Cloying as this ritual may seem, many alumni remember the verses fondly. One admits that he still says his morning verse while shaving.

The solemnity of the verses sets the tone for the morning "main lesson," an intense two-hour class. (Coincidentally, carving out large blocks of study time like this has become a popular reform in all sorts of schools today.) Waldorf teachers are supposed to avoid reading from books when presenting their lesson material and to prepare original oral presentations virtually every day. The emphasis placed on these presentations does occasionally fill

class time with more droning lectures than engaging student projects—
a borrowing from traditional education's more oppressive practices. But
there are compensations. Teachers are taught to present lessons as topics for
open discussion and to create a dramatic atmosphere in which the moral
principles involved in a given subject can be not only pondered but felt. First
graders, for example, will pretend that they are gnomes in a fairy tale that
posits concepts of good and evil. Fourth graders may act out Nordic myths,
fiercely stomping their way through a poem's iambic and dactylic rhythms.
The poems also talk about Norse gods who symbolize pride, loss of innocence, and the power of the intellect—issues that Waldorf teachers believe
are just beginning to dawn on fourth graders.

Waldorf's assorted lessons in goodness (the schools also ask students to
do regular community service) seem to have their effect. "A lot of optimists
come out of here," says Damon Saykally, a recent Sacramento Waldorf senior, who entered the program as a sophomore and describes himself as a ni-
hilist. "When I first came here, I was shocked at how much they think they
can help the world. It's the most beautiful thing ever. I don't believe it. But
there are a lot of happy people here." There is also a remarkable absence of
conflict. "You will never find a fight here. Ever," Saykally says, an observation I heard from students at most other Waldorf schools as well.

Waldorf's philosophy of teaching through living out stories may be unusual, but it comes out of a long tradition, from the folkways of ancient cultures to the modern-day theories of child psychologists such as Bruno
Bettelheim and Robert Coles. In his well-known books on the development
of a moral and spiritual intelligence in children, Coles stresses an immersion
in moral stories.[15] Waldorf teachers go even further. They believe that when
students go through school without such stories, their ability to develop a
sense of empathy is inhibited and that this limits their capacity to find
meaning in life. Pointing to the psychologist Jean Piaget's famous theories
about a youngster's gradual stages of development, Waldorf teachers argue
that traditional schools aggravate this problem by imposing intellectual demands on students before they're ready for them.[16] This only discourages
youngsters, they say, leaving them prone to become clever but unfeeling
cynics or, worse, simply apathetic.

One big plank in Waldorf's platform that is a bit difficult to get a grip on is
the exhaustive references to the *soul*. The word comes up, Saykally told me,
"*all* the time." (*Soul* occurs, for example, no fewer than four times in the
nineteen lines of the upper-school morning verse.) I was perplexed by the
ubiquity of this term and by the apparent lack of discussion of its meaning,
so I began asking students what it meant to them. "Regardless of what you

do, it's who you are," a San Francisco eighth grader said. "What you believe and think," one of her classmates said. "How you act with that in the world," another said. Pretty good answers, I thought. An hour or so later David Weber, the head teacher of their school, abruptly pulled me aside. "Don't interview them about that!" he said. "They're not at that level yet. It's too analytical. That's for the eleventh grade. Now they're just feeling it. It's just an experience. That's where it should stay." Later, when he had cooled down, Weber explained his concern more fully: Questions from a reporter might encourage eighth graders' tendency to be judgmental, a trait that Waldorf teachers try hard to temper. "How healthy is it for children to make judgments at this age?" he asked me. Eighth graders want to see everything as "black and white," he said. "It's cool or it sucks. Some never get beyond that. We're trying not to dignify this kind of self-absorbed judgment."

Though aspects of Weber's goal sound laudable in theory, they can prove elusive in practice. During my visits I saw many seventh and eighth graders roll their eyes at various exercises meant to feed the soul (a puppet show of a fairy tale in a school assembly; the relentless morning verses; and, once, a seventh-grade science lesson wrapped in a fable, in which a king ordered an alchemist to get the dirt out of his salt). When I asked students about these exercises, I got mixed but mostly respectful reactions. Some outsiders, however, are considerably more distrustful, having sensed a huge piece of Waldorf philosophy that teachers keep largely hidden from their students.

COVERT SPIRITUALITY

In early 1998 Dan Dugan, a disenchanted Waldorf parent in San Francisco, filed suit in federal district court, charging the Sacramento school district and another nearby for unlawfully introducing the Waldorf philosophy in two public schools in the mid-1990s. Dugan argued that the movement violates the Constitution's First and Fourteenth amendments with a secret agenda: the indoctrination of children into Waldorf's "religious doctrines of anthroposophy."

Anthroposophy is the name Rudolf Steiner gave to his theories about the evolution of human consciousness, drawn from a multiplicity of disciplines—anthropology, philosophy, psychology, science, and various religions, particularly Christianity. As Steiner wove these disciplines together with his own research, he created his own brand of spirituality, some of which complements the New Age movement. A number of Steiner's beliefs are now somewhat accepted—for example, the notion that virtually all fields of study, from the humanities to the sciences, share a foundation of explanation.[17] Yet many of his theories remain suspect—in large part, no doubt, because of the dreamy way in which Steiner expressed them. In a typical essay, "The Roots of Education," he argued, "If you observe man's development with the means of inner vision of which I have already spoken—with the eyes and ears of the soul—then you will see that man does not consist only of a physical body . . . but that he also has supersensible members of his being."[18]

These notions make Dan Dugan, who is a sound engineer, smile and shake his head. "I'm opposed to magical thinking; I'm a secular humanist," he told me as we chatted in an office stuffed with electronic equipment on one side and dozens of anthroposophy books on the other, all of which he claims to have read. In Dugan's view, Steiner's theories are simply "cult pseudoscience." After Waldorf began spreading into public school classrooms, Dugan formed a group called PLANS (People for Legal and Non-Sectarian Schools) to declare what he calmly calls "epistemological warfare." His goal, he says, is to sort out two questions: "What is reliable knowledge? How is it obtained?"

Waldorf teachers counter that they don't formally teach anthroposophy. This is true; in fact, their own rules prohibit them from doing so. They do study it, however—most intensively at Rudolf Steiner College, where virtually every text in use was written by Steiner or another anthroposophist. (This should not suggest that anthroposophy constitutes the whole of Waldorf teachers' preparation. The Steiner College expects student teachers to come to these studies after obtaining a standard bachelor's degree.) Waldorf teachers say they hide anthroposophy not because they see anything evil or dangerous in it but because they don't want to push their philosophy onto the students. The purpose of the anthroposophical studies, they argue, is to enliven their own sensibility and deepen their understanding of evolution. Only then, according to Waldorf theory, can they inspire students with the wonder and curiosity that make for profound learning. Steiner himself encouraged this distinction. "If I had my way," he wrote, "I would give anthroposophy a new name every day to prevent people from hanging on to its literal meaning. . . . We must never be tempted to implement sectarian ideas. . . . We must not chain children's minds to finished concepts, but give them concepts capable of further growth and expansion."[19]

Steinerian pronouncements of this sort have excited legions of Waldorf teachers. Ruth Mikkelsen, of the T. E. Mathews School, noticed this when she first observed Waldorf classes. "Why do they think these kids are so special?" she remembers wondering. "Thousands of times I've sat with teachers and heard them say, 'I want to kill Johnny' or 'I can't wait till I get home and can have a glass of wine.' At Waldorf they say, 'How can we help little Ronnie, who's, you know, killing puppies now?'" That attitude may be precisely the point. As Jerome Kagan, a developmental psychologist at Harvard, once told me, "In most of the curriculum changes schools make, if there's any benevolent effect on students, it's because the teacher is now motivated and passionate. And kids benefit from that, not from the curriculum."

But anthroposophy still "leaks into the curriculum," as Dan Dugan puts it. "They try to hide it, but they can't," Rebecca Bolnick, a recent graduate of the Sacramento Waldorf School, told me. Take, for example, Steiner's belief that each child's temperament matches one of the four medieval types: choleric (bold), phlegmatic (deliberate), melancholic (brooding), or sanguine (lighthearted). Steiner also believes that physical and spiritual development fall into distinct seven-year periods, the first beginning with the arrival of a child's permanent teeth. Suspect as these ideas may be to the uninitiated, the outside experts I spoke to consider them relatively innocent. "When you think of what the learning-disability people cook up, this is very mild," one prominent expert on early education told me. The court in Dan Dugan's case seemed to agree. In 2001, the federal judge who had been hearing the case disqualified his expert witnesses, then dismissed the case for lack of standing. Dugan promptly filed an appeal, which was expected to take at least a year to resolve.

Harmless or not, zealotry in the practice of Steiner's theories usually has a much simpler cause: bad teachers. Although this problem afflicts every school, Waldorf wrestles with an extra challenge by being one of the last refuges for the countercultural values of the 1960s. "A lot of people think Waldorf schools are the place for the kids of ex-hippies," says Eugene Schwartz, the director of teacher training at Sunbridge College, in Spring Valley, New York. That image, he said, often attracts teachers who are "dropping out from the world of competition or power." They can find great comfort in Steiner's spirituality, and become more devoted followers than even Steiner himself might have wished. The result is that students sometimes learn more about Steiner's scientific theories than about Isaac Newton's. Indeed, to meet district requirements at Urban Waldorf, Dorothy St. Charles found they had to add some muscle to the Waldorf curriculum, and more tangible measures of achievement. This especially pertained to the sciences, where Waldorf tends to favor the views of the eighteenth-century German writer and scientist Johann W. von Goethe. "It's a one-sided view, really," says St. Charles. Ironically, this public vetting of Waldorf's modern-day romanticism might return its pedagogy to its earlier, more fertile roots. "People often think Waldorf offers an easy way to teach the sciences," Eugene Schwartz says. "In fact it's just the opposite."

As public school officials collaborate with Waldorf leaders (who come to public schools by invitation only), the two camps are working out other interesting armistices in response to the "epistemological warfare" waged by Waldorf critics. There is no uniform system for Waldorf public schooling as yet, and given the diverse interests of the nation's school districts, there may never be one. Some schools follow Waldorf's practice of using the Old Testament in the early grades, in world-literature studies and for inspiration on student projects; others avoid it. Most adopt Waldorf's accelerated approach to basic arithmetic and some form of its relatively slow, layered approach to reading. In other communities, beyond Milwaukee, the initiatives show intriguing signs of success with underachieving minorities. For instance, although Waldorf schools' reading scores are often low in the early years, they generally rise dramatically by eighth grade, a point at which many traditional public school scores reach a plateau or fall. One school near Nevada City, California (one of the two named in Dugan's lawsuit), has been the recipient of a state award and some generous state grants to spread its work. But the partnerships have also presented challenges. Steiner's pedagogy and the class readings that result are heavily Eurocentric; public school teachers typically modify this ancient orientation to accommodate American literature and, increasingly, multicultural points of view. (In California, for instance, white students may be inspired by gardening, but Hispanics generally aren't.) And dramatic change in schools never proceeds smoothly. When teachers are asked to try, as adults, learning to sing, play music, and paint, many suddenly find their somewhat less adventurous old ways quite attractive. As for any broad troubles with religious indoctrination, the classes in public Waldorf schools have been pretty well stripped of explorations of the spiritual.

THE SECOND MOTHER

One of the most unusual aspects of Waldorf education is a system called looping, whereby a homeroom teacher stays with a class for more than a year—and in a private Waldorf school's case, from first through eighth grade. The practice has an intriguing combination of pros and cons and is attracting growing attention in education circles, both private and public.

Although Waldorf students work with other teachers each day in subjects such as music, foreign languages, and physical education, the main lessons are taught for eight years by the same teacher. The purpose of this is to build solid, long-term relationships and to teach students how to do that themselves. "If you get in an argument with someone, you have to work it out," says Karen Rivers, a Waldorf educator and consultant in California. (This is a fair point of pride—by all accounts Waldorf teachers do spend considerable amounts of time talking with students and their parents.) For students, looping offers a base of support. "I can't tell you how wonderful it is to have a second mom," Ivi Esguerra, a recent graduate, told the audience at the Steiner School open house in New York. "The caring went beyond the academics."

In Waldorf public schools, particularly those serving the underprivileged, looping holds special power. To begin with, it gives each teacher badly needed extra time to reach these children. "At private Waldorf schools, kids walk in ready to trust the teacher," Mark Birdsall, a former teacher at Milwaukee's Urban Waldorf School, told me. "Here, they don't. They learn to *not* trust, that they will get in trouble if they do." To Dorothy St. Charles, Urban Waldorf's former principal, the standard system of moving on to new teachers each year merely institutionalizes the mistrust. "The buck is always getting passed to the next year's teacher," she said. "With Waldorf, you don't teach for the now. When you have them for five years, you have to think, What do I want this child to be down the road?"

The downsides of looping, however, can be substantial. The task of preparing new lessons each day may keep material fresh for the teachers and students, but it also restricts the teacher's ability to perfect given lessons with repetition. Most important, perhaps, conflicts between teachers and students aren't always overcome, and even when they are, tension can remain. "Our teacher was great," Ben Klocek, the recent Sacramento senior, told me. "But it was way too much. By the eighth grade you're completely sick of each other." Perhaps most important, the holes in a given instructor's teaching aren't always readily filled later. Scott Embrey-Stine, a Waldorf high school teacher in Sacramento who has spent most of his career in public schools, says he could identify the strengths and weaknesses in each lower-school teacher just by the distinct characteristics of each class. "You see the imprint of the class teacher," he says.

A DIFFERENT CITIZEN

In the end the measure of any school lies in the graduates it produces. Overall, the Waldorf record seems pretty impressive. Consider students' scores on the Scholastic Aptitude Tests. Despite Waldorf students' unfamiliarity with standardized tests, their SAT scores have generally come in well above the national average, particularly on verbal measures. "The concepts, they've got," Kathleen O'Connor, a freelance college counselor who works with the Washington, D.C., Waldorf School, told me. "When they get direction on how to take multiple-choice tests, their scores soar." More important, considering the limited extent to which SATs measure ability, Waldorf students have a solid record in college admissions. Graduates from the New York and Washington schools are enrolled at many of the country's top private colleges, including Amherst, Stanford, Princeton, Swarthmore, Wellesley, and Yale.

Waldorf graduates have never been carefully tracked in this country; the only longitudinal study is a German survey, published in 1981, in which three independent researchers looked at 1,460 Waldorf graduates. They found that 22 percent had passed a rigorous German achievement test— triple the rate for state-school students.[20] Evidence here in the United States is anecdotal but encouraging. And alumni rosters are replete with professional acclaim in fields as varied as industry and the arts, medicine and the military. An illustration of the resourcefulness that makes for these successes may be the account of two Sacramento Waldorf graduates, Jeff Dorso and Kai Schneider, who took a year abroad to study law at American University in Cairo.

Their professor, Tim Sullivan, had been teaching in Cairo at that point for twenty-five years. During that time, Sullivan told me, he'd grown accustomed to seeing his students struggle with suddenly being a minority in a land with a different language and strange cultural norms. But the Waldorf graduates, he said, seemed to adjust "without the contortions others went through." In class, which apparently included 120 top students, many of them aggressive Ivy Leaguers, Sullivan said Dorso and Schneider more than held their own. "They had learned how to learn, how to think independently. You could pull them out of their normal frame of reference and they could still function and think their way through the problem." When I met Dorso, I too noticed his humble confidence and unusual versatility. Tall and soft-spoken, Dorso told me he was slow to pick up reading as a child and didn't perform particularly well on his SATs—substantially worse, in fact, than most of his pre-law classmates. However, when he took the notorious LSAT exam, his scores came in well above average. Dorso recalls that in the LSAT preparation class, which trains students in analytical reasoning and argument, "everyone else was sort of stuck in the material, writing every single thing down. For me, it was very easy to grasp the main point. I think that comes from having the broad base." What's particularly interesting about Dorso's stint in Egypt is that it occurred in 1996, another time of considerable turmoil in the Middle East. At the end of the semester, most of the class chose to leave. Among the few who had the courage to stay for another term were Dorso and Schneider.

—

Waldorf education remains dogged by a persistent fear—that its non-competitive approach doesn't prepare students to fit in and succeed in a dog-eat-dog world, a criticism that some Waldorf leaders acknowledge is sometimes justified. Indeed, many students choose hard-nosed schools after leaving Waldorf, precisely because they, or their parents, want more pressure and rigor in their lives. Karen Rivers, who talks frequently to worried parents in her role as a Waldorf consultant, thinks these families miss the point. "We're not trying to teach them to fit in," she told me. "They already know how to fit in. We're trying to educate them to create a better world." But what about those who don't change the world—those who, like most people, don't even rise to the top? At a Steiner School alumni gathering in New York, Deborah Grace Winer, now a freelance writer, recalled that her mother always told her, "Life is not a horse race." Because someone will always beat you? I asked. "Yes," she answered. "And when someone does finally beat you, you have nothing."

Winer's comment reminded me of my visit to the Mathews School for juvenile offenders, where students begin each day already behind, with little of the foundation that Winer now has. A feel for music is but one example. "Our kids have no sense of rhythm," their teacher, Evelyn Arcuri, told me. As the students master a musical instrument, Mathews teachers say, their sense of rhythm grows. This seems to provide an anchor that strengthens their confidence in other work. "The recorders are just excellent," Thomas, the outgoing seventeen-year-old, told me. "It calms you down, helps you think better." Thomas was kicked out of his previous school for getting into fights. Now, his grandmother says, "he's different when he's in that school. He doesn't come home as frustrated as he did." As I watched several Mathews students practice playing their recorders one morning, I understood what Thomas's grandmother meant. When the students hit a difficult section, some gave up and a few stomped out of the room. Most soon returned. "I screwed up too," the teacher told them, "but I don't let that stop me. Just play through. Persevere. That's what this is about." They tried again and then again, did better, and smiled.

Conclusion

After decades of disappointing experience with education's quick fixes, from new math to new technology to new standardized tests, it should now be easy to take a long, sober look back to see what counts in the class-room—and what doesn't. One state that affords one of the clearest hind-sight views is, not surprisingly, California—arguably the nation's most adventurous state, and unarguably the birthplace of the personal computer. Curiously, one of the most comprehensive looks at what computers have done, or not done, for California's schools was produced some time ago, in 1996, by the *San Jose Mercury News,* whose Silicon Valley headquarters puts the paper at ground zero of technology trends. That winter, reporters ex-amined test scores at a range of schools up and down the state—227 in all. About 10 percent were "model technology" institutions—schools that won big state grants for intensive technology programs. "In general," the paper said, "the analysis showed no strong link between the presence of technology—or the use of technology in teaching—and superior achieve-ment." The newspaper's study, which went to great pains to control for out-side influences such as family income, parents' education, and language background, found two exceptions to the flat pattern.

One was that the schools that did best, when compared with their peers, were in fact the model technology schools. But this wasn't true of the group as a whole, only those that serve unusually poor students. (Educators evalu-ating the study hypothesized that poor students' success with technology could come from "the motivation of having nice tools," the sense of freedom that technology unleashed, and the general jolt of novelty.) The other excep-tion involved non-model middle schools with big technology budgets. This group actually scored worse than middle schools with smaller technology budgets. Computer promoters tend to jump on such findings, saying they only prove that merely having technology will do nothing unless it's intelligently woven into the curriculum. Knowing this, the *Mercury* controlled for this argument, too. Schools that had gone to the trouble of making computers part of the daily work still underperformed when compared to other schools.[1]

Among the state's thousands of schools, one might have served as an exceptionally radiant object lesson of the *Mercury*'s findings. In fact, it could have done so almost a decade before the paper embarked on its study. In the late 1980s, the Belridge Elementary School in McKittrick, a small, cookie-cutter subdivision near the southern trough of California's agricultural heartland, took a huge step into the future. Flush with cash from the local oil field, Belridge invested $4.3 million in computer technology over a four-year period for a student body of no more than sixty children. The investment filled the school with futuristic gear of all kinds—laser-disk players, television production studios, shiny new Apple computers, piles of software, even e-mail accounts at a time when most schools hadn't even heard of the Internet. Teachers modernized their instruction methods too. They got students collaborating on projects to challenge them to think. They had students produce their own television news shows and simulate a computer-based presidential election. "We bought the very best money could buy," recalls Steve Wentland, a teacher at the time and later the school's combination principal and district superintendent. "I have not heard of one thing, even today, that another school is doing that we didn't do." Visitors soon poured in from all over the country.

Several years after everything appeared to be in place, it all came crashing down. When the annual district test scores were reported, they showed that students' performance had actually declined during the computerization years, falling slightly below the national average. Outraged parents picketed the school and elected a new school board. The new board promptly hired another principal, who cut back the computer program by selling off many machines and shoving the rest in a corner. "It was a dismal, miserable failure," Wentland recalls. "And they did everything right."

So what went wrong? "Technology will not fix what's wrong with schools," Wentland now says, sounding very much like his supplier, Steve Jobs, during that brief period of candor when Jobs had no affiliation with Apple. Wentland is a man unusually confident in his own judgment—so much so, in fact, that he's occasionally gotten into some local trouble for aggressively pursuing his own agenda.* But he knows technology and is well

---

*At various points, Wentland has been accused of muscling his underlings, trying to secretly purchase religious textbooks, making unauthorized use of school funds, and swinging a

traveled by now in the education-conference world. Perhaps most important to the residents of Belridge, ever since the school abandoned its high-
end approach to computing, test scores and other measures of academic
performance have risen substantially.[2] The school accomplished this by
doing little more than return to the basics, a move helped considerably by
yet another simple solution: small classes.

It will be tempting to read these stories, and the many that preceded them,
as a dismissal of classroom technology, a biased selection forming another
jeremiad in the thin but long line of Luddite literature that sees nothing but
evil in machinery. To do so would be off the mark—and unfair to our
schools. If any generalization can be made, it would be that technology is
used too intensely in the younger grades and not intensely enough—in the
proper areas—in the upper grades. Like it or not, computer technology is
also here to stay in some fashion. The challenge for schools, therefore, is to
be smarter about how and when they use technology, and how they separate its wheat from its chaff.

Most educators know this and believe they are doing so. But the computer industry has managed to survive on such a plethora of hype, habitu-
ating all of us to accept such a string of unfulfilled promises that we've long
since lost the ability to see what new inventions really can and cannot do.
Schools as a result have become industry's research-and-development labs
as well as its dumping ground—while asking very little in return. Considering the sacred public trust that we bestow upon our schools, they have every
right to expect more from this machinery, or any other innovation, before
they let it in the door.

Before tying up this indictment, let's be clear about the good things that
computers can do for schools.

Obviously, many programs—such as computerized vocabulary exercises
and foreign language drills; graphing software for geometry; data managers
and scientific simulations; and basic word-processing software—are already
capable of being useful supplements. The same is true of diagnostic software, which, in select cases, is capable of offering unusual portraits of how

---

sweetheart deal that got the school board to pay for his doctoral education. See a series of front-
page articles by Steven Mayer in *The Bakersfield Californian:* "School District Got Warning on
Textbooks," September 1, 1999; "Belridge OKs Cash for Superintendent's Tuition," September
10, 2000; and "Report Thrashes Wentland," May 11, 2001.

different students are handling their classroom challenges. These devices now join the long sequence of tools that have helped teachers throughout time—the tablet, the pencil, the pen, the ruler, the slide rule, the calculator, the overhead projector. All of these can be effective when they are used only as needed, when students are at the right age for them, and when they are kept in their place. This won't be easy. As Steve Grineski, the interim dean of the College of Education and Human Services at Moorhead State University, in Minnesota, put it, "It's hard to find a balance when you spend half a million dollars and then you say, 'Well, you're only going to use this minimally.'" But the challenge will not go away. The priority in each classroom is not the technological process but the human one. Those teachers who sit back and delight, as Napa's New Technology High School and scores of its followers do, in the way the computer lets the students "take over" their own learning are merely fooling themselves. Worse, they're fooling their students. As we've seen, the students aren't taking over in most of these classrooms. The computer is.

Obviously, certain programming languages (such as BASIC, LOGO, and, today, C++, among others) open fascinating windows of opportunities for students who are inclined toward math and the sciences. But school administrators need to remember that computer programs are nothing if not transitory, and that students with an aptitude for the technological must learn its fundamentals, rather than hot programs of the moment that are likely to be passé by the time the students enter the workforce. Those fundamentals are best learned in the upper grades, through following the example of some of the schools in this book. I'm speaking in particular of those few that bother to teach students enough of the principles of digital technology that they're able, among other things, to build their own computers and computer programs. Schools must also realize that activities like this are not interesting, or even helpful, for everyone. Equally important, those who enjoy technological challenges need to be guided with a wisdom and balance that schools have for the most part forgotten. The members of this crowd—who used to be called math nerds and are now referred to as computer geeks— seem to be increasing in number. And they are typically drawn to high technology's horizons with a passion. The schools' job, therefore, is to infuse the rest of their curricula with enough power and relevance that those students who are obsessed with the technical sciences will develop varied interests and skills. As the world grows increasingly technological, and increasingly strained by social inequities and human suffering of all kinds, we are going to need a different kind of employee in the technology industries. We'll need people, in short, who are as sensitive to the culture's humanistic needs as they are to its electronic possibilities.

And obviously, the World Wide Web—the über-program of the modern age—is a useful if not invaluable research source for all of us. But we all must realize that opening the Internet's door to youngsters also requires teachers to accept additional responsibilities. This does not just involve watching out for pornographic or violent material; that's the easy part. It also concerns watching what values and beliefs students develop about what knowledge is; how it's built; how it's used; and what it demands of them, as students and as citizens. Downloading a captivating live software applet from a NASA site, which some Web designer has loaded with a few earnest questions to satisfy somebody's grant requirements, does not a satisfactory lesson make. Nor does simply writing a paper about this material, based on some extra Internet "research."

This is not real work in today's high-speed, "global" society. It's where real work *starts*—for both students and teachers. The Internet, as we've seen, is filled with such a myriad of sites—many of which don't last long (and go on for pages and pages when they do)—that it is completely unreasonable to expect teachers to check every Internet source. A teacher's job today is therefore very different from what it used to be. Actually, it's somewhat like it was in the old days, but even more so. Ken Komoski, the longtime director of EPIE, the educational-products watchdog group, puts it this way: When a boy turns in a paper today, he asks, "How would you know if he knows *anything* until you *talk?*"

In the end, the legions of education critics who incessantly pester the schools to make dramatic changes would do well to remember one central fact: At its core, education is a people process. Yes, youngsters need tools, but most of all they need people. This is particularly the case with society's most disadvantaged children—the group supposedly suffering from this cruel "digital divide" and which educators are desperate to supply with gizmos. Survey after survey indicates that schools that serve the poor are doing fine as far as supplies of computer gear are concerned. They're not doing so well when it comes to teaching. From California to Harlem, from the hollows of poverty in West Virginia to the polished suburban corners of Montgomery County, Maryland, the presence of state-of-the-art technology is in general making matters worse. During the final years of the twentieth century and the opening years of the twenty-first—a time when computer technology has reached record levels in the schools—student performance on national and international achievement tests in subjects such as math, science, and history has either declined or remained flat.[3] School policy makers could easily attend to these troubles by other means. If they did so, those who suffer from education's divides—intellectual or digital—might have a much easier time closing the gaps on their own.

When confronted with criticisms of this sort, technology promoters incessantly point out that it doesn't have to be this way, that all kinds of sophisticated uses of the computer are possible, if only schools would pursue them. Those pursuits involve sufficient funding, proper teacher training, sufficient classroom control—the list goes on and on. In theory, the technovangels are right. But as we have seen, they have been making this case for years—for decades, in fact. At a certain point, everyone—teachers and taxpayers, parents and policy makers—has the right to stop and invoke the famous ad line "Where's the beef?" If computers are so great, why aren't we seeing great things by now in our schools?

THE PRIMACY OF TEACHING

During high-minded discussions about what matters in education, nearly every conversation suddenly gets wonderfully focused and simple when someone issues the following challenge: Think of a memorable moment from your old school days. What was most inspiring? Most helpful? Nearly everyone suddenly recalls that it revolved around a great teacher.

This is not news. Education insiders have understood and preached this boring truth since the beginning of formal education. Yet in some bizarre act of cultural sadomasochism, we continually pretend it isn't true. We let teachers twist in the breeze seemingly forever. For decades, we have taken people whom we hold responsible for the intellectual and moral development of our children, put them in chaotic, overcrowded institutions, robbed them of creative freedom and new opportunities for their own learning, imposed an ever-changing stream of rules and performance requirements that leave them exhausted and hopeless, and paid them about $40,000 a year for their trouble—far less, proportionately speaking, than teachers earn in most other industrialized societies. (Those societies include such economic middleweights as Spain, Portugal, Greece, Ireland, and Mexico. In countries where the GDP per capita begins to compare with U.S. levels, South Korea being one example, teacher pay in relation to average national income is nearly three times what it is in this country.) To make matters worse, during the economic boom of the 1990s, U.S. teacher salaries declined. Meanwhile, our teachers have had to carry almost a third more classroom hours than their foreign counterparts.[4] Then, when our children seem aimless and turn to machines and violence to feel some sense of power and self-expression, we wonder why. No we don't, actually. We blame the teachers.

Or we forget about them. In 1984, when *Forbes* magazine engaged in an internal debate over its coverage of school computing, senior editor Stephen Kindel, who was responsible for the magazine's technology section, wrote a cautionary memo. If computers let students do more and more of their work by themselves, Kindel asked, "what would happen to class discussion—and, more important, the sense of rubbing against other minds? I think that the best schools will eventually recognize a fact that's been apparent since Plato sat on Socrates' knee: Education depends on the intimate contact between a good teacher—part performer, part dictator, part cajoler—and an inquiring student." Kindel concluded with a comment that was noted in the second chapter of this book. "In the end," he said, "it is the poor who will be chained to the computer; the rich will get teachers." The author of the story in question, *Forbes* senior editor Kathleen Wiegner, made an equally passionate case supporting computers. This machine, she said, was merely taking its place in history's long line of world-changing machines. The printing press, the steam engine, the car, the telephone—each of these machines has empowered the individual, she argued, and thus helped dethrone centralized authority. "The day of the high priest in data processing is already waning in corporations, as the masses of employees become adept," she wrote. "Why not in the schools as well?" The editorial staff ultimately agreed with Wiegner, concluding, as the editor put it, that "computers will change the world."[5]

The magazine was right, of course, but only in one sense. As *Forbes* and most of the media joined in high technology's hype, they continually forgot that schools are not like the rest of the world. Youngsters need a quality of guidance that data processors don't—guidance that, as we have seen, is not much of a fixture in most classrooms, especially those that are heavily computerized. And as the family structure has weakened, or has at least been diluted by modern-day distractions, the only dependable place to which students can turn for such guidance is a teacher. There is even evidence on this score for those who worship test-score gains: In Tennessee, exhaustive longitudinal studies over the years have indicated that good teachers can raise students' test scores by as much as 50 percentage points. Interestingly, the Tennessee data also indicate that those gains last long after students have left a good teacher's classroom. Having more teachers might help as well, since studies have fairly conclusively proven (despite some occasional equivocation) that students learn more in smaller classes.[6]* Steve Wentland, the veteran of technology's rise and fall at Belridge School, puts the argument boldly. "Ninety percent of what a kid learns," Wentland says, "he learns from the teacher."

The lengths to which this country's leaders will go to ignore this simple fact are remarkable. Some of the latest examples come from the policies of the George W. Bush administration. The president has gotten tremendous mileage out of his incessant pledge to "leave no child behind." While Bush has, as we've seen, made some long overdue moves to build up the teaching force, his primary route for arriving at this state of grace—standardized testing for students and harsh accountability for their schools—is rather curious in today's age. Educators now have volumes and volumes of knowledge at their disposal about what really makes youngsters excel. One would think the nation's policy makers, armed with this information, could come up with something better than a lengthier sheet of multiple-choice questions, millions of new test essays, and a corps of evaluators who don't have the skill, or the time, to do their job.

One sample of the wisdom that's readily available is a book written nearly two decades ago, in 1985, a year after Kindel issued his warning at *Forbes.* Entitled *Developing Talent in Young People,* the book was the 550-page result of an intensive four-year examination of some of the nation's most accomplished citizens. The researchers were a team of professors and Ph.D. candidates from the University of Chicago, directed by Benjamin S. Bloom, a professor emeritus at that university and a professor of education at Northwestern. Their study focused on 120 stars in a handful of fields—specifically, musicians, artists, athletes, mathematicians, and scientists. How, they wondered, did these people rise to the top? In assembling their answers, the authors arrived at an interesting combination of new and old truths.

---

*From time to time, research surfaces suggesting that smaller classes do not make much difference. The studies making those claims have, however, been generally discredited. As but one indication, after California reduced class sizes in the late 1990s, test scores in some of the state's poorer, high-minority schools, especially in Los Angeles, fell. The reason, researchers discovered, is that the reduction required more classes and thus more teachers. This increased the prevalence of unqualified teachers—and gave good teachers new job opportunities in wealthier schools. And while other factors may have played a part, across the state's large urban districts as a whole, test scores did generally rise for low-income students after smaller classes were initiated. See "Some Calif. Test Scores Fall Along with Class Size," *Education Week,* July 10, 2002, p. 12.

The new discovery was that very few of these stars exhibited unusual natural gifts before embarking on their course of mastery. Many showed promising proclivities, and, of course, all possessed sufficient interest in the field and enough drive to carry them through many long years of relentless practice and study. Beyond that, however, these masters started out in life as average children. These facts, and Bloom's prior research, led him to hypothesize that "what any person can learn, *almost* all persons in the world can learn, *if* provided with appropriate . . . conditions for learning." The old news was what those appropriate conditions were: "a long and intensive process of encouragement, nurturing, education, and training." The concert pianist, for instance, grew up in a home that prized music and the arts; that stressed the values of hard work and self-discipline; that carefully staged the child's study and practice to progress from basics to gradually more sophisticated challenges; and that sought out master tutors and trainers all along the way. When this staged style of instruction is practiced in schools, it's sometimes been called "mastery learning," because students are taught to thoroughly master each step before progressing to a more advanced task. (Students who learn this way, Bloom noted, outperform 85 percent of the students taught through conventional instruction.) The scholastic version of the last piece of this process—the mentor—is even more common. It's called tutoring. In study after study, whenever tutoring is matched against some competing pedagogy, including technology, tutoring wins handily. In his own research, Bloom found that tutored students outdistance 98 percent of those taught in conventional group instruction.[7]

The message here is pretty plain. Education's opportunities lie primarily in the teachers' hands, not in technology. In a world that, by a 1995 count, produced 17,000 newspapers, 12,000 periodicals, 40,000 new book titles each year, 400 million television sets, and 500 million radios, it is clear that education's frontier does not consist of more information.[8] We may think it does when we see students become glued to computer screens. But just as we've learned with television, youngsters need to be taught how to evaluate what they see on the screen. The fact that very few of us, young or old, exercise much judgment in this direction suggests that media guidance is in short supply all around. It also suggests that some students may be drawn to computers partly because teachers and parents aren't giving them much attention.

One phenomenon that continually struck me while I worked on this book was how frequently I found people who shared this worry, and several others like it. Even among people who are favorably inclined toward computers, many sense that this is not an innocent innovation; that, with only a few exceptions, computer technology has become one more feature on an already crowded landscape of high-stimulus consumer items—TV, video games, pop music, action films, high-caffeine coffee shops on every urban corner, the list goes on and on. The primary function of that topography is to keep people buying; a side effect is that it keeps people perpetually hyped up and distracted from activities that might be more soothing and reflective. We have become, in a sense, a society of masochists. We bemoan youngsters' turning to violence while pouring millions into making suffering human beings the stuff of their entertainment. We criticize them for their poor self-discipline and short attention spans; then our commercial enterprises do everything possible to crowd and fragment their minds still further.

"We need *less* surfing in the schools, not more," David Gelernter, a professor of computer science at Yale, once wrote in *The Weekly Standard*. "Couldn't we teach them to use what they've got before favoring them with three orders of magnitude *more?*" Other educators, responding to policy makers' continual urgings that schools invest in what some were now calling "netricity," bemoaned the repetitive emptiness of these suggestions. One foundation invented another term for the schools' state of affairs in 2003: "technology fatigue."[9] Sentiments like these are much of what motivated Theodore Roszak, a history professor at California State University, to write *The Cult of Information*, his well-known "Neo Luddite Treatise," as he called it, "on High-Tech, Artificial Intelligence, and the True Art of Thinking." Roszak argued that learning operates on successive levels—information being the most elementary. Following from there are the demands of imagination, then insight, then knowledge and judgment. To propel this process, information must be put through constant synthesis and analysis—which is done best through projects that are complicated (not simulated), lots of writing, and face-to-face discussion. Roszak's last stage is wisdom, which is supposed to round out the process with deep and varied experience.[10] Computers can certainly be helpful devices throughout this evolution. But the most effective tools are likely to be much simpler things—books, field trips, test tubes, paper notebooks, microscopes, hammers and nails, conversations, and energetic teachers.

REAL HELP

After spending five years researching and writing this story, and many hours struggling painfully with its meaning, I have boiled down my feelings about the subject into a small set of hopes for schools. I hesitate to turn these hopes into formal recommendations for a reason. For decades, teachers and administrators have been battered with such advice—pretentious edicts from governmental commissions, business leaders, aspirants for national office, congressional panels, all manner of "experts" who do not spend their days cooped up in a room with dozens of unruly youngsters, some of whom will dedicate their entire classroom hour to getting under your skin. These teachers are doing God's work. Politicians and the media have long been telling us that this work is America's top priority (at least until September 2001). Yet it is work that very few of us have been willing to take on. The irony is that if we are going to avert more international violence, the solution lies in teaching youngsters how to deepen their human relations—which are very different interactions than the faux relationships conducted over the Internet. The teachers we depend on to teach these lessons could use some help. I therefore offer them these hopes.

I hope that at some point, the public breaks its habit of amnesia when it comes to promises that are sold to schools. One would think that adults—all of whom have gone through many difficult years of experience in school and most of whom have children of their own—would pay more attention when politicians and school administrators start buying in to quick fixes for education's troubles. But people rarely think unless they are forced to. And education doesn't require the same concentration of thought as would a business, whose failures create oil spills or drops in stock prices. No, the price of education's failures is conveniently amorphous, spectacularly delayed, and of little consequence to all but the poorest among us.

In particular, I hope that the next time teachers and administrators hear an expert making predictions about what school will be about in the future—especially concerning technology—the first thing they do is hold on to their wallets. While they're holding tight, they might pause a moment to review the accuracy of the soothsayer's past predictions. Because the record in the prediction market—not only in education but also in politics, in business, in any sphere where these storytellers peddle their wares—is not a glowing one.

With schools, and with technology in particular, the pattern has become relentless. Every few years, right around the time that educators have forgotten yesteryear's predictions, the schools are treated to a whole new definition of the landscape. All those old computer programs were no good anyway, they're told. Now we've finally got something that's truly useful. It's easy to handle; it's less expensive; it finally opens up some powerful learning opportunities. On and on it goes. The message is so seductive—no wonder schools fall for it. A few years and many millions of dollars later, here come the computer hucksters again with yet another offering. But what about that last generation of "educational" software? Oh, the computer promoters say, it turned out to be harder to use than we thought. It was difficult to integrate into the curriculum. It was too expensive. It taught the wrong material. It didn't coordinate with the new state tests. It was too demanding. It wasn't demanding enough. The list of excuses is endless. The schools hear them again and again, year after year. And they fall for them again and again, year after painful year.

It's a lethal combination, this alliance between education and technology, because it joins two domains in which people are particularly gullible. With both schools and consumer technology, people—particularly American people—are especially susceptible to idealistic pitches. The visions of what might happen with a new style of teaching or a new computer look so fabulous, so promising, so irresistible. Sometimes, as we've seen with the sophisticated sleights of hand devised by Renaissance Learning and other companies, the promoters of these visions are self-interested manipulators. Most of the time, however, the salesmen—be they software vendors, telecommunications company officials, or education's very own technovangels—fervently believe in their products. But that's half of what makes the educational-technology phenomenon so seductively effective—and thus so sad. When everyone in the game is being duped, everyone is both guilty and innocent. (To fight this syndrome, I certainly hope that when schools are tossed fancy research claims, they get in the habit of thoroughly checking them out.) The onslaught of fraudulent educational pitches is steady, and it is exacerbated by their salesmen's inexperience with the institutional and daily classroom realities their buyers face. By the time a school has spent a few years trying in vain to adjust to its new purchase—a laptop program or special reading software, a new distance-learning network, a "comprehensive" education reform model, or some combination thereof—the salesmen are long gone. So are their real consumers, the students, who must limp toward the next phase of their education on a flimsy crutch. By then, of course, some new prospect has captured everyone's attention and the potential lessons in this pattern are obscured yet again.

Perhaps all this gullibility is unavoidable—the flip side of the American coin, the dark part of our innate spirit of adventure and ingenuous, relentless optimism. If so, I hope it's not long before we realize that we have lived as reckless teenagers on the world stage long enough. Maybe this is one of education's great unmet challenges. Maybe it should fall to schools to lead the way in showing all of us how to grow up. Maturity is based, in part, on the ability to handle conflicting information. When truly wise souls confront a choice that poses both positive and negative consequences, they can comfortably stare its mixed reality in the face, feeling no need to dismiss one side or the other. That mixture defines computer technology. But if school policy makers have not learned enough to shrewdly pick their way through its obstacle course, they have no right to pass that task on to the nation's students.

I also hope that before schools sink much further into the computer world's unpredictabilities they at least attend to their basic responsibilities. Those obligations start with fixing leaky roofs and crumbling playgrounds and erecting enough buildings to offer uncrowded classrooms. They move on from there to include funding the many valuable curricular priorities visited throughout this book—music and the arts, books, physical education, field trips, "wet" science laboratories, modern-day shop classes, additional teachers—all of which have been cut back to make way for technology. In today's rushed, work-oriented world, school is often the only place where students can engage in some of these experiences. Once our basic responsibilities on these fronts have been met, schools can begin thinking about computing—an activity, it should be remembered, that is clearly not in short supply outside of school. But here, too, educators should do their homework. No school has a right to stuff classrooms with computers unless it also has an equal amount of money set aside for smart teacher training and technical support. That support involves far more than mechanical maintenance. It also means at least one staff member who knows educational software thoroughly enough to help trusting teachers steer clear of the junk.

To pay for these multiple obligations, I hope that at some point politicians start funding schools more generously. In 1995, investment in public education, kindergarten through college, made up a minuscule 4.99 percent of the gross domestic product. By 1998, as our economy rolled in wealth and schools were filling with a record number of students, the funding level actually fell slightly, to 4.82 percent. (In the following years, federal investment in schools did not much improve; in fact, despite President Bush's fervent promises to "leave no child behind," he actually cut funding for poor schools in 2003 by $6 billion, or 30 percent.)[11] When these figures are compared with the portion of GDP that other developed nations devote to public education, the United States comes in below average—stingier, for instance, than governments in Canada, all the Scandinavian countries, Portugal, Poland, and a half-dozen other nations.[12] This is why teachers, despite their sorry salaries, must continually reach into their own pockets to buy classroom supplies—an act of generosity that is steadily growing, averaging $521 per teacher in 2001, or more than $1 billion nationwide.[13]

It would be nice, of course, if this sorry trend could begin to reverse. But education activists have pushed for significant expansions in education funding for decades, mostly in vain. (Perhaps if their myriad competing camps got together and pushed in unison, politicians might start listening.) Should the stinginess continue, state and federal governments could at least devise a method of school funding that is more equitable than what they have now. Strangely enough, property taxes remain the schools' primary revenue source, even though everyone knows that these taxes are far more bountiful in rich communities than in poor ones. Everyone in education also knows about the government's primary mechanism to offset this imbalance: Title I, a federal subsidy program started during President Lyndon Johnson's War on Poverty that sends nearly $9 billion a year to schools with low-income children. However, through a magnificent shell game of tax loopholes and other governmental favors, wealthy communities continue to squeeze more school money out of Washington than their poor cousins get. One recent study found that in 1989 (the most recent census year available at the time), tax outlays that lean to wealthy communities in New Jersey, for example, were $1,257 per student. Those that concentrate in poor New Jersey communities were only $237. "There is something perverse," wrote *The New York Times*'s Richard Rothstein, "about both parties proclaiming that they wish to leave no child behind, when the federal government plays so big a role in pushing affluent children farther ahead."[14]

In the midst of this gaping landscape of school poverty, perhaps the saddest irony of all is that schools keep on purchasing fancy new gear that continually needs fancy new upgrades and repairs. In the face of this devil's bargain, schools, and the many different people and institutions involved in schools, will have to keep finding ways to live with halfway measures. They could do so if they simply scaled back their technology campaign and promised schools nothing more than a set of last year's computers and an assortment of recycled machines. If these commitments could be coupled with today's level of technical support—and if teachers and computer maintenance staffs could be trained on equipment that wasn't upgraded as soon as they mastered it—then schools might finally reach a long-needed level of equilibrium. Technical support would match the equipment. Reality would match politicians' promises. And education reform, at least on this front, might achieve a goal that has always been elusive: stability.

Whatever we do about school funding, I hope the country someday offers teachers a decent living. One longtime technology activist, Bob Albrecht, casually suggested that if we really wanted to solve education's troubles, we'd double teacher salaries. Hyperbolic as that sounds, it would merely put those salaries in the $80,000 range—a figure comparable to average pay for engineers, lawyers, and many other strivers in the private sector.[15]* Such an increase may be a bit slow in coming considering the country's myriad competing priorities, not the least of which is the bill for the massive defense buildup that followed the 2001 terrorist attacks. Additional local financial distractions further cramp school administrators. These expenditures include not only fancy computer systems but also high-priced reform plans that fly in and out of the schools like cafeteria trays. The many schools profiled in this book that have gone nowhere with these reforms, and the many that have made giant strides without them, should be proof enough that the keys to good learning don't reside in some huckster's seminar kit. They are everywhere, throughout education's long, abundantly documented history. And they are not expensive.

One of those keys, in the absence of money for big teacher raises, is to give teachers psychic raises. Society is full of professions that demand sophisticated work but don't pay well. These include social work, nursing, even architecture and politics. They also include the vast majority of careers for people in the arts—musicians, independent filmmakers, writers of all kinds. The institutions that do this work know full well that if the money is thin, the work has to be thick with something else. Often, these people toil away based on the faith that they're helping to save the world—a satisfaction that certainly graces the teaching profession. But successful institutions that are short on cash have learned to offer more than this—a sense of power or autonomy, ample room for creativity, an opportunity to learn, or just pure fun. Many offer some combination of all of these. Not so in most schools.

"The big problem is: *Good people don't take and stay in jobs that don't entrust them with important things*," says Theodore Sizer, a former school principal, the chairman emeritus of the Coalition of Essential Schools, and a leading

---

*The salary prospects for teachers are so bad that in the fall of 2000, Harold O. Levy, chancellor of the New York City public schools at the time, wrote an op-ed column for *The New York Times* pointing out that teachers between the ages of 22 and 28 earn $7,894 less a year than their college-educated counterparts in other professions. "The gap increases threefold by the time they are 44," Levy said. See "Why the Best Don't Teach," by Harold O. Levy, *The New York Times*, September 9, 2000.

voice in school reform, speaking with his own emphasis. "Smart college graduates look at the way the system works now and say, 'Well, maybe for a few years, Teach for America or something, but the system doesn't trust me, and there is no way I am going to make this a lifelong career.' So any solution to the teacher-quality problem has to reflect the movement of authority *downward.*"[16]

MAKING CITIZENS

Immediately following the September 2001 terrorist attacks on the East Coast, Richard Rothstein visited with a handful of high school students in central Florida. All of them were high performers and members of a church youth group, with well-educated, middle-class parents. If adolescents anywhere had the skills to discuss the meaning of the attacks and the complicated message they sent to America, Rothstein figured these should be some of them. But that's not what he found. When he asked students why they thought the nation had been attacked, one said it was because people elsewhere were jealous of Americans' freedoms, a comment that provoked wide agreement. Another said that Palestinian schools had brainwashed their children; a third said the terrorists didn't know the facts because they lacked the freedoms that Americans have.

When Rothstein tested out how the school's teachers were making use of America's freedoms to give their students the facts, the answers weren't encouraging. All the English teacher could say was that the attacks stemmed from crazed hatred. "She had no further explanation," Rothstein wrote in his weekly education column. When the school's history teacher tried to offer some material on Afghanistan, all she had was a fifteen-year-old film strip made when the Soviet Union still occupied the country and a video on world religions with fifteen minutes devoted to Islam. Nor did matters much improve in the years after the attacks. In a survey conducted of eighteen- to twenty-four-year-olds in late 2002, roughly half drew a complete blank about Afghanistan's geographical location.[17] It is not surprising, therefore, that the Florida history students did not know that Israel was a relatively new nation; nor did they realize that any compromise to achieve Middle East peace would likely displease both Palestinians and Israelis. Absent for many weeks—from this class and from leading voices in the national media (especially television news anchors and commentators)—was information that might help explain some aspect of the terrorists' motivation. This mattered. As experts on the Middle East continually pointed out at the time, simply blasting terrorist organizations might help a little. But it wasn't going to stop terrorism; there would always be more terrorists behind these angry souls until we somehow becalmed their motivation, or at least becalmed the sympathies of the societies that surround them. One might justifiably wonder how youngsters are going to learn this kind of multisided perspective when the adults around them lack the knowledge and wisdom to do the same. But that's what social evolution, and school, are all about: arming the next generation with deeper perceptions than the previous generation had. This requires an entirely different approach to social studies—a subject that many students in this Florida school weren't even taking. In fact, it requires a different concept of learning in general.

"Critical thinking," as Rothstein argued, "requires sources with conflicting viewpoints." To illustrate, he recalled the historic moment in 1971 when *The New York Times* and *The Washington Post* jointly published what came to be known as the Pentagon Papers. These were classified documents showing that policy makers had knowledge of Vietnamese motives that was far more sophisticated than the simplistic lines about Communist invaders that American officials were publicly proclaiming. "Thousands of lives might have been saved," Rothstein observed, "if ordinary Americans better understood the other side."[18]

The point here goes beyond the importance of balanced, sophisticated understanding. It revives an issue that's the bedrock of our country's foundation: the need to question authority. "We hold these Truths to be self-evident," states the Declaration of Independence, introducing America's familiar bedrock principles, "that all Men are created equal," and "that they are endowed by their Creator with certain unalienable Rights." It goes on to say that "whenever any Form of Government becomes destructive of these Ends, it is the Right of the People to alter or to abolish it, and to institute new Government . . ."

Students cannot responsibly answer this charge unless they're given the tools to do so—intellectual tools, not mechanical ones. And the work that needs to be done with those tools goes somewhat beyond what passes for critical thought today. One form is the polite, mildly informed, but ultimately superficial discussions that university professors increasingly observe in their classes, where students with a "whatever" attitude and a consumer's approach to education are unsettled and often offended by discussions that challenge their fundamental beliefs.[19] Almost equally pervasive is the cynical tendency to reflexively challenge any idea based on nothing more than one's instinctive reaction. Real questioning of authority—whether it be of classic figures in literature or of current leaders in government—breaks through both of these habits. It comes from a charged base of knowledge, a historical appreciation of the fine points, implications, and contradictions in history, in science, or in any other field. Those capabilities are difficult to acquire, however, when teachers are all rushing in one direction to satisfy the government's increasingly standardized definitions of skill. "There is less and less interest in preparing people who have the intelligence and the habit of mind to ask the unfamiliar and perhaps painful questions," says Theodore Sizer. "Our long-term economy depends on the informed skeptic, that person who says, 'That's interesting—it seems to work, but gee, if we looked at it in a different way, it might work better.' So it's the increasingly standardized values that trouble me the most. Feisty people are the people who have made this country special."[20]

I hope, in short, that the many different people involved in schools, and school policy, can someday find their way back to education's basics. Those basics do not mean years of feeding youngsters little more than facts and procedures related to the mythical three R's, then fawning over regurgitations that produce high test scores. I'm talking about an educational philosophy that was first mentioned in this book's Introduction, one that might be called enlightened basics. For at issue here are nothing less than the foundations of learning—building blocks that are increasingly important yet increasingly ignored.

These blocks can be broken into three simple parts: The first is an atmosphere of high expectations, tied to sophisticated, creative inquiries in the real world. To accomplish this, schools can follow some version of the gentle, artistic models of the Waldorf schools and New York's P.S. 234; or they can choose the grittier, no-nonsense approaches we've seen at the Expeditionary Learning Schools and Urban Academy High School. What is important, though (and occasionally missing in the experimental schools), is a kind of teaching that makes sure students' creative inquiries are backed and amplified by a broad base of knowledge. This leads to the second missing building block: a national collection of teachers who are not only well trained but also sufficiently well paid to attract the world's best and brightest—that is, people who can put good training to efficient, creative use. The third and final new element would be an educational culture that is first and foremost about people—and that trusts people, rather than numbers, to be the primary judge of a youngster's progress.* Ideally, this school-

---

*While it may seem idealistic if not heretical for a state to evaluate its students through some method that goes beyond standardized tests, it is not impossible. In late 2002, New Jersey Governor James McGreevey did just that, kicking off a five-year plan whereby teachers would

is-about-people message would be broadcast so clearly that students and teachers aren't the only ones to get involved in schools. America's parents will too.

———

It would be easy to characterize popular criticism of computers as merely another chapter in the world's oldest story—humanity's natural resistance to change. But that would minimize the forces at work in today's technological transformation. This is not just the future versus the past, uncertainty versus nostalgia. It is about encouraging a fundamental shift in priorities—institutional and personal. "In a very real sense," wrote Theodore Roszak, "the powers and purposes of the human mind are at issue."[21] I don't know why this lesson must be learned again and again. The only explanation I could come up with is that there is something about the nexus of technology and those untapped powers of the human mind that continually sets people to dreaming. Over the years, however, as technical reality has continually taken its toll, the more realistic of those visionaries have conceded defeat.

The pattern is perhaps best illustrated by the outer reaches of education's visionary history—its chronic dreams of wired Super Kids computing their way to the heights of human ability. One such visionary was George Leonard, the prolific chronicler of the human potential movement, a veteran education writer for *Look* magazine, and the author of *Education and Ecstasy*, a 1968 bestseller that envisioned a utopian learning environment, set, coincidentally, in 2001. The new schools Leonard described were going to be made of arboreal geodesic domes and computerized touch screens, complete with advanced CAI software that could communicate with children's brain waves.[22] Looking back, some thirty years after making this prediction, on society's inability to bring such a world into being, Leonard was now struck by technology's inherent limitations. "It's not that computers are so dumb," he told me. "It's that we've discovered that the human brain is much more complex and beautifully organized than we'd ever dreamed."

Some, unfortunately, have not discovered this fact. In late 2002, the departments of Commerce and Education jointly issued yet another report

---

start using student projects and other "performance" measures to assess scholastic progress. In endorsing the plan, which was partly developed by the state's chamber of commerce, McGreevey said tests have their place, but merely as "diagnostic" guides to help teachers adjust to students' needs. See "Governor Takes N.J. Down Testing Road Less Traveled," by Catherine Gewertz, *Education Week*, December 4, 2002, p. 20.

that dared to outline education's high-tech future. Written by a collection of scholars and technology experts and entitled "2020 Visions: Transforming Education and Training Through Advanced Technologies," the report sounds very much like Leonard's old predictions for 2001. It describes students learning through a variety of digitized media, such as simulations, game playing, and "tele-immersion" environments that would completely replace classroom teachers and make school buildings obsolete.[23]

Interestingly, two decades after composing his own breathless vision of edutopia, Leonard, by then a man in his sixties, wrote an essay for *Esquire* magazine that took a much calmer approach to this question of human potential. While Leonard didn't spell it out, there was another message here for the institution of education, a coda of sorts to University of Chicago professor Benjamin Bloom's findings on mastery. In Leonard's essay, which drew from his arduous years of experience learning the martial art of aikido (and which was later expanded into a book entitled *Mastery*), he divided people into four categories: dabblers, hackers, obsessives, and masters. His point was to delineate the different ways each of us deals with significant challenge, be it in a job, a sport, a relationship, or whatever. In Leonard's view, when people reach moments of great frustration, many unnecessarily give up and turn to a new pursuit—a different sport, a new lover, another job, and so forth. Though Leonard didn't question it, his theory could even include education's approach to the art of teaching, dominated as it's been by a continual search for new tricks. Whatever the pursuit, Leonard classifies those who bounce through them as society's dabblers. Hackers tend to be on the lazy side; they stop struggling altogether, contenting themselves with mediocre experiences. The obsessives take what feels like, and often looks like, the bravest approach: They begin pushing harder. Before long, they've injured themselves on the field, ruined perfectly good relationships, or spoiled prospects for career advancement; if they are in positions of authority, they often damage their professional institutions as well. (Grave illustrations of the obsessives' pattern in the business world occurred with the accounting scandals of 2001 and 2002, especially the Enron collapse, many of which were led by a corps of impetuous financial "stars.")[24] The master, meanwhile, avoids all these pitfalls by understanding one simple truth: Excellence is not about peak experiences; rather, it's defined by how we handle life's plateaus. Because that, after all, is where people spend most of their time. When masters feel progress stall, they see challenge for what it is—unavoidable, ubiquitous, and a gift. They know their task is to simply keep working, pushing gently and patiently toward the next momentary step up on life's endless series of plateaus.[25]

Learning, obviously, is not like a sport or a marriage or a job. But the fundamental lesson here—the virtue in achieving a balance between diligent effort and patience—applies to any difficult task. Education might even be one of society's most difficult, most complicated, and most troubled undertakings. One would think that its leaders might therefore approach incessant offerings of reform with an air of sobriety—and an appreciation for the long art of mastery.

═

In the end, the scenes described throughout this book come down to a set of unsettling truths. Computers can, in select cases, be wonderfully useful in school. But over and over, as we've seen, high technology is steering youngsters away from the messy, fundamental challenges of the real world—and toward the hurried buzz and neat convenience of an unreal virtual world. It is teaching them that exploring what's on a two-dimensional screen is more important than playing with real objects or sitting down to a conversation with a friend, a parent, or a teacher. By extension, it downplays the importance of listening carefully to people and of expressing oneself with acuity and individuality. And this leads all of us to sideline activities that have long helped youngsters develop fundamental human capacities, particularly the imagination, that sustain society over the long haul.

To get some final, visceral sense of the stakes in the computer era, it helps to recall what's known about the rest of electronic media. By now, most people understand the limitations of the vast bulk of material broadcast on television and in the movies. As for video games, educational technology's most vigorous ancestor, the harmful effects of the more violent products in this genre (boosting children's propensity to hostile behavior and constricting their imaginations) are well documented by now, as we've seen. But how many decades of gullibility did it take for us to get here? How many rounds of damage did we have to endure? One would think that the many warnings we've heard about our increasingly short attention spans—from teachers, from parents, and from employers—would have given education's policy makers some pause about expanding electronic media's influence even farther, into one of our most hallowed halls—the public school. One would think that the steady encroachment of the consumer culture, to the point where schools consider it perfectly acceptable to pepper textbooks with brand names and to make lucrative deals with companies like Coca-Cola and ZapMe!—the firm that promised schools free computers in exchange for the freedom not only to put advertising on their computer screens but also to sell students' consumer data to companies—would provoke real alarm.[26]

One would certainly think society's increasing turn to violence, especially among the young, many of whom commit horrific acts without showing the slightest sense of their gravity, would have stopped national leaders, or educators, or someone, in their tracks. If these trends are not enough to move us to rebuild the boundaries around our institutions of learning, one can only wonder what, if anything, will be. Maybe in the end, in the true American tradition, it will be money—misspent money, lots of it. The computer certainly makes for that.

It would be nice if books that sound stern warnings could save schools from years of costly mistakes. But they don't. Perhaps the final piece of this argument needs to be a submission to one of its own themes—that wisdom can come only through rich experience. And experience becomes rich only when it is fertilized with mistakes.

Like all of us, I suppose, schools have to fall for the latest thing, make blunders, and learn from there. If educators are swayed by a new mantra—that computer technology can be treated as "just a tool"—perhaps they'll also remember an old one. At the outset of this book, the campaign to put computers in schools was described as a *crisis* in the Chinese sense of the word, defined by two characters—one standing for danger, the other for opportunity. Thinking back on that duality, and everything I've seen while exploring it, I'm reminded of another ancient pairing of powerful forces. In an eighteenth-century book entitled *The Marriage of Heaven and Hell*, the poet William Blake wrote, "You never know what is enough unless you know what is more than enough."[27] Let us all hope that it is not much longer before that time comes, when technology's road of excess will have led our schools, and the rest of us, to a new palace of wisdom.

Acknowledgments

To write a book is an act of almost unbearable presumption—a search for large, elusive truths, which one dares argue that most of the world has been missing. To the extent that this book succeeds at some of that mission, much of the credit must go to my editor at Random House, Jonathan Karp. As this story was evolving, Jonathan continually saw possibilities for a longer reach and a more solid argument. For that, I am eternally grateful. I must also thank the family of expert editors at *The Atlantic Monthly*, which published the original article on which this book is based (and a follow-up story about Waldorf schools, an expansion of which became the book's final chapter). In the process of composing this story, one particular editor, William Whitworth, *The Atlantic*'s editor emeritus, generously read through multiple early drafts of the manuscript with painstaking care. Whether his suggestions were small or large (and there were plenty of both), his comments were always laced with a kind of literary judgment that has become almost extinct and which left me with conversational memories I will not soon forget.

During the lonely toil of book writing, often is the time when all a writer wants to do is step outside the door to run a few pages, or just a sentence, past someone who has sharp eyes and an understanding ear. Fortunately, I have been able to do exactly that throughout this project because of the existence of the San Francisco Writers Grotto. This collective, where my office sits, houses a number of insightful authors and artists, who have advised and supported me in this endeavor in countless ways. Sometimes, of course, an author craves outside assessment of an entire chapter. I occasionally inflicted this pain on fellow Grotto writers Po Bronson and Mary Roach; two former colleagues, Garrett Epps and Steve Schewel; Jonathan Rowe, another fellow scribbler; and Judah Schwartz, professor emeritus at Harvard and MIT and the former co-director of Harvard's Educational Technology Center. Each of these people provided just the right touch of encouragement and steerage, and at just the right time. Steve Schewel provided particularly useful insights as a reader of the final galleys. His fixes, which I was by then too close to the book (and too exhausted) to see, helped give numerous sections in this story some badly needed extra speed. I also thank Michael Rogers, my former editor at *Newsweek*, whose advice and support were invaluable; the Mesa Refuge, which generously housed me one summer as I pounded out drafts of several difficult chapters; and Grotto member Rodes Fishburne, whose ingenuity helped conclude a seemingly endless search for the perfect title for this book.

Underneath the structure and style of any book is its factual content, for which a collection of people deserve recognition. Todd Price, an assistant professor at National Louis University of Madison, Wisconsin, contributed prodigious early spadework on the telecommunications industry's history with the schools, and many hours of fruitful discussion, all of which lent valuable context to chapter 8. Sanaz Mozafarian brought a relentless diligence that helped pry a number of facts and figures out of obscure corners of the mazelike bureaucracy that defines education today. Several other researchers—Devon Kaylor, Tim Kingston, and Leena Pendharker—jumped in at other moments of deadline pressure to help document important details in this story. Others lent informal assistance that was equally invaluable—leading me to useful contacts and, in many cases, suffering through a series of long interviews. Foremost among these generous guides are Linda Carthage, Ann Cook, Scott Mace, John Markoff, Paul Reese, Gary Stager, and Andrew Trotter. Heavy thanks must also go to Random House's senior copy editor, Veronica Windholz, whose exacting questions and fixes brought extra precision to these pages.

But no intense, long-term project is completed without the people who inspire it. In this case, that inspiration has come, first, from my wife, Anh Crutcher Oppenheimer, whose understanding, careful readings, and gentle counsel fueled the writing of this story over the course of several long years; second, from my agent and good friend Rhoda Weyr, whose insights and wisdom kept this project on course; third, from my longtime friend Barbara Callander, who in a 1995 conversation planted the seed that led to this book; and, last, from the dozens of teachers I met throughout my travels. When writers describe teachers, it has become their cliché to couple the word *teacher* with the adjectives *dedicated, caring,* or *energetic.* During my tour of many kinds of classrooms across the country, the genesis of those clichés became very clear. I've examined many fields during my years as a journalist. Never have I met a group of professionals who face stiffer odds yet who approach their jobs with more commitment, and more heart.

Endnotes

Introduction

1. "That Sinking Feeling/The Pundits: I Goofed, but Not As Much As the GOP," by Laura Ingraham, *The Washington Post*, Sunday "Outlook" section, November 8, 1998, p. C1; "The Winners: See? Guess They Told You," *The Washington Post* "Outlook," November 8, 1998, p. C1.
2. "Welcome to Cyberspace," by Philip Elmer-DeWitt, *Time*, special issue, Spring 1995, p. 4.
3. Nicholas Negroponte, *being digital*, Vintage, 1995, pp. 6–7.
4. Exact figures on technology spending in schools are nearly impossible to compile because tabulations vary, even among authoritative sources. Among the many organizations that attempt this task, the most often cited is Quality Education Data, Inc., which compiles annual estimates based on annual surveys of 2,500 school districts. According to QED's most recent compilation, "Technology Purchasing Forecast 2001–2002," the schools spent $55 billion between 1991 and 2001. These figures are not markedly different from those compiled by a similar organization, Market Data Retrieval. However, the figures from both groups are considered by most experts to be very rough approximations, and probably on the conservative side. (When schools respond to surveys like QED's, they typically count only instructional hardware and software, and perhaps some staff training. This leaves out huge expenditures for items such as computer system management and maintenance, technical support, and, largest of all, administrative systems. Furthermore, districts often don't include every source of computer technology or funding—categories such as corporate donations, special state disbursements, or onetime grants.) One organization that does attempt to reflect these grand totals is the Software and Information Industry Association (SIIA). In its "Trends Report 2001" (http://www.trends report.net/education/1.html), SIIA estimated that the federal government was spending about $4 billion annually on educational computing. Charles Blaschke, an SIIA member who tracks these figures, estimates that other sources, such as industry, and state and local governments, contributed an additional $3.5 to $4 billion that year—for a total of $7.5 to $8 billion. Through-

out the 1990s, Blaschke said, the totals range from as low as $5 billion to as high as $9 billion. That makes for an average of $7 billion a year, or $70 billion over the course of a decade. In more recent years, additional expenses were added to this total, as administrators scrambled to automate their assessment systems to meet President George W. Bush's requirements for school account-ability.

5. The estimate that $70 billion in technology spending could have given the schools approximately 170,000 teachers over the last decade was calculated as follows: First, if one were to spread this fund equally throughout the 1990s, that would leave $7 billion available each year for teacher salaries. The average public school salary during this time hovered slightly above $40,000, accord-ing to a National Education Association report, "Rankings and Estimates," 2000–2001, April 8, 2002. (Specifically, teacher salary rates rose by no more than 0.3 percent a year during the 1990s, reaching $43,335 by 2001.) At those rates, $7 billion would cover the annual salaries of somewhere between 160,000 and 175,000 teachers—nearly 10 percent of the new recruits that the Department of Education has anticipated it will need by 2010.

6. The $4.67 trillion figure covers federal, state, and local spending on public ele-mentary and secondary schools, from 1990 through 2001. The tally comes from the Department of Education's *Digest of Education Statistics*, 2001, p. 34. (Those who are sticklers for detail may want to add another $20 to $40 billion a year over the last decade—the amount that the Department of Education esti-mates was spent on education indirectly during the 1990s, through property tax deductions, federal tax subsidies, and other diversions not reflected in the education budget. This item is reported in the Department of Education's *Fed-eral Support for Education: Fiscal Years 1980 Through 2001*, pp. 13–14.) The fig-ures indicating that more than half of the spending on school supplies goes to technology comes from "The Complete K–12 Report: Market Facts & Segment Analysis, 2002," Education Market Research, also cited in "Is Our Children Learning?" by Julie Landry, *Red Herring*, August 2002, p. 38. (The EMR report estimates, for instance, that in 2000–2001, $5.89 million was spent on school technology; meanwhile, $5.83 million was spent on books and supplementary materials. Roughly the same proportions, with slightly smaller totals, occur in previous years, from 1996 forward.)

7. Among the dozens of journal articles and books that describe education's addiction to fads—evident in any stroll through the stacks of a university library—some of the most commonly cited include the following: *Tinkering Toward Utopia: A Century of Public School Reform*, by David Tyack and Larry Cuban, Harvard University Press, 1995; *Revisiting "The Culture of the School and the Problem of Change*," by Seymour B. Sarason, Teachers College Press (Colum-bia University), 1996; *The Manufactured Crisis: Myths, Fraud, and the Attack on America's Public Schools*, by David C. Berliner and Bruce J. Biddle, Perseus, 1995;

and *Left Back: A Century of Failed School Reform,* by Diane Ravitch, Simon & Schuster, 2000.

8. These figures are data for the year 2000 from the National Private Schools Association Group and, for public schools, from "Quality Counts 2001," an annual special issue of *Education Week*, January 11, 2001, p. 110. The data in "Quality Counts" are compiled from a variety of government reports, primarily the Department of Education's National Center for Education Statistics. Anyone searching for precise figures should know that the number of teachers I have noted—4 million—is an extremely rough approximation, since the public and private school reports count school staff differently. The private school reports include both teachers and support staff (1.7 million, in their case), whereas the public school reports count only teachers, at 2.9 million. The full total comes to 4.6 million, which I've dropped to 4 million—a rough effort to count only teachers.

Chapter 1. Education's History of Technotopia

1. *Motion Pictures As an Aid In Teaching American History,* by Harry Arthur Wise, Ph.D., Yale University Press, 1939, pp. 1–2. Note: Wise excerpts Edison's quotes from two magazine articles. Those who wish to read them in the original should refer, in the first case, to "The Story of the Motion Picture," by Hugh Weir, *McClure's* 54 (November 1922), pp. 81–85; and, in the second case, to "What Edison Would Like to Do with the Movies," by Hugh Weir, *Collier's* 75 (February 21, 1925), pp. 20–28. Edison's 1913 remark is from *Dramatic Mirror*, July 9, 1913. It was since cited in *A History of Instructional Technology*, by Paul Saettler, McGraw-Hill, 1968, p. 98, and later in *Teachers and Machines: The Classroom Use of Technology Since 1920*, by Larry Cuban, Teachers College Press, 1986, p. 11.

2. Wise, *Motion Pictures*, pp. 4–24, 26–27, 113–14, 142–43.

3. Cuban, *Teachers and Machines*, pp. 11, 19, 26, 28.

4. "Programmed Instruction Revisited," by B. F. Skinner, *Phi Delta Kappan* 68 (October 1986), p. 104, as cited in *Technology and the Future of Schooling*, edited by Stephen T. Kerr, National Society for the Study of Education, 1996, p. 133. The second Skinner quote comes from p. 110 of his *Phi Delta Kappan* article and is cited on p. 134 of Kerr.

5. Cuban, *Teachers and Machines*, pp. 28–33. Cuban draws his Samoan account largely from *Bold Experiment: The Story of Educational Television in American Samoa*, by Wilbur Schramm, Lyle M. Nelson, Mere T. Betham, Stanford University Press, 1981, pp. 48, 54–55, 81–89, 185.

6. "The Computer Delusion," by Todd Oppenheimer, *The Atlantic Monthly*, July 1997, pp. 45–62.

7. "The PC? That Old Thing? An Industry's Founding Father Has Better Things to Do," by Steve Lohr, *The New York Times*, August 19, 2001, section 3, pp. 1 and

12; "Check Out the 'Me, Reborn' Generation," by Peter Applebome, *The New York Times*, November 22, 1998, Business section, pp. 1 and 6.

8. The $1,298 price for an Apple II comes from the Apple Museum (www.apple history.com/aII.html). The price of a standard mini-computer system is based on the Digital Equipment Corporation's PDP-11, a standard at the time, which sold for $17,900 in 1972. DEC cited the PDP-11 as comparable to previous systems selling for roughly $20,000. www.village.org/pdp11/faq.pages/price. images/pdp11-20-apr-1972/page2.gif.

9. "Minnesota's MECC Educates Next Generation of Computer Users," by Scott Mace, *InfoWorld*, December 7, 1981.

10. *The Tipping Point: How Little Things Can Make a Big Difference*, by Malcolm Gladwell, Little, Brown, 2000.

11. "Here Come the Microkids," by Frederic Golden, with reporting by Philip Faflick and J. Madeleine Nash, *Time*, May 3, 1982, pp. 50–56.

12. "Instructional Use of Computers in Public Schools," National Center for Education Statistics, U.S. Department of Education, Washington, D.C., 1982, pp. 1–2.

13. Drawing from reporting done in 1984 and 1985 by *Education Week*, Larry Cuban, a historian of education at Stanford, offered some rough computer counts in his book *Teachers and Machines*. Cuban found that by 1984, the number of school computers in the United States had climbed to 325,000, meaning that 68 percent of the schools had at least one computer. This trend was roughly confirmed by *The Wall Street Journal*, which reported that schools had bought 274,000 computers by April 1983. By 1985, Cuban wrote, the number jumped again; there was at least one computer in 92 percent of the nation's high schools and in 82 percent of the elementary schools.

14. *The Computer Generation*, by Peter Stoler, Facts on File Publications, 1984, p. 56.

15. "California Computer Education History: A Very Personal Perspective," by LeRoy Finkel of the San Mateo County Office of Education, *The Computing Teacher*, December 1982.

16. The book was *Computer Methods in Mathematics*, by Bob Albrecht, Addison-Wesley, 1969. The book, which actually appeared in 1968, drew partly on an earlier work: *Introduction to an Algorithmic Language: BASIC*, by Bob Albrecht, Sylvia Charp, David C. Johnson, Bruce E. Meserve, John O. Parker, Dina Gladys S. Thomas, and William F. Atchison, National Council of Teachers of Mathematics, 1968.

17. "Machine of the Year: The Computer Moves In," *Time*, January 3, 1983.

18. This speech was delivered to a conference put on by the Human Resources Research Organization (HUMRRO), in Warrenton, Virginia, which took place September 16–18, 1975. It has been listed on Seymour Papert's website at: www. papert.com/articles/SomePoeticAndSocialCriteriaForEducationDesign.html.

19. *Mindstorms: Children, Computers, and Powerful Ideas*, by Seymour Papert, Basic Books, 1980, p. 37.

20. "Trying to Predict the Future," by Seymour Papert, *Popular Computing*, October 1984, p. 38.

21. "The Future of School," a discussion between Seymour Papert and the Brazilian philosopher and educator Paolo Freire in Brazil during the late 1980s. The discussion was sponsored by Pontifícia Universidade Católica, the Catholic University of São Paulo, and the *Afternoon Journal* TV show. It was broadcast in Brazil by TV PUC São Paulo and KTV Solucoes. In 2001, it was available on Papert's website at: www.papert.com/articles/freire/freirePart1.html.

22. "Obsolete Skill Set: The 3 Rs—Literacy and Letteracy in the Media Ages," by Seymour Papert, *Wired*, May/June 1993.

23. Papert, *Mindstorms*, p. 187.

24. "The Importance of a Methodology That Maximizes Falsifiability: Its Application to Research About LOGO," by Henry Jay Becker, *Educational Researcher*, June–July 1987, pp. 11–16; "Situational Effects in Classroom Technology Implementations: Unfulfilled Expectations and Unexpected Outcomes," by Nira Hativa and Alan Lesgold, *Technology and the Future of Schooling*, edited by Stephen T. Kerr, National Society for the Study of Education, 1996, pp. 138–40; "Does Learning to Program Computers Teach You to Think?" by Helen Featherstone, *Harvard Education Letter*, Focus Series 3: "Technology and Schools," 1997.

25. This notion—that the best pedagogy is one that is varied, including both old-fashioned didactics and more progressive, hands-on student projects—will be developed throughout this book. (See in particular chapters 4–7, 9, and 11–13.)

26. *Tinkering Toward Utopia*, by Larry Cuban and David Tyack, Harvard University Press, 1995; *Greater Expectations: Overcoming the Culture of Indulgence in America's Homes and Schools*, by William Damon, Free Press, 1995; *Revisiting the Culture of School and the Problem of Change*, by Seymour B. Sarason, Teachers College Press, 1996; Ravitch, *Left Back*.

27. "Many Schools Buying Computers Find Problems with Using Them," by Burt Schorr, *The Wall Street Journal*, April 7, 1983, pp. 27 and 38.

28. "Technology Counts, '99: Building the Digital Curriculum," a special issue of *Education Week*, September 23, 1999, p. 61; "Technology Counts, 2002: E-Defining Education," *Education Week*, May 9, 2002, p. 54.

29. "Teacher Preparation: The Anatomy of a College Degree," Southern Regional Education Board, Atlanta, Georgia, 1985, pp. 3–18.

30. Out of fairness (or dark humor), it seems only fitting to identify this photo. It was published in a special issue of *InfoWorld*, on April 25, 1983. The issue was entitled *The InfoWorld Guide to Computer Camps*, and it appeared under a mock cover photograph of a gawky girl sitting in front of a tree, grinning at the camera with a mouthful of braces. In front of her is a desktop Sony computer that, were it not for the screen, could be mistaken today for a microwave oven. On the

monitor she has typed, "Dear Mom and Dad, It rained all day. But I don't want to come home! Love, Hilary."

31. "The Uses of Computers in Education," by Patrick Suppes, *Scientific American* 215, 3 (September 1966), pp. 206–20.

32. www.stanford.edu/~psuppes/ Note: Suppes's "intellectual autobiography" was written in March 1978 and previously published in a book entitled *Patrick Suppes*, edited by R. J. Bogdan, D. Reidel Publishing Company, Dordrecht, Holland, 1979.

33. "Firm Helps Teach Kids a Thing or Two," by Lorna Fernandes, *The Business Journal*, July 18, 1997.

34. "Computer-Based Integrated Learning Systems in the Elementary and Middle Grades: A Critical Review and Synthesis of Evaluation Reports," by Henry Jay Becker, *Journal of Educational Computing Research* 8, 1 (1992), pp. 1–41; "Research on Computers and Education: Past, Present and Future," a report for the Bill and Melinda Gates Foundation by Jeffrey T. Fouts, February 2000, pp. 5–9; "The 2 Sigma Problem: The Search for Methods of Group Instruction as Effective as One-to-One Tutoring," by Benjamin S. Bloom, *Educational Researcher*, Vol. 13 (6), pp. 4–16, 1984.

35. "Computers," *IFG Policy Notes*, the Institute for Research on Educational Finance and Governance, summer 1984, p. 4. Citing a forthcoming report by Stanford professor of education M. Beatriz Arias, the publication notes that 80 percent of the 2,000 largest and richest high schools serving Hispanics had microcomputers in 1983; meanwhile, only 40 percent of "the smallest, poorest high schools" had them. In a National Science Foundation survey the same year, the numbers are much smaller, but the proportions remain the same. The NSF found that computers were used in 32 percent of the "urban rich" schools, but only 18 percent of the "ghetto" schools.

36. U.S. Census Bureau, *Statistical Abstract of the United States*, 2000, p. 420.

37. "The Computer Fallacy," a Q & A between Joseph Weizenbaum and Franz-Olivier Giesbert of *Le Nouvel Observateur*, December 2, 1983. It was reprinted in the March 1984 issue of *Harper's*.

38. "Contrary to Expectations, Computers Don't Necessarily Improve Students' Writing," by Colette Daiute, *Harvard Education Letter*, Focus Series 3: "Technology and Schools," 1997; *The Child and the Machine*, by Alison Armstrong and Charles Casement, Robins Lane Press, 2000, pp. 95–109; "Researchers Cast Skeptical Eye on Efficacy of 'Writing to Read,'" by Peter West, *Education Week*, August 1, 1990. (This article is a lengthy examination of an IBM literacy program that was popular at the time.)

39. "California School-Technology Plan Hangs in the Balance," by Peter West, *Education Week*, June 7, 1989.

40. "Planning for Technology: Few Matching Dollars with Foresight," by Peter West, *Education Week*, September 13, 1989.

41. "Videodisk to Compete with Textbooks for a Spot on Adoption List in Texas," by Peter West, *Education Week*, January 17, 1990.

42. "Tex. Videodisk Vote Called Boon to Electronic Media," by Peter West, *Education Week*, November 28, 1990.

43. The *San Jose Mercury News* ran a package of five articles on this topic on January 14 and 15, 1996. The most pertinent of them regarding achievement were the following: "Computers in School: Do Students Improve? High Technology Doesn't Always Equal High Achievement," by Christopher H. Schmitt and Larry Slonaker, January 14; "Two Schools of Thought—Computers Get More Praise at a Model Technology School with Low Test Scores Than One with High Scores: The Principal Gives Little Credit to Computers," by Larry Slonaker, January 14; "Classroom Computers: A Help or a Hindrance?" by Larry Slonaker and Christopher H. Schmitt, January 15.

44. "High Tech Teaching—What's the Payoff?" by Terry Crane, *San Jose Mercury News*, February 11, 1996, p. 7C.

45. "What Happens After ACOT: Outcomes for Program Graduates One Year Later," by four professors from Memphis State University: Steven M. Ross, Ph.D.; Lana J. Smith, Ph.D.; Gary R. Morrison, Ph.D.; Jacqueline O'Dell, Ed.D. ACOT Report #6, 1990, produced for Apple Classrooms of Tomorrow Advanced Technology Group, Apple Computer, Inc.

46. *Teaching with Technology: Creating Student-Centered Classrooms*, by Judith Haymore Sandholtz, Ph.D.; Cathy Ringstaff, Ph.D.; and David Dwyer, Ph.D., Teachers College Press, 1997, pp. 1–10, 96–103, 174–77, and throughout; *Education and Technology: Reflections on Computing in Classrooms*, edited by Charles Fisher, David C. Dwyer, and Keith Yocam, Jossey-Bass, 1996, pp. 51–65, 237–50, 266–76, and throughout.

47. "Power On! New Tools for Teaching and Learning," Office of Technology Assessment, U.S. Congress, September 1988 (order no. PB89-114276), pp. 6–8.

48. "A Bill of Goods: The Early Marketing of Computer-Based Education and Its Implications for the Present Moment," by Douglas D. Noble, in *International Handbook of Teachers and Teaching*, edited by Bruce J. Biddle, Thomas L. Good, and Ivor F. Goodson, Kluwer Academic Publishers, 1997.

49. "How Important is the Internet?" by Ted Landphair, *Voice of America News*, January 25, 2003. (This article refers to comments that John Perry Barlow originally made about the Internet in 1995.)

50. "Closing the Book on Classics: Educators Say Computer Skills More 'Essential,' " by Nanette Asimov, *San Francisco Chronicle*, February 14, 1996, p. 1. (This story drew from a report by the Public Agenda Foundation, a New York–based research group.)

51. "Report Assails State's Low-tech Schools/Task Force Says Computers Would Boost Achievement," by Sara Catania, *Los Angeles Daily News*, published in the *San Francisco Examiner*, July 7, 1996, p. B6.

52. These accounts of spending on technology in the early 1990s are pulled from five different *Education Week* stories by Peter West. Sequentially, they are: "Disputes over Control, Direction Slow Technology Initiative," June 5, 1991; "Law-

makers, Worried About Ky. Computer Plan, May Repeal Cap," September 16, 1992; "'Apples for Students': Computers for Schools, Profits for Marketers," October 23, 1991; "Technology Project to Award $10 Million in Grants," December 4, 1991; and "Investors Urged to Help Spur the Use of Education Technology," February 3, 1993.

53. "Steve Jobs: The Next Insanely Great Thing," by Gary Wolf, *Wired*, February 1996, pp. 102–63.

54. ABC *Nightline*, September 30, 1998; "N.J.'s High-Tech Myth; Innovations, Not PCs, Said to Boost Test Scores," by Jay Mathews, *The Washington Post*, June 22, 1996, p. A1; interview with principal Bob Fazio.

55. ABC *Nightline*, September 30, 1998.

56. "Technology Counts 2001/The New Divides: Looking Beneath the Numbers to Reveal Digital Inequities," a special issue of *Education Week*, May 10, 2001, pp. 10, 36, 38, 40, 56–61, 68.

57. "Greedy Clicks," by Todd Oppenheimer, *Salon*, February 2, 2000 (www.salon.com/news/feature/2000/02/02/digital).

58. Confirmation hearing on Charles E. Wilson as secretary of defense before the U.S. Senate Armed Services Committee, January 15, 1953.

59. "SIIA: Fewer Tech Companies Will Serve Schools' Needs/But Those That Remain Will Be More Stable," by Cara Branigan, *eSchool News*, November 2001, p. 1.

60. "Feds Give $10 Million to Online School for Teacher Ed," by Corey Murray, *eSchool News*, November 2001, p. 41. (Note: This article reflects only limited criticism of the online program at Western Governors University. The broader critique of online "distance" learning is in chapter 3.)

61. Branigan, "SIIA," *eSchool News*, November 2001, p. 1.

62. "On a Florida Key," by E. B. White, *Essays of E. B. White*, Harper & Row, 1977, p. 141.

Chapter 2. Fooling the Poor with Computers: Harlem, New York

1. *The Atlantic Monthly*, October 1997, Letters to the Editor, from Linda Roberts.

2. The accomplishments of the Central Park East schools have been thoroughly documented in numerous studies and books about education reform. Some of the most thorough are two reports published by the National Center for Restructuring Education, Schools and Teaching (NCREST), Teachers College, Columbia University: "Makers of Meaning in a Learning-Centered School: A Case Study of Central Park East 1 Elementary School," by Jon Snyder, Ann Lieberman, Maritza B. Macdonald, and A. Lin Goodwin, August 1992; and "Lives of the Graduates of Central Park East Elementary School: Where Have They Gone? What Did They Really Learn?" by David Bensman, October 1994. Deborah Meier, the founder of the CPE schools, also wrote a book about her experiences: *The Power of Their Ideas*, Beacon Press, 1995.

3. For an explanation of the basic principles here—of intellectual rigor and of getting a circle of adults, especially parents, involved in failing students' education—see Damon, *Greater Expectations*, especially pp. 143–88; and *Waiting for a Miracle: Why Schools Can't Solve Our Problems—And How We Can*, by James P. Comer, M.D., Penguin, 1997, especially pp. 45–73. (It's worth noting that Brooklyn's Clinton Hill Elementary School uses Comer's "School Development Program," which stresses parental involvement, in combination with E. D. Hirsch's conservative "Core Knowledge" program.)

4. "Report Calls Filters 'Hopelessly Flawed,'" by Elizabeth B. Guerard, *eSchool News*, November 2001, p. 1.

5. "Filtering Company 'Dotsafe' Becomes Another Dot-bomb," by Cara Branigan, *eSchool News*, June 2001, p. 16.

6. "Board Blocks Student Access to Web Sites: Computer Filtering Hobbles Internet Research Work," by Anemona Hartocollis, *The New York Times*, November 10, 1999; "Internet Filtering Is Balancing Act for Many Schools," by Rhea R. Borja, *Education Week*, January 16, 2002; "Report: Some Web Filters Might Reflect Bias," by Dennis Pierce, *eSchool News*, April 2002, p. 1; "Report: Filters Alone Won't Protect Kids Online," *eSchool News*, June 2002, p. 20; "ACLU Sues to Ask and Tell What Sites N2H2 Blocks," *eSchool News*, September 2002, p. 14.

7. "Jed Perl on Art: Seeing and Time," by Jed Perl, *The New Republic*, August 3, 1998, p. 31.

8. "Strike the Band: Pop Music Without Musicians," by Tony Scherman, *The New York Times*, February 11, 2001, section 2, p. 1.

9. "In the Great Outdoors to Learn About Nature, Students Are Leaving Their Desks Behind," by Tyra Lucile Mead, *San Francisco Chronicle*, December 22, 1998. See also "Life's a Beach (and a Lighthouse) to Redwood City Fifth Graders," by Julie N. Lynem, *San Francisco Chronicle*, November 17, 2000.

10. "The Stories Behind the Story," by James W. Michaels, *Forbes*, August 27, 1984, p. 4.

11. Cuban, *Teachers and Machines*, p. 93.

12. The influence of rewards on a youngster's achievement is dealt with more fully in chapter 9. See in particular note number 54 for that chapter.

13. *Technopoly*, by Neil Postman, Vintage, 1992, p. 5.

14. "New York Reveals Test Score Errors: Says Thousands Were Wrongly Assigned to Summer School," by Anemona Hartocollis, *The New York Times*, September 15, 1999.

15. "The Battle over School Funding Has Been Waged Before," by Joel Stashenko, Associated Press, as published in *Newsday*, June 27, 2002.

16. *Savage Inequalities*, by Jonathan Kozol, Crown, 1991, pp. 133–34, 237. The *Wall Street Journal* excerpts were drawn from a June 27, 1989, editorial, and special education supplements that were published on March 31, 1989, and February 9, 1990.

17. New York State Supreme Court, *CFE v. State of New York Decision*, January 10, 2001; "Court Reverses Finance Ruling on City Schools," by Richard Perez-Pena, *The New York Times*, June 26, 2002.

18. "The Funding Gap: Low-Income and Minority Students Receive Fewer Dollars," The Education Trust, August 2002; "Study Finds Inequity in Students' School Days," by Debra Viadero, *Education Week*, September 11, 2002, p. 6; "Researchers: School Segregation Rising in South," by Alan Richard, *Education Week*, September 11, 2002, p. 5. These reports concern three separate inquiries. The Richard article reports on a conference held by the Civil Rights Project of Harvard University and the University of North Carolina's Center for Civil Rights. The Viadero article concerns a study by Columbia University Teachers College and the University of Maryland, College Park. The Education Trust study, by Greg F. Orlofsky, is an analysis of demographic and financial data for the 1999–2000 school year from approximately fifteen thousand school districts. The Trust's figures were adjusted and weighted to account for the higher cost of educating students in certain areas, like large cities, and for the extra expense that special-education students require. The report further found that while a good many states try to make up for local funding shortages by giving more cash to schools in poor districts, twenty-two states actually go in the opposite direction. They send poor districts less money than they send wealthier districts, thereby exacerbating local government inequities.

19. "Ticket to Nowhere: Pataki Court Decision Cites Schools as Track to Service Careers," by Wayne Barrett, *The Village Voice*, July 3–9, 2002.

Chapter 3. Breaking Down Rural Isolation: Hundred, West Virginia

1. "Rural Schools Leading the Way in Technology," *Preston County Journal*, Kingwood, West Virginia, December 30, 1988.

2. "San Lorenzo Schools to Give Laptops to All," by Meredith May, *San Francisco Chronicle*, August 19, 2001, p. A20.

3. "Rutgers Study: Web Makes Student Cheating Easier," by Cara Branigan, *eSchool News*, June 2001, p. 14.

4. There's a long history of philosophizing about the fundamental vices and virtues of technology. While there are many voices in this debate, some of the more enduring treatises have been: on the pro-technology side, *The Virtual Community*, by Howard Rheingold, Addison-Wesley, 1993; and *being digital*, by Nicholas Negroponte. On the worrying side are accounts such as *Computer Power and Human Reason: From Judgment to Calculation*, by Joseph Weizenbaum, W. H. Freeman and Co., 1976; Postman, *Technopoly*; and *The Cult of Information: A Neo-Luddite Treatise on High-Tech, Artificial Intelligence, and the True Art of Thinking*, by Theodore Roszak, University of California Press, 1986, 1994.

5. "Illinois Education Board Approves Online High School Courses," *eSchool News*, October 2000 ("Newslines" section); "Michigan Virtual High School Goes On-

line," *eSchool News,* September 2001 ("Newslines"); "Bennett's K–12 Inc. Targets Elementary Schoolers Online," by Jennifer Patterson Lorenzetti, *eSchool News,* November 2001, p. 18.

6. "Lessons Learned at Dot-Com U: In the Rush to Turn Online Education into a Business, the Roof Caved In. From the Ruins, Some Try to Rebuild," by Katie Hafner, *The New York Times,* May 2, 2002, p. E1; "The E-Learning Curve," by Glen C. Altschuler, for "Education Life," a special supplement to *The New York Times,* August 5, 2001, p. 13. (Altschuler is a professor of American studies at Cornell University and dean of the university's School of Continuing Education and Summer Sessions.) "Technology Counts 2002: E-Defining Education," a special issue of *Education Week,* May 9, 2002, p. 8.

7. "Giving It the Old Online Try," by William C. Symonds, *Business Week,* December 3, 2001, pp. 76–80.

8. *The No Significant Difference Phenomenon* (5th edition), by Tom L. Russell, North Carolina State University, 1999.

9. "Research on Computers and Education: Past, Present and Future," a report for the Bill and Melinda Gates Foundation, by Jeffrey T. Fouts, Professor of Education, Seattle Pacific University, February 2000, pp. 23–25.

10. "Technology Counts 2002," *Education Week,* May 9, 2002, pp. 13–34.

11. Altschuler, *The New York Times,* August 5, 2001.

12. "Using a Model of Learner Readiness to Study the Effects of Course Design on Classroom and Online College Student Performance," an unpublished doctoral dissertation, University of California, Berkeley, by Cathleen Ann Kennedy, Ph.D., 2001.

13. Hafner, *The New York Times,* May 2, 2002.

14. "Controversy Flares over Public Funding of 'Cyber Schools': A Fast-Growing Offshoot of Charter Movement Uses E-Mail, Web Sites/Einstein's Teacher Shortage," by Robert Tomsho, *The Wall Street Journal,* April 5, 2002, p. 1.

15. "Report: eLearning Raises Thorny Policy Questions," *eSchool News* (staff and wire reports), July 2002, p. 12; "Pennsylvania Seeks Fix for Troubled Cyber Schools," by Corey Murray, *eSchool News,* August 2002, p. 12; "Cyber Learning Complicates Charter Funding," by Caroline Hendrie, *Education Week,* January 15, 2003; "States Debate 'Face Time' Requirement for Virtual Schools," *eSchool News,* January 2003, p. 8; "Old-School Rules Challenge Cyber Education in N.Y., Colo.," *eSchool News,* February 2003, p. 6.

16. "Take-Home Test: Adding PC's to Book Bags," by Lisa Guernsey, *The New York Times,* August 23, 2001, pp. D1 and D7.

17. May, *San Francisco Chronicle,* August 19, 2001.

18. "Beaming Data Holds Promise, with Limits, for Networking," by David F. Gallagher, *The New York Times,* August 23, 2001, p. D9.

19. Guernsey, *The New York Times,* August 23, 2001; "Maine Buys 36,000 Laptops for Students, Teachers," *eSchool News,* February 2002, p. 1 (plus author report-

ing); "Michigan Officials Pin Hopes on Teacher Laptops," by Jennifer Patterson Lorenzetti, *eSchool News*, November 2001; May, *San Francisco Chronicle*, August 19, 2001.

20. "Turning Hand-Helds into Handouts," by Lisa Guernsey, *The New York Times*, August 23, 2001, p. D7.

21. "Parents' Protests Sink School's Laptop Plans," *eSchool News*, January 2002; "Wireless Laptops' Downside: Not Enough to Go Around," by Cara Branigan, *eSchool News*, January 2001; "Handheld Computing: New Best Tech Tool or Just a Fad?" by Andrew Trotter, *Education Week*, September 26, 2001, p. 8; "As Gadgets Go to Class, Schools Try to Cope," by Jennifer S. Lee, *The New York Times*, August 15, 2002, p. E1.

22. "Student Laptops Are a Luxury," an editorial in *USA Today*, September 13, 2002, p. A16; "Lakeside Tsunami: Bill Gates' Alma Mater Erupts in Controversy over Mandatory Use of Laptop Computers," by Judy Lightfoot, *The Seattle Weekly*, March 22, 2001.

23. "Professors Vie with Web for Class's Attention," by John Schwartz, *The New York Times*, January 2, 2003, p. 1.

24. "West Virginia Story: Achievement Gains from a Statewide Comprehensive Instructional Technology Program," by Dale Mann, Ph.D., Carol Shakeshaft, Ph.D., Jonathan Becker, J.D., and Robert Kottkamp, Ph.D., a study for the Milken Exchange on Education Technology, 1999.

25. Fouts, "Research on Computers and Education," pp. 19–20.

26. Mann, Shakeshaft, et al., pp. 48–49. (In 2003, the annual salary for a teacher's aide in West Virginia was $21,300.)

Chapter 4. Money, Bureaucratic Perfection, and the Parenting Gap: Montgomery County, Maryland

1. Drawn from budget figures for Montgomery County Public Schools. The figures were based on what was known in the spring of 2001, which included projections for 2002. It includes district and state funding, along with all special grants from federal and private sources.

2. "QED's School Market Trends: District Technology Forecast, 2001–2002," a report by Quality Education Data, Inc., pp. 7–8. Specifically, QED calculated that the nation's school districts were spending an average of $97 per student on instructional technology (that is, hardware, software, networks, maintenance, and training).

3. *Beyond the Classroom: Why School Reform Has Failed and What Parents Need to Do*, by Laurence Steinberg, Simon & Schuster, 1996.

4. A number of Jerome Bruner's books outline this psychologist's theories about how youngsters make meaning out of what they study and what they do. Early examples include *Toward a Theory of Instruction*, Harvard University Press, 1966, and *Actual Minds, Possible Worlds*, Harvard University Press, 1986. A

more recent sample is *The Culture of Education*, Harvard University Press, 1996, especially pp. 150–59.

5. Any number of education histories elaborate on the confines of traditional schooling through the decades. For a neatly condensed version, see "Education and Democracy," a chapter by Diane Ravitch in *Making Good Citizens: Education and Civil Society*, edited by Ravitch and Joseph P. Viteritti, Yale University Press, 2001, pp. 15–29.

6. This line—that if we only put more money into school technology, everything would work fine—has become one of the technovangels' arguments of last resort. A typical illustration of this was reflected in "Technology in American Schools: Seven Dimensions for Gauging Progress, a Policymaker's Guide," from the Milken Exchange on Education Technology, 1998. This report, and many supporting materials from the Milken Exchange (a non-profit outfit launched by the former junk bond king Michael Milken), was widely circulated in education-policy circles. Among other things, it said, "To date the technology capacity of most schools has not been sufficient for educators to use as everyday tools for learning. As this situation improves, the added staff and budgetary requirements for maintenance, operation, upgrades and replacements will be tremendous."

7. "Corporate Customers Can't Get No Satisfaction: Survey Shows Many Firms Unhappy with Their Tech Suppliers," by David R. Baker, *San Francisco Chronicle*, October 16, 2002, pp. B1 and B5.

8. "Student-Built Computers to Save Mississippi Nearly $2 Million," *eSchool News*, September 2002, p. 20; "Technology Spreads Slowly but Surely in Miss.," by Alan Richard, *Education Week*, April 2, 2003, pp. 6–7.

Chapter 5. Starting from Scratch with a Computer on Every Desk:
Napa, California

1. "Technology Counts 2002," *Education Week*, May 9, 2002, p. 32.

2. " 'eLearning for Schools' Steals the Show at NSBA Technology Conference," by Cara Branigan, *eSchool News*, December 2000, p. 45.

3. "Minnesota High School Pilots Online Registration: System Saves Time, Removes Guesswork," by Elizabeth B. Guerard, *eSchool News*, March 2002, p. 28; "Second Annual Tech-Savvy Awards," *eSchool News*, March 2002, p. 14. Various Internet sites have been built to display school accountability measures, which became a heavy emphasis of President George W. Bush's administration. One of the most complete sites was set up by the Heritage Foundation: www.heritage.org/reportcards.

4. Tyack and Cuban, *Tinkering Toward Utopia*; *The Schools We Need, and Why We Don't Have Them*, by E. D. Hirsch, Anchor, 1996; Ravitch, *Left Back*.

5. "Former Education Secretary Starts Online-Learning Venture," by Mark Walsh, *Education Week*, January 10, 2001.

6. "Search and Deploy: The Race to Build a Better Search Engine," by Michael Specter, *The New Yorker*, May 29, 2000, pp. 88–100.

7. "Study Reveals Web as Loosely Woven," by Ian Austen, *The New York Times*, May 18, 2000; "As the Web Matures, Fun Is Hard to Find," by Lisa Guernsey, *The New York Times*, March 28, 2002, p. G1. The latter story includes a number of devastating remarks from former Web enthusiasts who have found the Web to be an increasingly uninspiring place.

8. "From Unseemly to Lowbrow, the Web's Real Money Is in the Gutter," by John Schwartz, *The New York Times*, August 26, 2002, p. C1.

9. "Too Often, Educators' Online Links Lead to Nowhere: Recent Study Highlights Prevalence of 'Link Rot,'" by Andrew Trotter, *Education Week*, December 4, 2002, p. 1.

10. Specter, *The New Yorker*, May 29, 2000.

11. "Relegating Student Research to the Past," by Kathleen Kennedy Manzo, *Education Week*, November 20, 2002, p. 1; "The Tests We Know We Need," an op-ed column in *The New York Times* by Louis V. Gerstner, Jr., chairman of the IBM Corporation and co-chairman of Achieve, Inc., a non-profit school-reform group, March 14, 2002. (The Manzo article reports on a national survey of high school teachers conducted by *Concord Review*, a periodical dedicated to publishing exemplary high school history essays.)

12. "Freelancers Win in Case of Work Kept in Databases," *The New York Times*, June 26, 2001, p. A1.

13. Vintage High School Program Planning Guide, 2000–2001; Napa High School Student Curriculum Guide, 2000–2001; "Riley Says It's Time to Rethink High Schools," by Joetta L. Sack, *Education Week*, September 22, 1999, p. 20.

14. "Implementation and Performance in New American Schools: Three Years into Scale-Up," a report by Mark Berends, Sheila Nataraj Kirby, Scott Naftel, and Christopher McKelvey, RAND Corporation, 2001; "Unrequited Promise," by Jeffrey Mirel, *Education Next*, Summer 2002, pp. 64–72.

15. "Student Thinking Processes: The Influence of Immediate Computer Access on Students' Thinking, First- and Second-Year Findings," ACOT report no. 3, 1989, by Robert J. Tierney, Ph.D., Ohio State University, p. 12.

Chapter 6. Computer Literacy: Limping Toward Tomorrow's Jobs

1. "Viewpoint: Shaping the Nation's Ed-Tech Agenda," *eSchool News*, June 2001, p. 60.

2. "Connecting K–12 Schools to the Information Superhighway," a report prepared by McKinsey & Company for the National Information Infrastructure Advisory Council, a presidential task force appointed by the Clinton administration, undated, p. 7.

3. *The Productive Edge: How U.S. Industries Are Pointing the Way to a New Era of Economic Growth*, by Richard K. Lester, W. W. Norton & Co., 1998. While Lester finds a flat trend in worker productivity, in a more recent account ("The Pro-

ductivity Mirage," by John Cassidy, *The New Yorker*, November 27, 2000), a few hard-nosed economists go much further. They argue that when viewed broadly, computers and the entire Internet economy have actually had little effect on the nation's gross domestic product or on its overall productivity.

4. "Report: 2002 Not Promising for High-Tech," by Daniel F. DeLong, *NewsFactor Network*, June 6, 2001. The article cites a study by the Washington, D.C., job-placement firm Challenger, Gray & Christmas (www.newsfactor.com).

5. Oppenheimer, *The Atlantic Monthly*, July 1997, p. 54.

6. "Bridging the Gap: Information Technology Skills for a New Millennium," a study conducted by the Information Technology Association of America, Arlington, Virginia, April 2000.

7. "When Can You Start? Building Better Information Technology Skills and Careers," a study conducted by the Information Technology Association of America, Arlington, Virginia, April 2001.

8. "Classroom Computers: A Help or a Hindrance," by Larry Slonaker and Christopher H. Schmitt, *San Jose Mercury News*, January 15, 1996, p. 1A.

9. "On the Waterfront," by Paul Goldberger, *The New Yorker*, December 13, 1999, p. 38. (Matteo Pericoli's drawings of Manhattan were later published as a book, *Manhattan Unfurled*, Random House, 2001.)

10. "Zap! Splat! Smarts? Why Video Games May Actually Help Your Children Learn," by Neil Gross, *Business Week*, December 23, 1996, pp. 64–71.

11. *Life on the Screen: Identity in the Age of the Internet*, by Sherry Turkle, Simon & Schuster, 1995, p. 69.

12. "Seeing Through Computers," *The American Prospect*, by Sherry Turkle, March–April 1997, p. 79.

13. "California Educators Plan 19 Computer Demo Centers," by Scott Mace, *InfoWorld*, November 15, 1982.

14. "Corporate Involvement in Public Schools: A Practitioner-Academic's Perspective," by Larry Cuban, *Teachers College Record* 85, 2 (Winter 1983), pp. 183–203.

15. Cuban, *Teachers College Record* 85, 2.

16. "Better Schools, Uncertain Returns," by Peter Applebome, *The New York Times*, "Week in Review," March 16, 1997, p. 5.

17. Cuban, *Teachers College Record* 85, 2, p. 187.

18. "What Work Requires of Schools," A SCANS Report for America 2000, from the Secretary's Commission on Achieving Necessary Skills, U.S. Department of Labor, June 1991, pp. v, vii, xv, 20–23.

19. Berends et al., "Implementation and Performance," p. xxi.

20. Videotape of "Policy Arena," a closing session of "Fusion: Global Learning Summit 2000," a conference in Glasgow, Scotland, September 27–29, 2000.

21. "Computers Key to Future," by Angus King, Independent governor of Maine, *USA Today*, September 13, 2002, p. A16.

22. In "The Changing Economic Landscape," by James Fallows, *The Atlantic Monthly,* March 1985, Fallows managed to redefine the terror that was seizing United States policy makers at the time, as the old rust-belt industries—primarily the steel and auto-manufacturing sector—were falling into steep decline. The article demonstrates that tumultuous change is an unavoidable fact of industrial life.

23. Lester, *The Productive Edge.*

24. "Get to Work!" by Jeff Madrick, a review of Lester's *The Productive Edge* in *The New York Times Book Review,* June 28, 1998, p. 17.

25. Weizenbaum, *Computer Power and Human Reason,* p. 280.

26. "Why Civics Is Going to the Dogs," by E. J. Dionne Jr., a syndicated column for *The Washington Post* Writers Group, November 30, 1999. Two years later, a twenty-eight-nation poll found American students' basic knowledge of government remained relatively superficial and unconnected to real life. Across all countries, while students were interested in civic involvement in some fashion, four out of five showed no desire to engage in traditional governmental politics. See "28-Nation Study: Students' Grasp of Civics Is Mixed," by Kathleen Kennedy Manzo, *Education Week,* March 21, 2001, p. 1.

27. "Service Learning Required," by Joel Westheimer and Joseph Kahne, a commentary article for *Education Week,* January 26, 2000, p. 52.

28. As the one-year anniversary of the September 2001 attacks drew near, newspapers, magazines, and Internet sites exploded with worries and recommendations about how to turn the anniversary into a teachable moment. (One organization that seemed to be coordinating and promoting interest in civics, and doing so with a balanced view, was the Washington, D.C.–based Participate America Foundation.) See "Educators Split over What to Teach Come Sept. 11," by David J. Hoff, *Education Week,* September 4, 2002, p. 1.

29. "Education and Democratic Citizenship," by Norman Nie and D. Sunshine Hillygus, a chapter in *Making Good Citizens: Education and Civil Society,* edited by Diane Ravitch and Joseph P. Viteritti, Yale University Press, 2001, pp. 30–57, especially pp. 38–43.

Chapter 7. Bulldozing the Imagination

1. "Beyond Machines," by Kevin Bushweller, "Technology Counts, 2001: The New Divides: Looking Beneath the Numbers to Reveal Digital Inequities," a special issue of *Education Week,* May 10, 2001, pp. 31–36.

2. "Computers in Class: A Waste of $50 Billion?" *USA Weekend,* February 14–16, 1997, pp. 10 and 12 (and author interviews with Union City, California, school officials); "Teach Carpentry, Not Hammer," a letter of testimony to the Mansfield, Massachusetts, school board from Michael Bellino of Boston University's Center for Space Physics, November 18, 1996; "Studying Computers to Beat the Band," *San Francisco Chronicle,* May 20, 1996; "PE Requirement Delayed

While State Shapes Rules," by Terrence Stutz, *Dallas Morning News*, September 8, 2001, p. 1A.

3. "'Cyberstart' Puts Pre-schoolers in Front of Computers," by Cara Branigan, *eSchool News*, October 2000, p. 46.

4. "Learning Can Be Fun, at Least for the Makers of Electronic Toys," by Sherri Day, *The New York Times*, November 27, 2002, Business section, pp. 1 and 4.

5. *Endangered Minds: Why Children Don't Think and What We Can Do About It*, by Jane Healy, Touchstone (Simon & Schuster), 1990, p. 341.

6. *Failure to Connect: How Computers Affect Our Children's Minds—for Better and Worse*, by Jane Healy, Simon & Schuster, 1998, pp. 212, 185–89.

7. "Too Much Emphasis on Computers," by Ron Haybron, Cleveland *Plain Dealer*, August 6, 1996, p. 8E.

8. *The Hand*, by Frank R. Wilson, Pantheon, 1998, throughout, especially pp. 277–96; "The Hand as a Perceptual System," by Susan J. Lederman and Roberta L. Klatzky, a chapter in *The Psychobiology of the Hand*, edited by Kevin J. Connolly, Cambridge University Press, 1998, pp. 16–35.

9. *Handbook of Children and the Media*, edited by Dorothy G. Singer and Jerome L. Singer, Sage Publications, 2001, pp. 128–32, 223–68. In 2002, researchers found additional evidence that television viewing—of both violent and non-violent programs—is tied to aggressive behavior among adolescents and young adults. See "A Study Finds More Links Between TV and Violence," by Gina Kolata, *The New York Times*, March 29, 2002, p. A25.

10. *The House of Make-Believe: Children's Play and the Developing Imagination*, by Dorothy G. Singer and Jerome L. Singer, Harvard University Press, 1990, pp. 188–89.

11. "Zap! Splat! Smarts? Why Video Games May Actually Help Your Children Learn," by Neil Gross, *Business Week*, December 23, 1996, pp. 64–71.

12. Healy, *Endangered Minds*, pp. 326, 329, and 345.

13. "The Effect of Computer Software on Preschool Children's Developmental Gains," by Susan W. Haugland, *Journal of Computing in Childhood Education* 3, 1 (1992), pp. 15–30.

14. *Silicon Snake Oil: Second Thoughts on the Information Superhighway*, by Clifford Stoll, Doubleday, 1995, p. 136 (Anchor paperback edition).

15. "Fool's Gold: A Critical Look at Computers in Childhood," a report by the Alliance for Childhood, edited by Colleen Cordes and Edward Miller, released September 12, 2000.

16. "Your Child's Brain: How Kids Are Wired for Music, Math & Emotions," by Sharon Begley, *Newsweek*, February 19, 1996, cover story; "The Power of Music," by Laura Elliott, *The Washingtonian*, December 1995, p. 74; "Music of the Hemispheres," by James Shreeve, *Discover*, October 1996, pp. 96, 98.

17. "The Arts Step Out from the Wings," by Jane Buchbinder, *Harvard Education Letter*, November/December 1999, p. 4.

18. "Mozart and the S.A.T.'s," by Ellen Winner and Lois Hetland, *The New York Times*, op-ed page, March 4, 1999. (Winner, who teaches psychology at Boston College, and Hetland were researchers at the time at Project Zero, an arts program at the Harvard Graduate School of Education.)

19. "The Food of the Gods," *The Economist*, June 1, 1996.

20. Profile of SAT and Achievement Test Takers from 1990–1995, The College Entrance Examination Board, Princeton, N.J.

21. "Learning Improved by Arts Training," by Martin F. Gardiner, Alan Fox, Faith Knowles, and Donna Jeffrey, *Nature*, May 23, 1996, p. 284.

22. "Scientific Myths That Are Too Good to Die," by Gina Kolata, *The New York Times*, December 6, 1998.

23. "The Effects of Three Years of Piano Instruction on Children's Cognitive Development," by Eugenia Costa-Giomi, *Journal of Research in Music Education* 47, 3 (1999), pp. 198–212.

24. "Does Studying the Arts Enhance Academic Achievement? A Mixed Picture Emerges," by Ellen Winner and Lois Hetland, *Education Week*, November 1, 2000, p. 64.

25. "Maple Lane School, Centralia, WA," *Harvard Education Letter*, November/December 1999, p. 3.

26. "Beyond Finger Paint," by Deborah Solomon, *The New York Times Book Review*, May 17, 1998, p. 24.

27. "The Happy Meeting of Multiple Intelligences and the Arts," by Howard Gardner, *Harvard Education Letter*, November/December 1999, p. 5.

28. *Frames of Mind: The Theory of Multiple Intelligences*, by Howard Gardner, Basic Books, 1983.

29. "Teachers, Music, Libraries in Peril as Schools Retrench: Economic Woes Force Districts into Painful Classroom Cutbacks," by Elizabeth Bell, *San Francisco Chronicle*, March 18, 2002, p. 1; "Survey Rates States' Use of Learning Technologies: Despite a Sluggish Economy, 2002 Was a 'Good Year' for Ed Tech, Researchers Say," *eSchool News*, January 2003, p. 20; "Budget Crises Lead to Delays for Technology: Computer Replacements, Upgrades Put on Hold," by Andrew Trotter, *Education Week*, May 7, 2003, pp. 1, 16.

30. "School Based Expenditure Reports, Systemwide Summary," Board of Education of the City of New York, 1998–1999, 1999–2000 (p. 9), 2000–2001 (p. 7) and throughout.

31. Landry, *Red Herring*, August 2002, p. 41.

32. *Toward a Psychology of Being*, by Abraham H. Maslow, Wiley & Sons, 1968.

Chapter 8. The Spoils of Industry Partnerships

1. "Distance Learning Project Employs Fiber Optic Network: Voinovich Demonstrates New Education Project," a press release from the office of Governor George V. Voinovich, September 25, 1991.

2. "Power Trip: The Coming Darkness of Electricity Deregulation," by Alan Weisman, *Harper's*, October 2000; "Once Braced for a Power Shortage, California Now Finds Itself with a Surplus," by Timothy Egan, *The New York Times*, November 4, 2001, p. A17; "Collapse May Reshape the Battlefield of Deregulation" (an article about Enron's fall), by Joseph Kahn and Jeff Gerth, *The New York Times*, December 4, 2001, Business section, p. 1.

3. "Telecom's Pied Piper: Whose Side Was He On?," by Gretchen Morgenson, *The New York Times*, November 18, 2001, sec. 3, p. 1. (This article, a lengthy profile of Jack Benjamin Grubman, a fallen Wall Street analyst who was perhaps the biggest booster of telecommunications stocks in the late 1990s and 2000, also traces the telecom industry's dramatic and debt-ridden fall.)

4. "Phone Rate Cut Urged in State Memo," by Matt Pommer, *The Capital Times* (Madison, Wisconsin), May 11, 1994, p. 1A.

5. "Phone Rate Cut Backed," by Matt Pommer, *The Capital Times*, May 17, 1994, p. 1A. (While Ameritech's offer initially included a promise of at least $500 million, at the time Ameritech filed its formal agreement, on October 31, 1994, the company was promising to invest "a minimum of $700 million during the period between 1995 and 1999.")

6. "Wisconsin Bell, Inc.: Decreasing Infrastructure Investment Trend," a report by Scott Cullen, Administrator, and Glenn Unger, Chief Engineer, Telecommunications Division of the Public Service Commission of Wisconsin, May 20, 1994. (Note: During the period discussed here, Wisconsin Bell was a subsidiary of Ameritech, which was in turn later purchased by SBC Communications of Texas.)

7. "Ameritech Lobbies Hard," by Jeff Mayers, *Wisconsin State Journal*, August 2, 1994, p. 1A. Figures on 1993–1997 contributions to Governor Thompson were compiled by Michael Jacob of the Wisconsin Democracy Campaign of Madison, Wisconsin, on October 20, 1997.

8. According to reports from Ameritech's office of Community Relations, the company's donations to school technology, state by state, were as follows: Ohio: $20.7 million; Wisconsin: $16.8 million; Michigan: $27.7 million; Indiana: $30.3 million; Illinois: $2.2 million. These numbers, pulled from the company's website, were as of May 28, 2000. For an update, see: www.ameritech.com/community/education/investment/class.html.

9. This critique of Ameritech's proposal was made by Rodney Stevenson, professor in the school of business at the University of Wisconsin at Madison and executive director of the Wisconsin Public Utility Institute (which is partly funded by the utility industry). Stevenson's assessment is quoted in two articles: "Phone Shift Bill Spurs New Fears," by Matt Pommer, *The Capital Times*, June 7, 1994, p. 1A, and "Superhighway Blues," a *Capital Times* editorial, June 8, 1994, p. 9A.

10. "Technology for Educational Achievement in Wisconsin (TEACH) Board," a report by the Wisconsin state Legislative Audit Bureau, February 2002.

11. "Wiring the World: Ameritech's Monopoly on the Virtual Classroom," by Todd Alan Price, a chapter in *Campus, Inc.*, edited by Geoffrey White, Prometheus Books, 2000.

12. "High-Technology Stew: D.S.L. Service for Linking to Internet Is Problem Ridden," by Simon Romero, *The New York Times*, December 28, 2000, p. C1.

13. "Disconnected, Disillusioned," by Mike Ivey, *The Capital Times*, September 30, 2000, p. 1A.

14. Annual compilations of utility profit statements, as reported by the Wisconsin Public Service Commission.

15. Ivey, *The Capital Times*, September 30, 2000.

16. "Investigation into the Quality of Telecommunications Services Provided by Wisconsin Bell, Inc., d/b/a Ameritech Wisconsin, Stipulation and Consent Order," as ordered by the Public Service Commission of Wisconsin and signed by James Nelson, president of Wisconsin Bell, Inc., October 24, 2000.

17. The account of Ameritech service problems and various states' responses comes from a sequence of articles: "Complaints on Ameritech Soar 117%," by Lee Bergquist, *Milwaukee Journal Sentinel*, September 3, 2000, p. 1; "Ameritech Listens to Customers' Vast List of Grievances," by Nicole Ziegler Dizon of the Associated Press, *Wisconsin State Journal*, September 7, 2000, p. 2E; "State Tired of Ameritech's Act," by Jennifer Sereno, *Wisconsin State Journal*, September 15, 2000, p. 1A; "Regulators to Investigate Ameritech," by Lee Bergquist, *Milwaukee Journal Sentinel*, September 15, 2000, p. 1; Ivey, *The Capital Times*, September 30, 2000, p. 1A.

18. "eRate Update," a special publication of *eSchool News*, September 1998, p. 2.

19. "Cuts Possible in On-Line Plan for U.S. Schools and Libraries," by Seth Schiesel, *The New York Times*, June 11, 1998; "House Republicans Craft Bill to Kill eRate," by Dennis Pierce, *eSchool News*, March 1999, p. 1.

20. "Huge E-Rate Project Runs into Problems," by Andrew Trotter, *Education Week*, May 12, 1999, p. 1.

21. The scope of the San Francisco scandal was spelled out in a three-part, front-page series in the *San Francisco Chronicle*, November 11–13, 2001. Its findings are particularly well summarized in the opening story's headline: " 'A Grave Injustice Against the Children,' S.F. School Officials Squandered Millions of Bond, Tax Funds, Concealed Deficits from Voters While Seeking Millions More."

22. "S.F. Schools Can't Afford to Accept Grant," by Julian Guthrie, *San Francisco Chronicle*, April 2, 2001, p. A13.

23. *The Pentagon Catalog: Ordinary Products at Extraordinary Prices*, by Christopher Cerf and Henry Beard, Workman, 1986, pp. 14–17 and throughout.

24. "eRate Audit Triggers Fraud Inquiry: FCC Refuses to Identify Target," by Elizabeth B. Gerrard, *eSchool News*, March 2002, p. 1.

25. Semiannual report by the Office of Inspector General, Federal Communications Commission, October 31, 2002; "E-Rate Plans Involving IBM Draw Scrutiny," by Andrew Trotter, *Education Week*, December 11, 2002, p. 3; "Internet Com-

pany Accused of Fraud in School Program," by Benjamin Weiser, *The New York Times*, December 19, 2002; "eRate Bust Signals Crackdown," *eSchool News*, February 2003, pp. 1, 28; "E-Rate Audits Expose Abuses in the Program," by Rhea R. Borja and Andrew Trotter, *Education Week*, February 12, 2003, pp. 1, 18–19; "E-Rate Program Put Under Numerous Microscopes," by Andrew Trotter, *Education Week*, April 9, 2003, pp. 27, 31; "Old Foes Target eRate: Fraud Charges Open Congressional Probe," by Cara Branigan, *eSchool News*, March 2003, pp. 1, 32.

26. These items are drawn from the initial specifications in San Francisco's request for proposals on its first e-rate project, launched in early 2000. It was titled as follows: "Bid Package for E-Rate Subsidy at San Francisco Unified School District, for Infrastructure Conduit, 24-strand multi-mode fiber optical, category 5 and category 6 wiring and cabling, for purchases of equipment and services for Data, Internet, Advanced Telecommunications Networks Capable of MPEG-1/MPEG-2 to classroom and desktop."

27. Documents submitted as part of a bid, later approved with only slight modifications, by San Francisco Unified School District and the NEC Corporation. The bid was filed with the Universal Service Administration Company as Form 471 under NEC's Service Provider Identification (known, ironically, as its "SPIN" number), 143008317, on January 16, 2000. It should be noted, for the record, that NEC did not respond to numerous requests for comment on its San Francisco e-rate bid.

28. "Suit Alleges S.F. Schools' Kickbacks, It Claims Money Was Steered to District Official," by Chuck Finnie and Julian Guthrie, *San Francisco Chronicle*, November 17, 2001, p. A1.

29. "Ed. Board Computer 'Tax' Puts Big Byte on Schools," by Carl Campanile, *New York Post*, June 10, 2002. It is possible that this "tax" netted a good deal more than $6 million for New York's school bureaucracy reported by the *Post*. A partial reporting of computer expenses for all of 2002 showed that the city's school board had spent $10.02 million that year on 19,261 computers. This yields an average price of $520 per machine. But the prices that individual schools reported paying were two and three times that high, which would yield a profit for the district of $10 to $20 million. These inconsistencies could never be resolved, however. Repeated inquiries about them to the city's school board, over the course of more than a year, were rarely answered.

30. "Philly Creamed by $36M School-Software Scandal," *eSchool News*, December 2000, p. 24; "Qwest Probe Rocks Ariz. Wiring Project," *eSchool News*, April 2003, pp. 1, 30; Audit Report of Madison County, Arkansas, by the Legislative Joint Auditing Committee, Division of Legislative Audit, Little Rock, Arkansas, June 30, 1997; "Arkansas Probes Superintendent's Computer Sales to Own District," by Rebecca Flowers, *eSchool News*, December 1998/January 1999; author interviews with Bill Baum, deputy legislative auditor in the Arkansas legislative audit office, and Terry Jones, Arkansas state prosecutor.

31. *The School-to-Work Revolution: How Employers and Educators Are Joining Forces to Prepare Tomorrow's Skilled Workforce*, by Lynn Olson, Perseus, 1997, throughout, especially pp. 1–10, 87–112, 191–203. It's worth noting that Olson, a reporter for *Education Week*, started her book as a skeptic about school-to-work programs, seeing them as a tricked-up version of the deadening old vocational education routine. Months of fieldwork convinced her, however, that a valuable and durable revolution was actually occurring. Since 1997, school-to-work programs have continued their generally healthy growth, according to a March 2002 report by Peter Cappelli of the Wharton School at the University of Pennsylvania.

32. *Giving Kids the Business: The Commercialization of America's Schools*, by Alex Molnar, Westview Press, 1996, pp. 53–71, 78–79, 84–96.

33. "Woes for Company Running Schools," and "Edison Schools in Settlement with S.E.C.," both by Diana B. Henriques and Jacques Steinberg, *The New York Times*, May 14 and 15, 2002, pp. 1 and C1 respectively; "Public Schooling for Profit," a *New York Times* editorial, May 26, 2002; "Trouble for School Inc.," by Rebecca Winters, *Time*, May 27, 2002, p. 53; "Edison Buffeted by Probe, Loss of Contracts," by Catherine Gewertz, *Education Week*, September 4, 2002; "Flunked by Investors, Edison Schools Scorn Talk of Failure," by Charles Forelle, *The Wall Street Journal*, October 22, 2002, p. B1. This stream of bad news on Edison is doubly odd, considering the company's "core values." These are heavily publicized on Edison school walls as follows: "wisdom, justice, courage, compassion, hope, respect, responsibility, integrity."

34. "Philadelphia to Privatize Schools," *eSchool News*, June 2002, p. 1.

35. "Teaching Quality Viewed as Crucial," by Mary-Ellen Phelps Deily, *Education Week*, July 10, 2002.

Chapter 9. The Research Game: Faith and Testing in Las Vegas

1. "Accountability Systems: Implications of Requirements of the No Child Left Behind Act of 2001," by Robert L. Linn, Eva L. Baker, and Damian W. Betebenner, *Educational Researcher* 31, 6 (August/September 2002), p. 3; "Galileo's Dilemma: The Illusion of Scientific Certainty in Educational Research," by Douglas B. Reeves, *Education Week*, May 8, 2002, p. 44.

2. The volume of research looking for links between technology use and academic achievement is so large that a full listing would overwhelm these pages. To cite but a few examples, in 1972, J. F. Vinsonhaler and R. K. Bass published an article in *Educational Technology* (issue 12, pp. 29–32) entitled "A Summary of Ten Major Studies on CAI [computer-assisted instruction] Drill and Practice." Fifteen years and many studies later, Henry J. Becker, one of the leading researchers in this field, presented a paper at the 1987 annual meeting of the American Educational Research Association in Washington, D.C., entitled "The Impact of Computer Use on Children's Learning: What Research Has Shown

and What It Has Not." Since Becker's presentation, there's been a record-breaking abundance of these studies throughout the 1990s, which are dealt with later in this chapter.

3. "Effectiveness of Computer Based Instruction: An Updated Analysis," by Chen-Li Kulik and James. A. Kulik, *Computers in Human Behavior* 7 (1991), pp. 75–94; "Research on Computers and Education: Past, Present, and Future," a report to the Bill and Melinda Gates Foundation by Jeffrey T. Fouts, February 2000, pp. 6–9 and throughout.

4. "Pennsylvania Tests Essay-Grading Software," by Cara Branigan, *eSchool News*, January 2001, p. 1; "NRC Panel: Rethink, Revamp Testing," by Lynn Olson, *Education Week*, April 11, 2001; "School Spending to Soar on Test-Prep and Assessment," by Cara Branigan, *eSchool News*, October 2001, p. 12 (in this article, Eduventures.com projects technology spending in schools to be near $15 billion in 2002); "Business Intelligence: Insights from the Data Pile," by Leslie Berger, *The New York Times*, January 13, 2002.

5. "The 1992 National Reading Study and Theory of Reading Practice," 1992, The Institute for Academic Excellence, Madison, Wisconsin.

6. "National Study of Literature-Based Reading: How Literature-Based Reading Improves Both Reading and Math Ability," 1993, The Institute for Academic Excellence, Madison, Wisconsin.

7. "The Impact of the Accelerated Reader on Overall Academic Achievement and School Attendance," a paper given at the National Reading Conference, *Literacy and Technology for the 21st Century*, Atlanta, Georgia, October 4, 1996.

8. "Report of the National Reading Panel: Teaching Children to Read: An Evidence-Based Assessment of the Scientific Research Literature on Reading and Its Implications for Reading Instruction," National Institute of Child Health and Human Development, April 13, 2000, as commissioned by a 1997 congressional directive.

9. "Reading Achievement: Effects of Computerized Reading Management and Enrichment," by Janie Peak and Mark W. Dewalt, *ERS-Spectrum* 12, 1 (Winter 1994).

10. "The Effects of Incentives on Reading," by Jeff McQuillan, California State University, Fullerton, *Reading Research and Instruction* 36, 2 (Winter 1997), pp. 114–20.

11. "Computerized Self-Assessment of Reading Comprehension with the Accelerated Reader: Action Research," by Stacy R. Vollands, Keith J. Topping, and Ryka M. Evans, *Reading & Writing Quarterly* 15 (1999), pp. 197–211.

12. According to the National Assessments of Educational Progress (1971–2000), American fourth graders are reading slightly better than they were in 1971, but there's been no improvement among older students. According to the most recent International Education Assessment (1992), American nine- and ten-year-olds have been outperforming all but the Finnish students. Meanwhile,

American thirteen- and fourteen-year-olds lag behind those in approximately a dozen different countries.

13. "The Learning Effectiveness of Technology: A Call for Further Research," by T. H. Jones and R. Paolucci, *Educational Technology Review*, Spring/Summer 1998, pp. 10–14.

14. "The Kept University," by Eyal Press and Jennifer Washburn, *The Atlantic Monthly*, March 2000. In May of that year, the Associated Press reported that Dr. Marcia Angell, editor of *The New England Journal of Medicine*, recently "wrote a withering critique of the research system, saying science was being compromised by the growing influence of industry money." See "Harvard Keeps Strict Rules on Outside Research Work," *The New York Times*, May 27, 2000.

15. "Critical Thinking and Literature-Based Reading," a report from the Institute for Academic Excellence, November 1997.

16. Vygotsky, *Mind in Society*, p. 86.

17. Internet archives for Accelerated Reader in LM_Net, a discussion forum for librarians: www.ericir.syr.edu/Virtual/Listserv_Archives/LM_NET.shtml; "Accelerated Reader: What Are the Lasting Effects on the Habits of Middle School Students Exposed to Accelerated Reader in Elementary Grades?" by Linda M. Pavonetti, Kathryn M. Brimmer, and James F. Cipielewski, *Journal of Adolescent & Adult Literacy*, published by the International Reading Association, December 2002.

18. Pavonetti, Brimmer, and Cipielewski, *Journal of Adolescent & Adult Literacy*, December 2002.

19. "That Book Isn't on My Level: Moving Beyond Text Difficulty in Personalizing Reading Choices," by Jo Worthy and Misty Sailors, University of Texas, Austin. Published in *The New Advocate*, Summer 2001, based on a paper presented at the National Reading Conference in Scottsdale, Arizona, December 2000.

20. Internet archives for Accelerated Reader in LM_Net.

21. Of all the literature taking public schools to task for their failings, the most heavily promoted is the 1983 report "A Nation at Risk." In the years since the report's publication, a solid body of opposing literature has proved that the alarms it sounded were quite hyperbolic. (See, for example, *The Manufactured Crisis: Myths, Fraud and the Attack on America's Public Schools*, by David C. Berliner and Bruce J. Biddle, Perseus, 1995.) Hyperbole aside, a good portion of this report, and many others, have had solid points to make. As noted elsewhere, one of the best arguments on this score, narrow as it may be, is Ravitch, *Left Back*.

22. "Schools Taking Tougher Stance with Standards," by Tamar Lewin, *The New York Times*, September 6, 1999, p. A1; "Academic Standards Eased as Fear of Failure Spreads," by Jacques Steinberg, *The New York Times*, December 3, 1999, p. A1; "Soccer Moms vs. Standardized Tests," by Charles J. Sykes, op-ed column, *The New York Times*, December 6, 1999, p. A29.

23. "Right Answer, Wrong Score: Test Flaws Take Toll," by Diana B. Henriques and Jacques Steinberg; "When a Test Fails the Schools, Careers and Reputations Suffer," by Jacques Steinberg and Diana B. Henriques, *The New York Times*, May 20, 2001, and May 21, 2001, respectively, p. 1.

24. "Testing Reasoning and Reasoning About Testing," by Walt Haney, *Review of Educational Research* 54, 4 (Winter 1984), pp. 627–28.

25. "A Technological and Historical Consideration of Equity Issues Associated with Proposals to Change the Nation's Testing Policy," by George Madaus, *Harvard Educational Review*, Spring 1994, pp. 76–95.

26. "Promotion or Retention: Which One Is Social?" by Jeannie Oakes, *Harvard Education Letter*, January/February 1999.

27. "The Growing Revolt Against the Testers," a column by Richard Rothstein, *The New York Times*, May 30, 2001.

28. "Dukakis' State Miracle: Long on Jawboning," by James Risen, *Los Angeles Times*, August 7, 1988, p. 1; "Dukakis' Miracle Losing Luster," by Nicholas M. Horrock, *Chicago Tribune*, September 4, 1988, p. 1.

29. *USA Today*, March 14, 2000, p. 14A.

30. *The Boston Globe*, June 10, 1999, p. 1A.

31. "The Myth of the Texas Miracle in Education," by Walt Haney, *Education Policy Analysis Archives* 8, 41 (August 19, 2000); "Revisiting the Myth of the Texas Miracle in Education: Lessons About Dropout Research and Dropout Prevention," by Walt Haney, Lynch School of Education, Boston College, a March 2001 revision of a paper prepared for a conference sponsored by Achieve, Inc., and the Harvard University Civil Rights Project, January 13, 2001, Cambridge, Massachusetts.

32. During the months of litigation prompted by the TAAS case, in 1999 and 2000, a considerable amount of literature was generated that attempted to sort out the claims and counterclaims about the fairness and effectiveness of Texas's standardized testing system. One of the more exhaustive reviews of the story, albeit one weighted toward the state's arguments, was compiled by S. E. Phillips, who had served as one of the state's expert witnesses. The compilation became a package of nine articles published in the academic journal *Applied Measurement in Education* 13, 4 (2000). One of those articles ("GI Forum v. Texas Education Agency: Psychometric Evidence," pp. 343–86), written by Phillips, summarizes each side's main arguments and the court's findings on each count.

33. In 1996 and 1998 NAEP scores, Texas fourth and eighth graders placed ahead of almost every other state in math and writing. According to the Education Trust's report ("Real Results, Remaining Challenges: The Story of Texas Education Reform," a report commissioned by the Business Roundtable, April 2001), minorities did particularly well, trumping most or all of their peers across the nation. Texas black students led the pack, scoring even better than white students in seven states in the NAEP writing test. There has been good news to

report in international measures as well. In the 1999 Third International Math and Science Study (TIMSS), Texas scores were only average in science, but they shone in math. Despite having the most low-income and minority students of all thirteen participating states, according to the Education Trust, Texas essentially led them all on math scores. (On one math measure, Michigan topped Texas by one point among the participating states. However, on two other measures—those scoring internationally in the top 10 percent and those in the top quartile—Texas students led the field by several percentage points.)

34. "Real Results, Remaining Challenges," April 2001.
35. "Bush's 'Texas Miracle' in Schools? TAAS Tells," editorial, *The Sacramento Bee*, March 15, 2000.
36. "The Test Mess," by James Traub, *The New York Times Magazine*, April 7, 2002, pp. 46–78, especially pp. 49–50.
37. "States Teeter When Balancing Standards with Tests," by Richard Rothstein, *The New York Times*, May 1, 2002, p. A21.
38. " 'Texas Miracle' Doubted: An Education 'Miracle' or Mirage?" by John Mintz, *The Washington Post*, April 21, 2000, page A1.
39. Annual TAAS Participation Reports, Texas Education Agency, www.tea.state. tx.us/perfreport/aeis.
40. "The Harmful System of the TAAS System of Testing in Texas: Beneath the Accountability Rhetoric," by Linda McNeil, Rice University, Houston; and Angela Valenzuela, University of Texas, Austin, Harvard Civil Rights Project, 2000.
41. Mintz, *The Washington Post*, April 21, 2000.
42. Mintz, *The Washington Post*, April 21, 2000.
43. Editorial, *The Sacramento Bee*, March 15, 2000.
44. "Real Results, Remaining Challenges," April 2001.
45. "Rigorous School Tests Grow, but Big Study Doubts Value," by Greg Winter, *The New York Times*, December 28, 2002, p. 1. The article reports on a study financed by the National Education Association and conducted by Arizona State University's Educational Policy Research Unit and its Center on Education Policy. As might have been expected, soon after the study's release, it was criticized by another research team, from Stanford University, which released its own findings that test pressure was actually improving achievement. See "Researchers Debate Impact of Tests," by Debra Viadero, *Education Week*, February 5, 2003, pp. 1, 12.
46. The National Assessment of Educational Progress, 1992–2000; "Gap Between Best and Worst Widens on U.S. Reading Test," by Kate Zernike, *The New York Times*, April 7, 2001, p. 1.
47. According to Tennessee's annual state report cards, from 1996 to 2001, most students in grades three through eight have fallen in reading skill over the years, in relation to national norms. Specifically, third graders have gone from the 59th percentile to the 51st, fourth graders from the 58th to the 52nd, fifth

graders from the 53rd to the 55th, sixth graders from the 51st to the 52nd, seventh graders from the 54th to the 52nd, and eighth graders from the 56th to the 54th (www.state.tn.us/education/mstat.htm).

48. "Learning from Past Efforts to Reform the High School," by Thomas James and David Tyack, *Phi Delta Kappan*, February 1983, p. 406.

49. Madaus, *Harvard Educational Review*, pp. 78–79.

50. "Consequences of Assessment: What Is the Evidence?" by William A. Mehrens, *Education Policy Analysis Archives* 6, 13 (July 14, 1998), p. 1.

51. Traub, *The New York Times Magazine*, April 7, 2002, pp. 46–60; "How U.S. Punishes States with Higher Standards," by Richard Rothstein, *The New York Times*, September 18, 2002.

52. *Punished by Rewards: The Trouble with Gold Stars, Incentive Plans, A's, Praise, and Other Bribes*, by Alfie Kohn, Houghton Mifflin, 1993.

53. McQuillan, *Reading Research and Instruction* 36, 2 (Winter 1997), pp. 111–25.

54. As with many areas of educational research, there are mounds of studies on this topic. One of the most consolidated presentations of the main arguments on both sides was published in the *Review of Educational Research* 66, 1 (Spring 1996). The issue included four articles by eight leading writers and researchers on the subject of rewards. On the critical side were Mark R. Lepper, Mark Keavney, and Michael Drake; Richard M. Ryan and Edward L. Deci; and Alfie Kohn. Defending rewards were Judy Cameron and W. David Pierce. In 1999, Deci, Koestner, and Ryan responded with an exhaustive re-examination in *Psychological Bulletin* that criticized rewards once again. (See "A Meta-Analytic Review of Experiments Examining the Effects of Extrinsic Rewards on Intrinsic Motivation," *Psychological Bulletin* 125, 6 [1999], pp. 627–68). Judgments obviously can be subjective on this topic. But in terms of depth, detail, and scientific rigor, it certainly looks like the critics of rewards have carried the day.

55. A number of studies have looked persuasively at the basis, and the effects, of the Cognitive Tutor program. Among the most tangible are: "Intelligent Tutoring Goes to School in the Big City," by K. R. Koedinger, J. R. Anderson, W. H. Hadley, and M. A. Mark, *International Journal of Artificial Intelligence in Education* 8 (1997), pp. 30–43; "An Effective Metacognitive Strategy: Learning by Doing and Explaining with a Computer-Based Cognitive Tutor," by V. A. W. M. M. Aleven and K. R. Koedinger, *Cognitive Science* 26 (2002), pp. 147–79.

56. "Hold the Applause! Do Accelerated Reader and Electronic Bookshelf Send the Right Message?" by Betty Carter, *School Library Journal*, October 1996, pp. 22–25.

57. "Reading Rewards: Program's Popularity Overrides Criticism," by Jennifer Packer, Fort Worth *Star-Telegram*, April 21, 1997, p. 1.

58. For those who enjoy tracking studies of technology's effects on achievement, several additional examinations may be of interest. One, reported in late 2002, was conducted by two University of Chicago economists, who reviewed the results of the e-rate program in California between 1998 and 2000. The re-

searchers found that despite the massive infusion of Internet services that the program had brought to schools (particularly poor schools), those Internet services had done nothing for test scores in math, reading, and science. A five-year study of Internet use in one district, given the pseudonym Waterford, Pennsylvania, came to similar conclusions. (See "Narrowing the Digital Divide," *Business Week*, December 9, 2002, p. 28; *Bringing the Internet to School: Lessons from an Urban District*, by Janet Ward Schofield and Ann Locke Davidson, Jossey-Bass, 2002, especially pp. 9–13, 309–13.) Yet another study, released in early 2003, was conducted by James A. Kulik, the University of Michigan researcher and well-known meta-analyst of educational technology studies. As with his previous reviews, Kulik concluded that simple computerized tutorial programs were more effective than experimental programs such as simulations. But the gains he found were minimal in some cases, and inconsistent in others. Furthermore, as with Kulik's previous work, this review failed to account for poor research designs in the sample of studies he was examining. And since the drilling programs and tutorials that Kulik favored are less and less in use, Kulik's findings were dismissed by some technology experts as being out of date. (See "Study Probes Technology's Effect on Math and Science," by Cara Branigan, *eSchool News*, February 2003, p. 14; and "More Grizzly Than I Can Bear," a column by Gregg Downey, publisher of *eSchool News*, February 2003, p. 6.) An earlier study by the Educational Testing Service came to the opposite conclusion. Published in 1998, this study, which has been widely circulated by technology advocates, found that the standard "drill-and-practice" computer programs were actually having a negative effect on achievement in elementary grades, while simulations, spreadsheets, math learning games, and other innovative programs were stimulating achievement. (See "Does It Compute? The Relationship Between Educational Technology and Student Achievement in Mathematics," by Harold Wenglinsky, Educational Testing Service, 1998.) Unfortunately this study failed to account for the most obvious possibility: the absence of a level playing field. That is, students using innovative computer programs were compared to students who weren't doing anything that was innovative, with or without computers.

59. Berends et al., "Implementation and Performance," the RAND Corporation, 2001, pp. 79–133.

60. "Unrequited Promise," by Jeffrey Mirel, *Education Next*, Summer 2002, pp. 70–72.

Chapter 10. Education's Holy Grail: Teacher Training

1. "Preparing Teachers for the Digital Age," by Andrew Trotter, "Technology Counts, '99: Building the Digital Curriculum," a special issue of *Education Week*, September 23, 1999, p. 37.

2. Cuban and Tyack, *Tinkering Toward Utopia*, pp. 7–10, 20–22, 67–68; Sarason, *Revisiting "The Culture of School,"* pp. 37–44, 185–214.

3. "District to Teachers: All Hands on Tech," by Joshua Benton, *The Dallas Morning News*, September 8, 2001, p. 1A.

4. "Teacher Quality: A Report on the Preparation and Qualifications of Public School Teachers," U.S. Department of Education, National Center for Education Statistics, January 1999 (http://nces.ed.gov/pubsearch/pubsinfo.asp?pubid=1999080); "Technology Counts 2001: The New Divides," a special issue of *Education Week*, May 10, 2001, pp. 49–54, 60–64.

5. The National Commission on Teaching & America's Future, 1996 (www.tc.columbia.edu/~teachcomm); "State Indicators of Science and Mathematics Education 1999," a biennial report by the Council of Chief State School Officers, as described in "More Students Take Math, Science, While Many Teachers Unprepared," by Kathleen Kennedy Manzo, *Education Week*, March 1, 2000, p. 12; "Quality Counts 2001: A Better Balance," a special issue of *Education Week*, January 11, 2001, p. 97.

6. "1 in 4 Teachers Is Not Trained in Field," the Associated Press, August 21, 2002 (based on a random survey of teachers by the Department of Education); "The Great Divide," by Lynn Olson, in "Ensuring a Highly Qualified Teacher for Every Classroom: Quality Counts 2003," a special report by *Education Week*, January 9, 2003, pp. 7 (executive summary), 9–18 (Olson's story), and throughout.

7. "Failing Teachers," a series by Becky Beaupre, Kate Grossman, and Rosalind Rossi, Chicago *Sun-Times*, September 6, 7, and 9, 2001.

8. The National Commission on Teaching & America's Future, 1996. While no formal update of the commission's findings had been done by press time on this book, other available data from the nation's teachers' unions and other organizations indicate that these trends had not much changed.

9. "Money Can't Buy Good Teachers," by John Merrow, an op-ed column in *The New York Times*, August 23, 1999; and an update from the National Center for Education Statistics, as reported in "Getting Tough on Teachers," by Randal C. Archibold, "Education Life," a special supplement of *The New York Times*, November 1, 1998, p. 25.

10. "Building a Better Teacher," by Susan Black, *The American School Board Journal*, April 1999; "States Move to Improve Teacher Pool," by Bess Keller, *Education Week*, June 14, 2000, p. 1; and Archibold, "Education Life," *The New York Times*, November 1, 1998, p. 23.

11. "California Definitions of Qualified Teachers Rejected by Ed. Dept.," by Joetta L. Sack, *Education Week*, September 4, 2002.

12. "Flaws Appear as Companies Turn to Computer-Based Training," *The Wall Street Journal*, July 3, 2001, p. 1.

13. Market Data Retrieval, "Technology in Education 1999" and "Technology in Education 2000," as reported in "Technology Counts 2001: The New Divides," and "Technology Counts 2002: E-Defining Education," special issues of *Education Week*, May 10, 2001, and May 9, 2002, respectively (for 2001, p. 52; for

2002, pp. 11 and 54); The CEO Forum School Technology and Readiness Report, June 2001, p. 30, recommends that 30 percent of school technology budgets be spent on training. Other industry reports, such as those from the Gartner Group, have recommended much higher figures, to account for maintenance demands as well.

14. "WorldCom Fall Imperils Ed. Tech Aid," by Andrew Trotter, *Education Week*, September 18, 2002, p. 1; "WorldCom's $6 Million 'Miracle' to Save MarcoPolo," by Cara Branigan, *eSchool News*, January 2003, p. 10.

15. "Technology Counts 2002," *Education Week*, May 9, 2002, pp. 29, 42.

16. "The Psychopathic School," a speech given by John Taylor Gatto on January 31, 1990, in accepting the New York state senate's teacher-of-the-year award. This speech, and some others of Gatto's, appear in *Dumbing Us Down: The Hidden Curriculum of Compulsory Education*, by John Taylor Gatto, New Society Publishers, 1992. (For this quote, see p. 33.)

Chapter 11. Getting Real at New York's Urban Academy High School

1. "An Inquiry High School: Learner-Centered Accountability at the Urban Academy," by Jacqueline Ancess of the National Center for Restructuring Education, Schools and Teaching (NCREST), Teachers College, Columbia University; Foreword by Linda Darling-Hammond, March 1995, p. ix.

2. "Proficiencies: Graduation Assessment at Urban Academy High School," an Urban Academy video, 1999.

3. "Making School Completion Integral to School Purpose and Design," a paper by Jacqueline Ancess and Suzanne Ort Wichterle, delivered to "Dropouts in America," a January 13, 2001, conference sponsored by Achieve, Inc., and the Harvard University Civil Rights Project. (The report uses 1999 data.)

4. *Teaching as a Subversive Activity*, by Neil Postman and Charles Weingartner, Dell, 1969, pp. 2–3.

5. *Horace's Hope*, by Theodore Sizer, Houghton Mifflin, 1996, p. 67.

6. Ancess, "An Inquiry High School," p. ix.

7. Ancess, "An Inquiry High School," pp. 6–12, 17–19.

8. Ancess, "An Inquiry High School," p. 12.

9. "Proficiencies," Urban Academy video.

10. "Proficiencies," Urban Academy video.

Chapter 12. A Word from the Army: KISS

1. *Breaking the News: How the Media Undermine American Democracy*, by James Fallows, Pantheon, 1996, p. 4.

2. "Home Language and Literacy Environment: Final Results," by Patton O. Tabors, Kevin A. Roach, and Catherine E. Snow, in *Beginning Literacy with Language*, edited by David K. Dickinson, Ed.D., and Tabors, Ed.D., Paul H. Brookes Publishing Co., 2001, pp. 111–38.

3. *The Aims of Education and Other Essays*, by Alfred North Whitehead, Macmillan, 1929, p. 17.
4. "New Dell Program Gives At-risk Kids a Technology Boost," by Elizabeth Guerard, *eSchool News*, September 2001, p. 34; "Students Build Their Own High-speed Computers," *eSchool News*, May 2001.
5. "Experts Debate Effect of Whole-School Reform," by Joetta L. Sack, *Education Week*, January 30, 2002.
6. "Chess Makes Kids Smart. And, Indeed, It Really May. Read On," by Anne Graham, *Parents*, December 1985, pp. 113–16; "Chess as a Way to Teach Thinking," by Dianne D. Horgan, Department of Psychology, Memphis State University, *Teaching, Thinking, and Problem Solving* 9 (3), 1987, pp. 4–9; "Chess Improves Academic Performance," a report by Christine Palm for the New York City Schools Chess Program, 1990; "The Effect of Chess on Reading Scores: District Nine Chess Program Second Year Report," a report for The American Chess Foundation by Stuart Margulies, Ph.D., 1992; "Chess in Education Research Summary," a paper presented at the BMCC Chess in Education Conference by Dr. Robert Ferguson, Jr., executive director, American Chess School, January 1995, pp. 12–13.
7. *More Like Us: Putting America's Native Strengths and Traditional Values to Work to Overcome the Asian Challenge*, by James Fallows, Houghton Mifflin, 1989.
8. "Beyond Fourth-Grade Science: Why Do U.S. and Japanese Students Diverge?" by Marcia C. Linn, Catherine Lewis, Ineko Tsuchida, and Nancy Butler Songer, *Educational Researcher* 29, 3 (April 2000), pp. 4–14.
9. *Science Research Lessons in Japan*, a video of grade five at Shizuoka University, Japan, available through Catherine Lewis, Mills College, Oakland, California.

Chapter 13. The Human Touch

1. California state demographic statistics 1997–2001. The statistics are compiled annually in the "California County Data Book," a report published by Children Now, a child advocacy organization based in Oakland, California.
2. "Evaluation Report: Thomas E. Mathews Community School," by Ryan Babineaux, Stanford University, School of Education, 1999, pp. 32–33.
3. *Humboldt's Gift*, by Saul Bellow, Viking, 1973, pp. 270–71.
4. As quoted on the frontispiece of *Education as an Art*, by Rudolf Steiner, Rudolf Steiner School Press, 1979.
5. "The Origins of the Waldorf Movement and Its Current Challenges," by Henry Barnes, *Renewal: A Journal for Waldorf Education* 1, 1, pp. 4–7.
6. The tuition comparisons come from figures regularly compiled by the National Association of Independent Schools, the Council for American Private Education, the National Catholic Education Association, and the U.S. Department of Education's National Center for Education Statistics.
7. Tables provided by Milwaukee Public Schools, covering the years 1996–2001. The testing data are the results of the Fourth Grade Wisconsin Knowledge and

Concepts examination, which has been administered in Milwaukee schools since 1996.

8. This too comes from tables provided by Milwaukee Public Schools, covering the years 1996–2001, as cited above. It should be noted that comparing different years and different schools can be a fungible science—especially since not all students are tested each year. To compensate for this, I have focused on years when roughly equivalent percentages of students at each school took the state tests. As an example, in the 1999–2000 academic year, Starms excused between 6 and 10 percent of its students from the test. Urban Waldorf, meanwhile, did not excuse anyone that year (it did in other years). However, in the 1999–2000 year, 54 percent of Urban Waldorf students tested in reading as "proficient," and 10 percent at the top as "advanced" (these are the two crowning categories); in math, 31 percent tested as proficient, and another 31 percent as advanced; and in science, 21 percent tested as proficient and a full 46 percent tested as advanced.

9. Among the many ongoing re-examinations of human senses and abilities, the most widely known has been the work done by Howard Gardner of Harvard University. (See *Frames of Mind: The Theory of Multiple Intelligences,* by Howard Gardner, Basic Books, 1983.) It should be noted that the distinctions and connections that Gardner draws are seen by some leading psychologists to be rather facile and artificial; nonetheless, most of these experts acknowledge that Gardner's work has provided a badly needed broadening of common definitions of personal and intellectual ability. Beyond Gardner, many other academics have added to the literature on this front. Among them are Martin Hoffman of New York University, Peter Salovey of the psychology department at Yale University, and Eric Schaps and Catherine Lewis at the Developmental Studies Center in Oakland, California.

10. "Fairy Tales as a Learning Tool for Young Offenders," by Richard Rothstein, *The New York Times,* July 24, 2002.

11. *Experience and Education,* by John Dewey, Touchstone, 1938, pp. 25–50 and throughout.

12. The scientific basis for the theory that physical activity, particularly tactile complexity, builds the powers of the brain is treated more fully in chapter 7. Readers may wish to refer to those pages, and specifically to endnotes 5 and 8 on page 431.

13. "Chinese Parents' Influence on Academic Performance," by Shu Ya Zhang and Angela L. Carrasquillo, *New York State Association for Bilingual Education Journal* 10 (Summer 1995), pp. 46–53; "Changed Lives: The Effects of the Perry Pre-School," a monograph by John R. Berrueta-Clement, et al., High Scope Press, 1984.

14. *The Hurried Child: Growing Up Too Fast Too Soon,* by David Elkind, Addison-Wesley, 1988 edition (originally published in 1981), pp. xiv, 32–36, 103–10; *Miseducation: Preschoolers at Risk,* by David Elkind, Knopf, 1987, pp. 141–43.

15. *The Uses of Enchantment: The Meaning and Importance of Fairy Tales*, by Bruno Bettelheim, Vintage, 1977; *The Moral Intelligence of Children*, by Robert Coles, Random House, 1997, pp. 1–12, 99–102, and throughout.

16. "Jean Piaget and Rudolf Steiner: Stages of Child Development and Implications for Pedagogy," by Iona H. Ginsburg, *Teachers College Record*, Winter 1982, pp. 329–37.

17. *Consilience*, by Edward O. Wilson, Knopf, 1998. A condensation of Wilson's argument was published as a cover story in the April 1998 issue of *The Atlantic Monthly* under the title "The Biological Basis of Morality," pp. 53–70. "Moral reasoning," Wilson wrote, "is at every level intrinsically consilient with—compatible with, intertwined with—the natural sciences. (I use a form of the word 'consilience'—literally a 'jumping together' of knowledge as a result of the linking of facts and fact-based theory across disciplines to create a common groundwork of explanation. . . .)"

18. *The Essential Steiner: Basic Writings of Rudolf Steiner*, edited by Robert A. McDermott, HarperSan Francisco, 1984, p. 343.

19. *The Child's Changing Consciousness and Waldorf Education*, by Rudolf Steiner, Anthroposophic Press, 1988, pp. 23–24.

20. As reported in *Der Spiegel*, December 14, 1981.

Conclusion

1. "Computers in School: Do Students Improve? High Technology Doesn't Always Equal High Achievement," by Christopher H. Schmitt and Larry Slonaker, *San Jose Mercury News*, January 14, 1996, p. 1A.

2. State test scores, California Department of Education, 1980–2002, Belridge School District.

3. National Assessment of Educational Progress, 1999 Long-Term Trend Assessment, National Center for Education Statistics; "Progress Lacking on U.S. Students' Grasp of Science," by David J. Hoff, *Education Week*, November 28, 2001, pp. 1 and 14; "U.S. Students Prove Middling on a 32-Nation Test," by Diana Jean Schemo, *The New York Times*, December 5, 2001, p. A21; "Students, Especially 12th Graders, Do Poorly on History Tests," by Diana Jean Schemo, *The New York Times*, May 10, 2002.

4. "Education Study Finds U.S. Falling Short / Teachers Are Found Not Benefiting in Era of Economic Expansion," by Jodi Wilgoren, *The New York Times*, June 13, 2001, p. A28. (This article was based on data compiled by the Organization for Economic Cooperation and Development.)

5. "The Stories Behind the Story," by James W. Michaels, *Forbes*, August 27, 1984, p. 4.

6. "The Mystery of Good Teaching," by Dan Goldhaber, *Education Next*, Spring 2002, pp. 50–56, especially p. 54.

7. "The 2 Sigma Problem: The Search for Methods of Group Instruction as Effective as One-on-One Tutoring," by Benjamin S. Bloom, *Educational Researcher*,

Vol. 13 (6), pp. 4–16, 1984. This study by Bloom, who helped found the Head Start program, has become something of a gold standard on the power of tutoring.

8. *The End of Education: Redefining the Value of School,* by Neil Postman, Vintage, 1995, p. 43.

9. "Less Surfing, More Learning," by David Gelernter, *The Weekly Standard,* November 4, 1996, p. 14. "Benton: America's $40 Billion Ed-Tech Investment at Risk," by Corey Murray, *eSchool News,* February 2003, p. 12.

10. Roszak, *The Cult of Information,* pp. xiv–xvi and throughout.

11. Annual budget documents, the U.S. Department of Education; "Education Reform Left Behind," a *New York Times* editorial, February 8, 2003.

12. "Education at a Glance," a report published by the Organisation [*sic*] for Economic Co-Operation and Development (OECD), 2001, pp. 80–81.

13. "Teachers Dig Deeper to Fill Gap in Supplies," by Abby Goodnough, *The New York Times,* September 21, 2002, p. 1.

14. "How the U.S. Tax Code Worsens the Education Gap," by Richard Rothstein, *The New York Times,* April 25, 2001.

15. "Adding Up the Impact of Raising Salaries," by Steven Greenhouse, *The New York Times,* August 8, 1999; "Rankings and Estimates," 2000–2001, National Education Association, April 8, 2002 (www.nea.org/publicized/edstats/rankings/02rankings.pdf). The report finds that throughout the economic expansion of the 1990s, teacher pay remained nearly stagnant, rising by a meager 0.3 percent a year. By the boom year of 2001, the average salary of a public school teacher was $43,335, a level not reached by school districts in more than thirty states.

16. "School on a Hill: On the Design and Redesign of American Education," a roundtable discussion published in the "Forum" section of *Harper's,* September 2001, pp. 52 and 60. See also two *New York Times* op-ed columns: "Getting Better Teachers," by Robert E. Riccobono, November 22, 1999, and "How to Train—and Retain—Teachers," by Vartan Gregorian, July 6, 2001. (At the time of their writing, Riccobono was a visiting scholar at the Taub Urban Research Center at New York University; Gregorian, former president of Brown University, was president of the Carnegie Corporation of New York.)

17. "Afghanistan? Young Americans Can't Find It on Map, Survey Finds," by Bess Keller, *Education Week,* November 27, 2002, p. 11.

18. "Teach Students More Than Where to Put the H in Afghanistan," by Richard Rothstein, *The New York Times,* September 19, 2001, p. A24.

19. "On the Uses of a Liberal Education: I. As Lite Entertainment for Bored College Students," by Mark Edmundson, *Harper's,* September 1997, pp. 39–49; "Debate? Dissent? Discussion? Oh, Don't Go There!" by Michiko Kakutani, *The New York Times,* March 23, 2002, pp. A17, 19. Edmundson's essay is paired with an answering essay by Earl Shorris, entitled "II. As a Weapon in the Hands of the Restless Poor," pp. 50–59. Both essays are extremely thoughtful and inspiring.

20. "School on a Hill," a Forum discussion, *Harper's*, September 2001, pp. 40–63.

21. Roszak, *The Cult of Information*, p. xv.

22. *Education and Ecstasy*, by George Leonard, North Atlantic Books, 1968 and 1987, pp. 139–74.

23. "Visions of Learning in 2020 Will Help Shape Ed-Tech Policy," by Cara Branigan, *eSchool News*, November 2002, p. 34.

24. "The Talent Myth: Are Smart People Over-rated?" by Malcolm Gladwell, *The New Yorker*, July 22, 2002, pp. 29–33.

25. "Mastery," by George Leonard, *Esquire*, May 1987, pp. 149–52; *Mastery*, by George Leonard, Penguin, 1991.

26. "District Rethinks a Soda-Pop Strategy," by Constance L. Hays, *The New York Times*, April 19, 2000; "Free Computers to Schools: An Offer Too Good to Last," by John Schwartz, *The New York Times*, November 2, 2000, p. A1. As a fitting epitaph, it should perhaps be noted that in the fall of 2000, the ZapMe! deals apparently collapsed under their own commercial weight. The company says it never did sell the data it collected on student buying habits and other demographic information. But when the company failed to draw sufficient backers and advertisers, it resorted to another option in its contract—the right to charge schools for all the computer equipment it had promised free of charge.

27. "Proverbs of Hell," by William Blake, *The Marriage of Heaven and Hell*, 1790.

Index

West Virginia Northern Community
College, 106, 107
Western Governors University, 59,
422n60
Westside Community School (New
York City), 374–75
White, E. B., 61
Whitfield, Scott, 11
Whitfield, Shawn, 11–12
Whittle, Chris, 235–39, 237n
Whitwell Elementary (Ironton,
Ohio), 213–14, 220, 222,
226
Wiegner, Kathleen, 397
Williams, Brenda, 117–18
Williams, Valorie, 78
Wilson, Charles E., 58
Wilson, Edward O., 447n17
Wilson, Frank R., 199
Windows on Science (videodisk series),
43–45
Winer, Deborah Grace, 389
Winer, Toba, 378
Winn, William D., 202
Winner, Ellen, 208
Winter, Greg, 440n45
Wired magazine, 20, 52
Wirth, Tim, 37
Wisconsin, 50n, 215–20, 222,
223–27, 433n8, 433n9
Wisconsin Bell, Inc., 216, 217, 223,
433n6

Wisconsin Public Service
Commission (PSC), 216, 217,
222
Wise, Harry Arthur, 3–4, 6, 61,
417n1
WONDER (network), 226n
Worcester, Massachusetts, xii–xiii
word-processing programs, 41, 48,
52, 86–87
WorldCom, Inc., 315
Worthy, Jo, 272
writing skills, xiv, 157, 164, 185,
203, 208, 301, 352, 355, 356,
365–66, 366n, 439n33

X
Xchange program, 148

Y
Y2K, 41
Yocam, Keith, 47
York, Pennsylvania, 238–39
young children, computers for,
195–205, 348
Ysleta, Texas, 231

Z
Zamora, Ramon, 14
ZapMe!, 449n26
zone of proximal development (ZPD),
266, 267, 301
Zornes, Ken, 237

TODD OPPENHEIMER, a freelance writer based in San Francisco, has been working as a journalist since the late 1970s. The publications he has written for include *The Atlantic Monthly, Newsweek* (where he served as associate editor of its new-media division for electronic publishing), *The Washington Post, Columbia Journalism Review,* and an assortment of local newspapers (his favorite being *The Independent,* of Durham, North Carolina). This book, Oppenheimer's first, expands on one particular article—"The Computer Delusion," his July 1997 cover story for *The Atlantic,* which won the year's National Magazine Award for public interest reporting. Oppenheimer has won a variety of national awards for his writing, particularly in the field of investigative reporting, and has twice served as a judge for the annual awards conferred by Investigative Reporters and Editors, Inc. Oppenheimer also has a long history of volunteering in schools and in 1998 was honored as San Francisco's School Volunteer of the Year. Oppenheimer lives in San Francisco with his wife, Anh, and his son, A.J. He works at the Grotto, a local writers' collective.

ABOUT THE TYPE

The text of this book was set in Photina, a typeface designed by José Mendoza in 1971. It is a very elegant design with high legibility, and its close character fit has made it a popular choice for use in quality magazines and art gallery publications. The display font is Nofret, a typeface designed in 1986 by Gudrun Zapf-von Hesse especially for the Berthold foundry in Germany.